# Encyclopedia of
# Motherhood

# Encyclopedia of Motherhood

Andrea O'Reilly, GENERAL EDITOR

*York University*

1

SAGE | reference

Los Angeles | London | New Delhi
Singapore | Washington DC

*For information*

SAGE Publications, Inc.
2455 Teller Road
Thousand Oaks, California 91320
E-mail: order@sagepub.com

SAGE Publications Ltd.
1 Oliver's Yard
55 City Road
London EC1Y 1SP
United Kingdom

SAGE Publications India Pvt. Ltd.
B 1/I 1 Mohan Cooperative Industrial Area
Mathura Road, New Delhi 110 044
India

SAGE Publications Asia-Pacific Pte. Ltd.
33 Pekin Street #02-01
Far East Square
Singapore 048763

Printed in the United States of America.

*Library of Congress Cataloging-in-Publication Data*

Encyclopedia of motherhood / Andrea O'Reilly, general editor.

   v. cm.

 Includes bibliographical references and index.

 ISBN 978-1-4129-6846-1 (pbk.)

 1. Motherhood--Encyclopedias. I. O'Reilly, Andrea, 1961-

 HQ759.E52 2010

 306.874'303--dc22                    2009047934

This book is printed on acid-free paper.         Photo Credits: Page 1428.

10 11 12 13 14 10 9 8 7 6 5 4 3 2 1

 A Golson Media Production

| | |
| --- | --- |
| President and Editor | J. Geoffrey Golson |
| Director, Author Management | Susan Moskowitz |
| Layout Editors | Stephanie Larson |
| | Mary Jo Scibetta |
| Copyeditor | Stephanie Larson |
| Proofreader | Joyce Li |
| Indexer | J S Editorial |

 Published by SAGE Reference

| | |
| --- | --- |
| Vice President and Publisher | Rolf A. Janke |
| Senior Editor | Jim Brace-Thompson |
| Project Editor | Tracy Buyan |
| Cover Designer | Ravi Balasuriya |
| Marketing Manager | Amberlyn McKay |
| Editorial Assistant | Michele Thompson |
| Reference Systems Manager | Leticia Gutierrez |
| Reference Systems Coordinator | Laura Notton |

# Contents

# About the General Editor

**Andrea O'Reilly**, Ph.D., mother of three, is Associate Professor in the School of Women's Studies at York University and is founder and director of the Association for Research on Mothering, founder and editor-in-chief of the *Journal of the Association for Research on Mothering*, and founder and editor of Demeter Press, the first feminist press on motherhood. She is cofounder of the Museum of Motherhood to open in Seneca Falls in 2011 and is cofounder of the International Mothers Network, the first international consortium of motherhood organizations now with 120 plus members worldwide.

O'Reilly is author *of Toni Morrison and Motherhood: A Politics of the Heart* (2004) and *Rocking the Cradle: Thoughts on Motherhood, Feminism and the Possibility of Empowered Mothering* (2006) and is editor/co-editor of 14 books on motherhood including *Motherhood at the 21st Century: Experience, Identity, Policy, Agency* (2010); *Textual Mothers/ Maternal Texts: Motherhood in Contemporary Women's Literature* (2010); *Maternal Thinking: Philosophy, Politics, Practice* (2009); *Feminist Mothering* (2008); *Maternal Theory: Essential Readings* (2007); *Mother Outlaws: Theories and Practices of Empowered Mothering* (2004); *From Motherhood to Mothering: The Legacy of Adrienne Rich's Of Woman Born* (2004) and *Mothers and Sons: Feminism, Masculinity and the Struggle to Raise our Sons* (2001). She is currently at work on a monograph on "Mothers in the Academe" and completing two edited collections: one on the Motherhood Movement and another on Sarah Palin.

She has received 16 Social Science Humanities Research Council of Canada grants and is the recipient of several awards and honors including: the Atkinson Deans Award for Research Excellence; the Lillian Robinson Fellowship at Concordia University; York University "Professor of the Year" award (in 1998 and 2009); and the Canadian Association of University Teachers Sarah Shorten Award in recognition of outstanding achievements in the promotion of the advancement of women in Canadian universities and colleges.

# Introduction

In 1976, author Adrienne Rich wrote, "We know more about the air we breathe, the seas we travel, than about the nature and meaning of motherhood." By 1998, some 20 years after the publication of Rich's landmark *Of Woman Born*, many academic disciplines, from anthropology to women's studies, were engaged in some form of motherhood research. And while scholarship on motherhood in some disciplines still struggled for legitimacy and centrality, there was the recognition that motherhood studies was emerging as a distinct field within the larger disciplines of feminist scholarship or women's studies. In the last decade, the topic of motherhood has emerged as a distinct and established field of scholarly inquiry. Indeed, today it would be unthinkable to cite Rich's quote on the dearth of maternal scholarship.

A cursory review of motherhood research reveals that hundreds of scholarly articles have been published on almost every motherhood theme imaginable. The *Journal of the Association for Research on Mothering* alone has examined motherhood topics as diverse as sexuality, peace, religion, public policy, literature, work, popular culture, health, carework, young mothers, motherhood and feminism, feminist mothering, mothers and sons, mothers and daughters, lesbian mothering, adoption, the motherhood movement, and mothering, race and ethnicity to name a few. In 2006, the General Editor of this encyclopedia, Andrea O'Reilly, coined the term *motherhood studies* to acknowledge and demarcate this new scholarship on motherhood as a legitimate and distinctive discipline, one grounded in the theoretical tradition of maternal theory developed by scholars such as Rich, Patricia Hill Collins, Sharon Hays, Paula Caplan, Susan Maushart, Fiona Green, Miriam Johnson, bell hooks, Patrice DiQunizio, Susan Douglas, Meredith Michaels, Alice Walker, Marianne Hirsh, and Sara Ruddick. Indeed, similar to the development of women's studies as an academic field in the 1970s, motherhood studies, while explicitly interdisciplinary, cross-disciplinary and multidisciplinary, has emerged as an autonomous and independent scholarly discipline in the last decade. The publication of this encyclopedia on motherhood—the first ever on the topic—helps to both demarcate motherhood as a scholarly field and an academic discipline and to direct its future development.

In *Of Woman Born,* Rich distinguished between two meanings of motherhood, one superimposed on the other: "the *potential* relationship of any woman to her powers of reproduction and to children," and "the *institution*—which aims at ensuring that that potential—and all women—shall remain under male control." In motherhood studies the term *motherhood* is used to signify the patriarchal institution of motherhood, while *mothering* refers to women's lived experiences of mothering as they seek to resist the patriarchal institution of motherhood and its oppressive ideology. An empowered practice/theory of mothering, therefore, functions as a counter-narrative of motherhood: it seeks to interrupt the master narrative of motherhood to imagine and implement a view of mothering that is *empowering* to women. Empowered mothering may refer to any practice of mothering that seeks to challenge and change various aspects of patriarchal motherhood that cause mothering to be limiting or oppressive to women. Or, to use Rich's terminology, an empowered maternal practice marks a movement from motherhood to mothering, and makes possible a mothering against motherhood.

In the decades since the publication of Rich's landmark book, motherhood research has focused upon the oppressive and empowering dimensions of mothering and the complex relationship between the two. Stemming from the above distinction, motherhood studies may be divided into four interconnected themes or categories of inquiry: motherhood as institution, motherhood as experience, motherhood as identity or subjectivity, mothering as agency. While scholars who are concerned with the ideology or institution investigate policies, laws, ideologies, and images of patriarchal motherhood, researchers who are interested in experience examine the work women do as mothers, an area of study paved with insights from Sara Ruddick's concept of maternal practice. The third category, identity or subjectivity, looks at the effect that becoming a mother has on a woman's sense of self; in particular, how her sense of self is shaped by the institution of motherhood and the experience of mothering, respectively.

Since the turn of the millennium, a new theme in motherhood has emerged which scholars have termed *agency*. Motherhood scholarship, whether its concern is mothering as an institution, experience, or identity, has tended to focus on how motherhood is detrimental to women because of its construction as a patriarchal entity within the said three areas. For example, scholars interested in

experience argue that the gender inequities of patriarchal motherhood cause the work of mothering to be both isolating and exhausting for women, while those concerned with ideology call attention to the guilt and depression that is experienced by mothers who fail to live up to the impossible standards of patriarchal motherhood that our popular culture inundates them with. In contrast, little has been written on the possibility or potentiality of mothering as identified by Rich. This point is not lost on Fiona Green who writes, "still largely missing from the increasing dialogue and publication around motherhood is a discussion of Rich's monumental contention that even when restrained by patriarchy, motherhood can be a site of empowerment and political activism." More recently however, agency has emerged as a prevailing theme in motherhood scholarship. Specifically, the rise of a vibrant and vast motherhood movement in the United States over the last decade has paved the way for more meaningful exploration into the emancipatory potential of motherhood in the 21st century.

## The Encyclopedia

The intent of the encyclopedia is to introduce readers to and provide information on the central terms, concepts, topics, issues, themes, debates, theories, and texts of this new discipline of motherhood studies as well as to examine the topic of motherhood in various contexts such as history and geography and by academic discipline. As with all scholarly fields, motherhood studies comprises a tradition or canon of theoretical texts that constitutes and directs the scholarship of that discipline. The encyclopedia includes an entry for all the influential theorists of maternal scholarship from the pioneering theories of Nancy Chodorow, Adrienne Rich, and Dorothy Dinnerstein of the 1970s; the leading African American maternal scholars such as bell hooks, Patricia Hill Collins, and Dorothy Roberts; to the more recent writings of Ann Crittenden, Judith Warner, and Ayelet Waldman. Additionally, the central and governing terms and concepts of maternal scholarship, such as daugher-centiricty, matraphopia, matroreform, cultural bearing, maternal thinking, motherline, mask of motherhood, intensive mothering, new momism, empowered mothering, homeplace, othermothering, to name but a few, are all included in the encyclopedia. All the principal motherhood poets and novelists are also likewise referenced in the encyclopedia. As well, this reference work provides an overview of the topic of motherhood in many and diverse disciplines, such as anthropology, sociology, psychology, and philosophy, as well it examines the meaning and experience of motherhood in many time periods from classic civilizations to present day. Finally, as the encyclopedia provides a history of motherhood, it also covers issues and events of our current times to feature entries on the mommy blog, the motherhood memoir, terrorism, reproductive technologies, HIV/AIDS, LGBT families, the 21st-century motherhood movement (including entries for contemporary motherhood organizations).

One particular highlight of the encyclopedia is its attention to geographical, cultural and ethnic diversity. The encyclopedia includes an entry for almost every country in the world as well as entries on Aboriginal, Latina/Chicana, South Asian, African American, lesbian, queer, immigrant, adoptive, single, nonresidential, young, poor mothers and mothers with disabilities as well as entries on topics such as motherhood and globalization and trans-nationalism. The creative writing entries likewise include authors and poets from numerous nationalities and ethnicities. As well, in recognition of the explicitly interdisciplinary, multidisciplinary, and cross-disciplinary nature of maternal scholarship the encyclopedia includes entries from a wide range of discipline as well it considers particular themes or issues from several disciplinary perspectives. Finally, while this is an encyclopedia on motherhood, the volumes, in their wide-ranging and far-reaching examination of the topic, cover material central to childhood, family and women's studies, and the larger disciplines of sociology and humanities.

Reading the entries in the encyclopedia, one could forget that maternal scholarship, as a discipline, is still in its infancy; coming into being in the late 1970s and only being established in the last 10 to 15 years. Returning to the words that close Rich's *Of Woman Born*: "We need to imagine a world in which every woman is the presiding genius of her own body. In such a world women will truly create new life, bringing forth not only children (if and as we choose) but the visions, the

thinking necessary to sustain, console and alter human existence—a new relationship to the universe. Sexuality, politics, intelligence, power, motherhood, work, community, intimacy, will develop new meanings; thinking itself will be transformed. This is where we have to begin."

This encyclopedia, in its examination of motherhood from A to Z—from aboriginal mothering to zines—shows that motherhood studies, while still a new discipline, has given new meaning to our usual and familiar understandings of sexuality, work, power, community and the like: indeed it has transformed thinking itself. It is our hope that this encyclopedia will likewise provide a "place to begin" for the study of maternal scholarship.

**Acknowledgments**

In the acknowledgments to my 2004 book *Toni Morrison and Motherhood: A Politics of the Heart*, I cite the narrator's words from Morrison's novel *Song of Solomon* when she comments upon the importance of othermothering for the character Hagar Dead: "She needed what most coloured girls needed: a chorus of mamas, grandmamas, aunts, cousins, sister, neighbors, Sunday school teachers, best girl friends and what all to give her the strength life demanded of her . . . the humor with which to live it." Scholars likewise, I wrote, need a "chorus of mamas" to think and write well. Fortunately, once again with this encyclopaedia I have been blessed with a symphony in my life. Indeed, as I spend these last few hours on the encyclopaedia, I realize that my "chorus of mamas" have done more than support my scholarship, they have given me the very words and music in which to write, or perhaps more appropriately, sing, it. This encyclopedia, the first ever on motherhood, is thus truly the work of many individuals; the many scholars who pioneered motherhood studies, the authors who wrote entries for the encyclopaedia, the scholars whose research informs this project, the many and diverse researchers on motherhood today, my extended kin of scholars and friends, and the many people at Sage Publications whose labor—in both thought and deed—made possible this encyclopedia of motherhood. So my words of thanks are many and wide-ranging.

Thanks first to the pioneers of motherhood scholarship without who this encyclopedia and all motherhood research would not exist; most notably Adrienne Rich, Nancy Chodorow, Sara Ruddick, Miriam Johnson, Paula Caplan, Barbara Katz Rothman, and Patricia Hill Collins. My deepest appreciation as well to the more recent scholars on motherhood who have sustained and enriched the intellectual tradition of maternal scholarship that both made possible and created the need for an encyclopedia of motherhood, including Alice Walker, Mary O'Brien, bell hooks, Audre Lorde, Baba Copper, Marianne Hirsch, Shari Thurer, Tuula Gordon, Sharon Hays, Valerie Walkerdine and Helen Lucy, Susan Maushart, Dorothy Roberts, Patrice di Quinzio, Ann Crittenden, Susan Douglas and Meredith Michaels, Daphne de Marneffe, Judith Warner, Chris Bobel, Ariel Gore, Molly Ladd-Taylor, Andrea Doucet, Bonnie Fox, Kim Anderson, Patrizia Albanese, Marilyn Waring, and Lauri Umansky. I owe particular thanks to the many members of the Association for Research on Mothering (ARM): my thinking on mothering, as always, was nourished and sustained by this fine community of scholars. Indeed, it was the knowledge that I had the scholarship of the Association of Research on Motherhood to draw upon that gave me the confidence to do this encyclopedia, and it was the support of ARM members—in both mind and heart—that enabled me to complete it. Particular thanks are due to Enola Aird, Sharon Abbey, Linn Baran, Chris Bobel, Petra Bueskens, Deborah Byrd, Paula Caplan, Deidre Condit, Christina Cudahy, Jeanette Corbiere Lavell, Deborah Davidson, Rishma Dunlop, Regina Edmonds, Linda Ennis, May Friedman, Nancy Gerber, Diana Gustafson, Fiona Green, Lynn Hallstein-O'Brien, Linda Lisi Juergens, Amber Kinser, Kandee Kosior, Dawn Memee Lavell-Harvard, Gayle Letherby, Jenny Jones, Brenda McGadney, Joanne Minaker, Mary Ruth Marotte, Beth Osnes, Elizabeth Pod-

nieks, Marie Porter, Ruth Panofsky, Joy Rose, Sara Ruddick, Lorri Slepian, Lorna Turnbull, Nicole Willey, Judith Stadtman Tucker, Linda Hunter, Serena Patterson, Gail and Sarah Trimble, Jodi Vandenberg-Daves, and Gina Wong-Wylie.

I am deeply indebted to the Social Science Research Council of Canada and its continued support of my research through various grants, most notably the Standard Research Grant. My deepest appreciation, as always, to Renée Knapp at ARM, whose brilliance, generosity, humor and grit, in work and play, make possible—and survivable—the scholarship I do. Special thanks are due to Geoff Golson and Susan Moskowitz at Golson Media. As someone who earns her income by writing, I am seldom at a loss for words, but in this instance language can not convey the deep appreciation I feel for all that Geoff and Susan have done to deliver this encyclopedia into our hands: tireless, talented, devoted, and diligent are but some of many superlatives that could be used to describe the superb and sustaining support and effort they provided throughout the long labor of this encyclopedia's birth. Finally, my love and gratitude, as always, to my family; in particular my mother Jean O'Reilly, my sister Jennifer O'Reilly, my children Jesse, Erin, and Casey O'Reilly-Conlin, and my life partner Terry Conlin. Thank you for always believing in the importance of my motherhood scholarship. Virginia Woolf once wrote that a woman needs "a room of one's own in order to write." While I would agree that space and time enables a woman to write; it is, at least for me, the respect and support shown by my family for my need to both think and live that makes my writing possible. So thank you for knocking and for coming in.

Andrea O'Reilly
General Editor

# Reader's Guide

## Motherhood and Health

Advice Literature for Mothers
AIDS/HIV and Mothering
Alcoholism
Anxiety
Artificial Insemination
Attention Deficit Disorder
Autism
Becoming a Mother
Birth Control
Birth Goddesses
Breastfeeding
Breastmilk
Cancer and Motherhood
Childbirth
Depression
Displacement
Domestic Labor
Doula
Drug Abuse
Eating Disorders
Emotions
Environments and Mothering
Eugenics
Fertility
Fetal Alcohol Syndrome
Guilt
Learning Disabilities
Maternal Alienation
Maternal Bodies
Maternal Desire
Maternal Eroticism
Maternal Feminism
Maternal Health
Maternal Power/Powerlessness
Maternal Practice
Miscarriage
Mommy Brain
Mother Blame
Mothering and Creativity
Mothering Children With Disabilities
Munchausen Syndrome by Proxy
Obesity and Motherhood
Obstetrics and Gynecology
Natural Mothering
Nursing (Profession) and Motherhood
Overwhelmed Mothers
Postmaternity

Postpartum Depression
Pregnancy
Prenatal Health Care
Reproduction
Reproduction of Mothering
Reproductive Labor
Reproductive Technologies
Sexuality and Mothering
Sons and Mothers
Sterilization
Stillbirth
Sudden Infant Death Syndrome
Surrogate Motherhood
Violence Against Mothers/Children
Wet Nursing

## Motherhood and Society

Activist Mothers of the Disappeared
Adoption
Angel in the House
Art and Mothering
Autobiographies
*Brain, Child*
Buddhism and Mothering
Carework
Caribbean Mothers
Chicana Mothering
Christianity and Mothers
Cultural Bearing
Demeter Press
DES Mothers
Dramatic Arts, Mothers in
Earth Mothers
Equatorial Guinea
Ethnic Mothers
European Union
Fairy Tales, Mothers in
Film, Mothers in
First Nations
Gift Economy
Hinduism
*Hip Mama*
Honduras
Immigrant Mothers
Islam and Motherhood
Jewish Mothers
Judaism and Motherhood
La Leche League

Papua New Guinea
Paraguay
Peru
Philippines
Portugal
Puerto Rico
Qatar
Romania
Russia (and Soviet Union)
Rwanda
Samoa
Saudi Arabia
Senegal
Sierra Leone
Singapore
Slovakia
Slovenia
Somalia
South Africa
Spain
Sri Lanka
Sudan
Suriname
Swaziland
Sweden
Switzerland
Syria
Tajikistan
Tanzania
Thailand
Togo
Tunisia
Turkey
Turkmenistan
Uganda
Ukraine
United Kingdom
Uruguay
Uzbekistan
Venezuela
Vietnam
Yemen
Zambia
Zimbabwe

## Motherhood in the United States

Alabama
Alaska

Arizona
Arkansas
California
Colorado
Connecticut
Delaware
Florida
Georgia
Hawaii
Idaho
Illinois
Indiana
Iowa
Kansas
Kentucky
Louisiana
Maine
Maryland
Massachusetts
Michigan
Minnesota
Mississippi
Missouri
Montana
Nebraska
Nevada
New Hampshire
New Jersey
New Mexico
New York
North Carolina
North Dakota
Ohio
Oklahoma
Oregon
Pennsylvania
Rhode Island
South Carolina
South Dakota
Tennessee
Texas
Utah
Vermont
Virginia
Washington
West Virginia
Wisconsin
Wyoming

## Motherhood Studies

Aboriginal Mothering
Academe and Mothering
Activism, Maternal
African Diaspora
Ambivalence, Maternal
Animal Species and Motherhood
Anthropology of Mothering
Antiracist Mothering
Association for Research on Mothering
Biography and Motherhood
Birth Imagery, Metaphor, and Myth
Capitalism and Motherhood
Communism and Motherhood
Civil Rights Movement and Motherhood
Consumerism and Motherhood
Cross-Cultural Perspectives on Motherhood
Dialectics of Reproduction
Ecofeminism and Mothering
Economics of Motherhood
Economy and Motherhood
Ectogenesis
Essentialism and Mothering
Feminism and Mothering
Feminist Mothering
Feminist Theory and Mothering
Future of Motherhood
Genocide and Mothers
Globalization and Mothering
Idealization of Mothers
Infidelity and Motherhood
Institution of Motherhood
Intergenerational Trauma
International Mothers Network
*Journal for the Association for
   Research on Mothering*
Maternal Abject (Kristeva)
Maternal Authenticity
Maternal *Künstlerroman*
Maternal Mortality
Maternal Pedogogy
Maternal Subjectivities
Maternal Thinking (Ruddick)
Matraphobia
Matricide
Matrifocality
Matrilineal
Matroreform

Mauritius
Mother/Daughter Plot (Hirsch)
Motherhood Endowment (Rathbone)
Mother Outlaws (Group)
Mother Outlaws (Rich)
Motherself
Nationalism and Motherhood
New French Feminism and Motherhood
Noncustodial Mothering
Paganism (New Paganism)
   and Mothering
Patriarchal Ideology of Motherhood
Philosophy and Motherhood
Postcolonialism and Mothering
Price of Motherhood (Crittenden)
Psychoanalysis and Motherhood
Psychology of Motherhood
Scientific Motherhood
Self-Identity
Semiotic, Maternal (Kristeva)
Sensitive Mothering
   (Walkerdine and Lucey)
Social Construction of Motherhood
Social Reproduction
Transnationalism
Waring, Marilyn
Warner, Judith (Motherhood Religion)

## Prominent Mothers

Adams, Abigail (Smith)
Allende, Isabel
Atwood, Margaret
Benjamin, Jessica
Bernard, Jesse
Blakely, Mary Kay
Bombeck, Erma
Brooks, Gwendeolyn
Buchanan, Andrea
Bush, Barbara
Caplan, Paula J.
Chodorow, Nancy
Cisneros, Sandra
Clifton, Lucille
Clinton, Hillary Rodham
Collins, Patricia Hill
Columbus, Christopher, Mother of
Crittenden, Ann
Danticatt, Edwidge

# List of Articles

Belarus
Belgium
Belize
Benin
Benjamin, Jessica
Bernard, Jesse
Beta Mom
Bhutan
Bible, Mothers in the
Biography and Motherhood
Birth Control
Birth Goddesses
Birth Imagery, Metaphor, and Myth
Birth Mothers
Bisexuality
Blakely, Mary Kay
Body Image
Bolivia
Bombeck, Erma
Bosnia and Herzegovina
Botswana
*Brain, Child*
Brazil
Breastfeeding
Breastmilk
Brooks, Gwendeolyn
Buchanan, Andrea
Buddhism and Mothering
Bulgaria
Burkina Faso
Burundi
Bush, Barbara

**C**
California
Cambodia
Cameroon
Canada
Cancer and Motherhood
Cape Verde
Capitalism and Motherhood
Caplan, Paula J.
Care Giving
Carework
Caribbean Mothers
Celebrity Motherhood
Central African Republic
Chad

Chicana Mothering
Child Abuse
Childbirth
Childcare
Child Custody and the Law
Childhood
Childlessness
Child Poverty
Children
Chile
China
Chodorow, Nancy
Christianity and Mothers
Cisneros, Sandra
Civil Rights Movement and Motherhood
Class and Mothering
Clifton, Lucille
Clinton, Hillary Rodham
Clytemnestra
Code Pink
Collins, Patricia Hill
Colombia
Colorado
Columbus, Christopher, Mother of
Communism and Motherhood
Community Mothering
Co-Mothering
Conflict Zones, Mothering in
Congo
Congo, Democratic Republic of the
Connecticut
Consumerism and Motherhood
Co-Parenting
Costa Rica
Crittenden, Ann
Croatia
Cross-Cultural Perspectives on Motherhood
Cuba
Cultural Bearing
Cybermothering
Cyprus
Czech Republic

**D**
Danticat, Edwidge
Dating and Single Mothers
Daughter-Centricity
Daughters and Mothers

North Carolina
North Dakota
Norway
Nursing (Profession) and Motherhood

**O**
Oakley, Ann
Obama, Michelle
Obesity and Motherhood
O'Brien, Mary
Obstetrics and Gynecology
Ohio
Oklahoma
Older Mothers
Olds, Sharon
Olson, Tillie
Oman
Onassis, Jacqueline Kennedy. *See* Kennedy
   Onassis, Jacqueline
Opt-Out Revolution
Oregon
Organizations
Ostriker, Alicia
Other Mothering
Outlaw Mothers. *See* Mother Outlaws (Rich)
Overwhelmed Mothers

**P**
Paganism (New Paganism)
   and Mothering
Pakistan
Palestine
Paley, Grace Goodrich
Palin, Sarah
Panama
Papua New Guinea
Paraguay
Parks, Rosa
Patriarchal Ideology of Motherhood
Peace and Mothering
Peace Movements and Mothering
Pearson, Allison
Pennsylvania
Peru
Philippines
Philosophy and Motherhood
Planned Parenthood
Plath, Sylvia

Poetry, Mothers in
Poland
Politics and Mothers
Pollack, Sandra
Popular Culture and Mothering
Portugal
Postcolonialism and Mothering
Postmaternity
Postpartum Depression
Poverty and Mothering
Pratt, Minnie Bruce
Pregnancy
Prenatal Health Care
Preschool Children
*Price of Motherhood* (Crittenden)
Pronatalism
Prostitution and Motherhood
Psychoanalysis and Motherhood
Psychology of Motherhood
Public Policy and Mothers
Puerto Rico

**Q**
Qatar
Queer Mothering. *See* Lesbian Mothering; LGBTQ
   Families and Motherhood; Transgender
   Parenting

**R**
Race and Racism
Reagan, Nancy
Refugee Mothers
Religion and Mothering
Reproduction
Reproduction of Mothering
Reproductive Justice/Rights Movements
Reproductive Labor
Reproductive Technologies
Republican Motherhood
Residential School and Mothers/First Nations
Rhode Island
Rich, Adrienne
Roberts, Dorothy
Romania
Roman Mothers
Ross, Loretta
Rothman, Barbara Katz
Royal Mothers

# List of Contributors

Abbey, Sharon M.
Brock University

Adams, Sarah LaChance
University of Oregon

Adeniran, Adebusuyi Isaac
Obafemi Awolowo University

Aird, Enola
Independent Scholar

Aksit, Elif Ekin
Ankara University

Alban, Gillian M.E.
Dogus University

Albanese, Patrizia
Ryerson University

Al-Botmeh, Fatima
Independent Researcher

Alcalde, M. Cristina
University of Kentucky

Alcalde, M. Gabriela
Kentucky Health Justice Network

Allen, Sonja M.
Queen's University

Allison, Jill
Memorial University of Newfoundland & Labrador

Altinay, Rustem Ertug
Bogazici University, Istanbul

Antolini, Katharine Lane
West Virginia Wesleyan College

Arista, Michele C.
Independent Scholar

Arreola, Veronica I.
University of Illinois at Chicago

Bailey-Fakhoury, Chasity
Wayne State University

Baker, Carrie N.
Smith College

Baraitser, Lisa
Birkbeck, University of London

Barlow, Constance A.
University of Calgary

Barnes, Diana Lynn
Center for Postpartum Health

Barnhill, John H.
Independent Scholar

Barry, Cheryl Leah
University of Calgary

Bastia, Tanja
University of Manchester

Bauer, Deborah L.
University of Central Florida

Bjørnholt, Margunn
University of Oslo

Bobel, Christina
University of Massachusetts, Boston

Bode, Rita
Trent University

Boon, Sonja
Memorial University of
Newfoundland and Labrador

Boslaugh, Sarah E.
Washington University School of Medicine

Bouvard, Marguerite G.
Brandeis University

Bowles-Adarkwa, Linda
San Francisco State University

Boyd, Susan B.
University of British Columbia

Brady, Geraldine
Coventry University

Branch, Nicole T.
Howard University

Brooks, Kinitra D.
University of Texas at San Antonio

Brown, Geraldine
Coventry University

Brown, Ivana
Rutgers University

Bueskens, Petra
Deakin University

Burkett, Jennifer L.
University of Central Arkansas

Burstrem, Jessica B.
University of Arizona

Burton, Wendy E.
University of the Fraser Valley

Busse, Erika
University of Minnesota

Butterfield, Elizabeth
Georgia Southern University

Byrne, Nan
Independent Scholar

Cade, Roshaunda D.
Webster University

Campbell, Arlene
York University

Canelo, Kayla S.
California State University,
Stanislaus

Caplan, Paula J.
Harvard University

Caporusso, Catherine
University of Illinois at Chicago

Caron, Sarah W.
Independent Scholar

Carranza, Mirna E.
McMaster University

Cash, Sherri Goldstein
Utica College

Cellio, Jen
Northern Kentucky University

Chaban, Stephanie
Independent Scholar

Chamberlain Froese, Jean
Save the Mothers

Cheney, Emily R.
Spelman College

Chernyayeva, Natalia
University of Iowa

Cohen, Rina
York University

Comerford, Lynn
California State University,
East Bay

Condit, Deirdre M.
Virginia Commonwealth University

Corfield, Justin
Geelong Grammar School

Coulter, Myrl
University of Alberta

Craig, Lyn
University of New South Wales

Crawford, B. Scott
Radford University

Cuomo, Amy
University of West Georgia

Daigle, Christine
Brock University

Davidson, Adenike Marie
Fisk University

Davidson, Deborah
York University

Davidson, Diana
University of Alberta

DeLap, Alpha S.
University of Washington

de la Porte, Susan Elizabeth
University of KwaZulu-Natal

Deutsch, James I.
Smithsonian Institution

DeWan, Jennifer K.
Independent Scholar

Dillaway, Heather E.
Wayne State University

Dombroski, Kelly
Australian National University

Doucet, Andrea
Carleton University

Drew, Patricia
California State University, East Bay

Duffy, Donna
University of North Carolina,
Greensboro

Duncan, Ann W.
University of Virginia

Dunnewold, Ann
Independent Scholar

Duquaine-Watson, Jillian M.
University of Texas at Dallas

Dymond, Justine
Springfield College

Edmonds, Regina M.
Assumption College

Eichler, Margrit
University of Toronto

Engeman, Cassandra D.
University of California,
Santa Barbara

Ennis, Jillian Davina
Independent Scholar

Ennis, Linda R.
York University

Esterberg, Kristin G.
Salem State College

Falvey, Kate
New York City College of Technology

Fancher, Jill B.
Washington State University, Vancouver

Federer, Lisa
University of North Texas

Feng, Yuan
ActionAid International China

Finn, Melissa
York University

Foster, Mira C.
San Francisco State University

Francis, Ara
University of California, Davis

Freiburger, Melissa A.
University of Kansas

French, Sarah W.
Washington State University

Friedman, May
York University

Froese, Jean Chamberlain
Independent Scholar

Froese, Thomas
Independent Scholar

Fumia, Doreen
Ryerson University

Gamber, Cayo
George Washington University

Garrett, Sarah B.
University of California, Berkeley

Gatrell, Caroline
Lancaster University

Gillespie, Gill
University of Northumbria

Goettner-Abendroth, Heide
International Academy HAGIA

Gordon, Kelly Carolyn
Brevard College

Gotlib, Anna
State University of New York,
Binghamton

Gott, K.C.
East Tennessee State University

Graham, Natalie
Michigan State University

Green, Fiona Joy
University of Winnipeg

Grewal, Indera
Royal Holloway, University of London

Griffith, Alison I.
York University

Grigorovich, Alisa
York University

Grzyb, Amanda
University of Western Ontario

Guerrina, Roberta
University of Surrey

Gurr, Barbara
University of Connecticut

Gustafson, Diana L.
Memorial University of Newfoundland

Hamil-Luker, Jenifer
University of North Carolina at Greensboro

Hant, Myrna
University of California, Los Angeles

Harper, Susan
Mountain View College

Hartsock, Ralph
University of North Texas

Hattery, Angela
Wake Forest University

Heitner, Keri L.
University of Phoenix

Henderson, Heike
Boise State University

Hernandez, Marcia
University of the Pacific

Herrera, Cristina
California State University, Fresno

Herzog, Shawna
California State University, Fresno

Hidalgo, Danielle Antoinette
University of California,
Santa Barbara

Hinton Riley, Michele
St. Joseph's College of Maine

Holstine Vander Valk, Donna
Independent Scholar

Hryciuk, Renata Ewa
Warsaw University

Huang, Yu-ling
State University of New York,
Binghamton

Hutner, Heidi
State University of New York, Stony Brook

Isgro, Kirsten
State University of New York, Plattsburgh

Jaeckel, Monika
Independent Scholar

Jennings, Miranda E.
University of Massachussets Amherst

Jolly, Natalie
University of Washington, Tacoma

Jones, Rita M.
Lehigh University

Justin, Shaista
Independant Scholar

Kaptan, Senem
Sabanci University

Kauppinen, Kaisa
Finnish Institute of Occupational Health

Kaur Sangha, Jasjit
University of Toronto

Kentlyn, Sue
University of Queensland

Kingston, Anna
University College, Cork

Kinser, Amber E.
East Tennessee State University

Koritko, Andrea
Independent Scholar

Korolczuk, Elzbieta
Polish Academy of Sciences

Kte'pi, Bill
Independent Scholar

Kutz-Flamenbaum, Rachel V.
University of Pittsburgh

Lang, Sharon D.
University of Redlands

Leane, Máire
University College Cork

Lee, Joon Sun
Hunter College
City University of New York

Lengel, Lara
Bowling Green State University

LeSavoy, Barbara
State University of New York, Brockport

Letherby, Gayle
University of Plymouth

Levine, Ronda Lee
Independent Scholar

Lewiecki-Wilson, Cynthia
Miami University

Lewis, Carolyn Herbst
Louisiana State University

Leyser, Ophra
University of Kansas

Li, Ke
Indiana University Bloomington

Little, Christopher A.J.L.
University of Toronto

Liu, Lichun Willa
University of Toronto

Lovett, Laura L.
University of Massachusetts

Lucas, Sheri
Queen's University

Lyons, Nyla P.
Howard University

Maätita, Florence
Southern Illinois University,
Edwardsville

Mackinlay, Elizabeth
University of Queensland

Magwaza, Thenjiwe
University of KwaZulu-Natal

Maher, JaneMaree
Monash University

Mahoney, Jill
Murray State University

Marksova-Tominova, Michaela
Independent Scholar

Marotta, Marsha V.
Westfield State College

Marotte, Mary Ruth
University of Central Arkansas

Marr, Elisha
Ferris State University

Mayseless, Ofra
University of Haifa

Melis Yelsali Parmaksiz, Pinar
Ankara University

Mennill, Sally
University of British Columbia

Mercado-López, Larissa M.
University of Texas, San Antonio

Miller, Kim
Wheaton College

Milligan, Eleanor
Griffith University

Minaker, Joanne C.
Grant MacEwan College

Monson, Sarah
Minnesota State University, Mankato

Morganroth Gullette, Margaret
Brandeis University

Morolong, Bantu L.
University of Botswana

Mortenson, Joani
University of British Columbia,
Okanagan

Muller, Vivienne
Queensland University of Technology

Murphy-Geiss, Gail
Colorado College

Musher, Sharon Ann
Richard Stockton College of New Jersey

Nagakura, Wakasa
Columbia University

Namaba, Edith G.
Howard University

Nemzoff, Ruth
Brandeis Women's Studies Research Center

Nichols, Tracy R.
University of North Carolina at Greensboro

Nowlan Suart, Theresa
Loyalist College

Oakley Torres, Shirley
University of Memphis

Oberman, Yael
Independent Scholar

O'Brien Hallstein, D. Lynn
Boston University

Ojong, Vivian Besem
University of KwaZulu-Natal

O'Reilly, Andrea
York University

Ortiz, Christi Marie
Aurora Behavioral Health

Ortiz, Fernando A.
Alliant International University

Osnes, Beth
University of Colorado,
Boulder

Panofsky, Ruth
Ryerson University

Pantea, Maria-Carmen
Babes Bolyai University

Pantuso, Terri B.
University of Texas, San Antonio

Parsons, Jacqueline Ciccio
St. Mary's University

Pearson, A. Fiona
Central Connecticut State University

Pernigotti, Elisabetta
Université Paris 8 Saint-Denis

Perry-Samaniego, Lenora
University of Texas, San Antonio

Peters, Carolyn J.
University of Manitoba

Petit, Joan
Portland State University

Plant, Rebecca Jo
University of California, San Diego

Podnieks, Elizabeth
Ryerson University

Polacek, Kelly Myer
Fielding Graduate University

Policek, Nicoletta
University of Lincoln

Porter, Marie
University of Queensland

Powell Wolfe, Andrea
Ball State University

Premo Steele, Cassie
University of South Carolina

Prono, Luca
Independent Scholar

Purdy, Elizabeth
Independent Scholar

Randall, D'Arcy Clare
University of Texas
at Austin

Reid-Boyd, Elizabeth
Edith Cowan University

Reuter, Shelley Zipora
Concordia University

Reviere, Rebecca
Howard University

Reznowski, Gabriella
Washington State University

Richards, Amy
Independent Scholar

Richter-Devroe, Sophie
University of Exeter

Robbins-Herring, Kittye Delle
Mississippi State University

Rodgers, Julie
National University of Ireland

Rose, Joy
Mamapalooza Inc.

Rosenzweig, Rosie
Brandeis University

Roth-Johnson, Danielle
University of Nevada, Las Vegas

Rottenbrg-Rosler, Biri
Haifa University

Royce, Tracy
University of California,
Santa Barbara

Ruah-Midbar, Marianna
University of Haifa

Samblanet, Sarah
Kent State University

Sanchez Walker, Marjorie
California State University, Stanislaus

Sanmiguel-Valderrama, Olga
University of Cincinnati

Sardadvar, Karin
University of Vienna

Schalge, Susan L.
Minnesota State University, Mankato

Schultz, Renée
Independent Scholar

Schwartz-Bechet, Barbara
Bowie State University

Schwartzman, Jayme
University of Connecticut

Shroff, Farah
Women's Health Research Institute

Siddique, Julie Ahmad
City University of New York

Smith Koslowski, Alison
University of Edinburgh

Smith, Earl
Wake Forest University

Smith, Tracy L.
Indiana State University

Sobie, Sherryll
Independent Scholar

Soliday, Elizabeth
Washington State University, Vancouver

Spigel, Sigal
University of Cambridge

Stackman, Valerie R.
Howard University

Stephens, Angela
Sojourner-Douglass College

Stitt, Jocelyn Fenton
Minnesota State University

Sulik, Gayle A.
Texas Woman's University

Sutherland, Jean-Anne
University of North Carolina, Wilmington

Tayeb, Lamia
High Institute of Human
Sciences in Tunis

Taylor, Tiffany
Kent State University

Theodor, Ithamar
University of Haifa

Thern Smith, Jessica
University of Tennessee

Thibodeaux, Julianna F.
Independent Scholar

Thomas, Alice K.
Howard University

Thompson, Mary
James Madison University

Tolley-Stokes, Rebecca
East Tennessee State University

Trammel, Juliana Maria
Savannah State University

Trevino, Marcella Bush
Barry University

Turnbull, Lorna A.
University of Manitoba

Turner, Tracy Zollinger
Independent Scholar

Vallance, Denise
York University

Vancour, Michele L.
Southern Connecticut State University

Vaughan, Genevieve
Independent Scholar

Villalobos, Ana
University of California, Berkeley

Villanueva, Karen Nelson
California Institute of
Integral Studies

Wadhwa, Vandana
Boston University

Wafula, Edith G.
Howard University

Walker, Susan
University of Cambridge

Walks, Michelle
University of British Columbia

Walls, Lori A.
Independent Scholar

Walters-Kramer, Lori
State University of New York, Plattsburgh

Wansink, Susan
Virginia Wesleyan College

Wasserman, Stephanie
Merrimack College

Watson, Alison M. S.
University of St Andrews

Watson-Franke, Maria-Barbara
San Diego State University

Weinberger, Margaret J.
Bowling Green State University

Wies, Jennifer R.
Xavier University

Wilkins, Agata
University of Warsaw

Willey, Nicole L.
Kent State University

Willey, Tiffany A.
Independent Scholar

Wilson, Corinne
Coventry University

Wilson, Maureen E.
University of Massachusetts Amherst

Wilson Cooper, Camille
University of North Carolina, Greensboro

Wong-Wylie, Gina
Athabasca University

Woods, Laurie E.
Vanderbilt University

Wright Miller, Gill
Denison University

Wright Williams, Dawn
Georgia Perimeter College

Wyatt-Nichol, Heather
University of Baltimore

Xu, Xueqing
York University

Zamir, Sara
Ben-Gurion University, Eilat

Žnidaršic Žagar, Sabina
University of Primorska, Koper

# Chronology of Motherhood

**1570 B.C.E.**—Queen Nefertari of Egypt defies cultural conventions by serving as adviser to her husband, King Ahmose, and co-rules Egypt with her son after her husband's death.

**1473 B.C.E.**—Queen Hatsheput, a co-regent of Egypt along with her minor stepson since 1479, declares herself Pharaoh. Her tenure as ruler is the longest in Egyptian history for a female.

**Circa 1250 B.C.E.**—The Romans begin celebrating mothers by honoring the Mother Goddess Cybele each March.

**350 B.C.E.**—Greek philosopher and empiricist Aristotle generates the theory that a woman's uterus travels throughout her body in response to internal forces that include the woman's own emotional state. Aristotle also posits that women are imperfect men who have never truly developed physically.

**1405**—French writer and single mother Christine de Pizan publishes *The Book of the City of Ladies* in an effort to rebut character attacks on women by presenting them as mothers, wives, and political and social leaders through the eyes of Lady Reason, Lady Rectitude, and Lady Justice.

**1533**—Anne Boleyn, the second wife of Henry VIII, becomes Queen of England. Later the same year she gives birth to Elizabeth I, who becomes one of the best-loved English monarchs of all time. Three years after Elizabeth's birth, Boleyn is beheaded for high treason. In reality, her only crime is that she fails to provide the king with a male heir.

**1568**—The first incidence of planned family colonization in North America begins with the arrival of 225 Spanish settlers in what is modern-day South Carolina.

**1587**—One day after her arrival at Roanoke Island, British immigrant Eleanor White Dare gives birth to daughter Virginia, the first English child born in America.

**1607**—Twelve-year-old Pocahontas, the daughter of Chief Powhattan, saves the life of Englishman John Smith. In 1614, Pocahontas marries Englishman John Rolfe and gives birth to a son.

**1608**—Anne Forrest and her maid, Anne Burras, are the first Englishwomen to arrive in Jamestown, Virginia. Forrest's fate is unknown, but Burras marries John Laydon and bears four daughters.

**1620**—Arriving on the *Mayflower*, 13-year-old Mary Chilton is the first English female to set foot on Plymouth Rock. Her arrival is depicted in the painting *The Landing of the Pilgrims*. Chilton marries fellow Pilgrim John Winslow and gives birth to 10 children.

**1630**—Nurse and midwife Tryntje Jones immigrates to the United States from the Netherlands and becomes the first female to practice medicine in America.

**1632**—Commonly known as "The Woman's Lawyer," *The Lawes and Resolutions of Women's Rights: A Methodical Collection of Such Statutes and Customes, With the Cases, Opinions, Arguments and Points of Learning in the Law, as Do Properly Concerne Women* becomes the first English-language book to be published on the rights of women. The author, who is known only as T. E., offers a detailed summary of marriage, divorce, courtship, and custody laws.

**1637**—A pregnant Anne Hutchinson, who ultimately gives birth to 15 children, is convicted of sedition in Boston because of her religious beliefs. She and her family are banished to Rhode Island.

**1650**—The poems of Anne Dudley Bradstreet, the mother of eight, are published without her knowledge in London, earning her a place in history as the first American female poet to be published in England.

**1680**—Robert Filmer's *Patriarcha* defends the divine right of kings and the patriarchal system, which withholds political rights from women and prevents mothers from having authority over themselves and their children.

**1689**—John Locke's *Two Treatises of Government* is published posthumously, refuting Robert Filmer's arguments. Locke contends that mothers have equal authority with fathers over the children they have created.

**1692**—The Salem Witch Trials begin in Massachusetts. Mary Easty, the mother of seven, is among the victims. She and seven other accused witches are hanged on September 22.

**1702**—After the death of her brother William III, Queen Anne succeeds to the English throne. None of her 17 children survive her, and her German nephew, George III, becomes the king of England when she dies in 1714. His subsequent actions lead the American colonies to rebel against the Mother Country in 1776, creating the United States of America.

**1704**—On February 29, mothers in the settlement of Deerfield, Massachusetts, watch in horror as French and Abenaki attackers kill 25 children. Many victims are infants who are killed by bashing their heads against hard objects.

**1716**—The State of New York issues its first licenses to midwives.

**1773**—After helping to disguise the men who take part in the Boston Tea Party as Mohawk Indians, Sarah Bradlee Fulton becomes known as the Mother of the Boston Tea Party. During the Revolution, Fulton serves as a courier for American troops.

**1776**—On March 31, as the Continental Congress considers the ramifications of creating a nation, Abigail Adams writes to her husband John, a delegate and future president, chiding him to "remember the ladies and be more generous and favorable to them than your ancestors." Four of the Adams's six children live to adulthood, and John Quincy became the sixth president of the United States in 1824.

**1776**—Although she never has children of her own, Mother Ann Lee becomes the matriarch and founder of the Shaker Colony in New York's Albany County.

**1776–1777**—During the desolate winter at Valley Forge, Pennsylvania, when American troops are starving, Catherine Littlefield Greene remains with her husband, Major General Nathanael Greene. Over the next eight years, Greene bears five children, naming the first two after George and Martha Washington.

1784—Midwife Martha Ballard, who gave birth to nine children, dies at the age of 77. She leaves a diary chronicling her lengthy career and depicting the daily lives of women in 18th-century America.

1789—Known as "Lady Washington," Martha Washington, who has survived both of the children from her first marriage, moves into presidential headquarters with her husband and two grandchildren when George Washington becomes the first president of the United States.

1790—Along with other women, mothers who meet suffrage requirements are enfranchised in New Jersey. Woman suffrage is rescinded in the state in 1807.

1792—Mary Wollstonecraft, a British writer living in France, publishes *A Vindication of the Rights of Women* to refute the patriarchal argument that women do not deserve political rights because they are inherently incapable of rationality. Five years later Wollstonecraft gives birth to daughter Mary who pens the classic *Frankenstein* in 1818.

1793—Catherine Littlefield Greene, the widow of General Nathanael Greene and the mother of five children, proposes that her boarder Eli Whitney invent the cotton gin. Whitney's invention revolutionizes the cotton industry and inadvertently increases the demand for slaves in the American South.

1797—Mother and daughter philanthropists Isabella Graham and Joanna Graham Bethune establish the Society for the Relief of Poor Widows and Small Children in New York City.

1800—Abigail Adams becomes the first in a succession of First Ladies to live in the White House. Her husband John loses the election to his friend and nemesis Thomas Jefferson, and the Adams family returns to Massachusetts after only a few months in Washington, D.C.

1805—Weeks after giving birth, Sacajawea, a Shoshone, begins serving as an unofficial guide for the Lewis and Clark Expedition. The nursing mother leads the explorers across thousands of miles from the Dakotas to the Rocky Mountains.

1811—During a 3,500-mile trek from Missouri to Oregon, Marie Dorian, gives birth to her third child while serving as a guide to fur-trading magnate John Jacob Astor.

1812—American missionary Ann Hasseltine Judson gives birth to two children while serving in Burma. Neither child survives.

1819—Kaahumanu, the favorite wife of King Kamehameha of Hawaii, inherits his throne, along with their son Liholiho (Kamehameha II). She establishes the first legal code of the islands, which include the right to trial by jury.

1821—Lucretia Mott, the mother of six children, is officially recognized as a minister by the Society of Friends. An active abolitionist, Mott soon realizes that women are discriminated against within the movement.

1821—A strong supporter of British writer Mary Wollstonecraft, Hannah Mather Crocker, a Bostonian mother of ten, publishes *Observations on the Real Rights of Women*.

1824—Mary Randolph, a member of the Virginia elite, publishes the first American cookbook. Of her eight children, only four survive to adulthood.

1826—Thomas Jefferson dies at Monticello after using his prodigious legal skills to write a will leaving his estate directly to his daughter Martha, bypassing the existing mandate that married women's inheritances become the property of their husbands.

1827—Former slave Sojourner Truth convinces a court of law that her son Peter has illegally been transported to Alabama as a slave in violation of New York's 1810 law ensuring gradual emancipation.

1828—Sarah Buell Hale, the widowed mother of five young children, begins publishing *Ladies' Magazine*.

**1832**—The Boston Lying-In Hospital is founded as a training ground for physicians. Unlike the poor women who become patients, the city's more affluent women continue to give birth at home.

**1836**—Angelina Grimké, who has relocated from Charleston, South Carolina, to Philadelphia, Pennsylvania, issues *An Appeal to the Christian Women of the South* in which she draws attention to the fact that large numbers of black children are sired by white slave owners. Southerners are so incensed by her accusations that postmasters ban the book throughout the South.

**1837**—Queen Victoria of England succeeds to the British throne at the age of 18. The mother of nine children, Victoria's reign of 64 years is the longest in British history.

**1838**—In Alexandria, Virginia, a slave woman strangles two of her four children to prevent their being sold into slavery. The other children are rescued before they suffer a similar fate.

**1843**—Dr. Oliver Wendell Holmes generates heated debate by arguing that many new mothers are dying from puerperal fever because physicians spread germs by not washing their hands between seeing patients.

**1847**—Scottish physician James Simpson is the first to use anesthesia to mitigate the pain of childbirth.

**1847**—In Vienna, a study is released indicating that the death rate in male-operated maternity rates is 437 percent higher than in a similar ward run by midwives.

**1847**—A daughter is born to abolitionists Abby Kelly and Stephen Symonds Foster. The couple agrees that she will continue to lecture on slavery and women's rights while he remains at home with baby daughter Alla.

**1848**—After meeting at the London Anti Slavery Convention where women are hidden behind a curtain and prohibited from voting, Americans Elizabeth Cady Stanton and Lucretia Mott make plans to hold a women's rights convention. The Seneca Falls Convention has significant impact on the life of mothers, demanding that public attention be paid to women's issues ranging from suffrage to the right of married women to control their own property.

**1848**—New York becomes the first state to pass a comprehensive Married Women's Property Act. The act is motivated not by a desire to extend the scope of women rights but by the desire of fathers to see daughters rather than sons-in-law inherit property.

**1849**—Elizabeth Blackwell, a graduate of New York's Geneva Medical College, is forced to attend classes for midwives and nurses when she arrives in Paris to begin postgraduate studies. In England, Blackwell is greeted cordially by the medical community with the exception of both males and females who work in the department of female diseases.

**1850**—Oregon passes the Land Donation Act, permitting a married woman to hold one-half of a couple's allotted 640 acreage in her own name. Single women are also allowed to hold 320 acres.

**1851**—British philosopher and economist John Stuart Mill and Harriet Taylor, who later becomes his wife, publish "The Enfranchisement of Women." Mill is a strong advocate of birth control and insists that men do themselves a disservice by subjugating women and depriving society of all that women have to offer.

**1852**—Abolitionist and mother of six, Harriet Beecher Stowe publishes the antislavery novel, *Uncle Tom's Cabin*. The book is credited with being a direct cause of the Civil War.

**1852**—Feminist Amelia Bloomer launches a campaign to win the right for wives of abusive husbands to obtain divorces.

**1854**—Elizabeth Cady Stanton testifies before the New York legislature about the need for married women to gain additional control of inheritances and any wages they earn.

**1855**—Known as "Jennie June," Jane Cunningham Croly, a *New York Tribune* reporter and the mother of five, becomes the first American woman to work behind the desk of a major newspaper.

**1855**—Physicians Margaret and Emily Blackwell open the New York Infirmary for Women and Children with an all-female staff. Located in the Eleventh Ward, their clients are mostly immigrants. Throughout its history, the infirmary serves as a significant training ground for female physicians.

**1862**—German-born Dr. Marie Zakrzewska opens the New England Hospital for Women and Children in Boston. As in the New York Infirmary for Women and Children, the staff of the Boston hospital is composed entirely of females.

**1867**—After losing her husband and four children in a yellow fever epidemic, Mary Harris Jones, who becomes known as Mother Jones, devotes her life to improving working conditions in the United States.

**1870**—Louisa May Alcott publishes *Little Women* in two parts. Volume I follows the lives of Jo March and her sisters Meg, Beth, and Amy through the trials of growing up without their father, who is serving as a Union chaplain during the Civil War. Volume II depicts the lives of the surviving sisters as the eldest marries and gives birth to twins. Two sequels further chronicle the adventures of the March family.

**1870**—On December 10, the Wyoming Territory grants women legal equality, giving females the right to vote, own property, sign contracts, sue and be sued, and serve on juries. The Utah Territory follows suit, and Eliza A. Swain becomes the first women in the entire world to cast her vote in a general election.

**1872**—Jane Wells invents the baby jumper, providing mothers with a means of entertaining babies who are not yet walking.

**1874**—Jennie Jerome, a member of New York's elite, marries Lord Randolph Churchill. Later that year, she gives birth to a son, whom she names Winston. He grows up to be one of the foremost statesmen of the 20th century.

**1879**—In Copenhagen, Denmark, Henrik Ibsen publishes the play, *A Doll's House,* in which his protagonist Nora Helmer challenges her husband's contention that her most important role in life is that of wife and mother by insisting that her chief purpose is to be "a reasonable human being, just as you are."

**1880**—Based on the rationale that mothers have a serious stake in the education of their children, the women of New York are granted the right to vote in school board elections.

**1881**—The first birth control clinic in the world opens in the Netherlands. Interested parties flock to the Netherlands to observe the clinic, which becomes the model for clinics in other countries.

**1881**—At Harvard, Williamina Fleming, a single mother, becomes the first female hired to do mathematical calculations. She is subsequently able to identify and classify some 10,000 celestial bodies.

**1889**—Jane Addams and Ellen Gates Starr open Hull House in Chicago to serve the needs of immigrant mothers and their children.

**1891**—Impressionist painter Mary Cassatt, an American, holds a one-woman show in Paris. Although she never became a mother, Cassatt's favorite subjects are mothers and children.

**1892**—Charlotte Perkins Stetson (Gilman) publishes the short story, "The Yellow Wallpaper," which is ostensibly based on her own experiences with postpartum depression.

**1897**—Led by Alice McLellan Birney and Phoebe Apperson Hearst, the National Congress of Mothers is held in Washington, D.C. Although the two women expect a turnout of only 500 or so, more than 2,000 people attend the conference. This group forms the foundation for the Parent–Teachers Association.

**1900**—According to government reports, one-half of all babies born in the United States at the turn of the century are delivered by midwives.

**1902**—Britain establishes a licensing and oversight board for midwives with the passage of the English Midwives Act.

**1905**—Dancer Isadora Duncan flaunts social mores by giving birth to a child out of wedlock. In 1913, she refuses to marry the father of her second child. Both children are later killed in an accident, and Duncan is killed in a freak accident in France in 1926 when her fashionably long scarf becomes entangled in an automobile wheel.

**1906**—New York public health official Dr. Josephine Baker encourages new mothers to breastfeed their babies in order to avoid exposing them to milk that may be contaminated.

**1907**—Women's rights advocates in Austria launch a campaign to win six weeks' maternity leave for new mothers and 10 weeks' leave for nursing mothers.

**1907**—After the death of her financier husband, Russell Sage, Margaret Slocum Sage, establishes the Russell Sage Foundation and spends the rest of her life being active in philanthropic causes and documenting the history of women.

**1908**—Julia Ward Howe, the mother of six and the author of "The Battle Hymn of the Republic," becomes the first woman to be inducted into the American Academy of Arts and Letters.

**1909**—Writer Charlotte Perkins Gilman publishes *Herland*, a female utopian novel in which the burdens of motherhood are ostensibly lifted by instituting communal nurseries and kitchens.

**1910**—Writer Kathleen Norris chronicles the living and working condition of Irish immigrants to the United States in *Mother*.

**1911**—The new social insurance program in Great Britain provides for maternity allowances in a limited number of cases.

**1912**—After 10,000 female mill employees join a strike in Lawrence, Massachusetts, 35 mothers are charged with "child neglect." Charges are later dropped, and the women are instrumental in the strike's success. Widowed mother Mary Heaton Vorse uses the strike to launch a career as an American labor journalist.

**1912**—Throughout the United States, debates rage concerning the rights of mothers to maintain custody in divorce cases, and legislators begin addressing the issue of government aid for mothers who are impoverished in cases of divorce and desertion.

**1912**—Although she never gives birth to a single child, Juliet Gordon Low finds a way to mother generations of young girls by founding the Girl Scouts in Savannah, Georgia.

**1914**—Congress establishes the second Sunday in May of each year as Mother's Day.

**1914**—Birth control activist Margaret Sanger, whose mother had experienced 18 pregnancies, is arrested for including information on birth control in *The Woman Rebel*.

**1914**—Katharine Anthony, a niece of suffragist Susan B. Anthony, reveals in her study of the impact of harsh working conditions on Philadelphia mothers that 370 mothers have experienced the deaths of 437 babies.

**1915**—Norway passes the Castberg Law, which provides for children born to "unmarried parents" to carry the father's name and inherit his property as long as paternity is not disputed.

**1916**—Margaret Sanger and her sister, Ethel Byrne, open a birth control clinic in Brooklyn, New York. After ten days in which they see more than 500 women, most of them poor immigrants, officials shut down the clinic.

**1916**—Russian-American anarchist Emma Goldman argues that her free speech rights have been violated when she is arrested for publicly advocating birth control.

**1917**—Government officials actively recruit American women to fill a variety of jobs necessary to the war effort when the United States enters World War I on April 6.

**1917**—The Delaware legislature creates the Mother's Pension Fund.

**1918**—The name of Margaret Sanger's organization is changed from the National Birth Control League to the Voluntary Parenthood League.

**1918**—The Maternity Center Association is founded to promote better maternity care in the United States.

**1919**—Divorce rates soar, and the number of single mothers in the United States rises drastically in response to incidences of soldiers infecting their wives with sexually transmitted diseases (STDs), which they have contracted abroad during World War I.

**1919**—World War I ends with an Allied victory, and acknowledgment of the numerous contributions of women during the war leads Austria, Canada, Ireland, Poland, and the United Kingdom to grant woman suffrage.

**1920**—The United States Congress passes the Nineteenth Amendment, guaranteeing American women the right to vote. Women in Germany, Luxembourg, and the Netherlands are also enfranchised.

**1921**—In an effort to reduce American infant mortality rates, Congress passes the Sheppard Towner Act, which appropriates matching funds for states to establish maternity clinics. The act is repealed six years later, but Franklin Roosevelt's New Deal includes programs that continue this battle.

**1921**—General Mills creates Betty Crocker, an idealized homemaker, as a marketing tool.

**1923**—Suffragist Alice Paul's proposal for an Equal Rights Amendment (ERA) to the United States Constitution, which would mandate equal rights for women, is introduced in Congress. The ERA is revived during the women's movement of the 1960s, but opponents manage to block ratification.

**1924**—The mother of four sons, Nellie Tayloe Ross, a Democrat from Wyoming, becomes the first female governor in the United States after her husband, Governor William Ross, dies of complications from an appendectomy.

**1925**—Studies indicate that high infant mortality rates in immigrant sections of Pennsylvania and in poor areas of the Deep South are often the result of expectant mothers being overworked, malnourished, and neglected by the medical profession.

**1929**—In October, the beginning of the Great Depression ushers in a period of intense stress for American mothers who are sometimes unable to feed their children and who are often separated from family members who hit the road to find work.

**1932**—Twenty-month-old Charles Lindbergh, the child of aviator Charles Lindbergh and writer Anne Morrow Lindbergh, is kidnapped and subsequently murdered, leading the United States government to make kidnapping a federal crime.

**1932–1945**—Eleanor Roosevelt, the wife of President Franklin Roosevelt and the mother of five children, assumes unprecedented duties as First Lady because of her husband's physical frailties that resulted from a bout with polio in 1921.

**1933**—Dr. Gracie Langdon becomes the Child Care Director of Franklin Roosevelt's Works Project Administration, undertaking the responsibility for establishing 2,000 government-funded childcare centers.

**1934**—A distinctly different kind of mother–daughter relationship is depicted when Fannie Hurt's *Imitation of Life* becomes a movie. The film focuses on a young biracial woman who rejects her African American mother in order to pass as white in a society that discriminates against those whose African American ancestry is discernible.

**1935**—The notorious criminal "Ma" Barker, who has formed a bank-robbing gang with her three sons, is gunned down in a shootout in Florida.

1936—Clare Booth Luce's play, *The Women*, addresses the issue of single mothers displaced in their husband's affections by younger women.

1938—Maria von Trapp escapes from occupied Austria with her husband, Captain Georg von Trapp, and seven stepchildren. Maria gives birth to three children after the escape. In 1959, a fictionalized version of their story is turned into a play, *The Sound of Music*, which in turn becomes an award-winning movie in 1965.

1939—Anna Mary Robertson Moses, better known as Grandma Moses, begins painting at the age of 80. Over the course of the next 20 years, she completes 1,500 works.

1940—In New York, Mary Margaret McBride begins hosting a radio show that targets mothers and other homemakers.

1941—Grieving mothers respond with outrage when the Japanese attack the American Naval Base at Pearl Harbor, Hawaii, on December 7, killing 2,403 people. Congress declares war on Japan on December 11, and the lives of American mothers change as their sons and husbands join the military, and American women enter the work world in droves.

1942—Rationing begins in May, and mothers lead the patriotic campaign to conserve essential war materials.

1942—The government begins actively recruiting nurses to serve in the military and intensifies efforts to identify women who chose to remain at home and raise families after graduating from nursing schools.

1943—Mothers who lose sons in World War II become known as Gold Star Mothers. Alleta Sullivan loses five sons at once when the *USS Juneau* is sunk during a naval battle in Guadalcanal. The following year, their story receives national attention with the releases of the movie, *The Sullivans*. The United States subsequently institutes a Sole Survivor Policy to protect surviving siblings after a family member is lost in war.

1943—Susan B. Anthony II, a journalist and niece of the noted suffragist, publishes *Out of the Kitchen—Into the Wars* chronicling the participation of American women, many of them mothers, during World War II.

1945—For the first time in American history, Congress holds debates on drafting women to serve as military nurses. The Nurses Selective Service Act passes Congress but becomes moot when the war ends in April.

1946—In order to reunite families, Congress passes the War Brides Act, allowing the foreign wives of American military personnel to enter the country.

1950—French feminist philosopher Simone de Beauvoir publishes *The Second Sex* in which she argues that women are always defined as "the other" because males are considered "the norm." During the following decades, this work continues to have significant impact on the emerging women's movement.

1952—Elizabeth II becomes Queen of England. She gives birth to Prince Charles, the heir apparent and the eldest of her four children, in 1948.

1952—Marion Donovan invents the disposable diaper. Her initial diaper is made from a folded-up shower curtain and absorbent padding.

1952—The Voluntary Parenthood Leagues changes its named to Planned Parenthood Association and continues to be a major force in family planning.

1953—On January 19, actress Lucille Ball becomes the most famous mother in television history by giving birth to Little Ricky on the popular sitcom *I Love Lucy*. The show garners a 72-percent audience share. That same night, Ball gives birth to her real-life son, Desi Arnaz, Jr.

1953—Ethel Rosenberg, the mother of two small children, is executed for espionage along with her husband Julius. The case continues to arouse controversy for decades, and many people believe Ethel, unlike her husband, was innocent of the crime.

1955—In August, 14-year-old Emmett Till is brutally murdered by segregationists while visiting relatives in Money, Mississippi. His mother, Mamie Till Mobley, allows *Jet* to publish photographs of her son's mutilated body so that Americans can understand the impact of violence against innocent African American children. Two men confess to the murder, but they are never brought to justice.

1956—In Illinois, a group of seven nursing mothers found the La Leche League to promote breastfeeding. The group, which evolves into an international organization, continues to promote the health benefits of nursing and provides advice to nursing mothers.

1957—Writer Better Friedan polls her former classmates from Smith College to determine whether or not they are fulfilled as mothers and wives. She finds widespread dissatisfaction, and identifies this phenomenon as "the problem that has no name."

1957—In Little Rock, Arkansas, Daisy Bates, a newspaper publisher, serves as a mentor for the nine African American students who integrate Central High School. Her civil rights activities earn her numerous awards and the eternal gratitude of African American mothers who dream that their children will be able to live in a more equal society.

1958—The Childbirth Without Pain Association introduces the Lamaze method of childbirth to the United States, encouraging American mothers to experience childbirth naturally.

1959—Lorraine Hansberry's play, *A Raisin in the Sun*, a tale of transitioning family life in the African American community, wins the New York Drama Critics Circle Award.

1959—At age 41, Phyllis Diller, the mother of five, launches a career as a stand-up comic and becomes one of the best loved American comediennes.

1960—The birth control pill is approved by the Food and Drug Administration. Since the pill is the most effective birth control method available to date, it promotes more efficient family planning.

1962—The publication of Rachel Carson's *Silent Spring* helps to launch the environmentalist movement in the United States, geared in large part toward making life safer for future generations.

1962—Europe experiences an outbreak of birth defects caused by pregnant women taking thalidomide to control morning sickness. In the United States, Dr. Frances Oldham Kelsey of the Federal Drug Administration manages to keep the drug off the market.

1963—Jackie Kennedy becomes the only First Lady in American history to be pregnant in the White House. She gives birth on August 7, but Patrick Bouvier Kennedy dies two days later.

1963—Betty Friedan launches the Second Wave of the women's movement with the publication of *The Feminine Mystique*, arguing that women are dissatisfied with their lives because their individual identities have been submerged by their roles as wives and mothers.

1963—President John F. Kennedy establishes the President's Commission on the Status of Women. States. The commission identifies major issues and concerns that affect the lives of American women.

1963—On Sunday, September 15, four African American mothers lose daughters to civil rights violence when a bomb explodes at a Birmingham, Alabama, church.

1965—Based on the grounds of privacy within marriage, the Supreme Court holds in *Griswold v. Connecticut* that married couples have a constitutional right to obtain birth control.

1967—Anne Moore invents the Snugli, which allows parents to carry infants close to their bodies while leaving their arms free. The young mother becomes a multimillionaire as sales soar.

1968—In Boston, Massachusetts, members of Mothers for Adequate Welfare campaign for increased aid to mothers of small children by chaining themselves to furniture inside a welfare office.

**1968**—On April 4, Coretta Scott King, the mother of four children, becomes a widow when civil rights leader the Reverend Dr. Martin Luther King, Jr., is assassinated in Memphis, Tennessee.

**1968**—Pope Paul VI announces that the only method of birth control supported by the Catholic Church is the rhythm method, which involves abstaining from sexual intercourse on days when women are fertile. Determined to engage in responsible family planning, many Catholic women ignore the dictates of the Church.

**1968**—Singer and actress Diahann Carroll, who plays a single mother on the sitcom *Julia*, becomes the first African American to headline a regular series on American television.

**1970**—Affectionately known as "the grandmother of the Jewish people," Russian-born Golda Meir, who grew up in Milwaukee, Wisconsin, becomes the prime minister of Israel.

**1971**—Congress passes new legislation that awards federal subsidies for both public and private child-care centers.

**1972**—In *Reed v. Reed*, the Supreme Court determines that fathers should no longer be given precedence over mothers when managing estates of minor children. The case clears the way for a new examination of legal discrimination on the basis of sex according to the Equal Protection Clause of the Fourteenth Amendment.

**1973**—In *Roe v. Wade*, the Supreme Court holds that the right of privacy guarantees pregnant women a constitutional right to obtain an abortion within the first three months of a pregnancy. *Roe* proves to be one of the most controversial cases in the Court's history, and so-called pro-life advocates launch a campaign to have the decision overturned.

**1975**—The year is proclaimed the International Year of the Woman, and international and national groups launch a series of programs aimed at improving the quality of life for women and their children.

**1975**—The first World Conference on Women is held in Mexico City, Mexico, aimed at improving the lives and status of women around the world. Future conferences are held at five-year intervals in a number of other cities.

**1976**—In *Planned Parenthood of Central Missouri v. Danforth*, the Supreme Court decides that a married woman does not have to obtain her husband's consent to obtain an abortion.

**1976**—In *General Electric v. Gilbert*, the Supreme Court upholds the right of employers to exclude pregnancy from benefit plans, legitimizing the practice of employers paying benefits for the pregnant wives of male employees but not for pregnant female employees.

**1976**—Congress passes the Hyde Amendment, stipulating that poor women cannot use Medicaid funds to pay for abortions except in cases of rape and endangerment to the life of the mother.

**1976**—The publication of Adrienne Rich's *Of Woman Born* opens debates on the differences between motherhood as experience and motherhood as an ideal espoused by the institution of patriarchy.

**1977**—The inauguration of Georgian Jimmy Carter draws public attention to his colorful mother, "Miss Lillian." At the same time, Carter's wife Rosalynn proves to be a hands-on mother to their young daughter Amy.

**1978**—Congress passes the Pregnancy Discrimination Act as an amendment to the Civil Rights Act of 1964, banning workplace discrimination against pregnant women and essentially overturning the Supreme Court's actions two years earlier in *General Electric v. Gilbert*.

**1979**—The United Nations General Assembly sponsors the Convention on the Elimination of All Forms of Discrimination Against Women, which produces an international bill of rights for women, specifying behavior that constitutes discrimination and offering solutions for dealing with violations.

**1979**—In the wake of a scandal over advertising of prepared infant formulas in developing countries, the International Baby Food Action Network (IBFAN) is created to force the manufacturers of baby food formulas to cease unethical practices.

**1979**—The groundbreaking film, *Kramer v. Kramer*, highlights changing perceptions of the roles of both mothers and fathers.

**1979**—China establishes a one-child-per-couple policy designed to limit population growth. The policy proves to be detrimental to female infants who become the victims of infanticide. Other girl babies are abandoned or put up for adoption.

**1980**—After her daughter is killed by an inebriated driver with three prior convictions, Candy Lightner founds Mothers Against Drunk Drivers (MADD), which becomes Mothers Against Drunk Driving in 1984. The group is devoted to keeping drunk drivers off the road and educating the public about the dangers of drinking and driving.

**1980**—The first in vitro fertilization clinic opens in Norfolk, Virginia.

**1981**—Republican Sandra Day O'Connor, the mother of three sons, becomes the first woman to serve on the United States Supreme Court. She finds her niche by becoming the important swing vote in a number of cases dealing with women and children.

**1981–1988**—The elections of Ronald Reagan and George H. W. Bush are marked by a period of strong conservatism in the United States. "Reaganism" results in significant cuts to programs designed to help poor women and their minor children, and views on abortion become a litmus test for federal judicial appointments.

**1984**—Running with Minnesota Democrat Walter Mondale, Geraldine Ferraro, a Democratic Congresswoman from New York and the mother of three children, becomes the first women in American history to be considered a viable candidate on a major party ticket.

**1984**—A group of Canadian feminists establish Mothers Are Women to celebrate a mother's right to decide to serve as the primary caregiver for her child.

**1985**—Congress passes legislation mandating the creation of state programs to collect child support from delinquent fathers.

**1985**—Divorced mother of two, Wilma Mankiller becomes the first female Chief of the Cherokee Nation.

**1986**—Teacher Christa McAuliffe, the mother of two young children, is killed when the space shuttle *Challenger* explodes shortly after liftoff.

**1986**—The issue of surrogate motherhood receives national attention when Mary Beth Whitehead, who has received $10,000 to serve as a surrogate for William and Elizabeth Stern, reneges on the agreement. Ultimately, a judge places "Baby M" with Stern, who is her biological father, and Elizabeth Stern adopts her.

**1987**—The World Health Organization launches the Safe Motherhood Initiative designed to slash maternal mortality in half by the year 2000.

**1988**—The State of California passes legislation guaranteeing job security for mothers who take maternity leave.

**1988**—Toni Morrison's *Beloved* wins the Pulitzer Prize. Based on a true story, the novel tells the story of Sethe, a slave woman who kills her daughter to prevent her from becoming a slave.

**1989**—In *Webster v. Reproductive Health Services*, the conservative Supreme Court allots states greater control over access to abortions without overturning *Roe v. Wade*, as had been predicted.

**1990**—For the first time, the term "mommy track" is used to describe professional women who choose a slower career track that allows them more time with their families over an ambitious fast-track to success.

1991—To celebrate and encourage the contributions of midwives to maternal and child health, the first International Day of the Midwife is held on May 5 and becomes an annual tradition.

1991—In *Rust v. Sullivan*, the Supreme Court upholds the Reagan/Bush policy of forbidding health care professionals receiving federal funds to inform clients about abortion rights. This so-called "gag rule" is one of the first conservative policies overturned by Democrat Bill Clinton when he assumes office in January 1993.

1992—The year is designated the Year of the Woman in the United States as women are elected to political office at all levels of government and begin using that power to fight for the rights of women and children.

1992—The first Take Our Daughters to Work Day is held on April 28 in the United States to encourage young girls to recognize that their career possibilities are limitless.

1993—Congress passes the Family and Medical Leave Act, which allows both parents to take time off to care for a new or adopted baby or a sick child.

1993—Ruth Bader Ginsburg, the mother of two, becomes the second woman to serve on the Supreme Court. A Democrat, Ginsburg tends to be supportive of women's issues.

1994—Abortion provider Dr. John Byard Britton and clinic escort Lieutenant Colonel James Barrett are murdered at a family planning clinic by radical pro-lifer Paul Hill.

1994—Congress passes the Violence Against Women Act, making it a federal offense to travel across state lines to commit violent acts against a spouse or domestic partner.

1995—The Fourth World Conference on Women is held in Beijing, China, generating the Platform for Action designed to empower women throughout the world.

1996—Democrat Madeleine Albright, the mother of three daughters, becomes the first female Secretary of State in American history.

1996—First Lady Hillary Rodham Clinton publishes *It Takes a Village* in which she argues that raising children should be a societal responsibility.

1998—The Association for Research on Mothering is established as the first feminist international organization exclusively devoted to motherhood.

2001—Former First Lady and popular grandmother figure Barbara Bush becomes only the second woman in American history to become both the wife and mother of a president.

2002—The Human Rights and Equal Opportunity Commission (HREOC) opens an investigation into the possibility of establishing a national policy on paid maternity leave.

2002—A group of mothers in New York found Mothers Ought To Have Equal Rights (MOTHERS) designed to promote economic security and political clout for mothers and others who serve as primary caregivers for children.

2004—Australia passes the lump sum Maternity Allowance and Baby Bonus to assist new parents at the time of a child's birth.

2005—The Save the Mothers Program establishes a Master's Degree Program in Public Health Leadership in Uganda under the leadership of the Intersave Canada Board in an effort to improve the experience of motherhood in developing countries.

2006—Author Leslie Morgan Steiner publishes the *Mommy Wars*, which includes interviews with 26 mothers who discuss their personal perceptions of motherhood in the 21st century.

2007—The World Health Organization celebrates the 20th anniversary of its Safe Motherhood Initiative as part of an ongoing effort to improve the health of pregnant women and decrease maternal mortality levels.

2007—Former First Lady and current Senator from New York Hillary Rodham Clinton announces her bid for the presidency and becomes the most viable female candidate for high elected office in American history.

2008—Governor of Alaska and the mother of five, Sarah Palin becomes the first Republican female to be considered a viable candidate for the office of Vice President.

2009—Michelle Obama, the mother of two young daughters, becomes the first African American First Lady of the United States.

2009—Senator Hillary Rodham Clinton, the mother of an adult daughter, is sworn in as the third female Secretary of State in American history.

Elizabeth Purdy
Independent Scholar

# Aboriginal Mothering

The term *mothering* was constructed to describe the caregiving role and work of female parents. Aboriginal refers to cultural groups that originated in certain geographic areas prior to the European settlers' arrival in the late 1800s, primarily in North America, New Zealand, and Australia, although there is evidence of some other locations. The word *Aboriginal* generally means "from the beginning," or the first inhabitants. Typically, Aboriginal people do not refer to themselves as first inhabitants by comparing themselves to European migrants. Aboriginal identity is not claimed by all who have an Aboriginal heritage. In some circles, an Aboriginal identity is thought to be a spiritual and cultural heritage; others believe it is an intrinsic connection to the land, nature, and animals, while still others believe that it is a biological and racial identity. Despite many different geographical locations, diverse histories, and distinct cultural norms, Aboriginal mothering does have common elements. Aboriginal mothering embodies some similar values, parallel histories of oppression, and enduring forces of womanhood, which integrate caregiving for dependents, indigenous knowledge, and the keepers of the environment.

## Demographics and Government Interaction

Demographically, Canada reports approximately 4 percent of its population as Aboriginal, which includes Inuit, Métis, and First Nations people; while in the United States, approximately 1.5 percent of the population is Aboriginal. In Australia, just over 2 percent of the population is Aboriginal, while the Maori in New Zealand represent 14 percent of the population. Reporting statistics may not be accurate, as some Aboriginal communities are remote and do not always report their census data, while other communities have reported being suspicious of governmental efforts to enumerate Aboriginal people. Two trends appear consistent in all locations. The reporting of Aboriginal identities seems to be increasing, and there is a trend toward urbanization among Aboriginal populations. Aboriginal mothers are usually at the heart of their communities and these trends reflect their life experiences.

A consistent experience across Aboriginal communities is the history of colonization and systemic, state-sanctioned oppression. Aboriginal mothers were at the center of these experiences because many governmental policies were aimed at children, families, and cultural practices. The European settlement brought with it new diseases, new treaties, and laws. In addition, a new community organizational structure was enforced, called *reservations* (reserves), which relocated Aboriginal people to live apart from the European settlements. By the early 1900s, Australia, Canada, and the United States had legislated acts that specified rights and restrictions of Aboriginal mothers, including the loss of the right to practice spiritual ceremonies. Compulsory, government-run educational programming, which in many cases meant children were removed from their families and communities to be educated in other locations, also contributed to the loss of indigenous knowledge, traditional medical practices, and language. Without the rights to teach, parent, and heal their own children and community members, Aboriginal mothers lost their roles and rights as community members.

In some regions, when Aboriginal women married non-Aboriginal men, they and their children lost their legal Aboriginal status. This legislation was not overturned in some areas until the late 1900s. Child welfare policies and practices authorizing Aboriginal children to be placed in non-Aboriginal families and communities also had devastating effects on entire generations. These policies are still in effect in some locations. Such child welfare practices have been widely criticized for providing a legal vehicle to continue to control and dominate Aboriginal mothers and their communities by essentially cutting children off from their culture and heritage. This, in turn, left a generation of children without guidance from their Aboriginal mothers—what is sometimes referred to as the *lost generation*. There continues to be lingering negative health effects, poor access to medical treatment in some communities, and shorter life spans for many Aboriginal people. There is also a greater threat of dying young because of higher risks of violence, higher rates of children in foster care, and higher rates of poverty.

### Shared Values Among Diverse Communities

There is a considerable diversity among Aboriginal communities, cultural practices, and values. However, there are also some parallels illustrating the beliefs and knowledge that are gradually being reclaimed throughout many Aboriginal communities. Historically, Aboriginal communities were frequently organized as collective cultures with cooperative values emphasizing sharing of resources and parenting roles among adults. Aboriginal mothering philosophy has been passed along the generations and has been preserved in some locations.

In Aboriginal communities, the relationship between adults and children is frequently multi-layered. In addition to daily caregiving, adults and elders are responsible to pass on lessons that take the long view of life. The life cycle from birth to death and the many lessons that can be learned or passed on throughout this journey are inherent in the way Aboriginal mothers guide their children. In many Aboriginal traditions, everything is connected. The life cycle lessons are linked to the environment with its four directions, respect for nature's animals, and the changing seasons.

Women and their spirituality have typically had a place of honor in traditional Aboriginal communities. A woman's menstrual period was frequently referred to as her "moon," and women were treated with special respect during their moon time. In some traditions, "dreaming" can be understood as a way of thinking or imagining, or a way of remembering ancestors or important historical events. Dreaming can also be a narrative of what matters or what is important to Aboriginal women as they pass on their stories and knowledge.

Aboriginal mothering values share some common principles. Parenting is based on non-aggressive, interpersonal respect, where relationships are understood to be collaborative and primarily nonhierarchal. Aboriginal mothering values frequently emphasize nonverbal teaching and learning styles that encourage children to explore their environment and make decisions while mothers show children what can be learned from their choices. Subtle humor and teasing are also integral to Aboriginal mothers' guidance practices. Some of these values are in sharp contrast to many modern social values, which often emphasize individualized competition and direct communication.

### Mother Roles

Historically, many Aboriginal people were hunters and gatherers. Some communities were also organized by gender, where women had specific roles and responsibilities that differed from men. There is also evidence that some Aboriginal tribes were matriarchies. These gender roles and the place of

*An early-20th-century Eskimo mother carries a child on her back. Aboriginal mothering philosophy focuses on the life cycle.*

**Bibliography**

Lavell-Harvard, D. Memee, and Jeannette Corbiere Lavell, Eds. *"Until Our Hearts Are On the Ground"; Aboriginal Mothering, Oppression, Resistance and Rebirth.* Toronto: Demeter Press, 2006.

O'Reilly, Andrea, Marie Porter, and Patricia Short, eds. *Motherhood: Power and Oppression.* London: The Women's Press, 2005.

Carolyn J. Peters
University of Manitoba

# Abortion

Abortion is illegal in Uganda; practically mandated in India and China, where there are one-child-per-family policies; a form of birth control in Russia; and perhaps the most contentious issue in the United States. In some countries, abortion doctors are criminalized, while in other countries, abortion providers as well as women who have abortions can be fined or jailed. In the United States, abortion doctors and clinic staff have been murdered, and recently in Brazil, a bishop excommunicated a 9-year-old girl and a doctor over an abortion. This girl was pregnant with twins after allegedly being raped by her stepfather; the doctor performed the abortion because he didn't think her 80-pound body could carry a pregnancy to term. Brazil allows abortion only in cases of rape and in order to save the life of the mother.

The vast array of circumstances with abortion around the world gives the impression that there is no consensus on the issue—yet, some protest that the shared goal among many of these practices and restrictions is a desire to control women. Abortion rights supporters believe that the decision to terminate a pregnancy should be the woman's alone (in consultation with medical professionals); supporters of the right to life publicly denounce abortion as murder.

## History of Abortion

Women have sought to induce abortions since ancient times, and medical recipe books dating from the colonial period in the United States commonly

honor women had in their communities changed dramatically when European settlers introduced trading, alcohol, and an organized legal system, which many scholars indicate continues to be oppressive. Some fear that there is too much reliance today on Aboriginal mothers to lead the healing and restoration work, risking a depletion of their vigor and capacities. Despite lingering oppressive conditions, Aboriginal mothering resilience is illustrated in how Aboriginal women are reclaiming indigenous knowledge and practices to pass on to future generations.

**See Also:** Community Mothering; First Nations; Native Americans; Race and Racism; Residential School and Mothers/First Nations.

included descriptions of herbal *abortifacients* (substances that cause abortion), sometimes couched in ambiguous terms such as "remedies to restore menstruation." In the early 19th century, laws prohibiting abortion began to appear, beginning with Connecticut in 1821, and such laws became common in the 1860s. By 1900, abortion was illegal in most American states, although some states allowed exceptions, such as in the case of rape or incest. Abortion remained widely restricted until the Supreme Court decision *Roe v. Wade* in 1973, which prohibited states from restricting women's access to abortion in the first trimester (three-month period).

### Roe v. Wade

In the United States, abortion policies are most synonymous with the 1973 Supreme Court decision *Roe v. Wade*, which determined that abortion should be legal in all 50 states and available up until the point of viability (around 24–28 weeks), which in the past had been a similar cutoff described as quickening. At the time of the *Roe* decision, pregnancies were dated from the time of conception; currently, the medical community uses a standard 40 weeks, dating all pregnancies from the first day of the last period, which means that what was once a 28-week-old fetus could now be labeled a 30-week pregnancy. This form of dating places more emphasis on number of weeks pregnant rather than the age of the fetus.

The *Roe v. Wade* decision is credited with allowing women to terminate a pregnancy, but it's equally a decision about determining pregnancy; giving women the right to decide if and when they want to carry a pregnancy to term. The decision is also highly regarded as a privacy case—women had the right to this private decision, and thus, some become supporters of *Roe* entirely because of protecting this right, separate of their feelings about abortion.

Since *Roe* became the law, there have been numerous attempts to reduce its power by creating state-based restrictions—which are allowed under *Roe*—such as parental consent laws, waiting periods, and limits on funding. Most of these challenges have come via the courts, but abortion issues have been equally mired in the legislative and executive branches. An example is the Hyde Amendment, which restricted public funding for abortions,

including those receiving Medicaid or using Indian Health Services, as well as U.S. Military families and Peace Corps members. According to the Guttmacher Institute, women who use Medicaid are more than twice as likely to seek abortions. There is also the Global Gag Rule, also known as the Mexico City Policy, which under the Bush administration prevented U.S. funds for international family-planning agencies that provided abortions or even offered counseling or referrals. *Roe* is far from a comprehensive decision. The Canadian equivalent, known as the Morgantaler Decision, legalized abortion and took it out of that country's criminal code—and it is respected for being a more straightforward decision and less vulnerable to the diminishment of *Roe*.

### Types of Abortions

Medically speaking, an abortion is a procedure that removes a pregnancy by emptying the contents of a woman's uterus. There are medical and surgical abortions; most abortions happen in the first trimester, within the first 12 to 14 weeks of pregnancy. Medical abortions are a newer invention and are less invasive. The only marketed medical abortion product is Mifiprex, popularly referred to as RU-486, which is prescribed by a doctor and requires a follow-up appointment, but can be administered at home and usually happens around the eighth week of pregnancy. Regardless, surgical abortion remains the most prevalent in nations where abortions are legal: 87 percent in the United States, according to the Centers for Disease Control and Prevention. There is a third type of abortion—unsafe methods such as drinking turpentine or bleach, inserting herbal preparations, or inserting foreign objects such as chicken bones or sticks. Worldwide, these abortions account for 48 percent of all abortions, thus a higher percentage than any other form.

Surgical abortions are either the more common, manual vacuum aspiration or other variations involving dilation of the cervix—either dilation and curettage (D&C), or dilation and extraction (D&X). The latter is sometimes referred to as *partial-birth abortion*, so called because the procedure requires the mother's uterus to contract and then expunge the fetus. In instances when the fetus is too large to be expelled otherwise, or because the doctor feels the need for greater precision, a doctor might induce labor and thus have the woman "birth" the fetus. These later-term abortions are often because a fetus died in utero (miscarried), or because a mother chose to terminate the pregnancy due to a detection of a fetal abnormality. These procedures account for about 1 percent of abortions and are used most often after 16 weeks of the pregnancy.

## Assisted Reproductive Technologies

With the increasing popularity of assisted reproductive technologies (ART), which includes in vitro fertilization (IVF) and inter-utero insemination (IUI), selective reductions are also increasingly used as a form of abortion. In this case, doctors reduce multiple fetuses to a lesser number. With most instances of IVF and IUI, women are given hormones to overproduce eggs that are later implanted into the uterus, or donor eggs are used. To increase the likelihood that a pregnancy results, doctors often implant more than one egg, sometimes as many as a dozen, on the premise that most of these eggs will naturally weed themselves out. Many countries limit how many eggs can be implanted; the United States has no restrictions. Because carrying more than two babies to term has inherent risks, doctors use selective reductions to reduce the number of fetuses. Though this procedure resembles an abortion, it is rarely described as such, both by the women choosing it and in the medical community. This is likely because at least one or more babies are preserved (countering the assumption that abortion ends a pregnancy) and these procedures are performed in hospitals or private practices with the guidance of hi-tech sonograms, which presents it as a legitimate medical procedure. It's also a much more costly procedure, and thus unlikely to become a more mainstream option.

The aftermath of selective reduction is an interesting challenge to pro-life supporters: there is no matter that is expunged from the uterus—whatever exists reattaches to the remaining placenta. Stem cell research is another new challenge to those ambivalent about abortion, as the stem cells culled from aborted fetuses and unused embryos from IVF procedures are used in research. Some interpret this government-sanctioned research, which is hailed as leading the way to a cure for diseases, as an endorse-

ment or even encouragement of abortion. Yet, supporters point to the number of annual abortions as proof that there would never be a need to abort simply for stem cells.

## Grounds for Legalization

Ultimately, abortion has been legalized in most countries on the premise that because it happened underground, it was unsafe and unsterile, and women were needlessly dying. It was considered medically imperative that the procedure be legalized; at least to the extent that it was available to save the life or health of the mother. Now, according to the Guttmacher Institute, "termination of pregnancy is one of the most frequently performed surgical procedures in the United States."

No correlation had been established between illegal or legal abortion laws and abortion rates; in other words, laws have not been a deterrent for most women who seeking an abortion. This is still true in countries where abortion is illegal or otherwise censored. The abortion rate in Africa, where abortion is predominantly illegal, is 26 abortions per 1,000 births; and in Europe, where it is available with few restrictions, the rate is 29 abortions per 1,000 births. But a woman's economic status did have some bearing on her choices and access to an abortion in the past: rich and middle-class woman could usually find a doctor, either through a private practice or by traveling to another country, while poorer women often resorted to abortions performed by questionable medical professionals, had self-trained people conduct the procedure, or they had the child. Some women used desperate techniques in order to self-abort, such as coat hangers, horseback riding, or throwing themselves down the stairs

In many countries, the legalization process contextualized the procedure as a public health concern. As of 2009, Ireland's attempt to invoke an international human rights standard posits that denying women access to abortion is denying them their human rights. Women on Waves, a Dutch organization that uses a human-rights-based approach, provides abortions and health care to women in nations where abortion is illegal by providing their services on a boat offshore. Many other countries have used the rhetoric of "rights" or "choice," which has more recently evolved into "justice." Most of the battles to preserve and confirm a woman's access to abortion have been fought legislatively through the state, federal, or national courts, but more recently using international courts. Most initiatives introduced over the past 30 years have attempted to further restrict women's access to abortion, thus putting abortion crusaders on the defensive and requiring them to advocate and lobby for women's access. In the United States, a somewhat new tactic is using ballot initiatives, which gives the vote directly to the people. Generally, U.S. polls in 2008 indicated that roughly just over half of Americans have confirmed that they feel the procedure should be legal in all or most cases.

## Health Care Systems

The issue is further complicated in the United States simply by dint of its primarily private health care system. Even with supportive laws, there are many obstacles, such as cost, insurance, finding a doctor, or clinic locations. Doctors are not mandated to provide abortions. Similarly, insurance companies can simply decide what procedures (if any) to cover. Other countries that offer a national system of health care may or may not include abortion.

## Religious Beliefs

One of the biggest opponents of abortion has been those of religious faith, particularly the Catholic Church, which argues that abortion is murder, so much so that some Catholic leaders oppose an exception to preserve a mother's health or life. There is some correlation between religious views on abortion and women who have them. In the United States, Catholic women have the same rate of abortions as women from the general public. Protestants have about 69 percent as many abortions as the general public, and born-again Christians have 39 percent as many. This religious deterrent also isn't consistent. For instance, it doesn't apply in China, with its one-child-per-family policy; nor in India, where abortion is strongly encouraged for anyone who has more than one child.

## Support and Opposition

Though there is much public outcry against abortion, many doctors and all major medical associations (including the American Medical Association) endorse the availability of abortion. Some doctors are uncomfortable performing the procedures, which is why in the United States there is a decades-old conscience clause that exempts doctors from performing abortions. But many doctors feel that the long-term benefits of abortion outweigh the impact of the undue stress of an unwanted pregnancy on mothers, and are also familiar with the affects of raising children who are diagnosed with severe impairments.

In the past, abortion was a less contentious issue, primarily because it was less discussed and less available. With the professionalization of the medical community—around the turn of the 20th century—there was a move to undermine women's medical expertise, especially midwives, who had administered the majority of women's health care. Confirming abortion as a medical procedure meant that it could be transferred from the hands of midwives and into a profitable venture.

## Pro-Life Movement

The pro-life movement in the United States was formed in opposition to the Supreme Court decision *Roe v. Wade,* which invalidated most state laws prohibiting abortion and made it a legal medical procedure available to most women for the first time since the early 19th century. Pro-life activists contend that human life begins at the moment of conception, and therefore, an embryo or fetus is a person; hence, performing an abortion means killing a person. Many but not all are Christians and find support for this point of view in the Bible. Although they have not been successful in overturning *Roe v. Wade* and thus prohibiting abortion outright, pro-life activists have succeeded in protesting abortion by picketing buildings where abortions are performed (discouraging doctors from performing an abortion and women from obtaining the procedure), promoting legislation that requires additional procedures before an abortion can be obtained (such as a mandatory waiting period), and requiring spousal notification for adults and parental consent for minors.

## Family Planning and Choice

One attempt at preserving and destigmatizing abortion politics has been to contextualize abortion under the larger and more comprehensive heading of family planning or reproductive rights, arguing that abortion is simply one part of women's reproductive lives—alongside birth control, prenatal care, maternal health, and menopause. And while it was initially true that abortion services occurred in clinics providing a fuller range of services, it's increasingly true that the procedure is marginalized into clinics that don't offer the full range of women's gynecological and obstetric care. There is an increasing push for abortion to be mainstreamed in family medicine, which would make it less vulnerable and marginalized, and represented as one piece of a woman's reproductive life. Under this system, nurses and midwives would again be allowed to administer abortions.

Ultimately, family planning didn't represent abortion heavily enough, so the language morphed into a "choice" framework, which postulated that women should be endowed with decision-making power and should also have a full range of choices available to them. However, "pro-choice" is often identified as being pro-abortion. This is partly a consequence of a very successful backlash against abortion, and partly a consequence of individuals coming to terms with their own complicated relationship with the issue. Increasingly, *choice* is a strongly decisive term that does not represent how most people feel. Today, the abortion battle is over the issues of "legal to what extent" and "for whom," which are harder issues to mobilize around when women find themselves at many positions on that spectrum.

The abortion debate has presented abortion and motherhood in conflict rather than as related, but a clear majority of women who have abortions are or will become mothers. According to the Guttmacher Institute, six in 10 U.S. women having abortions are already mothers, while more than half intend to have (more) children in the future. In fact, most women who have abortions are weighing the issues of motherhood more than the issues of abortion—if they are ready to be a parent now, if their relationship is where they want it to be, or if they are financially and emotionally confident enough to raise a child. For instance, a Guttmacher Institute poll in 2004 reported that 23 percent of women cited "not being able to afford a baby right now" as their primary reason for having an abortion.

## The New Rhetoric: Reproductive Justice

Today, *reproductive justice* is becoming the favored term, and is meant to reflect the interconnectedness of issues. While the abortion movement would likely be aided by aligning itself with other movements, such as environmental, prisoners' rights, and immigrants' rights, those movements in the process might be stymied. Asian Communities for Reproductive Justice, one group that has pioneered this linking, defines reproductive justice in this way: "We believe that by challenging patriarchal social relations and addressing the intersection of racism, sexism, xenophobia, heterosexism, and class oppression within a women-of-color context, we will be able to build the collective social, economic, and political power of all women and girls to make decisions that protect and contribute to our reproductive health and overall well-being."

This lens focuses building alliances with other organizations and movements by "place[ing] reproductive justice at the center of the most critical social and economic justice issues facing our communities, such as ending violence against women, workers rights, environmental justice, queer and transgender rights, immigrant rights, and educational justice."

## Second Thoughts and Regret

Many women who have had an abortion, whether their political beliefs are pro-choice or pro-life, describe it as a very difficult decision which left them with regrets, sometimes describing a period of mourning for the child that would never be born. Pro-life activists have used testimonials by these women to discourage others from seeking an abortion; for instance, the Website www.gargaro.com/regrets.html. However, a 2008 literature review conducted at the Johns Hopkins School of Public Health found that few women suffered long-term psychological distress following abortion.

## Still a Hotly Contested Debate

The political debate over abortion continues to rage. Opinions on abortion are often challenged by another person's choices. Abortion rarely means the same thing to two people—one woman's doctor-ordered termination is another woman's abortion. Each person has their own threshold, and thus it is often discussed purely in terms of legal or illegal.

Even determined pro-choice defenders are conflicted on how to best present the issues. For instance, they often argue that they are protecting access to abortion for those communities that are most vulnerable, but in the process they can often further expose those individuals and also present an assumption that abortion is primarily benefiting those communities. This is reminiscent of the fight for legal birth control for nonwhite women, which was funded in part by eugenics and thus muddled with racist associations. Besides the racial problems with choice, the abortion debate is further complicated by the use of ART, which is unregulated in the United States. This type of genetic manipulation is leading the way to cloning and other manipulations that will inevitably prioritize certain communities of people over others.

For decades there has been no consensus on this debate, and likely won't be in the foreseeable future. Thus, abortion supporters are left to prioritize protecting the procedure and to make it seem less vilified. People are divided because of religion, race, misogyny, and a host of other issues. Another obstacle is women's ambiguity about their own wants and needs (as are men), and thus often find it more comfortable to be told what to do rather than be in a position of acting out.

**See Also:** Adoption; Artificial Insemination; Central African Republic; Family Planning; Fertility; Reproductive Justice/Rights Movements.

**Bibliography**
Asian Communities for Reproductive Justice. www.reproductivejustice.org (accessed April 2009).
Ehrenreich, Barbara, and Deirdre English. *For Her Own Good: Two Centuries of the Experts' Advice to Women*. New York: Anchor Books Revised Edition, 2005.
Garago.com. "Abortion and the Regrets." www.gargaro.com/regrets.html (accessed August 2008).
Guttmacher Institute. "Reasons U.S. Women Have Abortions: Quantitative and Qualitative Perspectives." www.guttmacher.org/pubs/journals/3711005.pdf (accessed April 2009).
Mundy, Liza. *Everything Conceivable: How the Science of Assisted Reproduction Is Changing Our World*. New York: Anchor Books, 2008.
Mundy, Liza. "Too Much to Carry?" *Washington Post* (May 20, 2007).
PollingReport.com. "Abortion and Birth Control." www.pollingreport.com/abortion.htm (accessed April 2009).
Roberts, Dorothy E. *Killing the Black Body: Race, Reproduction and the Meaning of Liberty*. New York: Pantheon Books, 1997.
Sedgh, Gilda, Stanley Henshaw, Susheela Singh, Elisabeth Ahman, and Iqbal Shah. "Induced Abortion: Estimated Rates and Trends Worldwide." *The Lancet*, v.370/9595 (October 2007).

Amy Richards
Independent Scholar

# Absentee Mothers

An absentee mother is a woman who lives apart from her minor children on a temporary or permanent basis. The decision leading up to these formal and informal arrangements vary, but are often linked to women's social and economic disadvantages. The effect of absence on a woman, her children, and the mother–child relationship also differs depending on whether she was involved in the decision or had it imposed on her.

A mother's absence may result from a court decision that denies her some or all of her parental rights and restricts physical access to her minor children on a temporary or permanent basis. In the past, unmarried women felt social, economic, or religious pressures to surrender their newborns for adoption, thus permanently absenting themselves from their child's life. Many such women mourned, often in silence, the loss of their child and a life unlived together. Some adopted children grew up feeling bewildered, angry, or unlovable because of their birth mother's difficult decision. However, laws and social attitudes are changing, and many absentee mothers and their now-adult children are attempting contact. Depending on the life histories and expectations of mother, adult child, and their respective families, these reunions have varying outcomes: Some planned reunions are called off before they occur because of mistrust or mixed messages;

some reunions are one- or two-time events that satisfy one or both parties, or neither, leaving emotions raw and many questions still unanswerable; still other reunions end a mother's long absence and begin a more or less satisfying relationship between her and her adult child.

The courts may remove a child from a mother who is experiencing difficulty parenting because she lacks adequate economic or social supports or parenting skills, or because she is incarcerated, has poor mental or physical health, or problems with drugs or alcohol. A mother will be absent from her child's life as long as the courts deem that the state or another relative is better able to provide for her child.

When a marriage or civil union ends, the courts may decide in favor of paternal or joint custody. Depending on the living arrangements, a mother may be absent from her child's life for days or weeks at a time.

## Other Factors

Economic imperatives push many mothers in countries such as the Philippines and the Caribbean to migrate, leaving behind their own children to work as domestics or nannies caring for other people's children. An absentee mother's income provides education and health care for her children and greater financial security for her family at the expense of her own well-being during her long years of absence. Similarly, some women temporarily absent themselves from their children's lives to seek seasonal work that supports their families living in poor communities.

In other informal arrangements, a mother may live apart from her children because she feels physically or emotionally unable to care for a child or because she wants to pursue her education, career goals, or other personal aspirations.

There are widely held cultural, social, and religious beliefs in a woman's natural ability to nurture, love, and therefore, be present in her children's lives. An absentee mother challenges these beliefs and may be regarded as a selfish, irresponsible, or deviant woman regardless of whether her absence is by choice, circumstance, or court order.

Children were often believed to be negatively affected by a mother's absence, especially during their formative and adolescent years. However, other factors are more predictive of long-term child well-being: adequate household income, access to supportive social networks, a safe and stable physical environment, cooperation between parents, and absent parent involvement. Although parenting from a distance is difficult, absentee mothers are more likely than absentee fathers to stay in touch through letters, phone calls, and regular and extended contact, resulting in closer and more durable relationships with their children.

Some notable absentee mothers include Ann Dunham, mother of American President Barack Obama; Canadian singer-songwriter, Joni Mitchell; and CBC-TV host and journalist, Anne Petrie.

**See Also:** Adoption; Birth Mothers; Caribbean Mothers; Maternal Absence; Mothers Who Leave; Noncustodial Mother; Nonresidential Mother; Philippines; Unwed Mothers.

**Bibliography**
Cohen, Shellee. "Like a Mother to Them: Stratified Reproduction and West Indian Childcare Workers and Employers in New York." In F. Ginsberg and R. Rapp, eds. *Conceiving the New World Order*. Berkeley: University of California Press, 2005.
Gustafson, Diana L. *Unbecoming Mothers: The Social Construction of Maternal Absence*. New York: Routledge Press, 2005.
Petrie, Anne. *Gone to an Aunt's: Remembering Canada's Homes for Unwed Mothers*. Toronto: McClelland & Stewart, 1998.

Diana L. Gustafson
Memorial University of Newfoundland

# Academe and Mothering

In the United States, women were not admitted to college until 1837, and it took the Civil War, declining enrollments, and over 30 years for more colleges to expand their admissions to include women. By 1900, 70 percent of higher education institutions were coeducational, and women accounted for approximately 30 percent of the student body. Women typically pursued higher education to fulfill their hopes of teaching secondary and higher education. Even then, a college degree increased their chances of getting a better job; however, women could be hired for much less than men. Society viewed teaching as an appropriate female occupation. Throughout history, women continued to enter college in increasing numbers until World War II. The war and its aftermath resulted in a sharp decline in the admissions and graduation of women, which did not return to its prewar rate until 1970.

The 1970s were a time of change for women that involved rising aspirations, delayed marital and family development, and the feminist movement. This led to a drive for equal educational opportunities, and diversity in pursued major area of study; not just teaching any more.

In 1900 the proportion of women on college faculties was 20 percent. It took over 70 years to rise to 25 percent, but since 1970 the percentage of academic women has risen steadily. Currently, approximately 38 percent of academic positions are held by women. Initially, women faculty concentrated in the lower ranks and in less prestigious institutions, and in education, social work, home economics, and nursing disciplines. Now, there is more diversity in discipline, but women are still disproportionately represented at lower ranks. Nationwide, women currently make up approximately 46 percent of assistant professors, 38 percent of associate professors, and 23 percent of full professors, according to the American Association of University Professors (AAUP).

## Mothers in the Professoriate

Although most faculty women taking positions in academe in the early years were single and many women remain childless within academe today, with time mothers joined and continue to join the ranks. Being a mother in academe is said to present women with many challenges. Faculty women find it difficult to balance their careers with motherhood, which is likely due to the demands placed upon them in academia. There are increasingly excessive pressures to attract grants, conduct and publish research, advise students, participate in meetings, and implement creative teaching strategies. Further, university life requires tasks to ensure retention, tenure, and promotion; long hours, ser-

vice work, and an exemplary teaching record; and commitment to the profession and community. All of this is expected to be accomplished while simultaneously meeting the demands of motherhood, which involve childcare, educational activities (such as learning a second language, tutoring, or art classes), and opportunities for enrichment (including piano lessons, soccer camp, and storytelling at the library). In addition to the approximately 50 hours per week faculty women spend working in academia, they spend an additional 15 hours a week engaged in housework and 27 hours engaged in childcare, according to Mason and Goulden. According to Ann Crittenden, mothers also make most of the sacrifices in their lives when it comes to childcare, such as arranging for childcare, transporting their children to and from childcare, changing their work schedules to accommodate their children's needs, taking time off from paid labor to provide primary care, paying for childcare out of their own paychecks, declining promotions, and inevitably decreasing their total workload.

Further, academic mothers seem to disproportionately encounter other challenges, such as infringed boundaries at work and home due in large part to technological advances, such as e-mail; primary responsibility for elder care; and finding time for the pursuit of extracurricular activities that include health-promoting and protective behaviors, such as physical activity and stress management, compared to their male and childless female counterparts. As a result, academic mothers struggle to overcome obstacles to advancement as they maneuver through their careers at the expense of their own health. The combination of motherhood and paid work are competing demands, which often inhibit women's participation in health-promoting behaviors.

The plight of many contemporary women is their perceived failure to "have it all." As such, many women are choosing to opt out of their professions and become stay-at-home mothers, or exit the professoriate (or are expected to do so) in order to find better balance for themselves and their families. However, Leslie Bennetts's *The Feminine Mistake* posits that women can, as many do, have it all. Bennetts urges women to hold on tightly during the exhilarating roller-coaster ride that is having it all—a successful career and family.

## In Search of Balance

Giving up a job to spend more time with family would be downsizing roles to balance one's life. Some stress the implementation of programs, policies, and practices that would support academic mothers and their success. Women have campaigned for a climate change in favor of a more family-friendly environment that respects and provides ways for its employees to survive and thrive. In the same way, individuals and groups have worked toward institutional change and demand improvements.

Academic accommodations designed to recruit and retain academic women and mothers have been growing on a number on campuses across the country. Offering work-life initiatives has demonstrated a reduction in absenteeism, an improvement in accountability, an increase in positive results of recruitment and retention efforts, an increase in productivity, and a reduction in health insurance premiums.

Another important reason cited for changing academic accommodations is for the effect it will likely have on student mothers. Between 1970 and 2001 in the United States, women took the lead over men in their pursuit and attainment of higher education degrees, and currently represent over 56 percent of undergraduates. Further, there is an increasing trend toward more nontraditional students entering colleges and universities than traditional students. According to the National Center for Education Statistics, students may be considered nontraditional for several reasons, including delayed enrollment, enrolled in college part time, and married and/or having children. Frequently, women may be nontraditional for a combination of each of these reasons.

Many women delay entry into higher education or attend part time because they become mothers or are mothers already. Although women are encouraged to earn a college education in the United States, there are often insufficient supports for them to take full advantage of a higher education. For example, mothers may not be able to afford or find quality childcare for their children while they are attending classes.

When childcare centers are opened on college campuses, they typically are available to student parents as well as faculty and staff mothers. A climate of inclusiveness tends to affect student satisfaction, attendance, and success. Mothering in academe is a reality that is gaining popularity, and mothers across the country are urging to have their needs addressed to maintain their advancement in society.

**See Also:** Breastfeeding; Childcare; Childlessness; Daycare; Economics of Motherhood; Education and Mothering; Employment and Motherhood.

## Bibliography

Bassett, Rachel Hile, ed. *Parenting and Professing: Balancing Work With an Academic Career*. Nashville, TN: Vanderbilt University Press, 2005.

Bennetts, Leslie. *The Feminine Mistake: Are We Giving Up Too Much*. New York: Hyperion, 2007.

Crittenden, Ann. *The Price of Motherhood*. New York: Henry Holt, 2001.

Evans, Elrena and Caroline Grant, eds. *Mama PhD: Women Write About Motherhood and Academic Life*. New Brunswick, NJ: Rutgers University Press, 2008.

*Journal of the Association for Research on Mothering*. Mothering in the Academy [special issue], v.5/2 (Fall/Winter 2003).

Williams, Joan. *Unbending Gender: Why Family and Work Conflict and What to Do About It*. New York: Oxford University Press, 2000.

Michele L. Vancour
Southern Connecticut State University

# Activism, Maternal

Historically, women have found that they could take up a public political role—one often traditionally denied to them through the prevailing political process—by advocating for causes that had a social currency. Although such women did not take on causes merely to aid their own fight for equality, their voices became heard more strongly than ever in mainstream political discourse. In the case of mothers, this public role has been a particularly obvious one. The increasing delineation of gender roles during the 19th century—with males belonging to the public world of work while females inhabited the domestic world of the home—made it necessary for women to use their motherhood both as a tool

*Motherhood activism often revolves around health care and a better life for children. Mariama Diamanka (left) discusses the advantages of Kolda's new mutual health organization in Senegal with fellow women's activist Khady Balde.*

to establish their rights, and as a way of bringing about the possibility of social justice. Moreover, at the same time, government propaganda of the idealized mother as representative of the nation gave mothers a certain moral authority that other groups found more difficult to achieve, something that has also translated into the role of mothers as activists.

### Examples of Maternal Activism

Maternal activism crosses ethnic, class, and racial divides and may be the result of a direct assault on one's own family. An example is the work of the Mothers of the Plaza de Mayo in Argentina, who came together in an attempt to find their missing sons and daughters who had been abducted during the years known as the Dirty War (1976–83). Many of those sons and daughters had been tortured and killed, and the Mothers campaigned for the prosecution of those responsible. Similar examples

include Mothers Against Guns in London, who aim to prevent more young people becoming victims of gun crime; and Mothers Against Drink Driving, a campaigning organization founded by two mothers in the United States. The role of mothers has also been a recurring theme in examinations of the Palestinian conflict.

Some maternal activism is an extension of the mother's ethic of care in general. Often, it is mothers who are at the forefront of campaigns such as the improvement of the environment or of health care provisions, not only because it would aid their own child's development, but because they feel it would impact children in the community in general. Such everyday activism has also been greatly facilitated by the development of online blogs, not only because these often serve as a force for mobilization, but because they alert mothers who may not have a particular political goal to become active in a cause for the common good. An example of this is the Mama to Mama initiative developed by Amanda Soule at soulemama.com, where handcrafters are encouraged "to connect . . . with mothers, children and families in need of a little bit of handmade love," and whose projects include, amongst others, an initiative to send caps for newborn babies in Haiti.

## Blurring the Lines

What is striking about all of these initiatives—whether radical or everyday—is that they blur the lines between the public and the private spheres, and in so doing play very much into the notion of the personal being political, which has been critical to second-wave conceptions of feminism. The case of maternal activism is significant because the variety of roles inhabited by women actually enables them to speak with the moral authority and community engagement through which their goals will be realized. Moreover, while mothers may become activists whatever their educational, ethnic-racial, or class backgrounds, the tools they use in order to mobilize and realize their activism may be different depending upon each background. Mothers' use of online resources is more likely if they have the financial and educational circumstances to achieve such access, while community activism may be more difficult for those who do not have a recognized community around them.

Finally, it is important to emphasize the continuing gendered nature of maternal activism. Paternal activism is not discussed in any significant sense, and those groups that do exist, such as Fathers for Justice, are generally perceived not to be protesting the life conditions of children per se, but rather the impact of the relationship between men and women on them. In a very real sense, it remains the case that it is women, and often mothers specifically, who are usually assumed to be primarily qualified to advocate on behalf of a child.

It is not necessary to be a biological mother to be an activist mother, nor to be motivated primarily by concern for one's own children. Naples found that the concept of mothering extended beyond the actual family group among female African American and Latina community activists combating racism and classicism: Those with children of their own said they were motivated by concern for their chil-

dren's welfare, and those who did not have children of their own were motivated by a sense of responsibility for the community, including other women's children. Cheryl Gilkes and Patricia Hill Collins both found that such "other mothers" who help build the community were particularly important in inspiring young women to activism. Additionally, bell hooks emphasizes the responsibility middle-class African American mothers have felt, from the 19th century to today, to improve the health and welfare of African American mothers less fortunate than themselves.

**See Also:** Activist Mothers of the Disappeared; African American Mothers; Collins, Patricia Hill; hooks, bell; Mothers Acting Up (MAU); Mothers Against Drunk Driving (MADD); Mothers of the Intifada; Mothers Movement Online; Palestine.

## Bibliography

Bouvard, Margurite. *Revolutionizing Motherhood: The Mothers of the Plaza de Mayo*. Lanham, MD: SR Books, 2002.

Jetter, Alexis, Annelise Orleck, and Diana Taylor, eds. *The Politics of Motherhood: Activist Voices From Left to Right*. Lebanon, NH: University Press of New England, 1997.

Naples, Nancy A. *Grassroots Warriors: Activist Mothering, Community Work and the War on Poverty*. New York: Routledge, 1998.

O'Reilly, Andrea. *Feminist Mothering*. Albany: State University of New York Press, 2008.

O'Reilly, Andrea. *You Say You Want a Revolution?: The 21st Century Motherhood Movement*. Toronto: Demeter Press, 2010.

Kim Miller
Wheaton College

# Activist Mothers of the Disappeared

Activist Mothers of the Disappeared are groups of mothers who form collectives to seek reunification with their "disappeared" children. Also referred to as forced disappearances, abductions of young children and adults by both the state and the government opposition are common in countries embroiled in civil and political unrest. Though these disappearances are treated as kidnappings, it is generally assumed that the victim has been murdered, most likely after enduring a period of torture. Disappearances are currently more often associated with state terrorism, though they are also understood to be a tactic of other forms of systemic oppression. Activist mothers protest these disappearances by performing and projecting images of maternity in public spaces and challenging fixed constructions of maternal identity and motherhood.

## Cultural Expectations and Maternal Identity

Efforts to locate the "disappeared" have been catalyzed by mothers of all social and economic classes, though most organizations are more commonly associated with mothers from the working class with little social or political mobility. Many of these activist mothers are citizens of developing countries that are dominated by traditions of patriarchy and, in some cases, are still experiencing vestiges of colonial rule. Though women tend to be both formally and informally oppressed in these countries, mothers maintain a degree of reverence, especially in areas with more religious presence. Because the patriarchal culture in these countries expects that women become mothers, the activist mothers maintain some leverage and mobility in that they are acting within their culturally prescribed maternal identities. Though they have transgressed their expected gender roles by challenging the boundaries of the private and public spheres, activist mothers remain relatively protected by their maternal identity.

## Performances of Maternity as Tactic

Activist mothers are keenly aware of the extent of their power as mothers, and will draw from, and even emphasize, their maternal and gender identities to deploy their tactics. By projecting traditional characteristics of maternity, such as pain, suffering, and submission, the mothers deploy their identity in subversive ways. A famous example is the wearing of white shawls on the heads of the Mothers of the Plaza de Mayo as they marched in the streets to protest the disappearances during Argentina's Dirty War. The white shawls were worn to imitate

religious *mantillas* that were traditional, but were not owned by all the mothers, as a means of distinguishing the activist mothers from the other women. The shawls were also embroidered with children's names to symbolize the baby blankets of the disappeared children. Though other activist mother organizations have considered such practices, some reject the use of gender-encoded items such as *mantillas* and even shawls in their efforts to challenge traditional paradigms.

## In the Americas

Activist mothers of the disappeared have formed collectives around the world, but the most recognized of these mothers hail from South and Central America. The Argentine Madres de Plaza de Mayo organized one of the most documented movements to protest the disappearances of their own children as well as between 11,000 and 30,000 *desaparecidos* (disappeared) during a military dictatorship between 1976 and 1983. These activist mothers not only challenged the dictatorship, but also destabilized rigid cultural constructions of motherhood. Their desire to find their children necessitated that they transgress the expectations of "good" motherhood by, most of all, taking their struggle out of the private sphere and into the public sphere.

The Mothers of the Plaza de Mayo have become powerful archetypes for other activist mother organizations. In Juárez, Mexico, and along the U.S.-Mexico border, the estimated 500 disappearances and femicide of Mexican girls and women have prompted mothers to organize. Hijas de Regreso a Casa (May Our Daughters Return Home) and Justicia para Nuestras Hijas (Justice for Our Daughters) are two regional groups that have formed to seek answers and have continued the legacy of maternal activism. These groups are in solidarity with established activist mother groups in Mexico, such as Union of Mothers with Disappeared Children of Sinaloa.

Other activist mothers groups have organized to protest the disappearances of children during times of civil unrest and dictatorship in Latin American countries such as El Salvador, Guatemala, Honduras, and Chile. Since the beginning of the century, forced disappearances have occurred, and continue to occur, in many countries, such as India, Algeria,

Pakistan, Ireland, Sri Lanka, Iran, Iraq, Afghanistan, Chechnya, and Germany. Though nongovernmental organizations such as Amnesty International have worked to address this global problem, legal and cultural barriers in many of these countries impede formal organizing by mothers.

**See Also:** Activism, Maternal; Argentina; Genocide; Mexico; Mothers of the Intifada; Mothers of the Plaza de Mayo; Patriarchal Ideology of Motherhood; Social Action and Motherhood.

**Bibliography**

Amnesty International. "Middle East/North Africa: Day of the 'Disappeared'—Time to Tell the Whole Truth." www.algeria-watch.org (accessed July 2009).

Bejarano, Cynthia L. "Las Super Madres de Latino America: Transforming Motherhood by Challenging Violence in Mexico, Argentina, and El Salvador." *Frontiers: A Journal of Women's Studies*, v.23/1 (2002).

Fisher, Josephine. *Mothers of the Disappeared*. Cambridge, MA: South End Press, 1999.

Guzmán Bouvard, Marguerite. *Revolutionizing Motherhood: The Mothers of the Plaza de Mayo*. Lanham, MD: SR Books, 2002.

Portillo, Lourdes. *Señorita Extraviada*. Film, 2001.

Taylor, Diana. *Disappearing Acts: Spectacles of Gender and Nationalism in Argentina's "Dirty War."* Durham, NC: Duke University Press, 1997.

Wright, Melissa. "Urban Geography Plenary Lecture—Femicide, Mother-Activism, and the Geography of Protest in Northern Mexico." *Urban Geography*, v.28/5 (2007).

Larissa M. Mercado-López
University of Texas, San Antonio

# Adams, Abigail (Smith)

Abigail Smith (1744–1818) was born at Weymouth, Massachusetts, and married John Adams in 1764. While she was the first woman to be the wife a President and mother to another, she may be better remembered for her letter writing, especially to John during the Continental Congress of 1776. Her appeal to John to "remember the ladies" makes her one of the United States first feminist icons even among women who may scoff at the label: ". . . remember the Ladies, and be more generous and favorable to them than your ancestors. Do not put such unlimited power into the hands of the Husbands. Remember all Men would be tyrants if they could. If particular care and attention is not paid to the Ladies we are determined to foment a Rebellion and will not hold ourselves bound by any Laws in which we have no voice or Representation."

Regardless of whether John listened to her or not, women were not written into the Constitution until the Nineteenth Amendment granted women the right to vote. Abigail's letter has been argued to be the start of the American feminist timeline. She continued to be a vocal supporter of women's rights and abolition throughout her life, including during her duty as First Lady. The amount of travel that John performed during the early days of the United States instigated the letter writing that stands as a document to the country's birth. Abigail had been asked to publish her letters during her lifetime, but she felt her letters were too private for public reading. She confided to her daughter how stressed she was as First Lady.

Abigail would say one thing in public, complain to her daughter about the same thing, and then exhort her daughter to say that her mother was very happy. Her letters to John were finally published years after her death by her son, and was the first such publication focused on a First Lady. During John's travel, Abigail also raised their five children and managed the family farm on her own. However, she did not live to see her son, John Quincy, become President; she died in 1818.

Abigail was a trusted confidante to her husband throughout their marriage. Their correspondence during the war and his diplomatic journeys to Europe reveal that John sought out her advice. During John's Presidency, Abigail was both beloved and hated for her counselor role, much as Hillary Rodham Clinton was in the 1990s. In one instance during his Presidency, after John Adams had made an unpopular appointing in this wife's absence, he wrote to inform her: "O how they lament Mrs. A's absence. . . . She is a good counselor!" The dichotomy between Abigail and Martha Washington was night and day. Abigail espoused the role of First Lady as a Mrs. President, while Martha crafted the more traditional role of the good hostess. Abigail saw the role of First Lady as not just a hostess, but as a partisan defender of her husband's policies, which she did splendidly.

Abigail Adams's role in the birth of the United States was predominately featured in the HBO miniseries *John Adams* in 2008. Laura Linney received a Golden Globe award for her portrayal.

**See Also:** Clinton, Hillary Rodham; Kennedy Onassis, Jacqueline; War and Mothers.

**Bibliography**

Caroli, Betty Boyd. *First Ladies: An Intimate Look at How 38 Women Handled What May Be the Most Demanding, Unpaid, Unelected Job in America.* New York: Oxford University Press, 1995.

First Lady Biography. "Abigail Adams." http://www .firstladies.org/biographies/firstladies.aspx?biography =2 (accessed April 2009).

The White House. "Biography of Abigail Smith Adams." http://www.whitehouse.gov/history/firstladies/ aa2.html (accessed April 2009).

Veronica I. Arreola
University of Illinois at Chicago

# Adolescent Children

Adolescence is a developmental period within the human life span that separates childhood from adulthood. It is marked by multiple transitions such as the onset of puberty and its corresponding rapid developmental growth, cognitive gains, transitions in schooling, shifts in familial and social relationships, and increasing autonomy and choice. Adolescence is typically considered to begin when a child reaches age 13; however, many biological, social, and psychological changes have already begun in the preadolescent years.

Puberty refers to the physical changes that occur as a child's body becomes capable of reproduction. Pubertal changes include rapid physical growth; redistribution and/or increases in body fat and muscle tissues; acquiring secondary sexual characteristics, such as breasts and pubic hair; menarche (for girls); and spermarche (for boys). Other changes that occur with puberty include acne and increases in body odor, strength, and endurance. Overall puberty takes five to six years to complete for most individuals. While often thought of as a marker for entry into adolescence, hormonal changes begin in middle childhood (approximately 8 years old for girls and 10 years old for boys). However, the onset of puberty can vary greatly by individual.

The adolescent period is often divided into three stages: early adolescence, middle adolescence, and late adolescence/young adulthood. *Early adolescence* refers to children aged 11 to 14 who are still undergoing many of the physical changes of puberty.

Other transitions that can occur at this period include multiple school transitions, increased responsibilities in the home, and an increasing desire to conform to peer influences. The middle adolescent stage includes children aged 15 to 17 years old, while late adolescence/young adulthood is typically applied to individuals between the ages of 18 and 21. While these later stages involve multiple transitions as well—including school changes, initiation of intimate relationships, and paid employment—most adolescents have achieved their adult height and full reproductive capacity by this time.

The end point of adolescence is not well defined, and often differs by culture as markers for reaching adulthood status are culturally determined. Entry to adulthood can include independent living; the ability to perform certain functions within the society, such as voting or serving in the armed forces; parenthood; and/or full-time employment. In many Western societies, adolescence has been extended into the early 20s due to increased expectations of postsecondary education and monetary dependence upon parents.

### Adolescent Health

Adolescence, while a fundamentally healthy time in an individual's life, is also associated with an increase in unhealthy and/or risky behaviors that are associated with poor health outcomes later in life. Adolescence is marked by an increase in sedentary behaviors and the development of unhealthy eating habits, as well as experimentation with risky situations such as drug use and unprotected sexual activity.

Parents play a critical role in the formation of their adolescent children's health habits through role modeling, communication efforts, and the setting of household policies and practices. Stronger associations have been found for the intergenerational transmission of health habits and risky behaviors for mothers than for fathers, with the strongest effects occurring between mothers and daughters. Adolescent children talk more with their mothers than their fathers, in part because mothers are perceived as being more emotionally available and empathetic and in part because mothers are more physically available in the lives of adolescent children. Adolescent reports of frequency of sexual communication with mothers is associated with safer sex practices, such as more condom and other contraceptive use, fewer intercourse episodes, fewer days of unprotected sex, and delayed sexual initiation.

## Reproductive Timing

The timing of reproductive transitions, specifically whether a transition occurs around the same time as the rest of a cohort or off time (earlier or later than their cohort) has been found to affect adolescent health and well-being. Early maturation in girls is linked to greater alcohol, tobacco, and/or substance use; earlier initiation and possibly faster progression from cigarette and alcohol use to other drugs; and higher rates of substance abuse disorder by mid adolescence. Early maturing girls may also show higher rates of depression and conduct disorders than other girls. Early maturing girls, because they appear older, are often thrust into social situations for which they are not prepared. Therefore, deficits in social interactions may be a pathway from early maturation to subsequent externalizing symptoms and possibly drug use for girls. Reproductive timing effects have been found for the wellbeing of boys as well, but they are not as strong as the effects found for girls. Associations have been found between early-maturing boys and both depression and tobacco use. In addition, late-maturation among boys has also been associated with adjustment difficulties, including greater internalizing problems and more problems with school.

Like adolescence, the onset of menopause, or the perimenopausal period, is also defined by multiple transitions, including changes in body image, reproductive role, and social status, as well as hormonal fluctuations that may affect mood, sleep, and general well-being. Most mothers enter the perimenopausal period around the time their children are adolescents. The timing of both maternal and adolescent reproductive transitions within the family may play a critical role in the formation of risk behaviors for adolescents as well as affect mothers' health behaviors and stress levels. Mothers are facing new challenges in parenting and potentially changing feelings about their own bodies, reproduction, and health.

## Mother–Adolescent Relationships

Adolescent children undergo shifts in their relationships with their parents. Earlier developmental models viewed separation, or a break in the parent–child relationship, to be necessary for optimal growth and eventual individuation. Adolescence was seen as a stormy and difficult phase for the family. More recent research has supported the permanence of parent–child ties throughout the adolescent period and point to satisfaction in parent–child relationship as the norm in most families. However, parent–child conflict does increase during this timeframe, and is considered both developmentally appropriate and healthy. Conflict within families increases due to adolescents' emerging ability for abstract thought, which allows them to critically examine previously accepted rules and norms. In addition, adolescent's increased need for autonomy and interest in peer relations create fodder for parent–child disagreements with regard to daily routines and activities. Parent–child conflict occurs most frequently in early adolescence (11–14 years old) and is generally more common between adolescents and mothers, particularly between mothers and daughters.

Mother–adolescent relationships are often perceived as strained by both parties, in part due to the increase in conflict that is experienced. However, it is primarily adolescents who experience this dissatisfaction; while mothers may perceive more negative interactions with their adolescent children, they also report more positive interactions, resulting in a largely stable sense of relationship satisfaction. The daily stresses and strains that affect mothers' lives do not have a significant affect on their adolescent children, yet the hassles and mood shifts experienced by adolescents have been shown to have an affect on mothers' emotional states. The emotional well-being of mothers is related to the level of intensity of conflict between mothers and their adolescent children. This relationship has not been found for fathers.

On the far end of the continuum of parent–adolescent conflict is parental abuse. While parental abuse is not normative, it is also not inconsequential, with estimates ranging from 7 to 11 percent of the general population. This range may be an underestimation, since family abuse is often underreported. Abuse of parents by their adolescent children occurs primarily to mothers and is mostly perpetrated by sons, although daughters can be abusive as well. Explanations for parental abuse include adolescent substance abuse and/or psychiatric disorders, continuation of abuse originally modeled by the father after a separation, and a sense of entitlement by youth in a society that has become overly youth focused.

**Gender Differences**
Spending time with their mothers is an important protective factor for boys. This is particularly true for spending time alone and/or talking with their mothers. For girls, the amount of time spent with their mothers is not as important to their wellbeing as is the quality of the time they spend together. Attachments between mothers and sons tend to be less intense than those between mothers and daughters, and greater emotional enmeshment has been found in mother–daughter relationships than in mother–son relationships, with boys reporting more emotional autonomy from their mothers than girls.

Little research has been conducted on mother–son relationships in adolescence; however, a large body of literature exists on mother–daughter relationships at this developmental period. Mother–daughter relationships during adolescence combine a unique blend of closeness, conflict, and control. Mothers tend to be more critical of their daughters than their sons and have been shown to interrupt them more often. Due to differences in attachment and communication processes, mother–daughter conflicts occur more frequently and are of a longer duration than mother–son conflicts.

Gender-specific theoretical perspectives have claimed that adolescent girls' psychological development occurs through their connections with significant others and that they desire to maintain these connections, particularly with their mothers, throughout adolescence. Mother–daughter relations during adolescence may serve as either a risk or a protective factor for girls' engagement in a variety of health-compromising behaviors. The timing of reproductive transitions (puberty and perimenopause) between mothers and daughters may be particularly salient to mother–daughter relations. For mothers of adolescent girls, watching their daughters enter puberty while they are entering or anticipating menopause may play a unique role in their feelings toward their daughters' bodies and may alter how they interact with their daughter as well as the behaviors they themselves are modeling in the home.

Psychologist Carol Gilligan's studies detailed the loss of confidence often suffered by female adolescents just as they are preparing to enter adulthood. Elizabeth Debold and collaborators trace this loss to pressure girls feel in adolescence to discard their individuality and intellectual ambitions in order to fit a societal "mold" in which they are judged primarily by how well they meet narrowly focused definitions of beauty and personality. In *Mother Daughter Revolution* (1993), Debold argues that mothers traditionally play a primary role in encouraging their daughters to conform to societal norms while boys are encouraged to value their individuality and take their place in the world. This research has been criticized on many grounds: that it depends heavily on questionable interpretations of psychological interviews, that it primarily applies to the white upper-class girls who were Gilligan's initial subjects, and that it overemphasizes small difference among male and female adolescents.

**Changes to Maternal Practice**
Mothers play a unique role in the family system. The maternal role typically involves executive functions for the planning, organization, and delivery of daily household routines as well as family traditions and rituals. Mothers spend more time with their children than fathers and often act as the emotional support system for the family as well as the family's health care provider. Acting in these capacities, mothers tend to become more intimately involved with their adolescent children than fathers or other adult family members and, as a consequence, are

subject to more parent–child conflict over family routines and policies.

Developmental transitions experienced by adolescent children affect the family system as well as alter maternal roles and responsibilities. Due to their increasing autonomy and competence, adolescent children require less daily care than younger children, allowing mothers more time for their own pursuits and interests. At the same time, parenting adolescent children requires the acquisition of new strategies and skills to support adolescents' initial attempts at autonomy and independence as well as to assist them as they navigate adulthood status, including living independently.

While issues of childcare take a backseat once children reach adolescence, they do not disappear completely. The after-school hours have been identified as a critical time for adolescents' engagement in problem behaviors, such as drug use, delinquency, and risky sexual behaviors. Unsupervised time has been linked with greater engagement in problem behaviors. Although many adolescents are involved in extracurricular activities during the after-school hours, availability of these programs is highly dependent upon socioeconomic status and location, with poor and rural families having far fewer options. Many extracurricular activities do not cover all the hours needed for families with working parents, and many may require drop-off and pickup service. Families are often forced to create patchwork coverage to meet the needs of both the working parents and the adolescent. Making and sustaining these accommodations often becomes the work of mothers.

**See Also:** Adult Children; Children; Daughters and Mothers; Sons and Mothers.

**Bibliography**
Archibald, Andrea B., Julia A. Graber, and Jeanne Brooks-Gunn. "Pubertal Processes and Physiological Growth in Adolescence." In Gerald R. Adams and Michael D. Berzonsky, eds., *Handbook on Adolescence*. Malden, MA: Blackwell Publishers, 2005.
Kurz, Demie. "Work-Family Issues of Mothers of Teenage Children." *Qualitative Sociology*, v.23/4 (2000).
Larson, Reed, and Maryse H. Richards. *Divergent Realities: The Emotional Lives of Mothers, Fathers, and Adolescents*. New York: Basic Books, 1994.
Stewart, Michel, Ailsa Burns, and Rosemary Leonard. "Dark Side of the Mothering Role: Abuse of Mothers by Adolescent and Adult Children." *Sex Roles*, v.56 (2007).

Tracy R. Nichols
University of North Carolina at Greensboro

# Adoption

Adoption has been a part of parenting for centuries. The Babylonians, Egyptians, Hebrews, and Hindus of ancient times all made reference to adoption in their laws and codes, and adoption is also mentioned in the Bible.

### Early History of Adoption
Roman law permitted adoption, but unlike today, where it is usually done in the best interests of the child, earlier adoption occurred primarily to benefit those doing the adopting. Roman adoption law provided an opportunity for childless couples to maintain family inheritances by adopting sons who would carry on both the family name and religious requirements that families have sons. Adoptees were all male and usually adults. English law did not address adoption because there did not appear to have been a need, since inheritance could occur only through blood lineage.

### History of Adoption: 18th–19th Centuries
By the 17th century, adoption had become unnecessary, as orphaned children or those whose parents could not care for them were most often placed in other homes for domestic service, indenture, and apprenticeship. Children who were not yet old enough to be "put out" to homes for work were placed in almshouses—public institutions for children—until they were 6 or 7 years old.

The first American almshouses were built in the 1700s, but by the mid-1800s most of them were gone. Often, 80 percent of the people in the almshouses were mentally ill, and the remaining children were often abused and neglected. Nineteenth-century adoption laws were put into place in order to take better care of children who were dependents of the system. In 1851, Massachusetts became the first state to enact such a law, which contained the following provisions: (1) the natural parents or legal guardian must give written consent; (2) both adoptive parents must consent to the adoption; (3) an adoptive child 14 years or older must also consent to the placement; (4) the judge involved in the adoption must be satisfied that the parents were suitable to care for the child; (5) once the adoption was approved by the court, the child's status would be the same as if he or she were a biological child, and (6) the biological parents forfeited all legal rights and obligations to the child. This law was the precursor to much of adoption law as it exists today.

In 1853, the Children's Aid Society of New York City began a program to deal with orphaned, abandoned, and otherwise homeless children on the streets of the city. The society began sending children ages 2–14 to live with farm families for permanent placement to provide farm labor, in an effort to keep the children from falling victim to life on the streets. This program included the *orphan train movement,* where children were placed on a train in eastern cities and then shipped westward to be adopted by farmers. There was such a demand for the children that the train stops were announced in advance; farmers showed up to inspect the children, selected them, and take them home. Historians estimate that as many as 100,000 children were placed on farms throughout the Midwest during the time the orphan train movement existed from 1854 to 1904, although a few trains ran as late as 1929. Unfortunately, there was no follow-up to ensure that the children were formally adopted by the farmers; apparently, many of the children had parents who had not forfeited their rights nor knew that their children had been sent to the rural communities.

### History of Adoption: Early 20th Century

Another attempt to care for America's homeless, dependent children included foundling homes—public and private institutions that housed and cared for them. With the influx of immigrants to America and the problems of poverty and urban slums, the foundling homes soon became overwhelmed. Mortality rates in foundling homes were extremely high, due in part to the absence of the nursing mothers. Illnesses such as measles, influenza, and other child-

hood diseases, along with the overcrowded conditions, were particularly disastrous for the children who resided in the homes. The developmental delays that physicians saw in the children because of their lack of personal attention and nurturing contributed to efforts to find placements for them in private homes. Infants were adopted out to families in increasing numbers, often with inadequate supervision, little or no investigation of the adoptive families, and no follow-up with the children. Legislation to protect the children was greatly needed.

Eventually following the lead of Massachusetts, by 1929 all states had passed some sort of adoption legislation. The "best interests of the child" was foremost in the statutes of most states. By mid-century, secrecy, anonymity, and sealing of records became standard adoption practice. Minnesota was the first state to initiate such laws, enacted primarily to shield the proceedings from the public eye, rather than to protect the identities of those concerned. Initially, the statutes permitted access to the information only by involved parties and their attorneys, but eventually most states barred any and all persons from the ability to inspect records, unless ordered by a judge. The original birth certificate was sealed and any and all birth and adoption information was kept from the biological parents, the adoptive parents, and the child.

During the 1920s, following World War I and the nation's influenza pandemic, there was a decrease in the birthrate, which resulted in an increase in demand for babies. The result was an influx of what came to be called *baby brokers,* unregulated agencies that found homes for infants; and black market adoptions, babies who were sold to adoptive parents. Private adoptions became the norm. As a result, most states passed legislation requiring investigations of adoptive parents and their homes, as well as approval of a judge before an adoption could be finalized.

### History of Adoption: Post–World War II

After World War II came another period of high demand for adoptable infants, but during that time the number of available infants nearly matched the requests for adoption. More than half of the babies up for adoption were the offspring of unwed mothers, 40 percent of whom were teenagers. The remainder of the babies were available due to the many divorces that followed World War II. By the mid-1950s, the tide had turned again and the demand for babies far outweighed the adoptable infant population. This mismatch continued until the mid-1970s, when many agencies refused to accept new applications for white, healthy babies. The wait was often three to five years with both public and private adoption agencies. A number of factors probably contributed to the lack of available infants for adoption: birth control, an increased incidence of infertility, abortions following the 1973 *Roe v. Wade* decision, and finally, the increase in the number of unwed, white mothers who elected to keep their babies.

Although white infants were in high demand for adoption, children with physical, mental, or emotional disabilities; older children; and children of color were not. Individuals and families willing to adopt children with disabilities were in short supply. The numbers of older children, children with disabilities, and children of color continued to increase, and by the latter part of the 20th century, children with AIDS became part of that group of "special needs" children, children for whom adoption was highly unlikely. Many special needs children spent their early lives in foster care.

Also in the latter part of the 20th century, adoption rights advocates began lobbying for more openness in the adoption process. Professionals, caregivers, and other practitioners found that adopted children suffered from self-esteem issues, identity confusion, and other problems that they attributed to the secrecy surrounding their birth parents. As that same cohort grew to adulthood, they formed activist groups and challenged the lack of access to their birth records and other pertinent information. In 1971, adoptee Florence Fisher founded the Adoptees Liberty Movement Association (ALMA), and not long afterward, a group of birth parents formed Concerned United Birthparents (CUB). Opponents to the idea of opening birth records and losing their anonymity formed their own groups, one of which is called Association for the Protection of the Adoptive Triangle (APAT).

Organizations such as ALMA provide a central clearinghouse for adoptees and birth parents who are trying to locate each other. For a one-time $50 fee, persons wishing to register can provide pertinent information about themselves in the hope that the child or parent, as the case may be, is also looking. With the advent of the Internet, registration and searching has streamlined the process somewhat, and ALMA boasted 170 matches in the year 2008 alone.

In the mid-1970s, in part because of an effort to avoid the problems with closed adoptions, many private agencies began arranging "open" adoptions. In this type of agreement, birth parents and prospective adoptive parents meet one another; exchange information; and decide how much contact, if any, the birth parents will be permitted with the child. Advocates of open adoption believe that involving the birth parents in the adoption process can provide valuable medical and genetic information for the child, as well as giving the adopted child a sense of identity that the closed adoption prohibits.

## Adoption Home Study

All adoptions in the United States, whether public or private, special needs or international, require a home study. Home studies are conducted to determine the prospective parents' suitability for parenting, motivation to adopt, financial stability, family environment, physical and health history of the prospective parents, and criminal background of the potential adoptive parents. A home study can take from three to six months, but may take longer when conducted by a public agency. Education for prospective parents is also a part of the home study, and most agencies require that parents attend a series of training sessions before the home study can be completed.

## Current Adoption Practices

Today there are essentially four different types of adoptions: (1) domestic adoptions of newborns through public and nonprofit agencies, both open and closed; (2) private adoptions, usually open to some degree; (3) domestic adoptions of "special needs" children; and (4) international adoptions of various types and ages of children from as many as 75 different countries. The cost of adoption runs anywhere from no fees for a child adopted from foster care, to $40,000 for a private domestic adoption. International adoptions usually cost between $10,000–$25,000, but may run more than $35,000.

The following is a description of the practices and procedures of each type of adoption:

## Domestic Adoption Through Agencies

Domestic adoptions of newborns are becoming increasingly rare in the United States, in part because of the cultural acceptance of single mothers. Young women who previously would have placed their babies for adoption by prospective parents are now choosing to raise the children themselves. The availability of services for single teen mothers, including the right to remain in public schools, childcare in high schools, welfare programs, and medical benefits for dependent children have made the possibility of keeping their babies more realistic for unwed mothers. Older, single women who might otherwise have placed their babies for adoption are better able to take care of both themselves and their children and are more likely to keep them, regardless of their marital status or the presence of a father.

Most newborn adoptions in the United States, especially of white babies, are done through private or nonprofit agencies. Typically, parents place their names on waiting lists with one or more adoption agencies, depending on their ability to pay. The wait for a white baby can be as long as five years, although many agencies advertise that their average wait time is much less. The fees associated with the adoption include a charge for the home study, medical expenses for the birth mother, and the placement fee.

African American babies are available to adoptive parents at a reduced fee from many adoption agencies. Because there are more African American and biracial babies than white babies, the wait time is considerably less than for white babies, and infants as young as a few days old are often available. Parents who are not African American but wish to adopt children who are African American or biracial are usually required to attend seminars on the special issues that multiracial families face.

## Private Domestic Adoptions

Private (or independent) adoption is a legal method of building a family through adoption without using an adoption agency for placement. In private adoption, the birth parents relinquish their parental rights directly to the adoptive parents, instead of to an agency. Some of the advantages of a private adoption include the ability for the birth and adoptive parents to meet each other to discuss the future

of the baby, the ability to get firsthand information from the birth parents about their backgrounds and medical histories, the possibility for adoptive parents to take an infant directly home from the hospital after birth, and for some, a shorter waiting period. Disadvantages include the inability to select the sex of the child, unpredictable medical costs (versus set medical costs through most agencies), and the stress caused by concern over whether or not either party might change their minds.

In some private adoption cases, a birth mother will move in with the adoptive parents for a period of time before the birth, giving her an opportunity to get to know them better, while also giving the adoptive parents a certain amount of control over how the birth mother cares for herself. The adoptive parents pay the medical expenses of the birth mother, and once the infant is born, they leave the hospital with the newborn.

Some prospective parents use newspaper and Internet ads to search for pregnant women willing to place their babies for adoption. A typical ad might read: "We are looking to adopt a baby. We could give him or her a loving home and everything a child could want or need! Please consider us!" Websites are set up for prospective adoptive couples who can post lengthy essays about themselves and their backgrounds, along with photos, in the hope that they will be chosen to adopt a child from a willing birth mother. One such Website provided profiles of more than 300 potential adoptive parents, available to be read by prospective birth parents. Prices for these Web postings start at about $100 per month.

Although accurate statistics are not available, it is estimated that one-half to two-thirds of all infant adoptions that take place in the United State are private. Some jurisdictions require that birth and adoptive parents have direct contact with each other, and private adoptions must still be handled by adoption attorneys in order to file all the necessary paperwork with the appropriate courts, as well as protect both the birth and adoptive parents.

## Open Adoption

Because the term *open adoption* has so many interpretations, it has become somewhat meaningless and varies from state to state. According to the National Adoption Information Clearinghouse:

Open, or fully disclosed, adoptions allow adoptive parents, and often the adopted child, to interact directly with birth parents. Family members interact in ways that feel most comfortable to them. Communication may include letters, emails, telephone calls, or visits. The frequency of contact is negotiated and can range from every few years to several times a month or more. Contact often changes as a child grows and has more questions about his or her adoption or as families' needs change. It is important to note that even in an open adoption, the legal relationship between a birth parent and child is severed.

The goals of open adoption are:

- To minimize the child's loss of relationships.
- To maintain and celebrate the adopted child's connections with all the important people in his or her life.
- To allow the child to resolve losses with truth, rather than the fantasy adopted children often create when no information or contact with their birth family is available.

## Special Needs Adoption

A child is usually designated as "special needs" if he or she is older than 10 (this can vary by state); has physical, medical, or emotional issues that require medication or therapy; has AIDS or is HIV-positive; or is biracial or nonwhite. Sibling groups are also considered special needs, as they are typically more difficult to place. Most states have active social welfare agencies that work to place foster children in permanent homes, once the children become available for placement. Unlike an infant adoption, where the parents are searching for a child who will fit into their lives, older-children adoptions are handled to match the prospective parents to the child or children, with the needs of the children considered first.

Children may spend years in foster care while their birth parents deal with their own issues, and the children may go back and forth from the birth parents to foster care before the parental rights of the biological parents are finally terminated. Some children languish in foster care while waiting to be

*The National Adoption Clearinghouse, a nonprofit agency, helps place children and teenagers with U.S. families.*

adopted. Other children, when they reach a particular age, will be given the choice whether to make themselves available for adoption or to "age out" of the system. Sibling groups are particularly difficult to place, and while effort is made to place children together, it does not always occur. Siblings may be placed in different foster homes and eventually, permanently placed in different homes.

In most states, adoptions of special needs children through a state Department of Children's Services or similar agency, are done at no or very little cost to the adoptive parents. Additionally, special needs children usually qualify for adoption assistance payments—for medical expenses, psychological counseling, and other needs. These payments vary from child to child and from state to state. Most children are covered under a state's public medical and dental plans, if needed. In some states, medical expenses not covered by the adoptive parents' private insurance may be paid by the state.

Public agencies looking to find parents for foster children employ various methods to bring parents and children together. Many agencies partner with television and newspaper outlets to feature children in Wednesday's Child segments and the like. Children are featured on billboards, in advertisements, and on Websites. A *match party,* sometimes called an *adoption party,* is a carefully planned event designed to bring together children who are waiting to be adopted with families interested in adopting them. In some cases, this means only families who have been approved to adopt; in other cases, the party may be open to those who may have been thinking about adoption. The parties are designed to place children in an informal setting where they can meet prospective parents.

As a nonprofit agency that helps place older children and teenagers with families all over the United States, the National Adoption Clearinghouse's motto is, "There are no unwanted children, just unfound families." The organization was started in 1972 by two women who were both adoptive parents of hard-to-place children from the foster care system. Since that time, the organization has cooperated with the federal Department of Children's Services and operates a national program to find families for children around the country whose parents are unable to care for them. Although all states have public agencies that deal with children in foster care and their availability for placement in permanent homes, sometimes a match cannot be made in the child's home state. Occasionally, it is in the best interests of the child or children to be placed in a home geographically distant from their biological parents or other influences. Between 1972 and 2008, the National Adoption Clearinghouse placed or participated in the placement of more than 21,000 children nationwide.

Prospective parents wanting to adopt infants and younger children are increasingly looking to foreign countries. Each country that permits international adoption has its own criteria to determine whom they will permit to remove their children to the United States. Although many abuses of the adoption system have been reported in international adoptions, some systems have been put in place in an effort to standardize the process. One such system was the Hague Convention on Protection of Children and Co-operation in Respect of Intercountry Adoption (referred to as the Convention). The Convention is a treaty signed in 1993 in the Hague, Netherlands, and its principles are as follows:

> . . . to strengthen protections for children, birthparents, and prospective adoptive parents in the adoption process. The Convention provides a framework for Convention

countries to work together to ensure that adoptions take place in the best interests of children and to prevent the abduction, sale, or trafficking of children in connection with intercountry adoption.

The United States signed the Convention in 1994. Congress passed the Intercountry Adoption Act (IAA) in 2000, which provided a means for implementation of the tenets of the Convention. The United States Department of State oversees the regulations, policies, and acts to ensure that appropriate steps are followed in the intercountry adoption process for the more than 75 countries that are part of the Convention, which requires that adoption agencies be accredited. Most, but not all, countries from which prospective U.S. parents attempt to adopt are members of the convention.

Accreditation regulations require that intercountry adoption agencies have a written policy expressly forbidding the agency, its employees, or anyone who operates on behalf of the agency from giving money to a birth parent or anyone else as an incentive to release the child for adoption. Incentive fees paid to persons for locating children for adoption are also forbidden, but agencies without accreditation may not follow the same guidelines.

In fiscal year (FY) 1998 (October 1, 1997 through September 30, 1998), there were nearly 16,000 adoptions to the United States from other countries. In FY 2004, adoptions to the United States peaked at nearly 23,000, the majority of which came from China, Russia, and Guatemala. The three countries accounted for 71 percent of adoptions to the United States. By FY 2008, the number of adoptions had fallen to 17,438, with the highest number of adoptions coming from Guatemala, followed by China. Adoptions from Russia had dropped from 5,865 in 2004 to 1,861 in 2008, in part because of media coverage surrounding at least one adoptive child from Russia who was killed by an adoptive parent, and the resulting moratorium that Russia placed on adoptions to the United States. Nearly one-fourth of all adoptions to the United States came from Guatemala in 2008, with an additional 22 percent from China. Other countries providing a significant number of children for intercountry adoption were Ethiopia, South Korea, and Vietnam.

## Adoption Disruption and Dissolution

According to U.S. Department of Health and Human Services, the term *disruption* is used to describe an adoption process that ends after the child is placed in an adoptive home and before the adoption is legally finalized, resulting in the child's return to (or entry into) foster care or placement with new adoptive parents. The term *dissolution* is used to describe an adoption that ends after it is legally finalized, resulting in the child's return to (or entry into) foster care or placement with new adoptive parents. An estimated 10–25 percent of adoptions disrupt, and the older the adoptive child, the more likely a disruption will occur. Adoption dissolutions are less common, but accurate statistics are difficult to determine because children's names and social security numbers may be changed, their original birth certificates may be sealed, and follow-up information is unreliable.

## The Birth Mother's Point of View

Historically, interest in the adoption process has focused on the well-being of the child and their psychological adjustment. More recently, psychologists have become interested in the adoption experience from the point of view of the birth mother. A 1999 literature review by Askren and Bloom found that many suffered from long-term grief that often remained unresolved and had physical and psychological repercussions, and researcher Ajoi found that feelings of disenfranchisement played an important role in the grief of mothers who relinquished their children to adoption. Ge and coauthors report that open adoptions, in which the birth mother may maintain contact with the relinquished child, result in better psychological adjustment by the birth mothers.

## Controversial Adoptions

Recently, nontraditional adoptive parents, such as gay or lesbian couples or single people, have been allowed to adopt children in some states. A 2005 literature review by Tasker concluded that children adopted by gay and lesbian children have similar experiences of family life and comparable psychological and developmental outcomes as do children adopted by heterosexual couples. Feigelman and Finley found comparable psychological outcomes among children living with a single adoptive parent or single biological parent.

**See Also:** Abortion; China; Foster Mothering; Guatemala; Russia.

**Bibliography**
Adoptees Liberty Movement Association. www.almasociety.org (accessed April 2009).
BabyCenter.com. "The Truth About Domestic Adoption." www.babycenter.com (accessed April 2009).
Hague Convention on Intercountry Adoption. *A Guide for Prospective Adoptive Parents.* United States Department of State, Bureau of Consular Affairs, October 2006.
Hochstadt, N.J., P.K. Jaudes, D.A. Zimo, and J. Schachter. "The Medical and Psychosocial Needs of Children Entering Foster Care." *Child Abuse & Neglect*, v.11/1 (1987).
Maskey, Trish. *Our Own—Adopting and Parenting the Older Child.* New York: Snowcap Press, 1999.
National Adoption Clearinghouse. www.adopt.org (accessed April 2009).
National Adoption Information Clearinghouse. www.calib.com/naic (accessed April 2009).
Sokoloff, B. "Antecedent of American Adoption." *The Future of Children*, v.3 (Spring 1993).

Laurie E. Woods
Vanderbilt University

# Adult Children

Mothering adult children is used to describe mothering a child with mental retardation or other disabilities that require the mother to continue her daily caretaking tasks into the child's adult years. It is also often used in connection with mothering children who are alcoholics. However, the most common category of mothers of adult children, though relatively little has been written about this group, is the parent of a child who is gown and is now an adult person.

The use of this oxymoron adult child is necessitated by the lack of vocabulary in English to describe the relationship between parent and child once the child has matured. In the United States and Canada, defining when adulthood begins is difficult as graduations and marriage, the traditional markers of the end of childhood, no longer define a shift in life stage. Both children and parents go back and forth between work and education and between married and single life. When childhood ends and when adulthood begins is ambiguous. Mother and child do not know what their obligations are; they are a mixture of choice and obligation on both parties. This confusion is fostered by the government, since U.S. states have different ages for various financial obligations. Thus, in some states parents can claim their children as dependants on their health insurance until age 26, but in others they cannot.

In addition, there is no constancy among U.S. government agencies in marking adulthood. The Internal Revenue Service parameters are not the same as of those of the legal system. Canadian law is also marked by inconstancies, and like the United States, has few laws that require children and parents to remain connected after whatever age of maturity the law specifies. In any case, maternal affection and feelings of obligation and worry do not end when the child becomes an adult, by whatever definition one chooses to mark that stage.

With increasing life spans, this second stage of mothering, which is defined as being a relatively healthy parent to a grown child, extends for many more years than mothering a young dependent child—up to 50 years in some cases. Though similar to a friendship, this relationship cannot be entered into and disregarded at will. It persists over time and great distances; it is both involuntary and permanent. Even when mother and child have little contact with one another, the relationship remains an emotionally significant one. Mothers are no longer required by law to provide for their children's needs or safety; however, out of affection and habit, mothers often wish to be or are involved in their children's lives. Shared history connects parents and children, and social norms encourage the two generations to identify themselves with each other over the course of life.

Children and parents must balance competing loyalties of new family members and friends. Boundaries are ambiguous and are dependent on personal taste, subculture norms, and life events. The daily intensity of the relationship varies over the life course and is affected by life events. Spouses, significant others, and grandchildren can compli-

cate and enhance or detract from the intensity of the relationship. Differing expectations often confound communication. Thus, mothers and grown children must continually redefine how and when they wish to receive aid and emotional support from one another. Mothers who have maintained connections with their children are more likely to receive adequate elder care. Research also notes the stronger one's social networks, the lower one's mortality rate.

**See Also:** Daughters and Mothers; Midlife Mothering; Mother-in-Law; Postmaternity.

**Bibliography**
Coleman, Joshua. *When Parents Hurt.* New York: HarperCollins, 2008.
Fingerman, Karen. "The Role of Offspring and Children-in-Law in Grandparents Relationships with Grandchildren." *Journal of Family Issues,* v.25/8 (November 2006).
Gullette, Margaret Morganroth. "Postmaternity as a Revolutionary Feminist Concept." *Feminist Studies,* v.28/3 (2002).
Knoester, Chris. "Transitions in Young Adulthood and the Relationship Between Parents and Offspring Well-Being." *Social Forces,* v.81/4 (2003).
Marek, Lydia I., and Jay A. Manici. "The Mother-Child Relationship Quality and Support Patterns in Adulthood." Seattle, WA: National Council on Family Relationships Annual Meeting (1990).
Mayur, P., et al. "Unmet Need for Personal Assistance With Activities of Daily Living Among Older Adults." *The Gerontologist,* v.41 (2001).
Miller-Day, Michelle. *Communication Among Grandmothers, Mothers, and Adult Daughters.* Mahwah, NJ: Lawrence Erlbaum, 2004.
Nemzoff, Ruth. *Don't Bite Your Tongue: How to Foster Rewarding Relationships Between Parents and Adult Children.* New York: Palgrave Macmillan, 2008.
Nielson, Linda. *Between Fathers and Daughters.* Nashville, TN: Cumberland House Publishing, 2008.
Silverstein, Merrill. "Do Close Parent-Child Relationships Reduce Mortality of Older Parents?" *Journal of Health and Social Behavior,* v.32/4 (December 1991).

Ruth Nemzoff
Brandeis Women's Studies Research Center

# Advice Literature for Mothers

Advice literature for mothers includes books, magazine articles, newsletters, pamphlets, Websites, and other popular literature, typically written by professionals, aimed at instructing mothers in the care of children. In traditional societies, parenting advice is spread informally, passing through family and community networks. As literacy and geographic mobility spread, along with declines in the number of children per mother, advice literature became more popular in the United States through the 1800s.

Prior to the early 19th century, little advice literature was aimed specifically at mothers, as fathers—in their role as patriarchs—were seen as ultimately responsible for the education and moral upbringing of their children. Men were seen as possessing reason and authority, qualities women were considered lacking; thus, men were the natural audience for advice literature. Seventeenth-century philosopher John Locke (1632–1704) thus cautioned fathers to bring up their children with discipline so that they may develop into civilized adults possessing reason. A century later, Jean-Jacques Rousseau (1712–78), in his treatise *Emile* (1762), outlined a philosophy of education opposing routines, stressing children's natural goodness and the differences between the sexes.

## Separate Spheres and 19th-Century Advice

By the early 19th century in the United States, with the development of separate spheres for middle-class women and men, women were charged with taking primary responsibility for child rearing. Advice literature aimed at mothers began to develop, fueled in part by growing literacy rates and rising availability of print materials. One of the more popular manuals was *The Mother at Home*, published by Rev. John S.C. Abbott in 1833, and "written for mothers in the common walks of life." Early 19th-century advice literature, produced by physicians and members of the clergy, stressed motherhood as central to shaping children's character. Children's moral development was of great concern to these writers. Motherhood was seen as the central task of women's lives and key to the development of civi-lization. By producing virtuous children, women could rear virtuous citizens.

Some advice books were written by women as well, including Catharine Beecher's *Treatise on Domestic Economy*, aimed at providing a more scientific education for housewives and mothers; and Lydia Marie Child's *The Mother's Book*, published in 1831. *The Mother's Book*, dedicated "to American mothers, on whose intelligence and discretion the safety and prosperity of our republic so much depend," gave mothers "plain practical good sense" advice. Other books by women included Mary Palmer Tyler's *The Maternal Physician*, published anonymously in 1811, which provided the view that mothers had a duty to raise virtuous citizens and also criticized male physicians for giving women advice on topics such as nursing an infant, which they themselves did not have the capacity to do.

Through the 1820s and 1830s, middle-class women formed a variety of mothers' organizations, many of them religiously based, which gave support and advice to members, established libraries, and circulated advice literature and domestic novels to their members. Several published journals such as the *Mother's Magazine*, *The Mother's Assistant and Young Ladies' Friend*, and *The Mothers' Journal*. Throughout these decades and through the end of the 19th-century, middle-class women were increasingly seen as morally superior and the natural caretakers of children. The cultural suggestion was that women's calling lay in creating a moral home and nurturing children, who were increasingly seen as tender innocents in need of protection from the harsh, outside world. Women were advised to care for their charges lovingly, in sharp contrast to the advice that was to follow. Notably, this advice literature was aimed at native-born, literate women rather than the growing immigrant population.

## Rise of Scientific Motherhood

By the end of the 19th century, physicians began to predominate among purveyors of advice to mothers. As the medical profession gained standing, pediatricians became seen as advisers on children's growth and development, not just to upper-class women but to poor women as well. Increasingly, the view was that women needed to be trained in scientific motherhood—that women's maternal "instincts" were no longer sufficient to guide them in proper care of the young. Dr. L. Emmett Holt's *The Care and Feeding of Children*, the most influential of the period, was first published in 1894 and remained an important source of information for mothers through several revised editions. Focusing on the physical care and hygiene of children and drawing on new information about sanitation and health, the text appealed to mothers' desire for scientific advice about childcare.

In the 20th century, advice to mothers took a scientific turn. With the publication of books by G. Stanley Hall (1904) and John Watson (1928), mothers were urged to adhere to rigid schedules for feeding and toilet training and to carefully suppress any unwanted behaviors in children. Mothers were cautioned against "spoiling" their children with too much affection. Professionals urged women to beware of maternal indulgence, cautioning mothers against picking up their babies or comforting them when they cried, lest they develop undesirable habits. Watson advised against maternal kisses and hugs, suggesting instead a maternal handshake in the morning and, if necessary, a single kiss on the forehead at bedtime. Mother love was seen as potentially toxic by some, and women as in need of rigorous scientific training so that their children would become well-trained and self-regulated adults. Thus, child-rearing experts advised women to control their natural impulses and suppress their natural characteristics of emotionality, sentimentality, and weakness.

Another important source of advice for mothers in the early decades of the 20th century included *Infant Care*, a popular series of pamphlets published by the Children's Bureau beginning in 1914. Although early editions of *Infant Care* mirrored the rigidities of the times, advocating strict scheduling and early toilet training, the advice aimed to relieve the difficulties women experienced raising children in isolated rural areas and to reduce infant mortality. Thousands of women wrote to the Children's Bureau, which often replied with tangible assistance and personalized advice. Throughout this time, the greater mobility of the population led to increasing popularity of advice books and child rearing manuals. Although women still relied on family networks and friends, they began to turn to advice literature when extended family networks were no longer available, as evidenced both by the popularity of *Infant Care* and the volume of letters women wrote to the Children's Bureau.

## Rise of Permissive Child Rearing Strategies

The shift to more permissive child rearing strategies—still popular in the early 2000s, in revised form—began in the late 1930s, although they did not become ascendant until the postwar era. Dr. Benjamin Spock's famous *Baby and Child Care*, first published in 1946, is often credited with the rise of the permissive era; others were also influential. Anderson and Mary Aldrich's *Babies Are Human Beings*, published in 1938, suggested that infants have a "developmental plan," which parents—mothers—needed to study. This developmental approach suggested a more individualized method of child rearing, with mothers encouraged to pay attention to each individual child's wants and needs, and to follow—rather than mold—the child's developmental. In a similar vein, Yale psychologist Arnold Gesell, along with his colleagues Frances Ilg and Louise Bates Ames, popularized a series of books on infant and childcare that stressed a developmental approach. Ilg and Ames published a widely syndicated newspaper column from the 1950s to the early 1970s.

## The Ascent of Dr. Spock

Permissive parenting was labor intensive, a style firmly established by Dr. Spock (1903–98), who remained the most popular parenting expert for decades in the 20th century. *Baby and Child Care*, which by 2008 was in its eighth edition (updated and revised by Dr. Robert Needleman), sold three-quarters of a million copies in its first year of publication. As women in the postwar era invested heavily in family and children, Spock's advice, both in his book and in a popular magazine column printed during the 1950s and 1960s in *The Ladies Home Journal* and subsequently in *Redbook*, was that women knew more than they thought they did, and that all would be well if they followed their own instincts—and the advice of their pediatricians.

Spock was followed in the late 1960s and 1970s by two other popular childcare experts: pediatrician

T. Berry Brazelton, whose book *Infants and Mothers* was first published in 1969; and British psychologist Penelope Leach, author of *Your Baby and Child: From Birth to Age 5* (1977). Both Brazelton and Leach published copiously from the 1980s to the early 2000s. These three best-selling authors—Spock, Brazelton, and Leach—provided the main source of advice literature for parents throughout the last decades of the 20th century, with their books spinning off into television shows, advice columns, Internet sites, and parenting institutes.

## Modern Advice Literature

In more recent decades, the series *What to Expect When You're Expecting* (and its companion volumes, including *What to Expect the First Year* and *What to Expect the Toddler Years*) has rivaled Spock, Brazelton, and Leach in popularity. Written by mother Heidi Murkoff during her first pregnancy in 1984 (and co-authored with a medical writer and a nurse), this popular series has sold more than 27 million copies. Following the rise in the Internet as a source of information, this book, now in its fourth edition, also has a Website that connects women with each other, with advertisers, and with an array of services, products, and information.

The tone of contemporary advice literature is double edged. On one hand, women are reassured that they can, by following their baby's lead, learn to understand "what every baby knows." The tone is soothing, designed to give mothers confidence, yet mothers are still urged to consult pediatricians—true experts—with any real difficulty. Mothering is presented as an intensive occupation in which a primary caregiver is expected to follow the child's lead. Although the tone has changed over the decades—subsequent editions acknowledge that women work outside the home, that men may serve as primary caretakers of children, and that families may come in a variety of forms—the books are primarily aimed at women, for whom child rearing is seen as a core part of their identity.

In the last decades of the 20th century, a more fragmented advice literature developed, heterogeneous in form and aimed at mothers in a more diverse array of family types. Thus, advice books and Websites for stepparents helped mothers cope with the arrival of older children in a blended family. Adoptive parents were counseled on both the tangible steps needed to complete an adoption and on the special care of raising adopted children, and lesbian mothers were presented with a wide array of advice literature counseling them on steps toward family formation. *The Lesbian Parenting Book*, considered the "Dr. Spock for lesbian families," is only one of a wide variety of advice books, written predominantly by therapists and lesbian parents, aimed at same-sex couples. Christian parents are provided with a biblically based form of parenting in books such as *Dare to Discipline* by evangelical Christian and child psychologist Dr. James Dobson.

In the contemporary era, it is clear that parents are reading advice literature, and with greater frequency than earlier generations. At least some evidence suggests that the greater use of advice literature is related to a tendency to consult expert advice more generally. It is not clear that mothers follow the advice they receive uncritically. The use of Internet sites connecting mothers directly suggests that expert advice may be tempered by practitioners' own experiences.

**See Also:** History of Motherhood: American; Mother Blame; Republican Motherhood.

## Bibliography

Esterberg, K.G. "Planned Parenthood: The Construction of Motherhood in Lesbian Mother Advice Books." In *Feminist Mothering*, A. O'Reilly, ed. Albany: State University of New York Press, 2008.

Geboy, M.J. "Who Is Listening to the 'Experts?' The Use of Child Care Materials by Parents." *Family Relations*, v.30/2 (1981).

Graebner, W. "The Unstable World of Benjamin Spock: Social Engineering in a Democratic Culture, 1917–1950." *Journal of American History*, v.67/3 (1980).

Grant, J. *Raising Baby by the Book: The Education of American Mothers*. New Haven, CT: Yale University Press, 1998.

Hays, S. *The Cultural Contradictions of Motherhood*. New Haven, CT: Yale University Press, 1996.

Jones, K.W. "Sentiment and Science: The Late Nineteenth Century Pediatrician as Mother's Advisor." *Journal of Social History*, v.17/1 (1983).

---

Meckel, R.A. "Educating a Ministry of Mothers: Evangelical Maternal Associations, 1815–1860." *Journal of the Early Republic,* v.2/4 (1982).

Ryan, M.P. *The Empire of the Mother: American Writing About Domesticity 1830–1860.* New York: Harrington Park Press, 1985.

Shields, S.A. and P. Steinke. "The Double Bind of Caregiving: Representation of Gendered Emotion in American Advice Literature." *Sex Roles,* v.33/7 (1995).

Walker, S.K. "Use of a Parenting Newsletter Series and Other Child-Rearing Information Sources by Mothers of Infants." *Family and Consumer Sciences Research Journal,* v.34/2 (2005).

Weiss, N.P. "The Mother-Child Dyad Revisited: Perceptions of Mothers and Children in the Twentieth Century Child-Rearing Manuals." *Journal of Social Issues,* v.34/2 (1978).

Kristin G. Esterberg
Salem State College

# Afghanistan

Motherhood is a defining feature of women's lives in contemporary Afghanistan. Yet mothers in that country face a situation that is quite unique. As a result of decades of war, religious fundamentalism, gender ideology, widespread poverty, and limited access to health care and education, motherhood continues to pose serious risks for Afghan women. Although recent efforts by national and international entities alike have attempted to improve the situation of Afghan mothers, significant challenges remain.

Women's lack of basic human rights in Afghanistan has a profound influence on their maternal experiences. Afghan women had gradually gained rights throughout the 20th century. However, conflicts of the late 20th century resulted in those rights being systematically stripped away. These conflicts included the Soviet occupation of Afghanistan from 1979–89, followed by civil war and government collapse, and then Taliban control of the country from 1996–2001. The Taliban was especially significant as it enforced strict gender segregation and forbade women from attending school, working outside the home, leaving the home unless accompanied by a male relative, appearing in public without wearing the *burqa,* or seeing a male doctor. During Taliban rule, women's social roles were limited to that of wife and mother; those who stepped outside of these social roles could be stoned, beaten, and even executed. There are a number of documented instances where mothers were publicly beaten or jailed when their daughters were accused of extramarital affairs or other gender-related infractions.

## Plight of Mothers

Although the Taliban was removed from power in 2001, the situation in Afghanistan remains a difficult one as demonstrated by the plight of mothers. It is common for girls to be married as young as 15, and women are typically not allowed to divorce their husbands. Marriage may happen against a woman's will and may be used to secure tribal alliances. Contraceptive use is rare, largely because of religious influences. As a result, when a woman gets married, she is likely to find herself in a continual cycle of pregnancy and childbirth (or miscarriage) that continues until she dies or reaches menopause. The average birth rate is 6.7 live births per woman, the highest in the region.

Over half of the population in Afghanistan lives in absolute poverty. Consequently, many suffer from food shortages and lack access to even basic health care services. Prenatal care is rare, and it is common for pregnant women to suffer from malnutrition, anemia, severe morning sickness leading to dehydration, and psychological stress. During delivery, conditions such as obstructed birth, slow delivery, significant blood loss, and sepsis are common. Lack of prenatal care has also been linked to birth defects. The majority of births take place at home and are not attended by trained medical personnel. Access to emergency obstetric care is limited due to both poor health care infrastructure and geographical constraints. While women who live in urban areas may have better access to such care, those who live in rural areas may have to travel (often on foot, horseback, or being carried by relatives) for days to receive emergency obstetrical care. Despite the efforts of various international organizations, hospitals and clinics remain severely underfunded. As a result, medical facilities frequently lack supplies, medicines, trained staff members, and the ability to provide even basic emergency procedures such as blood transfusions and Ceasarean sections. The maternal mortality rate is 1,650 per 100,000 live births, one of the highest in the world. In rural regions, it can be as high as 6,500 per 100,000 live births, the highest ever recorded. Nearly 50 Afghan women die every day from pregnancy-related causes. Neonatal, infant, and child mortality rates are correspondingly high.

In recent years, the situation has improved slightly. The Safe Motherhood initiative, established in 1997 in order to promote maternal health care services, has expanded. In addition, midwifery schools reopened after the overthrow of the Taliban. Since 2001, the number of licensed midwives in Afghanistan has tripled. Yet inadequate funding, poor coordination of relief efforts, and lack of infrastructure have resulted in limited gains for the mothers of Afghanistan.

**See Also:** Maternal Mortality; Midwifery; Poverty and Mothering; War and Mothers.

**Bibliography**
Ahmed-Ghosh, Huma. "A History of Women in Afghanistan." *Journal of International Women's Studies*. v.4/3 (May 2003).
Bartlett, Linda A., et al. "Where Giving Birth Is a Forecast of Death." *The Lancet*. v.365/9462 (2005).
Brodsky, Anne E. *With All Our Strength*. New York: Routledge, 2004.
Currie, Sheena, et al. "A Bold New Beginning for Midwifery in Afghanistan." *Midwifery*, v.23 (2007).
Das, Minakshi. *Taliban's War on Women*. London: Asia Research Centre, 2006.
Mawji, Shairose. *Safe Motherhood Initiative in Afghanistan*. New York: United Nations Children's Fund (UNICEF), 2000.
Mojadidi, Sedika. *Motherland Afghanistan*. New York: First Run Features, 2006.
Waldman, Ronald and Homaira Hanif. *The Public Health System in Afghanistan*. Kabul, Afghanistan: Afghanistan Research and Evaluation Unit, 2002.
World Health Organization (WHO). *Afghanistan in the 21st Century*. Geneva: WHO, 2000.

Jillian M. Duquaine-Watson
University of Texas at Dallas

# African American Mothers

In North America, mothers are caretakers of their homes, their partners, and their children. In many ways, African American mothers are no different from mothers of any other ethnic group, race, religious background, or class. They struggle, like all mothers, to raise healthy children who will grow up to be productive citizens. Yet, in the contemporary United States, African American mothers have a history and challenges that are unique. From their arrival on American shores in 1619 through today, the African American woman has been the bedrock of the African American family. Several particular, key markers—slavery, civil rights (the Jim Crow era), and the prison epidemic—have shaped the experiences of African American mothers.

## Slavery

Although African American women were not legally able to form family unions during slavery, there is evidence that they performed the role of "wife" under the slave mode of production. Sociologist E. Franklin Frazier, in his magnum opus on the African American family, demonstrated empirically that the unjust system of slavery that African Americans lived under for over 300 years did not fundamentally break their belief in and reliance on family for survival. The research of historian Herbert Gutman verified Frazier's work, wherein he showed that at the first point of freedom, the most consistent act among African American men and especially women was to set out to find their love partner.

To describe the system of chattel slavery in the United States as antifamily would be an understatement. The system of chattel slavery, which allowed people of African descent to be bought and sold as cattle or hogs, was antifamily by design. African American women worked to create families within the system of slavery, overcoming severe barriers to doing so. For example, slaves were not legally able to marry; thus, they created the tradition of "jumping the broom," which signified their commitment to each other. However, this commitment was not recognized by their masters, and it was not uncommon for slave masters to sell one partner to another plantation. Slave masters not only refused to respect familial relationships between slaves, they also frequently detested them, because these relationships had the potential to make it more difficult for them to rape and impregnate these slave women, thus increasing their slave holdings. Yet, African American women, despite being raped by their masters, continued to forge relationships with their partners. Additionally, they raised their children, often the progeny of these rapes, as best they could. Noted African American orator Frederick Douglass writes of this experience. As noted, there is strong evidence that when the institution of slavery finally ended, there were many intact African American families who did everything they could to reunite with relatives who had run away or been sold off.

## Jim Crow Era

Immediately following emancipation, many newly freed slaves continued to work as sharecroppers on the plantations where they had spent their whole lives. Just as during slavery, African American women continued to work in the fields alongside the men as well as to work in the master's house doing cooking, cleaning, taking care of children, and even wet nursing. This tradition, coupled with the intense rules of segregation that barred African American men and women from most social, political, and economic institutions, created a widespread pattern that persisted well in the middle of the 20th century: the role of African American women as domestics.

During the 20th century, unlike many white women, the majority of African American mothers were employed, especially after they became mothers. African American families depended on women's wages primarily because there were so few job opportunities for African American men, and those that did exist often paid salaries that were much too low to maintain a family. And, although those who were able to be educated could work in the professions as nurses and teachers, which were set up by African Americans in an attempt to service their own segregated communities, the majority of African American women found work as domestics. As Judith Rollins and Patricia Hill Collins document, these women would work six and sometimes seven days a week, 12 to 14 hours a day in other people's homes—usually white homes. In some cases, these women, even when they were married and/or had children, lived with the families for whom

they worked. If they were married, they might "live in" all week long and be allowed to return to their own homes for a visit on Sunday. If they were unmarried—with or without children—and with no home, they "lived in" permanently. Janet Langhart Cohen, wife of former Senator from Maine and former Secretary of Defense William Cohen, writes in her memoir *From Rage to Reason: My Life in Two Americas* about her experiences living with white families in Indianapolis in the early 1950s while her mother was a domestic. Gregory Howard Williams, President of City College of New York, recalls in his autobiography *Life on the Color Line: The Story of a White Boy Who Discovered He Was Black*, watching the woman who raised him—Miss Sally—trudge home, her shoulders weighed down by stress and her legs heavy from exhaustion after working very long days as a domestic in a white home on the other side of segregated Muncie, Indiana.

This labor-intensive work often resulted in neglect in their own homes. Many black women writers recount their mothers coming home after long hours of domestic labor and somehow, miraculously, finding the energy to prepare hot meals for their own families and braid their daughters' hair. As adults they understood, but even as children, they remember knowing that the burden of caring for other people's homes and children somehow robbed them of the attention that their mothers should have been paying to them.

Black feminists have long argued that the backbone of the Civil Rights movement was really women. Many women, including Coretta Scott King, Fannie Lou Hamer, Shirley Chisholm, Angela Davis, Dorothy Height, Daisy Bates, and Ella Baker played key roles in the Civil Rights Movement. For example, the Montgomery bus boycott of 1955 was engineered almost entirely by women. Many of the famous leaders of the Civil Rights Movement, including Martin Luther King, Jr., Jesse Jackson, and Reverend Shuttlesworth had wives at home whose dedication to their homes and the raising of their children allowed these men to crisscross the country giving fiery speeches and being jailed for acts of civil disobedience. The women of the Civil Rights Movement—many of them mothers—have not only been neglected by history, but have often been rendered invisible.

## Drug/Prison Era

As much promise as the accomplishments of the Civil Rights era seemed to hold, the struggles for African American mothers have not diminished, only morphed. Beginning in the late 1960s, with the War on Poverty under way, a new trend developed: a steep decline in the number of African Americans getting married. In fact, by 2008, almost half (46 percent) of all African American women over age 18 had never married, as compared to only a quarter of white women. Low rates of marriage do have serious consequences, namely poverty and the stresses of single motherhood. In 2008, three-quarters (75 percent) of African American babies were born to single mothers. Though it is important to point out that the majority of these births—in contrast to mainstream media images—were to adult women, not teenagers.

*Future African American mothers have unique challenges— fewer eligible men, single and teen motherhood, and poverty.*

In fact, there has been a slow but steady decline in the rate of teenage pregnancy and childbearing among African American women. More than half of these single-mother households fall below the poverty line. And, the consequences of poverty are severe. Infant mortality rates among African Americans are twice the national average. Hunger and homelessness rates for African American children are more than double the national average, and African American children are three times more likely to be poor than white children. Thus, the consequences of living in households headed by single mothers are devastating. Thus, a major challenge African American mothers face in the 21st century is raising healthy children while living in severe poverty.

Why are African American women facing motherhood alone? There are many reasons, including some that are not unique to African American women. First, overall, rates of marriage are declining, and rates of single motherhood are rising across all populations. That said, African American mothers face challenges that are unique; namely, the lack of marriageable men—what William Julius Wilson refers to as the "marriageable pool"—which is a result of two key factors: unemployment and incarceration. Unemployment rates for African American men are double the national average at nearly 20 percent. And, in some of the hardest-hit communities like Detroit, the unemployment rate for African American men nears 50 percent. Unemployment tends to lower marriage rates; however, with unemployment rates so high, it is unlikely that marriage would improve these mothers' economic conditions.

Perhaps the greatest challenge facing African American mothers today is the overincarceration of African American men. The latest Bureau of Justice statistics reveal that of the 2.3 million Americans who are incarcerated in any given day in the United States, half—or more than 1 million—are African American men.

Mirroring the trend in declining marriage rates among African Americans beginning in the late 1960s, beginning in the early 1970s with the passage of the Rockefeller drug laws, incarceration rates began to soar to the heights we see today. There are serious racial disparities with regards to sentencing. For example, in March 2009, Human Rights Watch released a comprehensive state-by-state analysis that demonstrated that although rates of drug use are similar across racial/ethnic groups, rates for incarceration for drug possession—which account for 80 percent of all drug sentences—were 5.5–11.3 percent higher for African American men between 2000 and 2008. Today, approximately one-third of all African American men will be incarcerated, as compared to fewer than one in 10 white men. The impact of incarceration on African American mothers and their children is devastating.

## Effects of Incarceration

Clearly, incarceration brings financial challenges to families; a breadwinner or potential breadwinner is removed from the household. Or, in the case of single mothers, a source or potential source of child support is removed. Additionally, incarceration is expensive for families. In addition to court costs, there are the costs associated with legal defense, as well as the expensive collect calls from prison—often $3–$4 per minute—that mothers may feel are essential. Similarly, the cost to travel to visit partners and children's fathers can be extraordinary, as most inmates are moved far from the high-population areas of their residence to the low-density areas where many prisons are built. The cost to stay in physical contact with lovers, husbands and children's fathers, therefore, may become prohibitive. For example, in New York, the vast majority of incarcerated African American men had been living in New York City at the time of their incarceration, but the majority of state prisons are in upstate New York. Thus, most African American men incarcerated in New York are locked away hundreds of miles from their families.

Another side effect of overincarceration on African American mothers is the increasing role they play in raising their grandchildren. As they are often the only stable person in the families of incarcerated men, the burden of raising their children increasingly falls to their own mothers. Just as they are entering retirement, many African American mothers find that they are left to mother their grandchildren.

A recent study by Devah Pager showed only 3 percent of African American men with felonies are likely to find employment, which also increases the likelihood of domestic violence. Living with domes-

tic violence and escaping from its grasp is a yet another hurdle—and a very high one—facing many African American mothers.

The war on drugs has added a unique and difficult struggle to the role of mother in African American families. Removing African American men from their families and communities leads to lower rates of marriage and higher rates of divorce, and creates an overall instability in both African American families and communities. And, of course, it is African American mothers and grandmothers who are left to pick up the pieces.

## African American Feminist Studies

Early studies of African American mothering styles reported that compared to white mothers, African American mothers were more authoritarian, more punitive, less consistent, less affectionate, and more likely to use physical punishment. However, such studies are often confounded by the socioeconomic status of the mothers studied, as African American women are more likely to have children in adolescence, be a single parent, and be employed and be poor, relative to white mothers. They also are more likely than white mothers to rely on an extended kinship and community network to assist in child rearing. Recently, many African American feminists have challenged the evaluation of African American motherhood as deficient when compared to a white, middle-class model of a self-contained, two-parent household. They also argue that behaviors characteristic of African American parenting, such as demanding self-sufficiency at a young age and showing less affection to children, may be based in the practical necessity of preparing children for a hostile world.

## Conclusion

Although African American mothers are in many ways no different than other mothers, particularly with regards to the love they feel for their children and the goals they have in raising them, they have been and continue to be faced with enormous and unnecessary barriers to mothering. From slavery up to the present drug and prison epidemic, African American mothers have struggled to keep their families together and to raise healthy children to become productive citizens.

**See Also:** African Diaspora; Civil Rights Movement and Motherhood; Collins, Patricia Hill; Incarcerated Mothers; Motherline; Other Mothering; Poverty and Mothering; Single Mothers; Slavery and Mothering.

## Bibliography

Blades, Joan and Kristen Rowe-Finkbeiner. *The Motherhood Manifesto*. New York: The Nation Books, 2006.

Blassingame, John. *The Slave Community*. New York: Oxford University Press, 1979.

Davis, David Brion. *Inhuman Bondage: The Rise and Fall of Slavery in the New World*. New York: Oxford University Press, 2006.

Frazier, Edward Franklin. *The Negro Family in the United States*. Chicago: University of Chicago Press, 1939.

Hattery, Angela J. and Earl Smith. *African American Families*. Thousand Oaks, CA: Sage, 2007.

Langhart, Janet Cohen. *From Rage to Reason: My Life in Two Americas*. New York: Kensington, 2004.

Collins, Patricia Hill. "Shifting the Center: Race, Class, and Feminist Theorizing About Motherhood." In *Mothering: Ideology, Experience, and Agency*, E. Glenn, et al., eds. New York: Routledge, 1994.

Hull, Gloria T., et al., eds. *But Some of Us Are Brave: All the Women Are White, All the Blacks Are Men: Black Women's Studies*. New York: Feminist Press, 1982.

Rollins, Judith. *Between Women: Domestics and Their Employers*. Philadelphia, PA: Temple University Press, 1985.

Williams, Gregory Howard. *Life on the Color Line: The Story of a White Boy Who Discovered He Was Black*. New York: Dutton Publishing, 1995.

Wilson, William Julius. *When Work Disappears: The World of the New Urban Poor*. New York: Knopf, 1996.

Angela Hattery
Wake Forest University

# African Diaspora

The term *African Diaspora* is generally understood to refer to the forced migration of African peoples to the Americas, Europe, the Caribbean, and Latin America in the modern period from the 15th to the 19th centuries. The Atlantic slave trade, also known as the transatlantic slave trade, was a major conduit for the forced transportation of peoples from the African continent. An estimated 12–15 million Africans were captured and transported by slave traders across the Atlantic Ocean regularly over a period of about 400 years. The majority were taken to the Caribbean, Latin America, and the United States to work as slaves on agricultural plantations. African men were the majority of those captured and sold in the transatlantic slave trade. Ratio by gender is estimated to have been two men for every female. The uprooting of African women disrupted traditional African family life. However, under slavery, certain African child rearing practices, such as community parenting, other mothering, and fictive kin networks, were reinforced and became essential to the survival of the black family in the African Diaspora.

In precolonial West African societies, motherhood accorded the African woman a high degree of prestige and influence within the community. In both matrilineal and patrilineal African societies, the bond between mother and child was regarded as the foundation of all social and community life. In addition, within these African societies, the concept of mothering extended beyond an individual's biological offspring. Children belonged to the community and women as well as men were responsible for the day-to-day nurturing and well-being of every child. Mothering was an activity to ensure the health and continuance of the society. Under slavery, however, family life and mothering were directed toward the production of capital for the landed class of slave owners. Black women from Africa were valuable for their labor production as agricultural workers and also for their capacity to reproduce slave labor.

## Motherhood and Slavery

Enslaved women worked the same as slave men, clearing land, cutting trees, digging ditches, and planting and harvesting crops. In addition, they were encouraged or coerced to have many children in order to increase the slave labor population. Some slave owners allowed families to remain together if many children were produced. Thus, if the female slave wanted to keep her family united and remain rooted to a particular plantation with friends and family, motherhood became the primary method for her survival and well-being. Ironically, slaves were encouraged to have children, but ultimately the task of mothering was not seen as a central activity for enslaved men and women.

Women who had just given birth and had to return to work in the field, relied on other women to help with the task of motherhood. In slavery, community mothering was a way to assist with childcare, which was the responsibility of elderly women and men who did not work in the fields; of children who were too young to work as laborers; and of a variety of other women, including slave midwives, nurses, relatives, and friends. Communal motherhood also provided care for children whose parents were sold or had died. Females who were not blood relatives assumed the fictive-kin mother role. Similar to the extended family structure in Africa, where relatives were provided a safety net of care and security, in America the slaves relied on nonrelatives acting in various familial roles. The enslaved child could rely on this family network of related and nonrelated kin to look after his or her needs.

## After Emancipation

In the United States, slaves were emancipated in 1865. Former slave men and women searched for family members and children separated by slavery. Freedmen were eager to legitimize their family and children through registered marriages. African Americans formed stable families from the time of emancipation until the mid-20th century. Until the 1960s, 75 percent of African American families included both a husband and a wife. During these decades, cooperative mothering continued because many black women had to work outside the home to support their families. In rural areas, women depended on female relatives for assistance with childcare. Women who migrated to the larger northern cities beginning in the 1930s sent for relatives from the South to help with childcare. As well, African American clubwomen were professional, middle-class women who devoted their efforts to uplifting the black community. In urban areas throughout the country, they established orphanages and day nurseries to take care of orphans as well as children whose mothers worked.

## Contemporary Mothering

Since the 1960s, the negative effects of urbanization and other socioeconomic factors have impacted black families adversely. Current statistics on marriage and living arrangements indicate that only 45 percent of black families in the United States include a married couple. More than 50 percent of black households are headed by a single woman, and unmarried black women constitute a majority of childbearing black women. Black single mothers in the United States tend to live with members of their extended family who assist with childcare. The trend of African American grandmothers becoming "new mothers again" is increasing. Instead of providing occasional childcare, these grandmothers assume the role of primary caregiver to their grandchildren in cases where their adult children are unable or unwilling to take on the parenting role.

Motherhood in other regions of the African Diaspora is also characterized by a high representation of female-headed households. In addition, in regions such as the Caribbean, separation of mother and child occurs frequently as a result of mothers immigrating to North America and other countries to seek work or educational opportunities. In these cases, the children left behind are generally cared for by grandmothers and other female relatives.

Mothering in the African Diaspora is not universal. However, there are common historical and contemporary practices that have resulted from a shared history of slavery and oppression.

**See Also:** African American Mothers; Caribbean Mothers; Childcare; Grandmothers and Grandmothering; History of Motherhood: 1750 to 1900; History of Motherhood: American; Mammy; Other Mothering; Single Mothers; Slavery and Mothering.

## Bibliography

Gaspar, David Barry and Darlene Clark Hine. *More Than Chattel: Black Women and Slavery in the Americas.* Bloomington: Indiana University Press, 1996.
McAdoo, Harriette Pipes. *Black Families.* Thousand Oaks, CA: Sage, 2007.
*Journal of the Association for Research on Mothering.* Mothering in the African Diaspora [special issue], v.2/2 (Fall/Winter 2000).

Terborg-Penn, Rosalyn, Sharon Harley, and Andrea Benton Rushing. *Women in Africa and the African Diaspora*. Washington, DC: Howard University Press, 1987.

Linda Bowles-Adarkwa
San Francisco State University

# AIDS/HIV and Mothering

The acquired immune-deficiency syndrome (AIDS) is caused by the human immunodeficiency virus (HIV). HIV is transmitted by the exchange of bodily fluids through sexual activity, blood and plasma transfusions, injection drug use (IDU) and unsterile syringes, and mother-to-child transmission (MTCT). HIV/AIDS cannot be cured, but antiretroviral therapies (ARTs) can help prevent opportunistic infections that occur as a result of HIV's attack on the body's immune system. ARTs also help prevent MTCT and significantly delay the onset of fatal complications related to AIDS.

Today, women of reproductive age (15–49 years) are increasingly bearing the brunt of HIV/AIDS. In areas such as sub-Saharan Africa, women account for 60 percent of all cases. HIV/AIDS is often the result of war, where systematic rape is sometimes used as a tool of control. For example, during the Rwandan genocide (1994), Interahame militia raped hundreds of thousands of Tutsi women and girls, resulting in HIV infection and unwanted pregnancies.

Additionally, children in many parts of the world remain highly vulnerable due to difficult access to MTCT prevention therapies. The high vulnerability of women and children to HIV/AIDS raises many issues around the topic of mothering, including motherhood choices and mothering experiences of HIV-positive women and their placement in deviancy discourses. The latter refers to practices and preferences that diverge from the perceived ideal or norm dictated by society. Other relevant issues are the intensive care giving often required for persons living with HIV/AIDS (PLWHA), be it the mother or her child, and the shifting of the mothering role to persons other than the birth mother when HIV/ AIDS debilitates or claims the mother. This complex, multifaceted relationship between HIV/AIDS and mothering also raises many policy-related concerns that are considered in the last section.

## Impact of HIV/AIDS on Women and Children

AIDS was first identified in the United States in 1981, but later found to have existed in Africa at least since 1959. Stigma, lack of accurate understanding and awareness of the disease, and the unavailability of ARTs in many parts of the world quickly resulted in a global epidemic, or pandemic. By 2008, AIDS had already claimed more than 25 million lives worldwide. Over 30 million persons were living with HIV, over 90 percent of them in low- and middle-income countries with inadequate socioeconomic resources. Additionally, care-giving duties within the pandemic have fallen disproportionately on women, but in most traditional societies, HIV-positive women are not entitled to similar care. Globally, the overall rate of increase of the HIV/AIDS epidemic has slowed in recent years, but the absolute number of PLWHAs has increased partly due to growing numbers of new HIV infections, half of which occur in women and almost one-sixth in children alone.

## HIV-Positive Mothering Experiences

In most cultures of the world today, motherhood has become a social institution in itself and is considered central to women's sense of identity and self. Most women themselves perceive motherhood and related acts of nurturing and mothering as essential to realizing their core identity. Therefore, it is not unexpected that women with HIV/AIDS also want to experience this role and responsibility. However, whether HIV-positive women have children prior to infection, found out during pregnancy, or opted for motherhood despite their diagnosis, they often find themselves the focus of double binds and deviancy discourses.

## Double Bind

The double bind constitutes a situation where conflicting messages from an authoritative figure or institution present a no-win situation. HIV-positive women, like others, internalize and respond to the dominant social message that motherhood and mothering are vital to realizing their identity. However, unlike most others, they are caught in a double bind of a contrary message that to reproduce would be uncaring and selfish. At this point, deviancy discourses become relevant as well. Dominant discourses of mothering ascribe idealized attributes of self-sacrifice and selfless care giving to this role, diametrically at odds with discourses of deviancy that carry connotations of selfishness, cruelty, and lack of caring.

A recurrent deviancy discourse within mothering is that of mothers with HIV/AIDS, who often report feeling stigmatized. They are thought of as selfish and cruel, putting their need for experiencing motherhood ahead of the child's welfare due to risk of MTCT and the assumed inability of the HIV-positive mother to perform demanding mothering tasks. As with other discourses pertaining to social institutions and structures, deviancy discourses regarding HIV and mothering are also characterized by interstices of race, ethnicity, class, and HIV/AIDS-specific attributes such as IDU and other risk behaviors. Negative signals from society become more pronounced if the HIV-positive mother belongs to a marginal social category.

However, there are also discourses of resistance and resilience from the same margins, with many HIV-positive women looking to their cultural and family contexts for strength. For example, HIV-positive women with current or past histories of IDU face stigma as unfit mothers from society and the state. However, like other mothers, most of these mothers gain a connection and purpose to life through nurturing and everyday tasks associated with mothering.

In the developing world, additional and/or different double binds exist for HIV-positive women who find themselves caught in the conflicts between indigenous practices and Western understandings. For example, health professionals with Western viewpoints and experiences still encourage HIV-positive mothers to refrain from breastfeeding, despite evidence that the lack of potable water and sanitary conditions often means higher chances of morbidity and mortality for infants on breastmilk alternatives. Moreover, risk of MTCT is considerably offset by adopting modified breastfeeding practices and the use of appropriate ARTs such as nevirapine, which

can reduce risk of MTCT by 50 percent in a single dose. On the other hand, women who do not follow traditional mothering practices such as breastfeeding are often regarded as promiscuous, selfish, or deviant within their cultures.

**Disruption of the Mothering Experience**

Observations show that regardless of geography, HIV/AIDS has a definite and usually disruptive effect on mothering experiences, although the degree of disruption varies depending on social location, access to physical resources, and emotional support systems. Recurrent themes in mothering situations for HIV-positive women range from fearing that the myriad tasks associated with mothering might be a burden on their own health, to its reverse, such as their own ill health preventing them from undertaking these essential tasks, guilt at presenting risk of HIV/AIDS to their children, anxiety regarding the ability to shield them from stigma, and whether or not to share the burden of their diagnosis with their children.

HIV/AIDS undoubtedly takes a toll on the mother's health and energy. In such cases, role reversal might take place, sometimes to a significant degree, where the mother herself might require mothering. In developing countries, HIV-positive mothers are often aided in their care-giving and mothering roles by older siblings in the family who might perform household chores, care for younger siblings, and even undertake economically gainful activities to sustain the family. In Western societies, women also report such support, but emotional or psychological sustenance is more prevalent than functional help. The emotional and substantive ramification of this role reversal on women and children is an important strand of the deeply entwined HIV/AIDS-mothering relationship.

**Mothering HIV-Positive Children**

The greater need for care and self-care of HIV-positive mothers often does not diminish their mothering responsibilities in the eyes of society. Women parenting children with HIV/AIDS face additional challenges that become more intense in resource-strapped areas of the world, where mothers are often forced to make hard decisions between their own and their family's needs—decisions where usually neither emerge winners. Regardless of geography, ensuring adequate and appropriate ART regimens, the emotional task of explaining the situation to the child, dealing with issues of stigma, and procuring medical and social support for their children all fall under their extra mothering responsibilities.

Discussions on mothering typically, although not exclusively, allude to care giving to a dependent child, which is widely understood to refer to children under 18 years of age. As with other chronic illnesses, HIV/AIDS creates situations of emotional and at times physical dependency of adult children on their families of origin, particularly on their previous primary care giver, usually the mother. Since mothering involves emotional and practical dimensions, both aspects are often called into play in the form of moral support, acceptance, and care giving when dealing with adult children with HIV/AIDS. However, mothering capabilities, child rearing practices, and the mother' philosophy are often questioned and blamed for causing the situation, often to the point of mothers internalizing the guilt.

## Mothering When AIDS Claims the Mother
Globally, 15 million children have been orphaned by AIDS; sub-Saharan Africa accounts for over 80 percent of them. During 1997–2002, 6 percent of maternal mortality in Africa could be attributed to HIV/AIDS, directly affecting household structures and care-giving configurations. Despite the enormity of the issue, few official systemic and structural safety nets exist for these children, even in the most affected countries. AIDS orphans have so far usually been absorbed and fostered by the households of their uncles and aunts, particularly in Africa. However, there has been an increasing shift toward parenting responsibilities being taken up by grandparents, primarily grandmothers. Additionally, there is a growing trend of mothering roles being taken over by older siblings, signaling increasing strains on the extended family system.

The impact of HIV/AIDS on mothering does not stop here. Since women are often primary care givers even in extended family and community situations in many societies across the globe, children may face a loss of mothering toward them if their mother is tending to others, often the father or another relative with HIV/AIDS.

## Policy Considerations
Ironically, one of the reasons for the increase in PLWHAs has been the greater availability of ARTs. However, in the developing world, ARTs have only reached one-third of HIV-positive women. Infants remain highly vulnerable, with a vast majority succumbing to AIDS-related diseases before ever being diagnosed and treated. The first step to assuring safe motherhood and improved mothering experiences for HIV-positive women and children is the better provision of ARTs. Therefore, many countries have instituted mechanisms specifically targeted toward these demographics to allow for cheaper and easier access to ARTs, which has already resulted in better survival rates and health outcomes.

Fighting HIV/AIDS with ARTs is a necessary strategy for boosting women's health and mothering experiences, but is incomplete without addressing the inherent vulnerabilities of local communities, such as poverty, food shortages, violence, substance abuse, and lack of basic health care and survival resources. Other important strategies need to address increased inclusion of men in various care activities and greater sensitivity from health care personnel regarding the emotional and physical needs of HIV-positive mothers.

**See Also:** "Bad" Mothers; Care Giving; Disabled Mothers; Genocide; Grandmothers and Grandmothering; Maternal Health; Mothering as Work; Mothering Versus Motherhood; Rwanda; War and Mothering.

**Bibliography**
Arendell, Terry. "Conceiving and Investigating Motherhood: The Decade's Scholarship." *Journal of Marriage and Family*, v.62/4 (November 2000).
Coovadia, H.M. and R.M. Bland. "Preserving Breastfeeding Practice Through the HIV Pandemic." *Tropical Medicine and International Health*, v.12/9 (September 2007).
Ingram, Deborah and Sally A. Hutchinson. "Double Binds and the Reproductive and Mothering Experiences of HIV-Positive Women." *Qualitative Health Research*, v.10/1 (January 2000).
Moenasch, R. and J. Ties Boerma. "Orphanhood and Childcare Patterns in Sub-Saharan Africa: An Analysis of National Surveys From 40 Countries." *AIDS*, v.18/S2 (2004).

Sandelowsky, Margarete and Julie Barroso. "Mother-hood in the Context of Maternal HIV Infection." *Research in Nursing & Health,* v.26 (2003).

Thompson, Elizabeth A. "Mothers' Experiences of an Adult Child's HIV/AIDS Diagnosis: Maternal Responses to and Resolutions of Accountability for AIDS." *Family Relations,* v.49/2 (April 2000).

United Nations Joint Programme on HIV/AIDS (UNAIDS). "Caregiving in the Context of HIV/AIDS." http://womenandaids.unaids.org/documents/20081002_Caregiving_in_context_of_AIDS_EN.pdf (accessed August 2009).

UNAIDS. "Fast Facts About HIV/AIDS." http://www.unaids.org/en/KnowledgeCentre/Resources/FastFacts/ (accessed August 2009).

UNAIDS. "2008 Report on the Global AIDS Epidemic." http://data.unaids.org/pub/GlobalReport/2008/jc1510_2008_global_report_pp1_10_en.pdf (accessed August 2009).

Vandana Wadhwa
Boston University

# Alabama

The state of Alabama closely resembles the general U.S. population in some statistical indices of motherhood, but varies widely in others. For example, 49.7 percent of all Alabama households were married-couple families, and 39.6 percent of those families had children of their own under 18 years; the comparable figures for all households in the United States were 49.8 percent and 43.5 percent, according to the U.S. Census Bureau's American Community Survey (ACS) for 2005 through 2007. In Alabama, 14.5 percent of all households were headed by women with no husband present, and 57.8 percent of those households had children under 18. In the United States, those figures were 12.5 and 59.6 percent, respectively. The average family size in Alabama was 3.04 persons, just slightly lower than the national average of 3.19.

Although the rates of both marriage and divorce in Alabama have been steadily declining since the mid-1990s, women are more likely to be wed and divorced than their counterparts elsewhere in the country. In Alabama there were 8.6 marriages and 4.8 divorces per 1,000 persons in 2006, compared with national marriage and divorce rates of 7.5 and 3.6 per 1,000 persons, according to the U.S. National Center for Health Statistics.

**Fertility and Teen Mothers**
The ACS shows some similarities, but also significant differences, in fertility statistics between Alabama and the rest of the nation. In the case of women aged 15 to 50, the numbers are identical: 55 per 1,000 women gave birth during a 12-month period, both in Alabama and the United States at large. However, in the case of teenage births, the rate in Alabama was significantly higher: 37 per 1,000 women, compared with 27 per 1,000 women in the United States. The higher birth rate among teenagers might also account for the lower rate of abortions in Alabama: 10.2 abortions per 1,000 women aged 15 to 44 in 2005, compared to a national average of 19.4.

Most studies indicate that children born to teenage mothers have lower educational achievements. According to the ACS, the percentage of persons over the age of 25 who did not have a high school diploma was 20 percent in Alabama, higher than the U.S. figure of 16 percent. Poverty also affected educational attainment; according to the ACS, 20.3 percent of all Alabama families with related children under 18 had incomes below the poverty level, compared to 15.1 percent in the United States at large. Among Alabama families with related children under 18 and no husband present, 47.3 percent were below the poverty level, significantly higher than the figure of 36.9 percent for all such families in the United States.

As a result, Alabama has a higher percentage of families receiving public assistance than the national average. For instance, 5.6 percent of all Alabama households received Supplemental Security Income and 10.2 percent received food stamp benefits, according to the ACS. The comparable figures in the United States at large were 4 and 7.9 percent. On the other hand, fewer children in Alabama received Temporary Assistance for Needy Families in 2006 than the national average: 2.8 percent of all children in Alabama, compared to 3.9 percent of all children nationally, according to the U.S. Department of Health and Human Services.

Like the rest of the country, Alabama has made significant strides in motherhood since the mid-19th century. Diaries and letters from Alabama in the 1840s and 1850s report a continual pattern of maternal difficulties and child mortality. Improvements in medical technology have made childbirth considerably safer since that time. In 1850, 119 Alabama mothers died in childbirth (0.6 percent of all 20,375 live births) and 2,024 infants died before they reached the age of 1 (9.9 percent). In 2005, 10 maternal deaths in childbirth (0.01 percent) and 561 infant deaths (342 neonatal and 219 postneonatal, or 0.6 percent of 60,262 live births) were reported.

Numerous mothers in the state have been influential, but two deserve special recognition: Kate Adams Keller, who gave birth to Helen Keller on June 27, 1880, in Tuscumbia; and Leona Edwards Parks, who gave birth to Rosa Parks on February 4, 1913, in Tuskegee. When Helen became deaf and blind at 19 months, her mother resisted calls to institutionalize her, and helped arrange for Anne Sullivan to educate the child. As a reformer and advocate for persons with disabilities, Helen Keller became one of Alabama's most noted citizens.

Leona Parks was a schoolteacher who taught her children to be proud of themselves even while living under racist conditions. Her daughter Rosa always felt her mother gave her the strength, determination, and self-respect to confront the challenges of life. After Rosa Parks refused to give up her seat to a white man on a bus in Montgomery in 1955, she became known as the mother of the Civil Rights Movement.

**See Also:** Georgia; Mississippi; Parks, Rosa; Reproduction; Teen Mothers; Tennessee.

**Bibliography**

Alabama Center for Health Statistics. "Vital Statistics at a Glance." www.adph.org/healthstats (accessed May 2009).

McMillen, Sally G. *Motherhood in the Old South: Pregnancy, Childbirth, and Infant Rearing.* Baton Rouge: Louisiana State University Press, 1990.

Schwartz, Marie Jenkins. *Birthing a Slave: Motherhood and Medicine in the Antebellum South.* Cambridge, MA: Harvard University Press, 2006.

Wilkie, Laurie A. *The Archaeology of Mothering: An African-American Midwife's Tale.* New York: Routledge, 2003.

James I. Deutsch
Smithsonian Institution

# Alaska

Alaska is the largest and least densely populated state in the United States: about two-thirds of the state's 683,000 residents live in urban areas. The population of Alaska is unusually young compared to the United States as a whole: 26.7 percent of Alaskans are age 18 or younger, ranking fourth among the 50 states and the District of Columbia. Total fertility rate (an estimate of the number of children born to each woman) in 2003 was over 2.2, among the highest in the United States.

Poverty is a serious problem that impacts the quality of life of Alaskans. In 2007, 16.9 percent of Alaska's population lived below the poverty level: only five states had higher percentages of people living in poverty. Of Alaska families with children under 18 years of age, 11.2 percent of the families live in poverty; for families with children under 5 years of age, the figure is 10.9 percent. Female-headed households have a much higher rate of poverty: 28.6 percent of such families with children age 18 or younger live below the poverty line, as do 32 percent of female-headed families with children under 5 years of age. This is despite a higher-than-average rate of persons in the labor force: 71.4 percent of Alaskans over age 16 are in the labor force (66 percent of women) as opposed to 64.7 percent in the United States as a whole. In many Alaskan families with children, all parents are employed: 59.4 percent of families with children under age 6 and 70.3 percent of families with children ages 6 to 17 fit this description. Educational levels are also low: just 21.4 percent of Alaskans age 25 and over held at least a bachelor's degree in 2007, ranking the state 44th in the United States.

In 2006, about 5,300 marriages were conducted in Alaska, for a rate of 7.8 per 1,000 residents, which is slightly above the U.S. average of 7.5 per

1,000 residents; in the same year, approximately 3,000 divorces were finalized for a rate of 4.4 per 1,000 population, well above the U.S. average of 3.6 per 1,000. The marriage rate is higher for women in Alaska than for men, a reverse of the situation in the United States as a whole: 48.9 percent of men in Alaska age 15 or older are married, with 52 percent for women (in the United States as a whole, 52.6 percent of men over age 15 are married, with 48.5 percent for women).

**Maternal and Child Health**

Alaska ranks poorly on many measures of maternal and child health. For instance, the state's infant mortality rate in 2007 was 9.4 per 1,000 live births, ranking 4th in the United States: only Mississippi, South Carolina, and Maine have higher rates. Among the 26 states that report data to the Pregnancy Risk Assessment Monitoring Assessment System, Alaska mothers ranked poorly on many risk factors, including tobacco use (30.9 percent), alcohol use (53.3 percent), and experience of physical abuse (4.3 percent). Reported rates of postpartum depression (16.6 percent) were also higher than the average of the 26 states included in the reporting data. In 2005, 2,207 legal abortions were performed in Alaska (386 to women aged 19 years or younger), for a ratio of 211 per 1,000 live births and a rate of 15 abortions per 1,000 women ages 15–44.

**See Also:** Aboriginal Mothering; Alcoholism; Poverty and Mothering.

**Bibliography**

Centers for Disease Control and Prevention. "Reproductive Health: Data and Statistics." http://www.cdc.gov/reproductivehealth/Data_Stats/index.htm#Abortion (accessed May 2009).
D'Angelo, Denise, Letitia Williams, and Brian Morrow, et al. "Preconception and Interconception Health Status of Women Who Recently Gave Birth to a Live-Born Infant—Pregnancy Risk Assessment Monitoring System (PRAMS), United States, 26 Reporting Areas, 2004." http://www.cdc.gov/mmwr/preview/mmwrhtml/ss5610a1.htm (accessed May 2009).
U.S. Census Bureau. "The 2009 Statistical Abstract: The National Data Book." http://www.census.gov/compendia/statab/ (accessed May 2009).
U.S. Census Bureau. "State & County Quick Facts: Alaska." http://quickfacts.census.gov/qfd/states/02000lk.html (accessed May 2009).

Sarah E. Boslaugh
Washington University School of Medicine

# Albania

Albania is a country in the Balkans in southeast Europe, and has a population of 3.17 million (2008). Many Albanians live overseas, in neighboring countries, Italy, the United States, and Australia. Albania has a birth rate of 15.1 per 1,000, and an infant mortality rate of 20.7 per 1,000 live births. The crude divorce rate in the country is 0.95 divorces per 1,000 marriages. Traditionally, the population in Albania since the 16th century has been largely Muslim, and the population today is officially regarded as 70 percent Muslim, with 20 percent Albanian Orthodox, and 10 percent Roman Catholic—the most famous Albanian being the Nobel laureate Mother Teresa from an Albanian family from nearby Skopje, in modern-day Macedonia.

Historically, the major role of women in Albanian society was that of a homemaker, and few had much opportunity to leave their native villages or towns. The English traveler Edith Durham visited Albania from the 1900s, and she found an intensely tribal society. In one case, a man told her that if he married a "writing woman" (i.e., one who could read and write), "that king would not fetch wood and water" for him. In 1918, the average family size was 4.6 persons in Tirana, and 3.8 in Durrës. Under King Zog, his six sisters were used as role models in Albanian society; the younger three never married. The period of the Italian occupation saw a small change in the role of women, and a tenth of the Communist partisans during World War II were reported to be women.

Social mobility was transformed during the period of Communist rule from 1944 until 1992, as was medical care; education became compulsory (and enforced) for all girls as well as boys. The Faculty of Medicine at Tirana University helped improve health care, and there was a widespread availability of midwifery services. With one of the highest literacy rates in the world (99 percent for women), better access to hospitals and midwives led to a dramatic fall in the infant mortality rate. In spite of this, women's participation in the country's government remained one of the lowest in Europe (around 6 percent). This increased after the end of Communism, and with the provision of even better health care, the infant mortality rate continues to be reduced. There have also been many programs to reduce the rates of domestic violence against women. Although the country's fertility rate has fallen from 4.4 in 1975 to 2.1 in 1999, it has been the highest in Europe on both occasions.

**See Also:** Bulgaria; Macedonia; Mother Teresa of Calcutta; Religion and Mothering.

**Bibliography**
Douglas, Carol Anne. "Albania: Feminism and Post Communism." *Off Our Backs*, March 1994.
Gruber, Siegfried. "Household Structures in Urban Albania in 1918." *The History of the Family*, v.13/2 (August 2008).
Kolsti, John. "From Courtyard to Cabinet: The Political Emergence of Albanian Women." In *Women, State and Party in Eastern Europe*, Sharon L. Wolchik and Alfred G. Meyer, eds. Durham, NC: Duke University Press, 1985.
National Library of Australia. *The Albanian Woman: a Great Force of the Revolution*. Tirana, Albania: 8 Nëntori Publishing, 1978.
Prifti, Peter R. "The Albanian Women's Struggle for Emancipation." *Southeastern Europe*, v.2/2 (1975).
Whitaker, Ian. "A Sack for Carrying Things—The Traditional Role of Women in Northern Albanian Society." *Anthropological Quarterly*, v.54/3 (July 1981).

Justin Corfield
Geelong Grammar School, Australia

# Alcoholism

Alcohol is a culturally acceptable, legal drug that is part of the lives of many women. However, alcohol dependency can occur when alcohol is continually consumed despite negative consequences to one's overall health and well-being. The American Medical Association considers alcohol dependence, also commonly known as alcoholism, to be characterized by tolerance, the need to consume increasing amounts of alcohol to feel its effects, and the appearance of physical symptoms when alcohol use is discontinued. The *Diagnostic and Statistical Manual*, 4th edition, text revision (*DSM-IV-TR*) a standard for diagnosis in psychiatry and psychology, defines alcohol dependence as the repeated use of alcohol despite recurrent adverse psychological and physical consequences such as depression, blackouts, and liver disease. Two types of alcohol that are commonly abused are ethyl alcohol, found in beer, wine, spirits and liqueurs; and methyl alcohol, in household substances such as solvents, paint thinners, and antifreeze.

**Maternal Alcohol Addiction**
While the physiological effects of alcohol addiction are well-documented as potentially life threatening to both men and women, a primary focus of literature pertaining to maternal alcohol addiction is related to the effects on children. Maternal alcohol addiction not only affects children prior to their birth, but also impinges on their ongoing relationship with their alcoholic mothers and their functioning as adult children. *Fetal alcohol spectrum disorder* (FASD), *fetal alcohol syndrome* (FAS), *partial fetal alcohol syndrome* (p-FAS), *fetal alcohol effects* (FEA), *alcohol-related birth defects* (ARBD), and *neurodevelopmental disorder* (ARND) are terms used to describe the permanent physical and mental challenges faced by children who were prenatally exposed to alcohol. Postnatal risks are considered in relation to a compromised home environment resulting from maternal incapacity. The impact of paternal and maternal addiction is evident in the Adult Children of Alcoholics Syndrome (ACOA), based on the premise that, as a result of their childhood experiences, individuals who grow up in alcoholic families have similar characteristics.

**Intersecting Oppressions**
Women with alcohol addiction frequently inhabit a culture of silence that is perpetuated by complex, intersecting oppressions that act interdependently,

*Poverty compounds the stress levels of mothers with alcohol addiction, and exposes children to an increased risk of victimization. Addicted mothers fear the removal or loss of their children, which can dissuade them from entering a treatment center.*

simultaneously, and reciprocally. Societal silencing mechanisms imposed on mothers with addiction include marginalization, surveillance, and censure by child welfare authorities and lay members of society. Like most women in Western societies, mothers with alcohol addiction are influenced by discourses of motherhood that call for sacrificial, intensive mothering. The ideal image of the "good mother" is one who raises her children in the "right circumstances," meaning two heterosexual parents, preferably married, with the mother (not too young or too old) who is the caregiver and the father who is the breadwinner. There also exists an underlying assumption that the ideal mother is mentally stable, without any interference of abuse. When mothers with alcohol addiction exhibit socially unacceptable or stigmatized behaviors that challenge the ideal image, they are criticized and labeled "bad mothers" and face punitive and stigmatizing judgment.

In addition, mothers with alcohol addiction frequently suffer from mental health disorders. In response to the high rates of co-occurring substance abuse and mental health disorders, the term *dual diagnosis* was coined, which resulted in the integration of substance abuse and mental health services. However, for some women, dual diagnosis is further complicated by a history of violence in the form of childhood physical and/or sexual abuse, and is often followed by adult partner abuse. Current research supports the link between abuse histories and subsequent mental health problems as well as subsequent addiction issues. Often, women suffering from these challenges are faced with multiple barriers to effective mothering, such as inadequate income, as well as difficulty meeting basic needs such as food, housing, transportation, and adequate childcare. Exposed to severe, chronic stressors within their families and communities, women in poverty are especially vulnerable to psychological distress and problem drinking. They and their children are at increased risk of victimization due to their compromised living environment.

## Challenges to Recovery

Alcoholics Anonymous is a long-standing and highly regarded peer support program that is a crucial aspect of recovery for both women and men. In part, its efficacy is related to supportive and challenging relationships that facilitate breaking the silence of addiction, an important first step in recovery. Although few in number, professionally managed, publicly funded treatment programs for mothers have been developed in the larger societal context that equates the mother with an alcohol addiction to poor care for her children. Therefore, a justification for publicly supported treatment programs for mothers has been made, and is seen as the first step toward a comprehensive preventative program for children who are considered "at risk" for a wide range of problems. A common argument for enhanced, gender-specific recovery programs for women is that costs to the public are reduced when women recover from their addiction and are able to care for their children.

Historically, treatment programs for alcoholism focused almost exclusively on patterns of drug and alcohol use among men, with little attention given to the disparate social, emotional, and economic realities of women's lives. Justification for this partiality was based on men having higher rates of addiction with more visible social consequences and being more likely than women to access treatment, stay longer, and have better rates of treatment completion. Cultural beliefs that excessive drinking is more acceptable for men than for women, women's drinking was often treated as invisible. As a result, many women with alcohol abuse problems often concealed their addiction. However, with the women's movement and concomitant advances in research on women's issues, the traditional, male-centered recovery programs based on the premise that what holds true for men can also be applied to women was challenged, leading to the creation of gender-based recovery programs.

Though treatment plays a vital role in helping women with alcohol addiction stabilize and re-establish their lives, the number of custodial mothers who enter, stay, and complete residential recovery programs is low. Several factors contribute to this circumstance. The possible removal or loss of children is a powerful sanction that is feared by many mothers and can induce concealment and underlie their reluctance to seek help. Therefore, deciding whether to enter a recovery program is often poses a dilemma for the custodial mother. Although they feel unable to provide adequate emotional support while experiencing distress, and believe sobriety and mental health would contribute significantly to the ability to mother effectively, they soon discover that most treatment centers are unable to accommodate children: mothers are often required to relinquish their children to relatives or the state while undergoing treatment. The double-barreled stigma associated with addiction and voluntary relinquishment of child custody leads to feelings of guilt and failure and is often the greatest challenge for mothers in recovery. As well, entering a residential treatment program often elicits an overwhelming sense of grief stemming from multiple losses, including the loss of their parental rights and responsibilities, their role as a mother, and the meaning and significance derived from a relationship with their children.

## Treatment Programs

An examination of treatment needs for women in recovery suggests a general consensus that treatment should be gender specific with an acknowledgment of the differences for women in relation to the effects of substance use, the patterns of use, and societal responses to women's addictions. Given the multiple locations of women in relation to class and race, the context of their addiction and their experience in treatment is varied and complex. Finding common ground to support mothers with addiction remains an ongoing challenge to the development of effective recovery programs. Research indicates that vocational training, education, self-care strategies, nutritional information, support from family and friends, and access to community resources are factors that mediate recovery. Also, a growing body of literature suggests that many women who have also experienced childhood sexual abuse and/or domestic violence find that a supportive environment that enables the development of their spirituality provides a context for the development of hope.

In relation to programming, effective recovery centers also incorporate facilities for children as well as childcare, prenatal care, mental health programming, and workshops on women-centered topics. Treatment programs that honor the importance of the therapeutic relationship and mutual support as the cornerstone for the provision of ongoing emotional support is a crucial aspect of intervention.

Including children in the recovery journey is an evolving aspect of treatment efficacy. The children have witnessed the detrimental effects of substance abuse and other concurrent challenges while suffering the multiple consequences of these issues. Not only do children need to witness their mother's progress in treatment in order to reestablish trust in her and their relationship, they also need support to overcome the issues they face as a result of their mother's struggles. Where it is not possible for children to be on-site at the recovery center, having access to their children is a vital part of the recovery process for mothers.

However, a mother's access to her children depends on a variety of variables, such as physical distance between mother and child, schedule compatibility, custody orders, and agreements on behalf of the custodial parent. Visits maintain the mother–child relationship, help families cope with the transitions and changes that accompany recovery, and provide a base for transition back into the home, as well as reassure the child of the mother's continued interest in the their lives. Interventions such as mothering skills and including children in the recovery process can promote resiliency in the mother, the child, and the relationship as well as serve to link children to supportive services.

While recovery programs for mothers have yielded positive results, they may shroud the untenable life circumstances that have led to addiction. Therefore, in addition to recovery programs aimed at the individual, simultaneous effort is required to address the larger societal context that currently fails to address the more global stressors faced by women, such as family violence, sexual abuse, poverty, oppression, and mental health challenges. From a holistic perspective, the context of a woman's life—including her physical, emotional, and spiritual health, as well as the social and occupational components of overall wellness—must be deemed equally as important as symptoms, diagnosis, and individual counseling.

**See Also:** "Bad" Mothers; Drug Abuse; Fetal Alcohol Syndrome; Poverty and Mothering.

**Bibliography**
American Medical Association. *American Medical Association Complete Medical Encyclopedia*. New York: Random House, 2003.
American Psychiatric Association. *Diagnostic and Statistical Manual of Mental Disorders, 4th Edition*. Arlington, VA: American Psychiatric Publishing, 2000.
DeVault, M. L. *Liberating Method: Feminism and Social Research*. Philadelphia, PA: Temple University Press, 1999.
O'Reilly, A. *Mother Matters: Motherhood as Discourse and Practice*. Toronto: Association for Research on Mothering, 2004.

Constance A. Barlow
University of Calgary

# Algeria

Algeria, officially the People's Democratic Republic of Algeria, is the second-largest country in Africa, stretching from the coast of the Mediterranean Sea down into the Sahara. It became a socialist state in 1962, after winning independence from France, its former colonial ruler. Arabic is the only official language, though Berber dialects have received some recognition, and French is still used in education and in certain media. In the 1970s, improvements in the health system increased the fertility rate to 7–8 children per mother, though the rate has since decreased dramatically due to changes in society, reaching a yearly birth rate of 1.82 births/woman in 2008, with the number of children born per woman in her childbearing years projected to be 2.38 by 2010.

## Population Growth and Allowances
Before 1980, there was no official birth control program in Algeria; most people lived in extended fami-

lies, patriarchal and patrilineal, with an emphasis on producing as many children—particularly sons—as possible. The rapid demographic growth, however, led the government to establish a family planning program with the emphasis on "birth spacing" and family well-being. Maternal and Infant Protection Centers were created to provide advice and contraceptives to interested women. Religious authorities found birth control compatible with Islam as long as it was voluntary, and included neither abortion nor sterilization. By 1989, when the United Nations Fund for Population Activities set up a new program of education and health care in Algeria, it was estimated that 35 percent of Algerian women of childbearing age were using contraception. By 1990 the infant mortality rate had decreased to 67 per 1,000 live births. A system of family allowances for certain employed persons, begun by the French in 1943, has gradually been extended to more categories of workers, but still offers little for single or divorced mothers. In 2008, the population reached approximately 34 million, almost equally divided between males and females.

More than half of university students are women. Though women now represent some 70 percent of lawyers and 60 percent of judges in Algeria, as well as predominating in medicine, the movement of women into the general workforce is slow, in part because overall unemployment is high. Official statistics state that 25 percent of Algerians were out of work in 2004, for example, and some observers think that 50 percent of males under 30 are without full-time employment today. Many men immigrate to other countries to find work. In the cities, large groups of young men without jobs lounge in the cafés and plazas. In April 2007, a conference on women in the workplace was held in Algiers, concentrating on issues such as access to employment and sexual harassment on the job. Women currently make up only 15–20 percent of the workforce. Childcare providers are in short supply, and the recent increase in nuclear families living apart from relatives makes it difficult for mothers to work outside the home.

## Societal Standards for Algerian Mothers

Algerian women are expected to be quiet, modest, decorous, virgins until marriage, and faithful

wives afterward. A new bride traditionally lives with her husband in or near the bridegroom's family home; there is frequently a difficult relationship with her mother-in-law. New mothers, since they gain status by producing boys, favor their sons and often nurse them longer than they do daughters. The tie between mother and son remains warmly intimate, and is often the closest connection in the family. Even when a married woman has a house or apartment she is, as L. Massignon remarks, "a stranger in her own home," because there is no community property between husband and wife in Algerian law.

The legal system is a combination of French and Islamic law. The Algerian Family Code of 1984 reinforced fundamentalist attitudes toward women and actually restricted women's rights, despite the fact that women fighters, *porteuses de feu* (bomb carriers), played a significant part earlier in the War of Independence. Helen Metz finds that through their participation in the war effort, Algerian women "thus achieved a new sense of their own identity and a measure of acceptance from men that they had not enjoyed before." Whereas the French discouraged the practice of veiling, after independence the number of women wearing veils in public increased both because of social pressure to conform and the entry of more women into situations outside the home. The limited emancipation achieved by Algerian women gives them an uncertain status in society. Sociologists report that women today are both "more religious" and "more modern" than earlier generations.

The 2005 revision to family code paradoxically makes it easier for men to divorce their wives and avoid support payments. In the cities, there are numerous divorced women and children who are homeless. Reliable information on divorce rates is difficult to find; popular blogs state that "everyone" is getting divorced these days, but official reports vary. Additionally, civil wars and natural disasters have created many orphans, who may be assisted by such organizations as the Foundation Mahfoud Boucebi or the Algerian branch of SOS Kinderdorf International. Formal adoption in the Western sense is not permitted by Islamic law, but the government has established a program of foster parents to care for orphans.

## Algerian Literature

Modern Algerian literature, like culture, is divided between Arabic, French, and local dialects. The most famous writer from Algeria is Nobel laureate Albert Camus (1913–60), born of French-Algerian settlers in Mondovi. He hoped to find ways to establish a free and cosmopolitan society in Algeria. Despite political failures, his work is much appreciated by readers in the land of his birth that he describes so beautifully in *Noces* (Nuptials). Assia Djebar (1936) is another well-known Algerian writer of French expression; she is especially concerned with the situation of Algerian women before, during, and after the War for Independence from France. Motherhood is a recurrent theme in her fiction, and mothers, grandmothers, sisters, and female friends are important in her writings. She values the feminine culture of traditional Islamic societies, yet criticizes the restrictions placed on women by Islamic men. Ahlam Mosteghanemi is the first Algerian woman to publish a novel in Arabic, *Memory in the Flesh* (1985). Poet/singer/painter Houria Niati (1948) now lives in England where she works in French, English, and Arabic.

**See Also:** France; Islam and Motherhood; Postcolonialism and Mothering; Sons and Mothers.

### Bibliography

Carroll, David. *Albert Camus the Algerian: Colonialism, Terrorism, Justice.* New York: Columbia University Press, 2007.

Charrad, Mounira M. *States and Women's Rights: The Making of Postcolonial Tunisia, Algeria, and Morocco.* Berkeley: University of California Press, 2001.

Djebar, Assia. *Women of Algiers in Their Apartment.* Charlottesville: University Press of Virginia, 1992.

Hintz, Martin. *Algeria.* New York: Scholastic, 2006.

Metz, Helen Chapan, ed. *Algeria: A Country Study.* Washington, DC: GPO for the Library of Congress, 1994.

Phillips, John and Martin Evans. *Algeria: Anger of the Dispossessed.* New Haven, CT: Yale University Press, 2008.

Ringrose, Priscilla. *Assia Djebar: In Dialogue With Feminisms.* New York: Rodopi, 2006.

Kittye Delle Robbins-Herring
Mississippi State University

# Allende, Isabel

Isabel Allende, a Chilean American novelist/memoirist now residing in San Rafael, California, merges feminist political-social commentary with family sagas, myth, and personal history. Born in Lima, Perum in 1942, she says her mother Francisca is her greatest supporter. The caption of a photo of her mother and herself, viewable in Allende's current online album, reads: "My mother is the longest love affair of my life. We have never cut the umbilical cord." Letters to her mother form the basis of the memoir *The Sum of Our Days* (2008), and she frequently visits her in Chile. Earlier, while working for the United Nations in Santiago, Isabel married Miguel Frías. In 1963 she gave birth to her daughter Paula, and in 1966 to her son Nicolás.

## Reflections in Allende Literature

One of her first publications was *Grandmother Panchita,* a story she told her own children. In 1973 the assassination of her cousin Salvador Allende sent her into exile in Venezuela. When she got word her grandfather was dying, she began a letter for him that became her first novel, *The House of the Spirits* (1982). Her grandparents were the models for the two characters in the book, Esteban Trueba and Clara del Valle. Susan Dobrian notes: this novel established "a political stake in motherhood" and "a feminine genealogy that stands against patriarchal repression." Then came *Eva Luna* (1987) and *The Stories of Eva Luna* (1989). Her sensuous style and lyrical storytelling have been called magical realism, but Allende sees her novels "as just being realistic literature," imposing fictional order on chaos by a long, trancelike process like "an elephant's pregnancy."

The illness and death of her daughter led the author to reflect on her own childhood in her first openly autobiographical writing, *Paula* (1994). It begins: "Listen, Paula. I am going to tell you a story so that when you wake up you will not feel so lost." Allende paints herself as the character of Demeter and her daughter as Persephone. Pregnancy and parturition play a large role in her fiction, where bellies swell like watermelons, bodies are ruined by births and miscarriages, and a dead boy's ghost haunts his mother. The major maternal theme in these writings is mother–daughter relationships, but with significant attention to mother–son relationships as well. In *Tosca,* an opera-mad young wife leaves her newborn son at home while she follows a honey-voiced medical student out into the South American oilfields, yet she never loses the sense of visceral connection to her child: "the animal pain that sank its claws in her every time she thought of her son." Years later she wants to reconcile—but cannot—with husband and son.

In her short story "The Judge's Wife" in her book *The Stories of Eva Luna,* the evocatively named Juana la Triste hangs herself in shame because her outlaw son has abandoned her to the judge's public cruelties, thus indirectly bringing about her son's own death. In *The Sum of Our Days* (2009) Isabel recounts how she sought and found a second wife for her son Nico, a woman so perfect for him that the two fell in love at first sight. Daughters, stepdaughters, foster daughters, and daughters-in-law abound in these stories. Eliza in *Daughter of Fortune* (1999) is reared by two devoted foster mothers: the shrewd Victorian spinster Miss Rose, who educates her as a proper young lady, and the cook/housekeeper Mama Fresia, who gives the girl the physical affection and Indian wisdom that nurture her spirit. In contrast, Elena in *Wicked Girl* is neglected by her biological mother who, "exhausted by heat and the grind of running her boardinghouse, had no energy for tenderness or time to devote to her daughter." The heroine of *Inés of My Soul* (2006), however, becomes the founding mother of the whole nation of Chile. The mother knot, for joy or woe, ties each woman to her children.

**See Also:** Autobiographies; Chicana Mothering; Chile; Literature, Mothers in.

### Bibliography

Correas de Zapata, Celia. *Isabel Allende: Life and Spirits.* Houston, TX: Arte Publico Press, 2002.

Dobrian, Susan. "Writing in the Margin: Maternal and Indigenous Space in *Entrada Libre.*" *College Literature,* v.22 (1995).

Dulfano, Isabel. "The Mother/Daughter Romance—Our Life: Isabel Allende in/and Paula." *Women's Studies,* v.35 (2006).

Zeff, Jacqueline. "What Doesn't Kill You, Makes You Fat: The Language of Food in Latina Literature." *Journal of American and Comparative Cultures,* v.25 (2002).

Kittye Delle Robbins-Herring
Mississippi State University

# Alpha Mom

Originally coined by graphic designer Constance Van Flandern for the launch of a cable TV program *The Mommy Channel* in 2004, the expression *alpha mom* describes educated and well-off mothers who aim to reach excellence in motherhood. They believe that motherhood does not come naturally, so excellence in motherhood cannot be achieved simply by trusting their instinct. Alpha Moms believe motherhood to be like a job: they diligently and scrupulously look for the latest information on how to raise a child and regard their duty as similar to a manager in a corporate business.

As the mission of Alpha Mom Website reads, "Alpha Mom was started because, as counter-intuitive as it may seem, motherhood is not a natural instinct for many (many) women. Rather, connectedness is a new mom's first instinct. And, with nonjudgmental support and advice from other moms and parenting professionals, we try to help women embrace motherhood with confidence." Because of their influence on American society, Alpha Moms have become an important focus for the marketing campaigns of major corporations and have been described as "hyperactive purchasing agents." As so-called Soccer Moms and Yoga Moms before them, Alpha Moms have gained visibility as influential consumers and as an influential social group within American society.

Van Flandern's client was Isabel Kallman, herself a new mother and a former senior vice-president at Salomon Smith Barney, who decided to launch a cable channel on parenting when she could not find anything regarding motherhood on TV. The channel was launched in 2005, obtaining distribution deals with Comcast and Cox. Although the channel struggled in its early days, its name has come to designate a new conception of motherhood and its influence on American society has grown steadily. Important companies such as Nintendo, General Motors, and Procter & Gamble have increasingly recognized the power of Alpha Moms as trendsetters and highly social networkers. Part of the success of the Wii console game was due to the endorsement it received from Alpha Moms. General Motors decided to focus Cadillac campaigns—in the words of Liz Vanzura, one of its marketing directors—to "moms who wouldn't be caught dead in a minivan. . . . Type A moms who hit one goal, then are off to the next."

In their projected image as efficient, technologically expert, and successful mothers both inside and outside the home, Alpha Moms combine two crucial American values: the work ethic and domesticity.

**See Also:** Beta Mom; Consumerism and Motherhood; Intensive Mothering; Mommy Wars; Mothers Movement Online; New Momism; Technology and Motherhood.

### Bibliography

AlphaMom.com. www.alphamom.com (accessed August 2008).

Horovitz, Bruce. "Alpha Moms Leap to Top of Trendsetters." *USA Today* (March 27, 2007). http://www.usatoday.com/money/advertising/2007-03-26-alpha-mom_N.htm (accessed August 2008).

Patterson, Randall. "Empire of the Alpha Mom." *New York Times Magazine* (June 12, 2005). http://nymag.com/nymetro/news/features/12026/ (accessed August 2008).

Luca Prono
Independent Scholar

# Ambivalence, Maternal

The changes and emotions associated with the arrival of a new baby are usually love, joy, and happiness. While most women take pleasure in having a baby, they may also feel exhausted, overwhelmed by the responsibilities of childcare, lonely if they take care of their child without sufficient social support, or confused about their new identity. Yet cultural images of new mothers rarely present such feelings. The difficulties, stress, or feelings of aggression that can be triggered by the transition to motherhood thus take many women by surprise. The concept of maternal ambivalence captures the simultaneous experience of positive and negative feelings, beliefs, or thoughts about motherhood and the relationship between mother and child. While most mothers probably feel conflicted about their children and their motherhood role at some point, societal perceptions of ambivalence as somehow wrong or deviant make mothers feel guilty about their feelings. Ambivalence is generally defined as having both psychological and social components. Conflicting feelings, cognitions, and motivations appear on the subjective, psychological level, while contradictions between social roles, statuses, and norms emerge on the social-structural level.

### Psychological Perspectives

The psychological understanding of maternal ambivalence is based on a presence of loving and hating feelings between a mother and an infant. In the works of psychoanalytic theorists like Sigmund Freud, Melanie Klein, and Donald W. Winnicott, love and hate are rooted in the unconscious and can coexist. For the infant, feelings of ambivalence represent an important developmental step in the achievement of the separation from the mother. Mothers' ambivalence stems from the contradictory emotions that they experience in the relationship with the infant, from the process of their separation, and the fear of losing the child. According to the psychological theories, the contradictory feelings become problematic if they become unmanageable or if they are suppressed. A mother's awareness of the conflicted emotions can turn against her own self and result in an overwhelming sense of guilt and, possibly, depression.

The focus of traditional psychoanalysis, however, is primarily on the infant and the environment the mother creates for the child's psychological development. Contemporary psychotherapist Rozsika Parker, in her study on maternal ambivalence *Torn in Two*, extends this understanding and turns the attention to the significance of ambivalence for maternal psychological development. In this perspective, the achievement of ambivalence and a mother's awareness of the coexistence of love and hate for the baby can actually be beneficial, as it promotes a sense of concern and responsibility toward the baby and a mother's sense of self-autonomy.

Manageable ambivalence thus enables the mother to form a more fulfilling relationship with the baby. However, unmanageable ambivalence can develop into anxiety or depression due to cultural idealization of mothers. Since every mother has a desire to be considered a "good mother," and experiencing anger and negative emotions toward the child is not a part of the "good mother" image, awareness of the contradictory feelings can increase the anxiety and guilt mothers feel about motherhood. The psychological relationship based on love and hate is thus also shaped by social and cultural conditions of mothering and the internalized image of a "good mother," which women try to achieve.

### Behind the Mask of Motherhood

In contemporary Western society, the conflicted and negative aspects of motherhood are, in the words of author Susan Maushart, hidden behind "the mask of motherhood," which keeps maternal ambivalence concealed to non-mothers. The social pressure to be a "good mother" allows only for the expression of maternal ambivalence in the form of humor, as something that can easily be overcome. The negative aspects, doubts, or anger associated with mothering are culturally represented as a deviance or an illness that needs to be treated with therapy or medications—for example, as in postpartum depression. The mask of motherhood thus obscures the full spectrum of the mothering experience, leaving new mothers to face the discrepancy between the idealized expectations and the harsh realities of motherhood. Results of qualitative sociological research by Tina Miller, Martha McMahon, and Deborah Lupton suggest that this lack of preparation and understanding of the true reality of the motherhood experience represents one of the factors central to the presence of maternal ambivalence.

### Social and Cultural Contradictions

As mothers' relationships with children exist under particular historical, social, and cultural conditions that affect both how a mother feels about mothering and the role of mother, social theorists locate ambivalence not only in interpersonal relationships but also in conflicting social norms and expectations oriented toward the mothering role. Modern societal conditions are characterized by increas-ing choices, contradictions, and demands, as well as conflicting role-related norms and expectations. Mothers can thus experience maternal ambivalence as a result of the different norms and expectations connected to the mothering role.

Social theorists agree that social expectations for contemporary mothers are historically very high. Contemporary mothers are expected to mother according to the prevailing ideology of intensive mothering. *Intensive mothering,* as characterized by Sharon Hays, requires a mother to be the central caregiver to the child, follow the advice of experts, always put the child's needs ahead of her own, be fully absorbed emotionally with the child, and spend significant time and financial resources for the benefit of the child. Susan Douglas and Meredith Michaels refer to this set of norms promoted by media as *new momism* and posit that increasing standards of perfection make it difficult for mothers to either achieve the prescribed ideal or carve a space for individual identity. This creates anxiety, guilt, and ambivalence for the motherhood experience.

In the course of their mothering, mothers encounter numerous contradictory, cultural, and social expectations that have the potential to trigger ambivalent feelings. For example, while contemporary mothers are expected to devote a lot of time and energy to their children, there is also an opposite expectation that they remain women with their own identities, interests, or careers. The cultural debate of whether stay-at-home or employed mothers make better mothers, sometimes referred to as *mommy wars,* represents this cultural contradiction, which can leave mothers ambivalent about their mothering regardless of which direction they choose. Maternal ambivalence can also originate in the conflict between prevailing and internalized norms of immediate attachment between a mother and a baby, and a mother's actual experience of forming a bond with the child that does not involve falling in love at first sight. In this way, any mothering experience that contradicts the prescribed norms of mothering can create feelings of ambivalence.

### Intergenerational Ambivalence

Maternal ambivalence is often associated with new mothers or mothers with young children due to the intensity and dramatic changes related to the transition to motherhood and demands of the early childcare. However, many sources of conflicted feelings remain, and new contradictions appear, once the children are older or even grown up. The ambivalence and dilemmas in the relationships between adult children and their older parents are referred to as intergenerational ambivalence. Maternal ambivalence, in these cases, stems from the contradiction of the societal expectations on children's achievement and behavior (for example, achieving financial independence, taking care of the elderly parents) and their actual practices (not having a job, living with the parents).

## Social Structural Differences

Mothers also experience maternal ambivalence differently according to their position in social structures and the resources they have to resolve it. Structural conditions and relations (race, ethnicity, class position) differentiate how mothers in various social settings experience maternal ambivalence. For example, for white, middle-class mothers, issues of personal identity or balancing work and family can produce strong feelings of ambivalence. However, for low-income or African American mothers, who have historically high rates of participation in the paid labor force, ambivalent feelings can be produced by another set of conflicting social norms, such as an expectation to provide quality education to their children or keep them safe in neighborhoods that do not have satisfactory schools or safe streets. Social, structural, and cultural conditions of mothering thus also affect experiences of maternal ambivalence and need to be considered along with the traditional psychological view of maternal ambivalence.

**See Also:** Becoming a Mother; Freud, Sigmund; Intensive Mothering; Mommy Wars; New Momism; Postpartum Depression.

## Bibliography

Douglas, Susan J. and Meredith W. Michaels. *The Mommy Myth: The Idealization of Motherhood and How It Has Undermined Women.* New York: Free Press, 2004.

Hollway, Wendy and Brid Featherstone. *Mothering and Ambivalence.* New York: Routledge, 1997.

Lupton, Deborah. "Love/Hate Relationship: The Ideals and Experiences of First-Time Mothers." *Journal of Sociology,* v.36/1 (2000).

Maushart, Susan. *The Mask of Motherhood: How Becoming a Mother Changes Our Lives and Why We Never Talk About It.* New York: Penguin Books, 1999.

McMahon, Martha. *Engendering Motherhood: Identity and Self-Transformation in Women's Lives.* New York: Guilford Press, 1995.

Miller, Tina. "Is This What Motherhood Is All About? Weaving Experiences and Discourse Through Transition to First-Time Motherhood." *Gender & Society,* v.21 (2007).

Parker, Rozsika. *Torn in Two: The Experience of Maternal Ambivalence.* London: Virago Press, 1995.

Peskowitz, Miriam. *The Truth Behind the Mommy Wars: Who Decides What Makes a Good Mother?* New York: Seal Press, 2005.

Pillemer, Karl and Kurt Luescher, eds. *Intergenerational Ambivalences: New Perspectives on Parent-Child Relations in Later Life.* Maryland Heights, MO: Elsevier, 2004.

Ivana Brown
Rutgers University

# Androgenesis

The term *androgenesis* (from the Latin *andro,* meaning male, and *genesis,* meaning life) originates in biology but has recently emerged in popular culture to describe reproduction inside the male body. In the scientific literature, the term first appeared in a 1916 *Glossary of Botanical Terms* (3rd edition) and narrowly referred to the growth of a life form from a male cell. Over time, it has come to mean the development of an embryo with only paternal chromosomes, which results from the failure of the egg nucleus to participate in fertilization.

The resulting embryo is thus a parthenogenic offspring, or clone of the father. Most recently, however, androgenesis describes reproduction in the male body, exemplified by some species of fish, including sea horses, sea dragons, and pipefish, which reproduce through male pregnancy and gestation. Feminist scholarship has used the term to describe the process whereby human males might eventually reproduce their offspring in their own bodies, with the help of current and future reproductive technologies.

## Historical Interest

Academic discussions of the feasibility and desirability of human androgenesis note that evidence of human interest in and desire for male pregnancy litters our history. Aristotle described human reproduction in distinctly androgenetic terms, claiming for men the power to form life and leaving to women the menial task of gestation. Androgenetic folklore abounds in Western culture, including the story of Zeus birthing Athena from his head. In Norse folklore, the god Loki allegedly twice gave birth, once after transforming into the body of a mare and once in his original form after eating a burnt ogress. According to some interpretations, even the Christian virgin birth story displaces Mary as the agent of generation in favor of a wholly procreative male God. Seventeenth-century spermists explained human reproduction as a function of the transmission of an *homunculus*, or "little man," in sperm, that is then transferred into a woman to grow into a child.

The idea of human androgenesis has gained increasing traction in both popular culture and scientific research during the last third of the 20th century. Male pregnancy is the theme of several commercial films, including *Night of the Blood Beast (1958), A Slightly Pregnant Man* (1973), and *Rabbit Test* (1978). It was Ivan Reitman's 1994 blockbuster, *Junior,* featuring a pregnant Arnold Schwarzenegger, however, that ignited recent widespread interest in the possibility of pregnant men. Four years after *Junior,* artist Lee Mingwei's "World's First Pregnant Man" Website (www .malepregnancy.com) claimed to report in "real time" on the scientific breakthrough of the world's first pregnant man. The site sports a continuous fetal heartbeat rhythm, articles about the science of male pregnancy, and videotaped interviews with the pregnant mom/dad-to-be. Though repeatedly revealed as an elaborate fabrication, Mingwei's site, which he maintains and regularly updates, still receives numerous daily hits, 11 years after its

inception. Androgenesis is also the focus of recent science fiction literature as well, including Stanley Pottinger's *Fourth Procedure* and Sherrie Tepper's *The Fresco.*

Further evidence of keen interest in male pregnancy was demonstrated by the response to the 2008 announcement that transgender American Thomas Beatie was pregnant. Mr. Beatie became an overnight media favorite. He starred in a quickly produced Discovery Channel documentary, and Seal Press published his autobiography by the year's end. The public announcement of his condition ignited a worldwide conversation about the ethics and desirability of male pregnancy and gestation. For Thomas Beatie, conception, gestation, and birth were possible because he was born with female reproductive anatomy and only later, in adulthood, underwent the hormonal (but not surgical) transition required to become male. According to some researchers, however, the science of human male pregnancy may soon be technologically feasible for men born without the benefit of Beatie's female reproductive organs.

## Overcoming Challenges

Researchers are studying challenges once thought insurmountable for male pregnancy. Men have two key physical features that prevent human androgenetic reproduction: they lack a uterus, and produce a hormonal environment at odds with a growing fetus. Many infertile women share one or both of these barriers, however, and research aimed at solving these problems for them could be equally applied to men. For example, recent successes in uterine transplantation, using either a donated organ or an artificially grown organ, could potentially be applied to both men and women. Alternatively, mounting histories of some women's successful ectopic pregnancies challenges arguments about the need for a uterus altogether. Finally, looking into the future, some suggest that pre-implantation genetic interventions could allow parents to choose to have their male children grow a uterus—just in case they should some day wish to use one.

Science is also addressing the hormonal environment issue. New endocrinology reveals that the pregnancy itself produces hormones, possibly in sufficient amounts, to allow a "pregnant dad" to support a fetus in his otherwise testosterone-rich body. Other research has documented the presence of dramatic reductions in testosterone, and concurrent increases in estrogens, in the male partners of pregnant women during pregnancy and delivery. Scientists hypothesis that such hormone shifts occur naturally to bond father to baby, while the baby remains in the mother's womb. The well-documented phenomenon of *couvades*, or sympathetic pregnancy, may be the result of these dramatic shifts in men's biochemistry during their female partner's pregnancies. One possible outcome of such discoveries could be the realization of human androgenesis that has, up until this point, existed only in the spate of science fiction works that have tackled the ethics and political implications of such a turn in human history.

**See Also:** Aristotle; Artificial Uterus; Ectopic Pregnancy; Hormone Therapy; In Vitro Fertilization; Pregnancy; Uterine Transplantation.

**Bibliography**
Graves, Jen. "Getting Patrick Pregnant." *The Stranger* (July 11, 2007).
Hedtke, Shannon M., Kathrin Stanger-Hall, Robert J. Baker, and David M. Hillis. "All-Male Sexuality: Origin and Maintenance of Androgenesis in the Asian Clam *Corbicula.*" *Evolution*, v.62/5 (2008).
McKeen, Catherine. "The Female in Aristotle's Biology." *Philosophical Books*, v.48/1 (2007).
Morel, Jim. "Male Pregnancy: Seahorse Style!" *Science in Africa*, www.scienceafrica.co.za/2003/february/shorse.htm (accessed February 2003).
Polinski, Michael. "Feeling Her Pain: Male Pregnancy Experience." http://includes.iparenting.com/layout/article_print.php?aid=2045&type=1 (accessed May 2009).
ScienceDaily.com. "Male Pregnancy: Genetic Archaeology Offers Clues to Gender-Bending Mystery." http://www.sciencedaily.com/releases/2006/12/0612069536.htm (accessed December 2008).
Teresi, Dick and Kathleen McAuliffe. "Male Pregnancy." In *Sex/Machine*, P. Hopkins, ed. Bloomington: Indiana University Press, 1998.

Deirdre M. Condit
Virginia Commonwealth University

# Angel in the House

The Angel in the House was an idealization of womanhood embraced by Victorian society, especially the middle class. Its origins lie in the patriarchal belief that women, because of their sex, are reproductive and domestic beings. The term comes from Coventry Patmore's poem of the same title, published between 1854 and 1862, but the image of the domestic paragon who finds fulfillment and happiness in motherhood and family life was already well established by mid-century. Restricted to the home yet powerful through her moral influence, the Angel is a contradictory figure who reflects some of the challenges to women's social position in the Victorian period and beyond.

The domestic Angel emerges as loving, good and pure, always gentle, pious, submissive, and above all, selfless and self-sacrificing. Without troubling about self-identity, she consistently places others, especially her husband and children, first. In the privacy of the home, she creates a haven of peace and benevolence, and a sanctuary from the morally suspect public sphere. She submits to her husband, but her innate female goodness makes her superior to the male sex. She is her home's moral center, providing guidance and exerting influence on the entire household.

The Angel in the House, although popularized by Patmore, was familiar to the readers of novels and women's advice manuals by the time of his poem's publication. Charles Dickens privileges female characters like Agnes Wickfield in *David Copperfield* (1849–50) whom David deems his better angel and identifies with a church's stained glass window. In her popular conduct guides, like *The Women of England* (1838) and *The Mothers of England* (1843), Sara Stickney Ellis advocates domestic and maternal duties as the paramount means of fulfillment for womankind's angelic nature. The Angel also had an American counterpart in the 19th-century ideal of the True Woman.

In its insistent association of women with the private sphere, the Angel ideal placed significant limitations on the majority of women's lives, but the conduct manuals suggest that her domestic responsibilities could also prove empowering. Her duties in the home education of the very young, both male ing. Woolf's admitted difficulty in permanently banishing the persistent angelic presence reflects the power of the Angel into the 20th century.

**See Also:** Essentialism and Mothering; History of Motherhood: 1750 to 1900; Idealization of Mothers; Literature, Mothers In; Myths of Motherhood (Good/Bad); Nursing (Profession) and Motherhood; Patriarchal Ideology of Motherhood; Republican Motherhood.

**Bibliography**

Helsinger, Elizabeth, Robin Lauterbach Sheets, and William Veeder. *The Woman Question: Society and Literature in Britain and America 1817–1883*. Chicago: University of Chicago Press, 1983.

Langland, Elizabeth. "Nobody's Angels: Domestic Ideology and Middle-Class Women in the Victorian Novel." *PMLA*, v.107/2 (January 1992).

Poovey, Mary. *Uneven Developments: The Ideological Work of Gender in Mid-Victorian England*. Chicago: University of Chicago Press, 1988.

Rita Bode
Trent University

*Victorian photos capture the demure persona of the Angel in the House, who was expected to be gentle, pious, and selfless.*

and female, meant a role in the moral development of the nation's citizens. Her comforting, orderly home required strong managerial skills and also signified social status, which middle-class women, no less than their husbands, desired. Through shifting societal needs, her image came to benefit her unmarried, childless sisters; Florence Nightingale's vision of nurses as ministering angels, practicing the care and mothering associated with womanhood, helped promote nursing as an acceptable occupation for single women.

The Angel, however, casts a long shadow. Modernist writer Virginia Woolf records her personal struggles with the angelic presence. The character Mrs. Ramsay, in *To the Lighthouse* (1927), based in part on Woolf's own mother, personifies the intense appeal of selfless maternal care; at the same time, Woolf shows Mrs. Ramsay's husband and children as continually depleting her emotional and spiritual inner life to nurture their own. In addressing the subject of *Professions for Women* (1931), Woolf tells of the Angel's phantom urgings to display her feminine charms rather than her mind in her writ-

# Angola

Situated on the Atlantic, in southwestern African continent, Angola has a population of 12.3 million (2007), and a life expectancy of 39.8 for females and 37.5 for males. Its birth rate is 45.1 per 1,000, and an infant mortality rate of 180.2 per 1,000 live births, making it the highest in the world. The maternal mortality rate, at 17 per 1,000 births, is the fourth highest in the world. The fertility rate at 6.2 births per woman (2008) is the tenth highest in the world.

With the arrival of the European settlers in the 17th century, Queen Nzinga (1582–1663) became a heroine leading the resistance to the Portuguese, who had already devastated sections of Angolan society with the slave trade. The Portuguese, who occupied Angola until 1975, built little infrastructure in the country. Independence came after war, and was followed by a civil war between the left-wing government and right-wing rebels, which led to a further devastation of much of the countryside, and destruction of what little government infrastructure existed. As a result, when the war ended in 2002, the country's health care system was in disarray, with many societal problems.

### Access to Health Services

In traditional Angolan society, women had the role not only of taking care of children, cooking, and cleaning, but were also expected to plant and harvest crops and fetch water. Considered the property of their husbands, women remained illiterate and infant mortality rates were high. Access to health services and education was limited for all Africans in the country, and more so for women who, during the fighting that started in 1961, had the task of holding together families.

The revolutionary M.P.L.A. government of Agostinho Neto, which came to power in 1975, promoted itself on the basis of providing better health care for women; the Liga da Mulher Angolana (League of Angolan Women) was later established to help promote this. Since 1963, the Organização da Mulher Angolana (Organization of Angolan Women) had operated within the left-wing Movimento Popular de Liberatção de Angola (MPLA). In politics, there were 20 members of the National Assembly, and a number of women in mainstream politics such as Albina Assis as oil minister; Fátima Jarden as minister of fisheries; and Josefina Pitra Diakite as ambassador to the United States. Analia de Vitoria Pereira contested the country's 2002 presidential election.

**See Also:** Botswana; Congo; Congo, Democratic Republic of; War and Mothering; Zambia.

### Bibliography

*Angolan Women Building the Future: From National Liberation to Women's Emancipation.* London: Organization of Angolan Women & Zed Press, 1985.

Hunt, Simon. *Situation Analysis of Children and Women in Angola.* Oxford: University of Oxford, International Development Centre, Food Studies Group, 1992.

James, W. Martin. *Historical Dictionary of Angola.* Lanham, MD: Scarecrow Press, 2004.

Shapiro, Martin Frederick. *Medicine in the Service of Colonialism: Medical Care in Portuguese Africa 1885–1974.* Los Angeles: Ph.D. Thesis, University of California, 1983.

Justin Corfield
Geelong Grammar School, Australia

# Animal Species and Motherhood

Motherhood in animal species can be defined as those behaviors directed toward the care and maintenance of offspring and often the offspring of close relatives. These behaviors can start before conception in some species, and can continue well into the young animal's life in others species. Maternal behavior is very varied among the animal species and can fall anywhere along this spectrum of care. In some cases, the maternal behavior is aberrant and includes behaviors such as cannibalism. Biological, experiential, and environmental mechanisms can be used to understand the observed maternal behavior in animals. Additionally, the study of animal maternal behavior has been used to provide a model for human maternal behavior.

### Variation in Maternal Interaction

The spectrum of maternal behavior ranges from animals that never see their young to others that prepare for their offspring before and after conception. The digger wasp is an example of an organism that prepares for its offspring by digging a hole in the ground as a nest. She puts a food supply (such as caterpillars) in the nest with her egg and then closes up the nest. The wasp then leaves her offspring to develop on their own using the food supply she had provided. Birds are examples of mothers that alter their feeding and daily routine to create a suitable nest to incubate their eggs. Once their chicks have hatched, the mother bird and her mate will feed and care for them. Elephants also spend extensive time with their calves, which have been known to still sporadically nurse from their mothers at age 4.

### Normal and Aberrant Maternal Behavior

In animals that give live birth, such as dogs or cats, licking and nursing are the first maternal behaviors exhibited at the birth. In the case of dogs, the licking dries the puppy, stimulates its respiration, and guides it to nurse. The puppies usually nurse until they are weaned by the mother around 8 weeks. Although kittens are seen being carried by their mothers, puppies will return to their mother when she licks their head. These behaviors result in the retrieval of the babies so that they are moved back to the safety of the nest area.

Maternal behavior patterns can go awry in animals. Maternal aggression, aberrant retrieving, and cannibalism have been observed. Explanations for these behaviors range from biological or offspring characteristics to experiential causes. An elephant in the zoo may never have observed a birth before, so their own childbirth experience will be their first exposure. Explained as a result of inexperience and or confusion, the new elephant mother may demonstrate aggression, such as kicking, toward her newborn calf. The calf is temporarily removed from the mother and then later reintroduced.

In multi-dog households, a new mother dog may move her offspring from place to place in the house. She aberrantly retrieves them rather than settling down and finding a location to nurse the new puppies. This negative pattern can sometimes be corrected by isolating her from the other dogs in the house and changing her environment.

In a more extreme case, cats will sometimes kill and eat their offspring. They may reject offspring that is not the correct size (indicative of a health issue). In one example, a cat's offspring were removed at birth and brought back an hour later. The cat rejected the kittens that had been cleaned and no amniotic fluid was present. The non-cleaned kittens were accepted.

## Biological Basis of Animal Mothering

Mothering in animals is sometimes described as instinct, or of having a biological basis. From the field of ethology, Konrad Lorenz studied egg-rolling behavior in the graylag goose. He notes that a brooding goose will return an egg outside of her nest back into her nest by rolling it. The way in which the goose performs this behavior is mechanical, since the goose will roll items such as beer cans and balls. Additionally, if she starts to roll an egg and it is removed, she will still complete the roll-

ing pattern on the now missing egg. Lorenz hypothesized that the sight of any egg-like object outside the nest provides a sign stimuli that results in the fixed egg-rolling pattern. Another example of a sign stimuli is baby birds opening their mouths and for their mother to feed them. This behavior stimulates the genetically predetermined feeding behavior.

Another example of the biological basis of motherhood in animals is the presence of hormones in the mother before, during, and after pregnancy. These hormones are used to time the arrival of the offspring and start the appropriate maternal behavior. Studies of rats has shown that a cross-blood transplant between rats with new offspring and rats without offspring will result in maternal behaviors in the rat without offspring.

Imprinting has been defined as an animal following the first item/individual that it sees after birth. In the wild, imprinting allows a young bird to identify its mother. Researchers had believed that animals could imprint to non-species-related items (such as a teddy bear or ball). This understanding of imprinting was challenged by Gilbert Gottlieb in his study of waterfowl and other precocial bird species. Research in the field had reported that young birds were very drawn to a unique call used by various species. When tested in the laboratory, Gottlieb found that young birds were drawn to the maternal calls of members of their own species, even if they had never heard them before. The young birds would go toward these species-specific calls despite having previously been considered imprinted on an experimentally induced inanimate object. He later concluded that the prenatal auditory input the chick received (hearing the mother's call before hatching occurred) was more powerful than any visual-stimulus imprinting after being hatched.

## Animal Mothers, Research, and Humans

A scientist of note in the application of animal motherhood to human mother/infant relationships was Harry Harlow and his monkey love experiments. Harlow studied baby rhesus monkeys in order to gain insight into the infant/mother relationship. He removed infant rhesus monkeys from their mothers soon after birth and provided two types of surrogate mothers. The surrogate mothers—one made of wire alone and one made of wire with a terry cloth covering—were both able to dispense milk to the infant monkey.

In his series of experiments, Harlow found that maternal attachment was greater than meeting physical needs such as one of hunger/thirst. When able to choose, the baby monkeys preferred the terry cloth mother, even if all food was dispensed by the wire mother. Harlow then put the monkeys in with either a terry cloth or a wire mother. The baby monkeys raised with a terry cloth surrogate were better able to soothe themselves when compared to an infant monkey raised with a wire surrogate. Finally, Harlow placed monkeys in seclusion for the first 8 months of their life, during which time they received no exposure to any other monkeys or either type of surrogate mothers. They found that baby monkeys could only develop attachment and

normal social interactions if their period of solitary confinement lasted no more than 90 days. After that critical period, damage to the monkey was irreversible. In human infants, this critical period was estimated to be six months. Thus, the role of motherhood in monkeys was used to elucidate the role of motherhood in humans. The ethics of this research has been called into question due to concerns about animal welfare and the suffering the infant monkeys endured.

Leonard Rosenblum, a student of Harlow, also studied maternal deprivation. He found that pigtail Macaque monkeys were severely disturbed when removed from their mothers. The level of protest at removal from the mother, as well as the subsequent depression at the separation, was experimentally explored. The baby monkeys did show some effort to cope with the loss of their mother and would engage in foraging behavior, which was identified by Rosenblum as therapeutic. In the Bonnet monkey, the infants' status in the group hierarchy was a key factor in the ability of the foraging behavior to rehabilitate or reverse the partial isolation-induced, disturbed behavior.

## Animals and Their Amazing Mothers

Bats are the only mammals that can truly fly. Bats use echolocation to locate their food and their offspring. In captivity, a bat does fly until about five to six weeks postnatal, and will still nurse for three months. Before they are weaned, the mother bat will feed the baby bat the masticated food from their cheek pouches. The baby bats vocalize, as done in echolocation, to communicate with their mothers. A mother bat is able to identify her baby by their vocal signature, or unique isolation call. Even on first foraging flights, the baby bat may maintain vocal contact with their mother throughout the flight in this same fashion.

Opossum are the only North American marsupials and are nocturnal omnivores. In response to predators, they will freeze or "play dead." A baby opossum is born blind, deaf, and hairless. These tiny babies crawl into their mother's pouch where they nurse for three months. Even for a few weeks after they are weaned, the baby still rides in the mother's pouch while she hunts. The baby is then ready to leave the pouch.

*Horses are follower species and are always near their young; both mother and foal show extreme distress upon separation.*

Seahorse mothers are perhaps one of the most unusual animal mothers in that she deposits her unfertilized eggs into the male seahorse's pouch. After this, the male seahorse takes over and the female seahorse is no longer involved in the offspring's survival.

Dolphin mothers are considered to be some of the most dedicated mothers. They help their babies to learn how to breathe, eat, and swim. As the baby dolphin grows, the mother continues to protect and guide them about appropriate behavior in the pod.

Humpback whales stay with their offspring for up to a year, and usually wean the baby by 11 months. When with groups, the mother whale will position herself between the calf and any possibly aggressive juvenile associates.

An American black bear, which normally gives birth to two or three cubs at a time, may walk away from one born alone, calculating that it's better to wait for a multiple birth next year than exhaust herself with a singleton now. The mother bear protects her cubs, warms them, and nurses them, sometimes sitting and cradling them in her forelegs while licking their heads and nursing them. Foraging mothers come immediately when their cubs cry. Mothers continue to lead and protect their cubs until the cubs are about 17 months old, when the mother becomes ready to mate again. Then she suddenly becomes intolerant of her yearlings and threatens them by chasing them away.

Tasmanian Devil mothers put in a lot of effort to care for their young. The mother can give birth to about 20 or more, but only the four toughest will survive, as the mother has only four teats in her pouch. The mother carries her young in the pouch for about four months. When they are ready to leave, the mother puts them in a simple den to get accustomed to the outside world. She comes back regularly to feed them milk and teach them how to catch their own food. The pups are weaned at about 10 months and are mature when they are 2 years old. Tasmanian Devils only live about 5 or 6 years on average.

## Mothers of Precocial Offspring

These species are generally grazing animals such as horses and sheep, and live in huge social groups of more than one female with one male. Behaviors immediately after birth are directed toward recognition of the infants and formation of a bond between mother and infant. Intense maternal licking is done so the mother can form an olfactory memory of her young. Within this class of maternal behavior, there are two distinctive maternal strategies: hiders and followers.

The follower species, such as horses and sheep, are always near their young after giving birth. Both mother and young have separation issues and show extreme distress upon separation.

Hider species such as cattle and deer leave the young hidden (after birth and initial licking) to rejoin the social group. These mothers nurse their young a few times during the day, but mostly maintain large distances from their young.

Marine mammals are a diverse group of roughly 120 mammal species that are primarily ocean-dwelling or depend on the ocean for food. These animals consist of whales, dolphins, porpoises, manatees, dugon, seals, walruses, otters, and polar bears. Most of the marine mammals give birth to only one calf or pup at a time. Maternal care is very important to the survival of offspring that need to develop a thick insulating layer of blubber. Milk from the mother is more than 50 percent fat, which supports the development of blubber in their offspring.

## Marine Mothers

Mother polar bears are extremely protective of their young, willing to risk their own lives in their cub's defense. Polar bears stay with their mothers for up to 30 months, whether or not they are still nursing, as they depend on their mother for survival. When the cubs are 30 months old, the mother is ready to breed again and the cubs are chased away.

Harbor seal mothers leave their pups during the nursing period so they can forage at sea instead of fasting, which their bodies cannot handle. The seals are able to nurse on both land and at sea. The harbor seal mother is extremely attentive and noses the pup often while the pup is nursing. After weaning, the mother shows no more interest in the pup.

A mother sea otter aggressively defends her young against any intruders. The mother spends the majority of her time grooming her pup for the first three months. She carries her pup on her belly. When the mother dives for food, the pup is wrapped in kelp to keep it from drifting away. If the mother senses danger, she grabs the pup by the loose skin of the neck and dives until they get to safety.

Walruses are extremely protective of their calves. The mother walrus will defend and protect her calf and shelter it under her chest between her foreflippers. Typically, calves ride on their mothers' backs while they are in the water. Most calves are nursed for about two years or longer if the mother hasn't produced another calf.

## Animal Mothers in the Desert

Animals that live in the desert usually have special adaptations that allow them to survive the extreme temperatures and conditions. Some of the animals of the Sahara include the dromedary camel, fennec fox, addax, dama gazelle, and Saharan horned viper. Some of the animals of the Sonoran include the Sonoran desert toad, desert bighorn sheep, cactus wren, pronghorn antelope, and western diamondback rattlesnake.

Snakes stay close to their offspring. Since newborn snakes are not able to see well through their soon-to-be-shed skin and do not have a striking force yet, the mother stays nearby to deter predators and keep the young babies warm.

The Hairy Desert Scorpion's offspring (generally as many as 20) stay very close to their mother, where they molt. After a week or two, the young scorpions will disperse and leave the mother.

Desert bighorn sheep offspring stay constantly by their mother's side for five to six months until they are weaned. The ewes isolate their lambs for the first few weeks. Each mother remains the leader of her offspring.

Camels generally only give birth to a single calf. Calves remain close to their mothers until they reach maturity at 5 years of age. Mother camels will nurse their calves for one to two years.

## Animal Mothers in Australia

Australia is home to some of the most unique and interesting groups of animals, the marsupials. These are mammals that carry their babies in a pouch until the baby matures.

The koala is one of Australia's best-known animals. Females usually give birth to only one joey a year. In the pouch, the tiny joey—weighing less than 0.35 ounces attaches itself to one of the mother's teats, which swells in its mouth, preventing it from being dislodged from its only source of nutrition. The joey stays in its mother's pouch for about six or seven months. After leaving the pouch, the joey rides on its mother's abdomen or back and returns to the pouch to nurse until it is too big to fit inside the pouch. The joey leaves its mother's home range somewhere between 1 and 3 years of age.

The chudditch (Western quoll) is located in southwestern Australia. A chudditch is ready to breed at only 1 year of age. Females give birth to only one litter (which can include up to eight young) every year. About three months after they are born, the young leave the pouch but stay within the group.

The Australian dingo can be found in almost any part of the Australian mainland, which provides access to drinking water. The dingoes are mature at 1 year of age and take a lifelong mate at that time. The dingo will give birth to between one and eight pups during the year. Both dingo parents take part in raising the pups, which stay with their parents for up to three years. The mother nurses the pups for two months and then the mother regurgitates food for the pups until they are about 4 months old.

Kookaburras are birds that inhabit woodland areas of eastern and southwestern Australia. Kookaburras typically live in pairs or in small groups in open woodland. Both mother and father will incubate the eggs for a period of 25 days. The young leave the nest 30 days after hatching, but the parents continue to feed them for another 40 days.

## Animal Mothers in the Rainforest

Rainforests are located across the world, generally around the equator between the Tropic of Cancer and the Tropic of Capricorn. Central and south America, Africa, India, southeast Asia, parts of Indonesia, and Australia all contain rainforests. There are many different species of plants and animals in the rainforest, such as butterflies, beetles, spiders, ticks, snakes, lizards, frogs, parrots, toucans, sloths, and jaguars.

Orangutans, like humans, will give birth to one or two infants at a time. Orangutan mothers learn how to care for an infant by watching their own mother. Young orangutans have the longest maternal dependency period of all mammals. Newborns cling to their mothers for approximately 10 months and may continue to nurse up to age 5. Orangutan offspring generally leave the immediate vicinity of their mothers at around 5 years of age.

Bengal tigers typically give birth to two to four cubs, which will stay with their mother until they reach 2 years of age. The mother will nurse for eight weeks and then bring them prey to eat. The cubs will be able to hunt on their own in 11 months.

Spider monkeys produce one offspring at a time. The mother will carry her newborn around her belly for only the first month. After one month, the baby will travel on the back of its mother. Spider monkey mothers are very protective of their young and are considered good mothers. They grab their young and put them on their back for protection and assistance in navigating from tree to tree. Mothers will also groom their young. A young spider monkey relies exclusively on its mother for the first 6–10 months of its life.

Pink dolphins, which live in the Amazon rainforest in the areas of the Orinoco River systems in South America, are very protective mothers. The pink dolphin usually gets assistance from the other dolphins in the pod. The mother raises and protects the calf for up to three years. To protect the calf, the mother hides them by her side and covers her calf with her own body. Once the calf leaves its mother, it joins a pod or group with others about the same age. With this group, it protects itself from predators.

Toucans nest in holes in trees. Parents of toucans are very impatient and rarely sit on their eggs for more than an hour at a time. The parents will care for their young for about eight weeks. Both parents share the work of bringing food.

Golden lion tamarins live in the coastal lowland Amazon rainforest of Brazil. They are one of the most endangered mammals in the world. The father plays a dominant role in raising their young and is only with their mother while nursing and for the first few weeks of their lives. At 3–5 months old, the young are ready to be on their own, but will die of loneliness if they get separated from their family for a long period of time. When the female tamarin is about 15 months of age, the mother will send the female away so it will find her own family and avoid incest.

## Animals in Africa

Africa is very fortunate to have the largest variety of animals in the world. It is home to more than 800 bird species, 150 mammal species, about 50 snake and lizard species, 11 tortoise species, and thousands of invertebrate animals like insects and arachnids. Mothering skills are just as important as foraging or protection against predators. In the region of southern Kenya and for the period from July to October, the harsh environment provides an acid test for motherhood. Most water holes are dry, the grasses are dead, and only a very few shrubs produce fruit. The animals have to work very hard to survive.

The black rhinoceros is native to the eastern and central areas of Africa. There is only one calf born to a mother, which can follow its mother around after just three days. The calf is weaned at around 2 years of age and the mother and calf stay together for two to three years until the next calf is born. The female calves may stay longer and form small groups.

African lions are very protective of their young and will share the duties of protecting and nursing their cubs, as more than one female in the pride typically gives birth around the same time. Generally, a female will give birth to up to four cubs at a time. After giving birth in a secluded area, she then introduces the cubs to the pride when they are about 2 months old. Mothers will nurse for up to eight months, even though they begin to take their cubs on animal kills as young as 3 months old. When the cubs are almost a year old, they start learning to hunt with the pride. Mothers will take care of their cubs until they are about 2 years old, at which time the mother is ready to produce a new litter.

The giraffe lives in the savannahs of Africa. The mothers are protective animals and will stand over and defend her calf against predators. Even though they are very protective, half to nearly three-fourths of calves fall prey to lions and spotted hyenas in the first months. Within the first weeks of life, a calf will lie down half the day and most of the night guarded by its mother. The mother stays very close to her calf for the first two weeks, although the mother may stay over 100 yards from a calf (when the calf is hidden) and even leave it alone to get water. There is a maternity group that guards calves in a crèche, which increases security and allows a mother to go farther away and stay away longer. Calves are hardly ever left totally unattended. Mothers that leave typically return before sunset to nurse their calves and stay with them through the night. Giraffes are weaned and nutritionally independent at about 16 months, but the maternal bond lasts up until the young one is almost 2 years old.

The hippopotamus lives in western, central, eastern, and southern parts of Africa, living in lakes and rivers near grasslands. The hippopotamus mother will stay alone with her calf for 10 to 44 days before she rejoins the herd. The calves will begin grazing at about 5 months of age and become completely weaned by about 8 months of age. Small calves are often guarded by crèches while mothers go to pasture. The mothers will mob bulls that create a disturbance in their mist, as trampling is the main danger to calves during fights, chases, and stampedes that are generally caused by bulls.

Elephants are found in the southern portion of the Sahara, and are most commonly found in southern and eastern Africa. The elephant mother is one of the most tender and loving of animal mothers, and the bond between mother and daughter lasts up to 50 years. They are extremely protective of their young; rarely does a predator succeed in taking a baby elephant, as the whole group of elephants will defend and protect the babies. For the first year, a calf will remain in constant touch with its mother, and if it strays more than 20 yards away, the calf is retrieved. Gradually, the calf will assume the burden of staying close by, developing the leader-follower ties that bind an elephant herd. At 4–5 years of age, the young elephant is weaned, and at 9 years of age, the young elephant still spends half its time within a few yards of its mother's side.

## Animal versus Human Mothers

In her 1999 book *Mother Nature—Maternal Instincts and How They Shape the Human Species*, Sarah Hrdy argues that maternal instinct does not exist and that human mothers use a variety of practical strategies in dealing with their offspring that weigh the probability of their own survival as well as that of their children. For instance, widespread infanticide and child abandonment has been observed in contexts where adequate food is not available: Hrdy interprets this as mothers rationally choosing to not waste resources on a child that would be unlikely to survive anyway.

Hrdy's theory is based on sociobiology and is informed by her studies with langurs (a type of monkey) in which she observed competing evolutionary strategies (including infanticide and promiscuity) intended to increase the probability of survival-related offspring. Many scientists disagree with applying such studies to humans, arguing that it oversimplifies the motivations of human conduct and disregards the importance of cultural traditions and ethical principles.

**See Also:** Attachment Parenting; Association for Research on Mothering; Absentee Mothers; Child Abuse; Childcare; Childhood; Family; Maternal Absence; Maternal Health.

**Bibliography**
Abitbol, M.L. and S.R. Inglis. "Role of Amniotic Fluid in Newborn Acceptance and Bonding in Canines." *Journal Maternal Fetal Medicine,* v.6/1 (1991).
Bonner, Nigel W. *The Natural History of Seals.* New York: Facts on File Publications, 1990.
Brown, Patricia E., Timothy W. Brown, and Alan D. Grinnell. "Echolocation, Development, and Vocal Communication in the Lesser Bulldog Bat *Noctilio Albiventris.*" *Behavioral Ecology and Sociobiology,* v.13/4 (1983).
Carpenter, C.R. "Behavior of Red Spider Monkeys in Panama." *Journal of Mammalogy,* v.16/3 (1935).
Dewsbury, D.A. and Raymond Corsini, eds. "Animal Parental Behavior." In *The Encyclopedia of Psychology.* Hoboken, NJ: John Wiley and Sons, 1994.
Gottlieb, Gilbert. *Development of Species Identification in Birds: An Inquiry Into the Prenatal Determinants of Perception.* Chicago: University of Chicago Press, 1971.
Hanson, B.M., L.J. Bledsoe, B.C. Kirkevold, C.J. Casson, and J. W. Nightingale. "Behavioral Budgets of Captive Sea Otter Mother-Pup Pairs During Pup Development." *Zoo Biology,* v.12 (1993).
Harlow, Harry F. "Love in Infant Monkeys." *Scientific American,* v.200 (June 1959).
Houpt, K.A. "Small Animal Maternal Behavior and Its Aberrations." In *Recent Advances in Companion*

*Animal Behavior Problems*. Ithaca, NY: International Veterinary Information Service, 2000.

Lorenz, Konrad. *Evolution and Modification of Behavior*. Chicago: University of Chicago Press, 1965.

Milius, Susan. "The Social Lives of Snakes: From Loner to Attentive Parent." *Science News* (March 27, 2004).

Perry, Richard. *The World of the Walrus*. New York: Taplinger Publishing, 1968.

Rheingold, H.L. "Maternal Behavior in the Dog." In *Maternal Behavior in Mammals*. Hoboken, NJ: John Wiley & Sons, 1963.

Miranda E. Jennings
University of Massachusetts Amherst

# Anthropology of Mothering

The anthropology of mothering is the cultural study of mothering. In this field, as with all other topics of study, anthropologists focus on cultural beliefs and practices holistically and through cross-cultural comparison. This is similar but different from the sociological approach that focuses on social structures, social relations, and social interactions. Since anthropology is comprised of four fields—archaeology, physical anthropology, cultural anthropology, and linguistics—anthropological studies of mothering cross species as well as historical and geographical lines. The Anthropology of Mothering recognizes that while motherhood exists universally, practices of mothering vary worldwide and historically. Thus, the Anthropology of Mothering offers cross-cultural examples of different types of mothering, in addition to a plethora of ideas about who can mother, and what a mother can be.

## Perspectives of Mother and Mothering

The anthropological perspective acknowledges that mothering is not restricted to reproduction and the carework done by biological and legal mothers. Most anthropologists, in fact, acknowledge that mothering is not just done by women. Thus, the scope of who engages in mothering or who is considered a mother includes, but is not limited to nannies, fathers, grandmothers, aunts, sisters, foster mothers, adoptive mothers, surrogate mothers, step-mothers, coparents, females from the same human community or nonhuman primate group, teachers, and wet nurses. Consequently, mothering includes such behaviors as biological reproduction, breast-feeding, bathing and preening, language teaching, engaging in play, facilitating interaction within the community, and general care giving.

Due to this broad understanding of who and what a mother is, and the cross-cultural, historical, and cross-species evidence to support such scope, anthropological research related to mothering has influenced theories of human child rearing—such as the importance of mother–child bonding—particularly since the 1950s. Since then, such research has also become important in public discussions about who can or should count as a legitimate mother and family, with respect to new reproductive technologies (NRTs), and the rise of "alternative" family forms like same-sex parented families.

## Scant Anthropological Research on Mothering

Despite its current advocacy role regarding respect for diverse types of mothering, and anthropologists' concern for kinship, the explicit focus on mothering—and not just human reproduction or kinship—is a recent shift of gaze. In fact, less than five anthropologists are known to have explicitly researched mothering or motherhood before the mid-1990s. Published research on mothering has increased significantly since the turn of the millennium, and can be partially credited to the rise of Third Wave feminism. While most of this research has been conducted by cultural anthropologists, the work of archaeologists, physical anthropologists, and linguists has also been significant.

## Archaeology

Archaeology is the study of past cultures through material remains and environmental data, such as artifacts, architecture, landscapes, and biofacts. In terms of mothering, archaeological studies of artwork (i.e., paintings, pottery), artifacts (tools, jewelry), and biofacts (bones/bone structure), as well as archival and interview research (with descendants or others who can supply an oral history) are key. Despite the numerous potential sources of information, explicit studies of mothering are almost completely neglected in archaeology. Significant archaeological attention to female-bodied figurines, breastfeeding, and kinship/women's roles in houses and culture, have all implicitly considered "mothering," but the explicit, in-depth study of mothering has been limited to one book-length archaeological publication: Laurie Wilkie's *The Archaeology of Mothering: An African-American Midwife's Tale*. Patriarchal methods and gazes still dominate archaeological work, and an archaeology of gender has only emerged in the last 15 years.

## Misplaced Assumptions in Archaeology

Anthropologists' explanations or theories of "Others" often either explicitly support the status quo of the anthropologist's home culture, or directly challenge it by offering a utopian alternative. This is most problematic in archaeology, as no living person, and limited concrete evidence, is available to correct the misplaced assumptions. This is particularly exemplified in studies regarding the cultural roles of women, andmothers in particular.

Kathleen Bolen notes, "Women today are believed to be unequal, weaker, biologically inferior, and evolutionarily unimportant; under patriarchal, androcentric, and traditional archaeological frameworks, this ideology creates similar women in the past." Conversely, when feminist archaeology first emerged, "evidence" was found to demonstrate strong, equal, politically active women and mothers of past generations. The hope was that this research would foster equality between men and women in Western cultures. Archaeologists now have to develop theories surrounding their "evidence" more critically in order to withstand the controversy from both patriarchal and feminist archaeologists.

## Archaeological Fertility Symbols

The biggest archaeological controversy regarding the status of women and the importance of fertility and motherhood, prehistorically, has centered on statuettes depicting women, also known as the Venus figurines. Debates focus on the importance and role of these figurines (i.e., regarding fertility and women's cultural status), as well as if they were meant to physically represent particular people and/ or goddesses, or simply made to be representational of women in general.

## Breastfeeding and Archaeology

The other major area in which mothering has been studied implicitly relates to the practice of breastfeeding. Archaeologists study breastfeeding through skeletal remains, tooth enamel, archives, and art. While the cultural practice, significance, and attitudes toward breastfeeding cannot be completely known, some archaeologists have been able to determine, through studying tooth enamel, children's age at weaning and introduction of food. Others have looked to skeletal remains to study the process of lactation and weaning. Data has also been gathered through archives; for example, Norwegian archives on child mortality report breastfed children survived at three times the rate of non-breastfed children. Lastly, artwork depicting breastfeeding or wet nurses can be found in various parts of the world. Tomb carvings, paintings on vases and other pottery, and terra-cotta figurines from classical Greece all reflect the dominant cultural views that existed regarding mothering and breastfeeding. Elite mothers are depicted by the presence of naked male babies, which are depicted suckling on animals. Alternatively, wet nurses are depicted as ugly and large breasted, in contrast to the slim, small-chested, elite mothers. These images illustrate views of breastfeeding being animalistic and uncivilized, while also showing the social importance for women to become mothers by bearing male offspring.

## Physical Anthropology

Physical anthropology, also called biological anthropology, directs its attention to the evolution of human biology, and in particular the interaction of biology with culture. As with anthropological research in the other branches, physical anthropology is often interdisciplinary. Thus, psychologists or behavioral scientists often conduct work as physical anthropologists or simply conduct research relevant to the discipline. While there are multiple branches of Physical Anthropology, the two that have the most research relating to mothering are the study of human evolution and the study of nonhuman primates. Research and hypotheses in these areas include, but have not been limited to mother–son bonding, the invention of baby carriers (i.e., the sling), child "caches" and infant "parking," breastfeeding, co-sleeping, mother–child communication, and care giving by those other than biological mothers, also known as allomothering. Of these, the most prominent are allomothering and mother–infant bonding.

## Primate Research on Mother–Infant Bonding

Research on mother–infant bonding among primates has influenced human childcare theory and practice. Harry Harlow's 1950s psychological experiments with rhesus monkeys are the most notorious studies of primate mother–infant bonding. Infant monkeys were placed with wire "surrogate mothers," wire and cloth "mothers," or with no mothers. The monkeys "raised" with no mothers were not capable of forming affectionate, longterm social bonds, whereas the monkeys with cloth and wire "mothers" were. Moreover, the monkeys raised with no mother were incapable of copulating, and the female monkeys who were later forcibly inseminated neglected or reacted aggressively toward their offspring. This study, in addition to more recent studies of nonhuman primates in their natural habitat, demonstrates the importance of mother–infant bonding. For nonhuman primates in their natural environment, this bond is often lifelong, maintained through mother–child grooming as well as female offspring learning to be competent mothers. Infants who had experienced sensory and social deprivation, however, demonstrated social behavioral deficits and unusual, self-directed behavior (such as hugging oneself and rocking back and forth). As was demonstrated by the wire and cloth monkeys, the bonding required does not have to occur with the biological mother.

## Allomothering

Allomothering is also called aunt behavior, babysitting, alloparenting, fostering, adopting, or depending on the circumstances, kidnapping or infant stealing. In nonhuman primates, when the biological mother is still living, allomothering may be performed by female kin; biological or social fathers; juvenile females from within the biological mother's group or from a rival or different group; or, more rarely, an older female from within the group. Multiple hypotheses consider why allomothering occurs, as well as the possible benefits and detriments to those involved. In most instances,

allomothering is a consensual act, giving respite to the mother or allowing her to forage *sans enfant*, while providing a learning opportunity for juvenile females to gain mothering skills, or strengthening the pair-bond between mother and father when care is provided by the biological father. In other instances, when infants are kidnapped by either higher-status females from with the group or by a different group, the benefits are less evident; often, death of the infant and/or the mother results. It is hypothesized, however, that this type of alloparenting occurs when mothers are deemed by others to be incapable, and thus evolutionarily speaking, it benefits the group by eliminating the genes and/or socialization related to poor mothering.

## Linguistic Anthropology

Linguistic Anthropology is the study of language and its relation to culture. It encompasses, among other foci, the study of language acquisition, discourse analysis, pragmatics, and semantics. In relation to mothering, two particular areas are key: language acquisition, and the meaning and words attributed to reproduction and breastfeeding, as well as their effects on mothers and mothering.

Language acquisition refers to the learning of language both by infants gaining knowledge of their mother tongue, as well as by children and adults' learning of their first or additional languages. Mothers play a key role in language acquisition as the mother–child dyad is universally recognized as the primary locus of language acquisition. This relationship is recognized through the term *motherese*, which refers to infant-directed communication, although the term *caregiverese* is now gaining prominence. When mothers are not able to pass on their mother tongue due to various cultural circumstances, maternal grandmothers often fill in this role. One example of this is explained in Jenanne Ferguson's study of the Southern Tutchone of Yukon Territory, Canada. Here, a strong bond between grandchildren and grandmothers is culturally celebrated. Since today's parents were students of residential schools that successfully "Westernized" them, grandmothers play a pivotal role in teaching the *dän k'è* language and traditional culture to their grandchildren, through reading, singing, dancing, and sewing, among other activities.

Feminist anthropologists have studied the practices of childbearing, reproduction, and breastfeeding in various cultures, taking particular note of the language used with reference to these practices and how they differ cross-culturally. With respect to breastfeeding, Penny Van Esterik notes that Euro-American culture privileges a discourse that speaks of "prolonged breastfeeding rather than premature weaning," obviously placing a value on what is "good" mothering practice. Regarding human reproduction, various anthropologists have studied and critiqued phrases and words frequently used in relation to conception and birth in Western cultures. This includes narratives of conception expressing active sperm and passive ova; how gender and personhood is attributed to fetuses at earlier stages of gestation, through language; and the words that attribute physical and intellectual authority to medical personnel while situating birthing mothers as unknowing, incapable, vulnerable patients waiting for their child to be "delivered to" them, as opposed to "birthed by" them. Anthropologists have demonstrated the significance of these language practices in enculturating mothers, through exemplifying what is expected of them as mothers—passivity, obedience, humility, and self-sacrifice, to name but a few.

## Cultural Anthropology

Cultural anthropology focuses on present-day cultural practices. While research explicitly focusing on mothering in the past was sparse, as only three cultural anthropologists are widely recognized for English-language publications before 1995—namely Margaret Mead from the 1920s to 1970s, and Sheila Kitzinger and Ellen Lewin, both from the 1970s through the 1990s. Research focused on mothering became much more prominent after the 1995 publication of Rayna Rapp and Faye Ginsburg's edited volume, *Conceiving the New World Order: The Global Politics of Reproduction*. The anthology put forth "two agendas: to transform traditional anthropological analysis of reproduction and to clarify the importance of making reproduction central to social theory." A few of the chapters highlighted anthropological work on mothering or motherhood, and together with Jane Collier and Sylvia Yanagisako's 1987 anthology, *Gender and*

*Kinship: Essays Toward a Unified Analysis*, helped to develop an anthropological focus on mothering. In the last 15 years, mothering and motherhood research has evolved considerably to include studies of mothering's relationship to consumption and consumerism; the new or more visible roles of mothering made available through NRTs; the effects of race, ethnicity, geographic location, and class on mothering; the pressure to mother and the effects of being childless in varying cultures worldwide; the effects of globalization on mothering; and studies of the role of class, religion, immigration, disability, gender, sex, and sexuality on mothering. While diverse in their focus, much of this work addresses the universal pressure for women to mother.

## Cultural Expressions of Motherhood

While not many experiences of mothering or motherhood are universal, the pressure for women to become mothers is. This pressure, however, is expressed differently in each culture, and the understanding of who is or should be recognized as a mother also differs culturally. The necessity of motherhood is most predominantly expressed in research on infertility and childlessness. In Euro-American cultures, infertility usually centers on the notion of complete childlessness, as the concept of "subfertile" is nonexistent. In other cultures, however, the concept of "infertility" expands to include notions of not having enough children or not having enough male children, or simply not getting pregnant within a month or two of marriage. Western couples are not medically considered infertile until they have spent a year or two without use of contraceptives while actively attempting to conceive.

Conversely, in some societies in Chad and Cameroon, for example, newlyweds may be considered infertile after only a month or two of marriage; and in fact, before a year has passed, a lack of pregnancy—interpreted as a sign of infertility—can be grounds for divorce. Moreover, in some cultures, having only one or a few children may still not be enough to avoid the social label of being "infertile," especially if none (or only one) of them is male. Children, and sons in particular, are culturally recognized for their importance in carrying on family names; their ability to participate in warfare; the expectation that they will look after their parents economically and socially; and, in some cases, ability to ensure their passage to the next world via reincarnation. In some cultures, a lack of cultural recognition as a mother can result in her not being recognized as a woman (only as a girl); lead to divorce, poverty, or ostracization, and sometimes even legitimize her killing.

The universality of the pressure to mother is always associated with cultural concepts of who should and should not be a mother, and who makes a good mother and who makes a bad mother. While the specifics differ cross-culturally, women are often judged on their capacity to mother, and their capacity to be a good mother based on their class, race, ethnicity, politics, age, gender presentation, sexuality, marital or relationship status, geographic location, and disability.

Behaviors that are linked to good mothers and bad mothers change constantly both with time and as different cultures influence others. This is exemplified in Françoise Guigné's study of medical recommendations and the experiences of infant feeding among mothers with human immunodeficiency virus (HIV) in Saskatoon, Saskatchewan, Canada. Guigné found that mothers living with HIV were considered both "good" and "bad," as they navigated poverty, access to formula, stigmatization due to their HIV status, and different notions of what is healthier for themselves and their children.

While the current policy in Saskatoon for women with HIV is "no breastfeeding," Guigné argues that women there know "breast is best." Some of these women are also aware that in other areas of the world (i.e., where clean water is not as accessible), women living with HIV are told to exclusively breastfeed their infants. Tensions like these are not uncommon to discourses of "good" and "bad" parenting, as different expectations and standards are placed on women of different contexts. The anthropological gaze, though, is able to bring attention to these situations, with the hope of creating more understanding of and respect for diverse cultural practices.

**See Also:** Animal Species and Motherhood; "Bad" Mothers; Cross-Cultural Perspectives on Motherhood; Greece (and Ancient Greece); Lewin, Ellen; Mead, Margaret; Social Construction of Motherhood.

**Bibliography**

Bolen, Kathleen M. "Prehistoric Construction of Mothering," *Exploring Gender Through Archaeology: Selected Papers From the 1991 Boone Conference.* Madison, WI: Prehistory Press, 1992.

Fairbanks, Lynn A. "Reciprocal Benefits of Allomothering for Female Vervet Monkeys." *Animal Behavior,* v.40 (1990).

Fernandez-Duque, Eduardo, Claudia R. Valeggia, and Sally P. Mendoza. "The Biology of Paternal Care in Human and Nonhuman Primates." *Annual Review of Anthropology,* v.38 (2009).

Ginsburg, Faye D., and Rayna Rapp, eds. *Conceiving the New World Order: The Global Politics of Reproduction.* Berkeley: University of California Press, 1995.

Iqbal, Isabeau. "Mother Tongue and Motherhood: Implications for French Language Maintenance in Canada." *The Canadian Modern Language Review,* v.61/3 (March 2005).

Lewin, Ellen. *Lesbian Mothers: Accounts of Gender in American Culture.* Ithaca, NY: Cornell University Press, 1993.

Mead, Margaret. *Male and Female: A Study of the Sexes in a Changing World.* New York: William Morrow, 1949.

Ragoné, Heléna and France Winndance Twine, eds. *Ideologies and Technologies of Motherhood: Race, Class, Sexuality, Nationalism.* New York: Routledge, 2000.

Spencer-Wood, Suzanne M. "Feminist Gender Research in Classical Archaeology." In *Handbook of Gender in Archaeology,* Sarah Milledge Nelson, ed. Lanham, MD: AltaMira Press, 2006.

Taylor, Janelle S., Linda L. Layne, and Danielle F. Wozniak, eds. *Consuming Motherhood.* New Brunswick, NJ: Rutgers University Press, 2004.

Van Balen, Frank, and Marcia Inhorn, eds. *Infertility Around the Globe: New Thinking of Childlessness, Gender, and Reproductive Technologies.* Berkeley: University of California Press, 2002.

Van Esterik, Penny. "Contemporary Trends in Infant Feeding Research." *Annual Review of Anthropology,* v.31 (2002).

Wilkie, Laurie A. *The Archaeology of Mothering: An African-American Midwife's Tale.* New York: Routledge, 2003.

Michelle Walks
University of British Columbia

# Anti-Racist Mothering

Anti-racist mothering is an approach to childrearing used to combat the racial oppression of children by imparting in them a healthy self-esteem, a positive sense of racial/cultural identity, an awareness of societal racism, and strategies for resisting racism. Mothers employ this practice to help their children survive and prosper emotionally, psychologically, and physically despite any racial bias they encounter. Anti-racist mothering can also entail teaching children to accept, respect, and be open minded toward people who are racially and culturally different from them so they do not form racist ideologies or socially reproduce discriminatory practices. In addition, anti-racist mothering strategies can be used to care for women's biological or nonbiological children, and it can also be community based.

## Combating Racism

The harsh realities of societal racism have motivated mothers to engage in anti-racist mothering, particularly mothers of color like those of African, Asian, and Latino descent, as well as those from indigenous cultures, such as Native American and Australian Aborigine mothers. The racism that mothers strive to counteract can encompass general, day-to-day discriminatory practices faced by marginalized racial groups such as the legally enforced segregation that African Americans were subjected to in the United States prior to the mid-20th century.

Likewise, anti-racist mothering can combat discriminatory practices specifically targeted toward racial and cultural minority families. For instance, during U.S. slavery, from approximately 1619 to 1865, African American slave women were regarded as property and child breeders. Their children were customarily taken from them and sold to white male plantation owners. Whereas in Australia, from approximately 1869 to 1970, the Australian government allowed white Australians to forcibly remove Aborigine children from their families without any proof of maltreatment—a practice ratified under the Aborigines Protection Amending Act in 1915. In total, both implicitly racist social climates and explicitly racist public policies have influenced the racial consciousness and child-rearing practices of mothers of color around the world. Mothers of color in vari-

ous nations have fought to retain and protect their children and families from harm and exploitation.

Anti-racist mothering, which some scholars refer to as *racial ethnic mothering,* racially conscious mothering, or motherwork, is an important survival tactic for families of color. It is also an enduring tradition that has been modeled and passed down for many generations in marginalized racial and ethnic communities. Anti-racist mothering has helped children avoid or escape persecution, and it has helped preserve culture. Some Latino mothers have intentionally raised their U.S.-born children to be bilingual, thereby teaching them their family's native language in addition to English in order to resist expectations that their children be fully assimilated to English-speaking U.S. culture. Other anti-racist strategies entail mothers' passing on positive stories of racial history and resilience to their children in order to affirm their sense of cultural pride and defy stereotypic depictions of their racial group.

## White Mothers and Children

White mothers who raise biological, multiracial children or nonbiological, adopted children of color may also engage in anti-racist mothering that attempts to shield their children from the harmful effects of racial oppression. White mothers who engage in the anti-racist mothering of white children strive to raise their children's sociopolitical consciousness about the perniciousness of systemic racism so they, as members of the dominant racial group, will develop anti-racist ideologies, treat others fairly, and challenge inequitable power structures.

Given that mothering is a culturally relevant and socially constructed practice, various women's cultural norms and experiences with racism also influence their anti-racist mothering identities, consciousness, and strategies. The anti-racist mothering of women of color is not only informed by a maternal desire to protect and nurture their children, it is also influenced by their firsthand experiences with racism and their racialized identities that stem from being part of a racial minority group. White women's anti-racist mothering is informed by their membership in the dominant, white racial group. Critical white scholars and feminist theorists of color further contend that white women benefit from the social and political privileges that come with having dominant racial status, even if their children do not. Mothers of color and white mothers participate in anti-racist mothering with different degrees of social influence. Power dynamics is an important aspect of anti-racist mothering, since women perform anti-racist mothering in both private and public spaces. In total, anti-racist mothering is a form of cultural and political resistance most often linked to mothers' efforts to love, care for, protect, and nurture their children and families. Yet, anti-racist mothering can entail women working to uplift their communities through mentoring, social activism, institutional reform, and other means of communal care that are also referred to as *other mothering*. Anti-racist mothering, whether it assists individual children, families, and/or communities, can be empowering and transformative.

**See Also:** African American Mothers; Australia; Other Mothering; Race and Racism; Slavery and Mothering.

**Bibliography**
Aanerud, Rebecca. "The Legacy of White Supremacy and the Challenge of White Anti-Racist Mothering." *Hypatia*, v.22/2 (2007).
Australian Human Rights Commission. "Bringing Them Home—Part 2" (April 1997). http://www.human rights.gov.au/social_justice/bth_report/report/ch3 .html (accessed November 2008).
Collins, Patricia Hill. "Shifting the Center: Race, Class, and Feminist Theorizing About Motherhood." In *Mothering: Ideology, Experience, and Agency*, Evelyn Nakano Glenn, et al., eds. New York: Routledge, 1994.
Cooper, Camille Wilson. "School Choice as "Motherwork:" Valuing African American Women's Educational Advocacy and Resistance." *International Journal of Qualitative Studies in Education*, v.20/5 (2007).

Camille Wilson Cooper
University of North Carolina, Greensboro

# Anxiety

Anxiety is a feeling of apprehension that is a normal reaction to everyday life stressors. Feelings of anxiety are generally experienced in momentary instances due to the stress of daily life. When anxiety persists and affects the ability to function adequately in everyday activities, this is considered a sign of an anxiety disorder.

Motherhood is a life experience that is often accompanied by anxiety. Child rearing can create levels of worry, stress, guilt, and feelings of inadequacy, which are all precursors to anxiety.

When mothers venture off into new ways of mothering, there can be levels of guilt, stemming from the pressures to reach perfection. This guilt may be experienced by stay-at-home mothers who may not contribute financially to the household or feel they are not viewed as a strong role model as an at-home mother, or mothers who work outside the home and feel guilty because of the limited time available to spend physically with their children.

## Factors, Diagnosis, and Types

A large factor that contributes to anxiety in mothers is economics. Economics affect childcare and health care options for both mother and child. Economics often dictates housing location, living conditions, and education options for children.

Anxiety disorders are diagnosed based on characteristics such as performance of repeated acts or avoidance of particular activities in attempt to avoid feeling anxious. There are symptoms that are common to anxiety disorders, such irrational fear of death and insanity, fatigue, and irritable bowels. Depression often accompanies anxiety disorders. The most common feature of several anxiety disorders is panic attacks. Panic attacks are episodes of intense fear and panic that produce at least four or more of the following symptoms: sweating, shortness of breath, feeling of choking, dizziness, increased heart rate, feelings of confusion or detachment, fear of losing control or dying, chest pain, abdominal irritation, hot flushes, tingling, or chills. The main anxiety disorders, according to the *Diagnostic and Statistical Manual of Mental Disorders* (DSM-IV-TR), are panic disorder with or without agoraphobia, social phobia (also referred to as social anxiety), obsessive-compulsive disorder, generalized anxiety disorder, posttraumatic stress disorder, and specific phobias.

Panic disorder is reoccurring episodes of intense fear without a notable stimulus. This condition is

*Women who become mothers as teenagers or in their early 20s are more likely to suffer depression during pregnancy.*

diagnosed when four or more panic attacks are experienced in a month or one panic attack that produces prolonged fear of having more attacks. Panic disorder without agoraphobia is where one experiences panic attacks but remains active in day-to-day activities. Panic disorder with agoraphobia occurs when avoidance of certain activities or places happens out of fear of anticipating panic attacks. Agoraphobia is fear and avoidance of any trigger that may produce panic and panic attacks. Examples of some triggers are enclosed, public, and open spaces; and being alone or without a "safe" person, place, or thing. Agoraphobia can become so severe that loss of employment, family, and friends results.

Individuals with social anxiety have an excessive and irrational fear of social interaction and judgment by others. Social anxiety creates an extreme fear of humiliation and avoidance of situations that require social engagement, such as public speaking, interviewing, office meetings, interacting at social events, dating, and talking on the telephone and online chatting. The levels of anxiety and avoidance can become severe enough to jeopardize employment and social networks.

Obsessive-compulsive disorder has the double component of repetitive thoughts combined with repetitive physical behavior, usually the completions of rituals, where both are irrational and involuntary. Combined, these thoughts and behaviors monopolize the time and lives of those with this disorder, who find themselves engrossed in completing rituals to relieve anxiety produced by their irrational thoughts. This negatively impact their normal day-to-day activities.

The symptoms of generalized anxiety disorder are similar to panic disorder, although panic is not the primary feature. Excessive worry about day-to-day activities is the main focus. While those with this disorder are not paralyzed by worry, high levels of anxiety do affect them physically.

Posttraumatic stress disorder is the direct result of exposure to a traumatic event, either experienced directly or as a witness. The reaction is intense horror and can be triggered by dreams, smells, and visual images.

Specific phobias are limited to a specific object, such as animals or bridges. These usually do not impact the ability to function normally unless the phobia occurs in everyday situations such as the fear of elevators or birds.

Treatments for anxiety and anxiety disorders range from traditional treatments to alternative remedies. Medications like selective serotonin reuptake inhibitors (SSRIs) and cognitive behavioral therapy have proven effective for treatment of severe cases. As well, yoga, meditation, exercise, and diet modifications have all had positive results in the lowering of anxiety levels.

**See Also:** "Bad" Mothers; Depression; Emotions; Fears; Full Time Mothering; Guilt; Mental Illness and Mothers; Postpartum Depression; Working-Class Mothers.

### Bibliography

Castle, David, et al. *Mood and Anxiety Disorders in Women.* Cambridge, UK: Cambridge University Press, 2006.
Warner, Judith. *Perfect Madness: Motherhood in the Age of Anxiety.* New York: Riverhead Books, 2005.

Wilson, Robert R. *Don't Panic: Taking Control of Anxiety Attacks*. New York: HarperPerennial, 1996.

Dawn Wright Williams
Georgia Perimeter College

# Argentina

In Argentina, the third Sunday of October is the *Dia de la Madre* (Mother's Day). Mother's Day is a special day because in this culture, mothers are elevated to a position of respect and admiration. In the past, mothers were relegated to stay home with children. However, Argentina's history of motherhood shows a remarkable trend in mothers leaving the traditional role in the private realm to secure political platforms in the public arena. The cultural norms of motherhood have changed, and motherhood has become a more modern institution, one in which holds the role of worker, politician and activist, and currently, president.

Argentina is the second-largest country in South America. The population is roughly 40 million, and an estimated 92 percent are Roman Catholics. Approximately two children are born per woman, and the birth rate is approximately 18 births per 1,000 women, with an infant mortality rate of around 12 per 1,000 live births. Abortions are illegal in Argentina, yet an estimated 450,000 abortions are practiced each year. One of the most profound changes in motherhood in this country is in the area of birth control practices and laws. In 2009, the Argentine Congress passed a reproductive health law that provides for free birth control methods and advice to women nationwide. Promotion of birth control had been previously forbidden by the government of Argentina, although in 2001, the Chamber of Deputies originally passed the bill with slight modifications. In 1974, a government executive decree had ordered all family planning institutions to be closed, and oral contraceptive pills were prescribed only if a physician found absolute medical indications and then only on a special prescription in triplicate. This previous decree called for the Minister of Social Welfare to carry out a study in Argentina of all possible means to counteract the supposedly alarming demographic situation in Argentina. The current bill was opposed by the Catholic Church, an institution that holds much political power in Argentina, that based its opposition to the bill on the argument that it encouraged abortion, the use of "abortive" birth control methods, and state meddling in the question of sex education among minors.

## Famous Mothers

The Virgin Mary is perhaps the most famous of mothers in Argentina. December 8 is Día de la Inmaculada Concepción (Immaculate Conception Day), also known as Día de la Virgen (Virgin Mary's Day). A controversial figure in Argentina, Maria Eva Duarte de Perón was known by her union supporters as the Mother of the Nation, although she never had children. Revered as a saint by many Argentines, Evita died from cancer at the age of 33. Wife of Juan Domingo Perón, Argentine general and president, she was an activist who supported the poor, the working class, and marginalized groups like single mothers— all of whom became fanatical followers.

An interesting phenomenon of famous mothers in Argentina are the human rights activists and social movement, the Madres de Plaza de Mayo (Mothers of the Plaza de Mayo) in Buenos Aires. The Madres were formed during the military coup of the Dirty War (1976–83), when mothers began searching for their *desaparecidos*, or disappeared (people who were considered subversive to the government). The Madres de Plaza de Mayo officially formed in 1977, and the group splintered in 1986 when the Madres Línea Fundadora (Founding Line of Mothers) withdrew from the original group. The Asociación Madres was formed after the split, and Hebe de Bonafini became president. The Madres stopped their protest against the Argentine government in 2006, yet they continue to march around the pyramid in the Plaza de Mayo at 3:30 p.m. every Thursday, just as they have for the past 31 years. In 1992, the Asociación de Madres was awarded the Sakharov Prize for Freedom of Thought, and in 1999, the organization was awarded the United Nations (UN) Prize for Peace Education. The Madres' white scarves have become a trademark and symbol of mothers' love.

Another famous activist group in Buenos Aires is the Abuelas de la Plaza de Mayo (Grandmothers of the Plaza de Mayo), who were nominated for the

Nobel Peace Award in 2008. Group president Estela Barnes de Carlotto and the other grandmothers have fought for justice in *desaparecidos*, including children who were taken from pregnant women during the Dirty War. In 2003, Carlotto was awarded the UN Prize in the Field of Human Rights.

In October 2007, Cristina Fernandez de Kirchner became the first elected woman president in Argentina. She is the mother of two children and is a former senator and first lady (her husband is former president Nestor Kirchner). So far, President Kirchner has not decriminalized abortion or established equal rights and maternity pay in Argentina.

**See Also:** Activist Mothers of the Disappeared; Birth Control; Maternal Activism.

**Bibliography**

"Argentina Bans Birth Control." *American Medical Association*, v.229/2 (July 8, 1974).

Bouvard, Marguerite Guzman. *Revolutionizing Motherhood: The Mothers of the Disappeared*. Lanham, MD: SR Books, 2002.

World Health Organization. http://www.who.int/en (accessed April 2009).

Shirley Oakley Torres
University of Memphis

# Arizona

Arizona was inhabited by Native American peoples for centuries before the first European explorer came through the region in 1539; Spanish missionaries were later founded in the 1690s. However, it was not until the end of the Mexican–American War of 1847 when the region was ceded to the United States, gaining statehood in 1912. The population of Arizona is currently 6.5 million, with 60 percent of the population being European Americans.

There is much documentation to show that of the early settlers, mothers had to be resourceful to keep their family together. One of these families who settled in Arizona in the early years was that of Ellen (or Nellie) Cashman. Following the death of her father, her mother brought her and her sister from Ireland to the United States, settled in San Francisco, and looked after the two girls herself. Nellie managed to track down some missing troopers lost in the desert and brought them food, making herself a local hero. Years later, her sister's husband and then her own sister died, leaving her to look after their five children in the "Wild West" township of Tombstone—made famous by Wyatt Earp's gunfight at the O.K. Corral. In 1899, the year after Nellie Cashman left Arizona to search for gold in the Yukon, the territory passed a law to make education compulsory for all children between the ages of 6 and 16.

## Native American Traditions

Within the small Native American community, there are many documented instances of mothers passing down traditions to their children. The story of Nampeyo, from the Hopi who fled westward after the failure of the Pueblo Rebellion of 1860, illustrates how mothers have passed skills to their daughters for six generations. Born soon after this flight, Nampeyo was brought up by her paternal grandmother, who managed to persuade her to make pots and sell them in a local store. After her husband was employed by an archaeologist, collectors recognized her skills and started collecting her work. She managed to pass down her skills to her daughter, and her great-granddaughter, Dextra Quotskuya, born in 1928, continues to make pots in the traditional manner.

Arizona's birth rate is 16.6 per 1,000. The fertility rate is 2.4 children per women, the second highest in the country (after Utah). The two counties in Arizona (La Paz and Greenlee) that have the highest rates both do not have a hospital, with Santa Cruz and Coconino having the lowest infant mortality rates. The figures are slightly skewed, as nearly 80 percent of the population live in two counties, Maricopa and Pima.

## Notable Arizona Women

There are numerous other stories of women who have made successful careers in Arizona, including Hattie Josephine "JoJo" Goldwater (née Williams) who descended from John Williams (the cofounder of Rhode Island) and married a Phoenix shop owner —their son was the politician Barry Goldwater, who was born in 1909. Modern Arizona history is not without many important women. The state was the first to have had four female governors: Rose Perica Mofford from 1988 to 1991, Jane Dee Hull from 1997 to 2003, Janet Napolitano from 2003 to 2009, and Jan Brewer since 2009.

**See Also:** California; Native Americans; Nevada; New Mexico.

**Bibliography**

Arizona Department of Health Services—Division of Public Health Services. http://www.azdhs.gov/plan/report/cvs/cvs01/index.htm (accessed May 2009).

Brown, Wynne. *More Than Petticoats: Remarkable Arizona Women.* Helena, MT: Falcon Press Publishing, 2003.

Caiazza, Amy B. *The Statues of Women in Arizona: Politics, Economics, Health, Rights, Demographics.* Tucson: Southwest Institute for Research on Women and Women's Foundation of Southern Arizona, 2000.

Clayton, Robert Flake. *Pioneer Women of Arizona.* Self Published, 1969.

Health Profile. http://www.rho.arizona.edu/Resources/Dataline/Health%20Indicators/HealthIndicators.htm (accessed May 2009).

Johnson, Dee Strickland. *Arizona Women: Weird, Wild and Wonderful.* Phoenix, AZ: Cowboy Miner Productions, 2006.

Kelly, Rita Mae. *Women and the Arizona Political Process.* Lanham, MD: University Press of America, 1988.

Osslaer, Heidi J. *Winning Their Place: Arizona Women in Politics.* Tucson: University of Arizona Press, 2009.

Justin Corfield
Geelong Grammar School, Australia

# Arkansas

The state of Arkansas is in the southern region of the United States bounded by the great Mississippi River on its east, with the Ozark and Ouachita Mountain ranges nestled within its territory. Motherhood in Arkansas will be examined by looking at vital statistics, fertility, mortality, and health status in order to provide a detailed understanding of the status of women in the state. Famous Arkansan mothers include author and poet Maya Angelou, actress Mary Steenburgen, Watergate player Martha Mitchell, and composer Florence Beatrice Price.

Arkansas has a population of over 2.8 million, of which 96 percent are native-born Arkansans. The racial/ethnic makeup of the state is 80 percent white, 16 percent black, 1 percent Native American/Alaskan Native, 1.5 percent Asian/Pacific Islander, and 5 percent Hispanic/Latino. Eighty-one percent of those aged 25 or older have attained the level of high school graduate (or equivalent) or higher. The median household income for the state is reported as $37,555.

Females comprise 51 percent of the total Arkansas population with the majority being 18 years of age or older. Of females aged 15 years or older, 51.1 percent report their status as married and 51.3 percent of Arkansas households are married-couple family households. However, 7.8 percent of Arkansas households are identified as female-headed households with no husband present, and with children under 18. Forty-eight percent of these households have incomes below the poverty level. On average, the median earnings for female, full-time year-round workers are 75 percent of that of males. The divorce rate stands at 6.1 percent.

The mean age of an Arkansan woman having her first child is 23 years. The overall birth rate for the state is 14.6 percent, with a teen (15–19) birth rate of 62.3 percent. The fertility rate for women ages 15-44 is 72.2 percent. Eighty percent of mothers begin prenatal care in the first trimester and only 4.7 percent of mothers begin prenatal care late or not at all. The rate of caesarean delivery is 33.2 percent and 13.7 percent of births are delivered preterm. It is estimated that 9.2 percent of births are of low-birth-weight babies. The infant mortality rate stands at 8.3 percent.

When it comes to caring for mothers and their infants, the Arkansas Department of Health offers information on a variety of programs. There is in-depth coverage of breastfeeding, offering information, resources, and links to organizations where mothers can gain additional knowledge and assistance. Mothers are also provided with information regarding licensed midwifes, newborn screening, immunization, healthy eating for mother and baby, keeping children safe, and breast cancer screening. Mothers are also given information about government-funded programs such as Women, Infants & Children (WIC). Another service offered by the Arkansas Department of Health is the Mother/Infant Program. According to the department's Website, this program provides skilled home nursing visits for new mothers and infants to meet their medical, social and nutritional needs. Additionally, women are offered services such as family planning information, pregnancy testing, and sterilization options. Arkansas women are also supplied with a directory of abortion services available in each of the state's counties.

To get a better understanding of life for women and mothers in Arkansas, it is instructive to look at the Centers for Disease Control and Prevention (CDC) Behavioral Risk Factor Surveillance System (BRFSS). According to the CDC Website, the BRFSS was established in 1984 and collects monthly data on all 50 states covering topics such as health risk behaviors, preventive health practices, and health care access primarily related to chronic disease and injury. The current information available for Arkansas provides a wealth of information on women in the state. Of the women surveyed 62.2 percent rate their health as being "good" or "very good." Sixty-seven percent report that they have participated in physical activities during the past month. Only one-quarter state that they consume fruits and vegetables five or more times a day. Of the adult female respondents aged 18-64, 75.7 percent report that they have some type of health care coverage.

However, 17.5 percent of Arkansas residents are without health insurance and the per capita personal health care expenditures made by the state was $4,863. Of women respondents over the age of 40, 71 percent have had a mammogram in the past two years and 80.8 percent of female respondents over 18 have had a Pap test in the past three years. Additionally, 57.4 percent of the women surveyed were classified as being overweight or obese according to the body mass index (BMI). Only 2.6 percent of the adult female respondents report being heavy drinkers (consuming more than one alcoholic drink per day), while 60 percent of these respondents report never having smoked.

**See Also:** Abortion; Breastfeeding; Fertility; Midwifery; Obesity and Motherhood; Poverty and Motherhood; Pregnancy; Prenatal Health Care; Unwed Mothers.

**Bibliography**
Jacoway, Elizabeth. *Turn Away Thy Son: Little Rock, the Crisis That Shocked the Nation.* Fayetteville: University of Arkansas Press, 2008.
Moneyhon, Carl H. *Arkansas and the New South 1874–1929 (Histories of Arkansas).* Fayetteville: University of Arkansas Press, 1997.
State of Arkansas Government. "Parents and Kids." http://www.healthyarkansas.com/moms/moms .html#Infants (accessed July 2009).

Chasity Bailey-Fakhoury
Wayne State University

# Armenia

The population of Armenia in 2005 was just over 3 million, with a negative annual population growth rate (meaning more deaths than births occur per year) of minus 0.6 percent. The population is primarily urban (64 percent). The 1915–23 genocide killed approximately half of the Armenians living in Asia and drove the remainder from their homes. They settled in concentrated diasporas around the world where maintaining an Armenian identity through the birth of children and grandchildren was a priority. Today, there are about 9 million Armenians around the world.

## Motherhood and National Identity
Motherhood is central to the national identity of Armenia: the personification of the country is Mother Armenia, which symbolizes the ideals of strength and peace, honors important women in Armenian history, and recalls the important status granted to older women in the Armenian family. The most famous exemplar of Mother Armenia is a monumental statue in the national capital of Yerevan: it portrays a woman holding a sword, standing on a pedestal designed to resemble a traditional Armenian church (Armenia is predominantly Christian), which contains a museum to Armenia's war dead.

However, women in Armenia suffer from suboptimal health care due to national poverty and the disruption of economic and social life since Armenia became an independent country after separating from the Soviet Union in 1991. Although Armenia has enjoyed strong economic growth recently, this has not always translated into improved health services. Fifty-one percent of the population live below the poverty line, and Armenia as a country ranks 83rd out of 177 on the United Nations Development Program (UNDP) Human Development Index.

Literacy is high (over 99 percent) for both men and women, although girls reflect a decreasing enrollment in schools as the grade level rises: they are 95 percent of all enrollees in primary school, versus 90 percent in secondary school. In 2004, Armenia spent 5.6 percent of its Gross Domestic Product on health care expenditures, for an average per-capita expenditure (in U.S. dollars) of $321; most of the expenditure (78.7 percent) was paid out of pocket by private households, while 23.1 percent was paid by the public sector.

**Vital Statistics**

Life expectancy for males is 70 years and for women is almost 76 years. In 2004 there were 37,520 live births, for a crude birth rate of 11.15 per 1,000 population: 15 percent of births were to women in the 15- to 19-year-old age group.

Despite the fact that almost all births (99.5 percent) are attended by skilled medical personnel and 82 percent of women received at least one prenatal care visit, the maternal death rate in Armenia has been rising since 2002, and in 2004 was twice that of the World Health Organization (WHO) European Region: 37.3 maternal deaths per 100,000 live births. The lifetime chance of a woman dying from maternal causes is 1 per 1,200. The perinatal mortality rate per 1,000 births in 2004 was 14.4, about 1.5 times the European Region average. Only 22 percent of Armenian women reported using contraception in 2000, while abortion remains common: in 2004, Armenian women had 283.7 abortions per 1,000 live births.

**See Also:** Genocide; Poverty and Mothering; Russia (and Soviet Union); War and Mothering.

**Bibliography**
Bobelian, Michael. *Children of Armenia: A Forgotten Genocide and the Century-Long Struggle for Justice.* New York: Simon & Schuster, 2009.
Dolian, G., F. Ludicke, N. Katchatrian, A. Campana, and A. Morabia. "Contraception and Induced Abortion in Armenia: A Critical Need for Family Planning Programs in Eastern Europe." *The American Journal of Public Health*, v.88/5 (May 1988).
Fort, A.L. and L. Voltero. "Factors Affecting the Performance of Maternal Health Care Providers in Armenia." *Human Resources for Health.* v.22/2 (June 2004).
Payaslian, Simon. *The History of Armenia.* New York: Palgrave Macmillan, 2007.
World Health Organization. "Towards the European Strategy for Making Pregnancy Safer: Improving Maternal and Perinatal Health: Armenia." (2007). http://www.euro.who.int/document/MPS/ARM_MPSEURO_countryprofile.pdf (accessed April 2009).

Sarah E. Boslaugh
Washington University School of Medicine

# Art and Mothering

In addition to its aesthetic concerns, art is often a reflection of current social issues across and specific to gender, racial, and socioeconomic lines. Mothering as subject matter and the concerns of mother-artists are no exception, although historically, motherhood has been predominantly either sentimentalized or marginalized as a subject in art. Critics historically have paid less attention to women artists; women artists who are also mothers, and who deal with the topic of mothering in their art, were even more marginalized until the last few decades.

Since the feminist art movement, begun in the late 1960s and flourishing in the 1970s as an outgrowth of the second wave of feminism, mothering has become more acceptable as a subject in art, and mothers themselves have been less marginalized as artists, even as the feminist art movement has not always embraced mothers as artists as a reflection of the divisions and tensions regarding female identity within the movement itself.

Contemporary artists who are mothers now explore motherhood as institution and mothering as experience more directly and explicitly, allowing for a more substantive discourse about roles for women and giving greater credibility to artists who explore mothering as a theme in their art.

If art is truly a reflection of the time in which it is created, the image of woman as mother reflects society's comfort level at any given time. Artists have depicted many aspects of mothering—pregnancy, birthing, breastfeeding, child tending—from various perspectives: sometimes within the context of family, at other times within the context of working outside the home. While women increasingly explore mothering through the lens of lived experience as a means of witnessing themselves in the context of psychological theory and feminist practices and beliefs, prior to the second significant evolutionary period of feminism in the latter half of the 20th century, the notion of "mother" was more often explored as object and symbol rather than through the lens of subjective experience and psychosocial growth.

Ancient civilizations of Egypt, Cyprus, India, the Near East, Central and South America, and all cultures since, have depicted women primarily in the role of mother. Mother images have appeared across cultures and time periods in a variety of media, such as Mycenaean ivories, Egyptian wall paintings, Mexican stone carvings, Cycladic marble figurines, Athenian vase paintings, Indian terra-cottas, Chinese hand scrolls, African sculptures, Persian manuscript paintings, Japanese wood-block prints, Inuit stone carvings, and in works of Western art from the Renaissance through today.

From the Middle Ages (600–1350 C.E.) through the Renaissance, which began during the 14th century and continued through the 16th century, religious imagery was predominant in Western art. One of the central images of Christian art depicted by artists was the Virgin Mary, or the Madonna, and Christ, which spoke to the importance of the image both literally and symbolically. The Madonna was an archetype for the mother image: a chaste, nurturing figure. This archetype, which reflected the culture's preoccupation with the mother figure as all nurturing and unconditionally self-sacrificing, is still central to many cultures' beliefs about the role

of women as mothers—notions that are increasingly being challenged by contemporary artists across all artistic and literary disciplines.

Literally defined as "rebirth," the Renaissance is considered a period of great innovation in the arts, having been situated as pivotal to the art historical canon even as its histories continue to be revised by scholars from a feminist perspective. Prominent Renaissance artists such as Leonardo da Vinci (1452–1519), Michelangelo Buonarroti (1475–1564), and Raphael (1483–1520), often made religious imagery, including the image of the Madonna and child their subject matter. By contrast, women artists of this time were rarely recognized. If women did engage in creating art—as many in the upper classes were encouraged to do—they were not supported professionally and their work was not

*The Madonna has been an artistic symbol of motherhood, one who sacrifices unconditionally for her child.*

regarded critically. Earlier iconic imagery by male artists is contrasted with that of later artists, such as Marc Chagall (1887–1985), who interpreted the Madonna image of mothering more personally while retaining a sentimental, idealized view. Chagall's *Madonna of the Village*, for instance, reflects his own personal vision of woman as mother, both symbolically and literally. In the painting, Chagall depicts himself embracing the Madonna, who wears a flowing, white bride's gown, while in the background, angels cavort playfully.

Women in art most have often been objectified by male artists in both the roles of mother and as providers of sexual gratification. Such depictions often reflect deep-seated cultural, psychological, and sociological differences and conflicts with those beliefs and roles. Impressionists like Pierre-Auguste Renoir (1841–1919) painted women and children or scenes of domestic life, but these were often idealized. Post-impressionist artist Pablo Picasso (1881–1973) depicted women as either monstrous or distorted, while his images of women with children were idealized. English sculptor Henry Moore (1898–1986), by contrast, offered a more neutral view of the mother–child dyad.

## Female Artist Representations of Women

Female artists have generally depicted the mother–child relationship in a far more complex manner than their male contemporaries. Mary Cassatt (1844–1926) was among the first female visual artists to achieve critical recognition and success in the male-dominated art establishment, and much of her art addressed mothering. Cassatt, who was not a mother, pursued painting in a manner similar to her male contemporaries—she painted daily and involved herself in professional societies. Her subject matter was most often domestic, reflecting her personal interests and the prevailing practices of impressionists, who sought to capture scenes of daily life.

Cassatt's contemporary Berthe Morisot (1841–95), another preeminent female painter of the time, was perhaps the first painter in history to document her lived experience as a mother while pursuing a professional career as an artist. Morisot was ahead of her time in realizing that women would always struggle with their own creative needs and desires in tension with the demands of child rearing, and the desire to be with and nurture one's own children, and as such, foreshadowed mother art that sprung from the feminist movement even as it evolved in tension with that movement.

Morisot's paintings did not reflect sentimental ideas about motherhood, but, like Cassatt, offered an aesthetic perspective on domestic life and social practices grounded and yet departing from the dominant aesthetic trends. Morisot employed a wet nurse to care for her own daughter, which was a common practice during the time; her painting of the wet nurse with her daughter often has been misunderstood as painting of a mother and child rather than representing the economic transaction it was: a working-class woman hired to feed the baby of an upper-class mother. Both Cassatt and Morisot, formally accomplished and critically recognized artists, approached children and domestic life as legitimate subjects for art, suggesting that the lives of women and children had value and were not simply sweet or decorative.

Representing further departures, German painter, printmaker, and sculptor Kathe Kollwitz (1867–1945) explored mothering from a more personal perspective, expressing the emotional intensity of mothering as a fundamental aspect of the human condition, but without sentimentalizing it. This is contrasted with Paula Modersohn-Becker's *Reclining Mother and Child* (1906, oil on canvas), which depicts a nude mother and nursing child sleeping on a mat. The artist's intention was to convey the mother's selflessness and suggest she is a heroic figure for her sacrifice—ideas that today are the source of great tension and debate for women.

The contemporary painter Alice Neel (1900–1984), identified as a feminist artist, realized a prolific career despite the challenges of raising and supporting a family. Known for her wide range of portraits of women and men from all backgrounds, Neel painted portraits of her extended family, as well as a series of nudes that took on a female point of view rather than the predominant male perspective on eroticism. Neel became a role model for women during the feminist movement, and navigated the challenges of mothering and caring for her family while working as a professional artist, without silencing herself as a mother, as many artist mothers have felt compelled to do.

The artist Marisol's piece titled *Working Woman* (1987, wood, charcoal, and plaster) speaks to the tension between child rearing and working in the professional sphere, a conflict unique to middle-class and upper-middle-class women who may not work out of financial necessity, but either desire to do so or feel that working represents autonomy. In Marisol's sculpture, the mother is quite literally wooden: as she stands holding her briefcase in one hand and her child in the other, and her expression is cold and severe, as if she were an automaton. Images such as this speak to the postwar, second wave feminist trend toward women working outside the home, a trend that created many new tensions as well as freedom for women, and served as a precursor to the present-day "Mommy Wars."

While reverence for mothering and motherhood is far more prevalent than a critical perspective in art about mothering, and has historically been perpetuated by both male and female artists, contemporary, conceptual art reflects a shift toward exploring controversial and complex ideas about gender roles and issues of identity, particularly in the context of and as a reaction to the feminist art movement.

## The Feminist Movement

Corresponding with the trajectory of feminism, the feminist art movement, begun in the late 1960s, sought to bring more visibility to women artists, alter the foundations of art production and reception, and reflect upon an international movement of women artists making art that reflected their own lives and experiences. In the 1970s, during the heyday of the movement, the nation's first feminist art education program was established at California State University, Fresno, by Judy Chicago and 15 female students. Chicago, along with Miriam Schapiro, later founded the feminist art program in Los Angeles, the Feminist Studio Workshop, which led to the groundbreaking installation WomanHouse.

While the feminist art movement allowed for the emergence and more widespread critical discourse around many new types of work by women, it was criticized for its marginalization of mother artists, particularly those who sought increased support for women with children in the context of their art making practices. In reaction to this lack, a group of women artists began the Mother Art Collective in

1974. Helen Million-Ruby, Christy Kruse, Suzanne Siegel, Gloria Hajduk, and Laura Silagi, who met as students in the Feminist Studio Workshop in Los Angeles, began the collective with the intention of demonstrating that motherhood was a legitimate subject for feminist art.

The collective was one of the first to come out of the Woman's Building (1973–91), home of the Feminist Studio Workshop, as well as women's art galleries, artists' studios, and the Sisterhood Bookstore. Million-Ruby, in particular, wanted to bring art to the everyday woman, reflecting a belief that the feminist movement favored white, middle-class women and did not reflect the concerns and realities of women of color and lower socioeconomic status. Mother Art artists believed that diversity in mothering should be recognized as well, and that lesbian and adoptive mothers should also be included.

Active through 1986, the collective combined motherhood and activism as a means of helping women locate their own voices—a central tenet of the feminist art movement. Another important aspect of the movement was challenging the assertion that a woman would have to choose between her art and her children, a claim made by many feminist artists, including Judy Chicago, who was not a mother. Early in the feminist art movement, a separation was made between the sacred and unique childbearing qualities of woman and the actual children that resulted.

While efforts such as the Mother Art collective made incursions in to the male-dominated art world, even as mothers and the representation of motherhood at times continues to be marginalized by feminists and other female artists alike, a number of contemporary feminist artists have made inroads toward more widespread critical and cultural acceptance. As more artwork by mothers representing motherhood became critically recognized, a complex debate emerged surrounding issues of an innate, essential femininity versus a sexuality defined by culture, reflecting a larger debate within the field of psychoanalysis begun in the early 20th century.

Artist Louise Bourgeois (1911– ) explored over several decades the dynamic of mothering children from a psychoanalytic perspective, influenced by the theories of Melanie Klein. While feminists have often divided themselves along Freudian and Klei-

*Mary Cassatt's 1901 painting,* After the Bath. *Both Cassatt and Berthe Morisot, critically recognized female artists, treated the subject matter of women and children as legitimate rather than simply sweet or decorative.*

nian lines, Bourgeois, who is regarded as one of the preeminent contemporary artists of the postmodern era, was able to maintain a position of strength and high critical regard as a serious artist who continued to question and examine theoretical ideas in the context of a stylistically evolved and groundbreaking practice. Scholar Mignon Nixon credits Bourgeois with initiating a critical reworking of surrealism, a male-dominated movement, in relation to feminism. Bourgeois refutes the surrealists' characterization of the mother as a symbol of patriarchal law.

Conceptual artist Mary Kelly (1941– ), also a preeminent figure in the feminist art movement, created one of the best-known contemporary art pieces to directly face the experience of motherhood from a social and psychoanalytical perspective. *Post-Partum Document*, created between 1973 and 1979 and considered Kelly's groundbreaking work, explores Kelly's relationship with her son. In the form of a

diary, Kelly documents the significant stages of her son's development, and in doing so, expressed the experience of mothering in both a Freudian and a social context as she explored the relationship between mother and son. Kelly's work is considered central to the feminist discourse of the 1970s.

Like Bourgeois and Kelly, contemporary artists who are also mothers are increasingly suggesting that mothering is at once complex and worthy of recognition, both in terms of its importance and as a response to its continued devaluation in many cultures, and the paradox inherent in those extremes. These artists have created art about the experience of mothering and have also commented on motherhood and perceptions of motherhood through their art, while being faced with the continuing tensions between the demands and desires of mothering and the demands and desires of art making. The emotional intensity of such tension has often driven the creation of art—in a sense reconciling the two opposing conditions.

Sally Mann (1951– ) took photographs of her children simply because they were there: approaching mothering as a subject because it reflected her environment rather than as a statement or expression about mothering. Mann created an early series of photographs of her three children and husband entitled *Immediate Family*. Mann was featured on the PBS art documentary *Art 21*, a program that included notable contemporary artists who have broken new ground in terms of subject matter or approach. Janine Antoni (1964– ), also featured on the program, has made performance art dealing with the subject of self and identity, including the role of women as nurturers. In her photograph *Coddle* (1998), Antoni offered a different perspective on the nurturing relationship between Madonna and child by depicting herself as the Madonna, and instead of cradling a child, she cradles her own leg—offering an opposing view on the mother-child narrative that could be said to focus instead on a narcissistic obsession with the female body.

Nancy Spero (1926–2009), a prominent figure in the feminist art movement and the mother of two sons, explored female identity through images of the goddess throughout history. Spero appropriated mythical goddesses, fertility symbols, and contemporary imagery of women found in press photographs to parody the manner in which the female form has been represented by men, while at the same time celebrating the ancient, mythic attributes of femininity, including motherhood.

Two groundbreaking contemporary exhibitions, Maternal Metaphors I and II (2004 and 2006), curated by Jennie Klein and Myrel Chernick, explored questions surrounding what the curators termed "our normative cultural construction of motherhood." The first exhibition, Maternal Metaphors I: Artists/Mothers/Artwork, was premised upon questioning the institution and representation of motherhood and mothering in the west. While the artists included in Maternal Metaphors I were artists that resided and worked in the United States, Maternal Metaphors II included an international roster of artists in order to represent views that were not strictly American-culture-centric. This roster of artists included Camille Billops,

Monica Bock, Zofia Burr, Myrel Chernick, Patricia Cué, Cheri Gaulke, Denise Ferris, Judy Gelles, Judy Glantzman, Heather Gray, Rohesia Hamilton Metcalfe, Youngbok Hong, Mary Kelly, Ellen McMahon, Margaret Morgan, Gail Rebhan, Aura Rosenberg, Shelly Silver, Barbara T. Smith, Signe Theill, Beth Warshafsky, Sarah Webb, and Marion Wilson. The artists challenged the representation of motherhood as an institution that is primarily white, middle class, young, and heterosexual, while exploring their own ambivalence about becoming mothers after successfully establishing careers as artists. The work represents various mediums, including painting, drawing, photography, video, sculpture, installation, artist's books, and a Web-based piece.

Other exhibitions such as Doublebind, shown in Germany and Australia in 2003–04 and curated by Signe Theill, and Mother/mother-*, curated by Jennifer Wroblewski and presented in 2009 at A.I.R. Gallery in Brooklyn, New York, represent additional efforts to showcase art by mother artists exploring motherhood.

Critics and writers have been influential counterparts to the discussion and issues surrounding art and mothering and motherhood. Adrienne Rich's seminal critical work *Of Woman Born* coincided with the feminist art movement in the 1970s to challenge and encourage the ideas set forth by mother artists. The editors of art journal *M/E/A/N/I/N/G*, Susan Bee and Mira Schor, organized a forum on motherhood and art concerning the difficulty of balancing one's career as an artist with one's identity as a mother, beginning a discussion that is still ongoing. Theorists have explored film, popular culture, and literature alongside visual art in terms of maternal representation.

**See Also:** Birth Goddesses; Da Vinci, Leonardo's Mother; Feminism and Mothering; *Literary Mama*; Literature, Mothers in; Mommy Wars; Mother Goddess; Motherhood Memoir; Motherhood Poets; Mothering and Creativity; Myth, Mothers in; Rich, Adrienne; Second Wave of Feminism.

**Bibliography.**
Chernik, Myrel and Jennie Klein, eds. *The M Word: Real Mothers in Contemporary Art*. Toronto: Demeter Press, 2010.

Davey, Moyra, ed. *Mother Reader: Essential Writings on Motherhood.* Toronto: Seven Stories Press, 2001.

Edelstein, T.J. *Perspectives on Morisot.* Manchester, VT: Hudson Hills Press, 1990.

MamaPalooza.com. www.mamapalooza.com (accessed April 2009).

Moravec, Michelle. "Mother Art: Feminism, Art and Activism," in *Journal of the Association for Research on Mothering: Mothering, Popular Culture and the Arts* (York University, Spring/Summer 2003).

Nixon, Mignon. *Fantastic Reality, Louise Bourgeois and a Story of modern Art* (The MIT Press, 2005).

Pollock, Griselda. *Mary Cassatt: Painter of Modern Women.* London: Thames and Hudson, 1998.

Public Broadcasting Service (PBS). "Art:21." http://www.pbs.org/art21/ (accessed April 2009).

Rich, Adrienne. *Of Woman Born: Motherhood as Experience and Institution.* New York: Norton, 1995.

Tobey, Susan Bracaglia. *Art of Motherhood.* New York: Abbeville Press, 1991.

Julianna Thibodeaux
Independent Scholar

# Artificial Insemination

Also known as donor insemination or alternative insemination, artificial insemination is the process of injecting sperm into a woman's uterus or cervix during ovulation for the purpose of achieving pregnancy. The oldest and one of the most widely forms of assisted reproductive technology, artificial insemination may be carried out under medical supervision or independently, using artificial insemination with husband's sperm (AIH) or from an artificial insemination by a donor (AID), both known and unknown. Most artificial insemination is carried out under medical supervision, although self-insemination is also practiced.

## History of Artificial Insemination

The first human experiments with AIH in the United States were reported by gynecologist J. Marion Sims in the 1860s. Although only one of the six women he reported inseminating due to cervical abnormalities achieved pregnancy, none achieved a live birth. Using AID for male infertility was first practiced in 1884 by Philadelphia doctor William Pancoast, who was said to have arranged for his patient, a wealthy woman married to an infertile male, to be anesthetized under pretext and inseminated with the sperm of a medical student. According to the report, which was not published until after the turn of the century, the woman was never told how she became pregnant. Relatively few cases of artificial insemination were reported prior to the 1930s, and most were not successful because of an inaccurate understanding of women's fertility. It was not until the 1940s that AID was cited in the popular press as responsible for a number of births. Infertile couples in the United States during the 1950s and 1960s increasingly sought help from physicians. Although the true number of children born using donor insemination is impossible to ascertain, popular articles in *Time* and *Newsweek* suggested that as few as 10,000 and as many as 50,000 children were born using AID in the 1950s and 1960s.

The use of AID for treating male infertility increased in the United States over the 20th century, typically under secrecy and under physician control. Donor insemination was initially offered to heterosexual married couples, in which the male was infertile or had reduced fertility. Physicians matched physical characteristics of the donor with the husband and purchased sperm from medical students, residents, and other physicians. Donors were typically anonymous, and married couples kept their use of AID a secret. Sometimes couples were encouraged to engage in sexual intercourse around the time of insemination so that paternity might remain uncertain. With physician-controlled donor insemination, unmarried heterosexual women and lesbians (with or without partners) were generally excluded.

The first successful efforts to freeze sperm (cryopreservation), based on similar practices in animal husbandry in the 1950s, were reported in 1953. Yet the use of frozen sperm and the commercial development of sperm banking did not develop until much later. More effective techniques for freezing sperm were developed in the 1970s. This technological advance, coupled with concerns about transmitting human immunodeficiency virus (HIV) infection through the use of fresh sperm in the 1980s and 1990s, led to the use of frozen sperm for donor insemination, typically stored in a sperm bank (cryobank). Although estimates are difficult to obtain because of the secrecy involved and lack of regulation, in the United States some 30,000 children a year are currently estimated to be born as a result of donor insemination.

The development of cryopreservation and sperm banks enabled men to bank their own sperm prior to undergoing medical treatments that might affect their fertility (such as chemotherapy), for those undergoing major life events (such as mobilization for war), or for those who wished to preserve the option to have children following vasectomy.

Single women and lesbian couples gained access to clinic-based donor insemination on a limited basis in the United States and Canada, in South Africa, and in a few European countries beginning in the 1990s. Elsewhere, AID has been primarily restricted to heterosexual couples. Although donor insemination by lesbians is not prohibited in the United Kingdom (UK), physicians there are required to consider the welfare of the proposed child, including the child's need for a father. Thus, clinic-assisted AID for lesbians in the UK is somewhat less common.

Techniques for introcytoplasmic sperm injection (ICSI) became available in 1992, making donor insemination less attractive to some married couples. In ICSI, a single sperm is extracted from the donor and used to fertilize the egg using techniques of in vitro fertilization (IVF). Because the process allows a genetic tie where the male has a very low sperm count or weak sperm, it has to a certain extent supplanted donor insemination among heterosexual couples.

### Health Concerns With Donor Insemination

As frozen sperm increasingly became available and effective in achieving pregnancy in the 1980s, concerns about the spread of disease with the use of fresh sperm arose. To counter the risk of spreading HIV and other illnesses, sperm banks and commercial services screen donors carefully for HIV and an array of other infectious diseases. Donors are tested for chromosomal abnormalities and genetic diseases, such as Tay-Sachs disease and sickle cell anemia. The U.S. Food and Drug Administration (FDA) began regulating sperm donation in 1994, mandating screening of sperm donors for sexually transmitted infections and other communicable diseases. Current guidelines call for quarantining frozen sperm for six months prior to use. The American Society for Reproductive Medicine also provides guidelines for donor insemination. Sperm banks may also choose voluntary accreditation by the American Association of Tissue Banks, which provides strict standards for collection, storage, and transmission of sperm.

### Sperm Banking

The first sperm banks in the United States, typically small and private, developed in the 1960s. Commercial cryobanks—laboratories for screening, preparation, storage, and distribution of sperm—emerged as a for-profit industry in the 1970s. By the 1980s, there were 135 in the United States. One of the most notorious, created by entrepreneur Robert Clark Graham in the 1970s, was aimed at banking the sperm of Nobel laureates and other men who were deemed highly intelligent. This sperm bank, which closed in 1999, had a eugenic aim, and claims to have been responsible for producing over 200 children. Most sperm banks are for-profit enterprises, some of which provide services for single women and lesbians; others restrict themselves to heterosexual married couples.

Over the 1990s and 2000s, sperm banking and AID became increasingly commercialized in the United States. With the development of the Internet, potential parents can search catalogs of sperm donors online, with vials available for purchase and shipping, including shipping overseas. In the United States, this has also entailed a shift from doctor-selected/doctor-directed AID to consumer-directed selection and purchase of donor sperm. Commercial sperm banks are established across the world. With international boundaries easily crossed through the Internet, donated sperm is available for a fee worldwide. The largest sperm bank in the world is located in Aarhus, Denmark, which ships sperm to over 40 countries worldwide.

Sperm banks provide catalogs listing donor characteristics, ranging from health history, religion, personality characteristics, hobbies, race and ethnicity, and physical appearance (height, weight, hair and eye color, complexion, and build). As sperm banking has become commercialized, more donor information has become available, and Internet sites aimed at helping clients locate the "right" donor have sprung up. Sperm banks provide a range of services including donor screening, testing for sperm count and motility, and washing sperm to accommodate both vaginal and intrauterine insemination. Many sperm banks have begun to offer sperm from donors who agree to release identifying information once donor offspring reach adulthood. The number of donor programs offering open-identity sperm donors has increased in the United States since the late 1990s.

## Lesbians' Use of Artificial Insemination

Lesbians began to use donor insemination for family formation in the late 1970s and 1980s. Few physicians at this time or prior were willing to give lesbians and single heterosexual women access to sperm and clinic-based insemination. Because of the low technology involved, some lesbians conducted artificial insemination by themselves using fresh sperm collected from known donors or, with the assistance of intermediaries, unknown donors. The first "self-insemination" support group formed to find sources of sperm is thought to have been established in 1978. Since then, self-insemination has provided one avenue for parenting for lesbians seeking parenthood.

Clinic-based insemination services have been available to lesbians since 1982, when the Sperm Bank of California was founded as a nonprofit offshoot of the Oakland Feminist Women's Health Center. The Sperm Bank of California was the first publicly available sperm bank that openly catered to lesbians and single women. Insemination services have become more broadly available to U.S. and Canadian lesbians over the 1990s and 2000s and in a few other countries worldwide. In 1997, South African law permitted unmarried women—including lesbians—access to donated sperm. In 2002, the American Society for Reproductive Medicine issued Guidelines for Sperm Donation that specifically included females without male partners as eligible for donor insemination.

## Ethical and Legal Issues

Ethical issues surrounding the use of donor insemination include the question of children's rights to know their genetic origin and the identity of their genetic parents, the question of whether it is ethical to pay for sperm, and the legal parental status of sperm donors.

Laws regarding payment of donors vary. In 2004, the Assisted Human Reproduction Act prohibited the purchase of sperm from donors in Canada. Similarly, payments have been reduced in the UK to provide only minimal fees, and sperm donors in Australia may only receive reimbursement for modest expenses. In the United States, sperm donors may receive payment, which can vary widely.

The parental status of sperm donors has been an area of concern. In the United States, women who use a sperm donor to self-inseminate without a physician or clinic intermediary may find that the sperm donor has parental rights. Most U.S. states have adopted the Uniform Parentage Act, which states that a physician must be used in order to terminate the parental rights and obligations of the donor. In these cases, the offspring of a married couple are considered the "natural" child of the husband. This is the case in France as well. In other countries, offspring born using artificial insemination are not considered kin. According to Muslim tradition, a child born from donated sperm would be considered illegitimate.

The ethical question of whether children have a right to know their genetic origins and biological parentage has also been raised. Historically, most donor insemination was carried out in secret, and parents were urged not to disclose the origins of children born through AID. Physicians sometimes collaborated with parents in developing the myth that the infertile father "could have" been the biological father of the child. As genetics has increasingly become emphasized in medicine and treatment of disease, the trend to disclosure has developed. Open donation has become more common in Europe, Anglophone countries, and the United States. A number of countries specify that the identity of donors must be made available to offspring once the children reach the age of majority. Sweden, the Netherlands, the UK, Norway, New Zealand, and Austria all specify disclosure of donor identity. In the United States, no laws specify donor identification. There is a greater tendency toward open donation in the United States, however, with sperm banks offering increasing numbers of donors who agree to be contacted by their children. Some evidence suggests that lesbian couples and single heterosexual women are more likely to choose open donors than heterosexual couples. In most other regions, donors are usually not identified.

## Research on Artificial Insemination Children
Little research has considered the issues of the person conceived by donor insemination. Research on lesbian parents indicates that lesbians tend to disclose the donor-assisted origins of their children. In lesbian families, sperm donors may play a variety of roles, ranging from active parent to unknown donor. Research on single heterosexual women who give birth using AID also suggests a trend toward disclosure. Research on children of heterosexual married couples conceived using AID is limited. In New Zealand, qualitative evidence from small-scale studies suggests that most parents intend to tell their children. The majority of parents in a study of similar families in the UK did not intend to disclose. It is too early to tell how laws regarding open donation will affect parental disclosure.

## Religious Prohibitions
Some religious traditions forbid donor insemination; others permit assisted reproduction under certain circumstances. Jewish law has been flexible with regard to donor insemination; although it forbids the emission of sperm for any but procreative purposes, AID is used in Israel, and religious Jews may choose sperm from non-Jewish donors. Unlike in vitro fertilization, however, donor insemination in Israel is typically regarded with shame. Sperm donation is prohibited by both Sunni and Shi'a Muslim doctrine, although AIH and ICSI are acceptable. The Roman Catholic Church has opposed all reproduction technologies, including artificial insemination. In many Roman Catholic countries, such as in Latin America, donor insemination is prohibited, as it is in Italy. Although official Catholic teaching may prohibit donor insemination, as does Greek Orthodox teaching, many Catholics and Orthodox Christians practice assisted reproduction.

## Cross-Cultural Issues
Acceptance and availability of artificial insemination varies cross-culturally. Although infertility is prevalent in non-Western countries, especially in central and South Africa, fertility treatments are generally unavailable in poor and rural areas. Arti-

ficial insemination and other reproductive technologies are regulated in a number of countries, including Australia, Sweden, the UK, Canada, Germany, Israel, Greece, and the United States. By the early 1990s, over 100 reports on AI and reproductive technology had been produced by governments and nongovernmental organizations.

In some pro-natalist cultures, such as Israel and India, donor insemination is practiced with great secrecy. Generally speaking, outside of Europe, United States, and other English-speaking countries, physicians tend to exert greater control of artificial insemination and assistive reproductive technology, and donors remain anonymous. In almost all areas in which assisted reproductive technologies are practiced, in vitro fertilization has increased the chance of using genetic material from the male and thus, although a more physically intrusive procedure for women, has gained precedence over the lower-technology AID.

**See Also:** Infertility; Lesbian Parenting; Pregnancy; Reproductive Technologies.

## Bibliography
Bharadwaj, A. "Why Adoption Is Not an Option in India: The Visibility of Infertility, The Secrecy of Donor Insemination, and Other Cultural Complexities." *Social Science & Medicine,* v.56 (2003).
Blyth, E. and A Farrand. "Reproductive Tourism—A Price Worth Paying for Reproductive Autonomy?" *Critical Social Policy,* v.25/1 (2005).
Carmeli, Y.S., D.B. Carmeli, Y. Soffer, M. Matilsky, I. Kalderon and H. Yavetz. "Donor Insemination in Israel: Sociodemographic Aspects." *Journal of Biosocial Science,* v.33/2 (2001).
Daniels, K. and E. Haimes, eds. *Donor Insemination: International Social Science Perspectives.* Cambridge, UK: Cambridge University Press, 1998.
Daniels, C.R., and J. Golden. "Procreative Compounds, Popular Eugenics, Artificial Insemination and the Rise of the American Sperm Banking Industry." *Journal of Social History,* v.5/27 (2004).
"Guidelines for Sperm Donation." *Fertility and Sterility,* v.82/1 (2004).
Inhorn, M.C. and D. Birenbaum-Carmeli. "Assisted Reproductive Technologies and Culture Change." *Annual Review of Anthropology,* v.37/1 (2008).

Mamo, L. "Biomedicalizing Kinship: Sperm Banks and the Creation of Affinity-Ties." *Science as Culture,* v.14/3 (2005).

Murray, C. and S. Golombok. "Going It Alone: Solo Mothers and Their Infants Conceived by Donor Insemination." *American Journal of Orthopsychiatry,* v.75/2 (2005).

Scheib, J.E. and R.A. Cushing. "Open-Identity Donor Insemination in the United States: Is It on the Rise?" *Fertility and Sterility,* v.88/1 (2007).

Kristin G. Esterberg
Salem State College

# Association for Research on Mothering

The Association for Research on Mothering (ARM) is the first international feminist organization devoted explicitly to the topic of mothering and motherhood. Its mandate is to provide a forum for the discussion and circulation of research on motherhood, and to establish a community of individuals and institutions working and researching in the area of mothering and motherhood. ARM was formed to promote, showcase, and make visible maternal scholarship and to accord legitimacy to this academic field. Most importantly, ARM exists to provide a community for like-minded scholars who research and work in the area of mothering and motherhood.

ARM was founded and officially launched in September 1998 by Dr. Andrea O'Reilly, at a second annual mothering conference also co-coordinated by Dr. O'Reilly and sponsored by the Centre for Feminist Research (CFR) at York University, Toronto, Ontario, Canada. In its inaugural year, ARM attracted over 30 members; a decade later, in 2008, ARM had more than 500 registered members from over 20 countries.

During the first 10 years, more than 1,500 people at one time or another held memberships with ARM. ARM is concerned with both membership and research, with the inclusion of all mothers: First Nations mothers, immigrant and refugee mothers, working-class mothers, lesbian mothers, mothers with disabilities, mothers of color, and mothers of other marginalized groups. Members are mothers, scholars, writers, activists, social workers, midwives, nurses, therapists, lawyers, teachers, politicians, parents, students, or artists. They are individual members, or members of local and/or international government or social agencies and/or community groups that work for, and on behalf of, mothers.

## Joining Community and Research

To bridge the gap between community work and academic research on mothering, ARM provides various forums that draw and unite people to share their insights, experiences, ideas, stories, studies, and concerns on mothering and motherhood. ARM hosts a Mother Outlaws Speakers Series and Mother Outlaws community gatherings and potluck dinners in the Toronto area for women interested in discussing motherhood issues from a feminist perspective, and making the links between their own mothering practices and social change. ARM also hosts an annual international academic conference in October that draws its diverse membership to address varying themes and issues surrounding the experience of motherhood and mothering.

ARM meets its mandate to provide a forum for discussion and distribution of knowledge and research on mothering and motherhood by also publishing the *Journal of the Association for Research on Mothering* and housing Demeter Press. Both publications aim to produce the most current, high-quality scholarship on mothering and motherhood, and to ensure that this scholarship considers motherhood in an international context and from a multitude of perspectives, including differences of class, race, sexuality, age, ethnicity, ability, and nationality. This critical mass of scholarly work on mothering and motherhood generated by ARM has contributed to the development of maternal theory, Motherhood Studies, and a three-volume encyclopedia dedicated to the subject of motherhood.

**See Also:** Demeter Press; *Journal for the Association for Research on Mothering*; Mother Outlaws (Group); Motherhood Studies.

## Bibliography
Association for Research on Mothering, York University. www.yorku.ca/arm (accessed April 2009).

Kingston, Anna Karin. *Mothering Special Needs: A Different Maternal Journey*. London: Jessica Kingsley Publishers, 2007.

The Motherhood Website. "Association for Research on Mothering." www.themotherhood.com (accecssed September 2009).

Fiona Joy Green
University of Winnipeg

# Attachment Parenting

Attachment parenting is a specific parenting philosophy, initially articulated by parenting author Dr. William Sears. The philosophy has grown in popularity and has proponents worldwide.

This parenting style draws from attachment theory within developmental psychology, a theory that suggests that strong attachment between parents and offspring is a biological necessity. Attachment parenting maintains that certain key parenting behaviors encourage or assure strong attachment, resulting in children with increased confidence and sensitivity. These behaviors include breastfeeding on demand, co-sleeping, immediate skin-to-skin contact between mothers and infants in the moments following birth, and the avoidance of strollers in favor of carrying babies and toddlers.

Attachment parenting (often shortened to AP by both proponents and detractors), was initially made popular by Dr. Sears and his wife, Martha Sears, who is a registered nurse. They maintain that they did not invent this parenting style, but rather borrow from both indigenous cultures and parents' own instincts. Using almost exclusively anecdotal evidence, the couple maintains that in addition to fostering strong attachment, the behaviors of attachment parenting also result in children who are smarter and healthier, as well as easier to discipline, more empathetic, and less materialistic. While Dr. Sears generally provides disclaimers throughout his writing, suggesting that no aspect of attachment parenting is mandatory, he writes forcefully in favor of a commitment to all of the following core components.

Parents must ensure that immediate contact is made between mother and infant in the moments postdelivery. In order to encourage this, and to encourage lucidity of both mother and child, medical interventions in childbirth are generally discouraged unless absolutely necessary, and parents are strongly urged to empower themselves in pregnancy in order to ensure that all early components of attachment parenting are supported.

Attachment parenting philosophy views crying on the part of babies and young children as a critical cue of discomfort and/or displeasure and maintain that total responsiveness is required. To this end, attachment parents do not allow their children to sleep train (following the parenting philosophy of Dr. Richard Ferber) by crying for extended periods of time.

## Breastfeeding

Nursing is a critical component of attachment parenting with both physical and emotional benefits suggested. Babies are fed on demand (in keeping with the need for responsiveness outlined above). Sears suggests that breastfeeding is almost always possible and holds a lack of support within both medical and social contexts as well as the enormous impact of formula advertising responsible for low breastfeeding rates. Mothers who genuinely cannot nurse are encouraged to bottle-feed in a nursing way, by ensuring that mothers remain the primary food providers and through the maintenance of skin-to-skin contact.

## Babywearing and Co-Sleeping

Attachment parenting suggests that Western infants are generally held insufficiently. Through the use of various slings, pouches, and baby carriers, children are held the majority of the time, well into toddlerhood. Babywearing is meant to relieve some aspects of parental isolation, as babies who are "worn" can theoretically be taken into a number of different contexts, contributing to the socialization of infants and toddlers as well as their parents.

The family bed is a core concept within attachment parenting, wherein parents and children sleep in one bed until children are ready to move to a bed of their own. While this aspect of attachment parenting has garnered the most criticism (generally from the medical community on the basis of safety concerns), many attachment parents, as well as some medical research, suggest that co-sleeping is as safe as crib sleeping.

## Avoidance of Dogmatic Parenting Styles

Attachment parents are strongly warned against parenting styles that suggest rigid approaches to childrearing. Instead, attachment parents are meant to follow their children's own cues and tailor their parenting accordingly, in accordance with the principles laid out above.

## Followers and Critics

Attachment parenting has a large following of very passionate parents. Although Dr. Sears remains the movement's figurehead, there are a large number of local and international AP groups, including an umbrella group, Attachment Parenting International (API). At an institutional level, attachment parenting is often celebrated for its return to nature and natural instincts; more common Western parenting techniques and instruments such as bottles, cribs, and strollers are viewed as unnatural and harmful.

Attachment parenting is most often practiced within the context of heterosexual marriage, and followers tend to have middle-class or higher income levels; much of the literature on attachment parenting presupposes a family unit comprised of a mother and father with children, as well as flexibility with respect to employment, which is not always available to working-class families. Within the philosophy, mothers and fathers have very distinct roles; mothers are viewed as essential to healthy attachment, while fathers are meant to support the family unit to ensure that mothers may bond securely and completely. Fathers are viewed as essential to attachment, but the primary parent depicted in attachment parenting texts is unambiguously the mother.

Critics of attachment parenting view this style of parenting as overly demanding to parents, especially mothers, and suggest that attachment parenting is overly child-centered. In particular, Judith Warner, author of *Perfect Madness: Motherhood in the Age of Anxiety*, blames attachment parenting on creating an "age of anxiety" for mothers, while sociologist Sharon Hays argues that attachment parenting is a euphemism for intensive mothering.

**See Also:** Breastfeeding; Childbirth; Mothering as Work; Stay-at-Home Mothers.

**Bibliography**

Nathanson, Jessica and Laura Camille Tuley, eds. *Mother Knows Best: Mothers Talk Back to the Experts.* Toronto: Demeter Press, 2009.

Sears, W. and M. Sears. *The Baby Book: Everything You Need to Know About Your Baby From Birth to Age Two.* New York: Little, Brown, 2003.

Warner, Judith. *Perfect Madness: Motherhood in the Age of Anxiety.* New York: Riverhead Trade, 2006.

May Friedman
York University

# Attention Deficit Disorder

Attention deficit disorder (ADD) has become, in recent years, almost a childhood epidemic. Those diagnosed with the disorder exhibit difficulty paying attention, disorganization, impatience, forgetfulness, distractibility, fidgeting, excessive talking, and impulsiveness. Much controversy surrounds ADD—both in the diagnosis and in the treatment of the disorder. Treatment of ADD generally involves medication such as Ritalin® or Adderall®. Recent treatment options take a more holistic approach, focusing on dietary needs and restrictions rather than medications.

ADD first began to receive acknowledgment in 1980 by the *Diagnostic and Statistical Manual of Mental Disorders, Third Edition* (DSM-III). This diagnosis focused on two types of ADD: ADD with hyperactivity and ADD without hyperactivity. By the time the DSM-IV came out, psychologists assigned many nuances to the disease. For the initial diagnosis, six of the following nine criteria must be met:

1. Fails with attentiveness to details or careless mistakes are made in schoolwork, work, or other activities
2. Has difficulty maintaining attention to tasks or play activities

3. Appears to not listen when being directly spoken to
4. Difficulty following through with directions and fails to complete activities
5. Often demonstrates difficulty organizing tasks and activities
6. Avoids or dislikes activities requiring sustained mental focus
7. Loses important objects
8. Easily distracted by external stimuli
9. Forgetful in daily activities

For a diagnosis of ADD with hyperactivity, six of the nine following criteria must be met:

1. Often fidgets or squirms in seat
2. Leaves the room in situations where remaining seated is expected
3. Runs or climbs excessively in inappropriate situations
4. Has difficulty playing or engaging in leisure activities quietly
5. Often talks excessively
6. Appears to always be on the go or driven by a motor
7. Frequently blurts out answers before questions are finished
8. Has difficulty waiting
9. Interrupts or intrudes upon others

All of the above symptoms must be persistent for duration of at least six months, have an onset before the age of seven, be present in two or more settings, and must lead to a clear impairment in social, academic, or occupational functioning.

## Treatment of ADD

ADD is most often treated with medication. Stimulants are prescribed for patients. While it might appear to be counter-intuitive to prescribe stimulants to those already suffering from hyperactivity or inattention, studies have shown that these medications do help alleviate the symptoms of ADD. The two most commonly prescribed medications for those suffering from ADD are Adderall and Ritalin. Other pharmaceuticals prescribed for treating ADD include antidepressants and or anti-hypertensive drugs.

*Children with attention deficit disorder have difficulty concentrating on schoolwork. Controvery surrounds diagnoses.*

Another treatment option for those suffering from ADD is behavior modification therapy. For children undergoing behavior modification therapy, timers, clear rules, and schedules are of the most benefit. Parents might set a timer for the child getting ready for bed, or they might have a checklist of items to be completed before leaving the house in the morning. Other treatments focusing on behavior include maintaining an exercise program, therapy sessions, and parental training.

A third treatment option for those diagnosed with ADD is diet and environmental control. Parents who swear by this treatment option focus on a holistic diet, avoiding processed foods and sugars. Some additives that have been cited as causing ADD-like symptoms include tartrazine (yellow dye number 5) and monosodium glutamate (MSG). Low blood sugar has also been cited as a cause for ADD-like symptoms, causing mothers to increase the number of healthy snacks and decrease the number of sugary snacks and sodas. One of the most widely known anti-ADD diets is the Feingold Diet.

## Controversies

Many controversies surround both the diagnosis of ADD and the medicating of the disorder. One problem with ADD is the diagnosis. Many disagree over whether it is a mental disorder or not. Other arguments centering on diagnosis focus upon the research methodologies involved. Finally, some critics cite that foundations of this diagnosis have not been formally developed by neuroscience, genetics, or biology.

Controversies surrounding medication for ADD surround the safety of the medication and its effectiveness in treating the disorder. Critics often cite research showing the relationship between Ritalin and liver cancer in rats as one problem with medication. A second concern centering on medicating ADD is the fact that stimulants are often very addictive and misused. Finally, concern over the involvement of the pharmaceutical companies with mental functioning is cited as a possible problem.

A number of alternative therapies such as yoga, hypnosis, and dietary supplements have been proposed to treat ADD. The effectiveness of these therapies is unproven and many see them as simply a type of mother-blame, i.e., placing the blame for a poorly understood disease on inadequate mothering. This charge echoes Bruno Bettelheim's unsubstantiated (and now discredited) theory that autism was caused by a lack of maternal warmth.

**See Also:** Brain, Child; Depression; Discipline of Children; Home Schooling; Learning Disabilities; Natural Mothering.

### Bibliography

Armstrong, Thomas. "Attention Deficit Hyperactivity Disorder in Children: One Consequence of the Rise of Technologies and Demise of Play? In *All Work and No Play: How Educational Reforms Are Harming Our Preschoolers*. Santa Barbara, CA: Praeger, 2003.

Breggin, Peter R. *Talking Back to Ritalin*. Monroe, ME: Common Courage Press, 1998.

Brown, Thomas E. *Attention Deficit Disorder*. New Haven, CT: Yale University Press, 2005.

Feingold, Ben. *The Feingold Diet for Hyperactive Children*. New York: Random House, 1979.

Feingold, Ben. *Why Your Child Is Hyperactive*. New York: Random House, 1985.

Green, Christopher and Kit Chee. *Understanding ADHD: The Definitive Guide to Attention Deficit Hyperactive Disorder*. New York: Fawcett Columbine, 1998.

Phelan, Thomas W. *All About Attention Deficit Disorder: Symptoms, Diagnosis and Treatment: Children and Adults*. Glen Ellyn, IL: Child Management, Inc., 2000.

Ronda Lee Levine
Independent Scholar

# Atwood, Margaret

Canadian writer Margaret Atwood was born on November 18, 1939, in Ottawa, Ontario. As a poet, novelist, literary critic, author of children's books, feminist, and activist, she has had an impressive and lasting impact on feminist writing and literature. While her literary work has been characterized as "science fiction," she has insisted that "speculative fiction" is much more representative of her work.

In addition to poetry and short fiction collections, edited anthologies, children's books, and nonfiction, she has published a long list of novels, including *The Edible Woman* (1969), *Surfacing* (1972), *Lady Oracle* (1976), *Life Before Man* (1979), *Bodily Harm* (1981), *The Handmaid's Tale* (1985), *Cat's Eye* (1988), *The Robber Bride* (1993), *Alias Grace* (1996), *The Blind Assassin* (2000), winner of the Booker Prize (2000), *Oryx and Crake* (2003), *The Penelopiad* (2005), and *The Year of the Flood* (2009).

Described as a near-future dystopia, Atwood's *The Handmaid's Tale* (1985, winner of a number of prestigious awards) deals with the issues of feminism, environmental degradation, and political control wherein the issues of our time, and particularly issues that emerged out of the second-wave feminist movement are highly dramatized and problematized.

### Motherhood, Fertility, and Reproduction

Motherhood serves as a central issue addressed in *The Handmaid's Tale*, as those women who are fertile or handmaids are treated as an important commodity and are thus used by more powerful characters who do not have the luxury of fertility. In the society of Gilead, there are a number of central characters and categories of people that must maneuver within a world that is populated by a large portion of infertile women and ruled by a military dictatorship. Thus, these characters and categories of people are situated against the backdrop of a world that has become far more constraining for women.

For example, the protaganist, Offred, is a handmaid who is owned and used for her fertility by the Commander and his wife, Serena Joy. Both men and women have particular functions and duties to carry out, although women are hierarchically positioned below men. Women are not permitted to read and girls are not educated; women, in particular, serve a number of different functions, which are dependent upon their position as wives, daughters, handmaids, aunts, Marthas, econowives, unwomen, or jezebels, and always place them in positions of less power and prestige than men. Further, this long list of categories pits women against each other, positioning some women as far more valued and with more resources than others. In the case of handmaids, their sole social function is to provide wives with babies.

The final category that speaks to the central role of fertility and reproduction in this novel are babies. Unbabies, or "shredders," are babies that were born with a physical disability and are disposed of, while "keepers" are babies that are born without any physical disabilities. While wives such as the Commander's wife, Serena Joy, are hierarchically situated above handmaids via their ability (with their husbands) to use the handmaids for their fertility, the loss of control of other aspects of their lives is telling. Motherhood is the only option wives have; in the case of Serena Joy, for example, she is forced to give up her public role as a television preacher; thus, ironically, she formerly preached for the role that she now has and in which she is clearly unhappy.

Margaret Atwood's work, particularly *The Handmaid's Tale*, serves as social and cultural commentary on the issues of traditional values, motherhood, career choice for women, contemporary feminism (for example, antipornography feminists) and a number of other issues that have deeply impacted feminist writers and activists of both Atwood's and future generations.

**See Also:** Birth Mothers; Childbirth; Childlessness; Children; Fertility; Motherhood Poets; Poetry, Mothers in; Pregnancy; Reproduction.

**Bibliography**
Cooke, Nathalie. *Margaret Atwood: A Critical Companion (Critical Companions to Popular Contemporary Writers)*. Westport, CT: Greenwood Press, 2004.
Howells, Coral Ann. *The Cambridge Companion to Margaret Atwood*. Cambridge, UK: Cambridge University Press, 2006.
Tolan, Fiona. *Margaret Atwood: Feminism and Fiction*. New York: Rodopi, 2007.

Danielle Antoinette Hidalgo
University of California, Santa Barbara

# Australia

Australia is distinguished by a strong pro-natalist approach to women's roles, with considerable emphasis placed on reproduction as an important national good. This underpins Australian social policies in regard to mothers and children, except where issues of race or immigration arise. Australia's social policies to support women and children have varied in the two centuries since colonization, with limited success in supporting gender equity and care. Contemporary Australian women continue to carry key responsibilities for mothering and caring, while they are encouraged to contribute in the paid workforce, too.

### Australia's Colonial Past
Australia's colonial history is central to mothers' experiences and mothering practice within the country. When Australia was colonized in the 18th century, the mothering relationships of indigenous Australian women were interrupted, often brutally; this pattern continued into the 20th century, with the forced removal of children from indigenous families. There are still different welfare provisions for maternity payments, for example, for some groups of indigenous women. Indigenous mothers continue to experience significant social, economic,

and educational disadvantages, and the health and well-being of indigenous mothers and children is negatively affected. Indigenous infant mortality rates are twice that of other Australian children, although there have been some reductions in recent years. While indigenous mothers have more children on average than other groups of Australian women, they do so under considerably more difficult conditions.

This colonial past also shapes the national emphasis on the importance of women birthing and mothering children; Australia's geographic isolation and relatively small population have shaped national thinking about reproduction. Throughout Australia's history, there have been repeated national calls for women to produce children. In 1903, a Royal Commission on the Decline of the Birth Rate in NSW reported with concern that the number of children born to women had fallen from 7 to 4 children on average between 1870 and 1900. In the latter years of the 20th century, similar concerns were raised as fertility rates fell below replacement levels. Currently, Australia's birth rate is approximately 1.91 children per woman, which, while below replacement levels (2.1), compares favorably with birth rates in some other developed countries. In the past five years, birth rates have risen from 1.7 in 2000–01 to their current level. Immigration has been an important feature of Australia's population growth, and women coming from other nations generally experience higher fertility rates.

**Welfare and Incentives**
Mothering has attracted different forms of economic support from the government in Australia, with some mothers receiving much better support than others. Forms of support have varied from emphasis on a family wage to direct payments for mothers to support childbearing activities. In the middle of the 19th century, there was a payment of 5 British pounds made to mothers for each child born (although indigenous mothers were excluded).

The Harvester Wage Judgement in 1907 entrenched the importance of the national wage standard, which would allow a man to support a wife and three children on what he brought home. Broader forms of social support, including family allowances (support payments for children) and childcare benefits,

developed throughout the 20th century, particularly after World War II.

These have varied according to levels of economic prosperity and the ideological commitments of different administrations. There was a strong impetus in many of these policies to exclude well-off Australians, which resulted in means-testing attached to many forms of benefit. In the 21st century, a Maternity Allowance was instituted, which currently delivers $5,000 Austrailian dollars for each child at the time of birth. Many critics argue that Australia's welfare supports have not been generous, and recent decades have seen significant tightening of conditions; single parents face onerous conditions with disproportionate, negative financial impact on the nine out of 10 sole-parent households headed by women.

**Work and Family in Modern Australia**
In contemporary Australia, the means to balance work and family effectively have been identified as a key issue for mothers, fathers, and families, as women's paid work commitments have grown. Australia's framework of reconciliation policies for waged labor and care is not strong, and there is increasing evidence that families are under pressure. Deregulation of labor market policies, a feature of the Australian landscape since the 1980s, is seen to contribute to pressures in this area of employment regulation, as bargaining around family-friendly conditions becomes increasingly industry-specific. Australia is one of only two Organisation for Economic Co-operation and Development (OECD) nations without nationally mandated paid maternity leave, although unpaid maternity leave was established in the 1970s.

Federal employees were granted some funded maternity leave in 1973, and some individual organizations have developed provisions to support women in this way. Less than half of Australian women becoming pregnant, however, are estimated to have access to any form of paid maternity leave, which has led to a significant national discussion in the last decade. Several recent national reviews have supported the idea of universal paid maternity leave, and the growing numbers of Australian women with children in the workforce (currently more than 60 percent of women with children under age 12 undertake some form of paid employment) make this a vital issue for women and Australia more generally.

## Public Policy Support

In the latter decades of the 20th century, Australia developed some progressive policy platforms to support women's participation in public life. Anti-discrimination legislation prohibiting discrimination against parents and pregnancy emerged in the 1970s in the various state and national parliaments. The importance and specificity of women's role in Australia received formal recognition in the 1970s; Australia was the first country to appoint a Women's Adviser to the Prime Minister (Elizabeth Reid in 1973). The introduction of women's affairs offices at the state and federal level followed. Activism to support women refugees, no-fault divorce legislation (introduced in 1975), and maternal health in particular followed.

Australia's universal health care coverage has had important benefits for women and children. Since 1984, Australians have had access to free hospital admission and support for visits to general practitioners. Mothers and children are supported by a system of maternal and health centers, which offer primary care for women and infants during the early years (postpartum support, immunization, and basic health tests such as hearing and sight) and a system of referral to other practitioners. While there are pressures on these services, with access becoming tighter in the last several decades, this is an important feature of the Australian social landscape. There is general availability of contraceptive and family planning advice; access to abortion varies across state jurisdictions, with most requiring certification from a medical practitioner that it is necessary for the woman's health.

Although Australia's policy framework shows some support for mothering, Australia is often regarded as a strongly masculine culture, and reveals mixed attitudes around motherhood. Mothers are recognized as important for national well-being, but this does not always translate into cultural, social, or economic support. Research shows that women continue to carry the responsibility of child rearing and caring; they often work parttime, which allows the balance of work and care, but has impacts on lifetime earnings and workforce equity.

Although gains have been made, pay equity has not been achieved. While there is significant talk about the importance of Australia's mothers, this is not always reflected in the social and economic outcomes for women who have children.

**See Also:** Aboriginal Mothering; Anthropology of Mothering; Postcolonialism and Mothering; Public Policy and Mothers.

## Bibliography

Organisation for Economic Co-operation and Development (OECD). *Babies and Bosses: Reconciling Work and Family Life, Vol 1, Australia, Denmark and the Netherlands*. Paris: OECD, 2002.

Human Rights and Equal Opportunity Commission (HREOC). "Report of the National Inquiry Into the Separation of Aboriginal and Torres Strait Islander Children From Their Families." 1997. http://www.humanrights.gov.au/Social_Justice/bth_report/report/index.html (accessed April 2009).

Pocock, Barbara. *The Work/Life Collision: What Work Is Doing to Australians and What to Do About It*. Annandale, Australia: Federation Press, 2003.

JaneMaree Maher
Monash University

# Austria

Austria is situated in central Europe and has 8,200,000 inhabitants. It is a federal republic and member of the European Union (EU).

## Family Demographics in Austria

Women in Austria have an average of 1.38 children. The main fertility age is now 29.4 years of age; women's mean age at first birth is 27.7 years of age. According to the census in 2001, there were 3,483,719 women aged 15 years or older living in Austria, of which 29.6 percent do not have any children; 21.4 percent have one child; 27.6 percent have two children; 12.4 percent have three children; 5 percent have four children; 2.1 percent have five children; and 1.9 percent have six or more children.

In 2007, 20,516 marriages ended in divorce in Austria. On average, the number of children from the couples that divorced was 1.03. Divorces in 2007 involved altogether 15,031 children under the age of 18. Currently, there are approximately 352,000 single parents in Austria; about 143,000 of these single mothers have children below 15 years of age.

Education levels in Austria have been rising in the past two and a half decades. Differences between men and women are diminishing, but they still persist. In 2006, education levels in the population aged 25–64 were distributed as follows: 12.6 percent of men and 23.7 percent of women had compulsory school only 74 percent of men and 62.6 percent of women had a secondary education level, and 13.4 percent of men and 13.7 percent of women had a tertiary education level.

**Support for Mothers and Families**
For pregnant women who are employed, maternal protection, or *Mutterschutz*, starts eight weeks before the expected date of birth. During this time, mothers receive lying-in benefit, or *Wochengeld*, and are not allowed to be employed. Furthermore, working parents can take up to two years of parental leave, which encompasses protection against dismissal. Parents receive a parental leave benefit (*Kinderbetreuungsgeld*), which is currently not linked to employment status. Parents can share parental leave, but fathers' use of paternal leave is low.

Irrespective of employment status and earnings, parents also receive a national family subsidy (*Familienbeihilfe*) for each of their children. There are several other financial aids targeted at families, such as subsidies paid by the federal provinces for families with low income. The new Austrian government that formed in late 2008 planned crucial changes in the field of parental leave. Among them were plans for one month of paid leave for fathers after the birth of a child, and earning-related parental leave benefits.

Prenatal care in Austria is regulated in the *Mutter-Kind-Pass-Verordnung* (mother–child-passport-decree). When a pregnancy is stated by a medical doctor, the pregnant woman is handed the so-called *Mutter-Kind-Pass* (mother–child-passport). This document lists the medical checkups that a pregnant woman and her child are supposed to have,

from pregnancy to the child's fifth birthday. Having had the most important examinations in time is a prerequisite for receiving the full amount of the *Kinderbetreuungsgeld* parental leave benefit. This way, the state tries to encourage women to make use of prenatal and pediatric care. Prenatal care, as regulated in the mother–child-passport, consists of five medical examinations during pregnancy. Additionally, two ultrasound examinations are recommended. The examinations regulated in the *Mutter-Kind-Pass* are covered by Austrian health insurance. As a rule, they are cost-free for women.

The most popular contraceptive in Austria is the birth control pill. Emergency contraceptives are available in Austria, but they have to be prescribed by a medical doctor. In cases of emergency, however, pharmacies are allowed to sell the "morning-after pill" without prescription. Since 1975, abortion has been exempt from legal punishment until the 12th week of pregnancy, and later in the pregnancy to save the life or physical or mental health of the mother, if the fetus is severely deformed, or if the mother is younger than 14 years of age. In 2001, the abortion rate was 1.3 per 1,000 women. As of 2001, 71 percent of Austrian women age 15–49 reported using birth control.

**Religious Practices and Cultural Norms**
Over 73 percent of the people living in Austria (including the population without Austrian citizenship) are Roman Catholics. The Catholic tradition affects the cultural notion of motherhood, as do Christian conservative parties' political opinions and policies.

A strong cultural norm is the widespread attitude that young children should be cared for by their mothers. Therefore, parental leaves are rather long in Austria compared to other EU countries. Use and availability of childcare arrangements for children under age 3, and particularly under age 2, are low.

**Austrian Mothers in History and Fame**
The history of motherhood in Austria is marked by the Nazi era from 1938 to 1945 and the National Socialist motherhood ideology. The so-called *Fristenlösung*, the law exempting abortion from legal punishment until the 12th week of pregnancy, was implemented in 1975. Another important step was

the implementation of paid parental leave that began in the 1960s. In the 1970s, several amendments of parental leave and legal protection for expectant mothers were implemented, some of which still serve as the basis for today's legislation.

Famous mothers in Austrian history were the 18th-century empress Maria Theresia, who had 16 children; and the 19th-century empress Elisabeth "Sisi," who had four children. Other famous Austrian mothers were actress Romy Schneider, who had two children, one of whom died in an accident; and the skier Ulrike Maier, whose only child died in a skiing accident in 1994. Some well-known mothers are the Russian-Austrian opera singer Anna Netrebko, who had one child; Barbara Rosenkranz, a Freedom Party leader, who had 10 children; and Green Party leader Eva Glawischnig, who had one child.

**See Also:** Abortion; Birth Control; Childcare; Daycare; European Union; Employment and Motherhood; Fertility; Maternity Leave; Nationalism and Motherhood; Prenatal Health Care; Religion and Mothering; Welfare and Mothering.

### Bibliography

Austrian Government Website. www.help.gv.at (accessed April 2009).

Statistik Austria. *Education in Numbers. Key Indicators and Analyses.* Vienna, 2008.

Statistik Austria. www.statistik.at (accessed April 2009).

Karin Sardadvar
University of Vienna

# Authentic Mothering

See **Maternal Authenticity**.

# Autism

The complex neurological disorder autism, or autistic spectrum disorders (ASD) as it is most commonly known today, has been a cause for mother blame since the early 1940s. In the early days, professionals blamed mothers for lacking warmth and thereby contributing to children's lack of social reciprocity. Despite modern scientific knowledge, mothers of children with autism are still struggling to prove themselves guilt-free in the eyes of both professionals and society as a whole.

It was in 1943 that Dr. Leo Kanner, an Austrian-born child psychiatrist, first identified a unique group of children at his clinic at Johns Hopkins University in the United States. These children presented similar behaviors, such as failing to develop normal social relationships and being upset by changes in the environment; they also had marked language impairments.

Kanner pioneered the theory of the "refrigerator mother" in a paper in the 1940s, in which he attributed autism to a genuine lack of maternal warmth. Later, in a 1960 *Time* magazine interview, Kanner discussed the autistic child's withdrawal from other people as a result of highly organized and professional parents "just happening to defrost enough to produce a child."

It was, however, another American, psychotherapist Bruno Bettelheim, who gave the refrigerator theory widespread popularity. He compared autistic children to prisoners in Nazi concentrations camps, where human beings were deprived of healthy relationships, in particular with a mother figure. Bettelheim's articles in the 1950s and 1960s popularized the idea that autism was caused by maternal coldness toward their children. He consistently ignored the fact that a majority of these children had siblings who developed without these symptoms despite being mothered in the same way.

Modern knowledge and medical expertise have since abandoned the mother-blame theory. The cause of autism, however, still remains unclear and debated among experts. Most researchers, nevertheless, believe that it is triggered by a combination of genetic defects and environmental factors. Studies of the prevalence of autism differ from 20 per 10,000 individuals up to 60–70 per 10,000. While the exact figure is unknown, it is widely acknowledged that the incidence of autism has soared in recent years. This could be explained both by an increased polluted environment but also by a greater awareness and earlier diagnosis.

## Asperger Syndrome

A contemporary with Kanner was Dr. Hans Asperger, a pediatrician in Vienna, who in 1944 identified a consistent pattern of abilities and behavior in a certain group of children similar to that of Dr. Kanner. His group, however, included children with average intelligence and structural language disabilities. The pattern included a lack of empathy, little ability to form friendships, and one-sided interests and conversations. He also found that it predominantly occurred in boys. Asperger's pioneering work did not achieve any international recognition until Lorna Wing published a paper in 1981 using the term *Asperger syndrome*. It is now considered a subgroup within the autistic spectrum, and has its own diagnostic criteria.

## Methods and Therapies

Contemporary mothers of children with autism are often overwhelmed by methods and therapies promising to cure the child. They also face accusations of being responsible for their children's conditions by not following certain precautions. One heated debate among experts surrounds the argued link between vaccination of measles, mumps, and rubella and autism. Another involves not strictly following gluten- and casein-free diets.

**See Also:** "Bad" Mothers; Learning Disabilities; Mother Blame.

**Bibliography**

Attwood, T. *Asperger Syndrome: A Guide for Parents and Professionals*. London: Jessica Kingsley Publishers, 1998.

Fombonne, E. "The Changing Epidemiology of Autism." *Journal of Applied Research in Intellectual Disabilities*, v.18/4 (2005).

Kingston, A. *Mothering Special Needs: A Different Maternal Journey*. London: Jessica Kingsley Publishers, 2007.

Wallis, Claudia. "Inside the Autistic Mind." *Time* (May 7, 2006). http://www.time.com/time/magazine/article/0,9171,1191843,00.html (accessed November 2008).

Anna Karin Kingston
University College, Cork

# Autobiographies

Autobiographies, in which a person recounts their life history, have long been a popular literary genre. Autobiographies have increased in diversity and in volume during the 20th century, especially those written by women. Their style and subjects have also changed over time. Mothers have written autobiographies for a variety of reasons. Common motives include the demonstration of the impact of special circumstances on motherhood, the exploration of their personal relationship to cultural expectations of motherhood, the offering of advice or comfort to other mothers, or simply to share and validate their motherhood experiences. Childhood and coming-of-age autobiographies are another rich resource related to motherhood, as many adult autobiographers recall the formative impact of their childhood experiences. Autobiographies provide both scholars and general readers with important insights into places, times, events, social trends, or cultures, as well as the mothers who experienced them.

Autobiographies are most characteristically nonfiction prose writing with a first-person narrative style and chronological format, although they can include oral autobiographical traditions and sections of autobiographical material within larger works. They range from lengthy, detailed, or scholarly works meant to instruct or inform, to shorter, anecdotal, or humorous works meant to entertain. Some autobiographies chronicle the author's complete life history, while others, classified under the memoirs subgenre, chronicle a shorter time span. Some are serious and reflective, while others are lighthearted and humorous. Many autobiographies are organized according to a central theme, such as a person, place, or event. Other common characteristics are physical descriptions of settings and people, re-creations of spoken dialogues, and re-creations of the author's inner thoughts and feelings. Autobiographies provide the reader with a direct view of the author's experiences, as opposed to biographies, which are filtered through the eyes of another.

## Historical Autobiography

The most common early American autobiographical forms included narratives of spiritual conversion, Indian captivity, slavery, Civil War experiences, pioneer experiences, and the journey of the self-made man. Men wrote most early American autobiographies, although there are some notable exceptions. Literary scholars have noted that these early works largely reflected the American individual's self-identification through his or her relation to external circumstances as a result of the larger cultural movement to form a new life and a distinct national identity from the American wilderness. Autobiographies in the vein of Benjamin Franklin's classic also provided instruction for others wishing to improve their moral character and social conditions. Other common themes included the spiritual autobiography and conversion narrative detailing an individual's religious development, often ending with a spiritually transforming experience. These autobiographies were especially prevalent among the New England Puritans.

Autobiographies detailing pioneer life and its dangers offered more possibilities for the female author. Mothers authored several best-selling Indian captivity narratives of the 17th century, including Mary Rowlandson's *Narrative of the Captivity and Restoration of Mrs. Mary Rowlandson* (1682) and New England Puritan minister Cotton Mather's account of Hannah Duston's 1697 capture and escape. Duston watched her infant's murder as her group of captives marched through the forest, and she later received praise for her subsequent participation in the killing and scalping of 10 of her captors. Native Americans often took women and older children captive rather than killing them, and many children left accounts of the growing bond between them and their new Native American families. The Indian captivity narrative remained a popular format throughout the 19th century as westward expansion continued. Well-known autobiographical accounts of pioneer life include the *Little House* series by Laura Ingalls Wilder, which is based on her life and is historically accurate, even though its character simplification often leads to its classification as historical fiction.

A popular press capable of mass-producing books began to develop in the mid-19th century, increasing the market or autobiographies as well as other works. The public was interested in reading the autobiographies of notable individuals, such as political and religious leaders, which were public arenas not open to most women. The most common types of autobiographies of women in the public eye were those of actresses or activists such as the leaders of the women's suffrage movement. Another key autobiographical outlet for women during the 19th century was the Civil War journal and postwar memoir. The journals and memoirs written by women discussed the challenges of mothering during the male absences and economic hardships common during the wartime. One of the most well-known examples of the female Civil War memoir is white Southerner Mary Chesnut's autobiography, entitled *Mary Chesnut's Civil War*.

Slave narratives had emerged as an American literary genre by the mid-19th century. Most slave narratives followed a narrative formula tracing the journey from slavery to freedom. In addition to formal texts, slave narratives also took the form of journals, pamphlets, court testimony, and oral histories, among others. Most notable in this regard are thousands of oral histories collected by the Federal Writers' Project during President Franklin Roosevelt's New Deal. Although male authors were more common, there are a number of female slave narratives detailing slavery's impact on mothers and their children, as slave women emphasized family life in their writings. Mother Harriet Jacobs authored *Incidents in the Life of a Slave Girl* (1861), one of the most renowned female slave narratives, in which she recounted her struggle to free herself and her children from bondage. Slave narratives also exemplify the impact of historical autobiographies on their modern counterparts, as many modern African American autobiographies continue to reflect their race's collective experience as an oppressed minority.

## Modern Autobiography of Motherhood Roles

Autobiographies became a leading genre in American publishing during the 20th century. Many scholars believe that the dramatic rise in the number of autobiographies, many by first-time authors or in limited publishing runs, is a reflection of the increasingly difficult task of self-identification in a complex world as well as the late-20th-century cultural trend of introspection and self-examination. These trends were coupled with the cultural acceptance of formerly taboo subjects and the appearance of autobiographies written from a victim conscious-

*Israeli politician Golda Meir wrote of her earliest memories of her Russian childhood: cold, hunger, and fear of pogroms.*

ness and the increased interest in the experiences of ordinary people as well as leaders and celebrities. Female authorship in the genre also rose as women entered the public sphere. Many mothers who write autobiographies sought to connect with others who also felt isolated in similar situations or who may felt overwhelmed in a sometimes impersonal and overwhelming modern world.

Modern mothers have used the autobiographical genre to explore the impact of women's changing social roles and technological developments on the cultural expectations of mothers and motherhood. These works explore the impact of social expectations that women who become mothers will sacrifice their careers and personal interests to devote themselves fully to their families, and the labeling of "bad" mothers on those who do not follow such dictates. Some mothers recount their own experiences in order to challenge this idea, while others stress that feminist arguments against such gender roles are negatively impacting family

life. One notable autobiography challenging the "perfect mother myth" is writer and professor Jane Lazarre's *The Mother Knot*. Lazarre also articulated the ambivalence women sometimes feel at the prospect of motherhood that is often suppressed in the belief that such feelings will not be socially accepted. Some mothers write autobiographies to reaffirm their sense of self-identity as they navigate through motherhood.

### Autobiography of Motherhood Experience

Women have used autobiography to document and share their unique experiences of mothering within special circumstances, providing advice, support, and the acknowledgment that they are not alone. Themes include mothering within a certain race or ethnicity, mothering in poverty, mothering children with medical or mental disabilities, and mothers who themselves face medical or mental disabilities. Mothers such as nationally syndicated newspaper columnist and best-selling author Erma Bombeck have used autobiography to present a humorous look at the challenges of modern motherhood. The rise of the Internet has offered new outlets for mothers to share their experiences in an informal autobiographical form such as the mommy blog.

Many autobiographies not written by mothers or centered on the theme of motherhood explore motherhood issues as secondary themes. Some adult children have used autobiography to explore the prominent role their mothers played in shaping their adult identities. The mother–daughter relationship is often central to women's autobiographies.

Some mother portrayals are documentary, some are complimentary, and some are highly critical. Autobiographies of renowned leaders and celebrities remained popular in the 20th century as public interest in the private lives of popular figures grew. Children of some celebrities, such as actress Joan Crawford's daughter Christina in *Mommie, Dearest* (1978), detailed abuse or neglect at the hands of their famous mothers.

While many childhood and coming-of-age memoirs in this vein detail the effects of life in troubled families, a backlash gave rise to the nondysfunctional family memoir. In a few instances, mothers and children have created collaborative autobiographies exploring the mother–daughter or mother–son bond. For example, Tibetan spiritual leader the Dalai Lama wrote his mother's autobiography due to the fact that she was illiterate but had shared her stories with him through their culture's oral storytelling tradition.

## Controversial or Semifictional Autobiography

Another common theme among modern autobiographies has been the exploration of new and controversial topics that had previously been socially taboo. These topics have included issues related to motherhood, including dysfunctional family relationships, child abuse, incest, sexual orientation, drug use, incarceration, and physical and mental illness. Critics have noted that such autobiographies have made increasingly outrageous claims to attract readers who are progressively becoming inured to shocking family revelations, and that the authors may write out of the lesser motives of greed, attention, or revenge against those they feel have wronged them. Critics also note the often-negative personal effects on family members whose secret lives have been made public, especially if those members are children.

The autobiographical genre can also include autobiographical novels of fictional characters as well as autobiographies based on real people that openly or secretly blend autobiographical fact with fiction. Even those autobiographies based entirely on actual people and events are vulnerable to the unreliability of human memory, especially years after the fact, and the use of selective memory based on authors' conscious or unconscious desires to create positive self-portraits. Many autobiographers also commonly change the names of other people discussed in their work for privacy or legal reasons.

True autobiographies frequently borrow literary techniques from fiction, such as exaggeration and the inclusion of dialogue. Maxine Hong Kingston's autobiographical work *The Woman Warrior: Memoirs of a Girlhood Among Ghosts* (1976), in which her mother is a dominant figure, is a work of nonfiction that has elements of Chinese mythology. Another blend of autobiography and mythology is Audre Lorde's *Zami: A New Spelling of My Name* (1982). Some literary writers base their fictional works on their actual life experiences. For example, Doris Lessing's autobiographical fiction recalls

her childhood in Africa and the racial inequality she experienced, while Jamaica Kinkaid's autobiographical novels explore fictional mother–daughter relationships.

## Research of Motherhood Autobiography

Feminist, literary, and psychoanalytical theory scholars in the late 20th century began studying gendered differences in autobiographical writings, some from an interdisciplinary approach and others through a variety of separate fields. Some feminist scholars, such as Jane Lazarre and Julia Kristeva, have even written their own autobiographies. One notable characteristic of women's autobiographies that scholars have emphasized is the female author's search for self-identity through their relationship to others, both family and community. Motherhood is one such relationship bond. Many mothers who write autobiographies also identify themselves as part of a group consciousness based on their gender and race or ethnicity, emphasizing their collective as well as individual experience.

Twentieth-century scholars and readers have also showed an interest in the autobiographies of women and mothers living in underdeveloped nations, especially postcolonial minorities and revolutionaries. Many of these international autobiographies have multicultural and multigenerational aspects. Some scholars explore the connections between minority autobiographies written by women within and outside of the United States in the era of globalization. Such studies have linked modern autobiography to the field of postcolonialism, as developing countries and their peoples seek to cultivate postcolonial national and self-identities. These autobiographical works also exhibit the female tendency to link the individual struggle toward self-identity with the similar collective struggle of the minority or national group. Examples in these areas include the autobiographical writings of Guatemalan native Rigoberta Menchu and African American writer Maya Angelou.

Scholars emphasize the importance of women's autobiographies as reflections of their historical and cultural contexts as well as how cultural expectations of gender and motherhood have changed over time. Autobiographies record particular places and historical eras just as they record their authors' personal experiences. They have also debated whether female authors have used the public act of writing their autobiography to challenge or overturn gender ideology or whether their works fall within the existing gender ideology.

The inclusion of these characteristics reduces the tendency to view women as a collective body without enough recognition of their individual personalities, experiences, and interpretations. They are also important in studying the cultural impact of women's autobiographies, as cultural expectations also shape the public reception of an autobiography and its author.

**See Also:** Cross-Cultural Perspectives on Motherhood; Literature, Mothers in; Motherhood Memoir; Mommy Literature; Popular Culture and Mothering; Self-Identity.

**Bibliography**
Benstock, Shari. *The Private Self*. Chapel Hill: University of North Carolina Press, 1988.
Coleman, Linda S. *Women's Life-Writing: Finding Voice/Building Community*. Bowling Green, OH: Bowling Green State University Popular Press, 1997.
Cosslett, Tess, Celia Lury, and Penny Summerfield. *Feminism and Autobiography: Texts, Theories, Methods*. New York: Routledge, 2000.
Culley, Margo. *American Women's Autobiography: Fea(s)ts of Memory*. Madison: University of Wisconsin Press, 1992.
Eakin, John Paul. *Fiction in Autobiography: Studies in the Art of Self-Invention*. Princeton, NJ: Princeton University Press, 1985.
Foster, Frances Smith. *Witnessing Slavery: The Development of Antebellum Slave Narratives*. Second Edition. Madison: University of Wisconsin Press, 1994.
McKay, Nellie Y. "'We Got Our History Lesson': Oral Historical Autobiography and Women's Narrative Arts Traditions." In *Tradition and the Talents of Women*, Florence Howe, ed. Urbana: University of Illinois Press, 1991.
Morgan, Janice and Colette Trout Hall. *Redefining Autobiography in Twentieth-Century Women's Fiction: An Essay Collection*. New York: Garland, 1991.
O'Reilly, Andrea and Silvia Caporale-Bizzini, eds. *From the Personal to Political: Towards a New Theory of Maternal Narrative*. Selinsgrove, PA: Susquehanna University Press, 2009.
Podnicks, Elizabeth and Andrea O'Reilly, eds. *Textual Mothers, Maternal Texts: Motherhood in Contemporary Women's Literatures*. Waterloo, ON: Wilfrid Laurier, 2010.
Siegel, Kristi. *Women's Autobiographies, Culture, Feminism*. New York: Peter Lang, 2001.

Marcella Bush Trevino
Barry University

# Azerbaijan

Azerbaijan is a secular democracy of 8.12 million people, most (93.4 percent) of whom are Muslim. After it's separation from the Soviet Union in 1991, Azerbaijan's economic, social, and health indicators began to decline. Although the country has significant oil reserves and national wealth has increased recently, Azerbaijan spends very little as a nation on public health. Although expenditures increased 60 percent from 2002 to 2004, in 2004 it ranked the fifth-lowest in the world for public health expenditures, spending only 0.9 percent of its Gross Domestic Product on public health measures. Private expenditures make up about 78 percent of the funds spent on health care. Inflation is a serious problem: the consumer inflation rate was estimated at 21.6 percent in 2008.

**Vital Statistics**
Azerbaijan had a population of about 8.5 million in 2005, with 26 percent of the population under age 15 and an annual growth rate of 1.2 percent. It is a relatively poor country with a per capita income of $950 in 2004, and it ranked 101 out of 177 countries on the Human Development Index as of 2004. Life expectancy is 66 years for men and 70 years for women. Literacy is high for both men (99.5 percent) and women (98.2 percent).

There are about 129,000 births annually, with a total fertility rate of 2.9 children per woman in 2003, down from 3.3 per woman in 1993. Despite most births being attended by a person trained in health care (89 percent), and 74 percent of births taking place in health care facilities, the infant mortality rate is 43 per 1,000 live births, and the maternal mortality

*Children and their mothers peer into a health clinic in Azerbaijan, where they receive vaccines regularly, thanks in part to USAID. One-quarter of Azerbaijan children under 5 are stunted (too short for their age), which is an indicator of malnutrition.*

rate is 82 per 100,000 live births. Most (77 percent) of women have at least one prenatal care visit, 45 percent of women have at least four prenatal care visits, and 66 percent of women receive a postpartum visit within 3 days of giving birth. Few women (14 percent) use contraception, but the abortion rate is high (71 per 1,000 women of reproductive age).

Child immunization rates are high: 97 percent of children are immunized with three doses of diphtheria, tetanus, and pertussis (DTP), 98 percent with one dose, and 98 percent with three doses of hepatitis B vaccine. Azerbaijan is certified as polio free, so polio vaccinations are not given.

**See Also:** Islam and Health; Poverty and Mothering; Russia (and Soviet Union).

**Bibliography**

Centers for Disease Control and Prevention (CDC). "Prevalence of Anemia Among Displaced and Nondisplaced Mothers and Children—Azerbaijan, 2001." *Morbidity and Mortality Weekly Report*, v.53/27 (July 2004). http://www.cdc.gov/mmwr/preview/mmwrhtml/mm5327a3.htm (accessed April 2009).

Parfitt, B. "Health Reform: The Human Resource Challenges for Central Asian Commonwealth of Independent States (CIS) Countries." *Collegian*, v.16/1 (2009).

World Health Organization. "Highlights on Health in Azerbaijan." (2005). http://www.euro.who.int/document/E88388.pdf (accessed April 2009).

World Health Organization. "Towards the European Strategy for Making Pregnancy Safer: Improving Maternal and Perinatal Health: Country Profiles: Armenia." (2007). http://www.euro.who.int/document/MPS/ARM_MPSEURO_countryprofile.pdf (accessed April 2009).

Sarah E. Boslaugh
Washington University School of Medicine

# B

## "Bad" Mothers

The term *bad mother* is a moral, political, and social pejorative, applied to countless women in countless places. It is a label that is distinct from the case of bad parenting more generally, focusing in the specific task of mothering or, more precisely, on its failure. Because the mother–child relationship is burdened by cultural practices and sexual politics, the question of what makes a mother "bad" includes the issue of whether bad mothering is a legitimate category in the first place. It is therefore a distinctly difficult historical, philosophical, and psychological question. Although this discussion is limited to the Western (and especially American) 20th- and 21st-century preoccupation with good and bad motherhood, this is by no means a statement about the relative importance of other perspectives.

### Good Mothers

Most ideas of the good mother, like any value-laden term, are culturally bound and socially constructed. This is not to say that they lack social, political, or psychological staying power. There are some broad beliefs about good motherhood, which, while not necessarily universally shared, nevertheless tend to persist. Generally, the focus tends to be on two questions: first, who the mother is, and second, what she does. The former question is often translated into concerns about whether the mother is married, heterosexual, middle class, not too young or too old, and so on. The latter has, from about the 1700s, been interpreted as a concern with how domestic, doting, and successful in raising good children she is. A good mother protects her children and does not deliberately or neglectfully harm or abuse them. A good mother cares about being a good mother. More recently, a good mother listens to child-rearing experts, and is always aware of their latest advice.

The label of bad mother is applied to women regardless of their race, sexual orientation, religion, or socioeconomic status. However, these considerations have been key in furthering the stereotype. The following three categories provide an overview of modern bad motherhood.

### The Selfish Mother

The selfish mother puts her own needs before those of her children, either harming them by her absence or failing to protect them from harm. Even though historically, women—especially poor women and slaves—have worked both inside and outside the home, the focus since the 1950s has been on the

*Working mothers, or mothers who do not put their child's demands first, can be labeled as "bad" mothers.*

conflicts between the woman's role as a child's primary caretaker versus her role as a provider and someone with career interests and ambitions outside of the home. These working mothers are sometimes labeled as selfish or blamed for anything from their child's bad performance at school to autism to abuse. Sometimes, the label of bad mother seems to be applied without much regard for the reasons the mother is outside the home. As a feminist journalist and poet, Katha Pollitt has argued that this is used simply as a reactionary response to feminism. More recently, the "bad mother" label has been applied to women who have not placed the needs of their unborn child above their own, whether as a result of choice, addictions, poverty, or simply by not following the experts' advice about what it means to be a nurturing expectant mother.

### The Nontraditional Mother

The nontraditional mother comes in many different guises that deviate from a perception of the good mother of the traditional nuclear family. She not only fails to comply with a this perception, but is prima facie bad as a result of who she is perceived to be. She might be unmarried and welfare-dependent, and thus unable to provide what the experts deem essential for good mothering. If she is a minority parent, this criticism can also be rooted in stereotypes and prejudices. She might be an older mother, or an older mother who has conceived without a partner. She might be a lesbian or an otherwise non-heteronormative mother who parents with a same-sex partner, or with no partner at all. In these, and many other cases, she is perceived as someone who is unwilling and unable to provide the requisite stability, nurturing, and support.

### The Wayward Offspring Mother

This third kind of "bad mother"—sometimes also on the socioeconomic periphery—is one whose children seem to have lost their way. Specifically, her children might be incarcerated, constantly unemployed or unemployable, or are plagued by drug and alcohol problems. Even more so than the selfish and the nontraditional mothers, these women are offered as examples of the effects on children of certain choices and lifestyles. Studies and surveys are often used by experts as proof that certain kinds of mothers produce maladjusted, or even criminal, offspring.

### Bad Mothers or Flawed Labels?

This brief examination of the term *bad mother* is by no means definitive. While individual mothers can act in ways that are harmful to their children, serious disagreements remain about what defines good or bad mothering. A number of critics argue that the problem is not with the individual woman or classes of women, but with a society that does not confront its own economic and social injustices. In this sense, by vilifying bad mothers, there is a lack of consideration for the effects of a meaningful social safety net, as well as the presence of poverty, sexism, rejection of homosexuality, and racism.

**See Also:** Child Abuse; Lesbian Mothering; Sociology of Motherhood; Work and Mothering.

## Bibliography

Badinter, Elizabeth. *Mother Love, Myth and Reality: Motherhood in Modern History.* New York: Macmillan, 1980.

Eyer, Diane. *Motherguilt: How Our Culture Blames Mothers for What's Wrong With Society.* New York: Times Books, 1996.

Hequembourg, A.L., et al. "Lesbian Motherhood: Negotiating Marginal-Mainstream Identities." *Gender and Society*, v.13/4 (1999).

Jackson, D., et al. "Giving Voice to the Burden of Blame: A Feminist Study of Mothers' Experiences of Mother Blaming." *International Journal of Nursing Practice*, v.10/4 (2004).

Jacobs, J.L. "Reassessing Mother Blame in Incest." *Signs*, v.15/3 (1990).

Ladd-Taylor, Molly and Lauri Umansky. *"Bad" Mothers: The Politics of Blame in Twentieth-Century America.* New York: New York University Press, 1998.

Miller, M.L., et al. "Motherhood, Multiple Roles, and Maternal Well-Being: Women of the 1950s." *Gender and Society.* v.5/ 4 (1991).

Swift, Karen. *Manufacturing "Bad Mothers:" A Critical Perspective on Child Neglect.* Toronto, ON: University of Toronto Press, 2008.

Thurer, Shari. *Myths of Motherhood: How Culture Reinvents the Good Mother.* New York: Penguin, 1995.

Wegar, K. "In Search of Bad Mothers: Social constructions of Birth and Adoptive Motherhood." *Women's Studies International Forum.* v.20/1 (1997).

Anna Gotlib.
State University of New York, Binghamton

# Bahrain

Bahrain is one of the most densely populated countries in the world; about 89 percent of the population lives in the two principal cities of Manama and Al Muharraq. Approximately 66 percent of the indigenous population is originally from the Arabian Peninsula and Iran. The indigenous population is almost 100 percent Muslim.

Women are more publicly active in Bahrain than most other Arab countries. Many women choose not to be completely veiled. Bahrani women are highly educated and well represented in all of the major professions. More than 25 percent of Bahraini women hold jobs outside the home. Bahraini women were given the right to vote in 2002.

The most pressing issue for many Bahraini women is the need for a unified family law. The Sharia judges have the legal authority to decide divorce and child custody.

Gender roles in Bahrain show a variety of manifestations, and reflect the person's education and socioeconomic level, religious sect, urban or village background, and the degree of contact with local expatriates, as well as travel, study, or work abroad. Today many females are attending school, which is still noncompulsory. Due to strict family mores, some females still receive schooling only at home.

The sociological status of males and females as children, adolescents, and adults are clearly defined in the Koran and interpreted by the Bahrain legal system, which is based on a combination of sharia law and British jurisprudence, which are expressed through codes.

Bahraini women are able to sign their own operation permits in hospitals or use their thumbprints; however, due to local tradition, the husband, or even other relatives, tend to sign permits.

Women keep their family name after marriage, and all their property remains in their names, without becoming joint property or being held in their husband's name. Divorce is looked upon with strong disfavor in the Koran; however, divorce rates are escalating.

## Children and Contraception

Children are important in an Arab family. All men desire a boy to retain their name, and a woman will continue getting pregnant until she has a son to please her husband and herself. If a couple has difficulty conceiving, there are two in vitro fertilization (IVF) units in the country. The birth rate in Bahrain is one of the highest in the world, at 2.91 percent.

Contraceptives are legal, and free contraceptive aids are available for all Bahrain residents from the government at all the Primary Health Centers and government hospitals. Female and male sterilization are available and are being used more and more by older couples as a means of birth control. A few government publications report that approximately 50 percent of Bahraini families use contraception of some form. Abortions are allowed only under very strict religious regulations or if the pregnancy poses a threat to the life of the mother; otherwise, abortions are considered illegal. Bahrain's labor legislation protects women's right to work and paid maternity leave of 40 work days beginning from the first day of confinement. Women are also given one hour of breastfeeding leave each work day, up to four months from her delivery date.

**See Also:** Iran; Iraq; Islam and Motherhood.

**Bibliography**
Abdulla, Ahmed. *An Overview of Health Services in Bahrain*. Bahrain: Ministry of Health Report, 1995.
Badawi, Jamal A. *The Status of Women in Islam*. Plainfield, IN: Muslim Students Association of U.S. and Canada, 1980.
Curtis, Jerry L. *Bahrain: Language Customs and People*. Singapore: Tun Wah Press, 1977.
Ziskind, David. *Labor Laws in the Middle East*. Los Angeles, CA: Litlaw Foundation, 1990.

Miranda E. Jennings
University of Massachusetts Amherst

# Bangladesh

Traditionally, marriage and motherhood are of central importance to women's lives in Bangladesh. The two main religious traditions in Bangladesh, Islam and Hinduism, emphasize that marriage is a social and spiritual obligation, especially for women. As a result, there is strong cultural pressure for women to marry and have children, whereas unmarried, divorced, and childless women often experience social stigmatization.

Legally, the minimum age of marriage for women is 18; however, it is not strictly enforced. More than 50 percent of women are married by the age of 16, and 98 percent by the age of 24. Furthermore, Bangladesh has one of the world's highest rates of adolescent motherhood. One in three teenage girls is a mother.

The national fertility rate, which is 3.08 children per woman, is not particularly high. However, the fertility rate is unevenly distributed by socioeconomic class; poorer families tend to have more children than middle- and upper-class families. Approximately 60 percent of the population lives below the poverty line, and higher fertility rates among this population has significant consequences.

Ninety-two percent of childbirths occur at home and are attended by relatives or aides with minimal medical training. Lack of adequate health care contributes to high infant and maternal mortality rates. The infant mortality rate is 57.45 deaths per 1,000 live births, and the maternal mortality rate is more than 300 deaths per 100,000 live births. These numbers are unacceptably high, and the government is working to enact policies to ensure that trained medical providers are accessible to all women.

Poorer families may have more children due to cultural pressures or ignorance about family-planning strategies. Several nongovernmental organizations work to increase awareness about family planning. The contraceptive prevalence rate is currently more than 50 percent. Although some pregnancy termination, called menstrual regulation, is allowed up to 10 weeks of pregnancy, abortion is illegal.

**Patriarchal Effects**

Domestic violence is also a significant problem for mothers. Approximately 14 percent of maternal death is due to domestic violence. The Bangladeshi family law is based on religious law and favors men's rights. Domestic violence has not been criminalized, and women have unequal rights to obtain a divorce and retain custody of children. These legal barriers may help explain the very low divorce rate in Bangladesh.

Patriarchal cultural traditions also affect mothering. Since mothers recognize that their own status within the family is related to their sons, mothers often provide preferential treatment to boys. Similarly, boys are given more educational opportunities than girls. The male literacy rate is 53.9 percent compared to the female rate of 31.8 percent.

**See Also:** Birth Control; Hinduism; India; Islam and Motherhood.

**Bibliography**

Afsana, K., et al. *Discoursing Birthing Care*. Dhaka, Bangladesh: The University Press Limited, 2000.

Halim, Abdul M. *Women's Crisis Within Family in Bangladesh*. Dhaka, Bangladesh: The Bangladesh Society for the Enforcement of Human Rights, 1995.

Jahan, Roushan. *Hidden Danger: Women and Family Violence in Bangladesh*. Dhaka, Bangladesh: Women for Women, 1994.

Monsoor, Taslima. *From Patriarchy to Gender Equity: Family Law and Its Impact on Women in Bangladesh*. Dhaka, Bangladesh: The University Press Limited, 1999.

Rahman, Syed Azizur, Justin Parkhurst, and Charles Normand. *Maternal Health Review Bangladesh*. Dhaka, Bangladesh: Ministry of Health and Family Welfare, 2003.

World Bank. *World Development Report 2000/2001: Attacking Poverty*. Oxford, UK: Oxford University Press, 2001.

Julie Ahmad Siddique
City University of New York

# Becoming a Mother

Becoming a mother is simultaneously one of humankind's simplest and most complex identity development tasks. From a physical and social perspective, motherhood begins when a woman has a child. When and how women come to identify themselves as mothers, however, are complex processes that vary with each woman's unique personality and circumstances, including social demands, personal expectations, biological versus adoptive mothering, relationship roles, career/financial roles and status, health status, military status, and sexual orientation.

## Identity and Ideals

By definition, identity provides connections to established groups, and is constructed of a set of values and norms. Mothering values and norms are developed through the experience of having been mothered; community, social, and religious norms; and observing mothers in everyday situations and in the media. The specific impact of norms and values on a mother's identity will depend on how similarly she views herself in relationship to other mothers in her social group on factors such as age, locality, working status, and socioeconomic status. Further, the meaning individual women may assign to any social difference may vary. For instance, how a woman becoming a mother later in life might identify her maternal role depends in part on her judgments of other mothers.

Throughout life, an individual's identity constantly evolves—incorporating, adapting, and/or shifting between values and norms to create a working self-concept. Similarly, the mother's identity shifts and changes as her child transitions through major developmental phases—infancy to toddlerhood, preschool age, early childhood, adolescence, and into adulthood. Maternal identity changes associated with the growth of the child may depend on the social context of the child, the acquisition of new skills, and the development of confidence with each new mothering challenge. Mothering identity can also change as a result of partner status and/or the addition of more children.

The values and norms of "ideal" mothering can be in direct conflict with any number of other characteristics mothers value on an individual basis, such as autonomy, career identity, relationships to authority, femininity/masculinity, and so on. Androgynous women may have difficulty reconciling socially defined expectations of mothering as a feminine act with their own self-concepts, particularly if their partners hold traditional views of mothering and femininity. In Western cultures, women face a particularly daunting task of reconciling flexible gender roles and the independence of adulthood with the selflessness or self-sacrifice of parenting.

## A Mother's Identity: Biological and Adoptive

For biological mothers, self-identification as a mother can occur at any time from preconception through the postpartum period. Attachment with the developing fetus or newborn may have an impact on this identity shift. Nine events may impact attachment, including: (1) pregnancy planning; (2) pregnancy confirmation; (3) acceptance of the pregnancy; (4) experiencing fetal movement; (5) acceptance of the fetus as an individual; (6) birth; (7) seeing the newborn; (8) touching the newborn; and, (9) caring for the newborn. Through these nine events, the biological mother's bond with her child may shift and adjust with corresponding changes in her identification as a mother. In addition to personal events, social events such as baby showers, online mothers' groups, online pregnancy and child-development stage updates, telling family and friends about the pregnancy, "showing," the purchase or borrowing of maternity clothes, and other social experiences are likely to contribute to women's experiences of becoming mothers.

For adoptive mothers, the process can parallel that of biological mothers, depending on the reasons for adoption and type of adoption process. If adoption was chosen after failed fertility treatments or miscarriage, the mothering identity may have already begun to develop. If adoption was chosen as the initial parenting option, the motherhood identity may have started to develop with the mother's first exploration of adoption possibilities. The type of adoption—open or closed—can also impact maternal identity development. In an open adoption, the expectant adoptive mother may have a greater opportunity to experience anticipation of the birth and may even participate in prenatal medical visits and/or observe fetal movement. While each of these experiences can improve the attachment, like biological mothers, they may also serve to enhance the transition into motherhood.

## A Mother's Identity: Lesbian and High Risk

Lesbian mothers may face difficulty reconciling mothering roles within the context of dual-mother families. Along with the challenges of dealing with social responses to lesbian sexual orientation, further difficulties surround social understanding of each partner's respective role, such as in the case when one partner gave birth and the other partner did not. Sometimes, the nonbirthing partner is referred to as the "co-parent." Referring to the other partner as the "other mother" has been criticized within and outside the lesbian-gay-bisexual-transgender (LGBT) community because it emphasizes the role of "other" rather than that of "parent." Though special names may help clarify individual roles in the family, they may not be well liked by those to whom they are applied because they fail to adequately describe the relational bonds each parent has with one another and with her children.

Women with high-risk pregnancies and/or postpartum infant hospitalization in an neonatal intensive care unit (NICU) may experience additional challenges in developing their maternal identity. Some mothers may feel a hospitalized infant somehow belongs more to the hospital than to them, because hospital staff are charged with providing moment-to-moment care. This situation can also interfere with the development of a new mother's confidence in her ability to ensure her infant's survival, because she somehow feels she lacks necessary expertise to care for a vulnerable infant. Under these circumstances, the risk for difficulties in mother–infant attachment and problems in adjusting to the maternal role should be recognized.

Maternal illness may impact how women adjust to their parenting role as well. With an acute illness, a mother may require only temporary assistance and support, and if available, she may more easily maintain, albeit somewhat reduced, a mothering identity. With a progressive illness, some mothers may begin detaching or withdrawing, reducing their mothering expectations, and may ultimately facilitate the transition of major mothering/parenting roles to another. In relapsing/remitting illnesses, some mothers may experience greater guilt during relapses due to an inability to maintain their level of involvement and responsibility compared to their ability during remission periods. On the other hand, some mothers adapt more flexibly to the cycles of relapses and prepare the family for the sudden transitions.

## Cultural Expectations Versus Reality

In prevailing U.S. culture, an ideal conceptualization of "mother" often includes intensive, high-contact, and independent mothering. While the culture at large may seem to resist the concept of "supermom," the reality remains that for many mothers, the long-held traditional cultural influences within their own families and communities lead them to identify with the "highly involved mother" standard. Such a contrast between espoused cultural values and the mothering expectations may create identity stress and confusion for mothers. For women working outside the home, the expectations to fully commit and dedicate oneself to the work environment forces women to continually adapt to meet two conflicting sets of expectations.

Women married to military servicemen may also experience a difficult transition to motherhood. These mothers are often faced with numerous threats to their relationship stability, such as relative youth and inexperience in committed relationships, frequent and sometimes lengthy separation from their spouses, isolation from other mothers, frequent relocations, and limited financial resources. These factors relate not only to higher rates of depression among mothers with military spouses, but their children are also at considerably higher risk for child abuse and neglect. Programs to address this risk have shown to have positive, short-term effects.

When the reality of mothering fails to live up to one's expectations, significant distress affecting the transition to motherhood may result. Over time, some mothers simply adjust their expectations to more closely align with their respective realities. Others view their realities as consistent with their expectations, even if they are not. When mothers are unable to resolve their expectations in relationship to reality, they are at higher risk for depression, which can then feed into feelings of guilt for not living up to how they "should be." In addition, ambivalence toward the infant may develop, potentially disrupting critical early relationship development.

Becoming a mother is clearly complex. The specific course and trajectory for each woman is as unique as the woman herself. Nevertheless, when a woman becomes a mother, she can certainly expect profound changes in her identity.

**See Also:** Adoption; Ambivalence, Maternal; Guilt; Lesbian Mothering; Mask of Motherhood; Maternal Health.

**Bibliography**
Gabb, J. "Lesbian Mothering: Strategies of Familial-Linguistic Management in Lesbian Parent Families." *Sociology*, v.39/4 (2005).
Hartwick, G.A. "Women Who Are Mothers: The Experience of Defining Self." *Health Care for Women International*, v.18/3 (1997).
Johnston, D.D. and D.H. Swanson. "Cognitive Acrobatics in the Construction of Worker-Mother Identity." *Sex Roles*, v.57/5–6 (2007).
*Journal of the Association for Research on Mothering.* Becoming a Mother [special issue], v.5/2 (Spring/Summer 2001).
Maushart, Susan. *Mask of Motherhood: How Becoming a Mother Changes our Lives and Why We Never Talk About It. New York*: New Press, 1997.
Mercer, R.T. "Becoming a Mother Versus Maternal Role Attainment." *Journal of Nursing Scholarship*, v.36/3 (2004).
Schachman, K.A., et al. "Baby Boot Camp: Facilitating Maternal Role Adaptation Among Military Wives." *Nursing Research*, v.53/2 (2004).
Shin, H. and R. White-Traut. "The Conceptual Structure of Transition to Motherhood in the Neonatal Intensive Care Unit." *Journal of Advanced Nursing*, v.58/1 (2007).

Jill B. Fancher
Elizabeth Soliday
Washington State University, Vancouver

# Belarus

Belarus, a landlocked country in eastern Europe, formerly part of the Soviet Union, and became independent in 1991. The estimated population in 2009 was about 9.6 million, with 14.3 percent of the population under age 14, and 14.5 percent 65 years and older. Population growth is minus 0.378 percent, with about 9.62 births per 1,000. About 70 percent of the population lives in urban areas. The total fertility rate was 1.2 in 2003, down from 1.6 in 1993. Overall, the male/female ratio is 0.87 males per female.

Life expectancy at birth is about 65 years for men and 77 years for females. This has actually declined since the mid-1980s, particularly for men, and is largely attributable to a very high rate of heart disease. The population is about 80 percent Eastern Orthodox and 20 percent Christian, Muslim, Jewish, and other religions. Literacy is high for both males (99.8 percent) and females (99.4 percent). Belarus suffered less than other formerly Soviet countries in the years following independence, and today has a relatively even distribution of income, with a Gini coefficient (a measure of inequality) among the lowest in the world. Per capita income for 2008 was estimated to be $11,800, up from $9,900 in 2006, but inflation is a significant problem.

## Maternal and Child Health

Belarus's per capita expenditure for health in 2002 was estimated at $93, representing 10.5 percent of total government expenditures. Most health care costs (73.9 percent) are supported by the state, while 26.1 percent of health care expenses are privately funded, and about 0.1 percent comes from external resources.

Health care in Belarus is centrally organized and funded, but delivered at a local level. Excess hospital capacity is a problem retained from the Soviet years, and Belarus has a high number of health professionals, although they are unevenly distributed by geography and specialty. Health care is free at the point of use, and the government's goal is to provide universal access to care, which has been achieved in some categories of maternal and childcare. For instance, child immunization rates for common diseases such as measles and hepatitis B are nearly 100 percent, and nearly all births are attended by skilled health personnel. Modern contraception use among women is reported at 42 percent. Specialty clinics serving women's health are typical in polyclinics, and deliver abortion services and gynecological and obstetric care.

The maternal mortality in 2000 was 36 per 1,000 live births, the stillbirth rate was 6 per 1,000 live births, and the neonatal mortality rate was 5 per 1,000 live births; all are substantially lower than the average for comparable European countries.

A unique event that affected both maternal and infant health in Belarus was the Chernobyl accident in 1986, which contaminated 23 percent of Belarus with radiation. Various studies have found conflicting results in terms of birth defects or illness among children whose mothers were exposed to the radiation, and among the women themselves.

**See Also:** European Union; Infant Mortality; Russia (and Soviet Union).

### Bibliography

Petrova, A., T. Gnedko, I. Maistrova, M. Zafranskaya, and N. Dainiak. "Morbidity in a Large Cohort Study of Children Born to Mothers Exposed to Radiation From Chernobyl." *Stem Cells*, v.15/2 (1997).
Rytomaa, T. "Ten Years After Chernobyl." *Annals of Medicine*, v.28/2 (1996).
World Health Organization. "Belarus Health System Review." *Health Systems in Transition*, v.10/6 (2008). http://www.euro.who.int/Document/E92096.pdf (accessed April 2009).
World Health Organization. "Highlights on Health in Azerbaijan." (2005). http://www.euro.who.int/document/E88388.pdf (accessed April 2009).

Sarah E. Boslaugh
Washington University School of Medicine

# Belgium

Belgium is a country with diverse regional and cultural identities. The three main regions are Flanders, Wallonia, and Brussels. The main languages are Flemish and French, with a German-speaking minority. Belgium is a highly developed country, and mothers benefit from an extensive social support network; three phases of family policies support motherhood. Women also have high participation rates in all levels of education

The fertility rate is low and the divorce rate is the highest in the European Union, but children and family are important parts of women's identities. Many Roman Catholics in Belgium historically opposed legalization of divorce, abortion, and contraception, but there is currently a high use of modern contraceptives. The vast majority of births are attended by skilled personnel. Belgium's low rate of 1.65 children per mother has been below replacement rate since the mid-1970s, similar to the rest of northern Europe. Family size is small. Belgium has an explicit family-leave policy, with the regional governments responsible for family policies.

Government policies support the traditional family, with a generous child allowance. Universal, tax-free cash benefits, among the highest in Europe, are provided for employed families with a child under 18. Mothers are eligible for a 15-week maternity leave at 82 percent of income for the first 30 days, and 75 percent thereafter, up to an income ceiling; fathers have several days of paid leave around the birth.

Belgium has the highest divorce rate in the European Union. The total divorce rate was 18.4 percent in 1980, 30.6 percent in 1990, and 45.1 percent in 2000. The government provides a means-tested social assistance benefit for lone parents and guarantees three months of maintenance payments for up to three months if the noncustodial parent fails to pay support. Traditionally, Belgian men were the wage earners and women took care of the home and children. The traditional model has shifted; in most families, both parents work full time or the mother works part time. By 3 months of age, one-third of children are in regular care, and by 6 months of age, half of children are in regular care, 75 percent of whom are in publicly funded crèches or with daycare mothers; the rest are primarily with grandparents. Families receive tax credits for recognized daycare.

Most children go to school at age 3. Educational attainment is high, with 85 percent of girls enrolled in secondary education; women account for 66 percent of postsecondary enrollment.

While 75 percent of Belgians are Catholic, few practice the religion. The Roman Catholic identity was a deterrent to legalizing divorce, abortion, and the availability of contraception. Prior to 1973, the law forbade mention, advertising, or distribution of contraceptives. Abortion was legalized in 1990. Use of modern contraceptive methods is about 80 percent; condom use is increasingly popular among young Belgians. Prenatal care is covered by health insurance; virtually all births are attended by skilled personnel. Belgian family policies supporting motherhood were instituted in three phases. Family enabling (1930) focused on income maintenance for the traditional mother-at-home family. Service building (1960s–70s) focused on family planning education and childcare. Family empowerment (1980s–90s) focused on family-life balance and shifting childcare and housework to family responsibilities of men as well as women.

Famous Belgian women include Marie Terese Baird, mother of eight, who authored novels, including *The Scorpions, A Shining Furrow, A Lesson in Love,* and *The Birds of Sadness,* and Kim Clijsters, who became a mother in 2008 and was the youngest Belgian national tennis champion and the first Belgian woman to reach the number-one professional tennis ranking.

**See Also:** Abortion; Divorce; European Union; Family Values; Fertility.

**Bibliography**
Dumon, Wilfred. "Belgium's Families." In *Handbook of World Families,* Bert N. Adams and Jan Trost, eds. Thousand Oaks, CA: Sage, 2005.
Woodward, Alison E. "Belgium." In *The Greenwood Encyclopedia of Women's Issues Worldwide,* Lynn Walter, ed. Westport, CT: Greenwood Press, 2003.

Keri L. Heitner
University of Phoenix

# Belize

Flanking Guatemala to the east and Mexico to the south, Belize is a small, developing country with an agricultural economy. Sugar cane, which is raised on plantations, ranks as the country's chief crop; processed sugar is the main export. Unemployment in the cities and low farm production in rural areas are major problems, but Belizeans are working to develop their tourism. Belize is racially mixed; about half of the population has a full or partial black African ancestor. About a fifth are descended from Carib, Maya, or other Indian groups.

### Children and Childbearing
Belizean children between the ages of 6 and 14 must attend school. Belize has four colleges, but many students who seek career advancement must move to other English-speaking countries.

The vast majority of women rarely get Pap smears, which are done for a fee of $10 belize dollars at the Belize Family Life Association (BFLA)—but the fee is often waived. Abortion is illegal in Belize and thus not publicly financed. Many services such as magnet resonance imaging (MRI) and nuclear medicine simply are not available in Belize. Caesarean sections are performed very rarely: only if the baby has a transverse presentation, if the mother becomes eclamptic, or on a few other rare occasions when it is determined that the mother's life is at risk (it is not done for breech presentations or labor that fails to progress).

The impetus for Plenty International's Belize midwifery project grew out of Kek'chi and Mopan Maya people in the Toledo District. Spread out over approximately 48 rural villages, the Maya in this district have the poorest health indicators of any population in Belize. Mayan infants (birth–3 months) have a 45–55 percent mortality rate, which is about five times higher than that of the United States. A high percentage of Mayan women are anemic, which puts them and their unborn babies at risk during pregnancy and childbirth, and a high number of Mayan children suffer growth retardation due to malnutrition.

The majority of Mayan women birth their babies at home, and many of Toledo's rural villages are several hours' drive from the local hospital; transportation and communication systems are generally poor. The midwifery project helps train rural village women to assist their neighbors during pregnancy and childbirth and to provide emergency backup support.

### Agencies and Education

The Department of Women's Affairs and the National Women's Commission are among the key government agencies promoting the advancement of women in Belize. While the Belize constitution guarantees equality between men and women and defines discrimination, there are no acts that specifically define discrimination against women. Young women secure just over half of the available places in secondary schools, by virtue of selection based on academic merit. Women continue to be underrepresented in employment, especially skilled and professional positions more likely to deliver income equality. To date, the government has not pursued affirmative action provisions, especially for achieving improved gender equality in the labor force.

**See Also:** Guatemala; Infant Mortality; Mexico; Midwifery.

### Bibliography

McClaurin, Irma. *Women of Belize: Gender and Change in Central America.* New Brunswick, NJ: Rutgers University Press, 1996.

Wartinger, Lisa. "Midwifery Training Project to Begin in Belize." *Plenty: The Spring 2000 Bulletin,* v.16/1 (2000). http://www.plenty.org/pb16_1/PlentyMidwifery.htm (accessed May 2009).

Angela Stephens
Sojourner-Douglass College

# Benin

The Republic of Benin, one of the world's poorest countries, has a high birth rate and a low divorce rate; societal mores promote childbearing, and contraceptive use is low. Women in the formal work sector receive maternity benefits; government initiatives also focus on improving reproductive health. Most women have a primary school education. Vodum religious shrines are the unifying center of the family.

### Childbearing, Child Rearing, and Marriage

The typical woman in Benin who lives to 51 will birth more than seven children, higher than the World Health Organization rate for West Africa. Women in rural areas have a higher total fertility rate than in urban areas. Women employed in the formal sector are eligible for 14 weeks of maternity leave benefits, at 100 percent of pay. Most women work in the informal sector, and have six years or less of formal schooling. Girls represent about 35 percent of secondary enrollment.

Childbearing is an expected social norm. Yoruba and Goun are two Benin ethnic groups. Goun men are expected to provide a home and basic needs for their families; Yoruba women are expected to use the dowry as capital for their entrepreneurial activities and support themselves and their children. Yoruba women are more likely than Goun to be in polygamous marriages.

Vodum, recognized as an official religion alongside Christianity and Islam, is the dominant religion. Worship takes place at shrines, which are the center of the family, clan, or lineage. Introducing the child to the family community is the most important Vodum rite of passage.

Most women attend one prenatal visit, and about two-thirds attend at least four visits. Women seek prenatal care when they experience symptoms that are unusual or interfere with their daily tasks. About 50 percent of births are attended by a skilled assistant. The maternal mortality rate is very high.

Government protection of mothers is written into the Benin Constitution. The goal of the Ministry of Social Welfare and the Status of Women is to improve family health, including maternal outcomes. Divorce is legal, but different grounds apply to men and women. In some regions, divorce is not allowed

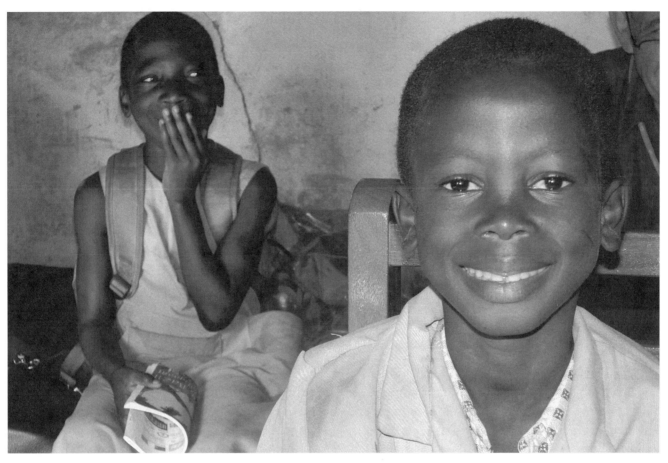

*Kamarou, a child in Benin (right), is happy that he will soon join his mother. USAID and the UNICEF-funded Le Bon Samaritain transit center rescued him from child traffickers. Benin's high birth rate and minimal formal education for women contribute to poverty.*

for any reason. Twenty-one percent of households are headed by females. The government authorized the creation of a Family Planning Association in 1971. Many women rely on withdrawal and lactation to space out the births of their children. Contraceptive prevalence for modern methods is 3.4 percent. Abortion is illegal but common; abortion-related deaths account for 23 percent of recorded deaths.

Famous Benin women include Marie-Elise Akouavi Gbèdo, a mother of two who ran for president of Benin in 2001 and 2006, and was the first female presidential candidate in West Africa. Anjelique Kidjo, mother of one, was one of the most successful performers in World Music in the 1990s and 2000s, and won a 2008 Grammy Award for her song "Djin Djin."

**See Also:** Education and Mothering; Postcolonialism and Motherhood; Poverty and Motherhood.

## Bibliography

Kneib, Martha. *Benin (Cultures of the World)*. New York: Benchmark Books, 2007.

Mandel, Jennifer L. "Mobility Matters: Women's Livelihood Strategies in Porto Novo, Benin." *Gender, Place and Culture*, v.11/2 (June 2004).

Keri L. Heitner
University of Phoenix

# Benjamin, Jessica

Feminist theorist, sociologist, and practicing psychoanalyst Jessica Benjamin is known for her work on intersubjectivity and recognition, and particularly the issue of maternal subjectivity and its implications for child development. Benjamin began her studies at Bard College and then at the University of Wisconsin at Madison. She went on to graduate work at the Frankfurt School in the late 1960s, where she became involved with the children's pedagogy movement. Upon her return in the early 1970s to the United States and influenced by both feminism and critical social theory, Benjamin continued her study of the connections between social theory and psychoanalysis.

She completed her doctorate in Sociology in 1977–78 at New York University (NYU). In 1980 she began postdoctoral training in psychoanalysis and psychotherapy, also at NYU, becoming an expert in British Object Relations and a major contributor to feminist debates on gender and sexuality. Benjamin's list of publications include *Like Subjects, Love Objects* (1995), *Shadow of the Other: Intersubjectivity and Gender in Psychoanalysis* (1997), and numerous articles in feminist and psychoanalytic journals. However, her ideas on the problem of maternal subjectivity are probably best captured in *The Bonds of Love: Psychoanalysis, Feminism, and the Problem of Domination* (1988).

## The Bonds of Love

In *The Bonds of Love*, Benjamin examines the structure of domination inherent in "ideal love" relationships and the self. Focusing on the pre-Oedipal and early mother–child relations, she explores the possibility that a child's awareness of the mother as distinct yet similar—as a separate subject in her own right—is both normal and desirable. She argues that it is only through recognition by the child of the mother as sovereign that the child's independent identity can emerge, leading to healthy object-love and a reciprocal, mutual relationship free from the distortions of domination and submission.

## Identificatory Love in Girls and Boys

In contrast with Benjamin's reading of this developmental phase is a traditional Freudian interpretation, where the mother and child are not separate but contiguous. Repudiated as the child's forbidden object of desire, she is relegated to the lesser status of Other. In this traditional interpretation, because of the mother's lack of independent subjectivity and the impenetrable attachment between mother and child, the child's sense of independence and separa-

tion from her can only be realized through the father, who represents agency and autonomy. He intervenes in their relationship of attachment, embodying what Benjamin refers to as "identificatory love." For boy children, father-identification results in the idealization of male power and a sense of independence and control. Rather than developing identificatory love with the mother, which would be a means to avoid domination or submission, instead the boy child rejects the mother if she does not offer him a "subject" with whom he can identify. In contrast, girls—who may identify only with the mother and then only if she has her own sense of self—a lack of identification with the father (who in fact does not invite it) results in girls' failure to see themselves as independent. This results in a tendency in adult relationships toward masochism, or the desire to submit to a strong man or master, and a final attempt by the ego to save itself from obliteration.

## Continued Tension

Of course, it is problematic for boys as well to have a mother without a sense of her subjectivity, and a father who insists on only his own; this requires choosing between domination and subordination. Benjamin advocates for a continued tension—both boy and girl children loving and identifying with *both* parents. However, as Benjamin further observes, in a cultural context of gender polarity and unequal responsibility for child rearing, the child's identification with both parents is not possible. In spite of Benjamin's progressive rereading of Freud and her assertion of the value of mothers' ability to maintain that tension between "I am here for you, and I am here for myself," for children, Benjamin's work has been subject to criticism. Within clinical circles, it has been said that her work lacks empirical evidence, relying too much on social theory (particularly postmodernism) and not enough on actual clinical cases (though she does cite many cases). Feminists have been critical of Benjamin's focus on heterosexual relationships without consideration of the possibility of healthy homosexuality, nor of the complicating factors of race and class in these processes.

**See Also:** Chodorow, Nancy; Maternal Subjectivities; Psychology of Motherhood; Sociology of Motherhood.

## Bibliography

Chodorow, Nancy. *The Reproduction of Mothering: Psychoanalysis and the Sociology of Gender.* Berkeley: University of California Press, 1978.

Dinnerstein, Dorothy. *The Mermaid and the Minotaur: Sexual Arrangements and Human Malaise.* New York: Harper & Row, 1976.

Shelley Zipora Reuter
Concordia University

# Bernard, Jessie

Jessie Bernard (1903–96) was an American sociologist whose pioneering work inspired the feminist movement of the mid-1960s and challenged the false aura of romanticism in which she considered motherhood to be enshrined, pointing out what she called its "hidden underside." In her seminal study *The Future of Motherhood* (1975), Bernard encouraged women "to fight those aspects of our society that make childbearing and child rearing stressful rather than fulfilling experiences."

Bernard was born Jessie Shirley Ravitch on June 8, 1903, in Minneapolis, Minnesota, the third of four children of Jewish Romanian immigrants David and Bessie Kanter Ravitch. She attended the University of Minnesota, where she earned a B.A. in Sociology in 1923 and an M.A. the following year with a thesis on *Changes of Attitudes of Jews in the First and Second Generation.* While at the University of Minnesota, Bernard also worked as a research assistant for sociologist and future American Sociological Association President Luther Lee Bernard, known as LLB, who became her husband in 1925. Several factors caused tensions in the marriage from the start: LLB was 21 years older than Bernard, and he was not Jewish, which caused Jessie's family to reject her. The marriage also hindered Bernard to develop her own career as she followed her husband to his different teaching positions. The couple finally settled down at Washington University in St. Louis in 1929. Jessie started to work on a Ph.D. there, which she obtained in 1935. In the late 1930s, she briefly separated from her husband and worked as a social science analyst for the U.S. Bureau of Labor Statistics in Washington, D.C. In

1940, however, Bernard gave up this job to start her teaching career at Lindenwood College for Women, St. Charles, MO, and eventually returned to her husband. In 1947, both LLB and Jessie were appointed at Pennsylvania State University. The couple had three children and remained together until LLB's death in 1951, when their third child was only six months old. Bernard retired from teaching in 1964, but that was hardly the end of her career. Of the 14 books that she authored, 10 were written after her retirement, and these are generally considered her most influential and classic works.

## Challenging Institutions

The encounter with the feminist movement was crucial for Bernard and, as she put it, made her see the world in a different way. After reading Betty Friedan's *The Feminine Mystique* (1963), Bernard realized that her life, characterized by single parenting and the difficult balancing of motherhood and work, qualified her as a feminist. The analysis of women's roles in a male-dominated society and the limited opportunities for women became her main line of enquiry. Bernard's later key books include *The Sex Game: Communication Between the Sexes* (1968), *Women and the Public Interest* (1971), *The Future of Marriage* (1972), *The Sociology of Community* (1973), *The Future of Motherhood* (1974), and *The Female World* (1980).

Families and social organization had been a main concern of Bernard's since her early career, but her feminist turn caused her to conceptualize the power imbalance between men and women in the institutions of marriage and motherhood. Thus, she claimed that men and women experienced marriage in a different way, and that the institution benefits more men than women. In addition, in *The Future of Motherhood,* she claimed that women should reject child caring as their only major activity and should also refuse the isolation "in which they must perform the role of mother, cut off from help, from one another, from the outside world." Bernard believed feminism should promote an unsentimental idea of motherhood and lead women to the discovery that their lives should not necessarily be centered on mothering.

**See Also:** Feminism and Mothering; Feminist Theory and Mothering; Sociology of Motherhood.

**Bibliography**

Bannister, Robert C. *Jessie Bernard: The Making of a Feminist.* New Brunswick, NJ: Rutgers University Press, 1991.

Howe, Harriet. "Jessie Bernard." *Sociological Inquiry* v.64 (1994).

Lipman-Blumen, Jean. "Jessie Bernard—A 'Reasonable Rebel.'" *Gender and Society,* v.2 (1988).

Luca Prono
Independent Scholar

# Beta Mom

Beta Mom types represent a reaction to Alpha Moms, the generation of college-educated women whose goal is to reach excellence in motherhood through the application of their experiences on the workplace to parenting. Contrary to Alpha Moms, Beta Moms do not desire to be perfect, overachieving mothers who have perfect, overachieving children. On the contrary, they believe that Alpha Moms' attempt to manage the home as a corporation may be ultimately damaging for the child. As TV journalist René Syler put it in her *Good-Enough Mother: The Perfectly Imperfect Book of Parenting*, a new type of mother is emerging, one that has learned to prize practicality over perfection and to reject the view of motherhood as a contest. Beta Moms also call themselves Slacker Moms to emphasize that they are more laid-back than Alpha Moms.

According to sociologists, the contrast between Alpha and Beta Moms is a new version of the Mommy Wars. While such wars used to be fought between mothers who wanted to stay at home and take care of their children and those who wanted to go out of the home and work, in the 21st century the battleground seems to have shifted on parenting styles. Supporters of the Beta Mom philosophy point out that mothers should build a new paradigm for motherhood that rejects the "perfectly good mother" that Alpha Moms value so dearly. According to psychologist Ann L. Dunnewold, the current age of "extreme parenting" causes women struggle to with increasing social pressure to do the right thing as parents. The stress on perfectionism that pervades cul-

ture and society often leaves mothers with the feeling that they are imperfect. Beta Moms advocate a relaxing of standards and the embracing of a less pressured life, which eventually benefits children as they learn to be independent individuals who do not feel the need to conform to the norms of perfection.

The debate between Alpha and Beta Moms makes it clear that in spite of social change and progress, 21st-century women are still considered more responsible than men for how children grow up. The pressure that this social belief puts on mothers and the different strategies women adopt to respond to it may be the cause of the distinction between Alpha and Beta Moms.

**See Also:** Alpha Mom; Mommy Wars; Soccer Mom.

**Bibliography**

Dunnewold, Ann L. *Even June Cleaver Would Forget the Juice Box: Cut Yourself Some Slack (and Still Raise Great Kids) in the Age of Extreme Parenting.* Arlington, VA: Health Communications, Inc., 2007.

Syler, René. *Good-Enough Mother: The Perfectly Imperfect Book of Parenting.* New York: Simon Spotlight Entertainment, 2008.

Luca Prono
Independent Scholar

# Bhutan

This isolated landlocked Himalayan country, sharing borders with China and India, has a population of 672,500 (2005 estimate), with a female life expectancy of 54.5, one of the few countries to have a lower life expectancy rate for females than for males. It has a birth rate of 33.6 per 1,000, and an infant mortality rate of 98.4 per 1,000 live births.

Abortion is illegal in Bhutan unless necessary to save the life of the mother, but it is widely believed that some women continue to obtain abortions from untrained providers. However, no reliable statistical data exist on this practice. Promotion of family planning by the government has helped raised the prevalence rate for contraception use from 18.4 percent in 1994 to 30.7 percent in 2000.

Infant mortality in Bhutan dropped from 162.4 per 1,000 live births in 1984 to 96.9 per 1,000 in 1994 and 84 per 1,000 in 2000. Maternal mortality declined from 770 per 100,000 live births in 1984 to 380 in 1994 and 255 in 2000. The under-5 mortality rate dropped from 164.2 per 1,000 live births in 1984 to 380 per 100,000 in 1994 and 84.0 per 100,000 in 2000. The nonprofit organization Save the Children was unable to assign Bhutan an overall rank on either the Women's Index and Children's Index due to missing data.

In recent years, the government has sought to achieve a greater role for women in its decision-making process. However, prevailing social attitudes in Bhutan have long led to discrimination against women, and as a result, they traditionally have not had the same access to education as men. This has meant that approximately 95 percent of women are illiterate, and many are still involved in agriculture. During the 1980s, less than 0.5 percent found work in the government bureaucracy. By 1989, a tenth of government employees were women, and more girls attend schools than ever before. The National Women's Association of Bhutan was established by the government in 1981, headed by Dasho Dawa Dem, one of the few women to receive the title "Dasho" from the king. There are also groups such as the Bhutan Women and Children Organisation (BWCO), which was established to help press for the rights of women and children, although much of the work of the BWCO takes place in refugee camps outside the country itself.

There is also discrimination against foreign wives, as the Marriage Act of 1980 states that foreign wives of Bhutan citizens do not gain Bhutanese citizenship. This was specifically introduced against the Lhotshampa minority, and is only really enforced against them; these wives were not permitted access to much medical care, and are also politically disenfranchised.

During the 1990s, the Bhutan government did much to change attitudes toward women, who now have the same civil rights as men, including the right to education and to vote. Furthermore, women have long been able to inherit land in Bhutan and decide on marriage. In this matriarchal society, a man goes to live with his wife's family upon marriage, and divorces are common and widely accepted. Fathers are required by law to pay a fifth of their salary for child support until their children reach the age of 18.

There have long been businesswomen in Bhutan, but there have been few prominent women role models. However, Kunzang Choden, born in 1952, became the first Bhutanese woman to write a novel in the English language. *The Circle of Karma* (2005) highlighted the country's restrictions on gender roles.

**See Also:** China; India; Nepal.

**Bibliography**
Armington, Stan. *Bhutan*. Oakland, CA: Lonely Planet, 2002.
Chakravarti, B. *A Cultural History of Bhutan*. Aylesbury, UK: Hilltop Publishers, 1981.
Mehra, G.N. *Bhutan: Land of the Peaceful Dragon*. Uttar Pradesh, India: Vikas Publishing, 1974.
Mittra, Sangh and Bachchan Kumar, eds. *Encyclopedia of Women in South Asia*. New Delhi, India: Kalpaz Publishing, 2004.

Justin Corfield
Geelong Grammar School, Australia

# Bible, Mothers in the

The Bible as a text contains a multitude of genres, stories, moral lessons, vivid imagery, and the basis for the Jewish and Christian faiths. Within this complex text, motherhood forms a central part of community life, represents a defining characteristic of women, and provides a metaphor for God's relationship with his people. Motherhood also acts as a source of maternal and birth imagery for describing the triumphs, difficulties, and developments of biblical figures and societies. Though these texts primarily center on the lives and perspectives of males, scholars and believers alike may find them instructive in understanding the lives of women living during these time period.

### Gender, Procreation, and Proper Motherhood
Beginning with the earliest passages of the Bible, gender differences and procreation are emphasized as central to both God's plan and the natural order

of humankind. In Genesis 2:23-24, with the creation of Adam and Eve, God creates woman out of man and ordains them to be married and united in this bond as spouses and parents. Later, when Adam names Eve in Genesis 3:20, he gives her a name that is loosely translated as "living," due to her role as mother of the human race.

These gender differences are furthered with the first reference to motherhood in the Bible. After Adam and Eve eat the forbidden fruit, God proclaims that Eve will have pain in childbirth and must live in subservience to her husband. Scholars have long debated the significance of this proclamation in Genesis 3:16, with some calling it a sign of punishment for Eve's disobedience and others seeing this as a statement of the realities of complex and difficult life as a result of the fall. Deuteronomy 21:18-21 and numerous Proverbs mandate respect for both parents and affirms the authority of both fathers and mothers.

As the population grew and societies formed, gender segregation and differentiation continues in the first books of the Hebrew Bible. Ritual purity concerns lead to segregation during times of menstruation in Exodus and Leviticus. In the latter book, the social roles of wife, mother, and homemaker define a woman's place in the world. The biological effect of the capacity for motherhood—menstruation—continues to be a concern in Ezekiel 8:14-15 and 13:17-23, passages that limit women's participation in religious ritual during that time of the month.

Yet, even as a negative stigma is attached to biological aspects of women's lives, these physical processes are also vital to the community's existence. In 1 and 2 Chronicles, the harsh reality of death during childbirth and child mortality demonstrates the need for women to bear many children. Thus, women are often defined by the household and family that she provides. Similarly, in the Old Testament, God is often represented as measuring the faithfulness of men by the character of their wives and the number of their offspring. This sense that God involves himself in the lives and fertility of his people continues in Malachi 2:10-16. In these passages, a message against intermarriage and divorce suggests that God limits fertility in these contexts.

One notable exception to this paradigm comes in Song of Songs. This text is the only biblical book in which a woman speaks without mediation and is the only book that does not mention God. This book embraces love, sensuality, and sexuality as defining elements of humanity, regardless of or in addition to procreation, thus adding another layer to the vision of womanhood and motherhood as defined by or limited by the bearing of children.

The Christian New Testament and the Gospels contain the life and teachings of Jesus Christ, who in these narratives leveled social, gender, and racial inequalities. In this vein, there is a definition of families by their women and children as well as their men, as in Matthew 12:50. In the letters of Paul, a more conservative view of the family is portrayed. Concerned with licentiousness and immorality and also assured of an imminent coming of the Kingdom of God, Paul questions the importance of marriage and sees it at best a place to stem sexual morality, not simply as a place for procreation (see, for example, 1 Corinthians 7:2-5).

## Mothers of Important Biblical Figures

A prevalent mention of mothers in the Bible comes in reference to the sons they have produced. One way they appear is in the long genealogical lists common in the first books of the Bible. As exemplified in Genesis 36 and 38, though these women may have had limited social standing, they are listed as part of this record of the continuation of mankind and as part of an attempt to codify the transmission of tradition and genetics through generations. Reflecting nonbiological maternal roles, various women are mentioned in Exodus in reference to the childhood of Moses. Mothers also guide their sons into morality or immorality. This theme can be found in Daniel 5:10-12, when it is the Queen Mother who advises King Belshazzar to consult Daniel. Though not an actor herself, the mother influences the action by imparting wisdom on her influential son. In Judges 17, Samson's mother guides him down the right path, while Micah betrays his mother who then encourages him into idolatry.

In the Christian New Testament, the obvious and most well-known mother is the mother of Jesus Christ, Mary. Her portrayal in the Gospels varies, as do interpretations of these portrayals by contemporary scholars. In the book of Matthew, Mary appears as relatively passive. Yet, motherhood remains necessary for this monumental event of God's birth as a human on earth. The child is conceived in Mary through the action of the Holy Spirit. Mary's constant and abiding devotion as a mother is demonstrated later in the book by her presence at Jesus's death. In Mark 3:31, Jesus's mother and brother are portrayed relatively negatively. Though it may have been an effort to save him, Mary attempts to capture Jesus after he is charged with insanity. She appears blind to the power Jesus in fact possesses.

In Luke, Mary appears obedient, quiet and nurturing, much like other women in that Gospel (see, for example, 1:38, 2:19, 51). Underscoring this more traditional portrayal, while the virginal conception of Jesus Christ is considered to be relatively definitive in Matthew, it is considered questionable by some scholars in Luke. In John, women generally form a crucial part of Jesus's life. In 2:2, the wedding at Cana, Mary is the catalyst for showing that Jesus can't be controlled by humans, even his mother. In this, the mother represents the prime example of discipleship.

In John 19:26-27, Mary is present at the cross, close enough to talk with Jesus. Here, she represents the continuation of Jesus's ministry after his death and the continuing importance of family.

## Mothers as Important Biblical Figures

The hardships that come from conceiving and birthing children play a recurrent role in the biblical text. Through telling the stories of women struggling with these concerns, lessons are learned about persistence and God's continual role in the life of his believers. Early in the Hebrew Bible is the story of Hagar, who serves as a surrogate mother to the patriarchs of Israel. Genesis 16 portrays the struggles of Rachel and Sarah to conceive and instances of trickery, such as Tamar's attempts to become inseminated by Judah. These stories, as well as stories surrounding the lives of Ruth and Naomi, demonstrate that a woman's position was determined by her husband and son and her value to society the bearing of a son. More than a determinant of a woman's place in society, motherhood also serves as a comfort for women with poor marriages. In 1 Samuel 1-2, Hannah's womb is said to be closed by God, here paralleling what happens to Rachel and Leah in Genesis 29-30.

Perhaps one of the most well-known stories about mothers in the Hebrew Bible is found in 1 Kings, Chapter 3. This story of two prostitutes who claim to mother a single child provides an opportunity for King Solomon to demonstrate his wisdom and justice as a leader, as he threatens to cut the child in half if the women cannot settle the dispute. Solomon hopes that the true mother will make herself apparent by stepping aside and sacrificing her own maternal claim to save the child's life. This is indeed what happens, demonstrating both Solomon's wisdom and a mother's self-sacrificing devotion.

In addition to the multitude of examples of parental advice aimed at both fathers and mothers in the book of Proverbs, the end of the book contains a remarkable portrayal of a mother. In 31:1-9, the mother of King Lemuel provides instruction to her young son, meant as wisdom for living a proper and devout life in the world. Carrying on the theme of woman wisdom throughout the book, these passages show motherhood as a source for wisdom to the young.

The Hebrew Bible also contains examples of mothering acts as indicators of the general welfare of society or the Jewish people. For example, Rachel weeps for her children in Jeremiah 31 and God mourns with and comforts her in her sorrow. This parallel action represents the consistency of God's presence and support and the rebirth of the society. Similarly, in Lamentations 2, mothers struggle with their hungry babies as an indicator of the horrors of wartime and the struggles of a society under stress. Here, as elsewhere, the well-being of this vulnerable part of society acts as a bellwether for the status of the society in general.

In the Christian New Testament, there are relatively few mothers as characters in the stories, beyond Mary, the mother of Jesus. However, a few examples are worthy of note. Beyond its portrayal of Mary, the book of Matthew demonstrates an appreciation of the maternal role, particularly in Chapter 2. Underscoring the subtle differences among the Gospels and the effects this can have on their interpretation is Matthew 20:20-28. Here, James's and John's mother calls for a place of highest honor for them, and Jesus repudiates her. In Mark and Luke, James and John call for this place of honor themselves, leaving the mother out of the picture. In the former, a mother's desire to have her sons as equal to Jesus is seen as distasteful and inappropriate; in the latter, the mother's perspective is left out of the picture. Another story of note comes in Mark 7:24-30. Here, the mother of a demon-possessed daughter turns to Jesus for assistance. While Jesus first rebukes her because of her shameful behavior, she persists, and he heals the daughter.

## Maternal and Birth Imagery and Metaphors

Perhaps the most powerful and prevalent use of motherhood in the Hebrew Bible is the use of maternal imagery and metaphor. Throughout the text, the language of birth, labor, and nurturing provide poetic descriptions of the struggles of the Jewish people. In Exodus 1, by refusing to kill the Jewish infants, midwives become the symbolic front lines in the birth of the Hebrew Nation. Later in the book, birth imagery such as the parting waters and allusions to labor pains point to birth as a metaphor for freedom and liberation. Throughout the book of Jeremiah (see, for example, 4:31, 6:24, and 13:21), childbirth imagery takes on a severe tone with a focus on the pain and intensity of the experience and its closeness to destruction in war.

Later, in Ruth, famine is associated with Moab and fertility with Bethlehem, connecting God's favor to the procreative fertility that assures the survival of societies. God's covenant with his people is directly paralleled to a nursing mother's devotion to her child or a pregnant woman's devotion to her unborn child in Isaiah 49:14-15. Later, in Isaiah 66:7-8, Mother Zion is said to give birth to the new nation. Yet, motherhood also serves as a metaphor for the proper and improper functioning of a society. In 2 Kings 6:24-31, the presence of cannibal mothers suggests that if even maternal instinct can be so easily violated, the world is in chaos.

The Christian New Testament contains a multitude of maternal and birth metaphors and a variety of familial language. In the Gospels and letters of Paul, Jesus and Paul are often compared to mothers, thus underscoring the attributes of a mother and the importance of this role for growth and development. For example, in Matthew 23:37-39, Jesus is compared to Rachel in mourning doomed children. Language of and concern for the family can be found throughout the Gospel of John, all in the context of creating new family within Chris-

tian community (see, for example, 3:3-10, 8:31-47, 14:1-3, 18-24, 16:20-24, 19:25-27, and 20:17).

In the midst of his aspersions on marriage, procreation, and women, Paul uses a wealth of maternal and birth imagery to describe his relationship with early Christian communities. In Romans 8:18-25, Paul uses the metaphor of labor pains to describe the emergence of these communities. Similar use is found in Galatians 4:19, Thessalonians 2:7, and 1 Corinthians 4:15. In the book 1 Corinthians 3:2, Paul describes himself as wet nurse; and finally, in Galatians 4:19, Paul describes himself as a mother to the Galatian Christians, using birth pain metaphors in 4:21-31 to hearken back to Sarah and Hagar.

The Bible contains a wealth of images, messages, and stories on many of life's questions and concerns, among them motherhood. The variety of stories and genres touch upon many of the concerns, realities, and preoccupations of motherhood. Though the broad spectrum of images and varieties of voices within the texts provide fodder for scholarly and theological debate, their past and continued influence on the lives of believers will continue.

**See Also:** Birth Imagery; Christianity and Mothering; Feminism and Mothering; History of Motherhood: 2000 B.C.E. to 1000 C.E.; History of Motherhood: Ancient Civilizations; Judaism and Motherhood; Myth, Mothers in; Patriarchal Ideology of Motherhood; Religion and Mothering.

## Bibliography

Bronner, Leila Leah. *Stories of Biblical Mothers: Maternal Power in the Hebrew Bible.* Lanham, MD: University Press of America, 2004.

Getty-Sullivan, Mary Ann. *Women in the New Testament.* Collegeville, MN: Liturgical Press, 2001.

Gruber, Mayer I. *The Motherhood of God and Other Studies.* Atlanta, GA: Scholars Press, 1992.

Meyers, Carol L. *Discovering Eve: Ancient Israelite Women in Context.* Oxford: Oxford University Press, 1988.

Rosenblatt, Naomi H. *After the Apple: Women in the Bible: Timeless Stories of Love, Lust, and Longing.* New York: Miramax Books, 2005.

Ann W. Duncan
University of Virginia

# Biography and Motherhood

Biography refers to the life story of an individual as narrated by someone other than the subject, as distinguished from autobiography, which is the story of one's self. Biography is associated with a Western literary tradition dating from the late 1500s, in which the lives or histories of notable subjects are recounted by biographers who trace, from birth to death, their subjects' personalities, relationships, and accomplishments.

## The Beginnings of Mothers in Biography

Career successes (or failures) and other feats of action take place within public or external spheres that have traditionally excluded women, who have been confined to private and domestic realms; therefore, both biographical subjects and their biographer-interpreters have historically been male. It was not until the late 19th and early 20th centuries that women's lives became a facet of biography, and even then it was only from the 1970s on that substantial inroads have been made into researching and documenting the stories of women. Feminist biography and its attendant body of scholarship have been addressing the maternal roles and identities of biographical subjects as well as that of the biographers themselves. This focus on maternity coincides with the growth of motherhood studies in the 1970s, a discipline whose scholarly legitimacy has only recently been solidified. In like manner, despite its privileging of representative male figures of the dominant Anglo-American culture, biography has also remained—until the late 20th century—outside the purview of academia. The improved status of both disciplines makes considering one in terms of the other especially possible and relevant.

## The Beginnings of Feminist Biography

According to scholars like Linda Wagner-Martin and Carolyn G. Heilbrun, the publication of Nancy Milford's *Zelda* (1970), a biography of the modernist artist, dancer, writer, and mother Zelda Sayre Fitzgerald, launched a renaissance in the field of women's biography. Sayre Fitzgerald had been known primarily as the wife of celebrated novelist F. Scott Fitzgerald. When Milford took her from the margins and placed her at the center of her own story, biographers were offered a blueprint for new designs in women's life narratives.

Feminist biography—a term referring to the theory and practice in which gender is foregrounded, and in which women's lives are examined from female perspectives—aims to recover the stories of "lost" or neglected women, and to reexamine those who have been deemed "minor." In addition, because women's lives have typically not unfolded in the same linear, action-oriented ways as those of men, and because women have had fewer role models in the public sphere, feminist biography relies less on formulaic strategies and seeks instead different patterns and structures for telling women's lives. In particular, feminist biographers and theorists redefine the criteria by which a subject is considered worthy of biographical pursuit in order to account for the complexity of women's experiences. They foreground not only outward accomplishments, but also the details of women's daily lives, such as their life cycles, interior worlds, domestic performances, and identities as daughters, wives, and—most significantly—mothers.

However, because of women's past treatment in biography, where they were judged specifically (and often negatively) in terms of their mothering, feminist biographers must negotiate how to reject age-old cultural assumptions about motherhood with the fact that today, mothering is gaining focus and value in society. For instance, the biographer who showcases maternity might be accused of capitulating to the expectations of traditional, stereotypical markers of female identity. But to downplay mothering may deprive the subject (and the reader) of perhaps the most important relationship in that subject's life. In addition, questions arise, such as can a biographer ever appropriately or adequately evaluate another person's mothering? And how does the biographer assess or weigh the input (from private papers, interviews, and published accounts) of the subject's children?

Joyce Antler, for instance, while writing her biography of educator Lucy Sprague Mitchell, wrestled with the negative attitudes displayed by Mitchell's three sons toward their mother. Further, ethical questions persist in terms balancing issues of academic integrity and insight with the increasing marketplace demands for private, and often salacious, revelations of a subject's life. Janet Malcolm has criticized the biographical treatment of poet Sylvia Plath's suicide, underscoring how prurient approaches to a life affect not only the construction of the subject as a mother, but also the lives of the children—implicated in the mother's behavior—and all future generations.

## A Story Within a Story

At the same time, theorists and practitioners ask questions about the biographer's role and stake in the enterprise. What, most significantly, are the biographer's motives for choosing a specific subject, and how do they impact her representation, particularly in the many cases where the biographer is the subject's daughter? Wagner-Martin points to the example of Eve Curie, whose biography *Madame Curie* is singularly attuned to her mother's outstanding career in science in order to restore her reputation sullied by her scandalous affair with a younger married man.

In other examples, the daughter's agenda is destructive rather than redeeming. Linda Gray Sexton, who was sexually abused by her mother, poet Anne Sexton, authorized biographer Diane Middlebrook to access and publish confidential tape recordings made by the poet while in therapy for mental illness. In a related manner, Christina Crawford published her memoir, *Mommie Dearest*, to expose her mother, actor Joan Crawford, as an abusive alcoholic.

The connection between memoir (a form of autobiography predicated on a subject's relationships with others) and biography is significant, for biographers often inscribe their own stories within their texts, just as autobiographers inscribe the stories of others within theirs. Scholars like Bell Gale Chevigny, Janet Beizer, and Jo Malin illuminate how biographers follow Virginia Woolf's dictum that "we think back through our mothers if we are women." In writing her biography of the 19th-century feminist Margaret Fuller, Chevigny came to identify with her subject by writing as a surrogate daughter to Fuller, while also calling up and even re-creating her relationship with her own mother within the text. Moreover, for Chevigny, the biographical subject and biographer may alike become metaphoric mothers: Fuller as mother to Chevingy, and Chevigny to Fuller as she maternally nurtures Fuller back to narrative life.

Beizer offers the most sustained scholarship on the topic in her examination of biographies of women like French authors George Sand and Colette, showing how contemporary female biographers seek spiritual foremothers while simultaneously engaging with their own biological mothers recreated in their biographies, producing a new genre that she coins "bio-autobiography." This term complements Jo Malin's hybrid form of an auto/biographical text in which every daughter who writes an autobiography (i.e., Sara Suleri, Kim Chernin, and Cherríe Moraga) necessarily embeds within it a maternal biography.

## The New Biography

Although biography has generally been associated with literary texts, today biography is disseminated in new media, like film (the biopic), TV (the Biography Channel; A & E's Biography series), and the Internet (www.biography.com, www.womenshistorynetwork.org), where interest in mothers is especially focused on celebrity culture. Biography.com, for example, features a section called TV Moms, in which mini-biographies of television characters such as June Cleaver are offered, along with the real women who played them, such as Barbara Billingsly. The Website is also producing a biography series called *Mothers and Daughters in Hollywood*.

In addition, the increased coverage of celebrity mothers and babies by tabloids and entertainment magazines like *Star* and *People*, as well as the spread of Internet blogs devoted them, has contributed to genres of print and electronic celebrity biography that draw attention to maternity while employing increasingly invasive and dangerous tactics. Meanwhile, the profusion of "mommy blogs" by nonfamous women means that the serial biographies of potentially millions of children are being registered and updated regularly.

According to scholars such as Nigel Hamilton, this is a "golden age" of biography. From tabloid tell-all bios to critically acclaimed and best-selling literary biographies, contemporary culture is consumed with the lives of others. As maternity becomes an even greater preoccupation for biographers within academia and popular culture alike, questions pertaining to gender, genre, and ethics become increasingly complex and vital.

**See Also:** Autobiographies; Celebrity Motherhood; Feminism and Mothering; Literature, Mothers in; Modernism and Motherhood; Mommy Blogs; Motherhood Memoir.

**Bibliography**
Antler, Joyce. "Having It All: Confronting the Legacy of Lucy Sprague Mitchell." In *The Challenge of Feminist Biography*. Champaign: University of Illinois Press, 1992.

Beizer, Janet. *Thinking Through the Mothers: Reimagining Women's Biographies*. Ithaca, NY: Cornell University Press, 2009.

Broughton, Trev Lynn, and Linda Anderson, eds. *Women's Lives/Women's Times: New Essays on Auto/Biography*. Albany: State University of New York Press, 1997.

Chevigny, Bell Gale. "Daughters Writing: Toward a Theory of Women's Biography." In *Between Women*, Carol Ascher, Louise DeSalvo, and Sara Ruddick, eds. Boston: Beacon Press, 1984.

Donnell, Alison, and Pauline Polkey, eds. *Representing Lives: Women and Auto/Biography*. New York: St. Martin's Press, 2000.

Gordon, Lyndall. "Women's Lives: The Unmapped Country." In *The Art of Literary Biography*, John Batchelor, ed. Oxford, UK: Clarendon Press, 1995.

Hamilton, Nigel. *How to Do Biography*. Cambridge, MA: Harvard University Press, 2008.

Heilbrun, Carolyn G. *Women's Lives: The View From the Threshold*. Toronto: University of Toronto Press, 1999.

Malcolm, Janet. *The Silent Woman: Sylvia Plath and Ted Hughes*. New York: A.A. Knopf, 1994.

Malin, Jo. *The Voice of the Mother: Embedded Maternal Narratives in 20th-Century Women's Autobiographies*. Carbondale: Southern Illinois University Press, 2000.

Rollyson, Carl. *A Higher Form of Cannibalism? Adventures in the Art and Politics of Biography*. Chicago: Ivan R. Dee, 2005.

Wagner-Martin, Linda. *Telling Women's Lives: The New Biography*. New Brunswick, NJ: Rutgers University Press, 1994.

Woolf, Virginia. *A Room of One's Own*. New York: Harper Collins, 1977.

Elizabeth Podnieks
Ryerson University

# Birth Control

Birth control encompasses a variety of methods designed to prevent pregnancy. Historical records dating back to 1550 B.C.E detail attempts to control fertility, which suggests that preventing conception and controlling population has been a prevalent and continuing issue facing individuals and societies for thousands of years. However, birth control has been the subject of controversy both in ancient and in modern times. Religious leaders in Jewish, Christian, and Muslim faiths have debated the morality of contraception. Additionally, the focus on population control in the latter part of the 20th century expands the morally and ethically charged birth control debate. Issues regarding involuntary sterilizations and state-controlled reproduction, such as China's one-child policy that began in 1979, continue to be matters of public concern.

A variety of methods are currently employed to prevent conception. These methods range from the natural to the pharmaceutical; each method varies in terms of its efficacy and invasiveness. From abstinence to barrier methods to sterilization, the type of birth control chosen by an individual is dependent upon medical factors and personal preferences.

## Abstinence
The oldest form of birth control is continued abstinence, which requires couples to refrain from sexual intercourse. Continued abstinence is the only 100 percent reliable form of birth control and has no risk of sexually transmitted disease. However, success is dependent upon individuals refraining from sexual intercourse and/or oral sex (sexually transmitted diseases). For many people this not a viable alternative.

## Natural Family Planning and Fertility Awareness
Natural family planning (NFP) and fertility awareness requires women to increase their awareness of their monthly cycle in order to recognize when they are ovulating. Women practicing NFP prevent conception during their fertile period by avoiding intercourse. Because NFP does not allow for other forms of birth control methods to be applied, it is considered "natural" and is sanctioned by religious groups such as the Catholic Church, which often disapproves of "artificial" methods.

Another "natural" method of birth control is breastfeeding. Women who consistently breastfeed their infants are less likely to become pregnant due to the body's release of hormones. However, breastfeeding usually protects against pregnancy only in the first six months and only if the woman breastfeeds exclusively.

Women using fertility awareness may choose to use a barrier method, such as a condom, when fertile. Fertility can be ascertained by taking the basal temperature each morning and by recognizing changes in cervical mucus. Some women also track hormonal changes with the aid of a home ovulation kit. It is important to remember that sperm can survive for several days, which increases the number of days that pregnancy is possible. Fertility awareness works better for women who have regular menstrual cycles than for women who have irregular menstrual cycles. If practiced perfectly, fertility awareness can be a successful birth control method. However, the rate of pregnancy increases significantly for a woman who does not abstain or use an alternative method of birth control on the day she is fertile.

## Coitus Interruptus

Coitus interruptus occurs when a man removes his penis from a woman's vagina before ejaculation. This method is dependent upon the man's ability to withdraw before ejaculating. It is not a recommended method, as sperm can be present in pre-ejaculate fluid on the tip of the penis.

## Barrier Methods

Barrier methods of birth control include condoms (male and female), cervical caps, and diaphragms. A male condom is a latex or polyurethane sheath that fits directly over the penis and prevents semen from entering the vagina. Male condoms may or may not include a spermicide. When used correctly, they have a 98 percent efficacy rating; if they are used improperly, the number drops significantly. For those with latex allergies, polyurethane condoms are an option. Because users often state they have increased sensation with the polyurethane condoms, polyurethane condoms tend to be more expensive.

Female condoms are also available; however, they are not widely used. Female condoms are a sheath, usually made of polyurethane, with two flexible rings at both ends. One end is closed and the other is open. The condom is inserted in the vagina with the closed end at the cervix and the open end covering part of the labia. Similar to the male condoms, the polyurethane provides increased sensitivity and decreases the chance of an allergic reaction. As with any form of birth control, there is a difference between perfect use and typical use. The female condom is about 95 percent effective when used perfectly and 75 percent effective in typical use. Male and female condoms provide an added benefit of protecting against sexually transmitted diseases. However, when used improperly or past their expiration date, condoms can break.

A cervical cap and/or diaphragm is individually fitted by a health care provider. The rubber cap stretches to cover the mouth of the cervix, which blocks the sperm from entering the uterus. Cervical caps are smaller and used less frequently than the diaphragms. However, the cervical cap and the diaphragm are used in combination with a spermicide, which, as the name suggests, kills sperm. The diaphragm has a 94 percent success rate when used properly, although improper use can significantly limit its effectiveness.

Also available is the sponge, which is a small, round, pliable barrier. The sponge works in a similar manner to a diaphragm and contains spermicide that is activated by water. Precautions are needed if one is sensitive to sulfa. Additionally, there is an increased risk of contracting toxic shock syndrome if the sponge remains in place too long (30 or more hours).

## Hormones

There is a wide range of hormonal birth control options, with their accompanying concerns; they carry with them the risk of blood clots, heart attack and stroke, and should never be used by those who smoke. The "Pill" is the most widely recognized, and is taken orally on a daily basis. Other methods of hormonal protection include injection, such as Depro Provera®; the Patch (worn on the skin); and the NuvaRing® (placed in the vagina monthly). Each option releases hormones that usually include a combination of estrogen and progesterone.

The Pill prevents the ovaries from releasing an egg. The hormones also cause the mucus located in the cervix to thicken, which assists to prevent sperm from entering the uterus. The pill is 99 percent effective when used properly.

Additionally, some types of hormone delivery can decrease the duration of or eliminate menstruation for several months. Hormones are gradually absorbed from a small, square patch worn on the skin, which is replaced monthly. The NuvaRing works in the same manner as the patch, but is placed in the vagina and removed monthly to allow for menstruation.

Finally, Norplant® is a hormonal delivery option that is less frequently used. Rods containing hormones are inserted into the female's forearm. This method is effective up to five years. The Norplant rods have to be inserted and removed by a health care provider.

### The IUD

Intrauterine devices (IUDs) consist of a small, T-shaped apparatus placed inside the uterus, and is more than 99 percent effective. The body recognizes the IUD as a foreign body and causes the level of white cells to increase. These white cells destroy the egg, whether it is unfertilized or fertilized. Recently, IUDs containing the hormone progesterone have been developed. While the IUD does not prevent sexually transmitted disease, it does carry a low risk of infection and may cause spotting between periods.

### Sterilization

Sterilization is considered a permanent form of birth control and, like the IUD and other forms of hormonal birth control, is 99 percent effective. While procedures such as a vasectomy (male sterilization) are sometimes reversible, it is advisable for those who consider having children in the future to choose another form of contraception. Tubal ligation (female sterilization) is not reversible. Surgically speaking, a vasectomy is a less complicated procedure than a tubal ligation. Additionally, the recovery time for a vasectomy is shorter. As with any surgery, complications can occur.

### Emergency Contraception

Emergency contraception refers to contraception used after intercourse and works by preventing fertilization or implantation. It works best when taken

*The most popular barrier method of birth control is the male condom. They have a 98 percent effiacy rating if used correctly.*

as soon as possible after unprotected sex. As the name implies, emergency contraception is usually used in the event that contraception failed or was not used, or in the case of sexual assault. Emergency contraception includes hormonal contraceptives such as Plan B® or the insertion of an IUD such as the Copper T®. Occasionally, a pharmacist will refuse to fill prescriptions for emergency contraception, in these cases, women can immediately contact a physician who will write a prescription.

### History: Genesis Through Medieval Times

In the Hebrew Bible, Genesis 28:7-10 tells the story of Onan, who spilled his seed upon the ground and was slain by the Lord. There is considerable debate regarding the sin of Onan. Some religious leaders have interpreted the text as a warning against masturbation, while others interpret the tale as a warning against contraception. There are other scholars who suggest that Onan's sin is his refusal to accept his brother's widow. In addition to its implications regarding contraception and religious dogma, the story has been interpreted to imply that once people in ancient societies realized the connection between coitus and conception, they began practicing withdrawal to prevent pregnancy.

One of the first written records containing a prescription for birth control is *Eber's Papyrus*, an Egyptian text that dates back to 1550 B.C.E. The papyrus contains a formula that combines lint, honey, and acacia leaves to act as a barrier to sperm when placed in the vagina. First-century Roman author Pliny the Elder in his *Natural History* provided a list of herbs that would cause sterility, and Soranos, credited as the first gynecologist, wrote of methods to prevent conception as well as medicines to produce an abortion.

In medieval times, the Roman Catholic Church condemned sex outside of marriage and asserted that the purpose of sex within marriage was reserved for procreation; any practice that interfered with conception was routinely condemned. However, according to historian John Riddle, women in medieval society would have passed on information regarding herbs that could act either to reduce the chance of conception or as an abortifacient. Common plants used in an attempt to prevent contraception included juniper, pennyroyal and Queen Anne's lace. In the East, the medieval physician Avicenna of Persia also wrote of herbal contraception in *The Canon of Medicine*, one of the most famous and influential medical texts in history.

## History: Renaissance Through the 1800s

With the arrival of the Renaissance, a new look at romantic love developed in western Europe. Reports regarding the use of condoms come from the writings of the Italian heartthrob Casanova, who used a lambskin sheath to prevent pregnancy and sexually transmitted disease.

By the 18th century, individual decisions regarding family and pregnancy became public matters of concern. Economist Thomas Robert Malthus's *An Essay on the Principals of Population* focused public attention on the relationship between population, resources, and economic development. Malthus posited that the increases in population could have an impoverishing effect on economies. Malthus's work would have a profound effect on those interested in population control in the 20th century.

Charles Knowles published *Fruits of Philosophy* in 1832. The text was influential in that it introduced birth control as a topic of discourse in the early 19th century. Knowles birth control information, however, was far from revolutionary, but it was his text that became the focal point for England's most famous birth control trial. In 1877 Charles Bradlaugh and Annie Besant were brought to trial for publishing *Fruits of Philosophy*, which was considered obscene. While Bradlaugh and Besant were originally sentenced to prison for refusing to give up their copies of the book, they appealed and were eventually exonerated.

Despite the social awareness of birth control, its efficacy did not increase substantially until manufacturers were able to vulcanize rubber, which allowed for the mass production of condoms. Initially promoted to prevent the transmission of sexual disease, the condom became an affordable and widely available form of birth control by the 20th century. Yet birth control still received social censure from Victorian moralists.

In the late 1800s in the United States, Anthony Comstock mounted a crusade against "vice," which included birth control. As a result, the Comstock laws prohibited the distribution of birth control information by mail. In England, specific law restricting access to birth control information did not exist; however, Victorian sensibilities regarding human sexuality made birth control information difficult to obtain.

## History: 20th Century

In the 20th century, Marie Stopes and Margaret Sanger became prominent advocates of birth control. Marie Stopes, a British scientist, worked to promote family planning. Her book *Married Love* provided information regarding human sexuality, and she opened first family planning clinic in the British Empire in 1921. Social activist Margaret Sanger dedicated her adult life to promote women's access to birth control. Sanger attributed her crusade to an event that occurred while she was a young nurse. Sanger was called upon to take care of a young woman, Sadie Sachs, who had performed a home abortion. As a result, the young woman developed an infection and nearly died; Sanger nursed her back to health. Once recovered, Sadie Sachs asked her physician how to prevent future pregnancies. The doctor responded sarcastically, telling Sadie to have her husband sleep on the roof. Sachs later became pregnant again, attempted to induce an abortion, and died. Sanger's devotion to the advocacy of birth control was unwavering. She was jailed for opening the first U.S. birth control clinic in 1916, but continued to work to change world opinion regarding contraception. She finally succeeded when the Supreme Court decided in *United States v. One Package* that the Comstock laws were unconstitutional.

Sanger also established the International Planned Parenthood Federation, worked to promote family planning, and supported research to develop an oral contraceptive. In the 1960s, the development of the birth control pill made contraception widely available in Western countries, and continued research has led to a wide variety of birth control options in recent years. However, birth control remains a political as well as personal and medical issue. Norman Himes, in his comprehensive *Medical History of Contraception,* noted that the future of birth control would be dictated by public and governmental support. Thus, perhaps it is not surprising that in many underdeveloped nations, women still do not have access to affordable, safe, reliable birth control.

## Population Control and Sterilization Abuse

The alliance between eugenics, population control and birth control proved a profoundly regrettable episode in history. Eugenics was a pseudoscience developed in the late 19th century that encouraged the breeding of "better" people. Therefore, people with physical deformities or those considered "feeble minded" were considered unfit. Countless numbers of people in mental institutions as well as institutions for those with developmental disabilities were sterilized without their consent. Both Margaret Sanger and Marie Stopes were involved to some extent with the Eugenics Movement; however, Sanger repeatedly reaffirmed her belief that birth control was a woman's choice. The Eugenics Movement declined after World War II, when people realized that the Nazi's adoption of several of the movement's tenets in their quest to create an Aryan world had resulted in the Holocaust and the devastation of Europe.

While a woman's reproductive autonomy is at the root of the second wave of feminism, individual's desires regarding reproduction were not always at the heart of efforts to slow population growth. In the latter half of the 20th century, many people in the West became alarmed at increasing global populations, particularly in what were considered "less developed" nations. Politicians in the United States restricted aid to poorer countries unless those countries agreed to implement some form of population control. For example, between 1975–77 in India, many impoverished people were coerced into "voluntary" sterilization.

Today in China, the one-child policy is still in effect. Instituted in 1979, women are allowed to bear one child; after her first child, if a woman becomes pregnant, she is strongly encouraged to abort. If a woman has more than one child, she is severely fined for the second child. The Chinese government for many years has been accused of using coercive population control, including cases of forced abortions; subsequently, U.S. funding for the United Nations Population Fund was cut off by President Ronald Reagan and President George W. Bush. President Barack Obama reinstated the funding in 2009, but the debate continues.

Because of the Chinese preference for sons, many girls have been abandoned. The availability of infant girls for adoption has had a dramatic impact on adoption in the United States, where many couples have opted to adopt Chinese infant girls. China is facing a series of problems connected with its one-child policy, including a higher percentage of men in the ratio between men and women, which may cause difficulties for men who wish to marry. In addition, Chinese economists and sociologists have become increasingly concerned about their rapidly aging population.

Decreasing birth rates in countries such as Japan and Germany also worry some economists, who ponder the effect of the increasing number of elderly who will need to be supported by fewer and fewer workers. Some countries have developed programs that allow for extended leave and monetary support in order to encourage women to have children. Access to safe and effective birth control and issues of population, economy, and birth control remain pressing concerns across the globe.

**See Also:** China; Eugenics; Germany; India; Japan; Pregnancy; Religion and Mothering; Reproduction; Reproduction of Mothering; Reproductive Labor; Reproductive Technologies.

## Bibliography

Bullough, Vern L., ed. *Encyclopedia of Birth Control.* Santa Barbara, CA: ABC-CLIO Publishing, 2000.

Connelly, M. "Controlling Passions." *The Wislon Quarterly,* v.23/3 (Summer 2008).

Glazer, Sarah. "Declining Birthrates." *CQ Researcher Online,* v.18/41. http://www.cqpress.com/product/Researcher-Declining-Birthrates-v18.html (accessed November 2008).

Himes, N.E. *Medical History of Contraception.* Philadelphia: Williams & Wilkins, 1936.

Hyatt, Jane, Kay Clark, and Mary Nelson. *Birth Control Facts.* Scotts Valley, CA: ETR Associates, 1986.

Purple, Matthew. "Flap Over China's 1-Child Policy Stirs." *Washington Times* (February 18, 2009). http://www.washingtontimes.com/news (accessed May 2009).

Amy Cuomo
University of West Georgia

# Birth Goddesses

Worship of the "goddess," defined variously as a deity or divine figure, idol, or a spirit or supernatural being, has existed throughout recorded history in various forms. Prior to the period of patriarchal dominance, a goddess-centered religion existed that continued beyond the advent of Judaism, Christianity, and other religions that were centered on a male God as supreme creator. This all-powerful goddess that is represented in many prehistoric cultures, the evidence for which exists in the form of pottery remains and other artifacts, was a universal symbol, considered the single source of all life.

While it is difficult to distinguish a birth goddess from this figure of the Great Goddess, as cultures developed their own mythological stories, individual goddesses emerged to represent aspects of the life cycle, including fertility, birth, death, and regeneration. The central theme of Goddess symbolism is the mystery of birth and death and the renewal of all life and earth, even extending to the entire cosmos.

In the religion of the Old European Great Goddess, which is included in the trajectory of Western religion and mythology, beliefs and realities surrounding fertility and birth resulted in the worship of the goddess.

## Goddess Symbols

Widely considered representative of the original birth goddess symbol, the Venus of Willendorf is a statuette of a female figure with pronounced breasts, vulva, and abdomen, estimated to have been created between 24,000 and 22,000 B.C.E. The statue, which is nearly five inches high, was discovered in 1908 by archaeologist Josef Szombathy at a site of Paleolithic remains near Willendorf in Lower Austria. A number of similar figures have been discovered since, predating the mythological figure of Venus by millennia, suggesting the importance and universality of the figure throughout many time periods and cultures. While there is no way to prove the original intent of creating the figures, the Venus of Willendorf's pronounced primary and secondary sexual characteristics, and the appearance of pregnancy, suggest a strong connection to fertility and birth.

The goddess-centered religion that has been identified through the excavated remains of ancient cultures suggests a Great Mother figure that is worshiped for giving birth to all things from her womb. She is documented as a figure of worship in tombs, frescoes, reliefs, sculptures, figurines, pictorial paintings, and other sources of representation, and is very often depicted in the act of giving birth.

## Roles of the Goddesses

The Old European deity of the goddess influenced classical Greek mythology, despite its transformation from a female worshiping to a male worshiping religion, whereby the male is the source of generation. The most important Old European goddesses—who became Artemis, Hera, Athena, and Demeter—found their way into the Olympic male pantheon of Greek mythology. These female goddesses, once parthenogenic (creating life without male participation), were now the brides, wives, and daughters of the Indo-European gods.

The role of goddesses changed over time, their attributes changing according to the religious or cultural beliefs of the time. The aspect of birth, as distinguished from mothering, is attributed to many goddesses at various times, while few goddesses are considered deities of birth as a single attribute. Goddesses associated with birth, from the Greek pantheon, include Hekate, Artemis, and Eileithyia.

Hekate (Hecate, Hera) descended from the Old European goddess of life, death, and regeneration. She remained powerful through Mycenaean and Greek time periods. In vase painting and sculptures she represented many phases of life: she was birth giver, mother-protectress, virgin, and crone. Hekate is still a predominant figure of worship for many, revered for her connection to the three archetypal aspects of a woman's life: virgin, mother, and crone. These aspects are analogous to the moon's phases—crescent, waxing, and full—that are also symbolic of the cycle of life, including life, death, and regeneration.

Artemis, particularly in Crete, was considered the birth giver, appearing at the birth of a child or animal. She was considered the goddess of spring, giving life to all of nature. The medicinal herb Artemisia (mugwort) was used to encourage delivery. Her Roman equivalent, Diana, was considered the "opener of the womb." In Thessaly, pregnant women sacrificed to her in the name of Enodia, in order to ensure her birth blessings.

Closely related to Hera and Artemis, both of whom bore epithets of her name, Eileithyia (or Ilithyia), daughter of Hera, is known as the goddess of childbirth and labor pains. Her Roman counterpart was Natio (birth) or Lucina (light bringer). Eileithyia was depicted in Greek mythology as a woman wielding a torch, representing the burning pains of childbirth, or with her arms raised to bring the child to the light. She had the power to further the birth, if she was of a kindly disposition; or delay it, if she was angry. These two aspects were originally attributed to two separate goddess figures, but eventually they were merged into one.

Cultures throughout the world worshiped goddesses related to fertility, pregnancy, and childbirth. In addition to ancient Greek and Roman cultures, Egyptian, Nordic, Mayan, Babylonian, Sumerian, Chinese, Indian, Eskimo, Japanese, and virtually every other culture have identified goddesses related to various aspects of fertility, birth, and mothering, speaking to the enduring belief in feminine divinity.

**See Also:** Greece (and Ancient Greece); Matriarchy; Mother Goddess; Myth, Mothers in.

### Bibliography

Gimbutas, Marija. *The Living Goddesses.* Berkeley: University of California Press, 1999.
Lerner, Gerda. *The Creation of Patriarchy.* Oxford: Oxford University Press, 1986.
Theoi Greek Mythology. "Eileithyia." www.theoi.com /Ouranios/Eileithyia.html (accessed April 2008).

Julianna E. Thibodeaux
Independent Scholar

# Birth Imagery, Metaphor, and Myth

Through language and imagery, birth has been used as a vehicle to elucidate other concepts, usually new, complex, or controversial. Often, representations of birth are metaphors for creativity or beginnings. Accordingly, birth metaphors appear in creation narratives and holy texts. Writers and other artists have also employed birth imagery to address issues such as feminism and even war.

Visual and oral symbols convey and shape a society's ideologies about the world, including the event of birth. The language and images chosen to represent the birthing experience echo and perpetuate the presumptions of a community of symbol-users. As a result, there is a relatively homogeneous comprehension of birth and birthing practices, which has been questioned by academics, practitioners, and parents.

### Birth in Religion

Scholars have drawn metaphor from religious texts, particularly the Bible, as well as used metaphor as a lens to interpret it. When reading the Hebrew Bible, it is easy to find metaphors for God such as King, Creator, and Rock. Although the Old Testament abounds with masculine language and imagery, the birthing metaphors that are present often symbolize

God's power. Additionally, there are references to God as a birthing attendant, as giving birth, and as providing nourishment through nursing. The text depicts the mother as one who engages in arduous work to bring life into the world; a life for which she will have never-ending love. On the surface, the corporeal struggles of birth are acknowledged. More significantly, the underlying meaning of this metaphor is that God's labor when creating the natural world was very strenuous, but that God, like all mothers, has unrelenting love for all life. Furthermore, when birth is evoked in the Old Testament, it invites readers to believe that God guides humans from darkness to light, just as the mother does when pushing a baby in utero out into the world. For both the baby who is being born and the person who is moving from a state of uncertainty or crisis to enlightenment or peace, the journey is difficult and can end well or badly. Despite the references to the discomforts of childbirth, the Old Testament portrays it as a source of both joy and power.

The birthing stories in the New Testament are about extraordinary births—namely, the virgin birth. Mary's experience giving birth to Jesus is not discussed in detail, but overall, is presented as a fairly serene event. In pre-Christian Rome, it was not uncommon for virgin births to be incorporated into myths, as these births were believed to symbolize divinity. In many cultures with a belief in a spiritual world, virgin births symbolized humans' closeness to the heavens while simultaneously conveying that the virgin was both pure and strong. In the New Testament, stories in which birth is referenced are often about Jesus's suffering in particular, and about temporary human suffering in general. The agony is deemed worthwhile, as it results in salvation.

## Birth in the Arts

Literature and film are outlets in which birthing myths can be challenged. In her feminist utopian novel, *Woman on the Edge of Time*, Marge Piercy envisioned a world full of artificially reproduced children, a world free of the very painful experience of childbirth. Artistic texts have also functioned to express one person's thoughts about birth. For example, Mary Shelley's novel *Frankenstein* is a Gothic novel in which the creation of a monster is the metaphor for birth. Other texts from which birth

metaphors and imagery have been excavated include Sylvia Plath's poetry, Kate Chopin's *The Awakening*, and Abraham Lincoln's *Gettysburg Address*.

## Birth in War

War is masculinized through discourses in which male virtues and characteristics are prized. Yet, birth-centered language is not absent from some war rhetoric. An example is the phrase "second birth," used to describe soldiers who live in fear of death while developing a deep love for their comrades. Instruments of war, particularly bombs, have been called "babies," suggesting the creator of the bomb is its mother. Antimilitarist artists have responded by including birthing women in depictions of war; juxtaposing life and death, and war and peace, to illustrate their perception of the absurdity of war.

## Birth in Medicine

The medical field has tremendous influence on how birth is conceptualized and enacted. In Western medical texts and discourses, women's bodies are represented as machines, a metaphor that emerged in 17th-century France. Once this metaphor gained hegemonic status, it functioned to transform the birthing experience. As a result, birth is seen as an event that demands the intervention of medical practitioners. Metaphorically, physicians are mechanics who replace midwives, and forceps are tools that replace hands. When a woman's body—specifically, a woman's uterus—is considered a machine, value is placed on production, efficiency, and control. Subsequently, if the person managing the birth believes the uterus is performing poorly, the process is interrupted; for example, by puncturing the amniotic sac, performing a caesarean section, or providing medication to quicken the progression of labor. The goal in birthing, as it is in manufacturing, is to have an uncomplicated, ordered process that ends with the creation of a first-rate product. The APGAR scores that range from 1 to 10 and are assigned to newborns one and five minutes after they are born illustrate how quality control is an established component of contemporary birthing experiences. As well, caesarean-section babies once were considered superior to babies delivered vaginally, resulting in a rise in C-section births. This trend appears to have reversed, as many hospitals now consider low numbers of these surgeries a point of pride. At the same time, the production-oriented rhetoric influences understandings of birth. The prevalent discourse in which a "natural" birth is idealized leads some women to craft unrealistic visions of their future birthing experience, only to be left feeling guilty when their actual experience is not in harmony with their anticipated one.

A child is affected by birth metaphors and myths even prior to his/her birth as the mother decides how and where the birth will occur, and who will be involved in the process. How the mother makes this decision is significant. She arguably has, over her lifetime, interpreted verbal and nonverbal symbols in multiple texts, all of which shape her understanding and expectations of birth and birthing practices.

**See Also:** Bible, Mothers in the; Childbirth; Film, Mothers in; Literature, Mothers in; Myth, Mothers in.

### Bibliography
Hammer, Margaret L. *Giving Birth: Reclaiming Biblical Metaphor for Pastoral Practice.* Louisville, KY: Westminster/John Knox Press, 1994.
Martin, Emily. *The Woman in the Body: A Cultural Analysis of Reproduction.* Boston: Beacon Press, 1992.
O'Reilly, Andrea. "Labour Signs: The Semiotics of Birthing." In *Mother Matters: Motherhood as Discourse and Practice.* Toronto: Association for Research on Mothering, 2004.
Ruddick, Sara. *Maternal Thinking: Towards a Politics of Peace.* Boston: Beacon Press, 1995.
Tong, Rosemarie. *Feminist Thought: A Comprehensive Introduction.* Boulder, CO: Westview, 1989.
Warner, Marina. *Alone of All Her Sex: The Myth and the Cult of the Virgin Mary.* New York: Alfred A. Knopf, 1976.

Lori A. Walters-Kramer
State University of New York, Plattsburgh

# Birth Mother

The term *birth mother* simultaneously acknowledges maternity and denies motherhood. A birth mother is a woman who gives birth to a child she then gives up for adoption. Although she is the biological mother, she will not be the child's mother. In societies that engage in collective mothering and regard raising children as the responsibility of a whole community, a phrase like birth mother may not be necessary. In societies that regard raising children as primarily the responsibility of the biological parents, the term *birth mother* points to what is widely considered an atypical family situation, although it is more common than popular perception recognizes.

### Adoptions
In adoption discourse, the phrase *birth mother* is relatively new, appearing as the rigid secrecy of the older, closed adoption system dissipates and the more inclusive forms of both closed and open adoption systems gain favor. Because more birth mothers now have some contact with the children they give up for adoption, both the official language around adoption procedures and the family networks involved in adoption required new ways to distinguish between the woman who gives birth to the child and the woman who becomes the child's mother. As noted in the glossary available on the Adoption Council of Canada Website, the term *birth mother* is largely preferred over awkward terms such as *real mother* or *natural mother*, both of which suggest that the status of the adopting mother is somehow artificial.

As the shift in adoption processes and attitudes continues, use of the phrase *adoptive mother*, with its implication that this mother is a substitute mother, has also faded. Socially, culturally, and legally sanctioned, mothers who adopt reject the qualifying connotations of the adjective *adoptive*. Although birth mothers have been granted certain cultural tolerance in recent years, they do not have wide social or cultural sanction. Thus, the distinction between the two mothers of an adopted child is made only in the phrase *birth mother*, the mother who is not the mother.

The term b*irth mother* also refers to pregnant women planning to give their children up for adoption. Today, before birth mothers sign the official documents, the open adoption process allows them to choose their children's families from portfolios provided by prospective parents. They can also make requests about their children's futures; for example, they may stipulate that education funds be established for them or that the chosen parents provide specific life experiences. They can even request, but not demand, particular names for their children.

### Open Adoption Contact by Birth Mothers

Birth mothers who enter into open adoption agreements even receive progress reports and are permitted specified levels of contact with their children. In these situations, birth mothers are also allowed short visits with their children at regular intervals for the first few years. As adopted children grow from infancy to early school age, the legal parents can choose to continue these visits if they feel their children are benefiting from them. They can also opt to diminish or cease them altogether. In some cases, birth mothers gradually fade out of the children's lives on their own, while in others, the birth mothers become part of their children's extended families.

### Adult Child Reunions

Women who reunite with adult children they relinquished to the closed adoption system decades ago now also fall into the category of birth mothers, even though their experiences are much different than those who remain in constant contact with their children and their families. Under the former closed adoption system, biological mothers were expected to simply disappear from their children's lives forever. These versions of closed adoption kept all identifying information secret. In some cases, secrecy was what the birth mothers wanted, but in other cases it was the only system available at a difficult time.

Since the advent of postadoption registries that provide opportunities for reunions between adult adoptees and their birth parents, women who gave their children up to the closed adoption system years ago are now finding themselves publicly acknowledged as birth mothers. Some women wear the label *birth mother* more easily than others. Whether they view the phrase positively or negatively, birth mothers rarely wear the term comfortably. The experience of being introduced as someone's birth mother is one that inevitably results in being on the receiving end of curious

glances and the focus of uneasy gaps in conversation. Polite society sometimes prevents further inquiries in public moments, but birth mothers who have come back into their children's lives after many years can expect some curiosity. Unlike the many books and guides available about being a good mother, there are as yet few instruction manuals about successfully managing an ongoing role as a birth mother.

**See Also:** Absentee Mothers; Adoption; Childbirth; Community Motherhood Denied; Mothering; Noncustodial Mothering.

**Bibliography**
"Birth Mother." *Adoption Council of Canada Glossary.* http://www.adoption.ca/AboutAdoption_Glossary.html (accessed February 2009).
"Birthmother Resources." Adoption.com. www.birthmother.com (accessed February 2009).
Turski, Diane. "Why 'Birthmother' Means Breeder." *"Birth—Mothers Exploited by Adoption."* http://www.exiledmothers.com/adoption_facts (accessed February 2009).

Myrl Coulter
University of Alberta

# Bisexuality

Bisexuality is generally defined as the ability to be sexually and emotionally attracted to person of both genders. This attraction can be expressed by maintaining multiple sexual and emotional attachments or through monogamous relationships where one is having sexual and emotional relationships with either gender exclusively.

### Bisexuality and Mothering

Bisexual mothers have no doubt existed in all historical periods, but generally their sexual preference becomes known only when the mother in question is a public figure. Famous celebrity mothers from the recent past include the German actress/singer Marlene Dietrich, the American dancer Josephine Baker, and the British author Vita Sackville-West.

Today, far more celebrity mothers are publicly acknowledging their bisexuality: examples include the American singer/actress Madonna (Madonna Louise Ciccone), the Portuguese/Canadian singer Nelly Furtado, the British Poet Laureate Carol Ann Duffy, and the American actresses Angelina Jolie and Anne Heche.

Noncelebrity bisexual mothers still face issues such as child custody (homosexuality can still be considered grounds to remove children from a home) and social stigma.

## Bisexuality Experiences

Throughout history there has been documentation of bisexual practice and tendencies. Alfred Kinsey was one of the earliest researchers to offer a scientific measure of sexuality. He created a point scale commonly known as the Kinsey Scale, where exclusive heterosexual behavior would be 0 and exclusive homosexual behavior would be 9. Bisexual behavior would place anywhere from 1–5, expressing varying degrees of bisexual attraction.

Bisexual experiences are vastly different, and there are many ways in which bisexuality is displayed. This ranges from situational experiences where one engages in homosexual liaisons as a result of isolation from the opposite sex, to transitional experiences where bisexuality is identified temporarily when moving from one sexual orientation to another. There are those who choose to identify as bisexual regardless of whether or not they are in exclusive relationships with one, both, or neither gender.

Bisexuality has long been a controversial topic since there is no common theory or agreed-upon understanding of the subject. Scholars have argued points ranging from the theory that everyone has the potential to be bisexual, to the idea that bisexuality is only a transitional phase that leads to changing one's sexual orientation, usually from heterosexuality to homosexuality. The latter theory is generally not accepted by most bisexuals, since it tends to promote invisibility and nonexistence.

Bisexuals sometimes find themselves rejected by heterosexuals because they "choose" to go against societal norms by not affirming exclusive attraction and relationships with one gender over another. They are frequently accused of being promiscu-

ous and are often categorized as gay or lesbian, disregarding their bisexual identity and orientation. Bisexuals are accused of not being able to be monogamous and promoting infidelity. Bisexuality has also been dismissed and rejected by some homosexual communities, again encouraging the idea that bisexuality does not exist. Bisexuals sometimes are not included in homosexual communities and events, even those that carry the labels LGBTQ (lesbian, gay, bisexual, transgender, queer). All of these accusations have assisted in producing an invisible, underground community of bisexuals. The pressures to conform to heterosexual or homosexual standards undoubtedly lead to frustration and issues of self-acceptance, where bisexuals feel forced to deny part of themselves to feel welcome in either or both societies.

## Woman and Bisexuality

Bisexual women in particular have expressed difficulty forging kinship and connections within lesbian communities. Bisexuality among women has often been viewed as an affront to feminism since it is generally assumed that a bisexual woman chooses to love and interact sexually with men. This negates and disregards any belief that a woman's bisexuality is not a choice, just as some homosexuals believe they are born gay or lesbian. There is much talk of bisexual women using their "heterosexual privileges" to fit in the mainstream heterosexual community, engaging in activities such as marriage to men in order to be viewed acceptable by society's standards, while engaging in lesbian relationships and sexual activities underground.

As a result of this invisibility and broad rejection by both the heterosexual and homosexual communities, there has been an emergence of bisexual organizations and communities. Within the media there has been a small increase of bisexual images that negate the preconceived stereotypes and offer a different perception of bisexuality and bisexual people. Various bisexual organizations have taken a vocal stand in combating discrimination and ensuring that bisexuals have a safe space to express and be themselves. The Internet has been a tool that has aided in forging connections with bisexuals as well as creating bridges that cross nationalities, ethnicities, gender, religions, and geographic borders.

There remains room for more research on bisexuality and women, since historically the focus of most research has been on bisexual men. There have been assumptions that heterosexuality and homosexuality is based on early-developing traits that extended over a person's lifetime. As research on women's sexuality increases, and women are becoming more self-accepting of their sexuality, this assumption has been found not as accurate for women.

Bisexual women express and claim their sexuality in a variety of ways, including marriage to either a man or a woman, or being in relationships with both. As bisexual mothers address their sexuality in relation to parenting, they also addressing their own confidence and challenges in their sexual choices.

**See Also:** Feminism; Feminist Mothering; Feminist Theory and Mothering; Lesbian Mothering; LGBTQ Families and Motherhood; Sexuality and Mothering; Transgender Parenting.

### Bibliography

Burleson, Williams. *Bi America: Myths, Truths and Struggle of an Invisible Community.* London: Harrington Park Press, 2005.

Hutchins, Loraine and Lani Kaahumanu. *Bi Any Other Name: Bisexual People Speak Out.* Boston: Alyson Publications, 1991.

Joslin, Mary. "A Bisexual Mom Comes Out." *Advocate* (May 25, 2004).

Dawn Wright Williams
Georgia Perimeter College

# Blakely, Mary Kay

Born in 1948, Mary Kay Blakely is a mother, teacher, author, journalist, and feminist who is also involved with multiple media outlets for women's issues. Many of her articles and books interweave topics such as politics, motherhood, and careers, and her novels chronicle the convergence of all three, resonating with contemporary women from a variety of backgrounds. In fact, she is often consulted for her views on women's topics, and her essays have appeared in the *Washington Post,* the *New York Times, Psychology Today,* and *Family Circle,* to name a few national publications.

### Numerous Organizations

Blakely has been involved with a number of organizations whose main objectives are to empower women to become the most productive members of society they can be. She is on the National Advisory Board for Women's Enews, which is a large Website covering news specifically tailored to women and women's issues. The main objective of Women's Enews is to allow women be completely informed in every aspect of life. Blakely is also involved with Journalism and Women's Symposium (JAWS), a group that brings together journalists, journalist instructors, and researchers from across the United States and abroad to empower women in journalism. She has served on the Board of the Directors for JAWS and currently serves on the Minority Mentor Program.

### Influential Editor

Additionally, Blakely has been a contributing editor to *Ms.* magazine since 1981. *Ms.* magazine, first published in 1971, was revolutionary in its ability to turn from an insert in *New York Magazine* into a worldwide feminist voice. *Ms.* magazine is credited with bringing feminist issues, women's rights, and women's points of view to conventional society. Another organization with which Blakely has an interest is the National Writer's Union, where she is on the advisory board. With 1,600 members, the National Writer's Union is the only union that represents freelance writers by providing assistance in all areas of life, including jobs and insurance.

Blakely is also a former "Hers" columnist for the *New York Times.* She was also on the board of directors for MOMbo, a radio broadcast that subsisted from 1990 to 2007; its goal was to discuss motherhood from various perspectives.

### Accomplished Writer

A prolific writer, Blakely writes her novels with moving prose and poignantly describe topics such as raising two sons after a divorce. Having married in the 1970s, Blakely humorously explores the crossroads of motherhood and feminism during the women's movement in *American Mom: Motherhood, Politics, and Humble Pie* (1994). She has also authored the critically acclaimed *Wake Me When It's Over: A Journey to the Edge and Back* (1989) which is Blakely's autobiographic account of the nine days she spent in a diabetic coma, at age 36, in a New York hospital. Mary Kay Blakely's *American Mom: Motherhood, Politics, and Humble Pie* (2004) was one of the first memoirs to concentrate on her experiences of motherhood. She describes raising two sons (Ryan and Darren) as a single mother (after a marriage of 10 years ended in divorce) and emphasizes the imperfect nature of her parenting. This is reflected in two of the rejected titles: *The Good Mother—Not* and *Raising Outlaws*. She emphasizes the practical difficulties faced by single mothers, from societal disapproval to too little money, as well as the ordinary problems of bringing up children.

Currently, Blakely teaches Advanced Writing in the magazine sequence in the Missouri School of Journalism, where she has taught since 1997. Blakely earned the prestigious William T. Kemper Fellowship for Teaching Excellence in 2004, as well as the Exceptional Merit Media Award and the Sigma Delta Chi Award from the Society of Professional Journalists.

**See Also:** Becoming a Mother; Divorce; Feminism and Mothering; Humor and Motherhood; Motherhood Movement; Politics and Mothers; Single Mothers; Sons and Mothers; Work and Mothering.

### Bibliography

Blakely, Mary Kay. *American Mom: Motherhood, Politics, and Humble Pie.* New York: Algonquin Books, 2004.

Blakely, Mary Kay. "Hers." *The New York Times* (March 19, 1981). www.nytimes.com (accessed December 2008).

Blakely, Mary Kay. *Wake Me When It's Over.* New York: Time Books, 1989.

"HerStory." *Ms.* http://www.msmagazine.com/about.asp (accessed February 2009).

National Writer's Union. "About the NWU." www.nwu.org (accessed January 2009).

University of Missouri. "2004 Kemper Fellows: Mary Kay Blakely." http://kemperawards.missouri.edu/fellows/2004/blakely.php (accessed January 2009).

Jennifer L. Burkett
University of Central Arkansas

# Body Image

Much has been written in the area of body image in pregnancy and postpartum. A person's body image is comprised of a multidimensional mélange of feelings and perceptions of their own body-filtered and reflected through sociocultural prescriptions of the ideal body size and shape. Body image fluctuates and is regulated by global self-esteem (the totality of thoughts and emotions regarding oneself). Societal prescriptions of size and beauty are intricately tied to global self-esteem. In fact, decades of research demonstrates a significant overlap between body image and self-image. In essence, body esteem arises out of a multidimensional experience, in which females compare their appearance against personal and social standards within their environment. Sanctioned by external forces and saturated with a barrage of the ultra-thin female body ideal, women's capacity to maintain a positive body image is threatened on a daily basis, particularly in the experience of pregnancy.

## Self-Esteem and Body Image

Researchers demonstrate the powerful connection between self-esteem and body image. Social comparison with fashion models and exposure to unrealistic media images of female beauty is shown to lower body satisfaction and body image. Overall, researchers reveal that in Western countries, lower self-esteem and higher body dissatisfaction are more evident among females than males, despite the fact that obesity rates are higher among males. Women feeling discontented about their bodies is pervasive enough, even 25 years ago, for the term *normative discontent* to be coined and commonly used to describe the experiences women have in relation to their bodies. Normative discontent implies that being unhappy with one's body and feeling too fat is so common for women in our culture, that it is now considered a part of the normal experience of being a woman.

The societal value of thinness and society's tendency to base much of a woman's value on appearance bear tremendous significance on women's relationships with their bodies. Societal messages impress upon women that their physical appearance is of utmost importance. Culturally, women are schooled to relate to their bodies as objects, tools, or weapons in the marketplace of social relations. A woman's identity is deeply intertwined with a sense of her body and her attractiveness. The current media standard for female beauty is a young, white, thin woman (with breast implants); the perpetuation of this construction has extraordinary implications for the relationship women have with their bodies. Increased rates of dieting, weight preoccupation, eating disorders, and cosmetic surgeries are associated with the prevailing messages of thin female ideal, and social comparisons with impossibly beautiful models and images are highly correlated with personal body dissatisfaction. As such, the development of a personal and stable body image is extremely problematic and precarious for women.

## Pregnancy and Body Image

Many women report being caught between two conflicting cultural messages: the standard of beauty requires a slim figure, and women draw self-esteem from being considered attractive. During pregnancy, body image may become an even greater issue for many women. Some women feel elated and embrace the changes in their pregnant bodies, while other women feel anxious, discontented, and have great difficulty accepting their changing body. Most of the time, a woman's experience vacillates between the two: disdain (feeling fat and ugly) and love (feeling pride) of her pregnant body. Notably, during pregnancy, a woman's body image may vary remarkably over the time period and continue postpartum. A positive body image may be more keenly felt in women who embrace the time in their lives when there is a socially accepted standard to have a larger belly and ample body shape. She may experience a renewed freedom to be heavier and enjoy signifying to the world that her body is producing life and that she will be a mother. For some women, the social status engendered with pregnancy induces further pride in identifying with the role that a maternal body inscribes.

Clearly, pregnancy affects every woman differently, and subsequent pregnancies in the same woman will also affect her body image differently. Women who are not happy, or who reject their pregnancy, may feel anger at their body changes and

their body image may be very low. Most women feel a myriad of feelings in association to their pregnant body, which can vary on a monthly, weekly, or even daily (even hourly) basis. One's body image during the trimesters of pregnancy also varies. Generally, in the first trimester women often report feeling fat when their clothes no longer fit well; however, they do not have the characteristic belly to indicate that they are pregnant. This can be a difficult time for a woman who feels she appears as if she's just put on some extra weight. The fear of being perceived as fat can greatly influence how a woman feels about herself. In the second trimester, often a woman's stomach begins to harden and protrude into the telltale pregnant shape. She may rejoice and celebrate in this distinct shape; however, she may also feel negatively about her body. Women may continue to struggle with feeling overweight, and may monitor the pounds as they increase. Voluptuous breasts and a larger stomach help some women to feel ultra-

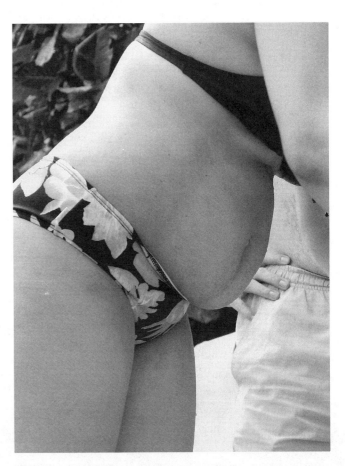

*The loss of elasticity in the midsection after pregnancy can affect how a woman feels about her body.*

feminine, strong, and sexual. Other women, however, simply abhor the added weight, stretch marks, and belly that pregnancy induces. Some women fight with their bodies continuously in order to control their weight.

## Cultural Factors Involved in Body Image

But there is also a societal expectation for women to become mothers, a process that involves radical change of the body during pregnancy and often results in weight gain that persists after delivery (the current medical recommendation is to gain 15–35 pounds, depending on previous body weight). Studies have found that over half of pregnant women are dissatisfied with their bodies, and many women feel social pressure to return to their pre-pregnancy weight soon after giving birth.

Studies have found that even women satisfied with their body image during pregnancy often feel overweight and dissatisfied in the postpartum period, feelings which are associated with depression and diminished desire to return to sexual activity. Dissatisfaction is highest among women of high socioeconomic status, who engage in more weight monitoring in the postpartum period and state greater belief that they will lose the pregnancy weight.

The rise in Hollywood celebrities glamorizing pregnancy and donning protruding bellies in a classic thin body, and the multitude of pregnancy books prescribing an exact amount of weight gain, promotes an ideal that may pressure women into a body surveillance project. A woman's body image may be affected greatly by these unrealistic standards imposed upon her, not only about the weight she gains and its placement, but also how quickly it is shed after birth.

Celebrity mothers themselves are not exempt from these expectations: for instance, Britney Spears (mother of two) was severely criticized for appearing on MTV's Music Video Awards in 2007 and showing off her no-longer-girlish figure in a bikini.

## Body Image in Postpartum

Body image postpartum is also an important consideration. Body weight gained during pregnancy, particularly in the belly, does not often disappear quickly after the birth of the baby. Often, immediately after birth, a woman may feel that she maintains much more body weight than she anticipated, which can be disheartening to the woman. Over the years, the loss of elasticity in her stomach due to multiple pregnancies, having stretch marks, and other body changes such as breast size and shape influences a woman's body image. These experiences of the female body evolution after having children often leave women feeling that they are an anomaly, when in fact, women with stretch marks and other body indicators of childbearing are much more the norm than the ultra-thin media images of women so flagrantly portrayed.

**See Also:** Depression; Eating Disorder; Emotions; Fears; Sexuality and Mothering.

### Bibliography

Goldman, Leslie. *Locker Room Diaries: The Naked Truth About Women, Body Image, and Reimagining the "Perfect" Body.* Cambridge, MA: Da Capo Press, 2007.

Norsigian, Judy and Boston Women's Health Book Collective. *Our Bodies, Ourselves: Pregnancy and Birth.* Clearwater, FL: Touchstone, 2008.

Wykes, Maggie and Barrie Gunter. *The Media and Body Image: If Looks Could Kill.* Thousand Oaks, CA: Sage, 2005.

Gina Wong-Wylie
Athabasca University

# Bolivia

Bolivia is a lower-middle-income country in South America with a population of just over 9 million and a Gross Domestic Product (GDP) per capita of $2,819 in 2005. It is one of the poorest countries on the continent. Life expectancy at birth is 64.7 years. According to official estimates, 32 percent of the population lives on less than $1 per day, and 65 percent of the population lives below the national poverty line. A high percentage of the population is of indigenous origins: 61 percent at the last census in 2001.

Bolivia signed the Convention on the Elimination of All Forms of Discrimination Against Women in

1990. However, gender-based discrimination continues to be widespread. Life expectancy for women is only 62.6 years, 4.3 years lower than men's. Women are also less likely to have attended school. Women's labor market participation has been increasing steadily, and 62.6 percent of all women are now in paid employment. Women on average earn just over half of men's average income ($2,059 as opposed to $3,584) and are overrepresented in the informal sector. According to one study, motherhood does not have negative effects on women's wages.

Most Bolivian women are mothers. Despite the fact that there has been a marked increase in the percentage of women who place education and paid work as their top priority, motherhood and marriage continues to be a fundamental part of women's identity. The fertility rate currently stands at 4 births per woman, down from 6.5 during the 1970s. According to a survey carried out in 2003, 12.6 percent of surveyed teenage girls already had a child, while 3.6 percent were pregnant.

## Maternal Health

Maternal mortality continues to be the highest in the region: 650 women die each year because of complications in pregnancy and birth. There are on average 230 maternal deaths per 100,000 live births, but in some rural areas, the rate reaches 887 per 100,000 live births. Maternal deaths are caused by hemorrhage, induced abortion, and hypertension. Abortions are illegal, except for a small minority of cases. Most women who decide to terminate their pregnancy have to do so illegally; between 27 and 35 percent of maternal deaths are abortion related. The remainder of maternal deaths depends on the availability and access to skilled birth attendants.

Between 1997 and 2005, only 67 percent of births were attended by skilled professionals. Access to and use of skilled birth attendants is strongly influenced by the mother's income. Rural and indigenous women are least likely to have access to modern health services. A major problem is that the national health system is not perceived to be sensitive to indigenous beliefs and practices. The United Nations Population Fund is currently working with the Bolivian government and Pan-American Health Organization to develop a culturally sensitive program for midwives. Bolivia celebrates Mothers' Day on May 27.

**See Also:** Abortion; Maternal Mortality; Poverty and Mothering; Teen Mothers.

**Bibliography**
Armstrong, Kate. *Bolivia (Country Guide)*, 6th Edition. Oakland, CA: Lonely Planet, 2007.
Koblinsky, Marjorie A., ed. *Reducing Maternal Mortality: Learning From Bolivia, China, Egypt, Honduras, Indonesia, Jamaica, and Zimbabwe (Health, Nutrition and Population Series)*. Washington, DC: World Bank Publications, 2003.
Spatz, Julius. *Poverty and Inequality in the Era of Structural Reforms: The Case of Bolivia*. New York: Springer, 2006.

Tanja Bastia
University of Manchester

# Bombeck, Erma

Erma Bombeck was a humorist whose column, *At Wit's End*, was published between 1965 and her death in 1996. She also wrote 15 books, most of which became best sellers. Bombeck's specialty was presenting a wry, humorous look at parenting, generally through the lens of her own middle-class, suburban life. She wrote about the challenges of both child raising and homemaking, often presenting these tasks as genuinely intolerable, yet always through humor. Like Betty Friedan, Bombeck unmasked the boredom, frustration, overall dreariness, and lack of respect and appreciation that many suburban mothers were feeling. Her ability to label and de-romanticize the mundane details of mother work was in stark contrast to other motherhood narratives that tended to emphasize the perceived selflessness and loving kindness of all mothers. Bombeck broke from the traditional, and in some ways stereotypical, version of motherhood in doing later activist work, most notably toward the promotion of the American Equal Rights Amendment (ERA).

Bombeck's mother, also named Erma, married Cassius Edwin Fiste at the age of 14 and gave birth to Erma two years later, on February 12, 1927, in Dayton, Ohio. Following Fiste's death in 1929, Bombeck's mother worked as a factory employee for two years until she remarried. For the years between Bombeck's mother's marriages, the two women lived in a much more industrial part of Dayton, with much of Bombeck's care being provided by her maternal grandparents. For these years, Bombeck's family structure differed notably from the nuclear families she was familiar with prior to her father's death. Watching her mother's entry into the work force galvanized Bombeck and clearly made an impression that women's abilities extended far beyond the home.

Following her graduation, Bombeck was hired as a full-time worker for the *Dayton Journey-Herald*, largely specializing in the "women's pages," articles on household tips for juggling priorities and ridding linens of stains. While at the University of Dayton, Bombeck met and married Bill Bombeck.

## Honest Humor

Bombeck struggled with infertility, and in 1954 became a mother to her eldest child through adoption; two subsequent children were born to Bombeck in 1955 and 1958. Bombeck left her job to work as a full-time homemaker between 1954 and 1963. As the mother of three young children, Bombeck wrote of being subsumed by her children's needs; while devoted to her family, she was nonetheless clear sighted about the many difficulties and frustrations of mother work. Her decision to return to paid employment centered on this frustration: Bombeck wrote a few sample columns laughing at the challenges of suburban motherhood and submitted them to a local paper. After a short time her column, which came to be titled *At Wit's End,* was picked up by the *Dayton Journey-Herald* and was subsequently syndicated worldwide. Her fame led her to a regular spot on *Good Morning America*, a short-lived sitcom, and numerous other projects.

Bombeck distanced herself from the women's movement, viewing it as elitist and condescending. Nonetheless, she did favor the advancement of equality for women. While refusing to discuss gender equality within her books and columns, Bombeck nonetheless began to take on a more political role. Between 1978–80 she toured the United States speaking in favor of the ERA, and during the Carter administration, she sat on the President's Advisory Commit-

tee for Women. In all her political work, Bombeck remained committed to a centrist position and argued fervently for both equality and tradition.

In 1996, Erma Bombeck died from complications of polycystic kidney disease.

**See Also:** Humor and Motherhood; Stay-at-Home Mothers; Teen Mothers.

### Bibliography
Bombeck, E. *Motherhood: The Second Oldest Profession.* New York: McGraw Hill, 1983.
Edwards, S. *Erma Bombeck: A Life in Humor.* New York: Avon Books, 1997.

May Friedman
York University

# Bosnia and Herzegovina

Bosnia, a country in the Balkans that was formerly a part of Yugoslavia, has a population of just under 4 million (2007 estimate), with a female life expectancy of 81.9. It has a birth rate of 8.8 per 1,000, and an infant mortality rate of 9.8 per 1,000 live births. The crude divorce rate in the country is 0.4 divorces per 1,000 marriages (2004 figures).

Abortion on request is available up to 10 weeks gestation; after that time, a committee must determine if abortion is necessary to save the women's life or health, if the child has a serious congenital defect, or if the pregnancy is the result of rape. After 20 weeks, abortion is legal only to save the life or health of the mother. Family planning services are available, but as of 2000 only 16 percent of women reported using modern contraception. Save the Children was unable to assign Bosnia and Herzegovina an overall rank on either the Women's Index and Children's Index due to missing data.

The employment-to-population ratio for women age 15 and over in Bosnia and Herzegovina is 51.6, lower than in other Balkan countries. Strict employment protection makes it difficult for women to re-enter the labor market after having children. One year of maternity leave is provided, and the employee is guaranteed to be rehired in the same job.

From late medieval times, Bosnia and Herzegovina was occupied by the Turks, and as a result Islam remains the majority religion in the country, with significant Serbian Orthodox and Croatian Catholic minorities. Historically, the vast majority of women in villages were homemakers; their role was heavily involved in caring for children and looking after the home. In the two major cities, Sarajevo and Mostar, as well as in more multicultural Bosnian societies, wealthier women managed to combine motherhood with involvement in the local political life, and encouraged others to do the same. This is reflected in the fictional character of Madame Daville in the town of Travnik, in Ivo Andric's *The Days of the Consuls* (1992). Andric emphasizes the role of the French Revolutionary and Napoleonic ideas in changing the perspectives of the wealthier citizens.

## War and Motherhood

In 1878 the Austrians annexed Bosnia, and there were even more dramatic changes in the provision of health care for women in cities, with more modern midwifery. Within the Kingdom of Yugoslavia during the 1920s and the 1930s, there were some further improvements, but much of the area's infrastructure was destroyed in World War II. It was not until the 1950s that the new Communist government of Yugoslavia started an organized program to reduce the infant mortality rate. Women were given more civil rights and were able to more easily gain access to government social security payments to help bring up children, and also gain easier access to divorce. Many women also managed to find paid work in farms and factories, and maternity leave was introduced.

The breakup of former Yugoslavia led to fighting throughout Bosnia during the 1990s. This conflict sparked numerous atrocities, including mass rape used methodically by some groups against others. Studies estimate that as many as one in seven Bosnian women were raped by Serb forces, and many were abused for months and prevented from obtaining an abortion. Women suffering from these experiences report high rates of depression, suicidal ideation, social phobia, posttraumatic stress disorder, and sexual dysfunction.

Since the end of the war in 1995, the new government has sought to improve the infrastructure of the country, again with funds provided by the European Union and elsewhere. The country's fertility rate has fallen from 2.4 in 1975 (one of the highest in Europe) to 1.2 by 1999.

**See Also:** Conflict Zones, Mothering in; Croatia; Macedonia; Serbia; War and Mothering.

## Bibliography

Andric, Ivo. *The Days of the Consuls*. Coleford, Gloucestershire, UK: Forest Books, 1992.
Commission for International Relations of the Federation of Women's Associations of Yugoslavia. *Women's Rights in Yugoslavia*. 1961.
Cuvalo, Ante. *Historical Dictionary of Bosnia and Herzegovina*. Lanham, MD: Scarecrow Press Inc, 1997.
Duric, Suzana and Gordana Dragicevic. *Women in Yugoslav Society and Economy*. Belgrade: Medunarodna Politika, 1965.
Malcolm, Noel. *Bosnia: A Short History*. New York: Macmillan, 1994.
Ramet, Sabrina, ed. *Gender Politics in the Western Balkans: Women and Society in Yugoslavia and the Yugoslav Successor States*. University Park: Pennsylvania State University Press, 1999.

Justin Corfield
Geelong Grammar School, Australia

# Botswana

In Botswana, motherhood is a central, multilayered role within the sociocultural institutions of marriage and the family. In this context, marriage, family, childbearing, and child rearing are intertwined. Traditionally, marriage was almost compulsory, and so was childbearing. However, the Setswana (the traditional people of Botswana), which was mainly founded on marriage, has been transformed into many different family forms: These include single parents; cohabitant families; and blended, adoptive, and foster families, with the single mother family as the most common and a growing phenomenon in Botswana.

African women marry at a much earlier age than women elsewhere. For Botswana, the average age at first marriage up to the late 1990s was 26 years for women, compared to earlier decades when girls married as early as 20 years of age or younger. Therefore, early pregnancies and early motherhood have become subjects of research and intervention programs in Africa. The mean age at first birth in Botswana is recorded at 18, and the majority of women aged 15–49 who have ever been pregnant have become pregnant for the first time at age 15–19. A decline is also indicated in the proportion of women currently married, concurrent to an increase in cohabitation relationships. With Botswana currently among the hardest hit by the human immunodeficiency virus (HIV) and acquired immunodeficiency syndrome (AIDS) pandemic, the problem of teenage motherhood is a great health concern. The transition in roles for young girls from child to mother without much preparation is daunting, and usually has serious psychological challenges. In spite of this, some of the proposed mechanisms for addressing it, such as sex education and use of contraceptives (which is only used by 32 percent of married women) are still facing sociocultural bottlenecks.

### Motherhood Desire and Privilege

While the cultural perceptions that value motherhood remain intact, the changed family forms show eroded importance of marriage as a precondition to motherhood. Premarital childbearing in Botswana is on the increase, and studies identify an almost universal desire for parenthood by Botswanian women, regardless of whether or not they are married. In the early 1980s, only 53 percent of women aged between 25–29 had ever been married, but 88 percent of those had at least one child. Both married and unmarried women obtain a positive sense of self worth from motherhood. It guarantees them dignity and respect for having fulfilled one of the key obligations particular to marriage.

Motherhood positions women well in the family hierarchies in Botswana and gives them certain powers and privileges, such as partaking in mother-directed cultural functions such as aiding in the delivery of a baby. The dichotomy of mother and nonmother is used in this context as a basis for intragender diversity and discrimination. While there is sympathy for the demise of barren women, this is still viewed with contempt and shame, mak-ing the issue of whether a bride-to-be will bear children a cause for anxiety for young girls. In spite of its reduced role in motherhood, marriage still legitimizes the identity of children born into it.

**See Also:** Becoming a Mother; Cross-Cultural Perspectives on Motherhood; Feminist Theory on Mothering; Future of Motherhood; History of Motherhood.

**Bibliography**

Arnfred, Signe. "Images of 'Motherhood'–African and Nordic Perspectives." *Jenda: A Journal of Culture and African Women Studies*, v.4 (2003).

Locoh, Therese. *Early Marriage and Motherhood in Sub-Saharan Africa*. Farmington Hills, MI: Gale Group, 2000.

Pitso, Joseph M.N. and Gordon A. Carmichael. "Premarital Childbearing in Thamaga Village, Botswana." *Journal of Population Research*, v.20/2 (2003).

Bantu L. Morolong
University of Botswana

# Brain, Child

*Brain, Child* is a quarterly magazine published in the United States. Subtitled "the magazine for thinking mothers," *Brain, Child* specializes in literary, scholarly, and self-reflective articles for mothers and other caregivers. Articles address a range of topics and are submitted by freelance writers. The magazine does not subscribe to any specific parenting philosophy and encourages a range of beliefs and opinions.

*Brain, Child* began in March 2000 as a collaborative venture between editors-in-chief Stephanie Wilkinson and Jennifer Niesslein. Within a matter of months, the magazine achieved industry success, receiving a prestigious Utne Independent Press Award as one of the five best new magazines in the country. The magazine is both well regarded and popular, boasting approximately 36,000 readers worldwide, three-quarters of whom subscribe to the magazine.

Each issue contains a number of components, including responses to research studies, legislative decisions, and other important news for mothers and families. In addition, each issue contains a debate in the form two articles taking competing positions on a topic, as well as book reviews and fiction. Personal essays and feature articles comprise the bulk of the magazine. These pieces maintain the diversity of the publication, representing a relatively wide range of positions and topics, including motherhood and homelessness, lesbian parenting, raising only children, surrogacy, the mothers' movement, and many more. Although the magazine does not privilege any one position with respect to political or controversial topics, there is an overarching focus on maternal empowerment as well as solidarity among mothers.

### Wealthy, Highly Educated Readership

While *Brain, Child* welcomes a diversity of opinion and parenting style, its readers are relatively homogenous. A readership survey undertaken in 2004 found that 90 percent of *Brain, Child* subscribers own their own home, and the median household income of readers was $125,000. In addition, *Brain, Child* readers are extremely well educated, with 96 percent holding undergraduate degrees and two-thirds of all readers having undertaken or completed graduate studies. Finally, the vast majority (95 percent) of mothers who subscribe to *Brain, Child* are either married or partnered. Given the uniformity of readers, it is therefore not surprising that while *Brain, Child* presents a heterogeneity of topics, within that range topics are generally those relevant to a middle-class, educated reader.

In terms of publishing philosophy, *Brain, Child* encourages respect and community within its pages, definitively rejecting the call toward intensive mothering. The foregrounding of personal narrative privileges a "life politic" approach that minimizes societal inequality and focuses on personal experience and resistance. This philosophy seeks to reach mothers who may find their personal privilege eroded as they parent. In terms of tone, the magazine is stylistically similar to *The New Yorker* and *Salon*, but, in its focus on mothers, stakes new territory for analysis.

The magazine's byline has generated some controversy, in terms of both the potential elitism of "thinking mothers" as well as the perceived exclusion of fathers. It should be noted that fathers are both reg-

ular contributors as well as readers of the magazine. Despite concern and debate, the magazine is flourishing as it enters its tenth year of publication.

**See Also:** Academe and Mothering; *Literary Mama*; Literature and Mothers.

**Bibliography**
*Brain, Child*. "About Us." http://www.brainchildmag .com (accessed May 2009).
Carchrae, Michelle. "Review of *Brain, Child* Magazine: Great Writing That Presents Complex and Emotional Parenting Issues." (June 19, 2008). http://parenting resources.suite101.com/article.cfm/review_of_brain_ child_magazine (accessed May 2009).

May Friedman
York University

# Brazil

The Federative Republic of Brazil, once a Portuguese colony, is an economic power with a diverse population and steadily declining birthrate. Mothers working in the formal sector are eligible for paid maternity leave. Traditional gender roles are shifting; formal unions are becoming less common, and divorce is legal. Most Brazilian women use some form of birth control, and most receive prenatal care and are attended at birth by skilled personnel. Brazilian law guarantees the right to family planning and free access to education through secondary school and the Brazilian Constitution supports the rights of working women. The overall birthrate in Brazil, which was 6.2 in 1960 and 4.7 in 1975, has decreased rapidly since the 1980s, to the 2008 rate of 2.2 children per mother. The decrease is partly attributable to a high sterilization rate. The fertility rate actually increased 20 percent between 1970–91 for women aged 15–19. Many teen mothers are from rural areas who lack access to education.

Under the Constitution, working mothers in the formal sector are eligible for a paid maternal leave of 120 days following the birth. Mothers have two nursing breaks each day. About half the Brazilian population works in the informal sector.

The number of legally sanctioned unions is decreasing in Brazil, and the number of female-headed households is rising. A quarter of families are female-headed, compared to 13 percent in 1970. Divorce was legalized in 1977; the divorce rate was 3.7 percent in 2002.

## Cultural Conceptions of Motherhood in Brazil

Colonization, slavery, and industrialization have influenced cultural conceptions of motherhood. From the colonial period through the 1970s, a mother's place was with her children. Gender roles were divided along the Mediterranean concept of *marianismo*, which attributes to women the central role of selfless mother; and *machismo*, reflected in the husband's dominance. The greater female autonomy in West Africa has survived in Afro-Brazilian communities, tempering the traditional model.

Other factors lessening the traditional split in gender roles include a weakening association between marriage and reproduction, and the industrialization of Brazil. Brazilian mothers remain in charge of the children and the home. If the mother is absent, another woman, often a relative, assumes this role.

Catholicism has influenced Brazilian attitudes toward reproductive rights, gender, and family issues. While 76 percent of Brazilians are nominal Roman Catholics, the religious influence of slaves from West Africa continues to be strong. Afro-Brazilian religious icons include many female role models of strong, defiant women. Brazilian mothers and wives resisted authoritarian military regimes, with support of the Catholic Church and leftist politicians.

## Family Planning, Education, and Prenatal Care

Family planning was declared a right in the 1988 Constitution, and the sale of contraceptive devices is not restricted. More than three-quarters of married women use contraceptives, but use is lower among women aged 15–24 and women in the rural northeast, where one-third of the population resides. An estimated 1.4 million illegal abortions take place each year, with a high rate among teenagers. Brazilian anthropologists have found that poor Brazilian Roman Catholic women distinguish the religious

prohibition against taking a life and the medical practice of preventing contraception. Sterilization is becoming increasingly common among younger women and poor women who may lack information about and have less access to other methods. Oral contraceptives are widely used.

Brazilian law guarantees free access to education through secondary school, and more girls than boys participate in secondary and tertiary education. White women are more than twice as likely as dark-skinned women to have 11 or more years of schooling.

Three-quarters of pregnant women attend at least four prenatal visits, and 84 percent receive some prenatal care; almost 90 percent of births are attended by skilled personnel. A Brazilian woman's lifetime risk of maternal death is similar to some of the poorest countries in Latin America. The infant mortality rate for white children is about 60 percent that of darker-skinned children.

Mothers benefit from legislation to protect women's rights. In the past, employers often asked women for a certificate of sterilization as a condition of hiring. Feminist activists succeeded in getting the Brazilian Constitution of 1988 to address women's workplace rights. The 1988 Constitution guarantees free access to daycare and preschool for all women, not just mothers.

Benedita da Silva, mother of two and the granddaughter of a slave, rose from a *favela* (slum) of Rio de Janeiro to become the first elected black woman deputy. Da Silva served in the Chamber of Deputies in the capital city of Brasilia and ran for mayor of Rio.

Ana María Machado, mother of three children, won the 2000 Hans Christian Andersen medal for Children's Literature. Her books have sold close to 8 million copies worldwide.

**See Also:** African Diaspora; Postcolonialism and Mothering; Poverty and Mothering; Teen Mothers.

## Bibliography

Lebon, Nathalie. "Brazil." In *The Greenwood Encyclopedia of Women's Issues Worldwide,* Lynn Walter, ed. Westport, CT: Greenwood Press, 2003.

Lúcia, Maria, and M. Afonso. "Brazilian Families in the Confrontation Between Hierarchy and Equality."

In *Families in a Global Context,* Charles B. Hennon and Stephan M. Wilson, eds. New York: Routledge/ Taylor & Francis, 2008.

Torres, Cláudio V. and Maria Auxiliadora Dessen. "The Brazilian Jeitinho: Brazil's Subcultures, Its Diversity of Social Contexts, and Its Family Structures." In *Families Across Cultures: A 30-Nation Psychological Study,* James Georgas, John W. Berry, Fons J. R. van de Vijver, Çigdem Kagitçibasi, and Ype H. Poortiinga, eds. Cambridge, MA: Cambridge University Press, 2006.

Keri L. Heitner
University of Phoenix

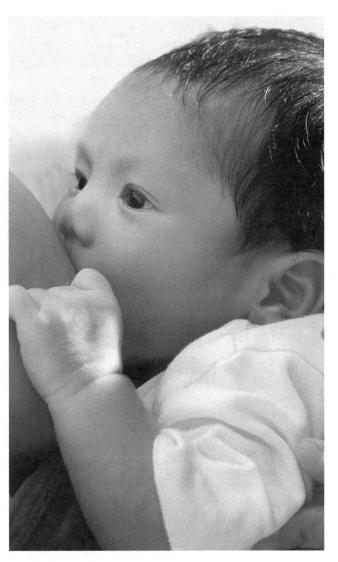

*Breastmilk is the perfect first food for babies, as it contains the precise levels of water, sugar, fat, and nutrients babies need.*

# Breastfeeding

Breastfeeding refers to the act of providing mothers' milk to infants for the purpose of nutrition. The most widely accepted definition of breastfeeding seems to accept infants/children extracting milk through sucking at their mothers' breasts for the health benefit of the infant and mother. The act of a woman expressing milk from her breast with the intention of feeding her infant is referred to as breast milk fed, according to Le Leche League International. Understanding breastfeeding history, biology, research, policies, resources, potential problems, treatments, and environmental supports is beneficial to gaining a full understanding of breastfeeding.

## Breastfeeding History, Research, and Policy

Breastfeeding can be traced back to the earliest societies where breastmilk was the only way to nourish infants, as is the case with other mammals. Breastmilk is produced during pregnancy. The baby's sucking stimulates the release of hormones (prolactin and oxytocin), which lead to breastmilk "coming in" and "letting down," respectively, three to seven days after birth. The milk is moved from the milk gland into the milk ducts and into the nipple, where is sucked into the baby's mouth. Until the milk comes in, babies will receive colostrum, which is low in fat but high in carbohydrates, protein, and antibodies. It is extremely easy to digest and an excellent first food for babies.

Current research and policy exist to support the importance of breastfeeding for the health of infants and their mothers. The World Health Organization (WHO), the American Academy of Pediatrics, and the American Academy of Family Physicians recommend that women breastfeed for at least one year (with exclusive breastfeeding for at least 6 months) to provide their babies with the best source of nutrition and antibodies to protect them from colds and infections. Breastmilk is easy for babies to digest, and it contains the perfect amounts of fat, sugar, water, and protein needed for growth and development. Studies have shown that breastfed children have slightly higher IQs than formula-fed children, as well as lower rates of sudden infant death syndrome (SIDS), type 1 and 2 diabetes, asthma, high cholesterol, overweight, and obesity. For new mothers, breastfeeding can help reduce the risk of certain breast and ovarian cancers, increase weight loss of pregnancy pounds, shrink the uterus (thus lessening bleeding), delay the return of ovulation and menstrual cycles, reduce the risk of hip fractures and osteoporosis after menopause, and provide opportunities for bonding and relaxation.

## Breastfeeding Techniques

How to breastfeed and express breastmilk involve many preferences of the mother and baby. There are several recommended positions (such as the cradle or football hold); schedules (alternating breasts during a feeding or one breast for a feeding, or alternating each time); and length of breastfeeding episodes (for example, 20 minutes or as long as the baby wants). Further, expressing breastmilk can be performed by baby-only, the hand, handheld manual pump, electric handheld pump, or institutional-grade electric pump. Among the many possible preferences, time and comfort may be the most common criteria among women.

## Work and Health: Benefits and Challenges

Employers can reap benefits, such as decreased absenteeism and increased productivity, if they invest in supporting lactation for their employees. Breastfeeding has also been associated with a reduction in health care costs. Healthier babies translate to fewer sick care visits, prescriptions, and hospitalizations. Further, breastmilk is inexpensive, convenient, and a natural way to nurture babies. For 2010, the U.S. Surgeon General has set goals to have 75 percent of babies breastfed when they leave the hospital; 50 percent of babies still breastfed at 6 months of age; and 25 percent of babies still breastfed at 1 year of age.

With advancements in research, policy, and technology, many mothers plan to breastfeed their babies. However, due to financial obligations, career aspirations, and societal/workplace constraints, these mothers encounter difficulties in achieving the goals and expectations set by the medical profession and lactation experts. The protection, promotion, and support of breastfeeding among working women is an important issue that requires greater attention as the majority of mothers plan to return to work. Despite the known benefits of breastfeeding, rates drop once women return to work due to a lack of support and knowledge regarding how to manage breastfeeding while at work, a nonsupportive work environment, and problems pumping breastmilk. Effective strategies for women to maintain breastfeeding until their babies are at least 6 months old include delayed return to work, working part time, improved conditions at work for breastfeeding, breastfeeding breaks during work hours, milk expression and storage options, and access to breastfeeding counseling.

In addition to the aforementioned potential barriers mothers may encounter, there are a few related specifically to women's health worth noting. It is common for women to experience some discomfort related to engorged breasts or pain from cracked nipples. Breast engorgement can occur from a delayed necessity to express breastmilk, or a baby's extracting less milk than is being produced. In other words, too much breastmilk can become contained within the mammary glands, frequently causing blocked milk ducts, which can be painful for women and may develop into mastitis (inflammation of the breast). In rare cases, untreated mastitis can develop into an abscess, which may involve surgery to remediate. Cracked or sore nipples occur when nipples become dry, and may result from improper latch-on by the baby or prolonged nursing. Correct latch-on involves the baby's mouth placed around the areola and his tongue under the areola.

Almost all breastfeeding mothers experience leaky breasts at some point. Breasts may leak on several different occasions, resulting from cues for milk letdown, like the sound of a crying baby, during lovemaking, overdue breastfeeding, and when weaning a baby from the breast.

Breastfeeding may continue for as long as the mother and infant/child desire. Some women wean their babies, and some babies wean themselves. Fortunately, there is a plethora of information on the Internet and in written resources for breastfeeding mothers, especially as provided by the Le Leche League International.

**See Also:** Academe and Motherhood; Breastmilk; Care Giving; Maternal Health; Wet Nursing.

**Bibliography**

Ferreira Rea, Marina and Ardythe L. Morrow, "Protecting, Promoting, and Supporting Breastfeeding Among Women in the Labor Force." *Advances in Experimental Medicine and Biology,* v.554 (2004).

Kantor, Jodi. "On the Job, Nursing Mothers Find a 2-Class System." *New York Times* (September 1, 2006).

Labbok, Mirriam. "What Is the Definition of Breastfeeding." *Breastfeeding Abstracts,* v.19 (February 2000).

Rabin, Roni. "Breast-Feed or Else." *New York Times* (June 13, 2006).

Michele L. Vancour
Southern Connecticut State University

# Breastmilk

In general terms, breastmilk is the liquid product of the lactating breast. Most commonly used to feed infants and children, breastmilk is also understood to have recuperative properties.

Numerous components comprise breastmilk, including proteins, fats, vitamins, and carbohydrates. Each of these elements performs a specific role, from aiding in digestion, developing infant immunity, and ensuring adequate nutrition. More controversially, breastmilk is thought to stimulate intellectual development.

## Liquid Gold

Breastmilk, as one of the only fluids to pass freely between humans, has powerful conceptual potential. Referred to in breastfeeding literature as "liquid gold," breastmilk has been understood as integral to the transmission of both physical and moral characteristics from mother to child. Historical texts counsel women to maintain not only their physical health, but also to cultivate a state of emotional equilibrium, as it was thought that violent emotions and passions could directly impact the moral, physical, and intellectual development of the child. More problematic still was the issue of class. The breastmilk of wet nurses, who were drawn overwhelmingly from the lower classes, was considered dangerous to upper-class infants, thus contributing to the significant scrutiny of wet nurses in surrogate nursing arrangements. More recent debates around the toxicity of breastmilk have focused not on the moral shortcomings of the mother or wet nurse, but rather on the environmental contaminants present in mother's milk. Research suggests that human breastmilk contains, among other things, pesticides, dioxins, and polychlorinated biphenyls (PCBs). Nevertheless, breastmilk can equally be understood to heal the body: the very toxicity of breastmilk suggests its potential to remove toxins from the body. This provocative theory was behind the establishment of the experimental 18th-century Vaugirard Hospital. Established in Paris in 1780 for the express purpose of treating syphilitic infants, the hospital imagined the breastmilk of syphilitic wet nurses as medical technology, using it as a vehicle to transmit mercury (the most common treatment for syphilis at the time) from syphilitic mother to syphilitic infant.

**See Also:** Breastfeeding; Care Giving; Maternal Health; Wet Nursing.

**Bibliography**

Bartlett, Alison. "Breastfeeding as Headwork: Corporeal Feminism and Meanings for Breastfeeding." *Women's Studies International Forum,* v.25/3 (2002).

Bartlett, Alison. *Breastwork: Rethinking Breastfeeding.* Sydney: University of New South Wales Press, 2005.

Giles, Fiona. "The Well-Tempered Breast: Fostering Fluidity in Breastly Meaning and Function." *Women's Studies,* v.34 (2005).

Huet, Marie-Hélène. *Monstrous Imagination.* Cambridge, MA: Harvard University Press, 1993.

Irigaray, Luce. "The Bodily Encounter With the Mother." In *The Irigaray Reader*, Margaret Whitford, ed., and David Macey, trans. Cambridge, UK: Basil Blackwell, 1991.

Kristeva, Julia. *Powers of Horror: An Essay on Abjection*, Leon S. Roudiez, trans. New York: Columbia University Press, 1982.

Shaw, Rhonda and Alison Bartlett. *Giving Breastmilk: Body Ethics and Contemporary Breastfeeding Practices.* Toronto: Demeter Press, 2010.

Sherwood, Joan. "Treating Syphilis: The Wetnurse as Technology in an Eighteenth-Century Parisian Hospital." *Journal of the History of Medicine and the Allied Sciences,* v.50/3 (1995).

Sherwood, Joan. "The Milk Factor: The Ideology of Breastfeeding and Post-Partum Illnesses, 1750–1850." *Canadian Bulletin of Medical History/Bulletin Canadian d'Histoire de la Médecine,* v.10 (1993).

Sussman, George D. *Selling Mothers' Milk: The Wet-nursing Business in France, 1715–1914.* Urbana: University of Illinois Press, 1982.

Young, Iris Marion. "Breasted Experience: The Look and the Feeling." In *On Female Body Experience: "Throwing Like a Girl" and Other Essays.* Oxford: Oxford University Press, 2005.

Sonja Boon
Memorial University of Newfoundland and Labrador

# Brooks, Gwendolyn

The first African American to win the Pulitzer Prize and the first black woman to hold the post of Consultant in Poetry to the Library of Congress, Gwendolyn Brooks was a poet who was admired for her linguistic acuity and use of established forms as well as free verse. A lifelong resident of Chicago, Brooks often wrote about the urban experiences of African Americans, including black women and mothers. Active in educating young people, Brooks gave readings in schools, prisons, and hospitals; established Poet Laureate Awards for Illinois students; and founded the Blackstone Rangers, a Chicago workshop for teenage gang members.

Born on June 7, 1917, Brooks grew up in a household that nurtured her early aptitude for writing poetry. By 1945, her first collection of poetry, *A Street in Bronzeville*, appeared, and Brooks quickly established her reputation as a poet of ordinary African Americans. In poems such as "Hattie Scott," "Queen of the Blues," "Ballad of Pearl May Lee," and "The Mother" section of "A Street in Bronzeville," Brooks also portrayed the lives of mothers struggling in a harsh urban landscape.

## Acclaimed Poems

Brooks's second collection, *Annie Allen*, which won the Pulitzer, traces the life of a young woman before and after World War II. The section titled "Womanhood" depicts Annie as a mother who has developed a wiser and more critical view of her life. By the time *Annie Allen* appeared, Brooks herself had married and become a mother when her son, Henry Blakely, was born in 1940. Her daughter, Nora Brooks Blakely, was born in 1951. In 1953 Brooks's first and only novel, *Maud Martha*, depicted "colorism," the discrimination against dark-skinned African Americans within the black community. Maud is a young mother whose husband regrets marrying a woman darker than he is.

In *The Bean Eaters* (1960), the Civil Rights Movement and motherhood were centerpieces of poems such as "A Bronzeville Mother Loiters in Mississippi." "Meanwhile, a Mississippi Mother Burns Bacon," which captures the tragedy of Emmett Till's murder through the perspective of a white mother married to one of his killers. The experience of mothers—in grief, poverty, and old age—mark poems such as "The Last Quatrain of the Ballad of Emmett Till," "Mrs. Small, Jessie Mitchell's Mother," and the widely anthologized "The Lovers of the Poor."

In 1967 Brooks found inspiration in Amiri Baraka (LeRoi Jones), founder of the Black Arts Movement. Brooks's next collection, the National Book Award–nominated *In the Mecca* (1968), features a mother's frantic search for her missing child in a rundown apartment building. The poem's portrait of poverty implicates the cultural and historical forces of slavery and white indifference.

Brooks's other honors include lifetime achievement awards from the National Endowment for the Arts in 1989 and the National Book Foundation in 1994, two Guggenheim fellowships, an American Academy of Arts and Letters Award in literature, and the National Medal of Arts award in 1995. In 1968, she was appointed the poet laureate of Illinois, succeeding Carl Sandburg, and in 1988 she was inducted into the National Women's Hall of Fame. She held the Gwendolyn Brooks Chair in Black Literature and Creative Writing at Chicago State University, and in 1994 was selected as the National Endowment of the Humanities' Jefferson Lecturer. Western Illinois University houses the Gwendolyn Brooks Cultural Center.

**See Also:** African American Mothers; Literature, Mothers in; Poetry, Mothers in.

**Bibliography**

Brooks, Gwendolyn. *Annie Allen*. New York: Harper & Row, 1950.

Brooks, Gwendolyn. *A Street in Bronzeville*. New York: Harper & Row, 1945.

Brooks, Gwendolyn. *In the Mecca*. New York: Harper & Row, 1968.

Brooks, Gwendolyn. *Maud Martha*. New York: Harper & Row, 1953.

Brooks, Gwendolyn. *The Bean Eaters*. New York: Harper & Row, 1960.

Kent, George E. *A Life of Gwendolyn Brooks*. Lexington: The University Press of Kentucky, 1990.

Melhem D.H. "Gwendolyn Brooks: An Appreciation." *Humanities*, v.15/3 (May/June 1994).

Watkins, Mel. "In Memoriam: Gwendolyn Brooks (1917–2000)." *The Black Scholar*, v.31/1.

Justine Dymond
Springfield College

# Buchanan, Andrea

American author Andrea J. ("Andi") Buchanan made her first mark on the scene of motherhood writing with her 2003 collection of essays, *Mother Shock: Loving Every (Other) Minute of It*. She subsequently edited three anthologies: *It's a Boy: Women Writers on Raising Sons*; *It's a Girl: Women Writers on Raising Daughters*; and, together with Amy Hudock, *Literary Mama: Reading for the Maternally Inclined*. Her 2007 collaboration with Miriam Peskowitz, *The Daring Book for Girls*, became a *New York Times* best seller and was followed by the publication of two Pocket Daring Books: *Things To Do* and *Wisdom and Wonder*.

## Expectations Versus Gut Feelings

In *Mother Shock*, Buchanan compares motherhood with a foreign country, where the rhythms of life are different and one is constantly sleep deprived. According to Buchanan, a new mother goes through four stages of adjustment, similar to the emotional dislocation of culture shock: initial euphoria, irritation, recovery, and finally, adjustment. In her essays, which roughly cover the first three years of her daughter's life, Buchanan talks freely about fears and insecurities, feelings of guilt and ambivalence, and finding joy in unexpected places. It is her stated goal to invite a dialogue about what mothers really feel, instead of what they should be feeling. The form (31 fairly short essays) also fits the lifestyle of mothers, both in regard to reading and writing.

*It's a Boy* and its companion piece *It's a Girl* are collective literary explorations of what it means to mother sons and daughters. The authors examine gender roles and gendered expectations. In her own contribution to *It's a Boy*, capturing the time in late pregnancy when almost everyone was asking her whether she was having a boy or a girl, Buchanan tries to come to terms with stereotypes like "boys are easier than girls," and also confesses her conflicted feelings about the prospect of having a boy. In *It's a Girl*, many of the writers struggle with how to shelter their daughters from damaging feminine stereotypes. Buchanan's introduction to the collection comments on how mothering daughters forces women to revisit parts of their own girlhood that they would rather leave behind.

*Literary Mama* is a collection of some of the standout pieces published on the widely successful Website with the same name, of which Buchanan was a founding editor. The site, launched in November 2003, was the brainchild of Buchanan and other women writers frustrated by what they perceived as a lack of readily available literary writing about motherhood. Speaking about their unique experiences in an unsentimental style, these writers reject the artificial binary of the mind and the body and prove that motherhood and creativity are not mutually exclusive. This ties in with Buchanan's own conviction that becoming a mother helped her become a real writer.

*The Daring Book for Girls* was conceived as a response and sequel to Conn and Hal Iggulden's *The Dangerous Book for Boys*. It attempts to strike a balance between doing and learning, offering a compendium of information and things to do from a time before computers and video games. Many of the activities are centered on sports and the outdoors; they include karate moves and yoga routines, instructions for mastering the jump rope and perfecting cartwheels, and rules of the game for basketball and netball. The book also includes more "girly" topics, like how to press flowers, as well as profiles of queens of the ancient world and today's real-life princesses.

**See Also:** Internet and Mothering; *Literary Mama*; Literature, Mothers in.

**Bibliography**
Buchanan, Andrea J. *Mother Shock: Loving Every (Other) Minute of It*. New York: Seal Press, 2003.
Buchanan, Andrea J. and Miriam Peskowitz. *The Daring Book for Girls*. New York: HarperCollins, 2007.

Heike Henderson
Boise State University

# Buddhism and Mothering

In Buddhist philosophy, mothering is symbolic of how to love all beings as a mother loves her child, without the attachment that leads to suffering.

A traditional Buddhist marriage in Japan is initiated with a vow to the Buddha followed by a wedding procession.

## All Beings as Mother
Buddhism posits that in the countless rounds of life, death, and rebirth, all beings have been one's mother, because time is beyond measure and each person has lived countless times before. This means that all people have the potential for a relationship with every being on the planet at least once and perhaps numerous times. A mother is viewed favorably for all the love and care that she gives her child. This relationship serves as an example of ultimate love and how Buddhists are to behave with one another as human beings. Having love toward all other beings is a necessary component for Buddhists in what they call the "path to enlightenment."

## Wisdom as the Source of Compassion
Mothering is also symbolic of wisdom, as Buddhists consider it the source of compassion and skill. Compassion and wisdom are so important in Buddhism that they are often called the two wings of Buddhism. For Buddhists, compassion begins with recognizing the suffering of all beings and wanting this suffering to end. Suffering is rooted in the attachment or desire for people and things that cannot, by their own nature, last forever. A mother's

attachment to her child may cause her to suffer because of the inevitability of change and the reality that everything has an ending. An example of the extreme of attachment is when a woman finds no meaning in her life outside of mothering.

For Buddhists, a mother exemplifies what it means to be compassionate toward another being, and for children specifically, by protecting her child from suffering, creating a stable environment to provide a sense of well being, and shielding her child from the inevitability of loss and death until the child is mature enough to handle this truth.

## Samsara
In Buddhism, *samsara*, life itself, is the realm of suffering; one means of escaping this suffering is through developing equanimity. This entails viewing all beings on a level playing field and recognizing that everyone equally desires happiness and the avoidance of suffering. The differences in relationships of

enemy, stranger, or friend are considered arbitrary, so that the happiness of someone held close is considered of no more importance than those kept at a distance. With a simple action or compliment in one's favor, an enemy can become an ally or a friend. In Buddhist theology, seeing that all beings experience suffering may cause one to feel empathy, which leads to compassion for all life.

Another means that Buddhists consider to escape suffering is through realizing what Buddhism considers the true nature of reality and the interconnectedness to all beings: emptiness. As self and loved ones are often seen as the center of the universe and more important than anyone else, Buddhists consider all to be equally important, connected, and affected by the actions of one another. The wisdom of emptiness, Prajnaparamita, is known as the Mother of All the Buddhas. Tara, the Tibetan Buddhist goddess, or meditational deity, is also known as the Mother of All the Buddhas.

### Mother as an Example of How to Love

In Buddhism, mothers and motherhood are considered as examples of how to love and may lead to the concept of *bodhicitta*, which is compassion for all beings and wanting them to be happy and avoid suffering. Buddhists may develop *bodhicitta* by training the mind by means of the sevenfold cause-and-effect instruction, which encourages compassion through the example of mothering. This method was used by many of the teachers of Mahayana Buddhism such as Atisha, Chandrakirti, Shantarakshita, and Je Tsongkapa, and was passed down through the Buddhas Maitreya and Manjushri. Beginning by thinking of one's own mother as a compassionate being, a Buddhist recalls all the ways in which one's mother was kind. These thoughts are extended to include the kindness of others in one's life and to contemplate the following: immeasurable equanimity, understanding all sentient beings to be one's mother, remembering and repaying their kindness, love through the force of attraction, compassion, altruism, and *bodhicitta*.

### The Bodhisattva Ideal

Once a Buddhist determines that she no longer wants herself or others to suffer and desires real and lasting happiness for everyone, she determines to become a bodhisattva. This is accomplished

through perfecting certain positive qualities such as generosity, morality, patience, willingness, meditation, and wisdom. In Buddhism, a bodhisattva loves all beings as a mother loves her child, without the attachment that leads to suffering.

**See Also:** Mother Goddess; Myth, Mothers in; Religion and Mothering.

### Bibliography

Paul, Diana. *Women in Buddhism*. Berkeley: University of California Press, 1985.

Powers, John, and Deane Curtis. "Mothering: Moral Cultivation in Buddhist and Feminist Ethics." *Philosophy East & West*, v.44/1 (January 1994).

Tsomo, Karma Lekshe, ed. *Buddhist Women Across Cultures: Realizations*. Albany: State University of New York Press, 1999.

Karen Nelson Villanueva
California Institute of Integral Studies

# Bulgaria

Bulgaria, in southeastern Europe, has long dominated much of the Balkans. It has a population of 7.3 million, and it has a birth rate of 9.6 per 1,000. Its infant mortality rate is 19.8 per 1,000 live births. The crude divorce rate in the country is 1.53 divorces per 1,000 marriages (2003). About 80 percent of Bulgarian women age 25–54 participate in the labor force, and over 67 percent are employed. Women are entitled to 315 days maternity leave.

For years Bulgaria had one of the highest abortion rates in Europe, due in part to availability of abortion on demand. However, abortion rates fell after the introduction of contraception, from a peak of almost 80 per 1,000 fertile women in 1980 to about 50 per 1,000 in 1995. Save the Children assigned Bulgarian a rank of 35 on the Mothers' Index (out of 41 more developed countries), 32 on the Women's Index, and 34 on the Children's Index.

### Mothers in Society

Prior to World War II, Bulgarian society was mainly patriarchal, and Bulgaria was a largely rural country with women mainly filling the roles of homemaker or farm worker. In fact, in the agricultural sector, women did most of the manual labor involved with crops, while men tended to work with animals. However, there were a few women, especially in Sofia, the capital, who did have careers. These were generally from the aristocracy, or the small middle class. In the countryside, the 1934 census showed that in one representative village, more than 15 percent of the population lived in family groups of 11 or more, and very few people over the age of 25 were unmarried.

During the period of Communist rule after World War II, there was an increase in female participation in the formal workforce, with more women having full-time or part-time manual or nonmanual work. Many women found work as nurses, teachers, pharmacists, and sales clerks. Health care in the country improved under Communist rule, and continued to improve after the end of Communism. This has resulted in a significant decline in infant mortality rates. An increase in female education has contributed to a progressive decline in the birth rate in the country, although the birth rates for ethnic Turks and Gypsies has continued to be much higher than that of ethnic Bulgarians. In an attempt to partly redress this situation, the Communist government instituted maternity leave with full pay and pension benefits, and also instituted a system of legal rights for women in the workforce. There were also income supplements to help mothers from poor families, although these were eroded by inflation in the 1990s. The fertility rate, 2.22 in 1975, fell to 1.23 by 1999, but the percentage of extramarital births during that time increased from 9.3 percent to 35.1 percent.

Famous women in modern Bulgarian history include the revolutionary Mara Buneva (1902–28); Nora Annanieva, who became the leader of the parliamentary group of the Bulgarian Socialist Party; and Reneta Ivanova Indzhova, who was Prime Minister of Bulgaria from October 1994 until January 1995, the only women to hold that position.

**See Also:** Albania; Communism and Motherhood; Romania; Rural Mothers; Ukraine.

**Bibliography**

Dobrianov, V., et al. "Bulgaria." In *Working Women in Socialist Countries: The Fertility Connection,*
V. Bodrova and R. Anker, eds. Geneva: International Labour Office, 1985.

Gancheva, Roumyana, ed. *Bulgaria as We Saw It.* Oslo: Sofia Press, 1981.

Kostova, Dobrinka. "Similar or Different: Women in Post-Communist Bulgaria." In *Women in the Politics of Postcommunist Eastern Europe*, Marilyn Rueschemeyer and M.E. Sharpe, eds. Self-Published, 1994.

Slabakova, Roumiana. "Research on Women in Bulgaria: The Hard Way Into the Future." *Women's Studies Quarterly* (Fall 1992).

Todorova, Maria. "Historical Tradition and Transformation in Bulgaria: Women's Issues or Feminist Issues?" *Journal of Women's History* (Winter 1994).

Vidova, Milanka. *Legal Status of Bulgarian Women.* Oslo: Sofia Press, 1989.

Vidova, Milanka. *Women's Legal Rights in Bulgaria: A Selection of Normative Acts with Annotations.* Oslo, Norway: Sofia Press, 1981.

Justin Corfield
Geelong Grammar School, Australia

# Burkina Faso

Burkina Faso is in west Africa, where poverty, illiteracy, economic difficulty, and traditionalism make motherhood a perilous state.

Burkina Faso's 13.3 million population is increasing at nearly 3 percent a year. Between 1996 and 2006 the increase was 341,000 per year. Education is compulsory but not enforced. In 2000, the illiteracy rate was 77 percent (66.8 male, 86.9 female).

In 2009 the first lady of Burkina Faso, Mrs. Chantal Compaoré, noted that 1,500 African women die each day, nearly half the world's maternal deaths. A Burkinabe woman and seven newborns die every three hours due to lack of adequate maternal and neonatal resources that promote prolonged labor, eclampsia, infection, and hemorrhage. Compaoré opened the women's house in Balé in 2005 to improve the life conditions for women, and is a fighter for women's literacy and improvement as well as an activist against human immunodeficiency virus (HIV) and acquired immunodeficiency syndrome (AIDS).

Infant mortality between 1996 and 2005 dropped only from 107 to 96 deaths per thousand. Acute malnutrition afflicted 35 percent of children under age 5 in 2007. Twenty percent of new mothers are malnourished, and only 56 percent had competent birth assistance in 2007. In 2003 Burkina Faso sent two obstetrician/gynecologists (OB/GYNs) to Uganda for clinical skills training, and one of the trainees provided training for 43 others. The Koupela District hospital had a surgeon trained in complications of pregnancy and labor, as well as in caesareans and other emergency procedures. These improvements were a small step in the ongoing effort to improve health care for mothers-to-be, and to save their lives.

## High Birth Rates, Maternal Deaths

The average Burkina Faso mother in 2004 had 6.7 children. High birth rates in these conditions weaken women's health and their ability to contribute to their society. The first official reproductive health clinic was established in 1985. Birth control was neglected, but health and reproductive services agencies reduced HIV/AIDS prevalence from 7 percent in the early 1990s to 2 percent in 2006. Just 14 percent of women use contraception, and in some rural areas the rate is 9 percent. The lower the use of contraception, the higher the maternal mortality rate. In 2006 the Burkina Faso government, assisted by USAID and the United Nations Population Fund, began a 10-year plan to promote contraception.

Divorce is uncommon, but more likely for the newer generations than for the older, and more likely for the first wife when a new wife joins the commonly polygamous household. A divorced woman cannot remarry within the same family or an allied family, so she has to seek a new spouse outside the village. Divorce is more likely in villages with better infrastructure (roads, communications, etc.) that provide access to a broader world.

Arranged marriages persist despite being illegal. Approximately half of Burkinabe women live in polygamous marriages, either forced or voluntary. Marriage of any sort is considered better than spinsterhood. Levirate marriage, where a widow has to marry her deceased husband's brother to keep the children, is illegal but practiced.

In 1996, Burkina Faso outlawed female genital mutilation (FGM), with penalties of up to five years in prison and fines of $1,500. FGM is a long-standing cultural practice in 14 provinces, regarded as a cleansing during initiation. It causes pain and bleeding as well as infection, difficulties in birth, and possible HIV/AIDS transmission. In 1996, FGM affected two-thirds of Burkina Faso women, but by 2008 that number had shifted to 16–43 percent, depending on region and group.

**See Also:** AIDS/HIV and Mothering; Education and Mothering; Islam and Mothering; Poverty and Mothering; Prenatal Health Care; Save the Mothers.

## Bibliography

AWARE. "Supporting Advocacy for Maternal and Neonatal Health in Burkina Faso." (2007). http://www.aware-rh.org/index.php?id=363 (accessed May 2009).

Brown, Kpakpo. "Burkina Faso Guide." OneWorld.net (2005). http://uk.oneworld.net/guides/burkina/development (accessed May 2009).

Social Institutions and Gender Index. "Gender Equality and Social Institutions in Burkina Faso." http://genderindex.org/country/burkina-faso (accessed May 2009).

Thiombiano, Bilampoa Gnoumou and Bruno D. Schoumaker. "Factors of Marital Disruption in Burkina Faso." Population Association of America (2008). http://paa2008.princeton.edu (accessed May 2009).

United Nations Integrated Regional Information Networks. "Burkina Faso: Female Genital Mutilation Declining, Says Minister." (May 26, 2003). http://www.aegis.com/news/IRIN/2003/IR030528.html (accessed May 2009).

Women Deliver. "Burkina Faso's First Lady Calls on Artists to Save Lives." (March 2, 2009). http://www.womendeliver.org/news/09_burkina.htm2 (accessed May 2009).

John H. Barnhill
Independent Scholar

# Burundi

Burundi, in central Africa, has a population of 8.4 million (2007), of which 93 percent live in rural areas. It has a birth rate of 42.2 per 1,000, and an infant mortality rate of 63.1 per 1,000 live births. The nation's fertility rate is 6.4 births per woman (2008), which is the seventh highest in the world. The maternal mortality rate at 1 per 100 births is also one of the highest in the world. The employment-to-population ratio for women age 15 and over was 83.5 in 2005. The law provides for 12 weeks of maternity leave paid at 50 percent of salary.

As of 2007, abortion was legally available only to save the mother's life or to preserve her mental or physical health. It is widely believed that there are high rates of death due to illegal abortions. Just over 15 percent of women age 15–49 use contraception, with 10 percent of those as modern methods.

In traditional society, houses in Burundi were constructed around the lifestyles of the people. The anthropologist Anne Stanford was able to point out the symbolism in their design and their connections to the female reproductive process. During the period of German colonial rule (1899–1924) and then Belgian rule (1924–59), life in the villages in Burundi (as in neighboring Rwanda) did not change significantly, and the colonial powers spent little on developing civil infrastructure in the countryside. After independence in 1962, attempts were made to help improve the life of villagers, and the hospital services in Bujumbura, the capital, were enlarged and modernized. Midwifery services were also provided in many towns and villages. However, inter-tribal strife between the Hutu and Tutsi flared up regularly; 100,000 Hutus were killed after an abortive coup attempt in 1972, and another 20,000 Hutus were killed in 1988.

**Attempts to Improve Maternal Health**
In spite of the regular internecine warfare, serious attempts have been made to improve the health of people in Burundi. There has been a slight decline in women's life expectancy compared to 10 years ago (now 51.6 years, compared to 52) and a slight rise for men (48 years compared to 50.1). This small change does not seem significant until considering the factor of the spread of human immunodeficiency virus (HIV) and acquired immunodeficiency syndrome (AIDS), which has had a particularly devastating impact on young mothers and children. Recent evidence shows that fertility rates for the country have not declined, unlike in many other African countries; and as the tribal warfare has ended, the conditions for bringing up children in Burundi have gradually improved, although about half of the children in the country under the age of 5 were classed as being undernourished. Among the 41 tier III or least developed countries, Burundi was ranked 15th on the Mothers' Index, 10th on the Women's Index, and 23rd on the Children's Index by the nonprofit organization Save the Children.

**See Also:** Congo; Congo, Democratic Republic of the; Kenya; Rwanda; Uganda; War and Mothering.

**Bibliography**
Kirk, D. and B. Pillet. "Fertility Levels, Trends, and Differentials in Sub-Saharan Africa in the 1980s and 1990s." *Studies in Family Planning*, v.29/1 (March 1998).
Krueger, Robert, Kathleen Tobin Krueger and Desmond Tutu. *From Bloodshed to Hope in Burundi: Our Embassy Years During Genocide*. Austin: University of Texas Press, 2007.
Lim, A. "Spotlight Burundi." *Population Today*, v.24/9 (September 1996).
Uvin, Peter. *Life After Violence: A People's Story of Burundi (African Arguments)*. London: Zed Books, 2009.

Justin Corfield
Geelong Grammar School, Australia

# Bush, Barbara

Barbara Pierce Bush was born in New York City, New York, on June 8, 1925, to Pauline Robinson Pierce and Marvin Pierce. Barbara was third of four children—one sister and two brothers. From 1940 until 1943, Barbara attended Ashley Hall, a boarding school in Charleston, South Carolina.

At a 1941 dance, when she was 16 years old, she met George Herbert Walker Bush, her future husband. In 1943, Barbara graduated from Ashley Hall and entered Smith College. At Smith, she made the freshman soccer team and served as captain. She worked during the summers, first at a Lord & Taylor department store, then at a nuts and bolts factory. One and a half years after their

*Nicknamed "The Silver Fox," Barbara Bush used her wit to trip up critics, particularly those of her husband or children.*

meeting, Barbara Pierce and George Bush became engaged, just before he left to serve in the Navy during World War II. When he returned on leave, Barbara dropped out of college and on January 6, 1945, they married.

After the war, George graduated from Yale University and the couple moved to Texas. Barbara gave birth to six children: George Walker Bush (July 6, 1946), Pauline Robinson "Robin" Bush (December 20, 1949), John Ellis "Jeb" Bush (February 11, 1953), Neil Mallon Bush (January 22, 1955), Marvin Pierce Bush (December 22, 1956), and Dorothy "Doro" Bush Koch (August 18, 1959). While Barbara was a stay-at-home mother, George built a business in the oil industry and then turned to politics.

Before becoming the 41st U.S. President, George Bush traveled often for business. This left Barbara with the traditional responsibilities of motherhood and housekeeping, as well as civic activities and volunteering. However, her role as mother would have later public impact. The death of the Bush's daughter, Robin, from leukemia in 1953 led Barbara to

support numerous cancer research and treatment programs. In addition, her son Neil's diagnosis as dyslexic began her lifelong interest in reading and literacy issues. In 1998, Barbara's third eldest child, Jeb Bush, was elected governor of Florida. Then, after serving as the Governor of Texas, her eldest son George W. Bush was elected President of the United States in 2000 and 2004. Besides Abigail Adams, Barbara Bush is the only other woman to be both the wife and mother of a U.S. President. Before the election, Barbara actively campaigned for her son, addressing both the 2000 and 2004 Republican National Conventions. She also traveled with the "W Stands for Women" fundraising tour that focused on the women's vote for George W. After his election, Barbara frequently defended her son's record as chief executive.

In interviews, Barbara Bush has attributed her popularity to her matronly figure and white hair, making her appear like "everybody's grandmother." Today, she continues her service at the Barbara Bush Foundation for Family Literacy, as AmeriCares ambassador-at-large, as a Mayo Clinic Foundation board member, and as a supporter of many organizations that include the Leukemia Society of America and the Boys & Girls Club of America. She has also authored four books. Barbara Bush lives with her husband in Houston, Texas, and at their estate in Kennebunkport, Maine.

**See Also:** Adams, Abigail (Smith); Lincoln, Abraham, Mother of; Politics and Mothers.

**Bibliography**

Bush, Barbara, *Barbara Bush: A Memoir*. New York: Scribner's Sons, 1994.

Bush, Barbara. *Reflections: Life After the White House*. New York: Scribner's Sons, 2003.

Gould Lewis L., ed. *American First Ladies: Their Lives and Their Legacy*. New York: Routledge, 2001.

Gutin, Myra G. *Barbara Bush: Presidential Matriarch*. Lawrence: University Press of Kansas, 2008.

Kilian, Pamela. *Barbara Bush: Matriarch of a Dynasty*. New York: Thomas Dunne Books/St. Martin's Press, 2002.

Jessica Thern Smith
University of Tennessee

# California

California is the most populous U.S. state, with an estimated population of 38,049,462 as of January 1, 2008. In 2006, 50 percent of the state's population was female. With regard to racial-ethnic background, 59.8 percent of state residents are white, 6.2 percent are African American, 12.3 percent are Asian American, and 35.9 percent are of Latino descent.

In California, the average family size is 3.54. Over 68 percent of households are family households, and 51 percent of those families have children under the age of 18. Of the family households, an overwhelming majority (73 percent) are married-couple families, 19 percent are headed by single mothers, and 8 percent are headed by a single father.

In 2006, there were 548,882 births in the state. Of those births, 29 percent were to non-Hispanic white mothers, 6 percent were to African American mothers, 12 percent were to Asian or Pacific Islander mothers, and 52 percent were to Latina mothers. That same year, the birth rate—the number of births per every 1,000 person in the state—was 15. The teen birth rate (ages 15–19) was 39. This rate has declined 47 percent between 1991 and 2005, which exceeded the decline for the national teen birth rate, which was 33 percent.

In 2005, 86 percent of California mothers began their prenatal care in the first trimester of their pregnancy, which is greater than the percentage of U.S. mothers (78 percent). Of these mothers, 89 percent of white women, 82 percent of African American women, and 84 percent of Latina mothers began their prenatal care in the first trimester of their pregnancies.

In 2006, California spent $124 on family planning for every woman in need, which was less than only two other states (Alabama and South Carolina). State programs, such as Family Planning, Access, Care and Treatment (PACT), offer teens and low-income couples easy access to free or affordable birth control. While pregnancies among teens have declined, that rate has increased among poor women in California. Overall, many laud this program for its success and the money it saves state and federal taxpayers from paying for unwanted pregnancies (more than $1.4 billion). However, many are concerned about the future of the PACT program because of the number of undocumented immigrant women who use these services. In September 2008, the Bush administration mandated that California change its system of determining the number of undocumented immigrants in its program, or risk losing its federal funding.

*California's Pacific coast is a draw for many families, the vast majority (73 percent) of whom are married-couple families.*

An estimated 80.8 percent of California residents aged 25 and older and 80.4 percent of women residents aged 25 and older hold at least a high school diploma or equivalent in 2006. Such percentages are lower than those for the U.S. population, as 85.4 percent of all residents and 85.9 percent of women residents have at least a high school diploma that same year. Moreover, 29.8 percent of California residents aged 25 and older and 28.8 percent of women residents aged 25 and older hold at least a bachelor's degree. These percentages are greater than those for the U.S. population, which are 28 percent for all residents and 26.9 percent for women residents.

The median income from families in California is $64,563, which is greater than the U.S. median family income ($58,526). However, 9.7 percent of California families lived below the poverty line in 2006. For married-couple families, 5.8 percent lived below the poverty line, and 8.3 percent of married couple families lived with children under the age of 18. Among single mothers, 24.0 percent lived below the poverty line, 31.7 percent of single mothers lived with children under the age of 18, and 35.2 percent lived with children under the age of 5.

## Liberal Cultural Norms in California

Given California's colorful history of Spanish missionaries and the Gold Rush, in addition to its high-tech and entertainment wealth and the beauty of the Pacific coastlines, people often consider Californians to be among the most liberal and progressive in the United States. One way to gauge cultural norms in California is to consider state legislation. For instance, in 1970, California passed the country's second no-fault divorce laws, which hold that neither party in a marriage has to admit fault for that relationship's dissolution. California has among the most progressive laws regarding breastfeeding: It is one of 40 states that allows women to breastfeed in any public or private location; one of 21 states that has laws related to breastfeeding in the workplace; and one of five states that has implemented a breastfeeding awareness education campaign.

Various parenting magazines, parenting Websites, and health organizations offer listings of the places to raise children or the best places to have a baby. *Fit Pregnancy* magazine identifies San Francisco as the second-best U.S. city to have a baby because of the high rates of breastfeeding, as well as more fertility clinics and doctors relative to population than almost any other city. *Best Life* magazine features 23 California cities as among the 100 best places to raise a family. San Diego, Santa Rosa, Los Angeles, and Corona are listed in the top 20.

California is the birthplace and/or home to numerous mothers. These mothers include entertainers, political activists, politicians, and authors: Isadora Duncan, dancer; Dorothea Lange, photojournalist; Nancy Reagan, actor and former U.S. First Lady; Shirley Temple Black, actor and U.S. Ambassador; Dolores Huerta, labor leader; Dame Elizabeth Rosemond Taylor, actor; Dianne Feinstein, Senator; Maxine Hong Kingston, writer; Alice Walker, author; Pat Benatar, singer and songwriter; Maria Shriver, journalist and First Lady of California; Ellen Ochoa, first Latina astronaut; Kristi Yamaguchi, Olympic figure skater; Lisa Leslie, professional and Olympic basketball player; and Angelina Jolie, actor and UNICEF Goodwill Ambassador.

**See Also:** African American Mothers; Birth Control; Breastfeeding; Divorce; Education and Mothering; Fathers and Fathering; Immigrant Mothers; Poverty and Mothering; Prenatal Health Care; Reagan, Nancy; Single Mothers; Teen Mothers; Walker, Alice; Welfare and Mothering.

**Bibliography**

Advisory Board Company and Kaiser Family Foundation. "California Could Lose Federal Funding for Family Planning Program Unless It Begins Verifying Immigration Status of Participants." *Medical News Today* (October 7, 2008). http://www.medicalnews today.com/articles/124459.php (accessed May 2009).

Best Life. "The 100 Best Places to Raise a Family." (April 4, 2008). http://www.bestlifeonline.com/cms/ publish/family-fatherhood/The_100_Best_Places_to_ Raise_a_Family.shtml (accessed May 2009).

California Department of Finance. "E-1 Population Estimates for Cities, Counties and the State With Annual Percent Change—January 1, 2007 and 2008." (May 2008). http://www.dof.ca.gov/research/ demographic/reports/estimates/e-1_2006-07 (accessed May 2009).

Centers for Disease Control and Prevention. National Center for Health Statistics: VitalStats. http://www .cdc.gov/nchs/vitalstats.htm (accessed May 2009).

The Henry J. Kaiser Family Foundation. "California: Percentage of Mothers Beginning Prenatal Care in the First Trimester, 2006." http://www.statehealth facts.org/profileind.jsp?rgn=15&cat=2&ind=44 (accessed May 2009).

U.S. Census Bureau. "Educational Attainment in the United States: 2006." http://www.census.gov/ population/www/socdemo/education/cps2006.html (accessed May 2009).

Florence Maätita
Southern Illinois University, Edwardsville

# Cambodia

The history of Cambodia since the 1970s has been marred by unrest, including bombings and invasions by the United States during the Vietnam War, extremely high civilian deaths during the Pol Pot regime, 10 years of Vietnamese occupation, and regular outbreaks of civil war. This meant many years of little or no economic development, and much of the population still lives in poverty. However, since 2004 the economy has grown about 10 percent per year, and the per-capita Gross Domestic Product in 2008 is estimated at $2,000, up from $1,800 in 2006. However, inflation is also high: consumer price inflation was estimated at 20.2 percent in 2008.

Population is estimated at about 14.5 million, with 36.6 percent under the age of 14 (an extremely high percentage, typical of a nonindustrialized country) and 3.6 percent over the age of 65. The population growth rate is about 1.8 percent, with a birth rate of 25.68 per 1,000 population and a total fertility rate (an estimate of the number of children which each woman has) of 4.7. Life expectancy is low for both men and women, about 60 and 64 years, respectively: one reason is a high rate of infectious diseases including human immunodeficiency virus (HIV) and acquired immunodeficiency syndrome (AIDS), food and waterborne diseases, and insect-borne diseases. The population is predominantly Buddhist (95 percent) and literacy is substantially higher for males (84.7 percent) than for women (64.1 percent).

Per capita health care expenditures were estimated to be $32, of which most (85 percent) was private rather than governmental. About 12 percent of Cambodia's Gross Domestic Product is spent on health care, and about 5 percent of the financing for health care comes from external sources. Standards of maternal and infant health care are much lower than in most countries of the world: for instance, less than 70 percent of children receive timely immunizations against measles, diphtheria, and tetanus, and tetanus immunization rates for expectant mothers are below 50 percent. Only 32 percent of births are attended by skilled health personnel and only 10 percent take place in health facilities; 44 percent of women receive at least one prenatal care visit, and 9 percent receive four or more. The maternal mortality ratios is 450 per 100,000 live births, the stillbirth rate is 37 per 1,000, and the neonatal mortality rate in 40 per 1,000.

Only 19 percent of women use modern methods of contraception, and although abortion has been legal in Cambodia since 1997, due to many barriers to providers a substantial number of women either seek to terminate their own pregnancies or seek the procedure from unsafe service providers. A randomized study in 2008 found that in 2005, over 30,000 Cambodian women were treated in health care facilities for complications of miscarriage or abortion, and 40 percent of these disclosed or showed strong evidence of prior termination attempts as well. The researchers projected a ratio of abortion/miscarriage complications to live births in Cambodia as 93 per 1,000.

**See Also:** Abortion; Buddhism and Mothering; Child Poverty; Laos; Malaysia; Poverty and Mothers; Thailand; War and Mothers.

**Bibliography**

Chaterjee, P. "Cambodia Tackles High Maternal Mortality." *Lancet*, v.366 (July 2005).
Fetters, T., S. Vonthanak, C. Picardo, and T. Rathavy. "Abortion-Related Complications in Cambodia." *BJOG: A Journal of Obstetrics and Gynecology*, v.115/8 (2008).
World Health Association. "World Health Statistics 2008." www.who.int (accessed July 2009).

Sarah E. Boslaugh
Washington University School of Medicine

# Cameroon

The Republic of Cameroon is a diverse West African country with customs that promote high fertility. Women in the formal sector receive maternity benefits. Tribal norms and religion influence gender roles and rituals. Contraceptive use is low; some prenatal care is common. Women's educational attainment is lower than men's, but women have been active in Cameroon's independence and pro-democracy movements.

Cameroonian mothers have an average of 4.41 children. Government pronatalist policies shifted in the late 1980s to raise awareness of problems of limited resources and a high birth rate.

Cameroon's labor legislation protects pregnant women's right to work and paid maternity leave of 14 weeks. Only a small percentage of women, those employed in the formal sector, are eligible.

The Civil Code recognizes fault-based divorce, and divorced parents have a say in child rearing and education. Young children typically remain with the mother, older children with the father. Less than 25 percent of families are female headed.

Cameroon was created by the unification of British and French colonies. Five regional cultural groups represent about 250 ethnic groups. Indigenous religions are pervasive. Marriages are monogamous or polygamous. The social imperative for motherhood is strong, with gender roles and rituals prescribed by tribal norms. Women are responsible for housework, childcare, and family duties. Islamic populations in the north practice circumcision rites, fertility rituals, and fertility masquerades. Traditional medical practices focus on reproduction. In some regions, Christians reject local rituals and rites.

## Contraception, Health Care, and Education

The sale of contraceptives is legal; almost all public health facilities offer reproductive health services. Contraceptive prevalence for all methods is less than 20 percent, 4.2 percent for modern methods. Cost and access to clinics are deterrents to use, but are free for indigent persons. Abortion is illegal except to protect the mother's health or for pregnancies from rape.

Public centers provide services to pregnant women. More than three-quarters receive some prenatal care; 62 percent of births are attended by skilled personnel. The maternal mortality rate is very high. Midwifery has almost disappeared and traditional healers are rarely consulted about reproductive health matters except infertility.

Cameroon has one of the highest literacy rates in Africa; primary education is compulsory. Girls' share in secondary enrollment is 44 percent.

Women actively participated in the struggle for independence, strikes, and pro-democracy demonstrations, and remain active in grassroots and nongovernmental organizations. In 1995, the government initiated a national plan and legal reforms for the advancement of women, including the right of pregnant girls to remain in school.

Ma Rose Fru Ndi was a mother and political activist who worked for women's empowerment and crusaded for peace, justice, and development.

**See Also:** Birth Control; Congo; Equatorial Guinea; Nigeria; Postcolonialism and Mothering; Poverty and Mothering.

**Bibliography**

Adams, Melinda. "Cameroon." In *The Greenwood Encyclopedia of Women's Issues Worldwide,* Lynn Walter, ed. Westport, CT: Greenwood Press, 2003.

Center for Reproductive Rights. "Women of the World: Laws and Policies Affecting Their Reproductive Lives—Cameroon." (2003). http://www.reproductiverights.org/pdf/benin.pdf (accessed May 2009).

Weigner, Susan and John Akuri. "Cameroonian Women's Perceptions of Their Health Care Needs." *Nordic Journal of African Studies*, v.16/1 (2007).

Keri L. Heitner
University of Phoenix

# Canada

According to quality-of-life indices, Canadians enjoy safe neighborhoods, universal access to health care, high education rates, and job opportunities. The United Nations Human Development Index (HDI), which examines the health, education, and economic wealth of 179 countries, ranked Canada third in 2008. Canada is characterized by great levels of diversity in terms of ethnicity, language, and culture, but also in terms of economic opportunity.

Quality-of-life indicators have therefore come under scrutiny in regards to how they pertain to certain segments of the Canadian population. Single mothers in particular are prone to disparities in quality of life and face obstacles related to housing, education, personal health, working conditions, and finances. First Nations mothers likewise face adversity related to several issues, including access to health care, poverty, food insecurity, domestic violence, adequate housing, and high rates of teen motherhood.

## Single Mothers

Single mothers in Canada face a variety of stressors related to securing gainful employment, managing childcare arrangements, and maintaining a reliable support network. Unemployed lone mothers are twice as likely to report a high level of distress compared with other groups; regardless of employment status, single mothers are more likely to report both high personal and chronic stress. Single mothers may have difficulty accessing affordable housing, as Canada's national rental vacancy rates totaled 2.2 percent as a national average in 2008. The lack of affordable housing has been attributed to the growing gap between the cost of home ownership and the affordability of renting. According to Statistics Canada, 38percent of lone-parent families headed by females had incomes below the poverty line, compared to 13 percent of lone-parent families headed by males.

## Health Care Quality and Access

Canadian mothers are guaranteed access to health care, independent of income levels, through Canada's public health care system. Health care policy comes under the jurisdiction of the provinces and territories, which may impose premiums based on earnings. According to a 2002 study, 26 percent of Canadians reported that access to health care had decreased in recent years, and lack of physician choice has been cited as a symptom of the system. Access to health care in rural areas can be problematic, particularly in remote northern communities, where evacuation for birth is common. Only 3 percent of obstetrician gynecologists practice in rural Canada, and physicians have cited both a lack of financial incentives and the lack of specialist backup as reasons for their reluctance to practice outside urban settings. Mothers in rural Canada deal with a host of issues related to health care, including separation from loved ones during hospitalization, arrangement of childcare to attend medical appointments, travel-related stress, and a weak patient/physician relationship due to high rates of provider turnover.

## Employment and Motherhood

Fifty-six percent of women in Quebec were in the paid labor force in 2004; in 2006, 73 percent of all Canadian women with children under the age of 16 in the household were employed. Despite increased participation in the labor force, mothers continue to bear the majority of domestic duties, and housework remains unequally divided. In Canada's competitive labor market, a working mother's prioritization of family responsibilities, such as child rearing, may contribute to a perceived lack of commitment in the workplace. Overall, working mothers earn 2 percent less in hourly wages than do working women without children. Many mothers experience stress in balancing work and domestic duties, and technology has further blurred the lines between the workplace and home. Of the over 50 percent of Canadian women in the work force, 69 percent are mothers with at least one child under the age of 3. Some mothers choose to work fewer hours, or leave the work force for long periods of time in order to meet family commitments. In 2006, 15 percent of female part-time employees stated that they worked reduced hours in order to care for children.

The universal health care system may be responsible for providing some Canadian mothers with the flexibility to be self-employed, and to work part time versus full time. Canadian mothers do not depend as heavily upon employer health care plans as would their American counterparts, and this may contribute to the fact that since 1989, Canadian women have consistently surpassed American women in the number of unincorporated businesses owned. According to a 2004 report by the Canadian Imperial Bank of Commerce (CIBC), 78 percent of Canadian businesswomen felt that entrepreneurship provided flexibility in balancing work and family commitments.

### Maternity Leave and Childcare

In 2000, parental leave in Canada was expanded from 10 to 35 weeks, which may be divided between the two parents. Women are also entitled to 15 weeks of paid maternity leave, at 55 percent of the employee's earnings. In 2000, only 3 percent of fathers used parental benefits, while in 2005, 11 percent did. Residents of Quebec have been able to receive maternal, paternity, parental, and adoption benefits since January 1, 2006, through the Quebec Parental Insurance Plan, which offers higher benefits but also requires workers to pay a higher tax to support it.

One impetus for the increase in leave was to provide nursing mothers with the opportunity to meet on-demand breastfeeding targets as set by the World Health Organization (WHO). Since the increase in maternity leave time, more mothers have continued to breastfeed exclusively for the duration of the first six months of life, as recommended by Health Canada and the WHO. It is possible that maternity leave may eventually be further increased in order to meet WHO breastfeeding targets, which recommend that children be breastfed a minimum of two years.

Federal and provincial programs provide some assistance in alleviating issues related to childcare and tax relief. All Canadian provinces and territories have childcare subsidy programs; however, qualifications for these programs vary widely. In 2003, 54 percent of Canadian children aged 6 months to 5 years of age were in some form of childcare. Childcare settings range from regulated centers and family childcare homes to unregulated, nonrelative care. Mothers who are employed, recently unemployed and seeking new employment, enrolled in job training, or enrolled in an educational program may apply for childcare subsidies, which are awarded according to income. With the exception of the province of Quebec, Canadian mothers navigate the social system to obtain childcare subsidies, and a wage increase may disqualify them from receiving assistance. Quebec residents, regardless of income, pay $7 (Canadian) per day for childcare. The Quebec program has resulted in an increase of working mothers; however, daycare spaces in large cities have also become scarce.

The Canadian government has recently developed incentive programs for employer-created childcare spaces, which include provincial and territorial funding to support childcare systems. Canada's federally funded Universal Child Care Benefit (UCCB) of $100 per month per child under 6 years of age is available to all families, regardless of their employment status. Canadian mothers may also be eligible to receive monthly child tax credits based on income. These payments vary according to provincial jurisdictions; however, in 2008, a two-child family earning less than $103,235 per year still qualified for a portion of the benefit.

### Birthrate and Divorce Rate

Canada's birthrate has been in decline since World War II, and continues to decrease. According to 2008 estimates, the birth rate stands at 10.29 births per 1,000 persons. Canada's fertility rate was 1.59 live births per woman in 2006. This figure represents a significant decrease from 1970, when the fertility rate was 2.3 live births per woman. As delaying motherhood translates to higher wages for working women, an increasing number of Canadian women are postponing childbirth in order to establish their careers. In 2005, the average age of women who gave birth for the first time was 29.3 years, an increase from 27.1 years in 1996. Contraception is widely available and practiced, and sterilization is also common among couples. Abortion is legal through all nine months of gestation and most abortions are publicly funded.

The fertility rate for Aboriginal women is 2.6, a decline from the 1960s average for Aboriginals of 5.5. Life expectancy for Aboriginal women at birth in 2001 was 76.8 years, higher than for aboriginal men (70.9 years) but lower than for non-Aboriginal women (just over 82 years). About 40 percent of Aboriginal women have not completed high school, and the most common reason for leaving school is pregnancy or the need to care for a child.

Canada's divorce rate is difficult to estimate due to the prevalence of common-law unions in the country, but divorce rates in 2004 reported 12.5 per 1,000 legally married females. According to 2001 Statistics Canada data, 16 percent of Canadian couples cohabitate; however, common-law unions are not included in Canada's divorce rate calculations. In 2002, the crude divorce rate was 2.2 per 1,000 people and the total number of divorces granted was 70,155.

## Education and Religion

Canada has the highest per capita postsecondary participation of any industrialized country. Education comes under the authority of the individual provinces and territories, and all major universities are publicly funded.

Major religious affiliations include Roman Catholicism, the United Church, and the Anglican Church of Canada. While 59 percent of the Canadian population identify with one of these religions, church attendance is comparatively low.

## Resourceful Canadian Mothers

Canadian mothers organize many opportunities for interaction through mothering and play groups sponsored by local organizations and community centers. Many of these programs are highly afford-

able, with low drop-in rates and shared responsibilities for snacks, cleaning, and toy donations. Such collaborative, community-based activities are used in part as an antidote to Canada's long and isolating winters. Historically, Canadian women have demonstrated resourcefulness and courage in spite of a precarious existence on a harsh landscape.

Margaret Atwood, born in 1939, is one of Canada's most popular contemporary writers. Her best-known works include the novels *The Handmaid's Tale* (winner of the Arthur C. Clarke Award), *Oryx and Crake,* and *Surfacing.* She has one daughter, Eleanor Atwood Gibson.

Laura Secord, a mother of seven children, is known as Canada's heroine of the War of 1812. She completed a journey by foot through enemy lines to warn British Lieutenant Fitzgibbon of a planned American attack. Laura Secord remains a recognizable household name; a popular Canadian chocolate company was named after her in 1912.

Harriet Nahanee (1935–2004), also a mother of seven children, was an activist for First Nations causes. She spoke out against the conditions in the residential schools, which she was forced to attend. She died of pneumonia at age 71 following incarceration for protesting the destruction of wetlands on Squamish lands.

**See Also:** Childcare; First Nations; Lone Mothers; Maternity Leave; Rural Mothers; Single Mothers.

**Bibliography**

Canadian Imperial Bank of Commerce. "Women Entrepreneurs: Leading the Charge." *CIBC World Markets* (2009).

Geissler, Shawna, Lynn Loutzenhiser, Jocelyn Praud, and Lessa Streifler, eds. *La Maternité au Canada: Voix Interdisciplinaires [Mothering in Canada: Interdisciplinary Voices].* Toronto: Demeter Press, 2010.

Statistics Canada. *Women in Canada: A Gender-Based Statistical Report.* Ottawa: Minister of Industry, 2006.

Sutherns, Rebecca and Ivy Lynn Bourgeault. "Accessing Maternity Care in Rural Canada: There's More to the Story Than Distance to the Doctor." *Health Care for Women International,* v.29/8 (2008).

Gabriella Reznowski
Washington State University

# Cancer and Motherhood

Every year, 700,000 women in the United States are diagnosed with cancer. Excluding skin cancers, breast cancer is the most frequently diagnosed cancer in women. In 2008, the American Cancer Society projected over 182,000 new cases. Although 80 percent of these cases were in women over age 50, nearly 33,000 diagnosed women were under the age of 45. Younger women with breast cancer face some issues that older women do not. In addition to frequently having more advanced cancers at diagnosis and higher mortality rates, these women potentially face infertility, early menopause, and implications for pregnancy after diagnosis. They are also likely to have dependent children and a greater responsibility for family care.

### Cancer Treatment and Fertility

Several common cancer treatments affect women's fertility, the ability to conceive and have children. Chemotherapy uses chemical agents to kill rapidly dividing cancer cells. Because the body has other cells that are constantly dividing (e.g., hair follicles, the gastrointestinal lining, and sperm and egg cells) these are also targets to chemotherapy drugs. Destroying these cells can cause side effects such as hair loss, diarrhea, premature menopause (when menstruation stops before the age of 40), and infertility (the diminished ability or the inability to conceive or have children). Chemotherapy-induced menopause occurs in 10–50 percent of women under age 40, and in 50–94 percent of women over age 40. Higher doses and longer duration of treatment cause the highest risk of infertility, and smaller doses result in infertility as age increases.

Hormone treatment, also called hormone therapy, can result in premature menopause that is temporary or permanent. Hormone therapy involves the use of drugs to "turn off" or "slow down" the body's production of the naturally occurring hormones, estrogen and progesterone, which have been found to promote the growth of some types of breast cancer. One of the most common drugs used in hormone therapy, Tamoxifen®, is often given along with chemotherapy and other breast cancer treatments to prevent estrogen from attaching to the cancer cells, thereby hindering their growth.

Because Tamoxifen inhibits the estrogen in the body that is needed for healthy menstruation, it increases a woman's chances of entering premature menopause and becoming infertile.

While radiation of the breast does not cause infertility, it does damage milk-producing glands, making breastfeeding difficult or nearly impossible. Depending on the type and extent of a woman's cancer diagnosis, treatment may also involve radiating or removing the ovaries, which produce eggs and female hormones. The aim is to reduce the amount of estrogen in the body in order to slow tumor growth. Removal or radiation of the ovaries causes infertility.

### Pregnancy After Cancer Treatment

Becoming pregnant following treatment for breast cancer poses health risks and ethical questions. First, a breast cancer diagnosis decreases a woman's life expectancy. How much it decreases depends upon the type of breast cancer, the stage at diagnosis, and the success of treatment. Ethically, some women do not want to risk having children when they may not live to raise them; others want to have a child regardless. Second, if there are microscopic cancer cells remaining in the body after treatment, the hormones released during pregnancy can make them grow faster, increasing the risk of recurrence. Cancer centers report no significant difference in overall survival between women who have had pregnancies following breast cancer and women who have not. Children born to women who have been treated for breast cancer do not appear to suffer harmful consequences as a result of the mother's treatment.

If early menopause is likely to result from treatment, there are options for fertility preservation. Most common is the harvesting and freezing of eggs or embryos prior to treatment. Women take fertility drugs to allow the release and collection of mature eggs. If the eggs are fertilized with sperm, the resulting pregnancy rate is 20–25 percent after the embryo is implanted. Unfertilized eggs are more sensitive to the freezing process, resulting in a 2 percent pregnancy rate. These low pregnancy rates result in even lower birth rates, depending on a woman's age, the number of embryos frozen and implanted, and other factors related to fertilization and the health of the reproductive system.

There are important issues for women with cancer to bear in mind if considering fertility-preserving techniques. First, they are expensive, and the majority of patients do not have coverage through health insurance. Second, they delay cancer treatment, sometimes for up to a year, which may not be a viable option. Third, there are no clear data on how safe fertility drugs are in the long term, or how they interact with breast cancer. If the risks of using fertility-preserving techniques outweigh the benefits, diagnosed women who want children may consider adoption or surrogacy.

## Mothers Aren't Supposed to Get Sick

The cultural image of the appropriate mother is one of an unselfish nurturer who provides family care. Despite changes in attitudes and women's workforce participation in recent years, women still perform the bulk of domestic work, are the childcare experts, and serve as caregivers and emotional managers for their families. When a mother gets sick, family roles and household routines usually need to change. Ideas about women's proper roles as family caregivers can influence a mother's capacity to get the support she needs to deal with cancer, treatment, and aftercare as well as to maintain her family and household routines.

Since mothers are often teachers of children, they must consider whether, what, and how to talk their children about cancer, and to think about what their children can reasonably understand. Demystifying what cancer is, explaining treatment, reassuring children that they will not be abandoned, and making promises one can keep are all ways to reduce children's anxiety. For mothers with teenage daughters, breast cancer can be difficult to discuss in part because their daughter's breasts are developing when their mother's breasts are the source of problems. Daughters may also be expected to fulfill their mother's traditional family role, causing resentment or guilt. Quality communication is critical for minimizing the negative effects of cancer, increasing mothers' access to social support, and sustaining the family system.

**See Also:** Artificial Insemination; Care Giving; Ethics of Care; Ethics, Maternal; Feminist Theory and Mothering; Guilt; Myths of Motherhood: Good/Bad; Reproduction; Surrogate Motherhood; Technology and Motherhood; Young Mothers.

### Bibliography

Coleman, P. *How to Say It to Your Kids: The Right Words to Solve Problems, Soothe Feelings and Teach Values*. Upper Saddle River, NJ: Prentice Hall, 2000.

Coyne, E. and S. Borbasi. "Holding It All Together: Breast Cancer and Its Impact on Life for Younger Women." *Contemporary Nurse*, v.23/2 (2006).

Love, S. *Dr. Susan Love's Breast Book*. Cambridge, MA: Da Capo Press, 2005.

Park, M., et al. "Preservation of Fertility and the Impact of Subsequent Pregnancy in Patients With Premenopausal Breast *Cancer.*" *Seminars in Oncology*, v.33/6 (2006).

Sulik, G. "The Balancing Act: Care Work for the Self and Coping With Breast Cancer." *Gender & Society*, v.21/6 (2007).

Vachani, C. "Female Fertility and Cancer Treatment." (October 6, 2006). Oncolink Abramson Cancer Center of the University of Pennsylvania. http://www.oncolink.com/coping/article.cfm?c=4&s=42&ss=90&id=990&p=3# (accessed August 2009).

Gayle A. Sulik
Texas Woman's University

# Cape Verde

Cape Verde became independent upon the unilateral declaration of independence for Guinea-Bissau on September 24, 1973, by the African Party for the Independence and Union of Guinea and Cape Verde (PAIGC) on July 5, 1975. In terms of human development, Cape Verde—classified "medium development" on the Human Development Index (HDI) 2007 Report—towers above its fellow west African countries such as Nigeria, which has comparatively massive natural resources. Cape Verde has relatively functional laws and policies that protect the interests of women when compared with other countries in Africa. The female literacy rate is quite encouraging; infant and maternal mortality have remained one of the lowest on the continent. Accessibility to health care has been quite encouraging, and hunger seems a rare phenomenon in the country of below half a million inhabitants (426,998 according to the 2008 headcount).

Although the human condition in Cape Verde has historically been unenviable, especially during Portuguese colonialism (when an estimated 55,000 citizens died of large-scale hunger and health-related problems between 1940–48), contemporary Cape Verde has been able to achieve remarkable progress in enhancing the standard of living of the entire citizenry, mothers included. Various birth control measures are indeed very potent in the country. Female reproductive education has not only been popular, but quite functional in both rural and urban areas. Accessibility to formal education across gender categories is among the highest in Africa, and compulsory for ages 6–14. This has enhanced mothers' capacity in taking up cogent, socioeconomic opportunities. Also, the state does make compelling incentives available in the form of social services to mothers and children. The sprawling incidences of early marriage and common childhood diseases prevalent among other larger, West African countries are quite rare in Cape Verde, with comparatively limited natural resources.

The rate of divorce on the island is quite lower when juxtaposed with the rest of the continent. Even when it occurs, divorce laws are designed to distribute the responsibilities of childrens' upbringing between mothers and fathers. Roman Catholicism is the most prominent religion in the country, which tends to influence the mode of relation within the family setting. That is, women are still expected to be submissive to their husbands; however, the nature of the societal structure is not designed to allow the men to hide under such submissiveness to manipulate women. Among such mothers were Simoa Borges, the adopted mother of Juvenal Cabral (father of the founder of the PAIGC, Amilar Cabral, and the country's first president, Luis Cabral); and Iva Cabral.

**See Also:** Burundi; Congo; Globalization and Mothering; Guinea–Bissau; Ivory Coast.

**Bibliography**
Adeniran, Adebusuyi. *Cabral, Amilcar (September 12, 1924–January 20, 1973).* New York: Wiley-Blackwell, 2009.
Fobanjong, J., and Thomas Ranuga. *The Life, Thought and Legacy of Cape Verde's Freedom Fighter Amilcar Cabral (1924–1973): Essays on His Liberation Philosophy.* Lewiston, NY: Edwin Mellen Press, 2006.
Human Development Reports. "2007/2008 Human Development Report: Cape Verde." (2008). hdrstats.undp.org (accessed May 2009).
Leite, Ana Mafalda. *Portuguese Literary & Cultural Studies 8: Cape Verde.* North Dartmouth, MA: Center for Portuguese Studies & Culture, 2002.

Adebusuyi Isaac Adeniran
Obafemi Awolowo University, Nigeria

# Capitalism and Motherhood

For both women and men, parenthood is a gendered experience. However, for women, the tasks of mothering, such as taking care of children and domestic responsibilities, are argued to provide women the opportunity to express biologically based behavior. Yet, scholars maintain that motherhood is like other social institutions and social statuses, and that family structure is flexible enough to respond to changes in the economy and politics. Researchers and activists contend that while different models of family life are sustainable and beneficial for all members, motherhood remains as an ideologically significant role for women in society.

Capitalism serves as the framework to understand the intersectional relationship of motherhood in different contexts and on multiple levels. Motherhood is simultaneously a cultural icon, an individual experience, and a social institution. As capitalism developed, it altered family life; for example, many of the roles and responsibilities of parenting are now commodities available for purchase. Depending on other statuses such as class and race, women may experience motherhood differently.

## Historical Connections
Scholars also note it is important to examine the influence of capitalism on motherhood at various historical moments to track how motherhood is defined and experienced at different points in time. Capitalism has supported the nuclear family model.

As industrialization indelibly altered market relationships, family life also changed in response to social, cultural, political, and economic trends. The growth of capitalism helped to fuel the creation of separate spheres of work and family life. As the gap between work life and family life grew, so did the distinct roles for mothers and fathers. The oft-repeated phrase, that family serves as a "haven in a heartless world," epitomized the belief that family life was disconnected from other social institutions such as politics and the economy.

In the separate-spheres model of family life, motherhood is a master status that defines women's lives in terms of their relationships with others. Feminist scholars note the idea of two distinct, separate spheres of home life and the labor market is a myth, as the two arenas have always intersected; the ideology of these separate spheres continues to have a powerful symbolic place in contemporary society. Motherhood is influenced by market forces, as it is increasingly seen as a service provided for someone else.

Although parenting of one's own biological children does not count as participation in the paid labor force, some activists and scholars argue that women should be paid for performing the tasks associated with motherhood. Barbara Katz Rothman contends that family life is best understood using the capitalist ideology of worker, resources, and power, particularly when analyzing the responsibilities that mothers are expected to fulfill. The emotional and physical labor of mothers' work, including the use of their bodies for reproduction, is necessary for society. However, the act of mothering has been cast as an emotional and biological imperative; therefore, women are expected to participate in the institution of motherhood without economic compensation. Just as in the paid labor market, within families, not all work or the workers themselves are considered of equal value or are compensated for their contributions.

## Class, Ethnic, and Racial Differences

Researchers argue that from the 18th century through the 1960s, the nuclear family was largely unchallenged until the second wave of the feminist movement. Although the social norms and expectations for mothers remained largely unchanged during this time, there were vast differences in how various groups of women were able to practice mothering or define motherhood for themselves.

For example, in the antebellum United States, black women who were enslaved were considered the property of their owners. If a slave owner was in debt, an enslaved mother could be sold without consideration of the consequences on her own family. Black women who were enslaved could also become mothers against their will, as this meant an increase of property for the slave owner. In this instance, enslaved women who were mothers provided additional property for their owners as the children born into slavery shared the designated status of slaves like their mothers. Enslaved women were also often responsible for the well-being of their owner's children, at the expense of spending time parenting their own. Motherhood for enslaved women was tenuous, yet for slave owners it was a desirable institution, as it provided them with new property.

Moreover, scholars note that while the nuclear family model and ideology of separate spheres strengthened during the antebellum period, motherhood was experienced differently whether a woman was enslaved or free, or from a poor, working family or a wealthy, merchant or land-owning family. The condition of being a mother and a slave highlights the contradictory status of motherhood. For enslaved mothers, the notion of separate spheres never existed as their labor; however, it was an important factor in the growth of capitalism in the United States and other countries, such as England and France, that profited from the transatlantic slave trade.

In the post–Civil War United States, upper-class and middle-class families sought domestics to care for their children. Social class differentiated women's experiences as they participated in a new market of the commodification of services once considered a natural part of women's roles as mothers. Although the ideology of the nuclear family model and separate spheres was entrenched in popular culture and political debates about family life, the burgeoning market for domestic servants in the late 19th and 20th century challenged the belief that motherhood and capitalism operated independent of each other.

Due to their position within the intersection of race, gender, and class in the United States and the institutionalization of gendered racism, African American women had very few careers choices prior to the Civil Rights Movement. Although historically black colleges and universities often accepted both male and female students, African American women were regulated into a limited number of professions. As a result, a domestic was a commonly held job. In their postions, African American domestics were expected to perform many of the duties associated with motherhood.

Domestic labor was common in European nations transitioning from rural and agrarian to urban and industrial economies, such as France and England in the 19th century. Rural families apprenticed their children as domestic help in cities. It was not uncommon to have children working as domestics doing work once considered appropriate for adults. Domestic service was also a popular option, among limited employment opportunities, for European immigrant women in the early 19th century in the United States. New immigrants did not disdain doing domestic labor as much their native-born counterparts. Instead, research demonstrates that in European countries and the United States, domestic work was often viewed as a temporary status for women as they transitioned from being single without children, to married with children. Domestic labor was viable employment that provided multiple benefits beyond money, such as the instruction of middle-class values and behavior and honing domestic skills prior to marriage. Having the ability to afford hired help to assist with domestic responsibilities was, and continues to be, a sign of affluence for middle-class and elite families.

## Feminist Critiques

During the second wave of the women's movement, activists and scholars emphasized the contradictions of mothering. Motherhood was challenged as the ultimate expression of femininity, as well as a "natural" role for women to hold. Some scholars and activists argued that if women's labor in the act of mothering was critical to a family's well-being, then they should be rewarded appropriately in a capitalist society with pay. Activists and scholars highlighted that motherhood, while not technically considered a profession, is one of the few jobs anyone is expected to enter without a labor contract that demands a large amount of physical, emotional, and psychological energy to perform.

The debate over wages for housework and mothering continues today. It speaks directly to the contradictions and tensions inherent in motherhood. Researchers also noted the tenuous situation a woman is in if she works only at home without pay or does not have another independent source of income. She must rely on her partner to provide food, clothing, shelter, and health care for her and her children. The movement to pay women for housework and mothering, while not successful, has helped to demonstrate that motherhood is not simply a natural phenomenon; it requires physical, emotional, and psychological labor. Instead, motherhood is argued to be a socially constructed phenomenon that benefits some groups at the expense of others in a capitalist society.

## The Commodification of Motherhood

Arlie Hochschild is among the most vocal scholars citing that contemporary forms of motherhood are intimately connected to capitalism. She posits that the family offers a new market niche for specialized services that were once considered only part of the unpaid elements of family life. In this process, motherhood and capitalism meet in a newly emerging "commodity frontier." For example, birthday planning was once considered a responsibility of mothers; however, in the commodity frontier, party planning is a new, emerging capitalist endeavor. For mothers with resources to purchase services, the commodity frontier provides multiple opportunities to highlight their affluence by consuming goods and services others provide to maintain their family's activities.

Scholars note that as capitalism and family life become increasing intertwined, motherhood takes on an even greater ideological and symbolic importance. Idealized notions of motherhood with an emphasis on caring, nurturance, and self-sacrifice are increasingly seen as necessary to provide a sense of stability, as other social institutions such as the economy become increasingly unstable. Families with sufficient resources are able to purchase elements of mothering that was once unpaid labor, providing an environment of comfort, safety, and security for their members.

*Mothers are not economically compensated for their domestic labor, even though their work is vital in a capitalistic society.*

Gender scholars argue that capitalism competes with family life, particularly motherhood, yet also complements the ideal family experience from services such as personal organizers, chefs, and party planners. As in the past, women from marginalized and disadvantaged groups, including racial and ethnic minorities, the working class, and poor, offer their domestic labor to families in the new commodity frontier. The previous centuries' labor patterns of domestic care and childcare remains within industrialized countries, although the labor base performing domestic duties varies more so than in the past. New waves of immigrants have replaced African American domestics in the American south, or Irish in the northeast. Social class relations have remained consistent so that motherhood, as an identity for elite and middle-class women, continues to provide a different set of opportunities and challenges than for women with fewer resources.

**See Also:** African American Mothers; Domestic Labor; Employment and Motherhood; Mothering as Work; Slavery and Mothering.

**Bibliography**
Coltrane, Scott. "Household Labor and the Routine Production of Gender." *Social Problems*, v.36/5 (December 1989).
Coontz, Stephanie. *The Way We Really Are: Coming to Terms With America's Changing Families*. New York: Basic Books, 1998.
Crittenden, Ann. *The Price of Motherhood: Why the Most Important Job in the World Is Still the Least Valued*. New York: Holt Paperbacks, 2002.
Ehrenreich, Barbara and Arlie Russell Hochschild. *Global Woman: Nannies, Maids and Sex Workers in the New Economy*. New York: Owl Books, 2002.
Hays, Sharon. *The Cultural Contradictions of Motherhood*. New Haven, CT: Yale University, 1996.
Hochschild, Arlie Russell. "The Commodity Frontier." In *Self, Social Structure and Beliefs: Essays in Sociology*, Jeffery Alexander, Gary Marx, and Christine Williams, eds. Berkeley: University of California Press, 2004.
Rothman, Barbara Katz. *Recreating Motherhood*. Brunswick, NJ: Rutgers University Press, 2000.
Steinberg, Stephen. *The Ethnic Myth: Race, Ethnicity and Class in America*. Boston: Beacon Press, 2001.

Marcia Hernandez
University of the Pacific

# Caplan, Paula J.

Paula Joan Caplan, clinical psychologist, researcher, lecturer, playwright, and actor, is known for her work on mother blaming. Her influential 1989 book, *Don't Blame Mother: Mending the Mother–Daughter Relationship* was revised in 2000 and renamed *The New Don't Blame Mother: Mending the Mother–Daughter Relationship*. In her writing, lectures, radio and television appearances, and keynote addresses, Caplan presents detailed data to substantiate the fact that within both the scholarly domains of psychological theory and the popular media, mothers are held primarily responsible for any difficulties their children manifest. Caplan has identified many of the pressures faced by mothers and categorized them into myths that perpetuate mother blaming. The unattainable standards of performance implicit in these myths and their profoundly harmful impacts give rise to personal as well as societal ills that further undermine the well-being of all. Ways to transcend these controlling, destructive myths and approaches to dealing with the injuries resulting from mother blaming are important elements of Caplan's work.

In addition to exposing the harm done by mother blaming, Caplan demonstrates her deep commitment to justice by articulating significant forms of bias against women found in the systems that mental health professionals use to diagnose psychiatric disorder, and the systems that the courts use to determine child custody. In numerous publications, Caplan critiques the lack of a scientific basis for many of the disorders found in the *Diagnostic and Statistical Manual of Mental Disorders*, the text used nearly universally to diagnose psychiatric abnormality. She focuses especially on those labels that pathologize women who experience distress as they negotiate the demanding expectations placed upon them by the cultural construction of womanhood.

Within the court system, Caplan regularly serves as an expert witness, often advocating for poor mothers in custody cases where their fitness to parent has been called into question by the application of problematic psychiatric labels, or as a consequence of other forms of institutionalized bias. These issues have mobilized Caplan to petition the U.S. Senate to address more effectively the rights of children and mothers in custody cases, especially those involving child sexual abuse.

Caplan's active life as a psychologist is creatively blended with her work in the theater as actor, playwright, and director. Her desire to artistically express some of the issues central to her work as a psychologist are reflected in several of her powerful plays, including *Call Me Crazy* and *What Mommy Told Me*, which have been successfully performed in a variety of venues.

Throughout her extensive career, Caplan has served in many professional capacities, such as professor of applied psychology and director of the Centre for Women's Studies at the Ontario Institute for Studies in Education, and as a Fellow at Harvard University's DuBois Institute. She is credited with teaching some of the first courses on mothering at the university level. Caplan is the recipient of many prestigious awards, such as the Distinguished Career Award conferred by the Association for Women in Psychology, and the Woman of the Year Award granted by the Canadian Association for Women in Science.

**See Also:** "Bad" Mothers; Child Custody and the Law; Mother Blame; Myths of Motherhood: Good/Bad; Public Policy and Mothers.

### Bibliography

American Psychiatric Association. *Diagnostic and Statistical Manual of Mental Disorders, 4th Edition*. Arlington, VA: American Psychiatric Association, 2000.

Caplan, Paula J. *Call Me Crazy*. Play. Self-Published, 1996.

Caplan, Paula J. *Don't Blame Mother: Mending the Mother–Daughter Relationship*. New York: Harper and Row, 1989.

Caplan, Paula J. *The New Don't Blame Mother: Mending the Mother–Daughter Relationship*. New York: Routledge, 2000.

Caplan, Paula J. *What Mommy Told Me*. Play. Self-Published, 2008.

Regina M. Edmonds
Assumption College

# Care Giving

Care giving is predominately used to describe the caretaking of someone who is chronically ill or disabled and is no longer able to care for him- or herself. Since this definition assumes that an individual was able at some point take care of him- or herself, it does not represent care of infants and young children. It does, however, include care giving for children with disabilities. The tasks associated in care giving of an infant, older child, adolescent, adult, or elderly person are basically the same. According to the National Family Caregivers Association, care giving consists of many emotional, financial, nursing, social, and homemaking services on a regular basis, including caring for someone who cannot dress, feed, go to the bathroom, or think for themselves; learning how to work with others on behalf of the cared-for person; worrying about what's wrong with this person, as well as wondering why no one ever asks how they are; and dreaming about being alone.

## Defining Care Giver

Defining *care giver* has included the type, amount, volume, duration, and intensity of care provided; the place it is provided; and the relationship of care giver to care receiver. The National Family Caregivers Association (NFCA) has conducted care giver surveys to define the link between all care givers, and they found in no uncertain terms that the common bond of care giving is its emotional impact. Additionally, care givers share the following characteristics: longing for the miracle of normalcy; frustration as a result of changing family dynamics; isolation from living outside the norm; disappointment over the lack of understanding of noncaregivers; stress over the increased and enormous responsibilities; and resourcefulness in problem-solving abilities.

Approximately 30 percent of caregivers are men. National projected demographic trends suggest that increased longevity among men and women will increase the number of male and female caregivers across their life spans in the immediate future. As the 65 and over age group continues to grow toward an expected 79 million by 2050, future demands for informal care will greatly increase.

Informal care is usually provided in a home environment, by family or friends, and for an unspecified amount of time. Spouses will become the likely care givers in many informal care situations. Men predominantly will become informal care providers as they tend to be married or remarried in greater numbers than women. Husbands play an important

role in caring for their wives with chronic illness. The choice of women and couples to remain childless or to have children later in life makes the need for care-giving spouses a growing priority.

## Different Types of Care Giving

The nature and type of care giving may differ among care givers. Primary care givers deal with the majority of care needs, while secondary care givers supplement care provided by others. Regardless, the requirements are taxing on care givers.

Although most researchers studying care givers do not consider parenthood to qualify as care giving, exceptions are made for parents with children who have disabilities or debilitating illnesses. However, similar to the common bond discovered by NFCA among care givers, mothers, especially new mothers, often share common characteristics. These characteristics include feeling overwhelmed, unprepared, and unsure of their identity, which can result in exhaustion with a strong sense of loss and aloneness. Studies have shown that new mothers used the following words to describe their experiences: misery, low confidence, low self-esteem, fatigue, frustration and confusion, lack of satisfaction, disorientation, depression, and despair. Other studies have shown that mothers frequently experience high levels of ambivalence and guilt, which can lead to more serious manifestations of stress, leaving women feeling overloaded, overwhelmed, and exhausted. Additionally, women frequently report factors such as not enough time to relax, financial problems, home responsibilities, and problems at work among their major stressors, which can manifest into physical symptoms such as neck and shoulder pains, difficulty sleeping, headaches, aches and pains, and upset stomachs. Psychological symptoms include irritability, nervousness, and sadness, and regular crying spells.

## Care Giving at the Expense of Health

Several factors influence self-care and health behavior, especially immediate competing demands, over which an individual has low control. Care giving and childcare can be competing demands vying for attention among women's other responsibilities. Once a woman becomes a mother or initiates a care-giving relationship, she likely perceives her life to be less controllable, predictable, and leisurely. This time may coincide with the onset of self-neglect to manage her multiple demands. Studies have shown that predominately women protect their priority role as mothers even at the expense of their health.

Women tend to perform the majority of care giving, regardless of whether the care is provided to children or a frail elderly friend or family member, and some women do both. These women are considered to be part of the sandwich generation. They find themselves in between caring for the young and the old. As a result, women eventually suffer from care giver's burnout. A care giver's burden encompasses daily adjustments, which prevent many care givers from attending to their own health needs. Feelings involved in care giving, which may include guilt, can impede an individual's well-being and health-promoting behaviors; specifically, eating a balanced diet and obtaining medical care. Care givers typically lack time and opportunity for maintaining a healthy lifestyle with routine participation in health-promoting behaviors, such as exercise.

### Societal Expectations of Care Giving

In today's society, the pressures surrounding care giving are growing in pace with other demands placed on individuals, and mothers are disproportionately susceptible, given the nature of their work. The responsibilities involved in care giving are equivalent to a full-time job that is performed in combination with other full-time jobs, which is why many care-giving women eventually burn out. Similar to modern mothering, care giving is an all-encompassing job, involving an unprecedented level of vigilance, knowledge, time, commitment, focus, concentration, productivity, and performance. For example, the mass media perpetuates images of elder abuse that dictate how vigilant and present women actually need to be as care givers to ensure the safety and satisfaction of their loved ones. Conquering all of the dangers is an insurmountable task, but yet women try. If nothing else, most women rise to the occasion and make a valid attempt to be the best, if not perfect, provider and caretaker. Societal expectations probably would not accept less.

**See Also:** Adult Children; Carework; Childcare; Childlessness; Children; Ethics of Care; Family.

### Bibliography

Kramer, Betty J. and Edward H. Thompson. *Men as Caregivers: Theory, Research, and Service Implications.* New York: Springer, 2002.

Koch, Tom. *A Place in Time: Care Givers for Their Elderly.* Santa Barbara, CA: Praeger Publishers, 1993.

Mccullough, Dennis. *My Mother, Your Mother: Embracing 'Slow Medicine,' the Compassionate Approach to Caring for Your Aging Loved Ones.* New York: Harper, 2008.

National Family Caregivers Association. *The Resourceful Caregiver: Helping Family Caregivers Help Themselves.* Philadelphia: Mosby-Year Book, 1996.

Michele L. Vancour
Southern Connecticut State University

# Carework

The term *carework* (specifically, here, maternal carework) refers to the physical and emotional labor invested by mothers in caring for and nurturing dependent children. In the labor market, carework refers to services delivered in a market-based economy, as opposed to care giving, which is generally provided without expectation of payment. The same type of work (e.g., caring for a child) may receive either label: the point is that carework recognizes that it is actual work, which costs the provider in terms of time and effort. The question of whether mothers should be primarily responsible for carework, especially during children's infant years, has been a focus of feminist scholarship for over 100 years. Even today, motherhood and the issue of maternal carework remains a site of intense sociological and political debate.

### Motherhood and the Labor Market

At the turn of the 20th century, the American writer Charlotte Perkins Gilman railed against the bodily confinement of (by implication, middle-class) married mothers within the home. Gilman noted how women's capacity for motherhood led to social assumptions that women were "naturally" suited to bear and nurture children. She contested embodying expectations about the gendered nature of "duty," which involved the provision of hands-on maternal carework, and which excluded mothers from the labor market.

The mid-20th century brought signs of social change in relation to maternal carework. During World War II in Britain and America (1939–45), while men were away fighting, women entered the labor market. Mothers were encouraged to combine the child rearing with paid work. Childcare was provided by the government, and during the War, the notion of outsourcing maternal carework was constructed by officials as good for children and useful to the war effort. When the war ended, however, women were expected to withdraw from the labor market, allowing homecoming men to reclaim available jobs. Mothers found themselves firmly back within the home, with maternal carework and domestic labor at the forefront of maternal identity.

## Challenging Gendered Labor Norms

During the 1950s, the influential sociologist Talcott Parsons portrayed a social norm whereby the division of labor within heterosexual households was gendered. Paternal identity was associated with paid employment and the external world, while maternal identity was seen internally within the family home. Women were expected to become mothers, to provide emotional and physical care for their children, and to undertake housework. Maternal carework and care of the home were thus seen to be almost indistinguishable, and were regarded as fundamental to the adult feminine role.

In 1963, Betty Friedan's seminal feminist text *The Feminine Mystique* questioned the social and embodying convention that a woman's place was in the home. Friedan challenged social assumptions that mothers should take sole responsibility for maternal carework and housework. Friedan's text led subsequent feminist writers to focus on the question of how far the bond between mother and child was biological (with mothers supposedly programmed to undertake maternal carework), and how far mothering could be seen as a socially constructed, institutionalized role.

## Controversial Assertions

During the 1970s and 1980s, maternal carework was a central focus of feminist research. Sociologists of motherhood explored women's work in relation both to birth, maternal carework, and paid employment. In 1970, the feminist scholar Shulamith Firestone argued that women should be freed from what she described as the "tyranny" of their biology. Firestone asserted that children should no longer be regarded as biological extensions of their mothers. She questioned the legitimacy of social assumptions that mothers should undertake the carework involved in nurturing and rearing children. Firestone suggested that maternal carework should be shared between groups of adults (not necessarily children's biological parents) within nationally regulated household units. Under this regime, mothers would no longer be obligated to perform maternal carework for their own children, but would join the labor market as paid workers.

Although Firestone's ideas sparked intense debate, not all feminist scholars agreed with her views. Responding to Firestone's vision, some writers on motherhood declared motherhood and maternal carework to be valuable female characteristics. These scholars rejected the idea that women should cease to bear and care for their own children. Feminist writers who sought to enhance women's labor market opportunities, while concurrently celebrating women's potential to bear children, often sympathized with the radical feminist movement.

## Two Advocates

Two famous scholars who advocated both motherhood and maternal carework, at the same time as campaigning for women's intellectual and occupational freedom, were America's Adrienne Rich and Britain's Ann Oakley.

Adrienne Rich identified two theoretical meanings of the concept of motherhood, one biological and the other socially constructed. Rich acknowledged the importance, for some women, of motherhood. She recognized the value, to mothers and children, of maternal carework involving the emotional and physical nurturing of infants. Rich believed that a special bond existed between mothers and their children. At the same time, however, Rich challenged assumptions that maternal carework should be the sole focus and responsibility of mothers. Rich identified the "institution of motherhood" as a social construction within a patriarchal society.

In this regard, Rich challenged two ideas. The first was the notion that supposedly maternal instincts would facilitate the natural performance of maternal carework. Rich positioned maternal carework as a form of labor that could be both demanding and lonely. Rich also challenged the conventional idea that, in order to be regarded as good mothers, women should prioritize maternal carework at the expense of personal ambition and social identity.

Similarly, in Britain, the feminist scholar Ann Oakley set a high value on childbirth. Oakley recognized the satisfaction that some women obtained from motherhood and maternal carework. Like Rich, however, Oakley confronted the social assumption that mothers should perform maternal carework full time. Oakley suggested that mothers should be encouraged to combine maternal carework with paid employment, without attracting social disapproval. Oakley further observed how motherhood and childcare work were conflated with domestic labor. She noted how, within heterosexual relationships, maternal carework was often extended beyond the nurturing of infant children to include housework and husband work. Oakley further argued that maternal carework was undervalued, with mother's contribution to society being regarded as less important than the contribution of breadwinner fathers.

### The Debate Continues

In the 1970s and 1980s, debates on motherhood and maternal carework were considered in relation to women caring for their own children at home. The group of mothers under consideration were by implication mainly white and middle class. Sociologists of motherhood were subsequently exhorted to consider the position of the working class, and black and ethnic minority women, in relation to maternal care work. In the 21st century, therefore, the role of nannies, nursery workers, and childminders, who are employed to perform maternal carework on behalf of others, has also been acknowledged within feminist scholarship, for example by Barbara Ehrenreich, Arlie Hochschild, and Caroline Gatrell.

These scholars note how, as more women enter the labor market, the number of jobs involving carework for other people's children increases. In comparison with other jobs, childcare work is poorly paid. For impoverished migrant women, undertaking paid work as a childcare provider in wealthier, Euro-American societies might even imply being separated from their own birth children. Some migrant women performing carework for the children of others may be employed without official residency, and/or they may be unqualified young adults. Women performing carework in such circumstances often work long hours for low pay and have little or no recourse to employment rights.

**See Also:** Childcare; Maternal Practice; Maternal Power/Powerlessness; Mothering as Work; Mothering Versus Motherhood.

### Bibliography

Ehrenreich, B. and A. Hochschild. *Global Women, Nannies, Maids and Sex Workers in the New Economy*. Chicago: Granta, 2003.

Firestone, S. *The Dialectic of Sex*. New York: William Morrow, 1970.

Friedan, B. *The Feminine Mystique*. New York: Penguin, 1963.

Gatrell, C. *Embodying Women's Work*. Maidenhead, UK: Open University Press, 2008.

*Journal of the Association for Research on Mothering*. Caregiving and Carework: Theory and Practice [special issue], v.10/1 (Spring/Summer 2008).

Oakley, A. *From Here to Maternity: Becoming a Mother*. New York: Penguin, 1981.

Caroline Gatrell
Lancaster University

# Caribbean Mothers

European, African, U.S., Latin American, and indigenous cultures contribute to the diversity of Caribbean mothers. Cuba and the Dominican Republic and Caribbean community (CARICOM) nations of Antigua and Barbuda, the Bahamas, Barbados, Belize, Dominica, Grenada, Guyana, Haiti, Jamaica, Montserrat, St. Kitts and Nevis, Saint Lucia, St. Vincent and the Grenadines, Suriname, and Trinidad and Tobago gained independence from British, French, or Spanish rule. The Commonwealth of Puerto Rico, the U.S. and British Virgin Islands, Aruba, Bonaire,

Curaçao, St. Martin, Martinique, and Guadeloupe are among the departments or territories of the United States, Britain, France, and the Netherlands. A majority of Caribbean women are the descendants of enslaved West Africans. The complexity of families is reflected in diverse forms—married, common-law, visiting unmarried couple, single-parent, and extended—that emerged in response to historical, economic, and social forces.

## Cultural Norms and Family Structure

Once a Caribbean woman completes her education, social norms begin to exert pressure on her to become a mother. Many young women lack knowledge about pregnancy and childbirth due to limited access to accurate information about human sexuality, contraception, and family life. Women with lower access to family planning tend to be poorer, less educated, and/or live in more rural areas. The average age at birth is increasing. Between 1980 and the late 1990s, the proportion of births to women under age 20 declined sharply, births declined to women age 20–24, and births increased to women age 30 and over.

Women have historically played an important role in the Caribbean economy, contributing to their motivation to achieve autonomy in their social and familial relationships. Across the Caribbean, the dominant cultural belief is that marriage does not have to precede motherhood. Caribbean women are the backbone of the family and often combine dual roles of primary parent and income earner. The maternal role carries more weight than marital status, and consensual unions are commonplace. Caribbean families reflect three stages of formation, beginning with the visiting union in which young women with children may live in their parental home, and blood relatives provide support. Up to three-quarters of Caribbean women under 25 have their first child prior to forming a residential union. The second stage is a common-law or nonmarital residential union. The third stage, representing most women in union from age 25 to 45, involves a gradual transition to legal marriage. After age 45, many women separate, divorce, or become widowed.

In 1995, between 22–44 percent of CARICOM women were single heads of households. Many women choose single parenthood, as reflected in a trend among middle-class professional women. Caribbean women may prefer to avoid permanent or semipermanent unions for financial reasons, or may fear losing their independence, subordinating to a male partner, or risking custody of their children if the union dissolves.

Migration patterns for employment, whether internal, between territories, or international (to the United States, Britain, Europe, and Latin America), have influenced formation of families that cross national boundaries. As a result of migration, families in the Anglophone Caribbean often incorporate cooperative, extended family arrangements that functioned in slave societies. Mothers who migrate for employment often hire another woman to provide childcare until the family is reunited.

**See Also:** Migration and Mothers; Postcolonialism and Motherhood; Slavery and Mothering.

## Bibliography

Caribbean Community Secretariat. *Women and Men in the Caribbean.* New York: United Nations, 2003.

Korrol, Virginia Sanchez. "Women in 19th and 20th Century Latin America and the Caribbean: Independence and Women's Status." New York State Department of Education CI&IT. http://www.emsc.nysed .gov/ciai/socst/ghgonline/units/ 5/documents/Korrol .pdf (accessed December 2008).

Stuart, Sheila. "Female-Headed Families: A Comparative Perspective of the Caribbean and the Developed World." *Gender & Development*, v.4/2 (June 1996).

Keri L. Heitner
University of Phoenix

# Celebrity Motherhood

Celebrities are those who have achieved fame as film and television personalities, athletes, musicians, politicians, models, and the like, as well as those increasingly ubiquitous figures from the late 20th century on who are, in Daniel Boorstin's terms, simply known for being famous. Celebrities who are also mothers or mothers-to-be have become, since the 1980s and more insistently in the new millennium, a cultural obsession. They are the mainstay of entertainment journalism—which includes print and electronic magazines, tabloid newspapers, TV news shows, and blogs—providing readers and audiences with weekly, daily, and even moment-by-moment updates about their lives.

## Celebrity-Driven Motherhood

Images of celebrity mothers are used not only to drive and to sell media content and programming, but also to promote, by way of association, products, services, and lifestyles related to all facets of maternity including pregnancy, birth, adoption, and childrearing. The popular media is perhaps the most powerful tool for constructing and disseminating ideologies of mothering, which it does most pervasively through both its fawning and critical treatment of celebrity mothers. Celebrities, in turn, are complicit in and resistant of the relentless attention they have been attracting as mothers. Because celebrities have high cultural status, how they are represented as mothers in and by the media has far-reaching implications for how mothers in general are regarded within their respective societies. Celebrity mothers have become the gauge by which countless women measure and judge their own maternal identities, skills, and practices.

Over the past decade, celebrity mothers (dubbed "celebumoms" in popular culture) like Christina Aguilera, Victoria Beckham, Jennifer Garner, Katie Holmes, Angelina Jolie, Nicole Kidman, Jennifer Lopez, Madonna, Demi Moore, Julia Roberts, Brooke Shields, Britney Spears, and Michelle Williams have become as, if not more, famous for being mothers as for anything else. In addition, their children have become household names and been catapulted to star status in themselves, a point underscored by the 2007 *Forbes.com* launch of an annual list of "Hollywood's Most Influential Infants"—based on print and electronic press coverage—who to date include, for example, Suri Cruise; Sean and Preston Federline; and Shiloh, Pax, and Zahara Jolie-Pitt.

## Celebrity Mothers, Children, and Media

Celebrity mothers and children are tracked, scrutinized, and judged by entertainment news, which since the late 20th century, has dominated the field of journalism and is disseminated in media such as: gossip magazines like *People*, *Star*, and *US Weekly*, along with their electronic counterparts (e.g., www. people.com); women's magazines like *Ladies' Home Journal*, *Good Housekeeping*, and *Redbook*; tabloid newspapers such as the *National Enquirer*, and the *Sun*; TV news shows such as *Entertainment Tonight*, *Access Hollywood*, *Extra*, and *Inside Edition*, as well as cable networks like A&E, The Biography Channel, and E! Entertainment Television; and blogs posted and maintained by corporate, in-house bloggers such as AOL's *TMZ* and Gawker Media's *Gawker* and *Defamer*, in addition independent blogs such as *Celebitchy*, *Jossip*, and *Perezhilton*. Celebrity mothers have even inspired noncelebrity mothers to create a new genre: celebrity mother and baby blogs, as in *Celebrity BabyBlog*, *Mamarazzi*, and *Babyrazzi*.

## Celebrity Mothers' Positive Influences

Public fascination with maternal celebrities was both reflected in and exacerbated by the emergence of a new genre—the celebrity mom profile—featured in women's and gossip magazines, in which stars speak candidly about the joys and blessings of motherhood. According to S. Douglas and M. Michaels, the profile came into prominence with the January 1981 issue of *Good Housekeeping*, which showcased singer and new mother Debby Boone. It was honed throughout the 1980s and 1990s by a media fixated on Diana, Princess of Wales. Through both studio and supposedly spontaneous photographs, Diana worked with the press to promote herself as a selfless, doting mother; her strategy not only won her the backing of the public during her bitter divorce, but also solidified her status as a maternal role model.

Celebrity mothers became especially influential in the 1970s and 1980s, Douglas and Michaels theorize, in part because they already had careers at a time when other women were just starting to enter the workforce in unprecedented numbers. The high-profile status of celebrity mothers meant they were in a position to inspire women to achieve success and reach goals in the public domain in a variety of ways. Diana, for instance, earned international recognition for her work with acquired immunodeficiency syndrome (AIDS) patients. Since then, singer Madonna has helped to build an orphanage in Malawi, and actors like Angelina Jolie, Nicole Kidman, and Reese Witherspoon have used their star power to bring attention to humanitarian issues and causes around the world in their respective capacities as United Nations High Commissioner for Refugees (UNHCR) Goodwill Ambassador, Goodwill Ambassador for UNICEF Australia, and honorary chair of the Avon Foundation. Political mothers like Hillary Rodham Clinton and Sarah Palin drew attention to their roles as working mothers during the 2008 U.S. presidential election campaign, while the new First Lady, Michelle Obama, has deliberately chosen to define her public duties in terms of motherhood, telling the media that her main title is "Mom in Chief."

Moreover, celebrities send the liberating message that mothers do not have to forfeit their sexual identities, as Diana refused to do. When actor Demi Moore posed nude and seven months pregnant for the August 1991 cover of *Vanity Fair*, she shattered assumptions that the pregnant body is de-eroticized. From the late 20th century on, celebrities have been routinely categorized by the press as "hot mamas" or "hot Hollywood moms," and, debunking traditional notions of the mother as angelic and pure, consistently testify that pregnancy and motherhood make them feel sexy.

## Celebrity Mothers' Negative Influences

If celebrities empower women, they also project a maternity predicated on fantasy. Sharon Hays points the concept of intensive mothering, dating from World War II, which mandates that women spend all their emotional, psychological, and financial resources on their children; and Susan Douglas and Meredith Michaels contend that celebrities are the most influential proponents of the new momism, a concept whereby women define themselves by and commit themselves entirely to their children. These two ideologies are taken to the unattainable extreme by the wealthy, beautiful, and privileged celebrity icon who has everything: time, money, and energy to spend on children; a fulfilling career; assistants to help with exercise, style, and childcare; and stable and loving relationships. Other than figures like Jodie Foster, Rosie O'Donnell, and Melissa Etheridge, celebrity mothering as covered by the media remains heteronormative.

Fans may regard celebrity mothers with envy, believing in and aspiring to the myth of the super-

mom, while purchasing the same designer maternity wear as well as baby clothes and products (baby slings, organic shampoos) used by the stars, or naming their children after celebrities. However, as celebrity culture scholars like Daniel Boorstin and Ellis Cashmore explain, celebrities are positioned in dichotomous terms, with the media either worshipping or debunking them, and audiences wanting to emulate or excoriate them. Therefore, it is perhaps not surprising to find that celebrity mothers are also the subject of an ongoing backlash. They are viewed, for instance, as satisfying their own cravings for attention in their outlandish, often embarrassing choices of baby names (e.g., Apple, Elijah Blue, Kal-El, Moon Unit, Sunday Rose, and Shiloh-Nouvel). Jolie has been criticized for "collecting" children (she has three biological and three adopted children, and plans on having more) in her self-construction as a global mother, just as Madonna received negative publicity for her adoption of Malawian David Banda. Ordinary women balk at celebrities' apparent ease of losing their pregnancy weight after parturition, recognizing that professional trainers and nutritionists were on hand. And when actor Gwyneth Paltrow uttered her now-infamous comment, "I would rather die than let my kid eat Cup-a-Soup," she was derided throughout cyberspace.

## Commodity Children

Perhaps most significantly, celebrity mothers and fathers are complicit in the increasing commodification of their children, as manifested in the growing trend of selling baby photos to the media for staggering sums. According to Forbes.com, since 2006, photos of the babies of Jolie (for her biological twins, and earlier for her first biological daughter); Jennifer Lopez, Anna Nicole Smith, Christina Aguilera, Jessica Alba, and Nicole Richie have fetched prices from $1.5 to $15 million. While Jolie has reportedly donated the money to charity, the practice raises ethical questions regarding the rights of the children. At the same time, selling photos allows celebrities to control the images that are disseminated, a justification that takes on greater resonance in light of the intrusive and often threatening paparazzi.

As editor of the tabloid-turned-glossy *Star* in the early 2000s, Bonnie Fuller put her reporters on "Bump Watch" duty, inaugurating the cultural phenomenon in which celebrity maternity is in a state of perpetual surveillance. If the media promotes the so-called "good" mothers as role models, it simultaneously ridicules, blames, and condemns the "bad" ones—those who are teen and/or single mothers, such as Jamie Lynn Spears; register ambivalent feelings about their children, such as Britney Spears; engage in questionable lifestyles, involving partying, substance abuse, and promiscuity (such as the now-deceased Playboy model Anna Nicole Smith); and exhibit little or no concern with their body weight or overall public image (such as actor/TV personality Rosie O'Donnell and actor Kirstie Alley).

A growing category of "bad" mother is the so-called "momager," the woman who interferes with her famous children's affairs, exploits them, and contributes to their tarnished reputations—for example, mothers Dina Lohan (Lindsay) and Lynne Spears (Britney and Jamie Lynn). When the "bad" mother is rehabilitated, however, she becomes a potentially even more inspiring role model for having overcome her problems, as witnessed by the positive press coverage of reformed drug addict Nicole Richie, as well as Britney Spears, who lost custody of her two sons in 2008 and has since regained visitation rights as her mental and physical health improves.

## Fan Connections

Audiences respond to celebrity mothers by embracing them uncritically; by recognizing that they promote unrealistic, unattainable, and untrue images of motherhood; or by negotiating the myths and ideals with their own realities, accepting the elements of celebrity mothering that empower them as "real" mothers and rejecting what does not. Realizing that fans formulate varying degrees of emotional and psychological connections to celebrities, the media portrays a level playing field between them, as exemplified in *US Magazine's* weekly section "Stars—They're Just Like Us!" which presents images of celebrities caught without makeup while taking a toddler to preschool, for example. Nonfamous mothers find maternity an equalizer, an aspect of life that humanizes celebrities, and so affords a seemingly more meaningful and more personal connection.

Concomitantly, celebrities are reaching out to audiences in apparently personal ways to reinforce

*Just two years after her 2003 National Mall performance, Britney Spears became a mother, and a subject of great criticsm.*

these connections. Nonfamous celebrity mommy- and baby-bloggers are slowly being joined by celebrities like Tori Spelling and Victoria Beckham, who use their own blogs to underscore that their mothering is "just like" their noncelebrity counterparts. Moreover, celebrities are contributing to another new genre, the celebrity "momoir": examples include Tori Spelling, who offers a lighthearted account of being a mother of two in *Mommywood* (2009); Lynne Spears, who recounts life as a "momager" in *Through the Storm: A Real Story of Fame and Family in a Tabloid World* (2008); Brooke Shields, who helped to destigmatize postpartum depression in *Down Came the Rain: My Journey Through Postpartum Depression* (2005); and Jenny McCarthy, who charts her battle with her son's autism in confessionals like *Louder Than Words: A Mother's Journey in Healing Autism* (2007).

Celebrity mothers can be considered in light of fan culture, in which people discuss celebrities as a way of understanding themselves, and to form networks with other like-minded people. In this context, celebrity mothers are used by everyday women as the springboard for nonfamous mothers to articulate, define, gauge, and legitimize their own maternal values and practices.

**See Also:** Consumerism and Motherhood; Film, Mothers in; Internet and Mothering; Media, Mothers in; Mommy Blogs; New Momism; Popular Culture and Mothering; TV Moms; Zines.

**Bibliography**

Boorstin, Daniel. *The Image: A Guide to Pseudo-Events in America.* New York: Random House, 1992.

Browne, Christopher. *The Prying Game.* London: Robson Books, 1996.

Cashmore, Ellis. *Celebrity/Culture.* New York: Routledge, 2006.

Douglas, Susan J. and Meredith W. Michaels. *The Mommy Myth: The Idealization of Motherhood and How It Has Undermined All Women.* New York: Free Press, 2004.

Holmes, Su and Sean Redmond. *Framing Celebrity: New Directions in Celebrity Culture.* New York: Routledge, 2006.

Howe, Peter. *Paparazzi: And Our Obsession With Celebrity.* New York: Artisan, 2005.

Ladd-Taylor, Molly and Lauri Umansky, eds. *"Bad" Mothers: The Politics of Blame in Twentieth-Century America.* New York: New York University Press, 1998.

Marshall, David. *Celebrity and Power: Fame in Contemporary Culture.* Minneapolis: University of Minnesota Press, 1997.

Turner, Graeme. *Understanding Celebrity.* Thousand Oaks, CA: Sage, 2004.

Elizabeth Podnieks
Ryerson University

# Central African Republic

The landlocked country of the Central African Republic, in central Africa, has a population of 4.4 million, a birth rate of 33.9 per 1,000, and an infant mortality rate of 85.6 per 1,000 live births.

In 2006, 70.5 percent of women age 15 and over in the Central African Republic were in the labor force, and their employment-to-population ratio in 2006 was 64.4. In 2006, women age 15 and over constituted 46.1 percent of the labor force, a percentage that has not changed substantially since 1985.

Abortion is highly restricted; even an abortion necessary to save the life of the mother is illegal, although in practice, such abortions are permitted on "grounds of necessity." Penalties are severe for providing an abortion, including a sentence of up to five years and a fine of up to $2 million Central African francs. However, contraception is not widely used, and illegal abortions are acknowledged to continue. Fourteen weeks of maternity leave is provided at 100 percent of salary. Men may take up to 10 days per year for "family events concerning their own home."

In traditional society, dowry played an important part in arranged marriages, and women were subservient members of society, effectively the property of their husbands. As slavery flourished, the lives of many women were similar to those of slaves. The French tried to change this from the start of their colonial rule in the region from the 1880s. There was an improvement in health care, but this largely affected the Europeans and the local elite in the capital, Bangui. However, scholar Marie-Ange Kallanda has argued that the Roman Catholic missionary nuns have done much to emancipate many women in the Lobaye district of the country, and this possibly was mirrored by events elsewhere. There were also problems with the spread of venereal diseases, which have led to higher levels of infertility, especially in women in the Nzakara tribe.

After independence in 1960, there was an extension of the hospital services, with midwives helping in the births of children in villages. Many of the doctors and midwives were either French, or trained in France or by the French, but the remoteness of some of the settlements made it hard for mothers to access these facilities. This, combined with the lack of access by many of the population to clean water, has led to high rates of maternal mortality—which at 1.1 per 100 births is one of the highest in the world.

Subsequent studies of the population have shown that there are major differences in primary infertility and secondary infertility—the first when there are no children after five years of marriage, and the other when there are no children born some five years after the birth of a previous child. Professor Larsen of the Harvard School of Public Health found that compared to Chad and Gabon, both of these infertility rates were the highest in the Central African Republic, and were unrelated to place of residence, occupation, or parental education level, or socioeconomic status.

The country became well-known internationally from 1977–79 when Jean Bebel Bokassa—himself one of 12 children—established the Central African Empire. He, as with many of the elite, practiced polygamy, and had as many as 17 wives. He fathered approximately 50 children.

**See Also:** Chad; Congo; Gabon; Rwanda: Uganda.

### Bibliography

Endjimongou, Patrice. *Evolution Psycho-sociologique de la Femme Centrafricaine: l'élite Future?* [The Psychosociological Evolution of the Central African Woman: The Future Elite?]. MA thesis, EPHE, Paris, 1975.

Kalck, Pierre. *Historical Dictionary of the Central African Republic.* Lanham, MD: Scarecrow Press, 2004.

Kallanda, Marie-Ange. *Les Soeurs Spiritaines de Mbaïki et l'évolution de la Femme en Lobaye 1931–1958* [The Holy Ghost Sisters of Mbaïki and Women's Advancement in Lobaye 1931–1958]. MA thesis, Bangui University, 1987.

Larsen, U. "Infertility in Central Africa." *Tropical Medicine and International Health*, v.8/4 (April 2003).

Pickanda, Fidel-Adoum. *L'enfant dans la Société Traditionelle Banda* [Children in Traditional Banda Society]. MA thesis, Université de Haute Bretagne, Rennes, 1981.

Justin Corfield
Geelong Grammar School, Australia

# Chad

Chad is a landlocked country in Africa—the fifth largest in the continent—and has a population of 9.9 million (2007). It has a birth rate of 45.73 per 1,000, and an infant mortality rate of 91.5 per 1,000

live births. The maternal mortality rate at 1.1 per 100 births is one of the highest in the world. Chad's fertility rate is 5.43 births per woman (2008), the 27th highest in the world, although this is down from 6.7 births per woman a decade earlier. These high fertility and infant mortality rates are partially due to the fact that 72 percent of the population marry before they turn 17 years of age, with many young mothers and fathers often trying to bring up families without a wider kinship structure.

The high fertility rate prompted a study by Professor U. Larsen of the Harvard School of Public Health, who found the infertility rates far lower than neighboring Central African Republic and nearby Gabon. This was ascribed to a slightly better system of health care, but also because of the remoteness of many villages. There was also not as much of a problem with venereal diseases, which have affected fertility in some neighboring countries, but the human immunodeficiency virus (HIV) and acquired immunodeficiency syndrome (AIDS) are a significant factor in the country; approximately 11,000 people have died of the disease since 2005, and approximately 57,000 children aged 16 and under have been orphaned.

## Poverty and Health Services

With desperate poverty in much of the country, over half the children in Chad are working before the age of 14. The employment-to-population ratio for women age 15 and over in Chad was 60.1, and labor force participation for women in that age group was 65.9 percent. Chad provides 14 weeks of maternity leave at 50 percent of the woman's salary, and there is also a prohibition against firing a woman while she is on maternity leave. Abortion in Chad is only permitted if necessary to save the mother's life. She must consent (unless it is impossible for her to do so), and the physician must have written approval from two other physicians, one of whom must be listed as an expert by the civil courts. It is illegal for a woman to induce her own abortion or to import drugs to induce abortions. However, illegal abortion remains common, and most cases of abortion are ignored by the legal system.

The French occupied Chad from 1897, but apart from some health services in the capital, N'djaména, mainly for the Europeans and the local elite, there was little effort to provide health care in rural parts of the country. After full independence in 1960, Chad's new government sought to improve the country's infrastructure, and to build clinics and establish a system of midwives in the countryside. However, as with many other parts of former French west Africa and French central Africa, the sheer remoteness of many isolated settlements make it very difficult for local mothers to access quality health and midwifery services. It has also been hampered by the lack of funds; Chad spends about $7 per head on health services, and there is still only one national hospital, 64 district hospitals, and 911 regional health centers. In 2004, there were only 345 doctors, 2,400 nurses, and 112 midwives for the entire country.

**See Also:** Algeria; Central African Republic; Egypt; Libya; Sudan.

**Bibliography**
Adler, Alfred. *"La Fillette Amoureuse des Masques: le Statut de la Femme chez les Moundang."* [The Little Girl in Love with Masks: The Status of Women Among the Moundang]. *Journal des Africainistes,* v.59/1–2 (1989).
Azevedo, Mario, ed. *Cameroon and Chad in Historical Perspectives.* Lewiston, NY: Edwin Mellen Press, 1988.
James, Valentine Udoh and James S. Etim, eds. *The Feminization of Development Processes in Africa: Current and Future Perspectives.* Santa Barbara, CA: Praeger, 1999.
Larsen. U. "Infertility in Central Africa." *Tropical Medicine and International Health,* v.8/4 (April 2003).

Justin Corfield
Geelong Grammar School, Australia

# Chicana Mothering

The term *Chicana* refers to a woman of Mexican descent, while Latina is a more general term, referring to a female from a Spanish-speaking household, born in a Spanish-speaking country, or choosing to identify as having Spanish ancestry.

Chicana motherhood varies across the social strata of Chicana mothers, and is irreducible to particular mothering practices or identities. As Chicanas, Chicana mothers negotiate the traditions and expectations of both U.S. and Mexican (Spanish and indigenous) cultures. Though Chicana mothers remain connected by their shared histories as subjects of colonization and the religious and cultural influence of Mexican maternal archetypes, the social, cultural, and generational differences among Chicana mothers have, in many ways, continued to evolve how Chicana motherhood is conceptualized.

**Chicana Mothering Roots**
Mirande and Enriquez trace the structure of the Chicano family back to its Aztec roots: distinctive characteristics include great emotional investment in family, assumption of the extended family, and emphasis on the mother as the center of family life.

Public health scholars such as Scribner and Dwyer have noted that Chicana mothers typically have excellent birth outcomes, although they are often poor, and that this advantage diminishes with acculturation or moving outside of Chicano enclaves. They are thus attributed to Chicana cultural practices, including social support for maternity, devotion to the maternal role, consumption of a healthy diet, and avoidance of negative behaviors such as smoking and alcohol abuse.

**Mexican/Chicana Maternal Archetypes**
The genealogy of Mexican maternal archetypes begins with the indigenous goddesses, Coatlicue and Tonantzín. Coatlicue, the goddess of birth and death, personifies duality, a concept foundational to Aztecan philosophy; this is evident in the visual representation of Coatlicue, in which her face is formed by two fanged serpents facing each other. Her hands also bear claws (destruction) and her breasts appear flaccid from nursing her children (life). A figure of duality, Coatlicue personifies the complex struggle of the mestiza, the racially mixed woman. From the origins of the mythology of Coatlicue also emerges the Mesoamerican Mother Goddess, Tonantzín. When indigenous Mexican Juan Diego claimed to have been visited by an apparition of a holy woman in 1531, the Spanish Catholic clergy in Mexico merged the long-revered indigenous

mother goddess, Tonantzín, with the Virgin Mary. This hybrid became Our Lady of Guadalupe, which missionaries used to convert the indigenous people to Catholicism. Because of Guadalupe's indigenous and Spanish lineage, she is sometimes considered to be the "first *mestiza*."

Though she embodies duality, Guadalupe also occupies one side of the duality of Mexican motherhood. Guadalupe, the "white" goddess, symbolizes goodness, while Tonantzín, the "dark" goddess, symbolizes deviance. This duality is subverted within Western culture, however, with the introduction of the legend of La Llorona.

According to the legend, Llorona is the woman who drowns her children in order to be with her lover, and now wanders along rivers at night wailing for her lost children. Llorona has come to represent maternal alienation and deviant motherhood, and is located opposite Guadalupe/Tonantzín within the motherhood dichotomy. Llorona is often compared to Malintzin, or Malinche, the indigenous woman who translated for Hernán Cortés and gave birth to his son. Malinche is recognized as the symbolic mother of the mestizo race, but is also held responsible for the Spanish conquest of Mexico. Malinche is also referred to as a derogatory term for intercourse, which suggests the conquest of Malinche's body symbolizes the conquest of the indigenous territory.

## Mothers, Nationalism, and the Public Sphere

Guadalupe/Tonantzín and Malinche/Llorona comprise the duality of motherhood that was actively imposed by Chicano nationalists during the civil rights movement of the 1960s and 1970s. From paintings and sculptures that frequently depicted Chicana mothers as Madonna figures to nationalist rhetoric that identified motherhood as the Chicana's duty to her race, the Chicana mother was encouraged to embrace the qualities of the good mother, Guadalupe. Those who transgressed the ideal of motherhood were called malinche or *vendida* (sellout). The concept of *marianismo*, a model of semi-divine womanhood that advocated purity (like the Virgin Mary), fidelity, self-denial, and submission, served the nationalist agenda by ensuring that mothers would remain bound to their husbands and *la causa* ("the cause").

In 1971, Chicana motherhood was recognized and politicized at the first national Chicana conference in Houston, Texas. Emerging from the two largest workshops, Sex and the Chicana and Marriage: Chicana Style, was a set of resolutions that called for an end to patriarchal practices within society and the home, and encouraged women to realize their potential to effect change within the family. In addition to asserting their "right to control [their] own bodies," the Chicanas declared that "Chicana motherhood should not preclude educational, political, social, and economic advancement." Recognizing the material struggle of Chicanas, the Chicanas also called for "24-hour childcare centers in Chicano communities." The resolutions encouraged Chicana mothers to end the cycle of female oppression by educating their sons in order to create new traditions of sex equality.

Following the national Chicana conference in 1971 was a succession of Chicana feminist movements in which mothers took active roles. Besides operating on the domestic front of the Chicano Movement, Chicana mothers participated in political struggles of their own. A notable community activist organization was the Mothers of East Los Angeles (L.A.). In 1985, Chicana residents of East L.A. formed the group in response to the state's plans to construct a prison near several neighborhood schools. Through their active involvement in the public sphere as mothers, the Mothers of East L.A. challenged traditional constructions and boundaries of motherhood, even when working within the parameters of the cultural expectations of Chicana/Mexican womanhood.

## Chicana Mothering

Like Mexican mothers, Chicana mothers traditionally have been expected to carry out the "double reproduction" of the Chicano people and culture. However, Chicana mothering is not exclusive to the birth mother; extended family members, such as grandmothers and close female friends or relatives called *comadres* (co-mothers), may frequently assist with the childcare responsibilities while the mother works. Chicana feminist scholarship reveals that this unique familial arrangement of surrogate motherhood and extended kinship poses challenges to canonical, psychoanalytic analyses of

Western motherhood that assume exclusive mothering practices.

Though many Chicana mothers have made great advancements in politics and the workplace, many others continue to struggle with the middle-class ideal of stay-at-home motherhood. This desire is prompted by the ideal of Western motherhood, as well as daughters' experiences with their absent working-class mothers who worked outside the home. The guilt experienced by working Chicana mothers is also a result of the struggle to negotiate multiple dualities of Mexican and Western motherhoods.

## Radicalizing Chicana Motherhood

Besides class and race/ethnicity, another intersection of Chicana motherhood is sexuality. Chicana lesbian writers such as Cherríe Moraga have written extensively about their mothers, as well as about their own experiences with maternity and motherhood. Such writings complicate traditional perceptions of Chicana motherhood and challenge heteronormative assumptions of *familia* that imbued Chicano Nationalist rhetoric, which continue to marginalize Chicana lesbian mothers. Chicana lesbian mothers, however, have taken steps to radically modify the concepts of *familia* and motherhood, proving that Chicana motherhood is socially, culturally, and historically dynamic.

**See Also:** Activist Mothers; African American Mothers; Cross-Cultural Perspectives on Motherhood; Feminism and Mothering; Lesbian Mothering; Mexican Spirituality and Motherhood; Religion and Mothering; Spirituality and Mothering.

## Bibliography

Alarcón, Norma. "Traduttora, Traditora: A Paradigmatic Figure of Chicana Feminism." *Signs: Journal of Women in Culture and Society,* v.7/1 (1981).
Castillo, Ana. "Toward the Mother-Bond Principle." In *Massacre of the Dreamers: Essays on Xicanisma.* New York: Plume, 1995.
Chabram-Dernersesian, Angie. "Encountering the Other Discourse of Chicano-Mexicano Difference." *Cultural Studies,* v.13/2 (1999).
Jenny, A.M., K.C. Schoendorf, and J.D. Parker. "The Association Between Community Context and Mortality Among Mexican-American Infants." *Ethnicity and Disease,* v.11/4 (Fall 2001).
McGlade, M.S., S. Saha, and M.E. Dahlstrom. "The Latina Paradox: An Opportunity for Restructuring Prenatal Care Delivery." *American Journal of Public Health,* v.12 (December 2004).
Mirande, Alfredo and Evangelina Enriquez. *La Chicana: The Mexican-American Woman.* Chicago: University of Chicago Press, 1981.
Moraga, Cherríe. *Loving in the War Years: Lo Que Nunca Pasó por sus Labios, Second Edition.* Cambridge, MA: South End Press, 2000.
NietoGómez, Anna. "La Chicana—Legacy of Suffering and Self-Denial." In *Chicana Feminist Thought: The Basic Historical Writings.* New York: Routledge, 1997.
Pardo, Mary. *Mexican American Women Activists.* Philadelphia: Temple University Press, 1998.
Scribner, Richard and James H. Dwyer. "Acculturation and Low Birthweight Among Latinos in the Hispanic HANES." *American Journal of Public Health,* v.79/9 (September 1989).
Smith, Silva Dorsia and Janine Santiago. *Latina/Chicana Mothering.* Toronto: Demeter Press, Forthcoming, 2011.

Larissa M. Mercado-López
University of Texas at San Antonio

# Child Abuse

Child abuse is a socially defined construct; as such, it does not lend itself to an easy definition. It is a highly controversial and complex concept, subject to constant change that is influenced by a range of political and cultural factors. Historically, the highly publicized case of the abuse of a young girl named Mary Ellen Wilson led to a public outcry resulting in the foundation of the Society for the Prevention of the Cruelty to Children in 1874, which ultimately initiated dramatic changes in society's treatment of children.

However, it was not until 1974 when formal legislation was passed in North America that clearly defined a mandate for the reporting of physical child abuse, sexual abuse, emotional abuse, and physical neglect. Estimates of child abuse in North America suggest that about one in every 10 children each year receive harsh physical treatment by a caregiver or parent that puts them at risk for injury and harm. By the age of 18, one in five girls and one in nine boys will experience some form of sexual abuse. Countless other children suffer from emotional abuse and physical neglect.

## Physical Child Abuse

Physical abuse involves any behavior by a parent that causes physical injury to a child. Physical abuse may occur even though the parent may not have intended to hurt the child, such as in the case of harsh punishment. Physical abuse typically involves a hostile, controlling, and aggressive parenting style. This parenting approach is characterized by a wide range of hurtful actions such as hitting, shaking, throwing, poisoning, burning, scalding, drowning, suffocating, punching, and other examples of physical harm. Prenatal exposure to damaging levels of alcohol or drugs may also be included. Physical harm also may be caused when a parent deliberately causes ill health to a child, commonly called Munchausen's Syndrome by Proxy.

The risk for physical abuse in childhood declines with the child's increasing age. Nearly half of all physical abuse victims are 7 years old or younger. Boys are generally at a slightly greater risk for physical abuse than girls. There is some evidence that vulnerable children may be at a greater risk for physical abuse, such as children born prematurely or children with physical or developmental disabilities. About half of all childhood deaths are a result of physical abuse. Most child deaths, whatever the age of the child, are the result of violence inflicted by males. Death may either be the result of one very violent act of aggression or the accumulation of chronic assaults. Head injuries are the main cause of death.

Younger parents are more likely than older parents to physically abuse their children. Physical abusers of very young children are more likely to be female, while abusers of older children are predominantly, though not exclusively, thought to be male. The histories of the majority of parents who physically abuse their children suggest that they have been physically abused themselves and have suffered maternal rejection and abandonment during their childhood. Typically, physically abusive parents have difficulty controlling their anger, demonstrate hostility and rigidity, have a lack of tolerance for frustration, exhibit low self-esteem, engage in substance abuse, and rarely show empathy. Compared with nonabusive parents, abusive parents have been found to have unrealistic expectations and negative perceptions of their children. They also view parenting as more stressful and dissatisfying and exhibit a number of deficits in child management skills.

Family and interpersonal difficulties such as isolation from family and friends, spousal conflict, and negative family interactions are more common among families of physically abusive parents than families of nonabusive parents. Single mothers are overrepresented among physical abusers; however, this appears to be more likely a function of poverty and stress in these families. In addition to low educational achievement of parents, low social economic status and elevated social stress are strongly associated with physical abuse. Physical abusers are more likely to live in dangerous circumstances and are likely to have experienced danger themselves in their past. Specifically, the probability that a mother will physically abuse her children is associated with three predictors of decreasing importance: being assaulted by her own mother as a child; a current abusive partner; and a previous abusive partner.

## Sexual Abuse

Sexual abuse occurs when a person uses power over a child and involves the child in any sexual act. The abuser is more powerful because of age, intelligence, physical strength, or control over the child. The activities may involve physical contact, including penetrative and nonpenetrative acts, or noncontact activities such as allowing children to watch pornography, involving a child in pornography or prostitution, and/or encouraging children to behave in sexually inappropriate ways.

Most children who are sexually abused are between the ages of 9–11, with girls being more likely to be abused than boys. However, the abuse of boys is often underestimated. Children with a disability are at almost double the risk of sexual abuse, with the risk increasing further when children are living in some sort of residential treatment center.

The age of perpetrators of child sexual abuse varies widely. Most sexual offenders develop deviant sexual interests prior to 18 years of age. The majority of perpetrators are male, representing all ethnic, racial, and socioeconomic groups. Although a minority of women have been identified as perpetrators, this phenomenon may be more common than data suggest due to lack of reporting. Most sexual offenders of children are known to their victims. However, rather than being family members, it is more likely that these individuals are outside the family sphere, such as friends or neighbors. Childhood sexual victimization also contributes to adult perpetration. Perpetrators may have experienced abuse directly in the past themselves, or they may have observed or been aware of the abuse of other family members. In addition, perpetrators of sexual abuse often lack the necessary social skills and interpersonal intimacy required for the development of empathy, possibly contributing to sexually abusive behavior.

Families with children who are sexually abused demonstrate significant levels of dysfunction; they are the least cohesive and the most disorganized. Frequently, one or both parents are involved in drug and alcohol abuse and possibly criminal behavior. There is often marital conflict, domestic violence, and divorce among these families. Mothers of sexually abused children are most likely to be co-conspirators rather than co-victims.

There is some evidence that mothers in incestuous families have childhood histories of sexual abuse in addition to being physically and emotionally abused by their children's perpetrators. Mothers who have been sexually abused in the past may gravitate toward men who are similar to their own abusers, or who do not make sexual demands on them because the men are sexually attracted to children. As well, maternal employment outside the home, maternal disability, or illness also is known risk factors for sexual abuse.

## Emotional Abuse

Emotional abuse involves any verbal or nonverbal behaviors by a parent that convey to the child that he or she is worthless or unloved, inadequate, or valued only insofar as he or she meets the needs of another person. It should be noted that some level of emotional abuse is inherent in all forms of child abuse; however, it may also occur independently. Six major types of emotional abuse have been identified, including: (1) spurning, which include hostile rejection and denigrating the child in verbal and nonverbal manners through criticizing, insulting and humiliating; (2) terrorizing, in which the parent threatens to abandon, hurt, maim, or kill the child unless he or she behaves or stops being needy; (3) isolating the child from other children from everyday activities, particularly those activities that are typically considered engaging or entertaining; (4) denying the child emotional responsiveness, such as ignoring the child's needs or failing to express positive affection toward the child; (5) exploiting or corrupting the child, such as encouraging inappropriate, antisocial, or criminal behaviors in the child; (6) failing to meet the child's medical and health needs.

The risk for emotional abuse of children increases with the age of the child. Children between the ages of 7 and 17 are more likely to be emotionally abused than children 6 years of age and younger. Findings are mixed regarding the association between gender differences and rates of emotional abuse. Some studies find no gender differences, while others find that girls compared to boys are at slightly more risk for emotional abuse by parents.

Mothers are slightly more likely to perpetrate emotional abuse than fathers. Emotionally abusive parents typically exhibit interpersonal and social difficulties, poor problem-solving skills, substance abuse, and deficits in child management techniques. They also may have a greater number of psychiatric symptoms and personality disturbances in addition to physical illnesses.

Families with lower incomes are significantly more likely than families with higher incomes to be characterized by emotional abuse. There is a tendency for these families to keep authority figures at a distance, as they are often wary of professional help. They avoid doctors and other health care professionals and often fail to visit clinics when pregnant. When health providers are involved, parents tend to miss appointments, ignore medical advice, and fail to administer medication to their children.

## Physical Neglect

Physical neglect describes the persistent failure to provide for the child's basic physical and/or psychological needs, which is likely to result in serious harm to the child's health or development. Neglect tends to be the most common form of abuse. Physical neglect typically includes not providing adequate food, clothing, housing, supervision, or education. It also involves failing to protect a child from physical harm or danger, or not providing access to appropriate medical care and/or treatment, as well as neglecting household sanitation and failing to meet basic standards of personal care and cleanliness of the child.

The risk for child neglect tends to decline with age of the child. It is estimated that over half of children who experience neglect are under 5 years of age, and of those, the majority are under 1 year of age. Children under 3 years of age are the most vulnerable and suffer the most significant consequences of physical neglect, such as failure to thrive, which is characterized by a cessation in growth during the first three years of life. In 2006, 41.1 percent of child maltreatment fatalities were associated with neglect alone.

Parents who are physically neglectful tend to be socially isolated and suffer from pervasive emotional numbness, feelings of hopelessness, and a sense of futility and apathy. This invariably leads to a caregiving environment that is characterized by both material and emotional poverty. Neglectful parents are typically unresponsive to the child's needs or distress; they also lack emotional involvement with the child. Mental health problems and psychiatric disorders, as well as severe developmental delays of parents, have been thought to contribute to child neglect. The histories of neglectful caregivers are often characterized by extreme neglect, such as parental depression or unresponsiveness, living in extreme poverty, or traumatic and unresolved physical and/or sexual abuse.

Families where neglect is high are generally characterized by low income, unemployment, and dependence on social assistance. Large families (four or more children), single-parent homes, and homes where mothers have a greater number of children during their teen years are at considerably higher risk for neglect.

## Additional Forms of Child Abuse

Substance abuse by parents, as well as parental mental health issues and the witnessing of domestic violence, are examples of caregiving environments in which the risks for child abuse increase. Furthermore, exposure to significant amounts of violence within communities is now considered a form of child abuse. Although institutional abuse is less common than other forms of child abuse, many children suffer all forms of abuse while in the care of institutional settings, which have been licensed to provide quality care for children. Other major forms of child abuse in which abuse is most likely to occur between a child and an adult who is not a family member may be through organized exploitation, such as child sex rings, child pornography, and child prostitution. Furthermore, as a means of mass communication, the Internet has proliferated these various forms of child abuse.

## Consequences Associated With Child Abuse

Children who experience child abuse are more likely than their nonabused peers to exhibit myriad physical, behavioral, cognitive, and emotional problems during childhood, which put them at risk for personality disorders, substance abuse, criminal behavior, and psychiatric disorders in adolescence and adulthood. The persistence of childhood difficulties into adulthood may contribute to the intergenerational transmission of the abuse. Recent evidence in the area of neuroscience has revealed how the emotional trauma associated with child abuse can negatively impact brain growth and development, which can result in enduring changes in all aspects of child development. Increased severity and duration of abuse, as well as the exposure to multiple forms of abuse, will increase the likelihood of a more negative outcome for children during childhood and in adulthood.

Posttraumatic stress disorder (PTSD) is a common, short-term symptom of trauma related to child abuse. In this case, the person is confronted with events that involve the threat of death to self or others, which provokes a response of intense fear and helplessness. Recently, complex posttraumatic stress disorder (C-PTSD) has been recognized by the psychiatric community as a condition that results from chronic exposure to extremes of social and/or interpersonal trauma, such as in cases of long-term child abuse. Specifically, C-PTSD is thought to arise from a prolonged state of victimization where the person is held in a state of captivity, either physically or emotionally, with no means for escape. While PTSD may be temporary, symptoms of C-PTSD may continue for years. C-PTSD is characterized by chronic difficulties in many areas of emotional and interpersonal functioning.

## Treatment

Child abuse treatment is typically directed toward the child victims, adult survivors, and/or the perpetrators. Few interventions have been developed that are unique to physical neglect and emotional abuse, as compared with those for physical and sexual abuse. Interventions focused on physical abuse typically aim to enhance the parenting skills of perpetrators, while programs focused on children aim to reduce the effects associated with the abuse. Relational-based interventions consider the healing of the parent–child relationship to be essential through facilitating the parent's ability to meet the child's needs for safety and protection. Community interventions often serve as adjuncts, based upon the view that there are multiple factors that contribute to child physical abuse, such as social isolation, financial stress, and excessive childcare demands. Research suggests that effective sexual abuse interventions for the child victims, adult survivors, or the perpetrators require an understanding of pre-abuse histories, the nature of the abuse experiences, and as available social supports and coping strategies so that services can be tailored to meet the specific needs of the client.

**See Also:** Absentee Mothers; Alcoholism; Anger; Anxiety; Bad Mothers; Caplan, Paula J.; Child Custody and the Law; Child Poverty; Daycare; Depression; Discipline of Children; Drug Abuse; Fetal Alcohol Syndrome; Incest; Infant Mortality; Infanticide; Mothering Children With Disabilities; Mothers Who Leave; Postpartum Depression; Poverty and Mothering; Single Mothers; Violence Against Mothers/Children; Welfare and Mothering; Work and Mothering.

## Bibliography

Cicchetti, Dante and V. Carlson, eds. *Child Maltreatment: Theory and Research on the Causes and Consequences of Child Abuse and Neglect*. Cambridge, UK: Cambridge University Press, 1989.

Corby, Brian. *Child Abuse: Towards a Knowledge Base, Third Edition*. Maidenhead, UK: Open University Press, 2006.

Howe, David. *Child Abuse and Neglect: Attachment, Development, and Intervention*. New York: Palgrave Macmillan, 2005.

Miller-Perrin, Cindy and Robin Perrin. *Child Maltreatment: An Introduction, Second Edition*. Thousand Oaks, CA: Sage, 2007.

U.S. Department of Health and Human Services. "Child Abuse and Neglect Fatalities: Statistics and Interventions." *Child's Welfare Information Gateway Factsheet* (June 2008). http://www.childwelfare.gov/pubs/factsheets/fatality.cfm (accessed May 2009).

Wolfe, David. *Child Abuse: Implications for Child Development and Psychopathology, Second Edition*. Thousand Oaks, CA: Sage, 1999.

Denise Vallance
York University

# Childbirth

While childbirth is certainly a biological event, it also has a sociocultural component that has changed over time to reflect particular historical moments. At varying times childbirth has been a private affair undertaken by a woman alone, an intimate experience shared by two partners, and a grand social event involving friends and family. This shift over time can be seen to correspond to changes in society; the status of childbirth is closely linked with dominant views on how a society sees women and to some degree reflects the overall social standing of women at that time. In the U.S. context, the changing nature of childbirth is apparent. During the 1920s, childbirth became increasingly medical, moving from the home to the hospital. Many have cited the "assembly line" style of care that attended this move, and birthing women became a major commodity in the health care industry. This shift mirrored women's widespread move from the home to the workplace and captured the overall tenor of the time—commodification of women's labor. A similar phenomenon can be seen during the 1950s, when idealized white, middle-class women were embracing domesticity and were striving for lives of suburban disengagement.

During this time, hospital birth became centered on complete pain management. With the advent of highly medical interventions, childbirth became a nonevent, perpetuating the cultural ideals of modesty, privacy and isolation. Gaining popularity during the early to mid-20th century, women were given scopolamine (an amnesiac) together with morphine (an opiate), resulting in a state popularly known as twilight sleep. This practice fell out of favor as its negative impact on mothers and babies was demonstrated (ranging from women's nightmare birth recollections to infant and maternal death) and as medicalized birth advocates championed the reclamation of unmedicated birth.

The ways that a society conceives of and approaches childbirth reflects its broader conception of women and speaks to the social standing of women at the time.

### The Landscape of U.S. Childbirth

Since the turn of the last century, childbirth has become increasingly medicalized. Beginning with birth shifting from home to hospital in the 1920s, medical management and oversight has become the paradigm of Western birth. Over the decades, the delivery room has become a site of advancing technologies, and laboring women have witnessed a birth process that reflects these rapid changes. As the field of obstetrics has grown more closely intertwined with developing medical technologies, childbirth itself has become more technological, which has allowed for the routine surveillance of women's birthing bodies through myriad devices. This ability to constantly monitor a woman's labor has fostered the entry of a growing number of medical interventions and has legitimized doctors' increased involvement in the birth process.

Today, with the overall social consensus that hospital birth is safest, this rising rate of obstetrical intervention is viewed as evidence of birth security. Particularly when attended by an obstetrician, a safe birth is seen as virtually guaranteed within the high-tech environment of the hospital delivery room. As a result, the vast majority of women continue to choose physician-attended (91.4 percent) or certified nurse midwife-attended (7.6 percent) hospital birth over other nonhospital alternatives (less than 1 percent). These statistics have remained relatively stable over recent decades. Today, over 99 percent of births take place in a hospital environment, and are subject to the procedures and treatments that accompany medicalized care.

### The Landscape of Childbirth Internationally

In many countries, childbirth remains a hazardous undertaking. The World Health Organization (WHO) estimates that about 529,000 women die in childbirth annually, almost entirely in low-income countries, and an additional 10 million suffer injury, infection, or disease. About half of women in developing countries give birth without the assistance of trained attendants or anesthesia. However, many developing countries have substantially reduced maternal mortality through low-cost methods, including training community workers to provide prenatal care and maternal education, providing basic medical supplies such as antibiotics to village clinics, and training nurse-midwives to assist at birth.

### Birthing Technologies

Most commonly, medical technologies are used to monitor the birthing woman and manage the delivery of the baby. It is routine practice for women to be constantly monitored through the use of an electronic fetal monitor (EFM), an instrument that measures the heartbeat of the baby, during the course of her labor. The rate of birthing women monitored during labor with EFM has climbed steadily since 1989, reaching over 85 percent, or more than 3.2 million live births, in 2003. EFM is the most frequently reported obstetric procedure, and may in fact be used to monitor an even higher percentage of births. According to their National Vital Statistics Report, the Centers for Disease Control and Prevention (CDC) has suggested that EFM statistics are often vastly underreported on birth certificates.

In addition to the EFM, it has become increasingly popular to employ internal fetal monitoring (IFM), where an electrode is attached through the vagina directly to the baby's head, to ensure constant monitoring of the baby's heart rate during labor. Both of these surveillance technologies require the body's connection to wires, electrodes, and sensors. Because of the growing evidence of false positive reports of fetal distress as a result of IFM, greater attention has been focused on curbing women's movement during labor and encouraging their immobility.

Labor monitoring is also carried out through detailed charting to ensure that cervical dilation is progressing along expected lines. It is a common obstetrical assumption that women will dilate according to the Friedman Curve, which stipulates 1.2 cm dilation for each hour of labor. Though many women do dilate in such a manner, as many as 20 percent of otherwise low-risk women do not progress at this rate. Slow or stalled labors are thereby quickly noticed, and more stringent courses of medical management are then adopted.

**Induced Births, Assisted Labor, and Caesareans**
A woman in labor is routinely supervised, and her medical caregivers regularly intervene into her labor and delivery. One-fifth of all birthing women will have their labor induced, a rate that has more than doubled from the 9.5 percent rate in 1990. This rising rate has been linked to a growing number of elective inductions (which have no medical or obstetric indication), and today, 25 percent of induced labors are the result of these "patient-choice" inductions. Labor contractions are also increasingly amplified with a variety of chemical stimulants, and 16.7 percent of labors in 2003 were augmented in such a way. This represents a 59 percent increase from the 1989 stimulation rate of 10 percent. Even when there is evidence that certain medical interventions are in decline—such as vacuum extraction and forceps delivery, which have dropped by 41 percent to only 5.6 percent in 2003, down from 9.5 percent in 1994—there is often a more complicated explanation for these trends, such as the drastic increase in caesarean births. Today the U.S. caesarean rate is above 30 percent—the highest rate ever reported. Driven by both the rise in primary caesareans (particularly for low-risk women) and the steep decline in vaginal birth after caesarean (VBAC), this represents a 5 percent rise from 2002 and a 25 percent rise from 1996. The rate of women having a vaginal birth after a previous caesarean (VBAC) fell 16 percent in the last year and has dropped 63 percent

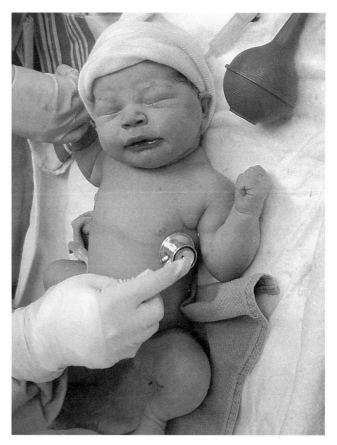

*Despite the increasing medicalization of childbirth, the alternative and natural childbirth movement is gaining momentum.*

since 1996. Because the majority of medical liability insurance providers no longer cover the procedure, it is increasingly difficult for women to choose a VBAC in a hospital environment. Thus, women who have an initial caesarean delivery must now deliver all subsequent babies via caesarean section. Also leading to the growing rate of caesarean deliveries is the rising number of women with very low-risk pregnancies delivering by caesarean, a trend that has risen 67 percent since 1990. A number of these are elective caesareans—surgical deliveries that were requested and scheduled by the woman herself rather than recommended by her medical team.

**Managing Pain**
Pain management plays a central role in childbirth today. The vast majority of women elect to use some sort of medication to alleviate the pain of childbirth. Most common is the epidural, a local or regional anesthesia or painkiller medication that is

injected through a tubelike catheter into the birthing woman's lower back. This technique of pain management numbs the body below the waist, and as a result women feel very little of the pain associated with childbirth. Analgesics are also given intravenously, and are commonly used to mitigate the pain of childbirth.

In addition, tranquilizers are administered (often in conjunction with analgesics) to calm and sedate birthing women who are unsuccessfully navigating the pain of childbirth. Another pain mitigation technique, one that has persisted since the beginning of the last century, is the administration of nitrous oxide (laughing gas) to laboring women. In some situations, birthing women are injected with opioids (narcotics), which can also be given intravenously to manage pain. In the hospital, enduring the pain of childbirth is believed to require a number of different medications, all of which are available and administered by the birthing woman's medical team. Even when women anticipate an unmedicated birth, many of them eventually request to one of the above-mentioned interventions for pain relief.

### The Critique of Childbirth Today

The medicalization of childbirth has not arrived without a small but vocal critique. Critics of medicalized birth have suggested that recent trends in the birth process are in many ways inhospitable, and are frequently hostile to the bodies and the experiences of birthing women. Growing out of the "natural" birth tradition of the 1960s, this approach extols the virtues of midwifery care, unmedicated labor, and even home birth. They have claimed that the increase in technological dependence and medical intervention have not resulted in the expected levels of safety and security, and may in fact be partially to blame for the United State's embarrassingly high rates of both infant and maternal mortality—26th in the world for infant survival in 1999, far below the rank of other developed (and a few less developed) countries. Though their ranks remain relatively small and their influence rather minimal, their rhetoric has empowered a growing number who are concerned with the current trajectory of medicalized childbirth. Their critical appraisal has occasionally garnered mainstream attention—particularly around the recent controversy over caesarean section—where it has led to a more general critique of obstetrical practices and the medical management of birth.

Ongoing childbirth activism has primarily focused on the character of medical care today. Particularly around issues of labor and delivery, the criticism has made a number of significant interventions into the nature of women's health care. This work has been instrumental in pointing out that some medical practices are unfriendly (and sometimes harmful) to birthing women, and are part of a larger tendency to see childbirth as a medical malady rather than a normal, biophysical process. Practices such as the pubic shave and enema were contested as inhumane and medically unnecessary, and have gradually faded away after years of protest. Partners and relatives are now welcome to attend the birth. Studies demonstrating the correlation between soaking in water and a decrease in pain during labor have been used to fuel a push for the installation of tubs in delivery wards. Childbirth advocates and birthing women have long promoted the efficacy of sitting, standing, and squatting during delivery, and have mounted an ongoing campaign to allow birthing women off their backs and into more comfortable positions. Though these critiques offer some amendment to the current birth idiom, the more general course of medical intervention and management continues unabated.

More recently, critics have wondered if medical practitioners can reasonably expect to follow their Hippocratic Oath of "first do no harm" in today's medical environment. Many childbirth activists and critics have suggested that health care workers (including labor and delivery nurses and obstetricians) are influenced by a variety of pressures that can complicate decision making. In a litigious field such as medicine, the specter of malpractice hangs heavy, and coupled with the profit motivation for hospitals and health maintenance organizations (HMOs), encourages a health care system that tends toward intervention rather than employing a more tempered approach.

### Medicalization of Childbirth Continues

Despite these critiques, the medical community continues to enjoy a high degree of legitimacy. The overall social consensus is that hospital birth is safest, particularly when attended by an obstetrician.

As a result, the vast majority of women (99 percent) continue to choose a medically managed hospital birth over other less medical alternatives. Medical intervention is seen as a normal part of the birth process, and medical technologies play a central role in the monitoring and management of labor and delivery. In fact, the increase in elective caesarean delivery demonstrates that today, more women than ever before are opting for a highly medicalized and indeed surgical birth. All of this occurs parallel to the mounting evidence suggesting that such a highly medicalized course of action may not offer the highest level of safety and security in childbirth. Many have begun to wonder why women continue to choose care that may compromise their goal of a smooth birth and a healthy baby.

Early critics of medicalized childbirth believed that women choosing such care for their pregnancy and birth were operating without full knowledge of the data and research. It was believed that once women learned that medicalized (including surgical) birth may not represent the pinnacle of health care, a paradigm shift would occur and more women would denounce medical birth in favor of a more natural experience. This dichotomy of natural versus medical is common in the alternative birth movement, as is a variety of other language that feminists and others have found problematic.

Instead, even as more research demonstrates the uncertain safety of medicalization during childbirth, women continue to choose hospital and even surgical birth in growing numbers. These rates demonstrate that women's birthing decisions are based on a number of different factors, of which overall safety of a procedure may play only a minor role. Women are not, in fact, operating under a sort of false consciousness assumed by early alternative birth critics, but are responding to a complex set of forces—both external and internal—that shape their decisions and inform their choices.

Much ink has been spilled debating the consequences of this medicalized childbirth trend. Arguments range from a profit- and fear-driven medical community to birthing women themselves who are actively requesting surgical birth and other medical interventions. The language of "elective," "on-demand," or "patient-choice" procedures is common. By couching the debate in terms of choice,

medical practitioners assert that they merely comply with women's delivery choices, even if medical evidence dictates otherwise. Critics suggest that such a choice is often fraught with social pressures—particularly when women opt for surgical birth to avoid the potential consequences of vaginal birth, including possible loss of vaginal tautness.

Others have wondered if birthing women feel alienated by the moral superiority that often permeates the alternative birth movement, which is often laced with condescension toward those who do not adhere to the tenets such as unmedicated delivery, breastfeeding, and co-sleeping. As a result, women who may have benefited from the critiques offered by the alternative childbirth movement do not explore its appraisal of medicalization and surgical birth. It has also been observed that women are often pleased with the pain reduction and convenience of surgical birth and choose it regardless of the risks, troubling the false-consciousness assumptions made by the alternative childbirth movement. Clearly, women's decisions about childbirth are influenced by a variety of social, economic, medical, and personal forces that shape the conclusions drawn about childbirth today.

## The Politics of Childbirth

The trend toward higher levels of surgical birth, and the rising rates of medical intervention more generally, has generated much commentary over the nature of childbirth today and its consequences. Many have pointed to the increased influence on medicine by HMOs, that have certainly shaped health care management and choice of procedures. The complex relationship between HMO, medical insurance, and liability has no doubt altered the practice of medicine, making it more susceptible to the pressures of the market. While there is evidence to suggest that such medicalization of childbirth has resulted in dramatic economic gains for HMOs, hospitals, and doctors, it is dangerous to assume that this is the only force pushing the trend toward surgical birth and an intervention model of care.

The medical community has been quick to respond to these claims, asserting that, in fact, this trend grows out of the demands made by birthing women themselves. There has been substantial evidence to support the argument that a growing number of women are choosing procedure such as caesarean, induction, and epidural before even interacting with their medical team. Women who have low-risk pregnancies and show no need advanced intervention are requesting medical procedures such as caesarean sections and labor inductions even before their waters break.

Such trends are particularly common among pop idols such as Madonna, Britney Spears, Jamie Lynn Spears, Angelina Jolie, Christina Aguilera, and Jennifer Lopez, who have been dubbed "too posh to push" and are increasingly opting for a "celebrity caesarean." Many doctors feel compelled to provide women with medical interventions whenever they are requested, even if such a demand puts woman and baby at a higher risk for complications. This debate has been presented as a matter of a woman's choice, which some (particularly alternative birth movement activists) have critiqued as being quite distorted. Critics have responded that the medical community has rarely been concerned with respecting a women's right to choice and have demonstrated the long history of restricting women's birth options, including harshly penalizing women who choose to birth at home, in a birth center, or with a midwife.

## The Debate of Choice

A more careful deconstruction of the elective caesarean section as an issue of choice has revealed that this choice may reflect a deeper social inequality that encourages women to make decisions that privilege others over themselves. A woman's choice to birth via caesarean section to preserve vaginal tautness or to prevent late-pregnancy weight gain, for example, reflects this tendency. Others have claimed that such reasoning strips a woman of her agency and undermines her autonomy. While both sides may have merit, it is clear that a debate around choice oversimplifies the complexity of the issue and escalates tension between the medical community, childbirth activists, and birthing women, all of whom find themselves defending a caricatured position in the face of mounting criticism.

The alternative childbirth movement has clearly played a role in the overgeneralization and occasional misrepresentation of the medical opposition. Although childbirth activists have advocated for greater social awareness around elective birth interventions since the 1960s, they have rarely managed to sustainably alter the direction of medicine, which they claim reflects the power held by a medical community working to systematically discredit and undermine critical opposition. Feminist critics have pointed to both the moralistic tone and language employed by the alternative childbirth movement, speculating that birthing women feel alienated by childbirth activists' intense and often polarizing views.

Furthermore, childbirth activists' criticism of medical intervention does not consider that many women find the use of pain-relieving drugs and medical interventions both empowering and fulfilling. However, while there is substantial research demonstrating the risk associated with a number of these practices, this ubiquitous denunciation does little to bring new women into the alternative childbirth movement.

## Loss of Midwifery

And yet, the kernel of their criticism remains valid—medicalization is often not the best practice in childbirth and does not promote the health of mothers and babies. Increasing levels of medicalization in obstetric care have resulted in shrinking midwifery units within hospitals and the decimation of out-of-hospital midwifery (also called direct-entry) care. In 15 states, including Illinois—where the American Medical Association is headquartered—practicing midwifery outside of a hospital environment is illegal, and direct-entry midwives operate through an informal, underground network without medical or legal support. In recent years, midwives have been tried and convicted of practicing medicine without a license, of manslaughter, and even of murder.

Such efforts have been largely successful, and the number of out-of-hospital births in the United States dropped to less than 1 percent in 2008. This drastic shift in the landscape of childbirth has not only normalized hospital births for nearly all women, it has also acted to diminish the voices that have long critiqued the medical establishment and has truncated the rich supply of evidence and documentation that supports it.

**See Also:** Birth Mothers; Homebirths; Maternal Body; Midwifery; Pregnancy; Prenatal Health Care.

## Bibliography

Arms, Suzanne. *Immaculate Deception II: Myth, Magic, & Birth*. Berkeley, CA: Celestial Arts, 2004.

Beckett, Katherine. "Choosing Caesarean: Feminism and the Politics of Childbirth in the United States." *Feminist Theory*, v.6/3 (2005).

Block, Jennifer. *Pushed: The Painful Truth About Childbirth and Modern Maternity Care*. Cambridge, MA: DaCapo Press, 2007.

Davis-Floyd, Robbie and Carolyn Sargent, eds. *Childbirth and Authoritative Knowledge: Cross-Cultural Perspectives*. Berkeley: University of California Press, 2007.

Eakins, Pamela, ed. *The American Way of Birth*. Philadelphia: Temple University Press, 1986.

Hay, Carla, Alice Kehoe, Krista Ratcliffe, and Leona VandeVusse, eds. *Who's Having This Baby? Perspectives on Birthing*. East Lansing: Michigan State Press, 2002.

Kitzinger, Sheila. *The Politics of Birth*. London: Elsevier, 2005.

Leavitt, Judith Walzer. *Brought to Bed: Childbearing in America 1750 to 1950*. New York: Oxford University Press, 1986.

Martin, Joyce, Brady Hamilton, Paul Sutton, Stephanie Ventura, Fay Menacker, and Martha Munson. "Births: Final Data for 2003." *National Vital Statistics Reports*, v.542 (2005).

Michaelson, Karen, ed. *Childbirth in America: Anthropological Perspectives*. South Hadley, MA: Bergin & Garvey, 1988.

Natalie Jolly
University of Washington, Tacoma

# Childcare

The past few decades have seen the rise in the number of young children in need of nonparental childcare. Much of this has been driven by changes in the world economy, which has resulted in an increasing number of women of working age employed outside the home. Many families find themselves seeking nonparental care, and most children are cared for in private, unregulated care situations. When regulated early childhood education and care is available, most children benefit. Studies show that local and national economies also benefit from high-quality education and care. At the same time, some have found that nonparental infant care, if begun too early and for too long, comes with some increased risks to psychosocial development. For all other children, including and especially children from disadvantaged families, high-quality childhood programming has been found to support children's social, emotional, and intellectual development. High quality is largely determined as having well-trained and well-paid early childhood education and care professionals. However, most early childhood education and care work continues to be underpaid and undervalued.

## Rising Need for Nonparental Childcare

It has been well documented that the past few decades have seen a fundamental restructuring of modern economies, driven by global economic change. There has been a move toward an information society, where the main sources of innovation, particularly in the most economically advanced nations, are derived increasingly from the production of ideas and not the production of goods. Economically advanced nations have seen a fundamental shift from goods-producing to a service economy, and the growth of professional and technical classes.

With globalization, many manufacturing jobs have been moving to parts of the world where labor is cheaper; a growing proportion of workers in the northern and western hemispheres are employed to work in service-sector jobs. While the knowledge-worker employment has increased in all regions of the world, the bifurcation within the service sector, and a polarization of jobs and earnings, is also well documented. Some of the new jobs are high skilled and knowledge based, but many are low paid, low status, and part-time (often with nontraditional work hours), or what some have colloquially termed "McJobs." In countries like Canada and the United States, some three-quarters of workers are employed in the service sector, where sales and services was the largest of the top-10 broad occupational categories. As a result of these shifts, family earnings instability and inequality grew throughout the 1990s.

With widespread worker displacement, an increasing proportion of families find themselves relying on individuals holding multiple jobs and/or having multiple incomes per household. While women's increasing labor force participation rates are related to women's rising levels of education and their desire for economic independence, families are increasingly dependent upon women's income to make ends meet. This trend is not new. Women have been entering the labor force in large numbers since the end of World War II, but some things are different today.

While fertility rates remain low across the most economically advanced nations, the proportion of women with young children in the labor force has been increasing steadily. By most recent accounts, more than two-thirds of all women of working age in the Organisation for Economic Co-operation and Development (OECD) countries—which are the most economically advanced in the world—are employed outside the home. In Canada, some 80 percent of women 25–54 years of age were in the labor force in 2005, as were about 72 percent of mothers with young children. In sum, one of the most striking changes in women's labor force participation rates across OCED countries has been among women with at least one child under the age of 6.

More women in the workforce improves a country's Gross Domestic Product (GDP), increases tax revenues, and reduces welfare cost. At the same time, new opportunities and new necessities for women with young children have resulted in new and more challenges surrounding childcare.

## Who Cares for Children

There is a growing trend toward out-of-home care for most children under the age of 6. On the other hand, there are significant differences in policies and practice across the most industrialized countries when it comes to the provision of early childhood education and care services. For example, all countries in the European Union now guarantee at least two or three years of preschool. While preschool is not a statutory right in the United States, more than 60 percent of America's preschool-aged children are in some form of early childhood program. Children not registered in early childhood programs are often cared for by relatives and nonrelatives in private homes, outside of daycare settings. Contrary to the belief that modern nuclear families are less dependent on extended family than they were in the past, recent research is showing that grandparents are increasingly relied upon to play a more significant role in the care of their young grandchildren. Some parents who can afford it have turned to hiring foreign- or domestic-born nannies for live-in care.

Today, much of the childcare sector, especially in North America, is private and unregulated, often with poor staff training and weak pedagogical programming. While some private, nonparental caregivers working outside a daycare setting may be well educated and knowledgeable about children's developmental needs, the majority do not have formal college or university training in early childhood education. In most cases, when children are cared for by relatives and nonrelatives outside of daycare centers, they are likely receiving custodial care (supervision) rather than developmental care. Developmental care involves an understanding of child development, which often widens the range of developmentally appropriate activities to which children are exposed.

## Undervaluing Care Work

Quality childcare entails well-trained and well-compensated early childhood education and care professionals, since the quality of care depends on the caregiver's ability to build and sustain strong relationships with children and their parents, and to provide secure, consistent, sensitive, stimulating, safe, and rewarding environments. The problem, however, is that caregivers and educators themselves also require stable work environments—and as it stands, many childcare professionals in most economically advanced countries have low wages, little job security, and few opportunities for career advancement. This results in high staff turnover rates, jeopardizing the quality of care. Staff with higher levels of education and specialized qualification provide more stimulating environments, and improve the quality of care; however, their pay and work conditions remain well below those of other educators and social care professionals.

## Early Childhood Education and Care

Given global economic changes, some have argued that preschool education is an investment in the future academic success and economic prospects of the world's children. Cost-benefit analyses of early childhood interventions have shown that the returns can be high for every dollar invested in early childhood care. Heeding this, countries such as Denmark, Sweden, Norway, and Finland have committed considerable energy and resources to establishing high-quality, universally accessible programs, particularly for children ages 3 to 5. Other countries, like Canada, Australia, and the United States, have invested considerably less.

Canada and the United States are considered welfare states. This means that the state accepts (some) responsibility for the protection and promotion of the economic and social well-being of its citizens, through the provision of things like unemployment insurance and access to basic health care and education. But not all welfare states are alike. In fact, scholars have established subcategories or classifications to distinguish states as either more or less magnanimous or noninterfering Canada and the United States have been classified as liberal welfare states, meaning that they are among the states that distribute benefits less freely, relying on the free market rather than extensive state support to families and social programs.

Within liberal welfare states, there is a shared basic assumption that the state will "step in" if citizens are in dire need, often with targeted rather than universal social programs; otherwise, they leave social welfare decisions to individuals. As such, decisions such as having children and using nonparental childcare are seen as personal lifestyle choices, and the responsibility of individual citizens and households. Of course, given that there are more magnanimous or social-democratic variants of welfare states, not all countries follow this model or agree with these basic premises—and this is obvious when comparing Canada and the United States to other developed nations when it comes to early childhood education and care.

For over 40 years, OECD has been collecting comparative economic and social data. Recently, it published *Starting Strong II* (2006), a report comparing early childhood education and care across its economically advanced nations. The report notes that there is a growing need for nonparental care across nations and increasingly, it is seen as

a public good. It identifies some of the challenges encountered in policy making and service coordination for early childhood education and care, compares availability and access to services, and provides a series of recommendations on how to improve quality and access to care. What is especially striking in the report is Canada's and the United States' showing compared to other developed nations. Of the 14 countries compared, Canada ranked the lowest—below the United States, which ranked 9th in public expenditure on early childhood education and care services as a percent of GDP. This means that while Canada and the United States are among the richest nations in the world, they also allocate the least in public spending on early childhood education and care. It also means that a larger proportion of the cost of care remains in the hands of individual families.

## Impact of Nonparental Care on Children

Studies of early childhood education and care in a number of countries uncover a strong relationship between quality early childhood programs and improved school performance. High-quality, early childhood programs support children's social, emotional, and intellectual development. They also have been shown to diminish the need for remediation in the school years, resulting in higher adult productivity later on, and reduction of antisocial behavior among high-risk populations.

Past and recent research has shown that early childhood education and related interventions contribute significantly to putting children in low-income families on a path toward success in school. Early childhood education programs targeting children in low-income families, like Early Head Start programs in the United States, have been successful at addressing some significant inequalities in the earliest years of children's lives. Early childhood education programs cannot fully compensate for poverty, but have proven to mitigate some of the effects of poverty and help compensate children from disadvantaged families.

Immigrant children, for example, have been found to be among the most destitute and disadvantaged in economically advanced nations like Canada and Germany. High-quality, early childhood education and care programs have helped immigrant children with their integration, improved their language skills, and reduced disadvantage on entry into formal education. In Germany, for example, children of immigrants are most likely to leave school early and least likely to go on to post secondary education. Those immigrant children who attended German preschools sufficiently improved their school record to compete with the same educational opportunities as low-income German families. Having said this, early childhood services alone cannot fully compensate for other social and structural problems faced by a nation's most disadvantaged; and not all services to all children are equally beneficial.

A number of studies have shown that infants who lack close interaction with parents and other significant adult caregivers have more poorly developed stress management systems, which can result in difficulties in responding to others. Some of these children have had longer-term problems, including depression, withdrawal, and inability to concentrate. As a result, concern has been raised over infants' exposure to nonparental childcare too early and for too long. Some have argued that the younger the child, and the longer the hours spent in childcare, the greater the psychosocial risk, particularly for children under the age of 1.

In response to this, some child advocates have pushed for, and some national governments have implemented, minimum parental-leave entitlements that would allow parents of newborns to stay home with their children for months, and years in some cases, with some income entitlement and job security. Increasingly, calls for high-quality, early childhood education and care programs have become coupled with calls for improved parental leave entitlements of at least one year, with significant salary compensation.

## Wider Social Benefits

There is ample international evidence to show that universal, community-based systems of high-quality, early childhood education and care are important components of strong economies, and are especially important when economies are contracting and in need of stimulation. Early childhood education and care has been found to have short-term, medium-term, and long-term economic and social benefits for children, their parents, the labor force, and local and national economies. Accessible, high-quality early childhood education and care programs help keep families out of poverty by supporting women's workforce participation, education, and training, which in turn builds stronger local economies. It helps support women already in the workforce and those who want to enter it. This in turn helps keep families out of poverty, increases tax revenue, and helps bolster national coffers.

**See Also:** Childhood; Children; Child Poverty; Grandmothers and Grandmothering; Nannies.

**Bibliography**
Baker, Michael, Jonathan Gruber, and Kevin Milligan. *Universal Childcare, Maternal Labor Supply and Family Well-Being.* Cambridge, MA: National Bureau of Economic Research, 2005.
Doherty, Gillian, Martha Friendly, and Jane Beach. *OECD Thematic Review of Early Childhood Education and Care: Canadian Background Report.* Ottawa: Her Majesty the Queen in Right of Canada, 2003.
Doherty, Gillian, Donna Lero, Hillel Goelman, Annette LaGrange, and Jocelyn Tougas. *You Bet I Care! Wages, Working Conditions, and Practices in Child Care Centres.* Guelph, ON: Centre for Families, Work and Wellbeing, 2000.
Fukkink, Ruben and Anna Lont. "Does Training Matter? A Meta-Analysis and Review of Caregiver Training Studies." *Early Childhood Research Quarterly,* v.22/3 (2007).
Immervoll, Herwig and David Barber. "Can Parents Afford to Work? Childcare Costs, Tax-Benefit Policies and Work Incentives." In *OECD Social, Employment and Migration Working Papers, No. 31.* Paris: Directorate for Employment, Labour and Social Affairs, 2005.
Organisation for Economic Co-operation and Development (OECD). *Starting Strong II, Early Childhood Education and Care.* Paris, OECD, 2006.
Prentice, Susan, ed. *Changing Child Care: Five Decades of Child Care Advocacy & Policy in Canada.* Toronto: Fernwood Publishing, 2001.

Patrizia Albanese
Ryerson University

# Child Custody and the Law

Despite the fact that women give birth to children and usually are expected to provide primary nurture and care, mothers have had an ambivalent relationship with child custody law. In some historical periods, custody laws have been inversely related to the biological and social ties between mothers and children. Child custody law regulates disputes about who has a) the legal authority to make decisions affecting a child's interests (usually termed *legal custody,* or sometimes *guardianship*, in North America); and b) the responsibility of taking care of the child (physical custody). Access and visitation are terms used to describe the contact between a noncustodial parent and a child. Parents may share legal custody (joint custody) and/or physical custody (shared parenting). Most parents arrive at consensual custody arrangements regarding their children. The main purpose of custody laws is to guide the resolution of disputes by judges or other decision makers, as well as provide a framework for the negotiation of disputes. Custody disputes arise most often between parents who are separating or divorcing, but others, such as adoptive parents, grandparents, aunts or uncles, sperm donors, or surrogate mothers, may also claim custody or access.

Until well into the 20th century, fathers held the primary rights to custody or guardianship of children. In most Western countries, decisions on child custody are now made according to the principle of the "best interests of the child," the primacy of which is affirmed in the 1989 United Nations Convention on the Rights of the Child. This laudable but indeterminate principle has been interpreted differently depending on time, place, and circumstances, as well as factors such as race, class, and sexuality. The modern sole custody/access paradigm under which mothers generally held custodial responsibility for children following divorce and separation has now given way to a normative model that favors joint custody and shared parenting. Concerns have been raised about the safety of women and children in shared care arrangements where there has been a history of abuse prior to separation and for the well-being of children who are exposed to persistent parental conflict. Others have commented on the continuing lack of fit between legal trends and the material realities of postseparation parenting. The lack of joint custody reforms with broader cultural and workplace changes has meant that fathers lack the opportunity to care for children in practice, and mothers are typically left with greater responsibility for childcare. A mismatch between legal norms and social patterns has arisen.

## Early History

Nineteenth-century English laws on guardianship and custody influenced many English-speaking countries such as the United States and Canada. Fathers initially held almost exclusive rights to the custody and guardianship of children born within marriage, including infants at their mothers' breasts. The first English statute to erode this paternal authority, Lord Talfourd's Act of 1839, resulted from a well-known crusade by Caroline Norton to gain access to, and the ability to communicate with, her three sons (one still a baby), who were in the custody of their father. Norton had left her husband after he subjected her to physical violence. Lord Talfourd's Act gave courts the ability to award a mother access to a child in the father's custody, or even award physical custody, until the child reached the age of 7. At that point, custody could revert back to the father, unless he decided otherwise. The father retained guardianship of the child throughout, and maternal rights remained exceptional.

## Proper Behavior of Mothers

During the course of the 19th century and into the 20th century, paternal rights were further eroded as the welfare of children was prioritized in law. However, a mother's enhanced ability to claim custody was usually conditional on her adherence to proper behavior as a wife and mother.

For example, mothers who were adulterous, or even those who were viewed as having left the marital home and/or their duties as wives for no good reason, quickly lost their parenting rights to an overriding paternal power. Given the strict moral expectations of mothers and the societal and legal resistance to seriously consider abusive behavior by husbands, mothers were vulnerable to fathers who chose to pursue custody claims. Some mothers returned to marriages to avoid the risk of losing their children.

## Maternal Presumption

The early- to mid-20th century saw the development of a "maternal presumption" in child custody law. This presumption took the form of the "tender years doctrine," which indicated that mothers should be favored for custody of a child during the period of nurture, namely until a child reached 7 years of age. After that point, fathers became entitled to claim custody. The tender years doctrine was not premised so much on female caregiving as on essentialist ideas that special ties exist between children and mothers, and that women's "natural" role lies in the domestic sphere. Scholars disagree about the extent to which the maternal presumption actually privileged mothers in situations where fathers seriously challenged them for custody. In several Canadian provinces, for instance, all other issues had to be equal between the parents in order for the presumption to apply. In many cases, they were not equal; for instance, if a mother was adulterous or had otherwise transgressed normative expectations. In some provinces, primary paternal rights prevailed well into the 1950s and 1960s.

## The Modern Ideology of Equality

By the 1970s, child custody law shifted toward a no-fault orientation, a more gender-neutral treatment of mothers and fathers, and a clear emphasis on the best interests of children as the predominant factor under consideration. Less weight was placed on adultery and on distinctions between the roles that mothers and fathers were meant to play in relation to children. Opportunities arose for lesbian mothers to claim custody of their children without denying their sexuality, although they typically had to be discreet in order to succeed. The "fathers' revolution" began, and movies such as the 1979 film *Kramer v. Kramer,* about fathers claiming custody of children, captured the public's imagination. The women's movement called for fathers to

*Shared parenting can be stressful on children as they transfer from one home to another, especially if there is parental conflict. Manipulative ex-spouses can use child custody disputes to exert control, which can cause mental and physical damage.*

increase their childcare responsibilities, especially as mothers increasingly participated in the paid labor force; fathers who did so were applauded. Blaming of mothers who entered the paid labor force, used daycare services, or left marriages also influenced the trend away from any preference for maternal custody.

In order to ensure that fathers maintained contact with children, novel court orders such as joint legal custody emerged. However, most children still resided primarily with their mothers after separation or divorce, reflecting the fact that women still bore the brunt of childcare labor. This fact also influenced privately negotiated agreements and court awards, which gave primary care of children to mothers in most cases. Joint legal custody typically meant that an access father would not share childcare, but would share in decisions about schooling, health care, or religious instruction. If the parents did not agree about such an issue, then joint custody effectively gave the father a veto over the mother's decision. Given the ongoing sexual division of labor in most heterosexual households, joint custody could be seen as granting mothers responsibilities for care whereas fathers gained rights to dictate decisions.

During the 1980s, the emerging fathers' rights movement gained in strength and exerted influence over law reform. Fathers' rights advocates typically argued that the legal system was biased in favor of mothers and against fathers, citing custody statistics on maternal custody awards. They suggested that mothers, and even judges, often denied fathers' contact with children, and argued that increased paternal rights would operate in children's best interests. They lobbied for joint custody presumptions, the use of mediation, and restrictions on the mobility of custodial parents. Psychological studies also began to suggest that children need two (opposite sex) parents, and to emphasize the importance of a paternal influence. Some jurisdictions adopted joint custody presumptions, meaning that mothers who were concerned about joint custody would have the burden of proving why a joint custody arrangement would not work or would not be safe for themselves or their children. Other jurisdictions opted for "maximum contact" legal provisions that enhanced contact with both parents and rewarded "friendly parents"—those who facilitated such contact between the child and the other parent. Unless a mother had clear evidence of serious abuse by a father or other safety concerns, she might be advised not to raise such concerns for fear of being labeled an unfriendly parent and losing custody. The legal push toward formal equality for mothers and fathers sat uncomfortably alongside the ongoing sexual division of labor in heterosexual families, where even employed mothers continued to assume greater responsibility for childcare. The ideology of motherhood still held women to stricter standards of responsibility in relation to children, but once parents separated, it was assumed that the tasks of motherhood could be taken over by others, such as fathers, new wives, or grandmothers. The new norms were also juxtaposed against the increasing awareness of woman abuse both during marriages and/or after the separation process.

## Shared Parenting

Throughout the 1990s and into the 21st century, the emphasis on the relationship between children's well-being and contact with their fathers continued to increase, despite research showing that the key determinants of children's well-being are a well-functioning, custodial parent and avoidance of parental conflict. Although continuing contact with each parent is also associated with positive outcomes, its benefit is diminished if the contact generates conflict between the parents. Shared parenting has been reported to work well when parents have a history of sharing parenting responsibilities, or when they are clearly capable of cooperating. Shared parenting arrangements can also relieve mothers from the constraints of full-time responsibility for childcare.

However, these arrangements can be damaging to both mothers and children when parents are in conflicted or abusive relationships. Custody disputes can be used by an abusive or manipulative spouse to continue an unhealthy relationship or to perpetuate control over a mother. Some fathers claim custody or shared time in order to reduce their child-support commitments, as increased time spent with a child may diminish the amount of paid support. Moreover, cases involving conflict between parents are most likely to end up in court, raising questions about the wisdom of court-ordered joint custody or shared parenting, as opposed to arrangements agreed upon by parents.

Debates about the merits of laws promoting joint custody and shared parenting have been lively. Many feel that the work of motherhood has never been properly valued in child custody law, and that the current trends exacerbate the extent to which mothers' caregiving labor is simultaneously reinforced and taken for granted in society. Modern trends also require sometimes unwanted ties between mothers and fathers, regardless of the parents' living arrangements or quality of their relationship. Even fathers who have never cohabited with a mother have sometimes been accorded generous custody or access rights, often based little more than their genetic tie with a child. For many judges, lawyers, and mediators, joint custody and shared parenting represent a useful compromise in difficult custody cases.

However, the empirical evidence suggests that workable, postseparation shared-care arrangements require high levels of cooperation and good communication between parents, indicating that a shared parenting regime is not appropriate for highly conflicted families that resolve their disputes through the legal system. Studies also indicate that there has been, over time, a considerable drift away from joint custody arrangements that have been ordered by a court, with children tending to return to live primarily with mothers. This drift indicates the difficulty of making genuine, shared-parenting arrangements work effectively for parents and children. The aspirational nature of shared-parenting reforms contrasts with the lack of government initiatives to support paternal caregiving on a broader scale.

### New Shared-Parenting Initiatives

Despite these concerns about the rise of shared parenting and alternative law reform proposals, such as presuming that the custodial parent should be the one who has provided past primary care (generally favoring maternal custody), new shared parenting initiatives appeared. In an effort to reduce conflict between parents and encourage cooperative post-separation arrangements, some countries have eradicated the property-laden terms of *custody* and *access* in favor of terms such as *residence, contact,* and *parental responsibility,* which would determine

where a child should live, the degree of contact with each parent, and who has responsibility for decisions. In 1995, for instance, Australia introduced these changes and vested children with the right to be cared for by both parents and to have regular contact with each, subject, of course, to the child's best interests.

Although judges were supposed to watch for the safety needs of children and other family members, the philosophy that children should have contact with both parents generally predominated. In 2006, after lobbying by fathers' rights groups and a three-year reform process, Australia went even further and introduced shared parenting amendments, including a presumption for "equal shared parental responsibility." This presumption that consultative decision making by parents is in a child's best interests does not apply if there is evidence of abuse, and can also be rebutted if evidence shows it is not in the child's best interests. Otherwise, a court must consider making an order for the child to spend equal time with both parents, and if not equal time, then "substantial and significant" time.

These amendments appear responsible for an increase in substantially shared care arrangements, but research indicates that a significant number of such arrangements are characterized by intense parental conflict. Worryingly, shared care of children appears to be a key variable affecting poor emotional outcomes for children, suggesting that it is not always in a child's best interests.

The shared-parenting trends, resting on the premise of maternal and paternal equality, may overemphasize formal genetic ties rather than caregiving ties with children, or the most appropriate arrangements from a child-centered perspective. These trends certainly pose challenges for heterosexual mothers who have a conflict-ridden or abusive relationship with their child's father.

But it is even less clear how paternal equality, premised on a man's genetic tie with a child, can be reconciled with the "lesbian baby boom," as children are increasingly born into lesbian-headed families through the use of assisted insemination. Although some jurisdictions now permit both lesbian co-mothers to be named as legal parents, the legal status of sperm donors often remains unclear. As a result, lesbian mothers remain vulnerable to custody claims by sperm donors who wish to claim paternal status. Custody claims have also arisen between lesbian co-mothers; the few existing judicial decisions tend to favor the birth mother and her genetic ties. Cases such as these challenge the legal system to prioritize either biogenetic ties or the caregiving relationship that mothers develop with children. Disputes between birth mothers and adoptive parents, or surrogate mothers and intentional parents, also raise difficult questions about the weight of genetic ties versus intentional-parenting ties.

## Ongoing Issues for Mothers

Mothers who "win" sole custody or primary care of children can nevertheless encounter problems related to both their children's nurture and their financial well-being. Although child support laws typically require the other parent to contribute to the children's expenses, enforcement can be difficult if payments are late, incomplete, or missing. Moreover, child support guidelines are not applied as strictly once a shared parenting arrangement is in place. Some fathers press for more time with a child, assuming they will have to pay less support. Some mothers relinquish claims to financial support or property in order to guarantee sole custody.

As well, modern custody laws expect that a custodial mother will facilitate contact between the children and their other parent (usually a father). If a mother is not willing to do so, citing concerns about a child's safety or well-being, she may be tagged as a "no-contact mother" and even lose custody. Ironically, as public consciousness about woman abuse and sexual abuse of children rose during the 1980s and 1990s, it became increasingly difficult for mothers to raise such concerns in the custody context. Requests to limit a father's contact with a child conflicts with the legal system's new objective to enhance contact with both parents.

Additionally, should a mother wish or need to relocate, for instance to rejoin her family or obtain better employment, she may encounter difficulties if the other parent objects. The direction that child custody law has taken in the name of children's best interests has caused maternal autonomy—or ability to make choices and decisions—has been constrained.

**See Also:** Essentialism and Mothering; History of Mothering; Law and Mothering; Lesbian Mothering; Violence Against Mothers/Children.

**Bibliography**
Boyd, Susan B. *Child Custody, Law, and Women's Work*. London: Oxford University Press, 2003.
Chesler, Phyllis. *Mothers on Trial: The Battle for Children and Custody*. New York: McGraw-Hill, 1986.
Fineman, Martha A. *The Neutered Mother, The Sexual Family and Other Twentieth Century Tragedies*. New York: Routledge, 1995.
Mason, Mary Ann. *From Father's Property to Children's Rights: The History of Child Custody in the United States*. New York: Columbia University Press, 1994.
Millbank, Jenni. "The Limits of Functional Family: Lesbian Mother Litigation in the Era of the Eternal Biological Family." *International Journal of Law, Policy and the Family*, v.22 (2008).
Rhoades, Helen. "The 'No Contact Mother': Reconstructions of Motherhood in the Era of the 'New Father.'" *International Journal of Law, Policy and the Family*, v.16 (2002).
Smart, Carol and Selma Sevenhuijsen, eds. *Child Custody and the Politics of Gender*. New York: Routledge, 1989.

Susan B. Boyd
University of British Columbia

# Childhood

When childhood is believed to begin and end varies from culture to culture, across time, and between institutions within every society. For example, at what age can children legally work for pay? When can a young person legally consent to have sexual relations? Who does child pornography legislation protect? When can a parent stop paying child support? The varying answers to these questions indicate that childhood is a social construct—a social creation subject to redefinition. Historically, differing philosophical approaches to understanding childhood exist, and childhood is experienced differently depending on a child's sex, race, and class background.

## Defining Children and Childhood

There is little consensus in how the terms *children* and *childhood* are defined, even among contemporary legal documents. For example, according to the 2006 Canadian Census Dictionary, children refers "to blood, step- or adopted sons and daughters (regardless of age or marital status) who are living in the same dwelling as their parent(s), as well as grandchildren in households where there are no parents present."

Here, child has nothing to do with physical maturation, chronological age, or level of maturity. Instead, it refers to the nature of the living arrangement, which is more likely to have something to do with dependency. This seemingly has its origins in the idea that economic adulthood begins with moving out of one's parental home.

Many of the current ideas about childhood are related to parental rights and obligations toward children. But the end of parents' legal obligations to children varies considerably, depending on its jurisdiction and type; therefore, childhood's span depends on the context in which it is used, the purpose it is intended to serve, and the type and nature of interactions it involves. Childhood can refer to a chronological age range, a level of maturity, a period of physical maturation, or of economic dependency. Our definitions largely reflect assumptions about ability, power, autonomy, and dependency, which vary over time and across cultures.

## Understanding Variations in Childhood

Because many children living in the past were silent or silenced by history, circumstance, lack of a public presence, powerlessness, and illiteracy, we are left with a considerable amount of speculation about the true lives of children and historical experiences in and on childhood. This has sparked theoretical debates about childhood, one of the more significant starting in the 1960s with Philippe Ariès's first book, *Centuries of Childhood* (1962).

## Medieval Indifference Toward Childhood

French historian Philippe Ariès, has been recognized by many as one of the first, best-known, and most influential and controversial historians of childhood in the 20th century. Ariès argued that "there was no place for childhood in the medieval world." He explained that he was not arguing that children were neglected or despised in the medieval world, nor that they lived lives devoid of affection, but rather that in the past people lacked the awareness of the distinctiveness of childhood apart from adulthood. He added that adults in the 10th and 11th centuries in Europe simply did not devote much time or special attention to them, as evidenced by their absence, marginalization, and adult-like depictions in portraits, and by their absence from the focus of religious festivals. He deduced that adults must not have had a distinctive conception of childhood as a separate stage in life since children were not given special emotional or legal allowances, and because they were depicted clothed as mini-adults or mingling with adults in everyday life for the purposes of work, relaxation, and sport. He also noted a lack of vocabulary in French and English for distinguishing children of different ages from one another. Children were either relegated to the margins or were fully integrated into the adult world because they were so much a part of adult life in work and leisure. An outcome of this supposition of the medieval world's indifference toward childhood was that it gave children more latitude, less monitoring, and more autonomy.

## The Development of Childhood

Ariès noted that at about the 13th century, images of children, at least in Europe, appeared closer to the modern concept of childhood. As a result, Ariès declared that "no doubt, the discovery of childhood began in the 13th century, and its progress can be traced in the history of art in the 15th and 16th centuries. But the evidence of its development became more plentiful and significant from the end of the 16th century and throughout the 17th. Among the elite of 17th-century Europe, there was a growing recognition of children's special need for attention, nurture, and guidance accompanied by increased attention to schooling. Birth rates began to drop, allowing parents the resources to pay more attention to individual children. The vocabulary relating to infancy appeared and expanded. He explained that with the passage of time, a more formal distinction was made between childhood and adulthood, especially among the elite who could afford to protect children longer.

While some scholars, like Albrecht Classen and Peter Stearns, note that Ariès's work was influential in kick-starting the historical study of childhood, they also note that a growing body of research indicates that Ariès's thesis was not always substantiated. Many have tried to prove, contrary to Ariès's views, that some medieval societies did have a view of childhood as unique and special. For example, Classen points to the writings of Jean Gerson (1363–1429), which suggested that parents pay more attention to their children's emotional needs; and to Mapheus Vegius (1406–58), who reprimanded parents for assuming that physical punishment was an ideal tool in education. Both Gerson and Vegius wrote in the period that Ariès claims reflected indifference to childhood. Others criticize Ariès for generalizing, overemphasizing, and misinterpreting on the basis of a limited and select amount of evidence.

Other scholars, like Colin Heywood, have argued that there was less homogeneity of experiences and thought about childhood than Ariès claimed. Heywood notes that "running like a red thread through the historical literature is the contradictory nature of ideas and emotions concerning childhood." Using evidence from diverse cultural traditions, he shows that at any given point, one can find competing themes in the treatment and understanding of childhood. Heywood shows that children have been concurrently written about as both innocent and wicked, products of nature and of nurture, needy and dependent, and unsupervised and independent. He also points to considerable variations in perceptions of childhood within Europe, at about the same periods in time as the work of Locke and Rousseau.

For some, the inventor of the concept of childhood was Jean-Jacques Rousseau (1712–78). The French philosopher has been credited with pushing the concept of childhood to mean something that was not only quantitatively different from adulthood, but qualitatively different as well. Others point instead to the work of John Locke (1632–1704), the English philosopher, for his pioneering work on childhood.

## Turning Points in European Thought

John Locke, the "father of English liberalism" in *Some Thoughts on Education* (1693), is believed to have provided Europeans with the first treatise or manifesto on a scheme for child-centered education. His work on governance refers to childhood as a distinct and unique period in the life of a person. Locke wrote about children as "citizens in the making" or incomplete versions of their future adult selves. While this may not seem especially significant to readers today, it was revolutionary for his time, when it was commonly believed that children were born either good or bad (born of original sin), a concept that could be twisted to relieve parents of a sense of responsibility over how children turned out.

His views that children have needs and interests different from adults required that children receive special attention and proper upbringing. He argued that children are born free of reason—as blank slates, and that experience alone, slowly acquired, stocked the mind. In other words, with proper education, children—who were not yet fully rational—were brought gradually to reason. Contrary to popular views of the time, he argued that children should not be driven into conformity and good behavior by being beaten or coerced. For Locke, education formed a child's ability to reason and function as a free and equal adult.

In contrast to Locke, as Rousseau expressed in the first sentence of his most famous work, *Social Contract* (1762), is the concept that "Man is born free but everywhere is in chains." Rousseau's political statement also expresses his views on childhood, which implies that a child is born carefree and innocent, but not "blank" and unequal, as Locke believed; and not "of sin," as many, especially priests and educators, believed. In another of his famous works, *Emile*, (1762), Rousseau exclaims, "God makes all things good; man meddles with them and they become evil." For Rousseau, childhood was uniquely a time of innocence and honesty, in sharp contrast to Locke's view of childhood as an "imperfect state." He believed that children had their own way of seeing, thinking, and feeling apart from adults; and while they did not reason as adults, they had their own form of sensitive or puerile reason that they should be free to explore and enjoy. He condemned Locke's advice that children should be reasoned with, explaining that they should be left alone to "be children" as nature intended, left to enjoy their social worlds before becoming stifled by life experiences.

Rousseau blamed educators and other adults for much of the stifling. While his views were highly controversial, they were extremely significant in challenging past European views on childhood. Ironically, Rousseau and his lifelong companion, Thérèse Levasseur, abandoned their own five children at the Paris orphanage soon after their birth.

Although these views seem very different, both had profound social consequences because their views laid the responsibility on parents and educators for how children turned out. While they did not agree on the type of attention needed, both recognized childhood as distinct from adulthood, and both expressed an underlying need for more adult attention to addressing children's needs. They also show that there was no single, unified view on what childhood was or how it should be treated.

## Cross-Cultural Variations

Across borders and within cultures, oscillations in the notion of childhood are caused by social, cultural, economic, and political diversity and change over time. Anthropologists hold that there are multiplicities of childhoods, each culturally codified and defined by age, ethnicity, gender, history, and location. Transnational variations exist in such assumed standards as the structuring of age categories and chronological age. Some, like Peter Stearns, have taken a world history approach in the study of childhood, and examine how the economic organization of diverse societies (hunting and gathering versus agricultural versus industrial) affects how childhood is understood and experienced. Stearns explains that nomadic peoples in hunting and gathering societies, with more temporary settlements, represent childhood as a period of dependency that potentially burdens the group. He cites anthropological evidence from the Americas, Australia, and India to show that in hunting and gathering societies, birth rates were kept relatively low through prolonged lactation, abortion, infanticide, or regulation of sexual contact.

Stearns notes that in agricultural societies, however, children of different ages quickly come to be seen as part of an essential labor force. With an expanded food supply, birth rates begin to grow. With more children in society, they gain attention in legal codes, have more peers, and are considered a distinct group. Their increased numbers, worth, and visibility also resulted in the rise of protective superstitions; in agrarian societies, it was important that children be protected so they could work.

Other interesting information has been uncovered about childhood and the treatment of children in early civilizations. The four great civilizations that emerged between 10,000 and 5000 B.C.E., close to large rivers—the Tigris and Euphrates Rivers in Mesopotamia (the Middle East), the Nile in Egypt, the Hindus River in Indus, and the Yellow River in China—all provide examples that counter Ariès's thesis that childhood did not exist as a concept before medieval European times.

For example, some of the earliest known codes of law, dating back to 4,000 years ago in ancient Sumer in Mesopotamia, reference the concept of parental responsibility toward children. Similarly, around 1792 B.C.E., the famed ruler Hammurabi created a code of 282 laws, of which 16 directly mentioned children. Some of these laws protected children from abduction (punishable by death), and from loss of rights resulting from a loss of one parent (through remarriage) or of both parents. Archaeological evidence of toys have been found buried with their affluent, young, prematurely deceased masters.

The notion of childhood has oscillated, taking on a more or less significant place within the life cycle depending on the economic, political, and cultural composition of any given group at any point in time. Childhood also varied along social class and gender lines; the same can be said about childhood today.

**See Also:** Adolescent Children; Care Giving; Children; Child Poverty.

## Bibliography

Albanese, Patrizia. *Children in Canada Today*. Don Mills, ON: Oxford University Press Canada, 2009.

Archard, David. *Children: Rights and Childhood*. New York: Routledge, 2004.

Ariès, Philippe. *Centuries of Childhood: A Social History of Family Life*. New York: Alfred A. Knopf, 1962.

Bentley, Kristina A. "Can There Be Any Universal Children's Rights?" *International Journal of Human Rights*, v.9/1 (2005).

Classen, Albrecht. "Philippe Ariès and the Consequences: History of Childhood, Family Relations, and Personal Emotions." In *Childhood in the Middle Ages and the Renaissance: The Results of a Paradigm Shift in the History of Mentality*. Berlin, Germany: Walter de Gruyter, 2005.

Colón, A.R. and P.A. Colón. *A History of Children: A Socio-Cultural Survey Across Millennia*. Westport, CT: Greenwood Press, 2001.

Heywood, Colin. *A History of Childhood*. Cambridge, UK: Polity Press, 2001.

Jalongo, Mary. "On Behalf of Children." *Early Childhood Education Journal*, v.30/1 (2002).

Jimack, P.D. "Introduction." In *Emile,* by Jean Jacques Rousseau. New York: Dent/Everyman's Library, 1974.

Locke, John. *Of the Conduct of the Understanding.* New York: Oxford Press, 1975.

Locke, John. *Treatise of Civil Government and A Letter Concerning Toleration*. New York: D. Appleton-Century, 1937.

Rousseau, Jean-Jacques. *Emile.* New York: Dent/Everyman's Library, 1974.

Rousseau, Jean-Jacques. "On the Social Contract." In *Collected Writings of Rousseau*, Vol. 4, R. D. Masters and C. Kelly, eds. Lebanon, NH: Dartmouth College Press/University Press of New England, 1994.

Statistics Canada. "Census Family Status." In *2006 Census Dictionary*. Ottawa, ON: Statistics Canada, 2007.

Stearns, Peter. *Childhood in World History.* New York: Routledge, 2006.

Stearns, Peter. *Growing Up: The History of Childhood in a Global Context.* Waco, TX: Baylor University Press, 2005.

Patrizia Albanese
Ryerson University

# Childlessness

In contemporary Western society, there are higher numbers of infertility cases than ever before. In addition, there are more women and men choosing to remain childless. Those who do have children have them later and have fewer; and increasing numbers of babies are born following some form of medical assistance, from self-administered donated sperm to medically sophisticated procedures such as egg donation. World fertility surveys and national censuses suggest that virtually all permanent childlessness in the developing countries is involuntary. Falling birth rates stimulate many concerns, and throughout the world, ideologies of motherhood (and fatherhood) and expectations to parent affect all women and men, whether or not they are parents. Arguably, these ideologies are more of an issue for women, as the ideal view of woman is synonymous with the image of the ideal mother.

One response to the disjunction between the ideology and the experience of motherhood is a focus on "the right to choose," which is defined in terms of the right not to have children. Yet, feminists and others have suggested that choice in this context is something of a red herring, because of the expectations and ideologies of ideal womanhood. In addition, even if it is possible to decide not to have children, it is not always possible to choose motherhood, which is often dependent on ideal biological and social conditions.

Yet, issues of kinship and the fear of genetic death are significant in contemporary Western society, which can be demonstrated by the rise of surrogacy and posthumous sperm donation. Furthermore, motherhood remains a primary expectation for women, which means that childless women are often defined as "other," although the terms *voluntarily childless* and *involuntarily childless* lead to different responses. Voluntary childlessness is often associated with selfishness, while involuntary childlessness can incur pity. Motherhood is associated with full adulthood; therefore, women without children are sometimes viewed as less than adult, like children themselves. There are many ways in which women have become mothers (biological and social), and there are many ways to have children in one's life; for example, as a teacher, aunt, godmother, and friend. However, there appears to be no description of the childless nonmother other than to refer to what she does not have.

### The Choice of Voluntary Childlessness
Some studies of voluntary childlessness argue that for some women, the choice not to have a child is a

fairly simple one. However, other research suggests that choice is this context is a complex experience, with childlessness being described by some women as an ongoing practice. Involuntary childlessness is a social experience, different from infertility. However, it is often experienced in conjunction with the medical condition of infertility, which is defined as the inability to conceive a child after a year or more of unprotected intercourse, or the inability to carry a pregnancy to term. Some writers refer to a continuum of voluntary or involuntary childlessness, which individuals move along at different times. Thus, a woman may at one time in her life define herself as certain she does not want children, but later in her life feels that choice has been taken away from her. Alternatively, a woman who begins by describing herself as desperate to have children may come to feel more voluntarily than involuntarily childless. Others may adapt, but still feel a sense of loss and exclusion from what some describe as the "motherhood club."

Feminists have argued for the recognition of and space for ambivalence within mothering, but less attention has been given to ambivalence and childlessness. Yet, ambivalence is significant to childlessness too. The voluntary childless are often believed to be ambivalent even if they claim the contrary, whereas the involuntary childless are assumed not to be serious about their desire for a child if they display any ambivalence at all.

Thus, the everyday understanding of voluntary and involuntary childlessness (and of infertility) are affected by medical, political, and lay discourses that are powerful and authoritative. Among other things, these discourses suggest that childless women lead barren lives, and medical solutions are available for those who deserve them. Ironically, the increased availability of techniques to assist to the involuntary childless has likely added to the pressure that some women (and men) feel. For these individuals, childlessness becomes a defining, stigmatizing condition. However, research in this area overwhelmingly suggests that just as the lives of those women and men who parent are complex and multifaceted, so are the lives of those who do not.

**See Also:** Ambivalence; Emotions; Fertility Maternal Absence; Maternal Desire.

**Bibliography**
Letherby, Gayle. "Childless and Bereft? Stereotypes and Realities in Relation to 'Voluntary' and 'Involuntary' Childlessness and Womanhood." *Sociological Inquiry,* v.72/1 (2002).
Letherby, Gayle and Catherine Williams. "Non-Motherhood: Ambivalent Autobiographies." *Feminist Studies,* v.25 (1999).
McAllister, Fiona, and Lynda Clarke. *Choosing Childlessness.* London: Family Policy Studies Centre and Joseph Rowntree Foundation, 1998.
Monach, James H. *Childless No Choice: The Experience of Involuntary Childlessness.* New York: Routledge, 1993.
Petchesky, Rosalind. "Reproductive Freedom: Beyond a Woman's Right to Choose." *Signs: Journal of Women in Culture and Society,* v.5 (1980).

Gayle Letherby
University of Plymouth

# Child Poverty

Although the United States and Canada are the most advanced industrialized countries in the world, they have some the highest child poverty rates in the industrialized world. Some children are poor because their parents are working, yet poor. Other poor children live with single mothers or recent immigrants. Children living in poverty experience increased strain on their physical, emotional, psychological, and social well-being. That said, there are some industrialized nations that have reduced child poverty rates through a number of programs and policies.

## Gap Between Rich and Poor

By many accounts, the poor in weathlier countries like Canada and the United States are getting poorer, and the gap between the lowest- and highest-income families has widened. Average incomes for the poorest in Canada, for example, have increased by about 18 percent over the past 10 years, while the wealthiest families experienced a 30 percent increase. Young couples with children experienced significant downward shifts, as their average wealth fell about 30 percent over the last decade. Inequality has worsened among families with children.

## Causes of Poverty
Children may be contributing to family poverty because they are a drain on family resources; however, research shows that in countries with more family-friendly policies, disposable income falls only moderately when families have children. In 2007, Wendy Sigle-Rushton, London School of Economics, and Jane Waldfogel, Columbia University School of Social Work, used data from seven Western, industrialized countries to compare gaps in gross and disposable family income between families with and without children. They found that differences in earnings and labor market participation of women were major drivers in the gap in gross and disposable income; taxes and government transfers also narrowed the differences. This means that poverty rates are strongly related to parents—especially mothers—having access to the labor force, the wages they receive, and government policies aimed at assisting families in obtaining and holding decent-paying, stable employment.

Many studies have documented the rise of precarious employment characterized by poor job quality, low wages, and few or no benefits. Over the past decade, Canada and the United States have lost hundreds of thousands of jobs in the manufacturing sector, resulting in the loss of higher-waged, permanent jobs with relatively low education requirements. Many of these displaced workers become employed in temporary, low-waged, precarious, nonstandard jobs. Recent immigrants to Canada and the United States, who often reside in large cities (with high cost of living) parachute into precarious labor markets. This has forced many recent arrivals and others to become multiple job holders in an attempt to make ends meet. This has also contributed to family instability, at a time of substantial cuts to social assistance.

Children are poor for many reasons—mostly due to their parent's relationship to the labor force. Some are poor because their parents earn low wages and/or work nonstandard jobs; others have parents with inadequate education or educational credentials that are not recognized in North America; some have experienced their parents' marital breakup and/or

live in lone-parent households; and others have been affected by government cuts in social spending. The most vulnerable children are those from recent immigrant families; from racialized groups, including Aboriginal children; children with disabilities; and (despite some improvements) those living in female-headed, single-parent families.

## Measuring Poverty
Countries like Canada have been publishing low-income rates based on a measure called the low income cutoff (LICO), but no common measure of poverty currently exists across developed nations. The LICO has been used to measure whether a family's basic food, clothing, and shelter expenditures are too large compared to other families. Today, LICOs are calculated using either/both after-tax and pretax income; a family is considered to be living in strained circumstances if it spends approximately 55 percent (the average of 35 percent plus 20 percent in the before-tax calculation of LICO, or 44 percent plus 20 percent in the after-tax calculation) or more on basic food, clothing, and shelter. This measure has been standardized and calculated based on family and community size (which typically affects cost of living).

The low income measure (LIM) is also commonly used and is based on a country's median income, which represents the middle value if all incomes in the country were ranked from highest to lowest. The LIM considers a family to be strained (poor) if it has a household income of less than half the country's median income.

LICO and LIM are considered to be relative measures that compare incomes and deduce that some are too low in relation to others. Noting this, some have argued that in countries like Canada and the United States, there is no absolute poverty, which is lacking the basic necessities of life—but rather relative poverty, implying that some only "feel" poor compared to others. But the negative effects of poverty on children are real and well documented.

## Emotional and Cognitive Impacts of Poverty
Studies show that as family incomes fall, risks of poor developmental outcomes in children's health, learning, and socialization increase. Analyses reveal that higher income, regardless of the measure, is

almost always associated with better child outcomes, with the relationship being most significant among younger children.

Young children depend on adults for their well-being, and their healthy development depends on access to basic nutrition and safe neighborhoods. Lower income contributes to limited access to adequate housing (more overcrowding, strained living conditions, residential instability, and poorer and less safe neighborhoods); decreased ability of parents to purchase children's learning assets; and decreased ability to afford recreational activities that promote child development.

Children living in low-income households exhibited delayed vocabulary development compared to children in high-income families, and household income was a significant predictor for many measures of 5-year-old children's readiness to learn. Early childhood poverty affects years of schooling, such that poor children are less likely to graduate from high school compared to children who are not poor or who experience poverty later in childhood.

Studies found that the physical environment of the home (with access to simulating materials and high levels of parental activities with the child) was the most important mediator in the relationship between income and children's applied problem scores. Family income was also associated with maternal emotional distress, parenting practices, and family stress, affecting parents' ability to cognitively stimulate children, which affected readiness to learn.

## Physical Impacts of Poverty

Studies show that child poverty negatively impacts physical outcomes: mortality, morbidity, accidents, and abuse. United Nations Educational, Scientific, and Cultural Organization (UNESCO) research reveals that while the majority of children born into today's developed nations enjoy unprecedented levels of health, the wealthiest nations are not the healthiest. The *Canadian Medical Association Journal*, for example, noted that despite a decline in the rate of unintentional injuries among Canadian children in urban areas, poor children were still twice as likely as children in affluent homes to die of an unintended injury. There is a noted association between several measures of low socioeconomic status and adverse birth outcomes across a

number of countries, including those with universal health care. Children in low-income families are over two and one-half times more likely than children in high-income families to have problems with vision, hearing, speech, or mobility. Poor parents, because of limited resources, often have a difficult time supplying their children with the best food, as well as adequate clothing and housing, resulting in exposure to harmful environmental conditions and increased stress. One of the most threatening outcomes of poverty is the risk of poor children growing up to be poor adults.

Children living in low-income families are not destined to live deprived lives. The effects of long-term poverty on children are mediated and moderated by neighborhood resources and social capital. Neighborhoods with more social supports have been found to positively modify the effects of long-term poverty. Poor children who live in families with constructive and supportive relationships also have an advantage. Children living in low-income families have been found to benefit from parental supports in the form of high-quality childcare, antipoverty programs, targeted welfare programs, and a host of other national- and neighborhood-based initiatives.

## International Comparisons and Initiatives

All industrialized countries have been exposed to global economic pressures, with surprisingly different results compared to Canada and the United States when it comes to child poverty. In 2005 UNICEF (2005) released its *Report Card 6—Child Poverty in Rich Countries*. While child poverty rates dropped slightly in Canada and the United States, Canada still ranked 19th and the United States ranked 25th out of 26 countries compared. English-speaking countries filled most of the bottom rungs of this ladder: Australia was one spot above Canada; filling the remaining bottom spots were the United Kingdom (UK), Portugal, Ireland, New Zealand, Italy, and Mexico. The report noted that in all countries, poverty levels were determined by a combination of social trends, labor market conditions, and government policies. But the report also found that while labor market conditions and social change played a key role in high child poverty rates, higher government spending on family and social benefits is associated with lower child poverty rates.

UNICEF's report shows that all nations in the study made significant efforts to reduce poverty through cash and other benefits to the unemployed and those living on low income. However, countries with the lowest rates of poverty, like Demark, Finland, and Norway, did a considerably better job when it came to government intervention. It found that the greater the proportion of Gross Domestic Product devoted to family allowances, disability and sickness benefits, formal day care provisions, unemployment insurance, employment promotion, and other forms of social assistance, the lower the risk of growing up in poverty. The report also explained that benefits that are universally provided (rather than targeting low-income families), though seemingly more expensive, actually work best to reduce poverty.

Canada, the UK, and the United States have made some attempts to reduce poverty; however, their initiatives reflect a patchwork of policies and programs. Compared to western European countries with low child poverty rates, Canadian, UK and U.S. policies reflect an individual-responsibility approach, in regard to families, which does not recognize a philosophy of society's shared responsibility for children. In contrast, western European nations with low poverty rates embrace a social-responsibility framework that assumes that children are the responsibility of both parents and the state. Unlike Canada and the United States, they have unified social and family policies that express society's shared responsibility for children, provide an adequate income floor for families with children, reduce gender inequalities, expand family time options for parents, and aim to ensure an adequate and consistent living standard for all children and families.

**See Also:** Aboriginal Mothering; Childhood; Childcare; Children; Class and Mothering; Divorce; Lone Mothers; Poverty and Mothering; Single Mothers.

**Bibliography**
Ackerman, B., E. Brown, and C. Izard. "Continuity and Change in Levels of Externalizing Behavior in School of Children From Economically Disadvantaged Families." *Child Development*, v.74 (2003).

Beiser, M., F. Hou, V. Kaspar, and S. Noh. *Changes in Poverty Status and Developmental Behaviours*. Ottawa, ON: Human Resources and Skills Development Canada, 2000.
Bradshaw, J. "Child Poverty and Child Outcomes." *Children & Society*, v.16/1 (2002).
Chung, H. and C. Muntaner. "Political and Welfare State Determinants of Infant and Child Health Indicators: Analysis of Wealthy Countries." *Social Science & Medicine*, v.63/3 (2006).
Organisation for Economic Co-operation and Development (OECD). *Society at a Glance: OECD Social Indicators*. Paris: OECD, 2005.
Sigle-Rushton, W., and J. Waldfogel. "Incomes of Families With Children: Cross-National Comparison." *Journal of European Social Policy*, v.17/4 (2007).
Stanwick, R. "Canada Gets a Marginal Grade in Childhood Injury." *Canadian Medical Association Journal*, v.175/8 (2006).
UNICEF. *Report Card 7—Child Poverty in Perspective*. New York: UNICEF, 2007.
UNICEF. *Report Card 6—Child Poverty in Rich Counties*. New York: UNICEF, 2005.

Patrizia Albanese
Ryerson University

# Children

The status and lives of children around the Western world have changed considerably over the past century. In fact, childhood as we know it is a relatively new phenomenon that is constantly evolving. As the family has changed—from being a unit of production to one of consumption—so has the status, role, and value of children within it.

Children have become a pivotal point of family aspirations for higher social status and cultural retention, among other things. As a result, since the 1950s and 1960s, a great deal of emphasis has been placed on ideas surrounding proper parenting and child rearing. This is evidenced by the growth in popularity of parenting manuals, journals, books, and Websites—all of which have transformed the meaning and expectations surrounding motherhood and fatherhood. With this, and growing international initiatives concerning children's rights, we have seen changes in the lives and experiences of children living in the North and West.

## What and Who Is a Child

Children exist in every society, but what is meant by child or children, and when childhood is believed to begin and end, varies from culture to culture, across time, and between organizations and institutions within societies. Even by legal definitions, a child can be anyone under the age of 6, 12, 14, 16, 18, or 19, or can be anyone, of any age, as long as they have a living parent. There is little consensus in how child, children, and childhood are defined, even among contemporary official or legal documents. Within any given time period or region, there are differing philosophical approaches to understanding children and childhood; and children of different genders, races, and social class backgrounds often experience childhood differently.

## Redefining Roles of Mother, Father, and Child

The post–World War II period, and especially the 1950s, was an anomalous period for families in North America. After the war and the return of soldiers, marriage rates soared, especially among younger women. In Canada, for example, for those aged 15 to 19, the marriage rate more than doubled, climbing from 30 marriages per 1,000 in 1937 to 62 marriages per 1,000 in 1954. The average age of brides at first marriage fell from 25.4 in 1941 to 22 years by 1961. Women married younger and had children at younger ages. The sharpest increase in birth rates occurred among women under 25. Not only were they having children at a younger age, they were also having more total children. What resulted was a baby boom—a bulge of births in the postwar period.

Changes in fertility rates contributed to the redefinition of motherhood and child rearing. Before this, particularly during early industrialization, a significant number of women (and children) were in the labor force or working the land alongside adult men; older children were expected to care for younger ones. To be a woman did not exclusively mean being a mother. Families could not afford to have women as childminders first and foremost. While women could not own property or vote, rural societies nonetheless needed women to work the land, and later, with industrialization, work in factories alongside their husbands. Like their husbands, women contributed to the household as producers. First in the Victorian period and then again with the end of World War II and the baby boom, womanhood was redefined and more closely equated to motherhood. It was expected that mothers should devote more time and attention to child rearing at the expense of other pursuits, including paid work. This put pressure on working-class mothers who were seen as neglectful if and when they needed to work for pay.

With these ideological and demographic shifts there was also the emergence of the traditional nuclear family as an ideal (while not always the reality), with the husband in the labor force, and wife/mother in the home caring for her growing family. This shift in thinking about family roles was reflected in the ever-expanding number of often contradictory magazine articles on parenting, and the rise in popularity of child psychologists and childcare experts. Many of these emphasized the importance of developing emotional bonds between mother (not father) and child; but with this increased emphasis grew mothers' anxiety about their abilities as parents.

Women got conflicting advice on feeding: follow a strict time schedule, like their mothers had, or feed when the baby demanded it? Breastfeed or bottle feed? The debates raged, and women were bombarded with conflicting views. North American women increasingly came to rely on books on how to parent. One of the most popular was Dr. Benjamin Spock's *Baby and Child Care*, first published in 1946, which sold more than 50 million copies by 1998, when he died at age 94.

Starting in the 1960s and 1970s, mothers' labor force participation rates increasingly raised fears of the effects of maternal deprivation on children, although those rates continued to rise. In fact, a profound, recent shift in parenting ideology was triggered by the rapidly growing number of women, and especially mothers of young children, in the labor force—resulting in more dual-earner couples. The "typical" North American family has become more difficult to identify among the growing number of family forms now legally recognized as families.

Political, economic, and other factors have also meant that young children residing in north America today are much more likely than ever before to be raised by mothers who are older, more educated, and working for pay. For some children, this has amounted to more economic stability, but child poverty rates remain high. More children are raised by single parents, especially single mothers, and some live with their same-sex parents. Contrary to popular belief, this has also meant that children are more likely to be surrounded by adults (because of more only-child families), and more likely to spend more time with their parents than in the past.

Today, the family adaptation model of parenting seems to prevail, where both mothers and fathers are expected to navigate paid and unpaid work, and adapt to complex schedules that include an

*Rather than simply adult perspectives on childhood, children themselves are increasingly becoming subjects for researchers.*

adequate amount of family time. With more mothers working for pay, more expectations have been placed on fathers (in heterosexual families) to get involved in parenting. Having said this, mothers are still more likely than fathers to spend more time in direct care of children.

## Changing Notions of Parenthood

Fatherhood has received less attention than motherhood, yet historical analyses suggest a number of periods of influence that have shaped our views of the father's role in child development over time, although fatherhood has generally been slow to change. Some have noted that in colonial times, father was seen as the disciplinarian, moral teacher, and head of the household. With industrialization, father was absent from the home and seen as provider or breadwinner. In the post–World War II period, fatherhood changed again to take on a more important role in gender socialization (daddy's little girl and playing sports with sons)—but he was generally not expected to be a primary caregiver or nurturer. Increasingly, literature shows that men are taking more responsibility for children's daily lives, embracing the role of the new, nurturing father. The increasing presence of fathers in parenting, and mothers' changing employment status, has in turn affected how women mother.

Employed parents with children under 12 spent more time with their children today than was the case even 20 years ago; but the time they spend with children is more goal-oriented, structured and saturated with activity. As North American culture places heavy emphasis on the value of paid work (where stay-at-home mothers and fathers are seen as anomalies), there is less social support for parenting, and increased expectations upon them. For many, parenting has come to involve finding and negotiating programs; registering children; paying fees; volunteering for fundraising; attending practices; driving children to games, classes, and recitals; speaking with teachers and coaches; monitoring practice; and praising them for their efforts. These kinds of shifts have altered parental beliefs about what are desirable characteristics in their children; for example, some parents have come to see dependent behavior in children as "clingy," worrisome and symptomatic of an underlying problem.

Today, parenting advice is abundantly available, through a variety of formats including the Internet, parenting magazines, advice columns, and books. Information is available on a wide range of topics, from breastfeeding, infant care, and healthy physical development, to divorce, stepfamilies, and parenting advice about terrorism. Analyses of parenting magazines have found a significant shift in emphasis from engaging in "fun" activities with children and fending off the "I'm bored" syndrome, to an increased focus on academic encouragement, choosing schools and programs, and children's cognitive development. Parents are increasingly encouraged and advised to foster their children's academic skills and stimulate their minds. Analyses have also found that parenting magazines, despite their names, are still primarily written for mothers and often reinforce traditional gender stereotypes and myths. Some change, however, has happened at national and international levels, with growing attention paid to the lives of children themselves, and to improving children's rights.

## Growing Emphasis on Children's Rights

Some have noted that historically, children's rights and the child liberation movement in the West was born of mid-20th century resistance to hegemonic racial, ethnic, gender, and economic oppression. With time, children's rights increasingly became the subject of legal theory, philosophy, political science, and social sciences, as children's rights became enshrined in global human rights declarations such as the United Nations' (UN) Convention on the Rights of the Child (CRC). Some studying children have identified a paradigmatic shift in the 1980s and early 1990s that resulted in children and childhood becoming a new locus of concern. This shift has coincided with increased attention placed on children's rights and autonomy.

In 1989, the United Nations General Assembly adopted the CRC, which includes a universally agreed-upon set of standards and obligations that are expected to be respected by the governments who have signed and ratified the agreement (the United States is one of only two nations, with Somalia, yet to ratify the agreement). The articles it contains are founded on the principles of respect for the dignity and worth of each individual, regardless of race, color, gender, language, religion, opinions, origins, wealth, birth status, or ability, and are expected to apply to every child everywhere. Its four main key commitments are: (1) the best interests of the child; (2) survival and development; (3) children's participation; and (4) nondiscrimination. Upon ratifying this agreement, governments are obliged to help improve conditions for children everywhere.

In 1990, at the World Summit for Children, world leaders made a joint commitment and issued an urgent, universal appeal to give every child a better future. This was the largest gathering of world leaders in history. Led by 71 heads of state and 88 other senior officials, the World Summit adopted a Declaration on the Survival, Protection and Development of Children and a Plan of Action for implementing the Declaration in the 1990s.

In 2002 the UN again called upon world leaders to join them in a global movement aimed at building "a world fit for children." This "new world" would be built on a commitment to uphold a large number of principles and objectives, including a commitment to put children first; eradicate poverty; leave no child behind; care for every child; educate every child; protect children from harm and exploitation; protect children from war; combat HIV/AIDS; listen to children and ensure their participation; and protect the Earth for children. At the international level, the 1990s was a decade of great promises to and for children and children's rights—at least on paper.

Even if only on paper, these international movements and initiatives have helped transform some of the theorizing about children and childhood. To begin with, it has amounted to a growing number of questioning and challenging of the notion of adult as "the being" and doer, and child as "becoming." Writing on this in 1994, Jens Qvortrup explained that adults are seen as human beings, while children are treated as human becomings—unstable, incomplete, incapable of independent thought. Qvortrup observed that it is the fate of children to be waiting: waiting to become adults, mature, become competent, get capabilities, acquire rights, become useful, have a say in societal matters, and share resources. This critique has contributed to the development of a new sociology of childhood—at least in the United Kingdom (UK) and a number of other locales.

## New Sociology of Childhood

What has come to be called the new sociology of childhood has been in existence for over a decade, and has been especially prominent in the UK and Australia (and recently gained prominence in Germany and Scandinavia). It arose symbiotically with the rise of the global children's rights agenda. Proponents of global children's rights movements and of the new sociology of childhood are committed to the view that children are more competent and autonomous than they appear or are allowed to be. They seek to overturn adult paternalism that refuses to recognize children's capabilities and rights. The goal of these "new" theorists is to provide a better understanding of childhood that recognizes the capacity of children for autonomy, competent decision making, and their role as social agents—this would in turn better inform policy and research.

The new sociology of childhood focuses on an appreciation of what children presently are, rather than what they will eventually become. This approach addresses dynamic, social, structural, relational, and interpretive dimensions of the state of childhood and status of "child," and emphasizes that children are active "doers" in and of their social worlds, lives, and activities. Children do not just passively adapt to and learn from the culture surrounding them, as assumed in developmental and socialization theories, but rather actively participate in the cultural routines offered to them in and by their social environments. Children are seen and treated as active reproducers of meaning, and are understood to be able to appropriate and reinterpret their situations and environments and so themselves contribute to cultural reproduction and change.

This approach seeks to highlight both the agency of children and their social, political, and economic status in contemporary societies—combining both macro/structure and micro/agency approaches. This means that children are seen and understood as participating actively in the construction of their own social situation, but children and childhood are also understood as being constituted in relation to the adult world in which they live. Through this theorizing, there is a new focus on the way that childhood has been constituted and reconstituted through the dynamic interplay of adult structures and children's social situations.

## Research on and With Children

So much of what is known about children today comes from adults, either reflecting upon their own experiences as children or reporting on the experiences of children responsibility—as parents, guardians, teachers, or other experts. This is not to say that this research is not valuable, insightful, or important. Many adults have contributed a great deal to our understanding of children and childhood by sharing their attitudes and experiences from when they were young, or as adults, on behalf of children. However, academics are increasingly involving children themselves as subjects, contributors, and participants—rather than objects—in the research process.

A great deal of emphasis has been placed on the ethics of research with children, and their protection from risks involved in participation in research. However, recent work in the area has focused on a general concern to empower children through the inclusion of their voices, views, and experiences. More child-centered methods have forced researchers to explore, reflect on, and understand children's social location; and at the same time, critically assess their own assumptions about children. As research, theory, and practice move forward, it is important to have high-quality and reliable research about children, but it is also important to have equally solid research with and by children.

**See Also:** Adult Children; Birth Control; Childlessness; Child Poverty; Childcare; Childhood; Family Planning; Fathers and Fathering; Fertility; History of Motherhood: 1900 to Present; Preschool Children; Pronatalism.

## Bibliography

Albanese, Patrizia. *Children in Canada*. New York: Oxford Press, 2009.

Daly, Kerry. *The Changing Culture of Parenting*. Ottawa, ON: Vanier Institute of the Family, 2004.

Daly, Kerry. "Reshaping Fatherhood: Finding the Models." *Journal of Family Issues*, v.14/4 (1993).

Handel, Gerald, Spencer Cahill, and Frederick Elkin. *Children and Society: The Sociology of Children and Childhood Socialization*. Los Angeles: Roxbury Publishing, 2007.

Howe, R. Brian and Katherine Covell, eds. *A Question of Commitment: Children's Rights in Canada*. Waterloo, ON: Wilfrid Laurier University Press, 2007.

James, Allison, Chris Jenks, and Alan Prout. *Theorizing Childhood*. Cambridge, UK: Polity Press, 1998.

Jenson, Jane. "Changing the Paradigm: Family Responsibility or Investing in Children." *Canadian Journal of Sociology*, v.29/2 (2004).

Lee, Nick. *Childhood and Society: Growing Up in an Age of Uncertainty*. Maidenhead, UK: Open University Press, 2001.

Moosa-Mitha, M. "A Difference-Centred Alternative to Theorization of Children's Citizenship Rights." *Citizenship Studies*, v.9/4 (2005).

Qvortrup, Jens, M. Bardy, G. Sgritta, and H. Winterberger, eds. *Childhood Matters: Social Theory, Practice and Politics*. London: Avebury, 1994.

Stasiulis, Daiva. "The Active Child Citizen: Lessons From Canadian Policy and the Children's Movement." *Citizenship Studies*, v.6/4 (2002).

United Nations Children's Fund (UNICEF). *Convention on the Rights of the Child*. New York: United Nations, 1990.

Wyness, Michael. *Childhood and Society: An Introduction to the Sociology of Childhood*. New York: Palgrave Macmillan, 2006.

Patrizia Albanese
Ryerson University

# Chile

The Republic of Chile has one of the lowest birthrates in South America; contraceptive use is high. Prenatal care is available at public hospitals and private clinics, and mothers are eligible for maternity benefits and breastfeeding breaks. Divorce was illegal until 2004 and remains rare, but marriage rates are decreasing and traditional gender roles are changing. The Catholic Church has influenced opposition to divorce and abortion. Thirty-six percent of Chileans complete secondary school. Women's involvement in formal employment increased during and continued after the Pinochet era.

The gopulation growth in Chile has been stable since the 1970s. Chilean women have an average of 1.95 children, compared to 5.3 in 1960. The low birthrate is attributed to increasing prosperity and urbanization. Maternity leave is available six weeks prior to and 12 weeks following childbirth. Mothers may leave work to breastfeed and to care for an ill infant under age 1.

Due to the influence of the Catholic Church, divorce is legally difficult to obtain and was illegal until 2004. As a result, Chile has one of the lowest divorce rates in the Western Hemisphere. Marriage rates are decreasing, and many children are born outside of marriage. Acceptance of nonformal unions is increasing.

Chile is comprised mostly of Spanish immigrants; most Chileans are of mixed Spanish and indigenous descent. Traditional gender roles are changing with women's increased education and labor participation, although household responsibilities fall largely on women. A culture of *Marianismo*, women as selfless mothers, supports traditional gender roles. Men are considered head of the household, although growing numbers of families are female-headed (30 percent in 2002).

Many Catholics accept premarital sex despite strong Church disapproval, and 81 percent accept usage of some form of birth control, which is widespread and available without a prescription. Most national family planning programs target mothers of at least one child or those who can pay. Access to contraception is more difficult for younger and poorer women. Abortion is illegal, but not uncommon; Chile's abortion rate is one of the highest in South America. Many women are familiar with infusions made from plant products believed to induce abortion. Maternity care is available at private clinics and public hospitals, where low-income and poor women receive free care. All births are attended by skilled personnel.

More than 36 percent of men and women completed secondary school. In 2000, 47.2 percent of students accepted into universities were women.

The regime of General Augusto Pinochet left more than 3,000 dead and missing in Chile, and many mothers became activists for the disappeared. During and after the Pinochet era (1973–89), women's involvement in formal economic activity increased to the point where women comprised more than half the workforce. The expectation under the Minimum Employment Program and the Occupational Program for Heads of Households was employment for all working-age family members, including mothers. The 1993 return to democracy and opening of new international markets meant even greater access for women to the economic world.

Famous Chilean mother Isabel Allende has had books translated into 27 languages. A memoir, *Paula*, focused on her daughter's illness and death. Michelle Bachelet, pediatrician and mother of three, was elected the first female president of Chile in 2006.

**See Also:** Activist Mothers of the Disappeared; Allende, Isabel; Postcolonialism and Motherhood.

**Bibliography**
Donoso-Maluf, Francisco. "Chile: New Bottle, Old Wine." In *Families Across Cultures: A 30-Nation Psychological Study,* James Georgas, John W. Berry, Fons J. R. van de Vijver, Çigdem Kagitçibasi, and Ype H. Poortiinga, eds. Cambridge, UK: Cambridge University Press, 2006.
Vergara-Mery, Alvaro. "Chile." In *The Greenwood Encyclopedia of Women's Issues Worldwide,* Lynn Walter, ed. Westport, CT: Greenwood Press, 2003.

Keri L. Heitner
University of Phoenix

# China

The role of motherhood is defined in China by cultural tradition and by the politics of the state. In China's long history, mothers were charged with the responsibility of nurturing, caring, and educating children, as well as looking after such domestic affairs as cooking and cleaning. Mothers were subjugated by a male-centered order in a traditional household, dominated by Confucian patriarchal culture. Their identity was defined by their obedience to their husbands and sons. Completely dependent on their husbands, both economically and psychologically, mothers were still expected to be role models for their offspring.

Beginning in the early 20th century, influenced by Western culture and communist ideology, some educated Chinese women began to break free of traditional values and fight for their rights. A dramatic change in Chinese motherhood took place

when the communist party gained power in 1949. Proclaiming the emancipation of Chinese women and improving both their social and family status, the government enacted policies that brought them into the workplace, for the sake of both mobilizing them as human resources to help construct socialism, and to promote political and economic equality. While opportunities opened up for women in education and various other professions, mothers as a result often were working the equivalent of two full-time jobs, both inside and outside of the household. This caused immense stress, especially when many daycare centers and kindergartens established in the early 1950s were discontinued. In rural areas, mothers engaged in even more exhaustive work, by farming, tending livestock, producing textiles, and processing food. Another significant obligation for Chinese mothers has often been taking care of elderly relatives.

Mothers' intensive load of bearing, rearing, and bringing up children was reduced by the onset of China's one-child policy in the late 1970s, which aimed to curb the rapid growth of population. China's economic reform and modernization has in some ways lightened household labor, although less so in rural areas, where the majority of mothers do not have the convenience of refrigerators, washing machines, and sometimes have insufficient water sources.

**Cultural Norms**
The term *mother* in Chinese culture is almost synonymous with the term *sacrifice*. For more than 2,000 years, its connotation was based on the Confucian code of women's conduct in the practice of motherhood. Numerous images of selfless, devoted, and sacred mothers have been portrayed in poems, plays, fictional works, and music, as well as by modern mass media, with an emphasis on their submission and self-sacrifice. In these works, a mother's sufferings from oppression are often hidden in the eulogy of her deeds. The mother is presented as goddess-like, without personal feelings or frustrations. During radical periods, such as the May Fourth Cultural Movement and the Cultural Revolution, along with the weakening Confucian patriarchal ideology, women gained some equality both in the family and society. Yet, their emancipation was interlocked with national reconstruction, their

devotion and sacrifice expected for the country's welfare. Since the economic reform starting late in the 20th century, followed by a revival of Confucianism, traditional views of mothers have in many ways been restored. Social expectations for mothers become imbued with modern content. Female virtue has again become the standard for judging a good mother. Contemporary Chinese culture, influenced by commercialism, further encourages the attributes of beauty and fashion in motherhood.

On the average, Chinese mothers have 1.6 children. Birth control has proved very effective since the one-child campaign became strictly enforced by the state. It limits urban families to one child, but is a little more flexible for rural families. If the first child is a girl, a second child is allowed. Just before the state intervened in 1979, the average birthrate in China was 5.7 children per mother. It fell to 1.8–2.0 in the 1990s, and 1.3 by 2005, while in rural areas the rate decreased from 6.4 to 2.0.

## Birth Control Practices and Laws

Efficiency, however, comes at the cost of an extreme invasion of women's autonomy and privacy. The imposed procedures (with and without a mother's consent) include intrauterine devices (IUDs), sterilization, and abortion, with X-rays and ultrasound tests for pregnancy. Many methods of contraception are provided free of charge, including sterilization and condoms, yet in practice are not accessible for many citizens. Between 1995 and 2003, the successful rate of pregnancy prevention for married women was 90.4–90.5 percent, dropping to 84.6 percent in 2006. These figures are much higher than the global average of 56 percent, with the level in developed countries at 66 percent. Forty-eight percent of women use intrauterine devices, and 33.9 percent have undergone sterilization. Among males, only 10 percent use condoms, and 5.3 percent have undergone sterilization. This highlights how birth control in China has largely been the responsibility of women.

While abortion in China has been decreasing since the 1990s, psychological damage to the mother is still a large concern. The government actively encourages sterilization as an alternative to abortion. In 1990, the number of abortions was 14.3 million. It decreased to 7.5 million in 1995,

and 7.14 million in 2004. As a percentage of total pregnancy preventative measures, abortion was chosen in 33.6 percent of cases in 1995, 37.6 percent in 2000, and 38.5 percent in 2004.

The enforcement of birth control includes both rewards and penalties. Policies for the employment of single-child parents are similar in all of China. They include financial assistance for daycare, and medicine provided up to age 18, and a one-time monetary compensation of over 1,000 Yuan for single-child mothers above age 55, and fathers above 60. In rural areas, single-child parents receive rewards for having only one child, and enjoy preferential treatment when being considered for retirement funds and housing. Parents with twins or other multiple-birth pregnancies, however, do not receive an reward, and only one parent receives a one-time compensation.

Pregnant women protected by the state's one-child policy enjoy routine prenatal care provided by the government. Monthly appointments are required during the first two trimesters, during which physical examinations and ultrasounds are conducted to detect any abnormalities. During the last trimester, weekly appointments are required.

Single-child parents in rural areas who are legally allowed to have another child, but indicate in writing that they will not, are awarded meritorious awards, as well as a monetary compensation of 500 Yuan. If the only child of a family becomes disabled or dies, and its parents choose not to have another, and if the mother and the father are at least 55 and 60 years old, respectably, they are each awarded 5,000 Yuan. Couples who violate the one-child policy receive penalties, such as having to pay the cost of giving birth without assistance, denying them any promotions or salary benefits during the mother's maternity leave, and paying a monetary fine. State employees and government officials may be demoted or even lose their positions.

In a society with a deep-rooted patriarchal tradition, Chinese mothers are under pressure to give birth to a son in order to fulfill the expectation of carrying on the family line. Many mothers in rural areas go into hiding when they have an unregistered daughter, in the hope that they might give birth to a son the next time. Infanticide and abandoned baby girls are a consequence of the one-child policy, which results in China's uneven gender ratio in general, and in mental trauma to the mothers specifically involved.

## State/National Financial Aid

It was not until 1995 that financial assistance to poor mothers, mostly in rural areas, came into practice. The Happy Project was set up by the China Population Welfare Foundation to help poverty-stricken mothers become literate and live more healthy lives. Since 2000, the Chinese government has run special aid programs to help impoverished mothers. Funds for medical training and equipment aim to lower delivering mother and infant mortality rates. They also subsidize the cost of hospitalization and of treating obstetric complications. However, these funds are not regularly accessible to every poor mother, and are available only in emergencies.

There are no aid programs or policies regarding the rights of unmarried mothers, though the law does entitle rights to children born out of wedlock. In recent years, the government has allowed nongovernmental organizations (NGOs) to provide medical aid. Unmarried mothers usually give their children to orphanages, individual adopters, or members of their own families. This is frequently done without using the proper official procedures. Unmarried mothers are discriminated against and ostracized in Chinese society, and government employees who have children outside of marriages are penalized and may lose their jobs.

China's education system has guaranteed basic education to the majority of girls during the last half century. The steadily increasing percentage of girls in primary school reflects the declining number of illiterate mothers. In 2005, literacy of Chinese girls aged 15–24 was 97.7 percent, a difference of less than 1 percent of that of boys. In rural areas, literacy in girls aged above 15 was 78 percent, compared to 92 percent for boys. The literacy gap between boys and girls varies in different provinces, and can range from 4 to 27 percent. Women still reflect a disproportionate number of China's illiterates

## Marriage and Divorce

Chinese marriage was relatively stable during its long history. Divorce was relatively uncommon, but some of the reasons for it, such as failure to produce a son, was discriminatory toward women. The stability of marriage has more recently been undermined by social and economic reform. Since 2000, there were over a million divorces in China annually. In 2007, the number rose to 2.1 million.

## Religious and Cultural Practices

Confucianism, Buddhism, and Daoism have played crucial roles in defining Chinese motherhood throughout history. Besides following Confucian teachings regarding codes for women's conduct, many Chinese mothers worship Buddhist and Daoist goddesses, such as Bodhisattva and Chen Jinggu, the goddess of Birth, in the hope of conceiving a son and receiving protection. Religion may manifest cultural expectations concerning goddesses, whose attributes are idealized and emulated by mothers. Such goddesses commonly possess traits traditionally attributed to mothers: being fertile, caring for the young, and the power to bless the family. Religion, whether Buddhist, Daoist, or Christian, also provides psychological support for mothers, as well as social support from others belonging to the same faith. In rural areas, it is common to find instances of female ancestor worship, where fertile elderly women are highly revered, and believed to be able to bestow good fortune to newborn children.

The tiny, matrilineal Mosuo culture—population approximately 40,000—of the Chinese Himalaya is very unique in China. The Mosuo live near the border between Yunnan and Sichuan Provinces, and participate in *zou huns,* or "walking marriages," whereby a man is invited to a woman's hut at night, but is required to leave in the morning. There are no formal marriages; women can change partners as often as they like without stigma, but typically retain partners for extended periods of time. Men help to raise children as a group, and as a result, have only limited relationships with their children. The previously isolated Mosuo culture has become a tourist attraction—primarily for curious male Chinese visitors. There are nearby brothels staffed primarily with non-Mosuo women, considered shameful by the Mosou. Their society is reported to be very stable, and Mosou village women head the households, make business decisions, and own property, which they pass on in a matrilineal fashion.

**Famous Mothers**

Three women stand out as the most revered mothers in Chinese history: Meng Mu, Xu Mu, and Yue Mu. Meng Mu, Mencius's mother, is celebrated for her efforts at single-handedly raising Mencius to become one of China's most eminent philosophers and thinkers. She is said to have moved her home three times, eventually to a plot beside a school, in order to provide the most beneficial environment for the upbringing of her son.

Xu Shu was a brilliant military strategist in the Three Kingdoms era of Chinese history. In order to make him betray his master, his mother, Xu Mu, was held hostage in a rival kingdom run by Cao Cao. Xu Mu, after seeing her son betray his master for her, committed suicide, thereby sending the message that her own safety was far less important than loyalty to one's country.

Yue Mu was the mother of Yue Fei, a legendary general and hero in the Song dynasty, who defended Han China against invaders. When the Jin kingdom invaded China, Yue Mu tattooed the words *Jingzhong baoguo*, meaning "honor and serve your country," on Yue Fei's back, constantly reminding him to fight for his country to the death.

Since 2007, a Mother Culture Festival has been held on Meng Mu's birthday in her hometown of Choucheng, Shangdong, to celebrate her devotion and service to both her son and the state.

**See Also:** Abortion; Angel in the House; Anthropology of Mothering; Birth Control; Birth Goddesses; Childcare; Communism and Motherhood; Cross-Cultural Perspectives on Motherhood; Employment and Motherhood; Religion and Mothering; Social Construction of Motherhood.

**Bibliography**

Bossen, Lauurel. "Women and Development." In *Understanding Contemporary China*, Robert E. Gamer, ed. Boulder, CO: Lynne Rienner, 2003.

Handwerk, Brian. "No-Fathers Day: Remote Group Has No Dads, and Never Did." *National Geographic News* (June 18, 2009). http://news.nationalgeographic.com/news/2009/06/090619-fathers-day-2009-no-fathers.html (accessed July 2009).

Office of Statistics of Society and Technology. *Women and Men in Chinese Society—Data and Facts.* Beijing: Office of Statistics of Society and Technology, National Bureau of Statistics of China, 2007.

Robinson, Jean C. "Of Women and Washing Machines: Employment, Housework, and the Reproduction of Motherhood in Socialist China." *The China Quarterly*, v.101 (March 1985).

Wolf, Margery, et al. *Women in Chinese Society*. Palo Alto, CA: Stanford University Press, 1975.

Xueqing Xu
York University
Feng Yuan
ActionAid International China

# Chodorow, Nancy

Sociologist, psychoanalyst, and professor Nancy Julia Chodorow is a leading scholar in the fields of feminist psychology, psychoanalysis, and sociology and has helped link these fields through her interdisciplinary approach. She has written numerous essays and groundbreaking books, including *The Reproduction of Mothering*, which is widely considered to be a classic in its field.

Topics she has helped bring to prominence include female psychology and the psychology of motherhood, psychoanalysis, the social construction of gender formation and identity, and object-relations theory. Her work offers both a critique and an alternative to patriarchal society and the belief that women are biologically predetermined to the role of nurturer, which she feels is the foundation for male dominance.

Nancy Chodorow received her B.A. from Radcliffe College in 1966 and her Ph.D. in sociology from Brandeis University in 1975. She received her psychoanalytic training at the San Francisco Psychoanalytic Institute. She has taught Women's Studies at Wellesley College and Sociology at the University of California at Santa Cruz and the University of California at Berkeley. She retired from teaching in 2005. Her influences include the work of Beatrice and John W. M. Whiting, Philip Slater, Karen Horney, and Melanie Klein. Scholars consider her work to be an essential contribution to the Second Wave of feminism, which lasted approximately from the 1960s through the 1980s. Her research into mothering fit within the Second Wave of feminism's emphasis on issues of equality, including the basis for social and cultural inequality and ways to change the patriarchal nature of society.

Chodorow's sometimes controversial work approached psychoanalysis as an essentially interpretive field. She has also blended theoretical approaches with the recognition of each person's individual differences in both her scholarly work and her private psychoanalytic practice. Her work emphasized the necessity of considering cultural and historical influences on the formation of gender identity rather than universal generalizations concerning this process. Her interdisciplinary emphasis on cultural and historical relativity blended well with the discipline of sociology while her emphasis on gender, and the development of gender identity blended well with the discipline of feminist theory.

One of Chodorow's main interests was the search for psychological explanations for most women's desire for motherhood and female centrality in childcare across cultures and historical eras. She explored alternative theories to the traditional scientific theory that it was biological differences between the sexes that predisposed women to the nurturing roles of infant care and childrearing. The absence of biological determinism provided a basis for feminist challenges to the patriarchal basis of society and its cultural perspectives on the functions of motherhood. She determined that the cultural belief that child rearing is a woman's responsibility is the foundation of male dominance and the social and political oppression of women.

Chodorow's work also offered groundbreaking new perspectives on the mother–child relationship and how that relationship differed depending on the child's gender. Chodorow's use of object-relations theory was a unique approach among American psychoanalysts. Object-relations theory is based on the importance of an individual's formation of relationships, beginning with that between mother and infant, and the belief that the desire to form such bonds is a prime motivation for individuals throughout the course of their lives. She believed that mothers felt a stronger sense of unity with daughters because they shared the same sex while they naturally felt a sense of "other" with sons despite the closeness of the maternal bond. Object-relations theory became central to her work because she believed that the individual's perception of these relationships, both on the conscious and unconscious levels, was the key determinant in that individual's ability to form and maintain a variety of intimate adult relationships.

## Self-Identity
Chodorow shifted from psychoanalytical theory's traditional emphasis on renowned Austrian psychologist Sigmund Freud's Oedipal Complex, which focused on the son's relationship to his father, to an emphasis on the pre-Oedipal stage and the child's relationship with the mother, who is the object of the child's first identification and love. She also notes that this identification continues for female children even after male children begin the process of separation and independence from their mothers during the Oedipal stage of development.

Thus, the male child develops his own self-identity, or ego, more readily than the female child. Emphasis on formation of self-identity in opposition to the mother places the mother as the central factor in child development. Placing the mother in a primary role represented a revision of Freud's earlier theories, which placed women in a subordinate role. Her work thus brought the formerly opposing fields of psychoanalysis and feminist theory together.

Chodorow's work explored the family's role in shaping the individual gender identity that reinforces social and cultural gender roles. She stated that children begin to unconsciously perceive their self and gender from infancy and that these perceptions develop differently depending on the child's sex. Children grow up within and internalize the socially prescribed framework of gender roles of their culture and this, rather than biological necessity, is what determines their gender identity. The ultimate result in patriarchal societies is female children who grow up to replicate the pattern of desire for motherhood and child rearing and male children who grow up to replicate the patterns of male dominance and difficulty with intimate relationships.

**See Also:** Feminist Theory and Mothering; Freud, Sigmund; Institution of Motherhood; Reproduction of Mothering; Psychoanalysis and Motherhood.

**Bibliography**

Chodorow, Nancy. *Feminism and Psychoanalytic Theory*. New Haven, CT: Yale University Press, 1989.

Chodorow, Nancy. *The Power of Feelings: Personal Meaning in Psychoanalysis, Gender, and Culture*. New Haven, CT: Yale University Press, 1999.

Chodorow, Nancy. *The Reproduction of Mothering: Psychoanalysis and the Sociology of Gender*. Berkeley: University of California Press, 1978.

Marcella Bush Trevino
Barry University

# Christianity and Mothers

Christianity has always held a largely positive view of motherhood, although not uncomplicated. Biblical mothers play mostly supporting roles, and are remembered more in relation to other, more central characters of the stories in which they appear. Theologically, because motherhood involves procreation and therefore sex, it has been associated with sin and impurity as well as blessing and life.

Historically, although mostly a private enterprise, Christian motherhood has also been active in highly public political movements, such as temperance and more recently, issues related to family values, such as abortion and gay marriage. Because Christianity is so diverse across cultures and denominations, teachings about motherhood vary. Most well known are two classic debates: one between Roman Catholics and others regarding the Immaculate Conception of Mary, and the other more long term and more popular, but less denominationally focused, about the Virgin Birth. There are a few common threads, however, including the image of mother as nurturer and healer; and though the theological details may differ, the centrality of Mary, the mother of Jesus, as model and principal image.

## Biblical Mothers

According to the Bible, the first mother was Eve, whose name means "mother of all living" (Genesis 3:20). Along with Adam, they appear in Genesis, not merely as the first people as literalists might claim, but also as representatives of humanity in general. The Bible records very little about Eve as a mother, noting only that she bore an unknown number of sons and daughters (Genesis 5:4), and that she claimed to do so "with the help of the Lord" (Genesis 4:1). Moreover, Eve is remembered for her participation in the introduction of sin into the world through a fall from grace, which was followed by specifically gendered punishments from God. For women, this included pain in childbirth, desire for one's husband, and wifely obedience to husbandly rule (Genesis 3:16). For centuries, some interpreters underlined Eve's role as the creator of sin, which they associated with sexuality and, by extension, childbirth.

A number of other notable mothers appear in the Hebrew Scriptures. Sarah, the first matriarch, was also the first among a number of "barren" women who eventually bore sons with the help of God. A complicated woman, she became jealous and even cruel when her maidservant, Hagar, bore a son before her, both caught in a patriarchal system in which women were only valuable as mothers of sons. In the end, both Sarah and Hagar bore sons who were valued by Abraham, and who went on to establish large and influential families, though it is Sarah's lineage that carries on the Judeo-Christian pedigree.

The mother of Moses, unnamed and described only as "a Levite woman" (Exodus 2:1), was a key player in saving her important son from the Pharaoh's edict to kill all male infants (Exodus 1:22). She placed the baby in a basket and hid him among the reeds along the Nile, which was soon found by the Pharaoh's daughter. Moses's sister Miriam, perhaps a third conspirator, happened along and suggested that she knew a Hebrew woman who could nurse the child, who was in fact Moses's mother. All three women participated in the lifesaving project, one as mother/wet nurse, one as daughter/sister, and one as a kind of adopted or foster mother, all with the motherly characteristic of compassion for a child.

The importance of the law of levirate, a dictate allowing a widow to procreate with the brother of her deceased husband so that she could produce an heir, is uniquely illustrated in the story of Ruth and Naomi. In this case, Naomi's husband and two sons all died, leaving her with no heirs. One of her daughters-in-law, Ruth, instead of striking out on her own in search of a new husband, stayed with the widow, and in levirate style, married one of Naomi's relatives. She eventually bore a son, Obed, whom Naomi nursed. Through Ruth's motherhood, Naomi maintained her place in the family lineage, and Obed eventually became the grandfather of King David. While the law of levirate may seem oppressive to modern readers, it was intended to maximize women's procreative potential, which gave them worth, while also providing for their care in families within a highly patriarchal society.

Black theologians have often read these stories somewhat differently. They have seen the biblical mothers as strong and powerful, not only doing God's work by passively bearing important males, but as responsible for raising their children and thereby bringing liberation in their own right. A mother's power is not then in her fertility, but in her power to influence the next generation.

### Mary, Mother of Jesus

The most famous mother in Christianity has always been Mary, the mother of Jesus. At one end of the theological spectrum, the Council of Ephesus (431 B.C.E.) gave her the name *theotokos*—mother of God. This was a radical notion, as critics claimed that God would not be found in a woman's womb. At the other end of the scale, Saint Francis, whose teachings focused on poverty and simplicity, preferred to envision Mary as a peasant mother, sitting cross-legged on the ground, holding her child.

Luke's account is the best known. An angel appeared to Mary, a virgin, and announced that she would conceive and bear a great son. Mary questioned the angel, asking how this could be, as she had no husband. The angel responded that other barren women had conceived (a common biblical theme), as nothing is impossible with God; and in this case, the Holy Spirit would "come upon" her (Luke 1:26-38). The birth then occurred while Mary was traveling with her fiancé, Joseph. No description of the birth is offered—only that she had to lay the baby in "a manger, because there was no place for them in the inn" (Luke 2:7).

Images of Mary as mother abound in Christian art, once the main conveyer of theological teaching to a largely illiterate populous. Early artistic depictions of Mary nursing the baby Jesus were common. Her milk was a metaphor for the gift of life, feeding not only her own child, but the entire Church. Just as Jesus displayed the wounds on his hands, connected with his saving act in the resurrection, Mary showed her breasts as a source of healing and a symbol of salvation as well. The nursing Madonna eventually disappeared in art, however, due to nursing's increasing association with the peasantry, a growing sense of modesty around the naked female body, and the way such images reminded people of the suffering in childbirth associated with sin, which was linked not to Mary, but to Eve. One remaining sign is *Liebfraumilch* ("dear lady's milk"), a sweet wine first produced at a German monastery.

Also common in art are depictions of the weeping mother Mary. Known as *pietàs*, (from the Italian for "pity" and Latin for "piety"), these sculptures and paintings show Mary mourning over the dead body of Jesus. These works became especially important during the Black Death of the 14th century, as mourning mothers were common, and many found solace in their association with Mary.

Depictions of the Virgin were used as religious decorations in homes as early as the 6th century. The mother of God has always been an important intercessory figure for women. For most of Christian history, infant mortality rates were high, and sterility was common and blamed on women, for whom successful childbirth was essential. Women's special concerns around fertility and health of children made Mary their most important intercessory figure, but some men appealed to her as well. For some, depictions of the holy family's domestic life became like a second trinity—one to which average people could relate.

Mary as mother has also been at the heart of two theological debates: the Virgin Birth and the Immaculate Conception. The Doctrine of the Virgin Birth, the belief that Jesus was miraculously conceived while Mary remained a virgin, was a universally held belief in Christianity by the 2nd century, largely uncontroversial, as accounts of virgin births had been common in explaining the origins of heroic figures. Through the Middle Ages that followed, the doctrine became central to how Christian women were defined—that is, as virgins or not. They were to be virgins before marriage and mothers soon afterward, as it motherhood was thought to redeem them from the sin of sex. Hence, the period between marriage and motherhood was problematic. Eve may have brought sin into the world through her disobedience, but Mary brought salvation, or its agent, into the world through exactly the opposite—her obedience. Motherhood was a way for all women to be obedient, not necessarily in bearing the son of God as in Mary's case, but in following God's command to "be fruitful and multiply" (Genesis 1:28) in general, crucial in an unstable world of constant disease and death.

Today, the Doctrine of the Virgin Birth is still accepted by Roman Catholics, Orthodox Christians, and many Protestants, though feminist theologians criticize the teaching as merely the theological interpretation of a highly patriarchal church, creating an impossible model for women—that of virgin and mother.

The Doctrine of the Immaculate Conception came much later, declared by Pope Pius IX in 1854, though widely believed and celebrated as a Roman Catholic feast day for hundreds of years before. This edict states that Mary, like Jesus, was born without original sin, though unlike Jesus, she was conceived through sexual intercourse. Again, feminist and other liberal critics of the teaching see it as further distancing Mary from real mothers who are neither virgins nor sinless.

Other than commentaries on these biblical models with Mary as primary, early Christian leaders had little to say about motherhood until the modern era. Most medieval writings about motherhood were authored by monks and nuns, focusing on their own spiritual growth as nurturers, or mothers of the church. Their texts were not read outside of their own circles, and had little basis in the reality of "earthly" mothers, illiterate and busy raising their children.

## American Protestant Motherhood

While Roman Catholics had an honorable alternative to motherhood through the monastic orders, Early Protestants did not—motherhood was the only respectable option for women. As a result, Puritan women married young and hoped for children early and often. While Puritan teaching relegated women to the domestic sphere, it also valued their work as Christian labor and an important contribution to Puritan society. Usefulness was a central Puri-

*Christian mothers teach their children the importance of prayer. They are also more likely to home-school their children.*

tan virtue, and mothers made themselves useful as they oversaw the increasingly isolated world of the home. Women were not permitted to teach adult men, but religious teaching of children and servants was expected. In addition, Puritan theology held that children were naturally sinful, and taught mothers to break each child's will and replace it with obedience.

As later waves of immigrants settled in the United States, homes became ethnic and religious centers, where mothers led in the maintenance of traditions. Mothers also sought support for their efforts, and formed maternal associations for that purpose. The first was organized in 1815 by Ann Louisa Payton, a Congregationalist minister's wife in Maine. She and other Christian mothers gathered regularly to pray and discuss the religious training of their children.

Another high point in Christian motherhood was the umbrella movement broadly known as Home Protection, led by Frances Willard and other First Wave feminists. They organized around temperance and suffrage, as well as other causes, in an attempt to guard the home from the evils of the world. Motherhood was hailed as second only to the church as the holiest institution, and was used in this case as a partner of the church in setting social morality. These early feminists also participated in the settlement house movement, bringing culture through Christian charity to the urban poor. Most of the social issues they addressed involved poor women and children, including fighting against prostitution and working to build the first urban playgrounds. As Republican Mothers, active in the political arena, suffrage was their crowning achievement. Participating fully in elections made it possible to make an impact on all of the various social issues that affected mothers and the children on whose behalf they wanted to vote.

### Contemporary Christian Motherhood

The two most prominent voices on contemporary Christian motherhood are the Roman Catholic Church and the conservative evangelical Family Values Movement, reflected in such organizations as Focus on the Family. Based in their belief that motherhood is natural and God-intended, they support policies that discourage abortion, enable childbirth, and maintain marriage as only between a man and a woman, the form they believe was created by God for the bearing and raising of children. A vocal minority have criticized women who work outside the home to the extent that they pursue their own fulfillment at the expense of their children's.

Many in the homeschool movement would also be included in these two groups. They feel that the public schools neglect the teaching of values, or teach against Christian values, so they place their children in Catholic or Christian schools, where their values are specifically taught; or, they teach their children at home, which in the large majority of cases means mothers.

Although Mother's Day is celebrated, or at least acknowledged in most Christian churches, there is no official connection between the two. The day was inspired as a way to hail the public efforts of mothers to clean up poor neighborhoods and to bring peace during wartime, but when it was proclaimed a holiday in 1914, it was announced as a celebration of the private home. Almost immediately, it became a market force for flowers, cards, and gifts. Because the day is so popular among Americans in general, and given the positive history of motherhood in Christianity, the recognition of Mother's Day in churches has become customary.

**See Also:** Family Values; Islam and Motherhood; Judaism and Motherhood; Religion and Mothering; Republican Motherhood.

### Bibliography

Bellis, Alice Ogden. *Helpmates, Harlots, and Heroes: Women's Stories in the Hebrew Bible*. Louisville, KY: Westminster/John Knox Press, 1994.
Hill Lindley, Susan. *"You Have Stept Out of Your Place:" A History of Women and Religion in America*. Louisville, KY: Westminster/John Knox Press, 1996.
Mellon, Joelle. *The Virgin Mary and the Perceptions of Women: Mother, Protector and Queen Since the Middle Ages*. Jefferson, NC: McFarland, 2008.
Warner, Marina. *Alone of All Her Sex: The Myth and the Cult of the Virgin Mary*. New York: Vintage, 2000.

Gail Murphy-Geiss
Colorado College

# Cisneros, Sandra

Sandra Cisneros, born in Chicago on December 20, 1954, is a Chicana writer and poet. She earned a Bachelor of Arts in English from Loyola University of Chicago in 1976 and a Master's of Fine Arts in Creative Writing from the University of Iowa in 1978. Her published and award-winning works include *Bad Boys* (1980), *The House on Mango Street* (1984), *My Wicked, Wicked Ways* (1987), *Woman Hollering Creek and Other Stories* (1991), *Hairs = Pelitos* (1994), *Loose Woman: Poems* (1994), *Caramelo* (2002), and *Vintage Cisneros* (2003). In addition to writing, Cisneros is a founder of the Macondo Foundation and Alfredo Cisneros del Moral Foundation.

Cisneros's childhood had a strong effect on her writing and the themes that permeate her work.

First, her father, Alfredo Cisneros de Moral, took a job as an upholsterer, which led the family to move multiple times between Chicago and Mexico City. Second, she is the only daughter in a household of six brothers. Finally, she looked at her mother, Elvira Cordero Anguiano—an avid reader—as her strongest female supporter. Each of these circumstances flavors Cisneros's writings as her characters often contend with their Chicana identities, female sexuality, and cultural boundaries.

Literary critics argue that Sandra Cisneros's focus throughout her work on feminist resistance to patriarchy indirectly stems from her relationships with her father and her six brothers. For instance, there is the preteen narrator, Esperanza Cordero, in *The House on Mango Street*. Esperanza understands that, in her culture, a woman's place is in the home, but that does not prevent her from looking for opportunities outside of what her culture allows. It is her mother who urges her to do well in school so that she can have the opportunities that transcend the notion that women should remain within the private sphere.

**Feminine Resistance**

To illuminate her focus on feminist resistance, Sandra Cisneros often writes about threefold representations of woman, what Gloria Anzaldúa referred to as "Our Mothers": La Llorona (the legendary woman who weeps for her children, whom she drowned); La Malinche (the Aztec woman who was interpreter and mistress to Hernan Cortés, thus paving the way for Spanish conquest in Mexico); and La Virgen de Guadalupe (the saintly and self-sacrificing woman). Each archetype is associated with a different notion of female sexuality, autonomy, and motherhood. Cisneros not only highlights each archetype in her writing, however; she reinvents them. An example of Cisneros rewriting a legendary image is in her short story *Woman Hollering Creek*. The heroine, Cleófilas Enriqueta DeLeón Hernández, is a mother of one with another on the way, and wife to an abusive husband. Without support from her female neighbors, she finds help from two women who work at a women's center. These women resolve to help Cleófilas return to her family in Mexico. As they drive across the arroyo on the way out of town, Felice, the woman who drives

Cleófilas to the bus station, releases a surprising and loud yell. Thus, in this story, Cisneros transforms La Llorana to a story of female empowerment, as the *arroyo* Felice and Cleófilas travel is not named so much after the "Woman Weeping" as it is about the "Woman Hollering."

One literary critic identified Cisneros as the most famous Chicana writer, which can be corroborated by the numerous awards she has won for her writing. *The House on Mango Street* won the Before Columbus Foundation's American Book Award in 1985. *Woman Hollering Creek and Other Stories* was presented the Quality Paperback Book Club New Voices Award and the Anisfield-Wolf Book Award, and was named a noteworthy book of the year by the *New York Times* and the *American Library Journal*. *Loose Woman* received the Mountains & Plains Booksellers' Award. *Caramelo* was named a notable book of the year by, among others, the *New York Times*, the *Los Angeles Times*, and the *Chicago Tribune*. Her other honors include a MacArthur Foundation Fellowship in 1995 and an honorary Doctor of Humane Letters from Loyola University, Chicago, in 2002.

In addition to the numerous accolades that Cisneros has received for her work, she is also lauded for her the services she provides for her fellow writers. She is the president and founder of the Macondo Foundation, a community of artists who serve their communities through their writing. Moreover, she established the Alfredo Cisneros del Moral Foundation in 2000. This foundation awards grants for writers who were born in Texas, live in Texas, or write about Texas.

Sandra Cisneros is a writer-in-residence at Our Lady of the Lake University. She continues to live and write in San Antonio, Texas.

**See Also:** Chicana Mothering; Literature, Mothers in; Mexican Spirituality and Motherhood; Mexico; Poetry, Mothers in; Texas.

**Bibliography**
Brackett, Virginia. *A Home in the Heart: The Story of Sandra Cisneros*. Greensboro, NC: Morgan Reynolds Publishing, 2004.
Cisneros, Sandra. *Bad Boys*. San Jose, CA: Mango, 1980.

Cisneros, Sandra. *Caramelo*. New York: Knopf, 2002.

Cisneros, Sandra. *Hairs=Pelitos*. New York: Knopf, 1994.

Cisneros, Sandra. *The House on Mango Street*. Houston, TX: Arte Público, 1984.

Cisneros, Sandra. http://www.sandracisneros.com (accessed December 2008).

Cisneros, Sandra. *Loose Woman: Poems*. New York: Knopf, 1994.

Cisneros, Sandra. *My Wicked, Wicked Ways*. New York: Knopf, 1992.

Cisneros, Sandra. *Vintage Cisneros*. New York: Vintage, 2004.

Cisneros, Sandra. *Woman Hollering Creek and Other Stories*. New York: Random House, 1991.

Jago, Carol. *Sandra Cisneros in the Classroom: "Do Not Forget to Reach."* Urbana, IL: National Council of Teachers of English, 2002.

Mirriam-Goldberg, Caryn. *Sandra Cisneros: Latina Writer and Activist*. Berkeley Heights, NJ: Enslow Publishers, 1998.

Florence Maätita
Southern Illinois University

# Civil Rights Movement and Motherhood

The grassroots Civil Rights Movement of the 1950s and 1960s had a profound and lasting impact on the mothers and families involved because of the often-profound experiences of activists. Some participants in the Civil Rights Movement separated their roles and parents and activists, others integrated these roles, and still others chose one role over the other. Some mothers active in the movement faced public criticism for neglecting their socially expected gender roles as wives and mothers. Children of civil rights activists continued to be affected by their parents' experiences into adulthood as they sought to establish their own identities. Adult children of renowned activists faced even more pressure due to their famous last names.

Activist parents, most often fathers, were absent from their families for long periods, which could result in marital tensions, financial difficulties, and distant relationships with children who had little memories of them. White activists sometimes endured estrangement from their own parents. Some parents introduced their children to the movement and their personal experiences, while others isolated their children and did not discuss their roles or emotions. Some children did not learn the extent of their parents' experiences until they had reached adulthood themselves. They were sometimes left with a sense of embitterment or a longing for missed parental affection. Activists sometimes also faced public criticism for their neglect of family life, especially mothers whose activism countered their traditional gender role as wives and mothers. Some, such as Black Panther leader Elaine Brown, faced challenges within her own organization due to her gender.

Some children were active in the movement themselves, participating in school integration, sit-ins, Freedom Rides, marches, and demonstrations. Even those who were not active participants still experienced the racism, taunts, and violence that accompanied the movement, such as viewing beatings and cross burnings, and in some cases the violent deaths of their parents. Interracial children whose parents were brought together by the movement faced discrimination and bullying.

Those whose parents introduced them to the movement often felt part of an extended family, as they frequently interacted with other participants. Some, such as children of Black Panthers members, attended communal schools and were raised according to a community-based parenting philosophy. Others could feel isolated if they lived in a neighborhood where their parents were among the only activists.

### Life After the Movement
The influence of the Civil Rights Movement on families continued after the movement reached its heights in the 1950s and 1960s. Mothers and fathers who returned to full-time parenting had to adjust to unfamiliar roles. Some struggled with depression, substance abuse, posttraumatic stress, or difficulties adjusting to life after the movement. Women who were raised within the movement became mothers and grandmothers themselves, facing the challenges of passing its lessons and goals on to the next generation. The language of the movement's history plays

on social definitions of motherhood, such as referring to female civil rights leaders Rosa Parks and Coretta Scott King as Mothers of the Movement.

Many adults whose parents were active in the Civil Rights Movement have felt a sense of the past in the present and a social and personal burden of carrying on the family tradition. They also feel a sense of duty to keep the memories alive in the public conscience. Some parents utilized summer camps and mentor networks designed to teach children to carry on the civil rights struggle, while others have encouraged their children to follow their own paths or discouraged them due to the physical risks of activism.

Some have become activists in civil rights or other causes, while others have rebelled against the expectations that they carry on the struggle. Some who choose different paths feel a sense of guilt or a fear of disappointing their parents and race. Children of segregationists face a different challenge as they become parents themselves: how to explain their parents' actions to their own children.

**See Also:** Activism, Maternal; African American Mothers; Anti-Racist Mothering; Community Mothering; Intergenerational Trauma; Politics and Mothers; Parks, Rosa; Race and Racism; Social Action and Mothering; Transracial Mothering; Womanism.

### Bibliography

Blake, John. *Children of the Movement*. Chicago: Lawrence Hill, 2004.

Collier-Thomas, Bettye and V.P. Franklin. *Sisters in the Struggle: African American Women in the Civil Rights-Black Power Movement*. New York: New York University Press, 2001.

Crawford, Vicki L., Jacqueline Anne Rouse, and Barbara Woods. *Women in the Civil Rights Movement: Trailblazers and Torchbearers, 1941–1965*. Brooklyn, NY: Carlson, 1990.

Ling, Peter J., and Sharon Monteith, eds. *Gender and the Civil Rights Movement*. New Brunswick, NJ: Rutgers University Press, 2004.

Olson, Lynne. *Freedom's Daughters: The Unsung Heroines of the Civil Rights Movement From 1830 to 1970*. New York: Scribner, 2001.

Robnett, Belinda. *How Long? How Long? African-American Women in the Struggle for Civil Rights*. New York: Oxford University Press, 1997.

Young, Andrew. *An Easy Burden: The Civil Rights Movement and the Transformation of America*. New York: HarperCollins, 1996.

Marcella Bush Trevino
Barry University

## Class and Mothering

A class is a group of people who share a similar economic position in a society. Classes differ in their political and economic interests and the power they have or lack over the lives of others. To identify classes, social scientists use quantifiable measures of household income, educational attainment, occupational status, property ownership, and wealth. Class distinguishes homeowners from the homeless, Ph.D.s from high school dropouts, lawyers from laborers.

In combination with gender, race, and ethnicity, class affects almost every aspect of people's lives. It distinguishes how groups of people behave, what they look like, how they speak, and the general quality of their lives. Class impacts whether, when, and who people marry, how they relate to family members, and what they can do for their children.

Although most people within a particular class face similar barriers and opportunities, classes do not represent monolithic groups. There can be as much diversity within a class as between classes. For example, members of the working class may be homosexual, heterosexual, transgender, or bisexual; male or female; or white, black, Asian, Hispanic, or Native American. Diversity within classes also emerges due to age, marital status, national origin, religious and cultural heritage, and other group affiliations.

### Working Class

There is no single accepted definition of working class: typically it is defined in opposition to the middle class by characteristics such as employment in a trade or semi-skilled occupation and coming from a family where college was not an expectation for every child. For women, working-class occupations include low-level, white-collar jobs such as clerks and secretaries (because of the low wages and lack of autonomy) as well as "pink collar" occupations like cosmetology and blue-collar occupations such as factory work. Most working-class families have less income and social capital at their disposal than middle-class families. The boundaries between upper-class, middle-class, working-class, and poor families are fuzzy and sometimes permeable, but the concept of class is integral to everyday thinking and social research on mothering.

## Impact of Class on Mothering

Women's educational backgrounds, occupational conditions, and economic resources interweave with their fixed characteristics and life experiences to shape their child-rearing strategies. Not all aspects of mothering are affected by class. However, women's access to resources shapes their sense and fulfillment of motherhood. More specifically, women's location in the class hierarchy impacts mothering through the availability of family forms, the ability to provide economic necessities and material comforts, performance of parenting styles, and investment in education.

## Family Forms

Not everyone has equal access to the broad range of family forms. Some restrictions on family formation are legally recognized, such as legislation prohibiting gays and lesbians from marrying or adopting children. Beyond state policy, class also influences one's ability to form families, and thus family structure. For example, poor, inner-city, African American women are the most likely to live in single-parent households. For young urban black mothers who wish to marry, they may be unable to find a mate living in neighborhoods with high levels of unemployment, incarceration, and mortality, which results in a shortage of marriageable men. Women's choice of partnering or remaining single is not solely an individual decision; it is shaped by their structural position in a class hierarchy.

Women's increased risk of living in mother-only households increases their and their children's risk of falling into poverty. According to the U.S. Census Bureau, 4.9 percent of married-couple families lived below the poverty line in 2007, compared to 28 percent of families headed by single mothers. But family structure is not the only differentiator between poor and nonpoor families. While 8 percent of white

children in married-couple families live in poverty, 10 percent of Asian children, 11 percent of black children, and 19 percent of Hispanic children do so. In single-mother families, more than half of black and Hispanic children live below the poverty line, compared to 32 percent of Asian children and 39 percent of white children living with single mothers. Because only one-third of African American children live in two-parent households, they experience the highest risk of living in poverty.

Class also influences the likelihood of other mothering. Poor children are the most likely to live without a biological parent, thus the most likely to be cared for by another relative, foster parent, or nonrelative. Among the 10 percent of black children who live with neither biological parent, 62 percent live with a grandparent, usually a grandmother. An additional 20 percent live with another relative.

## Economic Necessities and Material Comforts

A mother's class impacts their ability to provide basic necessities for her children. To estimate the economic costs for raising a child, the U.S. Department of Agriculture in 2007 calculated Americans' annual expenditures on children's housing, food, health care, clothing, and childcare. High-income married families (those earning at least $77,100 annually), will spend just under $300,000 to raise a child born in 2007 through age 17. This amount does not include education expenses beyond the age of 17. In contrast, low-income married families (those earning less than $45,800 annually), will spend less than half that amount ($148,320). Among single-parent households, child-rearing expenses are slightly lower, but consume a greater percentage of income. Poor families who paid for childcare in 2000, for example, paid 35 percent of their income on childcare, compared with only 7 percent spent by nonpoor families.

Even in the United States, physical survival of children is most uncertain in the lower strata of the class hierarchy. African American children face an infant mortality rate twice that of white infants, mostly attributable to the increased risk of black children living in poverty compared to whites. The lives of poor mothers and their children are threatened by hunger, malnutrition, domestic violence, infectious diseases, and crime.

Families living in harsh social environments are besieged by crime, violence, industrial pollutants, drugs, and poverty, all of which are severe obstacles to effective mothering. Poor neighborhoods have a limited tax base from which to provide adequate public services. Poor children are at risk for being homeless or living in dilapidated houses with leaky roofs, rodents, exposed wires, lead paint, and other health hazards. Poor children have higher rates of infectious diseases and mortality. Lack of cognitive stimulation in the home and harsh parenting styles contribute to developmental problems for poor children.

## Ability to Provide Well-Rounded Experiences

Beyond basic necessities, mothers in different classes vary in their abilities to provide their children with enriching experiences. Mothers less consumed by meeting their children's survival needs have more resources to devote to providing abundant, enriching environments. A 2000 Current Population Report reported that while 52 percent of school-aged children from families with a monthly income of at least $4,500 participated in enrichment activities, only 24 percent of children from families with monthly family incomes of less than $1,500 did so. Children from more affluent families take more music and language lessons and participate more frequently in sports, clubs, arts, and after-school programs.

## Parenting Styles

In the mid-1970s, sociologist Melvin Kohn wondered whether parents from different classes socialized their children to have different values and life outlooks. He interviewed 200 working-class and 200 middle-class couples with at least one child who was in the fifth grade. In this classic study, Kohn found that working-class parents wanted their children foremost to follow the rules, be clean, and conform to external authority. Middle-class parents, in contrast, valued characteristics that promoted independence, curiosity, and self-direction. What linked working and middle-class families was their desire to instill in their children the skills needed for future success. Divergent job demands and working conditions, however, shaped what skills parents believed were most important. Working-class occupations usually involve rigid schedules, standardized tasks, and close supervision. Thus, working-class parents

believed that their children's future occupational success depended on their ability to conform to authority. For middle-class parents whose occupations involved flexibility, discretion, and limited supervision, assertiveness and initiative were the keys to future occupational success.

Recent research has also concluded that class distinguishes parental behaviors and children's daily lives. For example, Annette Lareau and colleagues conducted an extended series of in-depth interviews and observations of 88 African American and Caucasian children and their middle-class, working-class, and poor families. Lareau found that mothers differed by class in the ways they perceived the nature of childhood and how they defined their own roles in their children's lives.

Middle-class mothers, both white and black, made deliberate efforts to stimulate their children's cognitive and social development. They attempted to transmit important life skills to their children by stressing the use of language and reasoning to solve problems instead of physical discipline. Middle-class mothers took their children's ideas seriously and often would acquiesce to children's requests. Middle-class mothers enrolled their children in numerous organized activities, which resulted in crowded family schedules carried out in a frenetic pace. While middle-class mothers' "cultivation" approach provided their children diverse life experiences, it did so at a cost. The activities dominated family life and created enormous labor for mothers. With an emphasis on children's performance, a focus on individualism and entitlement developed in these middle-class families.

Among the black and white working-class and poor mothers, childrearing strategies emphasized the "accomplishment of natural growth." Working-class and poor mothers believed that their children would thrive if they provided food, safety, and love, so they did not focus on developing their children's individual talents. Working-class and poor mothers established limits, then left the children free to structure their own activities within those limits. Although working-class and poor children participated in fewer organized activities, they used their additional free time to develop ties with extended family members. Similar to Kohn's 1979 study, contemporary working-class and poor mothers issued more directives to their children and were more likely than their middle-class counterparts to use physical discipline. They viewed children as subordinate to adults and rarely negotiated. Working-class and poor mothers taught their children to distrust institutions and avoid persons in authority.

Although not all mothers of a given class raise their child the same way, there are consistent, general tendencies that differ across classes.

## Education

Mothers' perceptions of how to prepare their children for school vary by race, ethnicity, and class. There is a strong relationship between family class and student academic outcomes. Once enrolled in school, middle- and upper-class mothers with superior levels of education, larger vocabularies, and confidence are more likely to criticize educational professionals and intervene in school matters. Working-class and poor mothers often view educators as their social superiors and defer to their authority. While offering emotional support to their children at home, working-class and poor mothers are less likely to directly contact school administration. As a result, middle- and upper-class students have greater access to better schools, challenging curriculum, and well-trained teachers. Affluent schools have better staff and more resources, which in turn help children from middle- and upper-class families gain access to higher education.

## Mechanisms and the Family Stress Model

Decades of research have documented that children with socially and economically disadvantaged mothers suffer above-average rates of physical, behavioral, and emotional problems. Economic disadvantage and hardship impairs parental functioning, which in turn may impair children's and adolescents' physical, emotional, intellectual, and social health. Two key theories attempt to explain the role of economic hardship on parenting practices: the Family Stress Model (FSM) and the Investment Model (IM).

The FSM proposes that financial difficulties adversely impact parents' behaviors, emotions, and relationships, which in turn affects their parenting abilities and strategies. For example, R. and D. Conger and colleagues studied Iowa families going through the severe economic downturn in agriculture in the 1980s. They found that families with low incomes and high debts faced economic pressures of unpaid bills, painful cutbacks, and unmet material needs. Economic pressures increased parents' likelihood of relationship problems, interparental conflict, depression, anxiety, and alienation. Parental distress heightened the likelihood of harsh, inconsistent parenting, which in turn led to children's and adolescent's elevated behavioral problems and impaired competence. In summary, the FSM hypothesizes that a cascade of influences connects parents' economic problems, disrupted family relationships, and poor child outcomes.

## Investment Model

In contrast to the FSM, which is primarily concerned with adverse consequences of low class, the IM focuses on advantages that accrue to those in higher classes. The IM proposes that while disadvantaged parents must invest in more immediate family needs, parents with economic resources invest more heavily in their children's development. Investments include learning materials in the home, specialized tutoring or training, higher standard of living, and residing in a location that fosters child development. By investing greater resources in children, more affluent parents promote a range of social and academic competencies in their children.

## Reifying and Resisting Class Hierarchies

As children acquire their parents' class at birth, families are a key mechanism transmitting life chances. Children raised in poverty have lower educational attainments and lower incomes as adults. Families at the top and bottom of the class hierarchy usually produce children who replicate their class. While upper-class mothers have the most opportunities to maximize their children's socioeconomic status, poor mothers have the fewest resources to help propel their children into a higher class.

Mothers are crucial to the reproduction of inequality but also to the resistance to hardship. Despite class limitations, mothers facing economic, health, or emotional hardship can play a positive role for their children by serving as teachers, role models, and confidants, as well as establishing extended care and informal networks to raise alternative sources of income and provide for their children. As disparities in socioeconomic status grow, it will be increasingly important to understand the ways in which class impacts mothering and how mothering shapes children's future class.

**See Also:** African American Mothers; Chicana Mothering; Consumerism and Motherhood; Economy and Motherhood; Family; Poverty and Mothering; Public Policy and Mothers; Welfare and Mothering; Welfare Warriors; Working-Class Mothers.

**Bibliography**

Conger, R.D. and K.J. Conger. "Understanding the Processes Through Which Economic Hardship Influences Families and Children." In *Handbook of Families and Poverty*, D. R. Heaton, ed. Thousand Oaks, CA: Sage Publishing, 2008.

Descartes, L. and C.P. Kottak. *Media and Middle Class Moms: Images and Realities of Work and Family.* New York: Routledge, 2009.

Gillies, Val. *Marginalized Mothers: Exploring Working-Class Experiences of Parenting.* New York: Routledge, 2007.

Lareau, A. "Invisible Inequality: Social Class and Childrearing in Black Families and White Families." *American Sociological Review*, v.67 (2002).

Jenifer Hamil-Luker
University of North Carolina at Greensboro

# Clifton, Lucille

Lucille Sayles Clifton is a major American poet, children's book author, and educator. Clifton was born in Depew, New York, in 1936 and attended Howard University and Fredonia State Teacher's College. She married Fred Clifton in 1958, and the couple had six children. She is a Distinguished Professor of Humanities at St. Mary's College in Baltimore, Maryland.

Clifton's maternal poetry is important for its frank, accessible, and deceptively simple portrayal of an African American woman's experience as mother and daughter, and for its expression of a woman-centered history and spirituality. Like the work of Anne Sexton and Alicia Ostriker, Clifton's poetry features women's lives of body, mind, and spirit, and contributes to women poets' revisionist readings of the Bible.

Clifton's honors include grants from the National Endowment for the Arts and the 2007 Ruth Lily Poetry Prize. Between 1979 and 1985, Clifton served as Poet Laureate for the State of Maryland. Two of her 11 poetry books were nominated for a Pulitzer Prize: *Good Woman: Poems and a Memoir 1969–80* (1987), and *Next: New Poems* (1987). *Blessing the Boats: New and Selected Poems, 1988–2000* (2000) won the National Book Award for Poetry.

Clifton's maternal poems show a vast thematic and tonal range compressed into a spare style. In "Poem in Praise of Menstruation," "Poem to My Uterus," and "To My Last Period," Clifton responds to the inconveniences, sorrows, and profundities of a woman's reproductive cycle, but she closes the sequence with "wishes for sons," which humorously imagines young men menstruating.

Other poems are known for their powerful maternal affect: "The Lost Baby Poem" speaks to the loss of a child to abortion or miscarriage. "Mercy" includes elegies for two of Clifton's children who died as young adults.

Clifton's work conjures strength from African American history and spirituality, particularly in *Two-Headed Woman*. *Generations: A Memoir* provides background for poems like "Ca'line's Prayer," told in the voice of Clifton's paternal great-great-grandmother, who maintained the spirit of Dahomey women through her experience as a slave.

Clifton also draws spiritual power from her maternal ancestry in poems like "Daughters," but she reflects a complex spiritual relationship with her mother, Thelma Moore Sayles (1914–59), in several elegies. Biblical revisions appear frequently in Clifton's work, and offer transformative readings of mothers in the Bible, from the Mary poems in *Good Woman* to "The Tree of Life" sequence featuring Eve and Lucifer in *Quilting*, to "Sarah's Promise" and "Naomi Watches While Ruth Sleeps" in *The Book of Light*.

**See Also:** African American Mothers; Bible, Mothers in the; Motherhood Poets; Ostriker, Alicia; Sexton, Anne; Teachers as Mothers.

**Bibliography**

Holliday, Hilary. *Wild Blessings: The Poetry of Lucille Clifton*. Baton Rouge: Louisiana State University Press, 2004.

Hull, Ashaka (Gloria T.) "Channeling the Ancestral Muse: Lucille Clifton and Dolores Kendrick." In *Feminist Measures: Soundings in Poetry and Theory*, Lynn Keller and Cristanne Miller, eds. Ann Arbor: University of Michigan Press, 1994.

Lupton, Mary Jane. *Lucille Clifton: Her Life and Letters*. Santa Barbara, CA: Praeger, 2006.

Ostriker, Alicia. *Feminist Revision and the Bible*. Oxford: Blackwell, 1993.

D'Arcy Clare Randall
University of Texas at Austin

# Clinton, Hillary Rodham

Hillary Rodham Clinton was the first viable woman candidate for the presidency of the United States, losing the 2008 Democratic nomination to Barack Obama. She was the first former First Lady to serve as a U.S. Senator and in the U.S. Cabinet, as Secretary of State in Obama's administration. Clinton has one daughter, Chelsea, born February 27, 1980. Clinton's contributions to the lives of children and women through political action are notable.

Hillary Diane Rodham, born October 26, 1947, to Hugh and Dorothy Rodham, was raised in Chicago, Illinois. In 1969, Clinton was the first graduating student to deliver the commencement address at Wellesley College. Clinton graduated from Yale Law School in 1973, and married William Clinton, 42nd U.S. president, in 1975.

As an attorney, Clinton's early years focused on children's rights, with a 1973 publication fostering changes in evaluating children's legal competence. Clinton was staff attorney for the Children's Defense Fund, and worked for mandatory teacher testing and state curriculum standards in Arkansas, universal U.S. health care coverage, the establishment of Arkansas's Children's Health Insurance Program, the U.S. Adoption and Safe Families Act, and the U.S. Foster Care Independence Act. Clinton and Attorney General Janet Reno co-created

In 2009, Secretary of State Clinton met with sexual violence victims in the Democratic Republic of the Congo.

the Office on Violence Against Women at the U.S. Justice Department. Clinton was Arkansas's 1983 Woman of the Year and 1984 Mother of the Year. Clinton's best-selling 1996 book *It Takes a Village (And Other Lessons Children Teach Us)* spoke to the responsibility to put children and families first at all levels of society and government. As a mother in the political limelight, on advice from former First Lady Jacqueline Kennedy Onassis, Clinton always worked aggressively to keep daughter Chelsea protected from the press. During her 2008 bid for the Democratic Party presidential candidacy, both Chelsea and Clinton's mother Dorothy regularly campaigned with her. Clinton spoke out, calling herself a "mother first," after an MSNBC correspondent (subsequently suspended) claimed Chelsea was exploited by her mother for campaign purposes.

Hillary Rodham Clinton cites her role as mother as influential in her political agenda. Her comments have brought attention to the difficulties of parenting, in itself and when balancing work–family demands. Clinton praised her skills learned through mothering as a way of paying tribute to the value of mothering for women and society. Clinton's focus on public policy, rather than traditional domestic pursuits, transformed the role of U.S. First Lady. A feminist trailblazer, Clinton is for some a role model, demonstrating that women can be attentive mothers while achieving career milestones.

**See Also:** Kennedy Onassis, Jacqueline; Law and Mothering; Obama, Michelle; Politics and Mothers; Palin, Sarah; Public Policy and Mothers; Violence Against Mothers/Children; Work and Mothering.

## Bibliography

Bazinet, K.R. and M. Saul. "Hillary Clinton Blasts MSNBC Over Chelsea 'Pimp' Comment." *New York Daily News* (February 10, 2008).

Clinton, H.R. *It Takes a Village.* New York: Simon & Schuster, 1996.

Clinton, H.R. *Living History.* New York: Simon & Schuster, 2003.

Coles, J. "Hillary Clinton Unplugged." *Marie Claire.* http://www.marieclaire.com/world-reports/news/latest/hillary-clinton-interview (accessed December 2008).

Ann Dunnewold
Independent Scholar

# Clytemnestra

Clytemnestra appears in Homer's *Odyssey*, and several classical plays including Seneca's *Agamemnon*, Sophocles's *Electra*, Euripides's *Electra* and *Iphigeneia at Aulis*. She is the title figure in a ballet by Martha Graham and is represented by painters such as John Collier and Lord Frederick Leighton. Clytemnestra is most famous, however, for her pivotal role in Aeschylus's dramatic trilogy, the *Oresteia*, as the murderer of her husband, King Agamemnon.

Daughter of Leda and Tyndareus, King of Sparta, Clytemnestra was also the half sister of Helen, who, unlike Clytemnestra, was immortal because her father Zeus seduced Leda in the form of a swan. Clytemnestra married King Agamemnon, but legends vary concerning the circumstances. For instance, in *Iphigeneia at Aulis*, Clytemnestra reveals that she was the wife of Tantalus when Agamemnon decided to take her for his bride. Apparently, Agamemnon murdered her first husband and then killed her son by dashing the child upon the ground.

Clytemnestra and Agamemnon lived in Mycenae of Argos and had several children, including Iphigeneia, Electra, and Orestes. When Paris kidnapped Helen, wife of Menelaus, Agamemnon's brother, it caused war to break out between Argos and Troy. Agamemnon then left home and Clytemnestra to join forces with his brother and other leaders from the Argive city states. At the straits of Aulis, the winds stilled and the army was stranded, unable to sail to Troy. A soothsayer told Agamemnon that he must sacrifice his oldest daughter, Iphigeneia, to Artemis if he wished to set sail. Deceiving Clytemnestra of his intentions, he sent her word that her daughter was to be married to Achilles, but upon Iphigeneia's arrival, Agamemnon had the girl sacrificed. According to Euripides, Iphigeneia is assumed into the heavens and a stag is sacrificed in her place; yet Clytemnestra, refusing to believe the messenger's tale, blamed Agamemnon for the death of her daughter.

Ten years passed before the Trojan War ended. In her husband's absence, Clytemnestra took a lover, Agamemnon's cousin, Aegisthus. In Aeschylus's *Agamemnon*, the most famous of the Greek plays that feature the Mycenaean Queen, Clytemnestra welcomes her husband home from the war. She convinces him to commit sacrilege by walking upon tapestries, an act reserved only for the gods. Once inside the palace, as Agamemnon disrobes, Clytemnestra mortally stabs her husband, thus avenging Iphigeneia's death. In addition, Clytemnestra murders his concubine, Cassandra, whose pitiable prophesy of the tragedy within, including her own death, is ignored by all on stage. As customary in classical Greek drama, where bodies are revealed after violence and death occur offstage, when the corpses of Agamemnon and Cassandra are displayed, Clytemnestra claims full responsibilities for her deed and Aegisthus acknowledges his role in the plotting of the murders.

In the second play of the *Oresteia*, *The Libation Bearers*, Clytemnestra meets her end. Following the death of Agamemnon, Electra and Orestes conspire to avenge the murder of their father. At play's end, first Aegisthus and then Clytemnestra die in the hands of Orestes, who subsequently flees from the palace to escape the vengeance of hideous gorgon creatures known as the Furies. In the final play of the trilogy, the *Eumenides*, Orestes is still pursued by the Furies, who are spurred to vengeance by Clytemnestra's ghost. Orestes flees to Apollo's sanctuary in Delphi. The ghost of Clytemnestra pleads for equal vengeance on her son for his crime, as now she resides in the underworld shamed and without honor. At the temple of Athena (goddess of wisdom), Apollo pleads for Orestes. The court consists of 12 Aegean citizens and the goddess herself presides as judge. Athena's diplomatic and persuasive pleas quell the temper of Clytemnestra's bloodthirsty Furies. The vengeful Furies become the judicious and honorable Eumenides. The court's decision, however, reinforces the supremacy of men as the head of the household and subjugates the role of the mother.

**See Also:** Birth Goddesses; Birth Imagery, Metaphor, and Myth; Demeter, Goddess; Greece (and Ancient Greece); Paganism (New Paganism) and Mothering; Mother Earth; Mother Goddess.

### Bibliography

Aeschylus. "The Orestia: Agamemnon and The Libation Bearers." In *The Harcourt Brace Anthology of Drama*, W.B. Worthen, ed. Berkeley: University of California Press, 2000.

Euripides. *Iphigeneia at Aulis*, W.W. Merwin and George E. Dimcock, Jr., trans. New York: Oxford University Press, 1978.

Guerber, H.A. *The Myths of Greece and Rome*. London: House & Maxwell, 1965.

Amy Cuomo
University of West Georgia

# Code Pink

Code Pink: Women for Peace is a political activist group founded in 2002 to protest the United States military involvement in Afghanistan and Iraq. With reference to the Bush administration's color-coded terrorist threat warnings, the group has used symbols of feminine sexuality and gender norms in its performance activism. Code Pink's campaigns are framed by both antiwar and feminist stances, though they do not exclude men. The group has expanded its mission to leftist social justice causes with multimedia products, Internet campaigns, targeted protests, travel programs, an online store, and an international network of local chapters.

## Symbols of Motherhood

In addition to intrinsically associating women with mothers by stating, "Women have been the guardians of life," they define war as a male activity and therefore its protest a female one. In addition to playing upon symbols of motherhood and femininity, many of their statements support both difference feminism and the social belief that maternalism is inherently pacifistic. Their 2009 Mother's Day protest outside of the White House was, "We will not raise our children to kill another mother's child," and included the unveiling of a knitted banner quilted by mothers and children all over the world. In their protest, Code Pink represents grieving mothers of dead children, and also include children dressed in pink in their photos. Their calls for peace are targeted toward mothers, grandmothers, and daughters, situating notions of motherhood's inherent moral connotation with a moral imperative to protest war.

Code Pink became a recognizable protest movement when a rotating group of roughly 100 women activists held a four-month peace vigil outside of the White House from November 2002 through March 2003. Through their book and public protests they have associated themselves with public figures such as Starhawk, Alice Walker, Diane Wilson, Maxine Hong Kingston, and Cindy Sheehan, and organizations such as the National Organization of Women.

## Expanding Nework, Causes, and Slogans

Medea Benjamin, head of the human rights organization Global Exchange; Jodie Evans, democratic staffer and former adviser to Jerry Brown; and peace activist Gael Murphy are the principal founders of what has since become an expanded network of groups and causes. These include protesting the wars in Iraq and Afghanistan, military recruitment in public schools, advocating for the closure of Guantánamo prison and unconditional negotiations with Iran, and publicizing the plight of Sudanese, Iraqi, and Pakistani refugees. Their web of causes continues to grow. By 2009, their campaigns had extended to an Israeli Ahava Cosmetics boycott, health care reform, "green" jobs, Congressional economic policy, and microfinancing.

Code Pink leads travel trips in coordination with Global Exchange to conflict zones, sell Code Pink–branded merchandise and their edited book through their online store, publish multiple blogs and a related radio show, stage loud, dramatic protests in sexy pink attire, and issue "pink slips"—scanty pink lingerie—to politicians who do not adhere to their demands. Their Web-distributed resources also include reading and movie lists, song sheets, logos, and party planning tips for events like a Valentine's Day "Make Love, Stop War!" fundraiser. Slogans such as "War Is SO Over!" "Remind Obama," "Counter-recruitment," and "War Is Not Green" reveal distinct campaigns with their own Web addresses, graphic designs, and potential activist populations.

**See Also:** Ethics, Maternal; Maternal Thinking; Peace Movement and Mothers; Sheehan, Cindy; Starhawk; Walker, Alice.

### Bibliography

Benjamin, Medea and Jodie Evans. *Stop the Next War Now: Effective Responses to Violence and Terrorism.* Maui, HI: Inner Ocean Publishing, 2005.

Code Pink. www.codepinkalert.org (accessed August 2009).

Collateral Repair Project. www.collateralrepairproject.org (accessed August 2009).

Kutz-Flamenbaum, Rachel V. "Code Pink, Raging Grannies, and the Missile Dick Chicks: Feminist Performance Activism in the Contemporary Anti-War Movement." *NWSA Journal,* v.19/1 (2007).

Women Say No to War. www.womensaynotowar.org (accessed August 2009).

Mira C. Foster
San Francisco State University

# Collins, Patricia Hill

Patricia Hill Collins, a sociologist, is one of America's leading black feminist scholars. Collins draws on diverse theoretical traditions, including Afrocentrism, feminist theory, standpoint theory, critical theory, poststructuralism, and postmodernism, and has published in a wide range of fields including sociology, philosophy, history, and psychology. She is Distinguished University Professor of Sociology at the University of Maryland, College Park; Charles Phelps Taft Distinguished Emeritus Professor of Sociology, University of Cincinnati; and the 100th president of the American Sociology Association.

The daughter of a factory farm worker and a secretary, Collins was born in Philadelphia in 1948. She received a B.A. in sociology from Brandeis University in 1969, an M.A. in education from Harvard University in 1970, and a Ph.D. in sociology from Brandeis University in 1984.

In 1990, Collins published the highly influential and widely cited book *Black Feminist Thought: Knowledge, Consciousness, and the Politics of Empowerment,* which won the Jessie Bernard Award of the American Sociological Association (ASA) for significant scholarship in gender; and the C. Wright Mills Award of the Society for the Study of Social Problems. In 1992 (with Margaret Anderson) she published *Race, Class, and Gender: An Anthology* (now in its seventh edition), widely read in undergraduate courses across the country and credited with shaping the concept of intersectionality (the interlocking of systems of oppression) and race, class, and gender studies. In *Fighting Words: Black Women and the Search for Justice* (1998), Collins emphasizes justice as a group-based phenomenon and identifies the ways in which elite discourses present white male ideas and actions as normative and superior to the oppositional positions of black feminist thought. *Black Sexual Politics: African Americans, Gender, and the New Racism* (2004), which received ASA's 2007 Distinguished Publication Award, examines racism from a global perspective and describes the ways in which racism and sexism intertwine. Collins's most recent book, *From Black Power to Hip Hop: Racism, Nationalism, and Feminism* (2006), explores the relationships between black nationalism, hip-hop, and feminism.

## Outsider-Within

Collins's groundbreaking article in 1986, *Learning From the Outsider-Within,* articulated Afrocentric feminist thought as rooted in a black woman's standpoint reflecting her race, gender, and social class as she moves across and within institutions (such as in domestic service, in which employees both do and do not have contact with the employers' worlds). The outsider-within has a sense of a dual (or plural) identity developed through the experience of having a position in which they are both included and excluded from a community. Collins highlights the role of power in this concept, because although the outsider-within can gain access to the knowledge of a particular community, at the same time they do not share the full power given to members of that group. Collins identifies black women as the "ideal" outsider-within because they are marginalized by gender and race, and are members of a wide variety of communities. She identifies this group boundary crossing as the black feminist standpoint, which "can produce distinctive oppositional knowledges that embrace multiplicity yet remain cognizant of power."

## Scientism

Collins' central thesis throughout her work is the idea that knowledge is connected to power. Methodologically, she critiques positivism, which she describes as "Eurocentric masculinist," for objectifying reality, creating static social categories, and separating information from meaning. Collins argues that knowledge must include values, interests, and feelings because all knowledge is value-laden. The politics of race, class, gender, and sexuality influence knowledge construction, and elites exercise disproportionate control over what ideas count as truth. Oppressed voices are denied under scientism, and Collins wants to "decenter" or unseat those who engage in power/knowledge by incorporating the voices from oppressed speakers into social theory. Black feminist epistemology requires an ethic of accountability, whereby probing into an individual's personal viewpoint is at the center of the knowledge-validation process. Collins argues that social theory is born of struggle, and examines the social, political, and economic justice concerns of specifically located groups of people.

## Intersectionality

Collins locates the solution to problems of "difference" in what she defines as intersectional analysis. Intersectionality is an "analysis claiming that systems of race, social class, gender, sexuality, ethnicity, nation, and age form mutually constructing features of social organization, which shape Black women's experiences and in turn, are shaped by Black women." Collins emphasizes the way in which intersectionality shapes experiences. She argues that the powerless have different viewpoints from that of the master narrative, but cautions that one should question hierarchical formulas that place one social category, such as race or class, for example, as more significant than other categories, such as gender. Because racism, sexism, homosexual discrimination, and classism are interrelated, it is senseless to suggest that one form of oppression is more important than another. Oppressions are not interchangeable or analogous; rather, dominations overlap and have points of convergence as well as areas of divergence.

Intersectionality, according to Collins, is a way of understanding social locations in terms of the ways in which systems of oppression crisscross. She argues that individuals are never exclusively either oppressors or oppressed. Rather, individuals may be oppressed because of race, class, gender, sexual identity, and so on; and, at the same time, be privileged (and oppress others) because of race, class, gender, sexual identity, etc.

However, she makes it clear that while intersectionality deepens individual analyses of experience, it does not elevate individual analyses over structural analyses. Intersectionality, she argues, "provides an interpretive framework for thinking through how intersections of race and class, or race and gender, or sexuality and class, for example, shape any group's experience across specific social contexts." Moreover, Collins stresses the importance of theorizing hierarchies within groups as well as between groups.

## Matrix of Domination

Matrix of domination refers to the overall organization of power in society. Collins describes the two features of any matrix: (1) every matrix has a particular arrangement of socially and historically specific intersecting systems of oppression; (2) intersecting systems of oppression are organized through four domains of power: structural, disciplinary, hegemonic, and interpersonal. The structural domain of power consists of social structures such as the economy, politics, law, and religion.

The disciplinary domain is made up of bureaucratic organizations that control and organize human behavior through surveillance, routines, and rationalization, and which hide the effects of racism homosexual discrimination, and sexism with arguments of efficiency, rationality, and equal treatment. According to Collins, segregation keeps marginalized groups outside the centers of power, and surveillance is used on individuals who move inside centers of power.

The hegemonic domain links the structural, disciplinary, and interpersonal domains and legitimates oppression. It consists of our values, language, thoughts, and the images we respond to: "Racist and sexist ideologies, if they are disbelieved, lose their impact." The interpersonal domain influences everyday life and is made up of our daily interactions. In a person's mind, their oppression has a tendency to become a master status. In the interpersonal domain, Collins highlights the contradictions of domination and the ways in which the oppressed becomes the oppressor: "Oppression is filled with such contradictions because these approaches fail to recognize that a matrix of domination contains few pure victims or oppressors." Through dialogue and the recognition of multiple standpoints, domination can be resisted.

## African American Mothering

Collins challenges attempts to hold up what she calls the white American notion of mothering as an ideal for African American families. She finds three main differences: in African American families, mothering does not take place exclusively within the private nuclear family; strict sex-role segregation and separate male and female sphere of influence do not generally apply to African American households; and there is not an expectation that women should remain at home with the children while men earn the money.

Collins notes African roots in African American mothering practices: for instance, in in the view that motherwork is a collective responsibility with fluid boundaries between biological mothers (blood mothers) and "other mothers" who share in childcare; that many women help raise children besides their own; and that this flexibility gives the community resilience and assists the blood mothers as well as the children. Motherwork includes both traditional nuclear family goals such as protecting and nurturing one's own biological children, but also teaching all children in a community how to protect themselves in a hostile world, embuing them with pride about their African and African American heritage, and assisting those whose own mothers have not been able to care for them.

According to Collins, work is an important facet of most African American mother's lives and is not a threat to their ability to mother their children. Providing for children's physical and practical needs is interdependent with providing for their emotional and affective needs, forced on families partly by the disruption of slavery.

Collins also notes that black women are often recognized as community leaders, with significant power and respect accorded older black women, and that perceived responsibility for community children was often an entrée into political organizing.

**See Also:** Essentialism and Mothering; Family; hooks, bell; Lesbian Mothering; LGBTQ Mothering; Morrison, Toni; Popular Culture and Mothering; Race and Racism; Sexuality and Mothering; Slavery and Mothering; Social Construction of Motherhood; Sociology of Motherhood; Transracial Mothering; Walker, Alice; Working-Class Mothers.

## Bibliography

Collins, Patricia Hill. *Black Feminist Thought: Knowledge, Consciousness and the Politics of Empowerment.* New York: Routledge, 2000.

Collins, Patricia Hill. *Black Sexual Politics: African Americans, Gender, and the New Racism.* New York: Routledge, 2004.

Collins, Patricia Hill. *Fighting Words: Black Women and the Search for Justice.* Minneapolis: University of Minnesota Press, 1998.

Collins, Patricia Hill. *From Black Power to Hip Hop: Racism, Nationalism, and Feminism.* Philadelphia: Temple University Press, 2006.

Collins, Patricia Hill. "Learning From the Outsider Within: The Sociological Significance of Black Feminist Thought." *Social Problems,* v.33 (1986).

Collins, Patricia Hill, and Margaret Andersen, eds. *Race, Class and Gender: An Anthology*, 7th Edition. Belmont, CA: Wadsworth Publishing, 2010.

Lynn Comerford
California State University, East Bay

# Colombia

The Republic of Colombia is a large, diverse South American nation with a moderate fertility rate that varies by ethnicity and urbanity. Mothers are eligible for maternity leave and breastfeeding breaks, and most women receive skilled prenatal care and birth support. Marriage rates are falling and divorce is increasing; meanwhile, traditional gender roles are changing. Women and men have similar educational levels. Family equality is written into the Colombian Constitution.

Fertility rates have been decreasing since the 1980s, but vary by urbanity and ethnicity. Colombian mothers have an average of three children; Pacific Afro-Colombians five to seven children. Indigenous women may feel pressure to preserve the culture by having many children. Maternity/adoption leave covers 12 weeks, with the husband or partner entitled to one of the weeks. Nursing mothers may take two 30-minute work breaks for six months.

Divorce has been legal since 1991, despite opposition from the Catholic Church. Family structures are changing due to a rising divorce rate, a large drop in marriage rates, and increasing numbers of domestic partnerships.

Colombia is one of the most racially diverse Latin American countries, with whites, *mestizos* (mixed race), blacks, and indigenous peoples. Despite constitutional familial equality, concepts of *Marianismo* (selfless motherhood) and *Machismo* (male dominance) influence traditional gender roles, which vary by a couple's age, education, poverty level, and employment status. Afro-Colombian families are the poorest and least educated. Girls are expected to complete 12 years of schooling, but the average

is seven years for both genders. Women comprise 60 percent of the university population.

The Catholic Church was an important institution in the colonial period and remains a social force. A child's *compadres* (godparents) provide guidance and financial support. More than 75 percent of Columbians use contraception; most use methods the Catholic Church opposes.

Sterilization is the most common contraceptive method; others are the pill, condoms, and intrauterine devices (IUDs). Spousal consent is not required. Most female sterilizations, insertions of IUDs, and vasectomies take place at government hospitals and PROFAMILIA, a private nonprofit organization. Illegal abortions are the second-highest cause of maternal mortality. Skilled personnel provide prenatal care, which 90 percent of women access; 86 percent of births are attended by skilled personnel.

In 1974 the Colombian Congress eliminated a husband's legal power over his wife's property, children, and decisions. Both partners have equal rights and obligations in family authority and expenses.

Ingrid Betancourt, mother and legislator, was kidnapped by the Revolutionary Armed Forces of Colombia (FARC) in 2002 while campaigning for president and was rescued in 2008. Her memoir, *Until Death Do Us Part: My Struggle to Reclaim Colombia*, was published in English in the United States in 2002.

**See Also:** Caribbean Mothers; Fertility; Postcolonialism and Motherhood.

**Bibliography**

Garcés de Eder, Elena and Adriana Marulanda Herrán. "Women in Colombia." In *Female Well-Being: Toward a Global Theory of Social Change,* Janet Mancini Billson and Carolyn Fluehr-Lobban, eds. London: Zed Books, 2005.

Safford, Frank and Marco Palacios. *Colombia: Fragmented Land, Divided Society.* New York: Oxford University Press, 2001.

Suárez, Juana. "Columbia." In *The Greenwood Encyclopedia of Women's Issues Worldwide,* Lynn Walter, ed. Westport, CT: Greenwood Press, 2003.

Keri L. Heitner
University of Phoenix

# Colorado

Colorado, in the western United States, has a population of 4.86 million people. Colorado is 89.9 percent white, compared with the national average of 80 percent, as of 2007. African Americans represent just over 4 percent of the population and Hispanics just under 20 percent, above the national 14 percent. More than 86 percent are high school graduates, above the national average of 80.4 percent. A third have college degrees, compared with one-fourth nationally. Income per capita in 1999 was $24,000, above the national rate of $20,500. The poverty rate is 11.5 percent, compared to the national rate of 13 percent.

In 2007, Coloradans gave birth to 68,453 babies. Births by unmarried women—divorced, single, and widowed—accounted for 17,971 of those children. The largest rate for unmarried women was for women aged 20–34, which was 101 per 1,000.

Colorado ranks 33rd in marriage stability with a 2001 marriage rate of 8.5 per 1,000 (the national rate is 8.4), but a divorce rate of 4.7 compared to the national rate of 4.0 per 1,000. Divorce increases the likelihood of domestic violence, child poverty, and other social problems.

## Laws for Controversial Practices

In 2008, when polygamists bought properties in Westcliffe, a community 2.5 hours from Denver, the neighbors were concerned about property values and curious about what to do about defecting members, but generally did not socialize with the newcomers. Polygamy is illegal in the United States but practiced in several states, Colorado being the newest. In 1996, State Senator Dorothy Rupert of Boulder first introduced a bill outlawing female genital mutilation (FGM), making it a child abuse crime; the bill took four attempts before passing in 2000. The bill affected the 20,000 Muslims in Colorado, particularly Ethiopians and Somalians, who retained the traditions of their native lands. There have been no prosecutions.

Domestic abuse is a problem for mothers and women in general. In 2007, Colorado had 38 fatal domestic abuse cases that resulted in 49 deaths. The victims were 18 to 84 years of age and the perpetrators 17 to 82; 25 of the victims were females killed by a male partner. Domestic abuse shelters had insufficient capacity in 2007 and had to turn away 6,341 people.

## Prenatal Care and Childbearing in Colorado

Prenatal care rates between 2002 and 2006 were 78.3 percent in Colorado, below the national rate of 83.9 percent in 2005. The Healthy People 2010 initiative set a target of 90 percent. Prenatal care in the first trimester was more likely for women 25 and older, while mothers aged 10–14 were least likely to receive early care. Teen fertility in Colorado has been declining since 1992, with the exception of Hispanic teens. The rate for teens aged 15–17 rose 11 percent over the same period. The rate for Hispanic teens in 2003 was over six times that for whites and double that of African Americans. Hispanic teens aged 13 and 14 had a 2003 fertility rate 10 times higher than that of whites, and five times the rate for African Americans.

Most of this childbearing is outside marriage. The latest census data indicates that 80 percent of births to those under 20 were out of wedlock; the 1970 rate was 44 percent. Teenage mothers are more likely to drop out of school, be single parents, and be poor. Their children are sicker, slower in cognitive development, more likely to have behavioral problems, and more likely to be teen parents.

Non-Hispanic mothers were most likely to receive first-trimester care. In 2004, 77.5 percent of Hispanic mothers nationally received first-trimester care; within the Hispanic culture, there is a strong, informal, prenatal care support system including family, friends, lay health workers, and community. The cultural norms are stronger for those who have spent less time in the United States. Hispanic women have lower rates of early delivery and low birthweight babies than the national average.

Although prenatal care rates are below the national rate, infant mortality in Colorado at 4.8 percent in 2006 is below the 6.4 percent national rate. Infant mortality is a significant indicator of a state's health because it is linked to maternal health, access to and quality of medical care, public health practices, and socioeconomic conditions. The 2007 eight-year average for Colorado was 6.1 per 1,000, better than the national average of 6.8 over the eight years. The United States and Colorado rates in 2007 were about 40 percent higher than the Healthy People 2010 goal of 4.5 per 1,000. Notable Colorado mothers include Frances Wisebart Jacobs, Colorado's "mother of charities," and Linda G. Alvarado, builder of a major construction company and a franchise empire, and the first woman owner of a baseball franchise, the Colorado Rockies.

**See Also:** Arizona; Birth Control; Chicana Mothering; Ethnic Mothers; Islam and Motherhood; Nebraska; New Mexico; Oklahoma; Teen Mothers; Unwed Mothers; Utah; Violence Against Mothers/Children; Wyoming; Young Mothers.

**Bibliography:**
Colorado Coalition Against Domestic Violence. "Domestic Violence Facts & Statistics." www.ccadv.org/facts.htm (accessed January 2009).
Colorado Community Based Abstinence Education Program. "WAIT Training." http://www.community basedabstinenceeducation.com/overviews_colorado _community_based_abstinence_education.asp (accessed May 2009).
Compass of Larimer County. "Infant Mortality." http://www.larimer.org/compass/infant_mortality_h_ph.htm (accessed February 2009).
Compass of Larimer County. "Prenatal Care." http://www.larimer.org/compass/prenatal_care_h_physical.htm (accessed June 2008).
National Women's Hall of Fame. Colorado. www.greatwomen.org (accessed May 2009).
Sallinger, Rick. "Colorado Town Gets Educated On Polygamist Group." (November 11, 2008). www.CBS4Denver.com (accessed November 2008).
Suleiman, Safa. "Efforts to End Violence Against Women." www.europrofem.org/contri/2_04_en/en-viol/50en_vio.htm (accessed May 2009).
U.S. Census Bureau. "State and County Quickfacts. Colorado." http://quickfacts.census.gov/qfd/states/08000.html (accessed May 2009).
Women's International Network. "Outlawing FGM in the USA: The States and the Federal Government." WIN News (Spring 2000). http://findarticles.com/p/articles/mi_m2872/is_2_26/ai_62140809 (accessed May 2009).

John H. Barnhill
Independent Scholar

# Columbus, Christopher, Mother of

Christopher Columbus's mother remains a mystery. Columbus's mother is cited as an Italian woman, Susanna Fontanarossa, the daughter of a wool farmer. There aren't any records of his mother prior to her marriage to Domenico Columbus, Christopher's father. Christopher Columbus was the first of five children: four boys (Christopher, Bartolomeo, Giovanni Pellegrino, and Giacomo) and one girl (Bianchinetta). However, some scholars claim that Susanna Fontanarossa was not the mother of Christopher Columbus, but rather that a woman named Maria Spinola was his mother. A third theory is that neither of these two women were Columbus's mother, and that a Jewish woman who had to change her name to escape persecution gave birth to the explorer.

### Questionable Lineage
The typical history of Columbus's mother begins when Susanna Fontanarossa married his father, Domenico Columbo, a weaver, in 1477. Before then, there is little to no evidence of her existence. According to scant records, she was a devout Catholic, and lived with Domenico in Genoa, Italy. However, because of the lack of documented proof, this "official" story is often questioned. Moreover, because there are many countries and cities wishing to claim this great historical figure, there are also many potential birthplaces.

One such alternative theory involves Christopher Columbus's family changing their names and being wealthy merchants. In his book, *The Life of Christoforo Colonne*, Professor Ensenat de Villalonga makes the claim that Christopher Columbus was actually a young man known as Christoforo Colonne. He states that his father, Dominico Colonne, changed his name from Scotto to Colonne while working for a wealthy merchant. The book also argues that there is a reason not much is known about Susanna Fontanarossa—because she is not the mother of Columbus, but rather, a Spanish woman named Maria Spinola is the mother of the famed sailor. Christoforo is recorded to have started his study of navigation at the age of 5, and also studied Latin in Portugal.

A second theory states the fact that Christopher Columbus never wrote in the Italian language, even though it appears he was born in Italy. This theory asserts that while he was born in Genoa, his mother and father were Jewish, and changed their names many times in order to escape persecution. When they escaped Spain, along with many Sephardic Jews, they continued to use the Spanish language at home rather than adopting the Italian language.

Yet another theory centers on their Catalonian origins. Supposedly, Christopher was a rebellious youth, and the name changes were made to protect his identity. Finally, and possibly the most obscure theory, states that Columbus's mother and father were Norwegian, with a last name of Bonde.

The fact remains that in the execution of his own estate, he cites Genoa as his birthplace. Unfortunately, little information exists of his mother, Susanna Fontanarossa. While she had five surviving children, it is very possible that she had more, and that they died young. In the records of the family, she is on three deeds with her husband. There is one further controversy—the question of whether or not Domenico and Susanna were ever married, and whether Domenico was Christopher's father. A document from when Susanna sold the family house implies that her son is Christopher Pelliegrino—not Christopher Columbus. This would imply that Susanna had children prior to her marriage to Domenico, and scholars are still debating Columbus's origins.

**See Also:** History of Motherhood: 1000 to 1500; Italy; Spain.

## Bibliography

Merrill, Charles J. *Colom of Catalonia: Origins of Christopher Columbus Revealed*. Spokane, WA: Demers Books, 2008.

Owen, Richard. "Spanish Lay Claim to Columbus." *Time* (May 6, 1999).

Taviani, Paolo Emilio. "Christopher Columbus: His Birthplace and His Parents." *Five Hundred Magazine*, v.1/2 (October/November 1989).

Williams, Mark. "Just Who Was Columbus Anyway?" *San Francisco Chronicle* (October 4, 1992).

Ronda Lee Levine
Independent Scholar

# Communism and Motherhood

Communism is a political ideology that aims to establish an egalitarian, classless society, in which the means of production are common property. According to Marxist theory, which constitutes the most prominent philosophical basis for modern communist thought, private ownership of the means of production is the primary cause of economic oppression and exploitation in capitalist societies. The word communism is also often used to denote a state that embraces some form of one-party or authoritarian government, in which the dominant ideology is Marxism-Leninism; however, such states are not properly considered communist societies, according to Marxist thought. Historically, the emergence of modern communism can be traced back to Thomas More's 1516 treatise *Utopia*, a description of a society without private property.

## Treatment of Women and Mothers

Communist theory and practice has often been paradoxical in its treatment of women in general and motherhood in particular. While Karl Marx and Friedrich Engels, in *The Communist Manifesto* and elsewhere, maintain that monogamous marriage functions as a means of the subjugation and exploitation of women, they focus primarily on husband-wife relations; motherhood receives little or no attention. However, Engels's historical materialist work *Origins of the Family, Private Property, and the State*, makes several claims that have been central to the communist understanding of the role of motherhood. Engels maintains that matrilineal societies, or those based on "mother-right," were very common at the stages of human development preceding the rise of civilization. In the conditions of group marriage present in those societies, paternity was often impossible to ascertain, but motherhood was immediately obvious. He then goes on to claim that "within prehistoric times," as a result of an unspecified revolution, the male line of descent was instituted in place of the female line, giving rise to modern patriarchal society and paving the way to the emergence of the oppressive bourgeois marriage. Again, mother–child relations are barely, if ever, mentioned, except when referring to bourgeois monogamy, where the phrase "production of children" is purposefully used.

The communist project for motherhood was to bring about the abolition of this form of bourgeois marriage and to liberate women from the subservient status of means of production. The prevailing doctrine was that this abolition would be a natural result of proletarian revolution, which was to be precipitated in large part by the introduction of women to the industrial workforce and their awareness of their economic oppression under capitalism. In a communist society, marriage would not be legally or religiously sanctioned, and childcare and education would be the responsibility of the entire community.

## The Baba as the Mother of the Revolution

The *baba* is an exclusively eastern European concept. It is a very common and pejorative term to describe a housewife or a woman in general. The *baba* is assumed to possess certain universal traits: she is overemotional, uneducated, narrow minded, and superstitious; at the same time, however, it is upon her that the functioning of a household depends. The *baba*, being ignorant and uneducated, lacks any knowledge of child psychology; according to communist dogma during and after the Russian revolution, she would need to be extensively educated and indoctrinated by her husband to become the Mother of the Revolution.

This education is extremely important, as, according to "scientific" Marxist theory of the time, it is the female's natural role to bring up children; however, without the requisite knowledge and awareness of class relations and class struggle, she is incapable of raising children who are immune to corrupting Western imperialist and capitalist influences. To the present day, the *baba* remains a very strongly entrenched stereotype. It is clear, then, that the Bolshevik party, after the revolution of 1917, employed in its propaganda the very same imagery pertaining to the role of women and mothers as the bourgeois marital institution it so fiercely criticized, taking advantage of the prevailing cultural assumptions about women. The Soviet state, despite its claims of full gender equality, as well as later communist regimes, became heavily invested in upholding traditional gender roles.

As a second path to becoming the mother of the revolution, the *baba* could embark on labor activity. This was mostly Party work—tasks such as mixing explosives, printing pamphlets, or performing the "naturally" feminine tasks of cooking and cleaning in the public sphere instead of on a domestic scale. Women were thus liberated from the private kitchen, only to be employed in the public one—in cafeterias or kitchens, distributing food and clothes or nursing.

To encourage women to perform Party work or enter the labor force and provide a second source of income for the family, Russian communists put a strong emphasis on state-funded daycare centers, such as preschools and kindergartens, as well as the legalization of abortion.

In the 1920s, there emerged a heated controversy centered on the issue of abortion. The legalization of abortion was often seen as a moral catastrophe, opening the doors for the corruption of women and children and the collapse of the natural role of motherhood. The first legal acts permitting abortion required that it be performed only by qualified (male) doctors and not midwives, and clearly labeled it as morally negative. The Party proposed establishing maternity centers, which were supposed to dissuade women from having abortions. The termination of pregnancy was legalized at a later date, but the complete absence of educational programs and the lack of availability of contraceptives, as well as a prevalence of very conservative attitudes about human sexuality within the Bolshevik Party, resulted in abortion as a necessity, not as a choice, for many women.

Throughout the Soviet era in Russia, women's organizations, periodicals, and Party committees were established to promote official ideology among the working classes, especially in rural areas. However, such enterprises were typically marginalized and given little attention, and beyond daycare centers, full communal childcare was never instituted. Despite efforts to the contrary, the patriarchal and patrilineal family was never truly challenged.

What is more, with time, the introduction of certain categories of women workers, such as pregnant women, mothers up to eight weeks after childbirth, mothers caring for a household of five or more, women taking care of an incapacitated person—

who were all treated as less capable of work than men—served to further consign women to their traditional domestic and "motherly" activities.

## The United States

In the United States, the emergence of communism gave rise to and was coupled with some feminist claims, and a certain amount of attention was given to the oppression of African American women and workers, unlike in eastern Europe. This is attributed to the gender differences in the Western world, which are less pronounced than class differences: the worker classes performed those same hard and dangerous jobs, regardless of sex, while the upper classes were uniformly idle. In eastern Europe, on the other hand, there persist strongly gender-based ideas, which are deeply ingrained in those cultures, of which the *baba* is just one example.

Women within the various communist movements of the late 19th and early 20th century, however, proposed measures and changes dramatically different from the bourgeois and upper-class women's suffrage movements; in fact, feminism, which was at the time synonymous with the middle- and upper-class suffrage movement, was denounced by Vladimir Lenin as a reactionary aberration. Instead, socialist and communist women focused their attention on labor-related legislation that would lessen the burdens on working-class women, and especially protective legislation for pregnant women. The rhetoric used to promote these claims, however, often stressed the natural and traditional caregiving roles of women, and the victories of such legislative projects can in large part be ascribed to this reinforcement of common cultural assumptions.

It was also in the United States that some of the Bolshevik ideas and dogmas were criticized or questioned by women activists. One of the examples is the Russian notion of *khoziaika*, a manager of the household, which met with strong opposition, as women claimed it glamorized housework. Socialist women generally held the view, reinforced by the Communist Party of America's official line, that housework should under no circumstances be viewed as productive.

The issue of housework in particular proved a significant point of contention and sparked many debates. In the 1940s, Mary Inman, a prominent activist within the communist movement, proposed that houseworkers should be considered laborers on par with industrial workers, despite the fact that they work at home. She argued that some women are simply unable to find a job in the industry, due to the burdens laid on them by the cultural assumptions of their natural maternal role, and their efforts cannot be denigrated or considered counterproductive. Inman was fiercely criticized by Party officials, generally on the grounds that her ideas would glamorize housework and prevent the emergence of an enlightened industrial proletariat; however, her ideas became quite popular among communist women. Arguably, Inman and other women working in the progressive and socialist movements in the 1920s and 1930s laid the groundwork for the feminist movement of the 1960s, which similarly questioned the assumptions about women's natural roles and the value of housework.

Unfortunately, despite the progressive claims of women's emancipation and liberation, any social and ideological changes that the Communist Party of America might have urged on or instituted, particularly in the area of childcare and mother-friendly legislation, were largely prevented by placing disproportionate weight on economical theories of oppression, instead of critical examination of the role of

*After the Soviet Union's collapse, village mothers near Uzbekistan had no drinking water until USAID established wells.*

motherhood and its social implications. The advent of the McCarthy era and the subsequent virtual dissolution of the communist movement in America put an end to its political influence, although much of the work done by communist activists would prove invaluable to the emergence of Second Wave Feminism and the Civil Rights Movement in the 1960s.

## The Legacy of Communism for Motherhood

While Soviet Russia, China, and many other communist countries used traditional gender stereotypes in their official propaganda, it should be noted that those countries have nevertheless made certain advancements to ease the lives of women, particularly working mothers. Despite the terror underneath Soviet communism, governments around the world are still incorporating many ideas introduced during that era, even those that avidly reject the socialist label. Among the advancements: the maternity leave, publicly funded daycare centers, and public medical assistance of pregnant and nursing women. One example might be Cuba, which still considers itself a communist and revolutionary state. According to the Cuban Law 1263, enacted in 1974, a mother is obliged to take a leave off work at the 34th week of pregnancy and has a right to a six-week postnatal leave, even when the child is stillborn or dies within the first few weeks after birth.

Countries of the former Eastern Bloc in Europe, such as Latvia, Lithuania, Poland, Slovakia, and Bulgaria, all ranked better than the United States in a 2007 United Nations study of the risk of death by pregnancy-related causes.

In many European countries, the right to a maternity leave has been extended onto fathers as well. In some, a nursing working mother also has a right to leave work daily for a certain period of time to breastfeed her infant. One of the latest developments, stemming from a socialist and communist grounding, is the establishment of private, corporate daycare centers. However, such practices are still relatively rare and considered an experimental novelty.

**See Also:** China; Cuba; Daycare; Employment and Motherhood; Housework; Maternity Leave; Russia (and Soviet Union).

## Bibliography

Center for History and New Media. "Women in World History." http://chnm.gmu.edu/wwh/index.php (accessed December 2008).

Engel, Barbara Alpern. *Women in Russia, 1700–2000.* Cambridge, UK: Cambridge University Press, 2003.

Fried, Albert. *Communism in America: A History in Documents.* New York: Columbia University Press, 1997.

Marxists.org. "Manifesto of the Communist Party." http://www.marxists.org/archive/marx/works/1848/communist-manifesto/ (accessed December 2008).

Marxists.org. "The Origin of the Family, Private Property and the State." http://www.marxists.org/archive/marx/works/1884/origin-family/index.htm (accessed December 2008).

Weigand, Kate. *Red Feminism: American Communism and the Making of Women's Liberation.* Baltimore, MD: Johns Hopkins University Press, 2001.

Wood, Elizabeth A. *The Baba and the Comrade: Gender and Politics in Revolutionary Russia.* Bloomington: Indiana University Press, 1997.

Enola Aird
Independent Scholar

# Community Mothering

Community mothering is a phenomenon based on communal responsibility, and is fundamental to sustaining the respectful and prominent role of the mothering institution. It defies traditional, dominant notions of child rearing and nurturing that tend toward individualistic maternal practice—that is, expecting one woman to assume full responsibility to care, love, and nurture biological children.

## Historical Overview

With kinship origins in early African societies, this collaborative maternal practice was promulgated by biological, or blood mothers, with other women, who in turn cared for biological children. In their seminal work, African American feminist intellectuals Bristow, Brand, and Collins assert that women who assist blood mothers are integral in the institution of African American motherhood.

Grandmothers, sisters, nieces, aunts, cousins, sister-in-laws and neighbors act as community mothers by taking on childcare responsibilities for one another's children. In many African American communities, these women-centered networks of community-based childcare have crossed borders to include "fictive kin" or extended family members. When relationships were not between kin or fictive kin, community norms traditionally were such that neighbors cared for one another's children. Based on a class commonality, everyone looked out for each other.

Community mothering has maintained a strong resilience and sustenance throughout the passage of enslavement, transmigration, and displacement of African people. It survived the African Holocaust and transplanted and adapted it's tradition on the slave plantations, when older women were essentially the caregivers to children of slave parents. These women, in turn, passed on African indigenous knowledge and taught their community mother role to the younger generation. As transplanted peoples, cultural traditions such as music, language, and cuisine were kept alive and sustained within their new communities.

As women of African descent, the community mothers applied their experiences to a hostile setting in response to the need to preserve their tradition and move the community forward. These relationships were based on caring, protecting, and resisting oppressive circumstances. Their work was critical to moral and spiritual uplifting of the "black family."

### Current-Day Implications

In contemporary society, community mothering has come to signify cultural resistance and a voice of liberation and transformation. Many African Americans could not rely on mainstream, traditional childcare systems, so this cultural practice of cooperative/collaborative childcare continued. Community mothering as a familial system helps to maintain a communal and interdependent lifestyle.

However, it also appears to be in a state of flux in present-day circumstances, due to economic and social upheavals within urban centers. In part, the infiltration of drugs within African American communities has led to a growing disconnect between elders and youth. Even under adverse conditions,

such as illness or drug or alcohol dependency, some African American women continue to engage in community mothering. The notion of a community of resistance is based on the idea of a resilient, sustainable network of elder, middle-aged, and young African American women who share power, agency, and authority to support, mentor, and communicate.

### Public Eye

Community mothering transcends the boundaries of home or the private sphere. It extends to restaurants, grocery stores, public transit, community centers, places of worship, town halls, libraries, and other public domains. It reinforces a collective responsibility, irrespective of social and geographic location. These activities are transferred to various occupations. Many African American women, especially social workers and teachers, reinforce community mothering for the social and academic betterment of children in the African American community. As community mothers, African American women teachers impart to African American children their commitment to the survival and wholeness of the communities' children.

### Vision

As community mothers, African American women envision themselves in relation to an extended family of African American children as a life skill and responsibility that teaches children to navigate successfully in a racist and sexist world, portray a community spirit, and exists as a source of empowerment and importance for African American women and ultimately for the community at large.

**See Also:** African American Mothers; Anti-Racist Mothering; Collins, Patricia Hill; Other Mothering; Poverty and Mothering.

### Bibliography

Brand, Dionne. *No Burden to Carry*. London: The Women's Press, 1991.
Bristow, Peggy, ed. *We're Rooted Here and They Can't Pull Us Up: Essays in African Canadian Women's History*. Toronto: University of Toronto Press, 1994.
Collins, Patricia Hill. *Black Feminist Thought: Knowledge, Consciousness and the Politics of Empowerment*. New York: Routledge, 2000.

Henry, Annette. *Taking Back Control: African Canadian Women Teachers' Lives and Practice.* Albany: State University of New York Press, 1998.

Mogadime, D. "Black Girls/Black Women-Centered Texts and Black Teachers as Othermothers." *Journal of the Association for Research on Mothering: Mothering in the African Diaspora,* v.2/2 (2000).

Arlene Campbell
York University

# Co-Mothering

Co-mothering is the experience of being a second mother to a child not biologically one's own. It is distinct from adoptive mothering or stepmothering in as much as the child's other parent is also a woman. In this respect the co-mother is not substituting for a missing parent so as to complete a heterosexual parent couple, but is in the position of an extra parent of the same gender as the child's mother. The term has assumed particular significance in the last 30 years with the visibility of lesbian couples and the increasing numbers of lesbian couples parenting children.

Within this context, a co-mother can be the female partner of a mother whose children were conceived in a previous heterosexual relationship. This situation is analogous to that of a stepmother. Alternatively, an established couple may jointly opt for parenthood. With advances in reproductive technologies, and changes to legislation governing these procedures, one partner in a lesbian couple may conceive using donated sperm, thus becoming a biological mother, while her partner becomes a co-mother. In this case, the co-mother is involved in the life of the child from conception. A co-mother may be the second parent of two (birth mother and co-mother), of three (birth mother, co-mother, biological father) or of four parents (birth mother, co-mother, biological father, partner of biological father) depending on the circumstances of conception.

In the United States and United Kingdom, the legal situation of a co-mother is not assured by her being the present partner of the birth mother.

In the United States, the situation is complex with different states adopting different approaches.

Within a minority of states, second parent adoption is possible, which allows the co-mother to become a legal parent without affecting the rights of the biological mother. This issue is highly politically contested and likely to change. Currently, a co-mother may apply through the courts for parental responsibility, which, if awarded, grants her the same rights and responsibilities of the child's biological parents. However, to become the legal parent of the child, she must apply to adopt the child. This will extinguish the legal parental status of the biological father and his family, and is therefore problematic in situations where more than two adults have parental involvement (see above). The parental rights of the biological mother are not affected. In a small United Kingdom study, co-mothers were found to be less likely to work full time than fathers, less likely to be earning more than their partners, and likely to be more involved in childcare and household duties than heterosexual male partners. These findings suggest that co-mothering is not identical to fathering in terms of division of household and childrearing labor, nor in terms of financial dependency of birth mothers upon the other parent.

## Types and Numbers of Co-Mothers
Co-mothers are heterogeneous group; it is not possible to generalize about the type or quality of parenting that they provide. Although concerns about the effects of having a co-mother as a second parent frequently form the basis of legal and political challenges to same-sex couples gaining legal rights over their shared children, no adverse behavioral or social outcomes have been found in children raised by co-mothers and their female partners. Co-mothers have been found to be more actively involved with their children than either biological fathers or fathers of children conceived by donor insemination (to overcome infertility) and born into heterosexual families.

It is difficult to know exactly how many women are co-mothers, because census data do not include this statistic. Extrapolating from Census 2000 data on co-habiting partners of the same sex who were forming a household with children under 18 years of age, one estimate for the United States was that 34.3 percent of lesbian couple households had children. The same data puts the number of lesbian couples in the United States at nearly 300,000, suggesting that at least 100,000 women are presently co-mothers, although this is likely to be an underestimate.

**See Also:** Adoption; Artificial Insemination; Lesbian Mothering; Other Mothering.

### Bibliography

Dunne, Gillian. "Pioneers Behind Our Own Front Doors." *Towards Greater Balance in the Organization of Work in Partnerships in Work, Employment and Society,* v.12/2 (1998).

Gay Demographics.org. www.gaydemographics.org/USA/USA.htm (accessed July 2009).

Golombok, Susan. "Adoption by Lesbian Couples." *British Medical Journal,* v.324/7351 (2002).

*Journal of the Association for Research on Mothering.* Lesbian Mothering [special issue], v.1/2 (Fall/Winter 1999).

National Gay and Lesbian Taskforce. "Map of Adoption Laws in the United States." www.thetaskforce.org/reports_and_research/adoption_laws (accessed July 2009).

Susan Walker
University of Cambridge

# Conflict Zones, Mothering in

Mothers in conflict zones must see to the basic needs of food, shelter, and protection for their children and themselves when danger and violence are perpetual. The mothering processes of nurturing and protection are almost impossible during a state of geopolitical and military conflict. Nonetheless, mothering does endure in occupied lands, refugee camps, and even in the case of "children born of war," the children of local women and occupying or enemy fathers. Rape has been a tool of war for centuries, and recent international conflicts have created sizable populations of children born of these war crimes and the rape victims who must raise them. Researchers have started to investigate the relationships between mothers and children in these contexts, their special needs, and their rights and treatment under international human rights law. In so doing, they have

verbalized a global sentiment that during war, the larger international society has a particular responsibility toward the care of children, in addition to the protection of their mothers.

## Basic Needs

The act of giving birth is the first major hurtle mothers face in conflict zones. Both infant mortality and maternal mortality can rise because of a shortage of health workers and infrastructure, as well as restricted access to hospitals because of curfews, checkpoints, and ethnic segregation. The consequences of unsafe childbirth can extend to dangerous, lifelong, or fatal maternal health problems. In 2005 the lifetime risk of maternal death in war-torn Afghanistan was as high as one in eight women, and most of the countries with highest risk are conflict or postconflict zones. In addition, the conditions available for providing infant nutrition are even more severe than finding food in general, as the stress of war and starvation can threaten lactation. However, decreased access to infant formula generally encourages breastfeeding, along with education campaigns by relief organizations such as the United Nations Children's Fund (UNICEF).

The absence of men in the society in which women reside can be difficult for civilian mothers and their children, not only because of the general danger, but also because some cultures restrict females from travelling without men. In the absence of male heads of households in some war-torn countries, mothers have no source of financial income unless they challenge social norms of acceptable women's roles. Organizations such as the Red Cross and Red Crescent help with basic needs such as food, water, shelter, and sanitation only if they are allowed access to victimized populations. Sometimes mothers' only option is to flee in search of humanitarian assistance.

## War and Genocidal Rape

According to the United Nation's High Commissioner for Refugees (UNHCR), there were 42 million refugees worldwide in 2008, including 26 million internally displaced persons (IDPs). One of the UNHCR's major policy priorities is the protection of women and girl refugees, who are particularly vulnerable to sexual assault. Whether in refugee camps, during capture and internment, or as an act of invasion, wartime rape is a common war crime; genocidal rape, forced pregnancy, and forced maternity are now considered crimes against humanity under humanitarian law. In fact, the Geneva Convention stipulates "special treatment" for women and girls because of their particular vulnerability to sexual assault and impregnation.

The UN Security Council Resolution 1325 of 2000 calls for a gender perspective in peacekeeping operations, along with attention to the "special needs of women and girls" in protecting civilians during war, displacement and reconciliation. While rape of any kind can cause pregnancy, countless recent conflicts reveal the use of rape and forced impregnation as tactics in ethnic cleansing. Genocidal rape is the systematic and repeated sexual violence for the purposes of destroying a target group by utter humiliation and impregnation of the group's women with the progeny of the persecuting army. Some recent conflicts where genocidal rape was common include Bosnia and Herzegovina (1992–95), Rwanda (1995–96), and the ongoing genocide in Sudan.

## Forced Maternity and Children Born of War

In the Bosnian war, forced impregnation was part of the Serbian army's systematic program in rape facilities, where women were held and raped until they became pregnant. In Rwanda, there were an estimated 2,000 to 10,000 children born from the 1994–95 rape campaigns. In Sudan, rape is a daily occurrence for women and girls gathering wood outside of refugee camps, and they are often forced to live away from their communities if they keep their babies. The physical and psychological impacts of forced maternity include dramatic increases in infanticide, suicide, the widespread abandonment of children, ostracization of mothers from their communities, and the emotional abuse and developmental hindrance of children.

Children themselves can become mothers prematurely, as in the case of Uganda, where "girl mothers" are abducted and must follow the Lord's Resistance Army as sexual slaves, child minders, and the bearers of child soldiers. To make matters worse, in modern conflict zones such as Rwanda and Sudan, the human immunodeficiency virus (HIV) and acquired immunodeficiency syndrome (AIDS) crisis hits this population at staggering levels (70

percent for Rwanda). The violence of rape spreads and increases the incidence of HIV infections and lasting physical wounds such as fistula, for which victims are rarely treated.

While mothering of intentional children is certainly a hardship in conflict zones, the mothering of children born of war rape provides additional and long-lasting challenges. Many children born of war do survive and are sometimes nurtured and protected by their mothers, but mothering well—given the emotional and physical circumstances—is the exception rather than the rule. Advocates of women and children in both civilian society and international organizations such as UNICEF have begun to discuss policies and services that may address this population of children and their mothers. Human rights groups have sought to grant them address and rights within the legal framework of the International Rights of the Child, and Organizations such as the International Network for Interdisciplinary Research on Children Born of War (INIRC) seek to fill the gap in research for these vulnerable children.

Women are victimized for their sexual anatomy during war, and as targets of international sympathy, are defined by their maternity with the common term *women and children* used to describe civilians in war. Mothering is a social construction and process that connotes protecting and preserving life, fostering growth, and ensuring a child's acceptability in society. Yet during a state of perpetual war and disruption of society, preserving and nurturing life is exceptionally difficult. When mothers are are victimized by their own maternity, the act of mothering is a daunting tastk. International scholars, activists, and intergovernmental organizations are working to provide a framework of justice and assistance so that mothers in conflict zones can mother effectively, and their children can grow as healthy and integrated members of society no matter the cause of their conception.

**See Also:** Bosnia and Herzegovina; Displacement; Refugee Mothers; Rwanda; Sudan; War and Mothers.

## Bibliography
Carpenter, Charli R., ed. *Born of War: Protecting Children of Sexual Violence Survivors in Conflict Zones.* Sterling, VA: Kumarian Press, 2007.

Coalition of Women's Human Rights in Conflict Situations. www.womensrightscoalition.org (accessed August 2009).

International Committee of the Red Cross (ICRC) Focus on Women and War. http://www.icrc.org/web/eng/siteeng0.nsf/htmlall/women (accessed August 2009).

International Network for Interdisciplinary Research on Children Born of War (INIRC). www.childrenbornofwar.org (accessed August 2009).

Mira Foster
San Francisco State University

# Congo

The Republic of Congo is a former French colony in sub-Saharan Africa with high poverty and birth rates. Women in the formal sector receive maternity leave benefits. Many women live in polygamous marriages; divorce is common. Christianity and indigenous African beliefs influence marriage forms and reproductive rites and rituals. Use of modern contraceptives is low. Many women lack skilled birth attendants and maternal mortality is very high. Government efforts support safe motherhood and women's advancement. An average of 5.9 children per mother reflects cultural and religious norms that encourage large families and discourage family planning. For rural traditionalists, having a large family and several wives is a sign of status and a way to support widows and orphans in a nation with 70 percent poverty. Employers provide women with 14 weeks of maternity leave at two-thirds pay.

Women are responsible for childcare, housework, planting, harvesting, and meal preparation. Extended families provide a social system of support and care. Divorce and polygamy are common. Polygamy is less desirable among urbanized, Western-educated Congolese and Christians, who comprise half the population. Islam and traditional religions are also observed. Traditional religious leaders call on spirits for fertility, pregnancy, and birth rites and rituals; Congolese fathers may perform purification rituals during and after a birth, although these practices are less common in urban areas.

Public education in public schools is free and compulsory until age 16, although many girls abandon their studies after primary school. Many leave to help take care of their siblings or perform domestic chores. French Christian missionaries encouraged educating girls, job training for women, and the importance of fathers in childrearing. Many Catholics partially observe the church's position against polygamy, divorce, abortion, and birth control.

The government disseminates family planning and birth control information through the media and provides family planning services through health centers. While contraceptive use is 44 percent, only 13 percent use modern methods. Almost three-quarters of women attend at least one prenatal visit, but fewer than 45 percent of births are attended by skilled personnel, contributing to a very high maternal mortality rate.

The government promotes training traditional midwives to use scans in maternity care. In 1999 the Congolese Government adopted a National Policy for the Advancement of Women, with a corresponding Plan of Action for 2000–02 to promote gender equality and women's empowerment. More than 500 women's groups, associations, and nongovernmental organizations partnered with the Ministry for the Advancement of Women to promote activities to address women's needs. Rosalie Kama, mother of three, is the Congo's Minister of Education. Jeanne Dabenzet, mother of six, serves as Minister for Public Administration and Women's Promotion.

**See Also:** Congo, Democratic Republic of; Postcolonialism and Motherhood; Poverty and Motherhood.

**Bibliography**
Edgerton, Robert. *The Troubled Heart of Africa: A History of the Congo*. New York: St. Martin's Press, 2002.

Gondola, Ch. Didier. *The History of Congo*. Westport, CT: Greenwood Press, 2002.

Groelsema, Robert. "Republic of the Congo." In *Worldmark Encyclopedia of Religious Practices*, Thomas Riggs, ed. Farmington Hills, MI: Thomson Gale, 2006.

Republic of the Congo. "Reply to the Questionnaire Concerning the Report of the Congo on Implementation of the Dakar Plan of Action and Beijing +10."

http://www.un.org/womenwatch/daw/Review/respons es/CONGO-English.pdf (accessed January 2009).

Keri L. Heitner
University of Phoenix

# Congo, Democratic Republic of the

The Democratic Republic of the Congo (DRC, formerly Zaire) is an African nation of almost 69 million people, with an astounding 46.9 percent aged 14 years or younger (the country's median age is 16.4 years). The population growth rate is 3.2 percent, with a rate of 43 births per 1,000 and a death rate of 11.9 per 1,000. Life expectancy at birth is 52.6 years for men and 56.2 for females; both are quite low by international standards due to death from infectious disease and warfare. The total fertility rate (the estimated number of children per mother) is 6.2, despite an infant mortality rate of 81.2 per 1,000 live births. The country includes over 200 African ethnic groups, with the Bantu in the majority; the population is 70 percent Christian, 10 percent Muslim, and the remainder other beliefs.

The DRC has a long history of political unrest and dictatorial rule, which prevented orderly economic development and impeded the established of even a basic system of health services delivery. It was first established as a Belgian colony and became an independent country in 1960, but in 1965 Joseph Mobutu (later Mobutu Sese Seko) seized power, which he maintained for over 30 years. The years 1996–2003 were marred by frequent civil warfare, in part sparked by unrest in neighboring Rwanda that spilled over the border: it is estimated that 5 million people died in the First and Second Congo Wars during these years. The continued internal warfare, along with wars in neighboring Rwanda, Burundi, and Uganda, produced many refugees and displaced persons: 2007 estimates are that the DRC harbors almost 200,000 refugees from neighboring countries and 1.4 million internally displaced persons.

Although the DRC is rich in natural resources (including cobalt ore, copper, diamonds, and tantalum), the continued warfare and political corruption mean that most of the population has yet to benefit from them. The per-capita Gross Domestic Product (GDP) in 2008 was $300, and the per-capita expenditure on health in the DRC was $4 in 2002, representing 4.1 percent of the total GDP. The government provides about 30 percent of spending on health, with external sources providing about 28 percent and private expenditures the remainder.

Women are a disadvantaged social class in the DRC due to a long history of discrimination, which has its basis in both tribal society and the colonial system. For instance, married women are required by law to have their husband's permission to take a job or open a bank account, and women have lower levels of education and are discriminated against. About 54 percent of women are literate, as compared to about 81 percent of men. Women also suffer disproportionately during the civil wars that are rampant in the DRC, often becoming victims of rape or kidnapping as sexual slaves. The DRC is on the Tier 2 Watch List of the U.S. Department of State for failures to monitor and combat human trafficking.

## Child and Maternal Health

Most indicators of child and maternal health in the DRC are very poor: childhood immunizations rates are below 50 percent for some common diseases, and only 4 percent of women use modern methods of contraception. Only 61 percent of births are attended by a skilled attendant, although 61 percent of women have at least one prenatal care visit. The maternal mortality rate is 9.9 per 1,000 births, the stillbirth rate is 42 per 1,000 total births, and the neonatal mortality rate is 47 per 1,000 live births. Despite the fact that the DRC was one of the first African countries to recognize human immunodeficiency virus (HIV) infection, HIV and acquired immunodeficiency syndrome (AIDS) remain a serious problem, with the adult prevalence rate estimated at 4.2 percent. Infection rates for women visiting prenatal clinics in the major cities are in the 4–6 percent range. HIV prevalence is higher among internally displaced persons and those living in war-torn areas than the national average, due in part to the use of rape as a weapon of war.

**See Also:** AIDS/HIV and Mothering; Child Poverty; Poverty and Mothers; War and Mothers.

**Bibliography**

Behets, F.M., et al. "Preventing Vertical Transmission of HIV in Kinshasa, Democratic Republic of the Congo: A Baseline Survey of 18 Antenatal Clinics." *Bulletin of the World Health Organization,* v.84/12 (December 2006).

Polgreen, Lydia. "Congo's Death Rate Unchanged Since War Ended." *New York Times* (January 23, 2008).

Traub, James. "The Congo Case." *New York Times* (July 3, 2005).

Weiss, Herbert F. "The Democratic Republic of the Congo: A Story of Lost Opportunities to Prevent or Reduce Deadly Conflicts." In *Responsibility to Protect: The Global Moral Compact for the 21st Century,* Richard H. Cooper and Juliette V. Kohler, eds. New York: Palgrave Macmillan, 2009.

Sarah E. Boslaugh
Washington University School of Medicine

# Connecticut

Connecticut, the Constitution State, joined the United States on January 9, 1788, and was the fifth state in the union. From the beginning, Connecticut enjoyed a vast measure of political independence, proclaiming in its Fundamental Orders of 1639 a democratic principle of government based on the will of the people.

The fertility rate of white women rapidly declined during the 19th century, partly as the result of using birth control and abortion to control family size. A woman's opportunity to have an abortion was illegal in the states during the latter part of the 19th century. Abortions, which increased markedly in the 1850s and 1860s, especially among middle-class white women, had been legal until the fetus quickened, or moved inside the uterus. Women who had abortions could be held criminally liable.

Title VII of the Civil Rights Act of 1964 was a huge step forward for women's rights, and prohibited employment discrimination based on sex, allowing women the ability to challenge the actions of employers or potential employers.

Currently, health insurance plans have to pay for at least 48 hours of inpatient care for women and newborn infants. Women who work for private employers are entitled to a total of 16 work weeks of unpaid leave during any 24-month period for the birth of a child. Those women are required to have been employed for one year and worked 1,000 hours during that year before their first day of leave. Permanent employees of the State of Connecticut are entitled to 24 weeks of unpaid leave in any 24-month period. An employer is prohibited from refusing to grant a "reasonable leave of absence for disability due to her pregnancy" or from terminating a woman's job due to her pregnancy. An employer must make a reasonable effort to provide a room or other location where a mother can breastfeed in private.

A woman is entitled to file for divorce. Connecticut is a "no fault" state, which means neither party has to prove the other was at fault in causing the marriage to break down.

There are 68,640 women of childbearing age that become pregnant each year in Connecticut. Sixty-three percent of these pregnancies result in live births, and 23 percent result in abortions; the remainder end in miscarriage. Connecticut's teenage pregnancy rate is ranked the 33rd highest of any state in the United States, with 7,420 teenage pregnancies every year.

In 1965, the U.S. Supreme Court's *Griswold v. Connecticut* ruling struck down state laws barring contraceptive use by married couples. There are 432,000 women in Connecticut who are candidates for birth control. Of these, 165,960 women have incomes below the poverty level or are sexually active teenagers. There are 56 publicly funded family planning clinics that provide contraceptive services; the federal and state governments spent $20,788,000 on contraceptive services and supplies in 2001. Connecticut teenagers are not required to consult with their parents prior to obtaining prescription contraceptives. Women with health insurance can get coverage for the cost of prescription contraceptives.

Currently, abortions are legal in Connecticut. Once a fetus is considered viable, abortions are only allowed to preserve a woman's life or health. Most health insurance policies will pay for the cost of having a surgical or medical abortion. A minor can consent to an abortion without notifying or obtaining permission from their parents. However, if the minor is under 16, a licensed provider has to discuss whether to involve the parents.

Since the 1980s, there has been a significant drop in the abortion rate. The abortion rate of women in their 30s did not change significantly, but the abortion rate for women in their 40s increased. Most of the abortions were performed on women in their 20s (nearly 60 percent). Abortions are far more common among unmarried women than married women. The numbers of legal abortions jumped threefold from 1973–84, with 6,770 abortions in 1973 to 21,490 in 1984. From 1985–2005, the rates declined from 21,850 to 16,780. Connecticut has added an "affirmative right to choose" into its state law. This law ensures women's access to previability abortions and would remain in effect even if *Roe v. Wade* (a woman's right to obtain an abortion) were overturned.

Women unable to conceive a baby and who want infertility treatment are covered by most insurance plans with certain limitations.

**See Also:** Abortion; Birth Control; Teen Mothers.

**Bibliography**
Connecticut Breastfeeding Coalition. www.breastfeedingct.org (accessed May 2009).
Connecticut Department of Labor. "Connecticut Family & Medical Leave." http://www.ctdol.state.ct.us/wg wkstnd/fmla/FMLAstatute.pdf (accessed May 2009).
Connecticut State Library Digital Collections. *A Guide to Women's Health Rights in Connecticut.* (2007). http://www.cga.ct.gov/pcsw/Publication%20PDFs/2007/Guide%20to%20Women's%20Health%20Rights%20in%20CT.pdf (accessed May 2009).
Guttmacher Institute. "Connecticut: Contraception Counts." (2006). http://www.guttmacher.org/pubs/state_data/states/connecticut.pdf (accessed May 2009).

Miranda E. Jennings
University of Massachusetts Amherst

# Consumerism and Motherhood

Consumption of goods and services constitutes approximately 70 percent of the Gross Domestic Product (GDP) of the United States. Consumerism, with its focus on consumption, has been one of the drivers of the country's economy. In many ways, it has also driven American society and its people. Mothers are no exception. When a woman becomes pregnant, or otherwise prepares to assume the status of mother through adoption or fostering, she becomes the target of advertisers and marketers selling her an ever-growing list of mothering products and services. When the child arrives, the targeting continues, expands to include the new addition, and follows them both through every stage of their lives. A steady stream of advertisements sends the message that there is a long and constantly increasing list of things that a mother must buy in order to be a good mother, and an equally long list of items that a child must have in order to be cared for properly.

Many activists contend that consumerism has profound negative implications for mothers, children, and the future of human beings. The economic crisis that began in 2008, which many in the United States partly attributed to consumerism propped by a culture of greed and a willingness to go into debt, led to cutbacks in consumer spending and calls for fundamental changes to place less emphasis on consumption. Only time will tell whether or not consumerism will continue to drive the economy of the United States, and with it, motherhood and childhood.

**The Mothering Market**
Mothers control 80 percent of U.S. household spending. They buy about $2 trillion annually in products and services, putting them at the top of the list of the nation's most powerful and sought-after consumers. Since the 19th century, mothers have been the primary purchasers of goods designed to meet household and family needs, including clothes, books, toys, and other commodities for children. In the United States, after World War II, companies that had manufactured prepared foods for the armed forces saw mothers as a substitute market. They redesigned their products and began advertising them to mothers as labor and time-saving devices. During the 1950s and 1960s, advertisers increasingly suggested that "taking care of the family" meant buying things for the family that had previously been homemade—especially food products like cake mixes and TV dinners.

In the 1970s and 1980s, a confluence of factors led to an intensification in marketing to mothers. Record numbers of women with children had entered the workforce and were spending many hours each day away from their children. Highly publicized reports about child abductions, child abuse, children's academic challenges, teen pregnancy, and other risks to children led to growing anxieties about children's safety and well-being, and their prospects for success in what seemed to be an increasingly dangerous and competitive world.

Families had more disposable income, but mothers' growing concerns about their children and varying feelings of guilt about being away from them combined to create fertile ground for advertiser appeals to mothers to buy their good and services. Products were offered as solutions to the problems mothers faced, and were promoted not just for their value in meeting children's basic needs and making mothers' lives easier; they were also advertised for their value in making children happier, enriching their lives, and meeting their developmental needs. Advertisers had all the right products to meet the growing needs they themselves were helping to create. Babies now needed more than the basic stroller and baby clothes. They needed a host of other products, including those with brand names, which were deemed to be of higher quality and thus could be sold at higher prices. Toddlers became a distinct target market. Toys were still sold as playthings, but they were also increasingly sold as tools for learning.

Broadcast and cable television and radio programs, catalogs, mothers' magazines and the child-rearing advice they featured, and the advertisements that supported all of these media carried the message that the good mother is also a good consumer of the array of new products deemed necessary for mothering. Until the 1980s, however, most advertisers treated mothers as the gatekeepers who had to be persuaded to buy products for their children.

That changed with the deregulation of the broadcasting industry. Under President Ronald Reagan, the Federal Communications Commission loosened broadcasting regulations, making it possible for producers to create television programs designed to market toys. The result was an explosion in the number of toy-based children's television programs. In addition, Congress restricted the Federal Trade Commission's authority to regulate marketing to children after the agency considered a ban on advertising to children under the age of 8. In the new deregulatory environment, advertisers set out to bypass mothers and target children directly.

## Childrens' Influence on Consumption

Each year, children and teenagers spend nearly $200 billion, and children under the age of 12 influence purchases worth $500 billion. Corporations spend approximately $17 billion each year marketing to children. It is estimated that children between the ages of 2 and 11 see more than 25,000 advertisements annually on television alone. They are also targeted through marketing on every form of communication including radio, the Internet, video games, cell phones, DVDs, movies, and MP3 players; in schools; and through educational videos and product placements in movies, and TV. Advertisers target children through brand licensing, in which television and movie characters are licensed to sell products; viral or stealth marketing, in which popular children are hired to promote products to other children; and cross promotions, when, for example, a fast food company promotes its meals by giving away a toy based on a movie character.

## Targeting Children

Children today are the targets of marketing not just for children's products. They are also sought after by hotels, car manufacturers, and other companies looking to establish brand loyalties with children that will continue throughout their lives. Children are a leading target demographic because, in addition to making their own purchases, they have a powerful influence over their mothers' and fathers' buying decisions, and they hold great promise as future adult consumers.

The surge in advertising and marketing directly to children began in the 1980s, when experts pointed out that if children were trained as consumers, they would be loyal customers for life. Marketers began what they call "cradle to grave" marketing, starting with children as babies and following them to day care, school, and all stages of their lives in order to shape their consumer appetites.

There has been a dramatic increase in marketing techniques designed to build brand loyalty in babies. Baby clothes routinely feature licensed characters, as do diapers, toys, food products, and a host of other baby items. This effort has been so successful that many babies request brands as soon as they are able to speak. Baby media companies promote their products as "educational," in spite of the fact that there is no reliable evidence to support claims that time spent in front of media screens is good for babies, and notwithstanding the fact that the American Academy of Pediatrics recommends no screen time for children under the age of 2. Toddlers are the targets of highly commercialized Internet sites such as Webkinz and Club Penguin, designed to get little children in the habit of shopping.

Schools are prime targets for corporate sales and the placement of corporate advertising. Marketing messages in schools are delivered to captive audiences of children and implicitly carry the schools' stamp of approval. Many schools sell sodas and low-nutrient snacks through onsite vending machines. Advertising messages, especially for soft drinks, snack foods, and a range of other products are routinely featured on textbooks and other teaching materials, school buses, school walls, gyms, scoreboards, and at sporting events. Every day, Channel One, a TV channel broadcast in approximately 10,000 schools to more than 6 million students, airs programs consisting of two minutes of ads for every 10 minutes of news content, in exchange for free video equipment for the school. Bus Radio delivers programming and marketing messages to school buses across the country. Scholastic, a company with a well-established reputation for selling books through school book clubs, uses its book clubs to sell a wide range of other products, including video games, makeup, and jewelry.

With a growing number of children carrying mobile phones, advertisers are stepping up their efforts to reach children on their cell phones—texting games and other activities to promote their products to children as they go about their daily activities.

The concept of Kids Getting Older Younger, or KGOY—an industry-promoted notion that children are growing up faster today than they did in the past—is used as a rationale for marketing toys designed for older children to toddlers, and highly sexualized clothing to little girls.

In developing their messages, advertisers and marketers rely heavily on the insights of psychology and other behavioral sciences and from children's peers. Psychologists are retained to help companies understand child development and to help them design marketing campaigns that encourage children to want to buy—and to nag their parents until they acquiesce. Anthropologists and other social scientists are enlisted to help companies capitalize on the children's market by doing extensive market research that often includes shadowing children, studying their habits, and recording their reactions to products and messages. Children are hired to advise companies about how to reach other children. The Girls Intelligence Agency, for example, hires popular girls as "secret agent influencer" to give advice to market researchers and to surreptitiously promote products at sleepovers sponsored by corporations.

## The Anticonsumerism Movement

There is a growing movement of activists and advocates raising questions about consumerism in general, and the onslaught of marketing to mothers and children in particular. Some critics of the intense marketing to mothers have argued that it contributes to what Sharon Hays called the ideology of "intensive mothering," and what Susan Douglas and Meredith Michaels described as a "new momism"—a cultural view of mothers that insists that they must be the primary, self-sacrificing caregivers for children, always focused on meeting their needs. Critics contend that this is a coercive ideal of motherhood that sets unattainable standards, unduly limits women's possibilities, and gives rise to profound tensions within mothers. They have called for maternal resistance to the notion that there is only one right way to be a good mother.

Corporate marketing to children has been the subject of increasing activism in recent years, with advocates arguing that it undermines the relationship between parents and children, damages children's health and undercuts their well-being, and contributes to a culture of materialism and greed. They argue that mothers and fathers alone cannot counter the negative effects of the onslaught of marketing and they have called for government regulation.

They point to evidence that suggests that marketing to children contributes to many of the most serious problems facing young people, including childhood obesity, eating disorders, the sexualization of childhood, youth violence, parent–child conflict, and materialism.

Most television ads for food are for products high in fat, salt, or sugar. A 2006 report by the Institute of Medicine found strong evidence of a link between television advertising to children and children's food choices, requests for products, and eating habits. Since the 1970s and 1980s, the rate of obesity among children has increased dramatically. In a study released in 2000, more than 50 percent of boys between the ages of 11 and 17 chose as their ideal a physique that is only attainable through the use of steroids. More than 40 percent of first-to-third grade girls report that they would like to be thinner.

A 2007 report of the American Psychological Association Task Force on the Sexualization of Girls concluded that the increase in sexualized images of girls in advertising and the media was damaging girls' self-image and undermining their healthy development. Young children who are exposed to violent programming are more likely to engage in violent or aggressive behavior as they get older than children who are not exposed to such programming. Parent–child discord has been linked to children's exposure to advertising. A strong and growing body of psychological evidence indicates that children, even preschoolers, who watch a great deal of television tend to be more materialistic than children who do not. Materialistic values are associated with anxiety, depression, substance abuse, and antisocial behavior—and can lead to a consumer identity focused on instant gratification and material things.

## Consumerism and Dehumanization

Activists argue that more than just selling products and services, consumerism promotes a way of looking at the world that emphasizes the material and encourages people to treat each other as objects.

Some scholars, notably Barbara Katz Rothman, have argued that with new reproductive technolo-

*Mothers are the prime target market, as they are the primary purchasers for households. U.S. children are targeted as consumers as soon as they can watch TV; before they are teenagers, they will influence $500 billion worth of purchases annually.*

gies, there is a growing dominance of consumer values in which people are increasingly seen as the sum of their parts. Pointing to examples such as the selling of women's eggs, prenatal testing that serves the function of quality control in the making of babies, surrogacy arrangements, and the prospect of designer babies, they contend that consumerist values are leading to the commodification and dehumanization of human beings. They argue that children are increasingly being seen as products produced by mothers through the work of mothering. They are asking crucial questions about whether we should allow motherhood and children to be redefined in this way, and whether we should as a society continue along this path. There is a growing effort among activists to increase public conversation and debate about the implications of these new reproductive technologies.

**See Also:** Activist Mothering; Capitalism and Motherhood; Economy and Motherhood; Intensive Mothering; Motherhood Project.

**Bibliography**
Bailey, Maria T. and Bonnie W. Ulman. *Trillion Dollar Moms: Marketing to a New Generation of Mothers.* New York: Kaplan Business, 2005.
Campaign for Commercial-Free Childhood. www.commercialfreechildhood.org (accessed July 2009).
Coffey, Tim, David Seigel, and Greg Livingston. *Marketing to the New Super Consumer: Mom & Kid.* Ithaca, NY: Paramount Market Publishing, 2006.
Douglas, Susan J. and Meredith Michaels. *The Mommy Myth: The Idealization of Motherhood and How It Has Undermined Women.* New York: Free Press, 2004.
Linn Susan. *Consuming Kids: Protecting Our Children From the Onslaught of Marketing and Advertising.* New York: Anchor Books, 2004.
Motherhood Project. *Watch Out for Children: A Mothers' Statement to Advertisers.* New York: Institute for American Values, 2001.
Rothman, Barbara Katz. *Recreating Motherhood.* New Brunswick, NJ: Rutgers University Press, 2000.
Schor, Juliet. *Born to Buy.* New York: Scribner, 2004.
Taylor, Janelle, Linda Layne, and Danielle F. Wozniak, eds. *Consuming Motherhood.* New Brunswick, NJ: Rutgers University Press, 2004.
Warner, Judith. *Perfect Madness: Motherhood in the Age of Anxiety.* New York: Riverhead Books, 2006.

Enola Aird
Independent Scholar

# Co-Parenting

Co-parenting is the law's attempt to adapt to the dissolution of a nuclear family and the changing legal status of women and children. The concept of co-parenting emphasizes shared parenting rather than a sole custody model. There is no consensus among legislatures or the legal profession regarding the definition of co-parenting. Co-parenting is also referred to as joint custody, shared parenting, shared custody, and co-custody. The "best interests of the child" standard remains paramount and tends to center on two factors that support co-parenting plans postdivorce/separation: (1) the child's ongoing contact with both parents, and (2) the parents' ability to cooperate in their continuing roles as parents.

Currently, over 2 million parents divorce annually, involving over 1 million children. Co-parenting acknowledges that divorce and separation do not end the legal relationship between parent and child, but rather rearranges the relationship among family members. The term *co-parenting* reflects legal self-determination, whereby both parents are equally empowered by the court, postdivorce/separation, to retain equal legal rights, authority, and responsibility for the care and control of their children.

### Historical Context of Co-Parenting
The concept of the nuclear family was supported during the social and economic upheavals of 19th century industrialization, when the transition to wage labor separated the home and the workplace and encouraged gendered parenting roles. When the early women's rights movement changed the status of women and children, new laws allowed women the right to own property; children came to be seen as developing human beings rather than small adults. The common-law preference for fathers in custody disputes gave way in the late 19th century to a preference for mothers and for children of "tender years."

The legal and social status of women and children again changed during the contemporary women's rights movement. The tender years preference gave way to a preference for gender-neutral custody decisions premised on "the best interests of the child" standard. The best interests of the child, in which mothers often received initial primary or sole custody, became the cornerstone of all state custody statutes beginning in the 1960s—at a time when children's rights became equated with their developmental needs in the areas of health, education, and welfare. The discourse of father's rights, which began to emerge in the 1970s, paved the way for co-parenting. Co-parenting statutes were implemented in the 1980s in response to the demands of fathers. Fathers' rights advocates argue that custody of children is a right of fatherhood, and that children benefit from the support of both parents after divorce.

### Benefits of Co-Parenting

Divorce and separation reconfigure families. When parents engage in co-parenting, children can continue to experience the feelings of love and concern from both parents. Co-parenting can provide stability and continuity of contacts with kinship networks and a better option than sole custody, which left many fathers feeling disenfranchised and many mothers overwhelmed. Co-parenting provides built-in breaks from parenting so those involved have more time for themselves and new relationships.

Co-parenting can provide parents the flexibility to personalize their parenting plan so that it fits the family's unique situation. There is evidence that co-parents are more likely to comply with parenting plans they co-create rather than state-imposed plans. Continuing contact with the other co-parent can provide opportunities for ongoing positive interactions. Successful co-parenting requires commitment, which suggests that co-parents ought to be able to negotiate differences, prioritize and accommodate children's needs, maintain a reasonable level of communication and cooperation, be flexible, and respect the bond between their child and the other parent.

### Co-Parenting Concerns

Research has identified many problems associated with co-custody. Numerous studies find that conflict between co-parents undermines child development and increases the chances for poor child adjustment. If there is continuing hostility, conflict, anger, and the desire to punish the other parent, co-parenting can be challenging. Additionally, a history of family violence (including the emotional and physical abuse of children), women violence, mental pathology, child neglect, and substance abuse have been found to negatively impact co-parenting.

If co-parents cannot trust one another or agree on how to the raise their children, co-parenting can be difficult. Courts can protect a child's basic right to see their noncustodial parent; however, the noncustodial parent is not in contempt of court if they do not follow through and spend their court-allotted time with their child. The court is powerless to order the noncustodial co-parent to pick up their waiting children. Ironically, the court can forcibly remove children, or imprison a custodial parent, if a custodial parent does not allow a noncustodial parent to spend their court-allotted time with their child (even if the custodial parent has legitimate concerns about the behavior of the noncustodial parent and/or if the child does not want to spend time with their noncustodial parent).

Research indicates that co-parenting obscures women's care work and gender-based violence. Battered women's advocates argue that revenge and control are the abuser's motivations for co-parenting. When there is evidence of woman violence, battered women's advocates strongly oppose co-parenting because it gives batterers continued access to their victims. When women separate from former abusive partners, violence often persists or, in some cases, escalates for them and their children. In these cases, co-parenting exposes children to violence and abusive power dynamics and gives the batterer control over the victimized parent. Research suggests that judges continue to fail to take domestic violence seriously and continue to award co-custody to violent men.

Co-parenting policy is premised on the idea that parents' access to children supersedes concern for the safety of women and children and has been applied without sensitivity to gender-based violence. Research on healthy child development has often been interpreted as suggesting that contact with both parents during postseparation is important in all families. Research suggests that contact with both parents postseparation may not meet the "best interest" standard if violence against women and children occurs. Violence against women and children are public health concerns and violations of human rights, and victim advocates have argued that co-parenting policies that enable the continued abuse of women and child should be amended.

**See Also:** Care Giving; Child Custody and the Law; Children; Co-Mothering; Divorce; Ethics of Care; Father's Rights Movement; Fathers and Fathering; Future of Motherhood; Intensive Mothering; Mothering as Work; Sociology of Motherhood; Violence Against Mothers/Children.

### Bibliography

Chesler, P. "Mothers on Trial: The Custodial Vulnerability of Women." *Feminism & Psychology*, v.1 (1991).

Featherstone, B. "Taking Mothering Seriously: The Implications for Child Protection." *Child and Family Social Work*, v.4 (1999).

Griswold, Robert. *Fatherhood in America: A History*. New York: Basic Books, 1994.

Hardesty, J. L. "Separation Assault in the Context of Post Divorce Parenting: An Integrative Review of the Literature." *Violence Against Women*, v.8 (2002).

Maccoby, E., C. Depner, and R. Mnookin. "Coparenting in the Second Year After Divorce." *Journal of Marriage and the Family*, v.52 (1990).

Mason, Mary Ann. *From Father's Property to Children's Rights: A History of Child Custody in the United States*. New York: Columbia University Press, 1999.

Mills, L.G. "Killing Her Softly: Intimate Abuse and the Violence of State Intervention." *Harvard Law Review*, v.113 (1999).

Varcoe, C., and L. Irwin. "If I Killed You, I'd Get the Kids: Women's Survival and Protection Work With Child Custody and Access in the Context of Woman Abuse." *Qualitative Sociology*, v.27/1 (2004).

Lynn Comerford
California State University, East Bay

# Costa Rica

Located in Central America, the Republic of Costa Rica was ruled by Spain until independence in 1821, joining the United Provinces of Central America, and becoming an independent republic in 1838. With an economy based on agriculture, and also textiles—and recently tourism, from 1870 until 1899 it was ruled by a liberal government, and in 1936 the government started establishing a social program which quickly made it the envy of the region.

Less than half (46.1 percent) of women age 15 and over in Costa Rica were in the labor force in 2006, and their employment-to-population ratio was 41.9. Women are entitled to four months of maternity leave at 100 percent of salary.

Abortion is legal in Costa Rica only if necessary to save the life of the woman or preserve her mental or physical health. The woman must consent to the abortion, and it must be performed by a physician or midwife. The punishment for providing an illegal abortion is up to 10 years imprisonment.

### Mothers' Roles

Traditionally, babies were born at home and the care of the mother and children was the responsibility of the immediate family, with help from the extended family. For the most part, women remain involved in bringing up children, preparing food, and looking after the house. This has come to be symbolized in the ideal of *marianismo*—where wives and mothers are expected to be loyal, submissive, and chaste, with a woman's virtue apparent through her self-sacrifice. However, in elite families, where intermarriage is probably the most extensive in the region, some women have been able to establish their own careers. The impetus for this was said to have started in 1903 with the establishment of the Colegio Superior de Senoritas, the first modern girls' school. Many of the former students then worked as teachers and care givers for the young, sick, and infirm, further encouraging the role of mothers sharing their domestic responsibilities with participation in the workforce. There have also been women running businesses and in politics. In recent years it has been estimated that a quarter of children in Costa Rica are born to parents who are not married, and about a fifth of Costa Rican families are headed by a single mother.

What distinguishes Costa Rica from so many other countries in Central America is its health care system. Tropical diseases have been largely eradicated, and 7.3 percent of the Gross Domestic Product (GDP) is spent on health. There are 132 doctors, 92 nurses, one midwife, and 140 hospital beds per 100,000 people. The death rate of 4.7 per 1,000 and a life expectancy of 79.7 for females are some of the best in the region. The infant mortality rate of 9.7 per 1,000 live births is about a third of that in neighboring Nicaragua. Save the Children ranks Costa Rica highly among tier II or less developed countries, placing it eighth on the Mothers' Index, 12th on the Women's Index, and 18th on the Children's Index.

**See Also:** Abortion; Nicaragua; Panama; Spain.

**Bibliography**
Lettinger, I.A. *The Costa Rican Women's Movement: A Reader.* Pittsburgh, PA: University of Pittsburgh Press, 1997.
Noonan, Rita K. "Gender and the Politics of Needs: Broadening the Scope of Welfare State Provision in Costa Rica." *Gender and Society*, v.16/2 (April 2002).
Palmer, Steven, and Gladys Rojas Chaves. "Educating Señorita: Teacher Training, Social Mobility, and the Birth of Costa Rican Feminism 1885–1925." *The Hispanic American Historical Review*, v.78/1 (February 1998).
Pearcy, Thomas L. *The History of Central America.* Westport, CT: Greenwood Press, 2006.

Justin Corfield
Geelong Grammar School, Australia

# Crittenden, Ann

Ann Crittenden is a journalist and author. She has written for *Fortune*, *Newsweek*, and the *New York Times*, and has published in many periodicals including the *Los Angeles Times*, the *Wall Street Journal*, and the *Washington Post*. Crittenden is best known for her book on the economic effects of motherhood, *The Price of Motherhood: Why the Most Important Job in the World Is Still the Least Valued.*

Born in 1937 and a native of Dallas, TX, Crittenden is part of the Texas tradition of strong women like journalist Molly Ivins and politician Ann Richards. She earned a B.A. from Southern Methodist University, an M.A. from Columbia University School of International Affairs, and left the Ph.D.

program in Modern European History at Columbia as ABD (All But Dissertation).

Crittenden's journalism background includes writing for a daily newspaper as well as weekly and monthly magazines. She worked for the *New York Times* from 1975 to 1983. Her series on world hunger was nominated for a Pulitzer Prize. She served as a foreign correspondent and financial writer for *Newsweek*, as well as a reporter for *Fortune*. Through these experiences, Crittenden learned the craft of writing and how to write quickly and thoughtfully.

Her academic background also provided opportunities for Crittenden. She served as moderator for a lecture series on economics in New York City, and led a seminar on the global economy at the Aspen Institute. Crittenden has also been a visiting lecturer at MIT and Yale.

**Crittenden's Mother Career**
With the birth of her son in 1982, Crittenden's career slowed drastically. She had to choose between 10-hour days at the *New York Times* and time at home with her son. Crittenden chose her son, and left her position at the *New York Times*. One evening at a party in New York, someone stopped her and asked if she used to be Ann Crittenden. At this point, Crittenden realized she needed to write about mothers and the workplace.

In *The Price of Motherhood*, Crittenden combines her research and writing skills with her personal experience. Her book brings to the forefront the issues of discrimination based on family responsibility. Crittenden exposes the discrepancies in work and economics for mothers and highlights the economic risks of motherhood. She proposes a dollar value for maternal work and introduces the idea of the "mommy tax," which is the amount of lifetime income lost by women after they have children. For college-educated women, this amount can be over $1 million, and for other women, it can range between $600,000 and $700,000.

Crittenden began writing *The Price of Motherhood* in the mid-1990s, when motherhood was not part of progressive feminism. Since the book's inception and publication, issues surrounding motherhood have become part of the feminist agenda as well as a focus of public policy. States now have paid family leave and insurance, whereas none did when Crittenden wrote the book. Another change came with the new attitude that motherhood should be considered serious work, a respected profession, and not something that keeps women from other things in life. Crittenden considers *The Price of Motherhood* her most satisfying work, because it resonates with so many women.

## Other Publications

In 2004, Crittenden published *If You've Raised Kids, You Can Manage Anything: Leadership Begins at Home*, a follow-up work to *The Price of Motherhood*. In this book, Crittenden highlights the similarities between working at home raising children and working in an office. She focuses on leadership lessons in caregiving and the transferable skills of child rearing.

Crittenden has also published other books. In 1988, she released *Sanctuary: A Story of American Conscience and the Law in Collision*, which was a *New York Times* Notable Book. *Killing the Sacred Cows: Bold Ideas for a New Economy* came out in 1993.

Crittenden also serves in organizations that pursue the type of change that inspires her writing. She has served as executive director of the Fund for Investigative Journalism in Washington, D.C., and was a member of the Council on Foreign Relations. She also serves on the board of the International Center for Research on Women. In 2002, she jointly founded MOTHERS (Mothers Ought to Have Equal Rights) with other advocates and the National Association of Mothers' Centers. MOTHERS is a nonprofit group dedicated to economic equality for caregivers.

**See Also:** National Association of Mothers' Centers; *Price of Motherhood* (Crittenden); Public Policy and Mothers.

## Bibliography

Ann Crittenden Website. www.anncrittenden.com (accessed December 2008).

Crittenden, Ann. *If You've Raised Kids, You Can Manage Anything: Leadership Begins at Home*. New York: Gotham Books-Penguin, 2004.

Crittenden, Ann. *The Price of Motherhood: Why the Most Important Job in the World Is Still the Least Valued*. New York: Metropolitan Books, 2001.

Mothers Ought To Have Equal Rights (MOTHERS). www.mothersoughttohaveequalrights.org (accessed December 2008).

Roshaunda D. Cade
Webster University

# Croatia

Croatia—until 1991 a part of Yugoslavia—has a population of 4.5 million (2008 estimate), with a female life expectancy of 78.5 years. It has a birth rate of 9.6 per 1,000, and an infant mortality rate of 6.7 per 1,000 live births. The crude divorce rate in the country is 1.12 divorces per 1,000 marriages (2004 estimate). In 2006, 44.6 percent of women aged 15 and older in Croatia were in the labor force, and their employment-to-population ratio was 38.3.

Croatia provides mandatory maternal leave from 28 days before the expected date of birth to 42 days following the actual birth; the leave may be extended until the child is 1 year old. After the 42nd day after birth, the father can take work leave in place of the mother. Mothers receive 100 percent of their salary until the child is 6 months old.

Abortion is available upon request in Croatia; the woman certifies in writing that she wants an abortion, and must receive counseling at least six days prior to the procedure.

In traditional Croatian societies, motherhood was a task shared by the mother and members of her extended family. Although help from midwives could be provided in towns, access was much more limited in the rural areas.

The Venetians managed to hold much of coastal Croatia, parts of which were later controlled by Austria. During the Napoleonic Wars, the French occupied the region, and health services were dramatically improved in the cities. From the 1750s, it has been possible to trace the rates of maternal mortality using parish records, which researchers Hammel and Gullickson were able to do. Their research showed clearly that women marrying into large extended families had a far greater chance to survive childbirth, a trend that continued through to the 1890s.

The role of mothers continued to center on bringing up children, preparing food, and looking after the house and crops, which resulted in few women able to develop careers of their own. A Croatian-born citizen with a Croation father, Josip Tito described how his mother, herself a Slovene, spent much of her time desperately trying to ensure there was enough food for the family; she herself was from a family of 14.

There was some attempt to improve the health care provision and midwifery services during the 1920s and 1930s, but this was largely restricted to cities. It was not until the 1950s and 1960s that the Yugoslav government was able to introduce measures to reduce the infant and maternal mortality rates. With better education for girls, and some women managing to enter professions with others taking factory or farm work, there was a trend toward having smaller families, which has continued to the present day. Despite Croatia remaining overwhelmingly Roman Catholic, it has a low fertility rate—in 2002 it was 1.4, only slightly higher in much of the rest of eastern Europe.

The percentage of extramarital births has risen during the same period from 4.9 percent, to 8.2 percent, the lowest in Europe. The divorce rate in 1999 was 0.13, also one of the lowest in Europe. Save the Children ranks Croatia 34h among 41 tier I or more developed countries on the Mothers' Index, 26th on the Women's Index, and 35th on the Children's Index.

**See Also:** Bosnia and Herzegovina; Eurpean Union; Hungary; War and Mothering.

**Bibliography**
Caldwell, John C. and Thomas Schindlmayr. "Explanations of the Fertility Crisis in Modern Societies: A Search for Commonalities." *Population Studies*, v.57/3 (November 2003).
Commission for International Relations of the Federation of Women's Associations of Yugoslavia. *Women's Rights in Yugoslavia*. Commission for International Relations of the Federation of Women's Associations of Yugoslavia, 1961.
Duric, Suzana and Gordana Dragicevic. *Women in Yugoslav Society and Economy*. Belgrade: Medunarodna Politika, 1965.
Hammel, E.A. and Aaron Gullickson. "Kinship Structures and Survival: Maternal Mortality on the Croatian-Bosnian Border 1750–1898." *Population Studies*, v.58/2 (2004).
Kohler, Hans-Peter, Francesco C. Billari, and Jose Antonio Ortega. "The Emergence of Lowest-Low Fertility in Europe During the 1990s." *Population and Development Review*, v.28/4 (December 2002).
Ramet, Sabrina, ed. *Gender Politics in the Western Balkans: Women and Society in Yugoslavia and the Yugoslav Successor States*. University Park: Pennsylvania State University Press, 1999.

Justin Corfield
Geelong Grammar School, Australia

# Cross-Cultural Perspectives on Motherhood

Motherhood is an important status recognized in all societies and a position most women hold. In many cultures, becoming a mother is a primary means to increase a woman's social status. However, tremendous cross-cultural variation exists in the meaning and practice of motherhood. Certain aspects of motherhood, such as childbirth, have a referent in biology; however, the meaning and practice of motherhood are mediated through culture. While mothering is often assumed to be a natural role determined by biology, it has developed in specific social contexts and in conjunction with various networks of other relationships, duties, and activities that influence the meaning and practice of motherhood.

There are no universal beliefs or practices of motherhood; from conception to childcare, the ethnographic record shows extensive diversity between different cultures. Even within specific societies, motherhood varies according to such groupings as race, class, and ethnicity.

## Conception and Childbirth
Motherhood is often viewed as a natural, universal role determined by biological processes. However, the meaning of such phenomena as childbirth varies cross-culturally. There are notable differences,

for instance, in how cultures define conception. Among Trobriand Islanders of the Pacific, a fetus is conceived from the mother's blood and the spirit of a matrilineal ancestor returning from the island of Tuma; fathers have no significant role in conception. In the West, the spread of assisted reproduction (e.g., in vitro fertilization, surrogacy, etc.) has challenged how motherhood is defined. Where conception once involved one man and one woman, as many as five individuals (social parents, egg donor, sperm donor, and gestational surrogate) may now be directly involved in conception, thereby complicating the definition of motherhood. For instance, in a famous 1998 California case, *Buzzanca v. Buzzanca*, Jaycee Buzzanca was deemed parentless when four of the five individuals involved in her conception refused legal and financial responsibility for her.

Beliefs regarding the appropriate manner of childbirth also vary cross-culturally. In some societies, childbirth is considered a time when the mother is temporarily "unclean" (as in Old Testament times, described in Leviticus 12:1-8). Alternately, the child may be polluted through birth, as the Hua of Papua New Guinea believe. In Japan, women are expected to be silent as they give birth; loud vocalizations or expressions of pain are considered shameful.

Gender stratification and stereotypes are reflected in each society's birthing beliefs and practices. Childbirth in North America has become medicalized, often treated as if it were a disease; hospital births managed by experts are the norm. Such expectations differ dramatically from the relatively solitary process of African Ju'hoansi women, as described in Marjorie Shostak's *Nisa* (1981). There, women gave birth alone or were attended by a small number of close kin. In each case, the act of giving birth reflects the core values and worldview of each society.

Varying childbirth experiences also impact infant and maternal mortality internationally, and the delivery of services through such programs as the Safe Motherhood Initiative. Poverty, limited access to health services, and reliance on potentially harmful traditional practices can lead to higher rates of maternal mortality in developing countries. The idea of motherhood maybe praised, but actual mothers may suffer due to poverty or stratification.

*The North American mothering ideal is of self-sacrifice and nurture, but mothering practices vary widely across cultures.*

## Mothering Ideology

In North America, good mothering is defined by intensive, child-centered caregiving, nurturing, and selflessness. Mothers are expected to love unconditionally and freely sacrifice for their children. Ethnographic research, however, shows that not all cultures define motherhood in the same way. Scheper-Hughes demonstrates in her 1992 account of women in a Brazilian shantytown that "[m]other love is anything *other* than natural and instead represents a matrix of images, meanings, sentiments, and practices that are everywhere socially and culturally produced." Scholars have argued that women are often defined in the West primarily as objects of infant attachment, rather than active subjects, but cross-cultural studies show that motherhood is linked to a variety of milieu. Kathleen

Barlow, in her 2004 article "Critiquing the 'Good Enough' Mother" in *Ethos*, states, "Anthropological studies have dramatically underscored the fact that women almost never devote their attention and energy solely to mothering, and that mothering needs to be understood in the context of other roles, relationships, and activities." Patricia Hill Collins highlights how mothering is affected by race and ethnicity. Motherwork occurs in specific times and places, thus, "racial domination and economic exploitation profoundly shape the mothering context, not only for racial ethnic women in the United States, but for all women."

### Mothering Practice

As primary caretakers of children, mothers play a key role in sustaining and transmitting culture. Practices vary widely and have a profound effect on childhood socialization. Ruth Benedict, in her 1989 book *The Chrysanthemum and the Sword*, demonstrated that how mothers treat their children and interact with them reinforces roles, values, and worldview; in short, culture. Mothers are taught core social values and they in turn relate those values and worldview to their children through such parenting practices as feeding, sleeping arrangements, conversation, and play. In *Maternal Thinking* (1989), Sara Ruddick sites practice as a key to defining motherhood cross-culturally; that is, women become mothers because they carry out the tasks of mothering. Therefore, where practices vary, motherhood does as well.

The amount of time that infants spend in close physical contact with mothers varies widely. Again, among Ju/'hoansi and Mbuti foragers of Africa, children are held constantly and feed upon demand. North American mothers interact and converse with their children regularly, but some child rearing experts warn of "spoiling" children or encouraging dependence by being too responsive to children's cries or co-sleeping. Mayan mothers did not spend time teaching, playing with, or talking to their infants. Their job was to simply keep infants safe and quiet. Japanese mothers, conversely, use teasing to instruct children and teach core values of restraint and conformity.

Subsistence strategies, access to resources, and poverty also impact the practice of motherhood.

Cross-culturally, mothers deal with challenges to their children's survival in various ways. Poor Brazilian mothers must learn to make difficult decisions about the distribution of scarce resources. Children who fail to thrive are neglected, allowing mothers to focus on family members more likely to survive.

### Work and Mothering

Women's entrance into wage labor affects maternal practice in multiple ways. For example, in many regions, matriarchal and female-headed households have increased in size and importance. Such households function without contributions from husbands or fathers, who migrate to find wage labor (as often happens in southern Africa) or abandon their families due to economic hardships. The international feminization of poverty creates environmental and material constraints to motherhood practice. In Tanzania, one must have dependants in order to achieve adult status; women most often do this through mothering. Today, becoming a mother can mean that a woman must take on the sole responsibility of providing for her children and grandchildren. Mothers work and devote their incomes almost entirely to the household. Throughout much of East Africa, mothers are expected to provide for all of their children's basic needs; therefore, work is closely bound to the definition of motherhood. Conversely, in the United States, work is generally defined as antithetical to, or in competition with motherhood.

The broad responsibilities associated with mothering demonstrate the diversity and multifaceted characteristics of motherhood cross-culturally. Motherhood is part of a triple burden (wage labor, domestic labor, and childcare) women carry as they negotiate rapidly changing economies, which requires them to meet traditional expectations and shoulder new burdens such as wage labor. Mothers must respond to a multitude of problems, from failing infrastructures and disease to globalization, in culturally specific ways.

**See Also:** Aboriginal Mothering; African American Mothers; Becoming a Mother; Class and Mothering; Collins, Patricia Hill; Economy and Motherhood; Employment and Motherhood; Ethnic Mothers; Globalization; Maternal Health; Maternal Practice; Matrifocality; Safe Motherhood Initiative.

## Bibliography

Arendell, Terry. "Conceiving and Investigating Motherhood: The Decade's Scholarship." *Journal of Marriage and the Family*, v.62 (2000).

Barlow, Kathleen. "Critiquing the 'Good Enough' Mother: A Perspective Based on the Murik of Papua New Guinea." *Ethos*, v.32/4 (2004).

Benedict, Ruth. *The Chrysanthemum and the Sword.* New York: Houghton Mifflin, 1989.

Collins, Patricia Hill. *Black Feminist Thought: Knowledge, Consciousness and the Politics of Empowerment.* London: Unwin Hyman, 1991.

Davis-Floyd, Robbie. *Birth as an American Rite of Passage.* Berkeley: University of California Press, 1992.

Glenn, E.N., G. Chang, and L.R. Forcey, eds. *Mothering: Ideology, Experience, and Agency.* New York: Routledge, 1994.

Hrdy, Sarah B. *Mother Nature.* New York: Pantheon Books, 1999.

Meigs, Anna. *Food, Sex and Pollution. New Brunswick*, NJ: Rutgers University Press, 1991.

Ragone, Helena and Frances Winddance Twine, ed. *Ideologies and Technologies of Motherhood.* New York: Routledge, 2000.

Ruddick, Sara. *Maternal Thinking.* Boston: Beacon Press, 1989.

Schalge, Susan. "Who Compares to Mother (Nani Kama Mama)?" *Journal of the Association for Research on Mothering*, v.6/2 (2004).

Scheper-Hughes, N. *Death Without Weeping: The Violence of Everyday Life in Brazil.* Berkeley: University of California Press, 1992.

Shostak, Marjorie. *Nisa.* New York: Vintage 1981.

Small, Meredith. *Our Babies, Ourselves.* New York: Anchor, 1998.

Susan L. Schalge
Minnesota State University, Mankato

# Cuba

The Republic of Cuba has the lowest fertility and highest rate of contraceptive use in Latin America. Social programs provide universal health care and access to daycare. Divorce rates are among the world's highest and consensual unions are common.

Women have primary responsibility for childcare and housework despite high labor force participation. Spanish colonialism and Catholicism influence traditional gender roles. Educational attainment is high. Social reforms guarantee women's right to education, work, paid maternity leave, childcare, and abortion, and marriage is an equitable partnership under the Family Code.

Cuba's rate of 1.4 children per mother is comparable to many advanced nations. Low fertility is attributable to high rates of labor force participation and educational attainment, free access to birth control, and legalized abortion. The government provides 18 weeks of fully paid maternity leave. Under the Family Code, poor mothers are guaranteed adequate food and access to daycare and family doctors. One of the world's highest divorce rates, early pregnancy, and consensual unions—which the most common type of partner relationship—contribute to a high number of female-headed households. Fewer than 60 percent of Cuban couples marry. Families are defined by blood relations and extended families are typical.

Spanish colonization and the Catholic Church influenced the ideology of *marianismo* (exalted selfless motherhood) in pre-revolutionary Cuba. After the Cuban Revolution in 1959, women were expected to join the work force. Marriage is an equitable partnership under the Family Code established in 1975, but traditional gender roles persist in respect to responsibility for childcare and the division of labor. The Family Code regulates all aspects of family life, including child support and child custody. Men are legally responsible for their children born in or outside of marriage, but many Cuban fathers do not support or raise their children.

Roman Catholicism is the dominant religion, but many West African religious traditions brought by slaves, such as *Santeria*, are practiced. Many Cubans, especially the poor, superimpose Catholic practices over West African religious traditions, such as reverence of the Virgin Mary. In recent years, more middle-class Cubans have embraced traditional practices.

Unlike elsewhere in Latin America, the Catholic Church's opposition to abortion and contraception has not influenced public family planning policies or practices. Cuban women have a legal right to obtain birth control and abortion. Widespread availability of contraceptives contributes to the highest rate of modern contraceptive use in Latin America and the Caribbean, at 72 percent. Under the universal health care system, all women have access to prenatal care and skilled birth attendants.

Girls are expected to complete 16 years of formal schooling; 88 percent of girls are enrolled in secondary education. Women comprise 61 percent of university enrollment. The creation of the Federation of Cuban Women (FMC) in 1960 and associated social reforms established women's rights to education, paid work and maternity leave, childcare, and abortion.

Vilma Espin played a prominent role in the Cuban Revolution and was the longtime head of the FMC. Ms. Espin, who was the wife of acting president Raul Castro with whom she had four children, was often described as Cuba's First Lady.

**See Also:** Activist Mothers; African Diaspora; Postcolonialism and Motherhood.

**Bibliography**

Estrada, Ana Vera and Teresa Diaz Canals. "Family, Marriage, and Households in Cuba." In *Families in a Global Context*, Charles B. Hennon and Stephan M. Wilson, eds. New York: Routledge/Taylor & Francis, 2008.

Roschelle, Anne R., Maura I. Toro-Morn, and Elisa Facio. "Families in Cuba: From Colonialism to Revolution." In *Handbook of World Families*, Bert N. Adams and Jan Trost, eds. Thousand Oaks, CA: Sage, 2005.

Keri L. Heitner
University of Phoenix

# Cultural Bearing

Nobel Prize-winning African American author, editor, mother, and professor Toni Morrison identifies four interrelated tasks and responsibilities of motherwork: preservation, nurturance, cultural bearing, and healing, according to Canadian feminist maternal scholar, mother, and professor Andrea O'Reilly. Morrison coined the phrase *cultural bearing* to name the specific consideration and attention that African American mothers give to promoting and ensuring the physical and psychological well-being and empowerment of African American people and the wider African American culture in their work as parents. Cultural bearing is essential to the thought and practice of a black motherhood that preserves, protects, and empowers black children in ways that affords children the ability to resist harmful racist practices. Cultural bearing is a form of nurturance that helps children develop a loved sense of themselves and to see themselves as worthy and deserving of love in society. By imparting positive and affirming images of black people and their history, mothers who practice cultural bearing assist in reducing their children's internalization of racist depictions, and foster a strong, healthy, and authentic sense of themselves as black people.

## Motherline

Cultural bearing is closely connected with the *motherline*, a term created by Anglo-American Jewish poet, author, feminist, and Jungian psychologist Naomi Lowinsky. The motherline connects mothers to their female ancestors and helps them understand how their life stories are linked with previous generations of women in their families and cultures. Motherlines help mothers gain female authority in various ways through exposure to an embodied knowledge of mothering; journeying back to their female roots through encounters with ancestor women who struggled with challenges of mothering; a life-cycle perspective and a worldview of interconnectivity; and opportunities of reclaiming female perspectives that consider how women and men are similar and different.

According to O'Reilly, within the context of African American mothering, black mothers pass on ancestral memories and ancient properties to their children and others through their motherlines. Motherlines help mothers teach children the skills of survival, independence, and the importance of remembering one's history and culture. Through their mother's stories, teachings, mentoring, advocating, and advising, children connect with their cultural, familial, and heritage traditions. Cultural bearing also serves to ensure African American people link with and retain their humanity in the world. Daughters develop and nurture their female subjectivity and creativity by identifying with their mothers and relating with their motherline. Sons nurture and sustain themselves in ways that enable them to transcend racism and grow into manhood whole and complete. While the relationship between a mother and her daughter is different from that with her son, the involvement of a child's mother and the presence of a motherline are crucial to both a boy's and girl's maturation.

Just as motherlines and the practice of cultural bearing help African American women claim authority and ground their knowledge and practices of mothering, motherlines and cultural bearing are equally germane to the motherwork and lives of feminist mothers. According to Fiona Joy Green, Canadian feminist mother, professor, and maternal scholar, feminist motherlines assist women in reclaiming their feminist mothering authority, uniting with agender-based worldview; grounding their knowledge and the knowledge of other feminist mothers; providing and strengthening a foundation for their ongoing political activism as feminist mothers; and creating a legacy of feminist mothering and motherwork for others.

Like African American mothers who practice cultural bearing by linking with and passing on their African American humanity, history, and culture to their children, feminist mothers practice cultural bearing by drawing upon their feminist motherlines to model feminist identities, culture, and strategies for living. These feminist maternal practices also include teaching children the crucial lessons and skills of critical awareness, survival, and independence.

**See Also:** Collins, Patricia Hill; Empowered Mothering; Feminist Mothering; Intensive Mothering; Maternal Thinking; Maternal Pedagogy; Morrison, Toni; Mothering Versus Motherhood; Motherline; Motherwork; Patriarchal Ideology of Motherhood; Ruddick, Sara.

**Bibliography**
Green, Fiona J. "Developing a Feminist Motherline: Reflections on a Decade of Feminist Parenting." *Journal for Research on Mothering*, v.8/1/2 (2006).

Lowinsky, Naomi R. *Stories From the Motherline*. New York: Jeremy P. Tarcher, 1992.
O'Reilly, Andrea. "Introduction." In *Maternal Thinking Philosophy, Politics, Practice*, Sara Ruddick, ed. Toronto: Demeter Press, 2009.
O'Reilly, Andrea. *Toni Morrison and Motherhood: A Politics of the Heart*. Albany: State University of New York, 2004.
Ruddick, Sara. *Maternal Thinking: Towards a Politics of Peace*. Boston: Beacon Press, 1989.
Wylie-Wong, Gina. "Images and Echoes in Matroreform: A Cultural Feminist Perspective." *Journal for Research on Mothering*, v.8/1/2.

Fiona Joy Green
University of Winnipeg

# Cybermothering

Cybermothering refers to the Internet-hosted exchange of stories and information about mothering and motherhood. Mothers who participate in cybermothering communities tend to be those with babies and infant children. They are termed *cybermothers*: mothers who use parenting Websites as a source of support and information about the health, rearing, and mothering of infant children. As well as seeking information, cybermothers around the world share stories and experiences with other mothers within online Website communities. An increasing number of women also post their stories and experiences on online blog sites called mommy blogs.

The increasing use of the Internet by cybermothers as a source of information, and a space in which mothers can exchange opinions, reflects the general increase in Internet use as a source of health and parenting information. Many Internet discussion spaces on cybermothering are designed and facilitated by major commercial organizations, which offer community discussion spaces for cybermothers, in addition to offering advice and advertising baby products. A rise has also been observed among more informal mothering Websites maintained by community groups, charities, and individual bloggers.

## The Expert Antidote

The advent of cybermothering has been identified as an antidote to traditional, "expert" parenting texts. Traditional guides on how to mother have been criticized for idealizing motherhood, and offering prescriptive guidance about how perfect mothers should behave. Expert texts on mothering have been identified by feminist scholars such as Jane Ribbens as a source of oppression for mothers. This is because such texts are argued to perpetuate notions that mothering should come naturally to women, failing to acknowledge that mothering can be tiring and challenging. Similarly, formal health advice offered by government agencies has been censured for failing to provide adequate information and support for new mothers, and for setting mothering standards that are argued to be impractical and oppressive.

By contrast, cybermothering has been defined as a source of empowerment for some mothers, partly because the Internet offers access to new and varied sources of support and information. As Caroline Gatrell has observed, cybermothering Websites and online discussion facilities enable the difficulties of pregnancy, and the sometimes problematic transition to motherhood, to be acknowledged.

In addition, cybermothering means that maternal correspondents can choose to remain anonymous, which allows mothers the freedom to share (sometimes negative) feelings and to express their parenting worries without fear of opprobrium from health visitors or other experts. Mothers are therefore more likely to seek reassurance online and talk about embarrassing issues than they might be in front of health professionals. Thus, as Clare Madge and Henrietta O'Connor have pointed out in their work on cybermothering, online discussion forums can allow participants the freedom to talk about motherhood away from the social gaze. Cybermothering is also seen as a positive way to reduce mothers' sense of isolation and feelings of loneliness when they are at home with infant, sick, or disabled children.

However, Madge and O'Connor have observed how mainstream commercial cybermothering Websites may be problematic in certain respects. For example, these writers note how mainstream Websites can perpetuate the conventional notion of mothers as heterosexual and in couple relationships. However, the growth of identity-based spaces, such as gay and minority ethnic communities, has been identified as a counter to traditional parenting and gender norms. It is also noted that impoverished women with no access to Internet facilities and/or without literacy skills cannot turn to the Internet for support.

## Yummy and Slummy Mummies

In addition to mainstream Websites, the number of mommy blogs available (either as part of commercial Websites or as independent initiatives) has proliferated. The idea of the Yummy Mummy is associated with middle-class motherhood and the notion that "good" mothers are able to perform the role of motherhood adeptly, while also looking elegant and taking responsibility for household labor, even if they are also engaged in paid work.

Mommy blogs often make fun of the figure of Yummy Mummy. Especially since the publication of Fiona Neill's book *Slummy Mummy*, women writing mommy blogs and women corresponding on (often informal) cybermothering sites enjoy sharing the embodied experiences of mothering babies and infant children. Slummy Mummy blogs and online discussion groups focus on the difficulties and humorous aspects of dealing with feeding babies and infants, diaper changing, childhood illness, and household clutter. While still often associated with middle-class women and heterosexual norms, Slummy Mummy Websites nevertheless resist idealized notions of good mothering. Instead of posturing for personal elegance and/or domestic perfection, Slummy Mummies celebrate practical and relaxed styles of clothing, and acknowledge the household clutter and chaos associated with infant children.

**See Also:** Childcare; Internet and Mothering; Mommy Blogs; Mothers Movement Online.

## Bibliography

Friedman, May and Shana Calixte, eds. *Mothering and logging: The Radical of the Mommy Blog.* Toronto: Demeter Press, 2009.

Madge, C. and H. O'Connor. "Mothers in the Making? Exploring Liminality in Cyber/space." *Transactions of the Institute of British Geography,* v.30 (2005).

Madge, C. and H. O'Connor. "Parenting Gone Wired: Empowerment of New Mothers on the Internet?" *Social and Cultural Geography,* v.7 (2006).

Neill, F. *Slummy Mummy*. New York: Penguin, 2007.
Phoenix, A., A. Woollett, and E. Lloyd, eds. *Motherhood: Meanings, Practices and Ideologies*. Thousand Oaks, CA: Sage, 1991.
Ribbens, J. *Mothers and Their Children: A Feminist Sociology of Childrearing*. Thousand Oaks, CA: Sage, 1994.

Caroline Gatrell
Lancaster University Management School

# Cyprus

Cyprus, a former British colony, became independent in 1960 following years of resistance to British rule. The island of Cyprus is divided into the Turkish Republic of Northern Cyprus and the Republic of Cyprus, and are separated by a buffer zone (the Green Line) controlled by the United Nations. This division has its roots in ethnic strife between the Turks and Greeks, and became solidified in 1974 after Turkey invaded and occupied about 40 percent of the island. Only the Greek-controlled Republic of Cyprus, a member of the European Union since 2004, is recognized internationally.

Cypriot life revolves around the central social institution of the patriarchal family with the father enjoying controlling power over the behavior of the other members of the family, especially women, as the preordained "order of things," legitimized by the religious attitudes and beliefs of the Greek Orthodox Church, which exercise a strong influence on the sexual attitudes and behavior of the people. Working wives and mothers are a relatively new phenomenon in Turkish Cypriot society. Until the post-1974 period, only a handful of women worked outside the home and even fewer had professional educations. After the 1974 war, this traditional arrangement lost its importance, and women's participation in the workforce became vital to meeting their families' needs. The male figure continued to have a strong decision-making role, as the wife became more involved in the family's economic and social choices.

Urbanization and modernization have altered Greek Cypriot attitudes toward marriage. The extension of education has meant that boys and girls meet from an early age and are exposed to modern ideas about social and sexual relations. The large growth in the number of women in the workforce also has released them from strict parental control.

From 1985 to 1989, the country's marriage rate was 9.5 per 1,000, the highest in Europe. Divorce was legal. During most of the 1980s, there was an increase in the number of divorces, from 149 in 1980 to 177 in 1987. The numbers of marriages went from 1,058 in 1981 to 1,162 in 1987.

## Population Growth and Contraception

At the end of the 1980s, Cyprus families had an average of 2.4 children, the highest in western Europe. In the 1970s, the reverse had been the case. Migration and a decline in the number of births resulted in a negative growth rate of minus 0.9 percent in 1973–76. From 1976 to 1982, while the economy was being restructured, population growth reached an average rate of 0.8 percent, and in 1984 it peaked at 1.4 percent. In the second half of the 1980s, the growth rate remained above 1 percent.

Contraceptives were available at conservative cost all over the island; abortions, widely carried out in private clinics, were seen not as matters of moral or religious controversy, but merely as a different means of family planning or as a last resort. Cypriot males believe that male contraceptives render lovemaking unnatural and unenjoyable. Thus, contraception ends up being the responsibility of women.

By 1995, women's employment was 38.6 percent of the total, as compared to 35.17 percent in 1985. In education, the ratio of girls was equal to that of boys, with some minor differences at the higher level.

Social insurance legislation enables a marriage grant payable to working women when they marry, as well as a maternity grant for birth mothers and a maternity leave allowance of up to 12 weeks. Reproductive health is integrated into the primary health care system, and is provided free of charge by athe state and at affordable rates by the private sector.

**See Also:** Birth Control; Postcolonialism and Mothering; Poverty and Mothering; Work and Mothering.

## Bibliography
Balswick, Jack. "Comparative Earnings of Greek Cypriot Women and Men." *Sex Roles,* v.4/6 (1978).

Czech Republic

House, William. *Population and Labour Force Growth and Development*. Nicosia, Cyprus: Department of Statistics and Research, Ministry of Finance. Cyprus: Intercollege, Research and Development Centre, 1996.

Papapetrou, S., and M Pendedeka. "The Cypriot Family: The Evolution of the Institution Through Time: Trends of Change." Unpublished paper presented at the Annual Conference of the Cyprus Sociological Association (1998).

Miranda E. Jennings
University of Massachusetts Amherst

# Czech Republic

The Czech Republic is characterized by a very high level of prenatal care, a high level of women's education, easy access to abortion, a high divorce rate, atheism, and many children born to unwed couples.

The fertility rate in the Czech Republic was 1.44 in 2007. Similar to other postsocialist countries, the birth rate declined sharply after the Velvet Revolution; in 1989, the rate was 1.87, with the lowest peak of 1.13 reached in 1999. The average age of a mother having her first child at that time was 27.1 years.

All mothers in the country are entitled to the same kind of support, although it is partially dependent on her previous employment and paid insurance. A birth mother receives a birth allowance as well as financial support in motherhood. Maternity leave lasts 28 weeks, has to start at least 6 weeks before the expected date of birth, is paid from sickness insurance, and represents 70 percent of her salary with an upper limit. After the maternity leave, a period of parental leave starts. The father or mother receives a parental benefit up to the fourth year of the child's age. If a family's income is below a certain level, they can receive a per child benefit.

Although the share of children born to unmarried women was 34.5 percent in 2007, there is not any special support for them; different social benefits depend on household income.

There is a widespread belief in the country that the mother should stay with the child at home they reach 3 years of age. Legally, an employer has to secure a job within the company for the parent up to the third year of the child's age.

Almost every second marriage is divorced. The average number of children in a divorced family in 2007 was 0.88. Families with one child represented 33.2 percent of all divorced couples in that year; families with two children, 23.1 percent; and families with three or more children, 2.8 percent.

According to 2001 census data, only 35.5 percent of women and 28.6 percent of men claim to believe in God. The country is considered one of the most atheistic in the world.

Contraception is available only with a prescription from a doctor and has to be fully paid for. A woman can undergo an abortion for any reason until the 12th week of pregnancy; until the 8th week, a so-called "mini abortion" (which is an ambulatory intervention) is possible. The abortion has to be paid for in full—the sum is about one-third of the minimum wage for the "mini abortion" and about half for the abortion until the 12th week. Abortions for health reasons is allowed until the 24th week.

The infant mortality rate was 3.14 per 1,000 live births in 2007, which is one of the lowest in the world. However, there is very specific situation concerning birthing: The Petition for Improving Maternity Care Services in the Czech Republic, called *Normalni Porod* (Normal Birth), points out that the maternity care standard in the country does not provide suitable alternatives for all mothers, since the Czech obstetrics standard considers birth outside large hospitals as unsafe, and independent midwifery is suppressed by state authorities.

**See Also:** European Union; Midwifery; Work and Mothering.

Czech Statistical Office. www.czso.cz (accessed January 2009).
Institute of Health Information and Statistics of the Czech Republic. www.uzis.cz (accessed January 2009).
*Normalni Porod* (Normal Birth). www.normalniporod.cz (accessed January 2009).

Michaela Marksova-Tominova
Independent Scholar

# Danticat, Edwidge

Born in Haiti, in 1969, writer Edwidge Danticat is renowned for her literary works, including novels and short stories, periodical articles, a Haitian travel book, a memoir, and two children's books. As one of only a small number of Haitians who write in English, which is not her native language, her controversial social commentaries describe life in Haiti.

Haiti is the poorest country in the Western Hemisphere, and has a long history of colonial exploitation, political turmoil, and more recently exploitation through globalization. Writing through her own experiences, interviews, and her insightful understanding of sociopolitical issues related to oppression, race, and gender, her work gives voice to Haitians in living in Haiti and abroad.

The daughter of working class parents, André and Rose Danticat, who had both immigrated to the New York by the time Edwidge was 4, Edwidge was not reunited with her parents until she left Haiti to join them at the age of 12. During the intervening years, Edwidge and her younger brother Eliab were raised by her father's brother, her beloved "second father" Uncle Joseph, a charismatic minister, and his wife her Tante Denise.

Educated at Barnard College, a women's liberal arts college affiliated with Columbia University, she earned a B.A. in French Literature, after which she completed her M.F.A. in creative writing at Brown University in 1993. Her thesis eventually became her first novel, *Breath, Eyes, Memory,* for which she won the 1994 Fiction Award from *The Caribbean Writer.*

Thus far, Danticat has won several other prestigious awards including the American Book Award for *The Farming of the Bones* in 1999, and the 2007 National Book Critics Circle Award for *Brother, I'm Dying,* a family memoir focusing on the relationship between her father and his brother Joseph, and her love for them both. Among Danticat's other works are *Krik? Krak!* (1996), a National Book Award finalist, and *The Dew Breaker* (2004). She also edited *The Beacon Best of 2000: Great Writing by Men and Women of All Colors and Cultures* (2000), and *The Butterfly's Way: Voices from the Haitian Dyaspora in the United States* (2001).

Danticat's powerful and passionate writing reflects and expresses her own and her family's experiences of political violence in Haiti during the oppressive François Duvalier regime, poverty, family love and loyalty, and the strength and resiliency of the Haitian people.

**See Also:** African Diaspora; Haiti; Intergenerational Trauma; Violence Against Mothers/Children.

**Bibliography**

Danticat, Edwidge. *Breath, Eyes, Memory.* New York: Vintage Books, 1994.

Danticat, Edwidge. *Brother, I'm Dying.* New York: Alfred A. Knopf, 2007.

Shaw, Denise R. *Textual Healing: Giving Voice to Historical and Personal Experience into the Collective works of Edwidge Danticat.* Roanoke, VA: Hollins University Press, 2007.

Deborah Davidson
York University, Toronto

# Dating and Single Mothers

In the United States, the number of single-parent households rose dramatically beginning in the late 20th century. The category of single mothers includes both those who have chosen single motherhood and those who did not. There are a large variety of single mothers with a variety of family situations, including those who have lost spouses to death or divorce, those who bore children out of wedlock for a variety of reasons, teenaged parents, abandoned mothers, and those who have adopted children. The rise of reproductive technologies and the lessening social stigma attached to divorce and single motherhood has increased both the number and visibility of single mothers. Since women most often have primary or full custody of their children postdivorce and head most single parent households, dating can be a more complicated issue for single mothers than single fathers. Research has shown that single mothers who date will face a number of issues related to their motherhood status and the physical, emotional, and psychological impacts their dating can have on their children.

Although dating is generally a normal component of the adjustment period for single mothers who lost a relationship through death or divorce, it raises many psychological and emotional issues. The first challenge for many single mothers who have determined they are ready to date is to determine when to tell a prospective date she has children, a fact that will make her less desirable to many men. Informing a date immediately can eliminate those potential partners who do not want children but may intimidate others who are uncomfortable with the idea. Modern single mothers have more support and guidance than their historical counterparts, who faced social stigma and isolation. Support groups, counselors, Internet sites, advice books, magazine articles, and groups such as the National Organization of Single Mothers can help single mothers connect and navigate the dating process.

Common male perceptions that can interfere with the single mother's ability to attract dates or develop a new long-term relationship include the belief that a mother will have less time to devote to a new love interest due to her primary commitment to her children. This fear is reinforced by cultural expectations of motherhood. Any mother is expected to sacrifice her own needs for those of her children, who are expected to be her top priority. Other issues include the fear of becoming an instant parent and adopting a ready-made family or blending two families into one, the lack of a genetic bond with the children, the economic responsibilities and time constraints of parenthood, and fears of the psychological difficulties on children and the effects of their potential behavior on a developing relationship.

Psychologists also recommend that single mothers considering dating should consider their own motivations and level of comfort with the idea. Some newly single mothers begin dating and enter a new relationship quickly, before the healing process is complete, out of a perceived need to replace the companionship or parenting help they lost. Other single mothers become overly sensitive to potential problems due to their past failed relationship and abandon a new relationship at the first sign of trouble. Sometimes they consciously or unconsciously use their role as mother as an excuse to avoid a new intimate relationship. Single mothers often experience strong feelings of guilt and emotional insecurity when they reenter the dating world, especially if they leave their children in the care of a babysitter while they are out. While they may consciously recognize the need to pursue their own happiness to be an effective mother, they may have difficulty overcoming guilt to follow through.

*Single mothers face challenges while dating, including finding someone appropriate for her children and securing childcare.*

Single mothers confronting the issues associated with any stage of the dating process must always consider the impact of their choice on their children's lives as well as their own. Research has shown that transitions such as a single parent entering a new relationship can be disruptive to a child's psychological well-being. One of the most important questions a single mother will have to decide is whether to tell her children she is dating. If she chooses to tell them, then she must decide how much information to share with them and when to share it. Key considerations include the child's age, comprehension level, and comfort with the situation. Single mothers of older children must also be prepared to answer the inevitable questions that children are likely to ask and realize that their children generally see them as role models. They must consider what message they wish to send their children about such issues as how romantic partners should treat each other or whether premarital sex is acceptable.

Children's reactions to a single mother's announcement that she is beginning to date can range from positive to negative, often within the same family. Influences on a child's reaction include their age and personality traits, the circumstances surrounding the family situation, the number of disruptions in a child's daily routines, and their mother's approach to the situation. Single mothers must achieve a balance between acknowledging their children's feelings and pursuing their own happiness, especially if the children express resentment or other negative reactions. A single mother's approach to dating will also shape her child's reaction, as a mother's emotions often consciously or unconsciously influence her children. Successful navigation of this difficult process can model healthy coping strategies.

Common fears among children of single mothers who begin to date include fears that a hoped for reconciliation with their father will not happen and fears that they will be abandoned or receive less attention due to their mother's new love interest. Dating may also increase an adolescent child's normal embarrassment over their parents. A child may also exhibit disruptive behavior or begin to do poorly in school based on their feelings of discomfort, unhappiness, and resentment over their mother's dating situation. Children who have been through numerous life transitions are more likely to exhibit such behavior than those whose lives have been less disrupted. Research reveals the best approach is a slow introduction of the dating process and the establishment of clear, firm boundaries between her children and her dates that can be expanded over time.

Single mothers who are dating a partner they feel may be right for a long-term commitment must consider the impact of a new person entering their child's life on a more permanent basis. Single mothers who feel guilty about dating often feel pressured that a sexual attraction turn into a relationship as justification for the time spent away from their children. A single mother must also make sure she is not pursuing a long term relationship for the sole reason that her children have become attached to her partner and she wishes to spare them the potential emotional issues of another separation. She must also consider not only what type of mate her partner will be but what type of parent they will be as well.

How single mothers navigate the dating process is an important determinant of how they will navigate the potential challenges of transitioning into a new home and stepfamily.

**See Also:** Divorce; Mother and Multiple Partners; Sexuality and Mothering; Single Mothers; Stepmothers; Unwed Mothers; Young Mothers.

**Bibliography**

Edin, Kathryn and Maria Kefalas. *Promises I Can Keep: Why Poor Women Put Motherhood Before Marriage.* Berkeley: University of California Press, 2005.

Engber, Andrea and Leah Klungress. *The Complete Single Mother: Reassuring Answers to Your Most Challenging Concerns.* Avon, MA: Adams Media, 2006.

Fisher, Ellie Slott. *Mom, There's a Man in the Kitchen and He's Wearing Your Robe: The Single Mother's Guide to Dating Well Without Parenting Poorly.* Cambridge, MA: Da Capo Lifelong, 2005.

Hertz, Rosanna. *Single by Chance, Mothers by Choice: How Women Are Choosing Parenthood Without Marriage and Creating the New American Family.* New York: Oxford University Press, 2006.

Marcella Bush Trevino
Barry University

# Daughter-Centricity

Daughter-centricity is a term used often in association with psychoanalytic theory to describe the narrative of the daughter/child that comes at the expense of the narrative of the mother. While the subject of the narrative may be the experience of motherhood, daughter-centric accounts are conveyed through the singular perspective of the daughter, thus skewing the position toward that of the daughter/child while marginalizing or ignoring the position of the mother. Daughter-centricity can be viewed as developing out of the oedipal theory of psychoanalysis, both processes that deny maternal subjectivity in favor of the child's sense of selfhood and independence. Striving for selfhood through maternal denial results in a negation of the mother, or as has often been found in myths, legends, and folklore, the demonizing of the mother into a monstrous figure.

Maureen T. Reddy uses the term *daughter centricity* to refer to the tendency of feminists such as Nancy Chodorow, Dorothy Dinnerstein, and Carol Gilligan to write about female experience from the point of view of daughters rather than mothers: they are more concerned with the experience of being mothered, rather than being a mother.

Feminist theorists have pointed out the inherent dichotomy of daughter-centricity, which would appear, on the surface, to advocate for women's individuation. Yet, the absence of the mother's sense of self through a focus on the story of the daughter is a divisive situation, since the mother is also a daughter. To escape patriarchally defined conditions of motherhood, scholars note that analysis by the feminist daughter must shift from the centrality of the daughter's experience to the marginalized locus of the mother's existence. While there are numerous publications across disciplines that detail, critique, praise, and analyze issues surrounding motherhood, very few perform their objective through the particular vision of the mother as an individual subject with personal agency.

**See Also:** Care Giving; Chodorow, Nancy; Collins, Patricia Hill; Daughters and Mothers; Feminism and Mothering; Freud, Sigmund; Girlhood and Motherhood; Jocasta; Kristeva, Julia; Mother/Daughter Plot (Hirsch); O'Brien, Mary; Sociology of Motherhood.

**Bibliography**

Daly, Brenda O. and Maureen T. Reddy. *Narrating Mothers: Theorizing Maternal Subjectivities.* Knoxville: University of Tennessee Press, 1991.

Hirsch, Marianne. *The Mother/Daughter Plot: Narrative, Psychoanalysis, Feminism.* Bloomington: Indiana University Press, 1989.

O'Reilly, Andrea and Sharon Abbey. *Mothers and Daughters: Connection, Empowerment, & Transformation.* Lanham, MD: Rowman & Littlefield, 2000.

Terri B. Pantuso
University of Texas, San Antonio

# Daughters and Mothers

Mothers and daughters are sometimes considered natural allies and sometimes considered natural enemies. What resolves the paradox of the coexistence of these views is recognition of the societal myths about mothers that have profound impact on the mother–daughter relationship, as well as understanding of the nature of power as it pertains to mothers.

It is not, of course, the case that mothers and daughters have more problematic relationships than do mothers and sons, fathers and daughters, or fathers and sons. In fact, the likelihood that both mother and daughter have been socialized to care about and become skilled at dealing with feelings and relationships often enriches the mother–daughter relationship beyond other parent–offspring relationships. So does the potential for understanding each others' sex- and gender-based dilemmas.

### Myths Interfering With Relationship

The first myths that can create or exacerbate problems between mothers and daughters are the four perfect mother myths, which establish standards that are difficult, if not impossible, for any human to meet. These myths are that good mothers raise perfect children, are endless founts of nurturance, naturally know everything necessary for raising perfect children, and never become angry.

The six bad-mother myths are sources of pressure on mothers, daughters, and others to take whatever a mother does—whether bad, neutral, or even good—and use it as evidence that mothers are bad. These myths are that mothers are inferior to fathers, they need expert advice to raise healthy children, they are bottomless pits of neediness, they are dangerous when they are powerful, mother–daughter closeness is unhealthy, and that mothers with paid work are bad mothers.

In the mother–daughter relationship, a great deal is at stake, because it has the potential to be wonderful and because they are likely to share many experiences and perceptions. Furthermore, since both are female, mother and daughter are likely, in most cultures, to have been socialized to be loving, empathic, and skilled at feelings and relationships. Set against this, however, are the pervasiveness of the two sets of myths about mothers, which increase the burdens on the mother–daughter relationship. If a daughter is influenced by these myths, the perfect-mother myths prime them to feel betrayed by and angry at mothers who are merely imperfect, and the

bad-mother myths prime daughters to pathologize their mothers. The two sets of myths, if believed, make it difficult for daughters to observe and evaluate their mothers realistically, because they tend to see them through the myths' distorting filters.

### Sexism and Stereotypes

The persistence of sexism in the form of negative stereotypes about women in general and mothers in particular increases the likelihood that mothers and daughters will blame themselves and each other, rather than understand the factors external to their relationship that often come between them. These factors also include the power imbalances that result from sexism, which are manifestated in the greater economic and political power that rests in the hands of men than in those of women, and the greater respect usually accorded men than women.

As often happens among those with less power and influence, mothers and daughters may be drawn closer by their shared, second-class circumstances, but may also be competing for the scarce economic and political resources allocated to them. This, at least in part, explains the socialization of both mothers and daughters to try to please the men in the family rather than each other.

The situation with regard to mothers, daughters, and power is more complicated and nuanced, however. The combined facts that mothers in most families still do the vast majority of child- and home-related care and are expected to be responsible for work related to feelings and relationships means that mothers often have a great deal of emotional power within the mother–daughter relationship—and sometimes, others within the family as well. At the same time, so much of childcare and housework is unacknowledged and even invisible—except when the mother neglects to do it—that the mother often experiences herself as utterly powerless within the family. This difference between what her children may experience as her significant power and her perception of herself as relatively powerlessness can cause serious miscommunications and other problems if the difference is not explicitly addressed.

### Trouble in the Mother–Daughter Relationship

Either party's lack of awareness of the ways that myths and power differentials work tends to increase the pain and bewilderment in mother–daughter relationships. The combination of often unarticulated assumptions about women, mothers, and daughters leads to such great expectations for their relationship that they are virtually impossible to meet. Consequently, mother and daughter can come to remind each other of their own and each other's failures to meet these impossible expectations, and no one likes to feel like a failure.

Further increasing the likelihood of trouble in the mother–daughter relationship is the labeling of females in general as selfish when they express a desire for themselves. Thus, a mother who is not constantly available to listen to her child is inclined to feel guilty or ashamed, and it is unpleasant to be in the presence of a person who is perceived as the source of one's guilt or shame.

Another major problem that is related to problems between mothers and daughters is the conundrum that the daughter is expected to have her mother as her primary role model, but that role model is often demeaned by society. The mother, in essence, is expected to socialize her daughter into a less valued role. This confronts mothers with a deeply conflicted dilemma: To the extent that they socialize their daughters conventionally, they must encourage them to defer to men, to put others' needs always ahead of their own, and to accept a relatively passive role (except when taking care of others' needs); but to the extent that they hold back from this socializing task, they risk raising daughters who will be rejected or at least struggle more as they swim against the tide.

Related to this is that daughters often express that they do not want to be like their mothers, which appears on it's face to be a dismissal of their mothers, but often turns out to reflect daughters' fear that they will be treated in the same, devalued way as their mothers.

A prevalent assumption is that the mother-daughter relationship is inevitably fraught with angst and anger, especially when the daughter is an adolescent. Mother–daughter problems arise, of course, as no relationship is problem-free. But for mothers and daughters, because both often have much at stake in the relationship, because of its potential benefits, and because of the special pains and fears involved in mother–daughter conflict, they often try

to tackle the biggest problems between them first. As in any relationship, this approach decreases the success of the effort.

Because of the societal expectation for females, such as dependency, politeness, and verbal abilities, it can be difficult for both mother and daughter to avoid seeing each other as deficient, weak, or manipulative, rather than to see each other's strengths, such as relational skills. Furthermore, this socialization leads them into conflicting situations. For instance, mothers are urged to raise empathic, nurturing daughters, but a mother who reveals some of her own problems—even when her revelations and the daughter's reaction is loving and appropriate—risks being blamed for role reversal, or expecting her daughter to take care of her. Similarly, if an adult daughter needs to temporarily move back with her mother for economic reasons, that mother risks being labeled as infantilizing her daughter if she does the daughter's laundry, as well as risks being blamed for allowing role reversal if the daughter reciprocates by cooking their meals.

When mothers and daughters experience conflicts or chasms between them, it is often especially disturbing to them for several reasons. As females, they have likely both have been raised to believe they should be able to fix relationships, so these problems diminish their positive self-identities; they may have a fear of losing their potentially greatest personal ally; the tantalizing images of impossibly perfect mother–daughter relationships make the reality of even good but less-than-perfect relationships seem devastating; and both mother and daughter have likely experienced at least some substantial benefits of the emotion- and feeling-oriented socialization of girls and women, so the risk that the relationship will completely disintegrate is frightening and sad.

## Three Steps to Healing the Problems

Three basic steps to mending mother–daughter problems have been found to be useful. The first is to establish or reestablish an alliance. Especially when the mother and/or daughter is experiencing a great deal of anguish, it is tempting to begin with accusations or threats, though these are nearly always destructive. Even a simple, true statement such as "I would like us to be more comfortable when we are together" can effectively create a basis from which to begin. That alliance can be strengthened if the mother and daughter work to understand the basis for and repercussions of the 10 myths about mothers. This process helps to make it clear how to what degree their difficulties are due to a society that devalues mothers, daughters, and their relationships.

A second step is to choose and define a specific, ideally a small, problem to start with, rather than the most painful and daunting of problems in the relationship. As with any kind of experience, starting small maximizes the chances for success at the initial level, giving the mother–daughter pair something to build on as they take the next step.

A third step—which is sometimes best as the first one—is for the daughter to humanize her image of her mother. A mother-blaming society presses the daughter to see her mother as less than she really is, yet the emotional power of many mothers within the family can make the mother loom larger than life. Most daughters know their mothers primarily as "my mother, the mother" and have never thought of their mothers outside of that role. To take this step, the daughter asks to hear her mother's life story, complete with asking questions such as "When you were in junior high school, what did you want to be when you grew up?" or "What did you think of your husband when you first met him?" Simply hearing about her mother's first day in school can suddenly shift a daughter's view of her mother onto a more human scale than before.

If nothing more, hearing the mother's life story can provide mother and daughter much more to talk about than the painful conflicts that sometimes become their primary topic of discussion. In addition, although many daughters are aware that physical and sexual abuse exists, many mothers have never told their daughters that they themselves have been abused in these ways. A daughter who learns this about her mother often experiences a sudden and dramatic shift in her interpretation of her mother's behavior, such as understanding that what she had thought was overprotective was actually concerned and loving.

See Also: Adolescent Children; Adult Children; Caplan, Paula J.; Daughter-Centricity; Mother Blame; Moth-er/Daughter Plot (Hirsch); Mother-Daughter Project; Motherless Daughters; Myths of Motherhood: Good/Bad; Self-Identity; Sons and Mothers.

**Bibliography**
Caplan, Paula J. "Mocking Mom: Joke or Hate Speech?" *Rejected Letters to the Editor,* v.1/4 (June 2007).
Caplan, Paula J. *The New Don't Blame Mother: Mending the Mother-Daughter Relationship.* New York: Routledge, 2000.
Caplan, Paula J. and Ian Hall-McCorquodale. "Mother-Blaming in Major Clinical Journals." *American Journal of Orthopsychiatry,* v.55 (1985).
Friday, Nancy. *My Mother/My Self: The Daughter's Search for Identity.* New York: Delacorte Press, 1977.
Howe, Karen. "Daughters Discover Their Mothers Through Biographies and Genograms: Education and Clinical Parallels." In *Woman-Defined Motherhood,* Jane Knowles and Ellen Cole, eds. New York: Harrington Park Press, 1990.
*Journal of the Association for Research on Mothering.* Mothers and Daughters [special issue], v.10/2 (Fall/Winter 2008).

Paula J. Caplan
Harvard University

# Da Vinci, Leonardo, Mother of

For centuries it was believed that the legendary figure Leonardo da Vinci, among the best-known artists to come out of the Italian Renaissance, was the son of a Florentine notary and an Italian peasant. Alternative theories have gained credibility in recent decades, suggesting that Leonardo's mother, Caterina, was in fact a slave of Arab descent, and that this heritage influenced Da Vinci.

Da Vinci, who was raised by his mother only until the age of 4, at which time he was sent to live with his father and his father's wife, had numerous half siblings from his father's marriages and his mother's marriage to a man said to have been handpicked by Leonardo's father after the birth of Leonardo.

Leonardo da Vinci embodied the notion of the Renaissance ideal, engaging in numerous fields of interest, including art, engineering, mathematics, philosophy, and science. Da Vinci's contributions to the arts and sciences are well known, and he is considered to be one of the greatest painters of all time. Two of his works, *The Last Supper* and *Mona Lisa,* are among the most famous paintings ever produced, and both have been reproduced and parodied extensively. Da Vinci's notoriety and subsequent fame resulted in part because of the diversity of his interests and the vigor with which he pursued them, in addition to his genius. For instance, although he was a vegetarian, and his love for animals was legendary, he also invented war machines and dissected cadavers to understand human anatomy.

### Mystery of Da Vinci's Birth

The relatively recent findings in the late 1990s and early 2000s by Italian researchers regarding the circumstances of Da Vinci's birth have challenged long-held assumptions about his origins. Papers discovered by the Museo Ideale Leonardo Da Vinci (Leonardo Da Vinci Ideal Museum), in the artist's hometown of Vinci, in Tuscany, coupled with 25 years of extensive research, resulted in the museum's assertion that Da Vinci's mother was not, after all, an Italian peasant as was believed for so many years.

While it is known that Da Vinci was born in Vinci, in Florence, Italy, on April 15, 1452, as the illegitimate son of the notary Piero da Vinci and a woman named Caterina, it is now disputed that Caterina was a local peasant. Rather, Da Vinci's father, Piero, is believed to have met Caterina through a friend who acquired her as a slave. In a tax record dating from 1457, when Leonardo was 5 years old, Leonardo's mother was identified as Caterina, at that time married to a man named Acchattabriga di Piero del Vaccha.

Researchers have said there is no other Caterina in Vinci or nearby villages who could be linked to Piero, Leonardo's father, other than the woman who lived in the house of Vanni di Niccolo di Ser Vann, a wealthy friend of Piero. Researchers have also claimed that Da Vinci's father, Piero, owned a slave called Caterina.

During the time of the Renaissance, a period of cultural rebirth that began in Italy in the 14th century and continued through the 16th, it was common for Florentines to take slaves from the Middle East and the Balkans. At the time of Leonardo da Vinci's birth, there were more than 500 slaves in Florence. Female slaves were commonly baptized and renamed, and the most popular names were Maria, Marta, and Caterina. While none of the evidence suggesting Caterina's Arabic background is definitive, it is highly suggestive of an alternative story. Further evidence of an Arabic lineage is suggested by a fingerprint analysis conducted using Da Vinci's notebooks and drawings, which were prolific. The patterns and ridges in Da Vinci's fingertips suggested a possible Middle Eastern heritage.

At age 60, and after the death of her husband, Caterina moved to Milan, where Leonardo was then living. Mother and son developed a relationship and continued to communicate by letter. These letters, contained in collections called the *Codex Atlanticus* and *Codex Forster II,* contain clues to Caterina's role in her son Leonardo's life, including suggestions of a Middle Eastern influence on Leonardo's work.

**See Also:** Art and Mothering; Italy; Columbus, Christopher, Mother of; Slavery and Mothering.

### Bibliography

Hooper, John. "Da Vinci's Mother Was a Slave, Italian Study Claims." *The Guardian* (April 12, 2008). http://dsc.discovery.com/news/2008/04/09/da-vinci-mother.html (accessed May 2009).
Lorenzi, Rossella. "Was Da Vinci's Mother a Slave?" *Discovery News* (April 9, 2008). http://dsc.discovery.com/news (accessed May 2009).
Vasari, Georgio. *Lives of the Artists.* New York: Penguin Books, 1965.

Julianna E. Thibodeaux
Independent Scholar

# Daycare

Daycare is the provision of care for a child through either a daycare center (nursery) or family-run, home daycare. Daycare differs from individual childcare by babysitters or nannies in that providers care for several children at one time. Daycare is typically used by working parents to care for children below the age of 5; however, many daycare facilities also offer before- and after-school care.

## Historic Background
Daycare emerged in the late 19th and early 20th centuries in Europe and the United States as a reflection of a variety of social and economic circumstances, including the industrial revolution and immigration of families. In the United States, nurseries and kindergartens were established to serve disadvantaged women, particularly widows and working women. During World War II, the first and only federal legislation that provided broad funding and support for childcare in the United States was the Lanham Act of 1941, which provided federal grant funding to states in order to create childcare facilities for women workers as they replaced men during the war. Federal funding was discontinued just weeks after the war.

## The Need for Daycare
Whether by choice or economic necessity, the increased number of mothers in the labor force highlights the importance of childcare. According to the U.S. Bureau of Labor Statistics, the participation of women with children under age 6 in the civilian U.S. labor force increased from 39 percent in 1975 to 63 percent in 2006. Similarly, the Organisation for Economic Co-operation and Development (OECD) reports that labor force participation rates of mothers with children under 6 years of age across selected countries in 2002 include Australia, 45 percent; Denmark, 74 percent; France, 58 percent; Germany, 52 percent; Italy, 46 percent; Spain, 43 percent; and the United Kingdom, 55 percent.

The National Association of Child Care Resource and Referral Agencies (NACCRRA) indicates that nearly 75 percent of infants and toddlers of working mothers are cared for by someone outside of their immediate family. The use of daycare typically depends on the work status of the mother, but household income and education influence the age at which families place their children in care. According to the National Institute of Child Health and Human Development, children are more likely to be placed in daycare at an earlier age when the family is more dependent on the mother's income.

In contrast, a low-income family's children who have not entered daycare by their first birthday are more likely to live in poverty and have mothers with less education.

Martha Davis and Roslyn Powell indicate the need for childcare has also been recognized globally through the International Convention on the Rights of the Child (CRC), adopted by the United Nations (UN) General Assembly in 1989. Article 18 of the CRC asserts that states have a duty to assist working parents in meeting the needs of childcare services. The CRC has been ratified by 191 countries—Somalia and the United States are the only UN members that have not ratified the CRC.

## Daycare Centers and Home Daycare
Daycare center providers include privately owned organizations, although some universities and churches also sponsor daycare programs. Smaller, private daycare centers tend to operate out of a single location; however, in recent years, publicly traded corporate daycare centers have emerged. For example, ABC Learning is listed on the stock exchange and has centers in Asia, Australia, the United Kingdom, and the United States.

Daycare centers are more likely to be licensed, subject to state inspections and regulation, employ trained staff, and provide a developmental curriculum. Licensed daycare centers separate children by age, meet specific caregiver and child ratios, and often provide age-appropriate cognitive and social development activities. However, the disadvantages of daycare centers include higher costs, staff turnover, and less individual attention. Home daycare providers offer care for children in their own home. The advantages of home daycare include lower costs and greater individual attention. Although most states in the United States require regulation among providers who care for more than four children, home daycare providers are less likely to be licensed and regulated.

## Regulation of Daycare
In the United States, daycare centers and homes are licensed by the states, and standards vary accordingly. The National Association for the Education of Young Children provides recommendations on the organization and structure of daycare centers. Features of quality care include small adult-to-child

ratios, group size, caregiver's education level, safe physical environment, and age-appropriate learning activities. It is important for parents to understand that not all providers are licensed. Within the United States, individuals can learn about specific providers and regulations by contacting their state. Many states use Health and Human Services departments to license and regulate daycare providers.

## Financing Daycare

A variety of methods are used to finance daycare, ranging from direct government sponsorship and provision of services to tax credits for parents who pay out-of-pocket expenses for daycare. The OECD reports that government support for formal daycare is highest among Nordic countries, where spending ranges from 1.5 to 2.7 percent of Gross Domestic Product (GDP), and lowest in Australia, Korea, Mexico, New Zealand, Slovak Republic, Switzerland, and Turkey. Nevertheless, most countries provide some form of subsidy for low-income families and many use a fee based on income approach.

In Finland, all children under 7 years of age qualify for daycare, which is funded by the local authority regardless of parental income. In France, *écoles maternelles* (nursery schools) are funded by the National Ministry of Education. Parents pay no fee, and children between the ages of 2 and 6 are eligible. There are also *crèches collectives* (home daycare), in which fees are based on income. Payroll taxes are used to finance both systems.

In the United States, low-income families often qualify for subsidies for childcare, while middle- and upper-income families receive tax credits. Federal support for daycare is provided to the states through Child Care and Development Block Grants to provide assistance to low-income families. Head Start is also a well-known program for low-income children. Britain adopted a similar approach through the National Childcare Strategy, which established Sure Start (modeled after Head Start in the United States) to assist low-income children. Britain also offers tax credits for childcare.

## Benefits of Daycare

Both children and mothers of young children can benefit from affordable, quality daycare. Many consider daycare to be an investment in the future of our children and a means to promote equality for disadvantaged children. Several studies have demonstrated positive effects of daycare on cognitive development, while the studies on behavioral performance have been mixed. The National Institute of Child Health and Human Development (NICHD) study found that children who attended daycare centers had better cognitive development and language skills, but were more likely to exhibit behavioral problems.

The National Institutes of Health also found that children who attended higher-quality childcare received higher scores on vocabulary tests in the fifth grade than children who attended lower-quality care. Studies of Head Start programs have also demonstrated positive effects of program participation on academic performance in early grade school; however, the effects diminish for minorities by age 10.

Day care also benefits mothers with young children by increasing labor force participation rates of women, promoting gender equality in the workplace, and raising household incomes. A 2004 OECD study found that government spending on public childcare increases full-time participation of women. Among those countries with less governmental support for daycare, such as the United States, high labor force participation rates of women with young children is partially explained by higher education levels and lower unemployment.

**See Also:** Childcare; Employment and Motherhood; Preschool Children; Work and Mothering.

## Bibliography

Dau-Schmidt, Kenneth and Carmen Brun. "Protecting Families in a Global Economy." *Indiana Journal of Global Legal Studies*, v.13/1 (Winter 2006).
Davis, Martha and Roslyn Powell. "The International Convention on the Rights of the Child: A Catalyst for Innovative Childcare Policies." *Human Rights Quarterly*, v.25 (2003).
National Association of Child Care Resource and Referral Agencies (NACCRRA). "Quality Infant and Toddler Care Promotes Greater Outcomes for Children and Helps Parents Go to Work." http://www.naccrra.org/policy/background_issues/quality_infant_toddler_care.ph (accessed May 2009).

Organisation for Economic Co-operation and Development (OECD). *Labor Force Participation of Women: Empirical Evidence on the Role of Policy and Other Determinants in OECD Countries*. Paris: OECD, 2004.

U.S. Bureau of Labor Statistics. *Women in the Labor Force*, Report 1011 (December 2008).

U.S. National Institutes of Health (NIH). *The NICHD Study of Early Child Care and Youth Development*. http://www.nichd.nih.gov/publications/pubs/upload/seccyd_051206.pd (accessed May 2009).

Williams, Fiona and Sasha Roseneil. "Public Values of Parenting and Partnering: Voluntary Organizations and Welfare Politics in New Labour's Britain." *Social Politics*, v.11/2 (2004).

Heather Wyatt-Nichol
University of Baltimore

# de Beauvoir, Simone

French existentialist philosopher and writer Simone de Beauvoir (1908–86) wrote what is considered one of the most significant feminist works of the 20th century, *The Second Sex*. In it, Beauvoir presents what appears to be a controversial view of motherhood, which has been very severely criticized as well as misunderstood.

Originally published in 1949, the work examines the "woman question." Beauvoir analyzes the concept of woman from multiple perspectives: biological, anthropological, historical, cultural, philosophical, and phenomenological. She bases her inquiry on the idea that while there is a myth of the eternal feminine, it does not constitute an essence to which one does or ought to correspond. She is dismissive of such essentialist positions.

In her chapter on biology, Beauvoir posits that the female biology determines a woman to serve the species—and while this is also true for the male, pregnancy is much more onerous for the female. Beauvoir presents a grim picture of pregnancy and childbirth, wherein the female experiences her body as other than herself; literally raped by the male and possessed by the species, she is "Tenanted by another, who battens upon her substance through-out the period of pregnancy, the female is at once herself and other than herself." Beauvoir describes the female body as radically altered by the sexual encounter and the pregnancy that ensues, and the female loses the sense of her own self. She feels alienated. Moreover, the fact that she has to provide care for the newborn has historically been the cause of her oppression, as she has been relegated to the household to perform these nurturing tasks.

In a later chapter of *The Second Sex*, Beauvoir examines the figure of the Mother as it has emerged historically and culturally, beginning with a discussion of birth control and abortion. In a world where abortion was illegal and often performed at great risk to the mother, Beauvoir writes in favor of, and later militates for, the legalization of birth control and abortion. She explains it is because she wants women to be able to freely choose to be mothers.

## Rewards of Motherhood

It is important for Beauvoir to express her opinion that motherhood can be extremely rewarding, if freely chosen, even if it is onerous for women—as well as charge that there is no such thing as a maternal instinct and that motherhood is not sufficient to fulfill woman. She presents these aforementioned ideas as patriarchal myths used to further oppress women and relegate them to a role where they cannot truly flourish, insisting that women who fail to perform such myths are made to feel unhappy and alienated. Such unhappy mothers become bad mothers who perpetuate such myths and seek to entrap their own daughters in turn. Beauvoir's goal is to demonstrate that these myths have no true substance: When women engage in motherhood as a freely chosen endeavor, they are better mothers and, by extension, better women. However, women do not need to be mothers to flourish as human beings.

**See Also:** Abortion; Becoming a Mother; Essentialism and Mothering; Feminist Theory and Mothering; Maternal Alienation; New French Feminism and Motherhood; Philosophy and Motherhood; Pregnancy; Self-Identity.

## Bibliography
de Beauvoir, Simone. *The Second Sex*. New York: Vintage, 1989.

Scarth, Fredrika. *The Other Within: Ethics, Politics, and the Body in Simone de Beauvoir.* Lanham, MD: Rowman & Littlefield, 2004.

Christine Daigle
Brock University

# Delaware

Delaware is the one of the smallest and most densely populated states in the United States. It ranks 49th in area and 45th in population, but sixth in population density. The population is predominantly white (76 percent in 2005) with the largest minority group (21.5 percent) being African American. 23.8 percent of the population is aged 18 or younger, placing Delaware 31st in the United States. In 2006, 11,988 children were born in Delaware, for a birth rate of 14.0 per 1,000 population and a fertility rate of 67.3 per 1,000 women aged 15–44. Total fertility rate (an estimate of the number of children born to each woman in her lifetime) in 2003 was 2.0, the same for the United States as a whole.

Overall, Delaware is a prosperous state, although there are pockets of poverty: 10.5 percent of people in Delaware lived below the U.S. poverty level in 2007, ranking 39th of all states. Median household income in Delaware was $54,610 in 2007, ranking 15th among the states, and per capita income was $40,608, ranking 12th. Educational levels are typical of the United States: 26.1 percent of Delaware residents aged 25 and over held at least a bachelor's degree in 2007, ranking the state 20th. Delaware has 250 doctors per 100,000 resident population, ranking 24th in the United States. However the state's general prosperity and reasonable supply of doctors does not translate to uniformly excellent health care: the infant mortality rate was 9.0 per 1,000 live births, ranking 5th in the United States; only Alabama, Louisiana, Mississippi, and South Carolina had higher rates. In such an industrialized country, this may indicate inequality of access to health care and/or a low priority placed on maternal and child health.

In 2006, about 5,200 marriages were conducted in Delaware, for a rate of 6.0 per 1,000 residents, slightly below the U.S. average of 7.5 per 1,000. In the same year, approximately 3,800 divorces were finalized for a rate of 4.5 per 1,000, well above the U.S. average of 3.6 per 1,000. In 2002, 82.2 percent of women in Delaware reported using contraception. In 2005, 5,150 abortions were performed in Delaware, for a rate of 28.8 per 1,000 women aged 15–44, substantially higher than the U.S. rate of 19.4.

Among the distinguished mothers from Delaware are the abolitionist Mary Ann Shadd (1823–1893), the second African American woman to earn a law degree; the actress and political activist Herta Ware (1917–2005), whose daughter Ellen Geer is also an actress; and Ruth Ann Minner, governor of Delaware from 2001 to 2009, which makes her the longest-serving female governor in U.S. history.

**See Also:** Abortion; Birth Control; Infant Mortality; Poverty and Mothering.

### Bibliography
Bensyl, Diana M., A. Danielle Iuliano, Marion Carter, and John Santelli. "Contraceptive Use—United States and Territories, Behavioral Risk Factor Surveillance System, 2002." *Morbidity and Mortality Weekly Report,* v.54/SS06 (2005) http://www.cdc.gov/mmwr/preview/mmwrhtml/ss5406a1.htm (accessed May 2009).

Centers for Disease Control and Prevention. "Reproductive Health: Data and Statistics." http://www.cdc.gov/reproductivehealth/Data_Stats/index.htm#Abortion (accessed May 2009).

U.S. Census Bureau. "State & County Quick Facts: Delaware." http://quickfacts.census.gov/qfd/states/02000lk.html (accessed May 2009).

Sarah E. Boslaugh
Washington University School of Medicine

# de Marneffe, Daphne

Daphne de Marneffe, Ph.D., clinical psychologist, feminist, and lecturer, theorizes a psychologically healthy and empowering-to-women form of maternal desire in her 2004 book, *Maternal Desire: On Children, Love, and the Inner Life.* In the book, de Marneffe explores mothers' relatedness to their children and defines maternal desire as a mother's desire to care for and relate to her children. As a feminist, de Marneffe is also interested in theorizing maternal desire in ways that are consistent with feminism and free from sentimentality and clichés. Most importantly, however, de Marneffe challenges the idea that women who desire to care for children are powerless and without agency, without the ability to influence their own lives. de Marneffe revises the classic psychoanalytic view of the mother–infant relationship as a psychologically unhealthy merger. In doing so, de Marneffe's core argument is that rather than a merger, the mother–infant and later mother–child relationship are best thought of as mutually responsive, with genuine relating at the core; thus, the interaction between a mother and her children gives both parties "a great deal more individuality than the somewhat swampy metaphor of merger evokes." As a result, de Marneffe suggests that maternal desire should be viewed as a sign of a woman's healthy desire to care for and relate to children and, equally important, as a symbol of women's agency and power within both the mother–child relationship and the mother's own life.

## Mutual Rather Than Merger

de Marneffe begins theorizing maternal desire by suggesting that contemporary women—who have taken advantage of the successes of 1960s and 1970s American feminism—have a "new problem" in terms of mothering. Specifically, contemporary women need to resolve how to take advantage of the changes in their lives without shortchanging their desire to mother. de Marneffe also suggests that maternal desire must be addressed, because the subject "gets the most simplistic public airing, even by its partisans, and the side that mainstream feminism has done the least to support." Thus, de Marneffe theorizes a more complex understanding of maternal desire that is consistent with the changes in women's lives brought about by American feminism as well as resists overly simple clichés both within feminism and culture.

With these goals in mind, de Marneffe begins by revising Nancy Chodorow's and Jessica Benjamin's class work on the mother–infant relationship. de Marneffe suggests that recent mother–infant research has shown that "the infant expresses his or her agency in encounters with the care giver, and that the care giver and baby are extraordinarily attuned to their unique interaction from very early on." As a result, even within the demanding first six months of an infant's life, more recent research suggests that the dynamic between mother and child is best thought of as a mutually responsive pattern of attentiveness with, again, genuine relating at the core of the relationship. Thus, de Marneffe also argues that viewing the relationship as mutually responsive also grants both mothers and children more agency and individuality than when the relationship is viewed as a merger.

Moreover, de Marneffe also suggests that viewing the relationship as mutually responsive fundamentally alters what counts as psychologically healthy interaction between a mother and her child. Drawing on recent attachment literature and, again, more current mother–infant research, de Marneffe argues that instead of physical separation as a sign of a mother's health, which is Benjamin's view, a care giver's self-reflective responsiveness to a child is far better indicator of a woman's health. Indeed, a mother's ability both to reflect on and communicate about her own childhood experiences and with her child are signs of the mother's own healthy sense of self and agency. A mother's ability to do so is also more crucial to a child's ability to develop both an independent sense of self and recognition of the mother's own individuality and agency. In other words, a mother's own internal or inner life and her ability to communicate that to and in relationship with her child is far more important to healthy mutual recognition of agency and connection for both the mother and child.

Consequently, rather than view a woman's desire to relate to and give care to her children as a potential sign of women's oppressive internalization of an oppressive role or a sign of bad health, de Marneffe argues for a psychological perspective that views this maternal desire as a potentially empowering form of agency for women and children. Finally, de Marneffe also argues that her understanding of maternal desire acknowledges and is consistent with women's progress in American culture.

**See Also:** Benjamin, Jessica; Chodorow, Nancy; Mothering and Feminism; Psychoanalysis and Motherhood.

### Bibliography

Benjamin, Jessica. *The Bonds of Love: Psychoanalysis, Feminism, and the Problem of Domination*. New York: Pantheon Books, 1988.

Chodorow, Nancy J. *The Reproduction of Mothering: Psychoanalysis and the Sociology of Gender*. Berkeley: University of California Press, 1978.

de Marneffe, Daphne. *Maternal Desire: On Children, Love, and the Inner Life*. New York: Little, Brown and Company, 2004.

Tucker, Judith Stadtman. "An Interview with Daphne de Marneffe." The Mother's Movement Online. http://www.mothersmovement.org/features/06/10/matenal_desire.html (accessed June 2009).

D. Lynn O'Brien Hallstein
Boston University

# Demeter, Goddess

Demeter was the Greek goddess of fertility, vegetation, and harvest, symbolized together with the life symbols of snakes and wheat (note: her Latin name *Ceres* is the root for the word "cereal"). She was particularly well known as the archetypal loving mother of her daughter, Persephone or Kore, meaning maiden, as recounted in the *Homeric Hymn to Demeter II*.

Demeter had many powers beyond being the goddess of the harvest: she also controlled the seasons, which meant that she could control all life on Earth. Demeter had a daughter named Persephone, who was abducted while picking flowers by Hades, the god of the underworld. A chasm in the Earth opened, and Hades emerged to abduct her down into the underworld by force. Demeter searched endlessly for her daughter, causing the Earth not to be fruitful. This initiated a period of famine, which could have destroyed Earth and its inhabitants, as well as depriving the gods of their sacrifices.

While Demeter was searching for her daughter, she traveled to the town of Eleusis, disguised as an old woman, where she was taken into the royal household to nurse their sons Demophon and Triptolemus. Demeter planned to make Demophon a god, and gave him ambrosia and held him in the fire to purge his mortality, but when his mother observed this and screamed, an angry Demeter stopped the process. Instead, Demeter taught the other son, Triptolemus, the art of planting and sowing crops.

Zeus wanted to put an end to the famine, and commanded Hades to return Persephone to her mother. There are many versions of the myth, but in all of them, Hades made Persephone return to the underworld for four months of the year, staying with her mother the other eight months, thus explaining the cycle of death and regeneration in nature, when Demeter the harvest goddess mourns her daughter's return to the underworld each winter.

Agreeing to this compromise, Demeter restored life to Earth and sent Triptolemus out to teach agriculture and the Mysteries of Eleusis, which were celebrated for nearly 2,000 years, offering its initiates the hope of eternal life, as seen through the pattern of death and rebirth in nature.

In other versions of the myth of Demeter, she was raped in the form of a mare by Poseidon, in the form of a stallion, thus sharing her daughter's fate. The roles of these two goddesses represented women's lives, from the fruitful Earth and their progeny, as well as their subjection to violence and death, with Persephone becoming an underworld judge.

Demeter protested against patriarchal forces as she sought after her beloved daughter, and although she finally made a compromise with Zeus, she first showed her tremendous power to give or deny life on Earth.

**See Also:** Demeter Press; Mother Goddess; Mother Nature; Myths, Mothers in; Rich, Adrienne.

### Bibliography

Baring, Anne and Jules Cashford. *The Myth of the Goddess*. New York: Penguin, 1991.

Dexter, Miriam Robbins. *Whence the Goddesses*. New York: Teachers College Press, 1990.

Evernden, Neil. *The Social Creation of Nature*. Baltimore, MD: Johns Hopkins University Press, 1992.

Foley, Helene P. *The Homeric Hymn to Demeter*. Princeton, NJ: Princeton University Press, 1993.

Gillian M.E. Alban
Dogus University, Turkey

# Demeter Press

Demeter Press was launched in 2004 in Toronto, Canada, by founder Dr. Andrea O'Reilly, and is the first-ever academic and feminist press to specifically focus on the topic of mothering and motherhood. The press is named in honor of the goddess Demeter, the Greek goddess of agriculture and fertility who unleashed her power when her beloved daughter Persephone was abducted and taken to the underworld by the god Hades. As history's most celebrated, empowered, and outraged mother, whose love and power were so great they undid rape and brought her child back from death, Demeter's triumphant resistance serves as model for the possibility—and power—of feminist mothering.

As a division of the Association for Research on Mothering (ARM), housed at York University in Toronto, Canada, Demeter Press supports ARM's mandate to promote feminist scholarship and to build a sustaining community of researchers by offering an array of writing on mothering and motherhood. The intention of Demeter Press is to contribute widely to and disseminate a range of theoretical and empirically oriented works and writings from poets, community activists, and feminist scholars regarding various aspects of motherhood and mothering. Demeter Press fills a void in feminist scholarship and writing on motherhood and mothering. It aims to contribute widely to the discussion and distribution of feminist, academic, and community grassroots research, theory, and praxis on mothering and motherhood. In its first four years of operation, Demeter Press published volumes on maternal theory, motherhood discourse, empowered mothering, aboriginal mothering, and poetry on mothers and motherhood.

**See Also:** Association for Research on Mothering; *Journal for the Association for Research on Mothering*; Mother Outlaws (Group).

### Bibliography

Dunlop, R., ed. *White Ink: Poems on Mothers and Motherhood*. Toronto: Demeter Press, 2007.

Friedman, M., and S.L. Calixte, eds. *Mothering and Blogging: The Radical Act of the Mommy Blog*. Toronto: Demeter Press, 2009.

Green, F. *Living Feminism Through Mothering*. Toronto: Demeter Press, 2012.

Latchford, F., ed. *Adoption and Mothering*. Toronto: Demeter Press, 2009.

Marotte, M.R. *Captive Bodies: American Women Writers Redefine Pregnancy and Childbirth*. Toronto: Demeter Press, 2008.

Nathanson, J., and L.C. Tuley, eds. *Mother Knows Best: Talking Back to the "Experts."* Toronto: Demeter Press, 2009.

O'Reilly, A., ed. *Mother Matters: Motherhood as Discourse and Practice*. Toronto: Demeter Press, 2004.

Fiona Joy Green
University of Winnipeg

# Depression

Depression, as a mental health disorder, is defined as persistent feelings of sadness that interfere with daily functioning. Depression is a continuum of mood disorders that include major depressive disorder, dysthymic disorder, psychotic depression, postpartum depression, and seasonal affective disorder. A related disorder, biopolar disorder, includes extreme mood swings that cycle from depressive to maniac states. Females outnumber males in major depressive disorders at a ratio of 2:1 during a woman's childbearing years. However, both prior to puberty and after menopause, rates of depressive disorders between males and females are similar.

Symptoms of depression can range from mild to severe, and not all women experience the same depressive symptoms. Symptoms can consist of persistent feelings of sadness, anxiety, and/or being "empty" as well as feelings of hopelessness, guilt, and being worthless. Women may also feel irritable and restless or may lose interest in their normal activities and hobbies. There can also be a loss of interest in sex as well as feelings of fatigue. Some women report difficulty in mental tasks, such as concentrating, remembering details, or making decisions. Depression can occur with either loss of appetite or increased eating patterns. It may also be associated with persistent aches and pains as well as headaches or digestive problems that are not alleviated by

*The stress mothers face in their daily lives—mothering, domestic responsibilities, and paid work—can have a critical impact on their ability to cope, and can leave them feeling overwhelmed and guilty. This distress puts mothers at particular risk for depression.*

treatment. Depression may also be associated with suicidal thoughts or attempts at suicide. Depression, along with stress and anxiety, can lead to self-medication and negative coping mechanisms such as drug and alcohol abuse. In fact, depression and drug abuse are frequently comorbid conditions.

### Types of Depressive Disorders

Approximately 6–17 percent of women suffer a major depressive episode (MDE) at least once in their life. MDEs are diagnosed by the occurrence of at least five of the depressive symptoms listed above occurring in a two-week period. One of the symptoms must include depressed mood or loss of interest in daily activities. In addition, the symptoms should occur nearly every day. Depression, even when treated, holds a high likelihood of recurrence. Over 80 percent of people suffering from depression have more than one episode. In addition, approximately

half of individuals who suffer from an MDE will experience a reoccurring episode within two years.

Dysthymia is a chronic mood disorder. It is considered less severe than MDEs, as it presents with similar but less intense symptoms. Dysthymia is defined by a duration of two years or longer. Diagnosis, as with MDE, includes experiencing depressed mood for most of the day on a nearly daily basis. However, with dysthymia, two of the depressive symptoms listed above must also occur for a diagnosis to be made, as opposed to the five required by MDE. While people who suffer from dysthymia are highly likely to experience MDE, a diagnosis of dysthymia requires its absence in the first two years of the illness. Psychotic major depression (PMD) affects approximately, 4 percent of the population. PMD is more severe than MDE. It is usually episodic, but some cases are chronic. PMD differs from MDE in that individuals suffer a break from reality, most commonly through delusions but sometimes through hallucinations. Paranoid delusions and delusions of guilt are most common. Another common delusion in PMD is the belief that something is wrong physically or with one's health. Most PMD hallucinations are auditory.

At least 13 percent of new mothers suffer from postpartum depression, with higher rates occurring among women of color, single mothers, adolescent mothers, and low-income mothers. Some degree of stress due to the adjustment to motherhood is normal, with "baby blues" estimated to occur in 50–80 percent of women during the first two weeks of motherhood. However, postpartum depression occurs when feelings of sadness, irritability, fatigue, and worthlessness overwhelm new mothers. Postpartum depression is more severe and longer lasting than the "baby blues." It typically begins about one month postpartum and can last up to a year. Postpartum depression is often undiagnosed and untreated, even though effective treatment is available.

Rarer still is postpartum psychosis; although it occurs in less than 1 percent of new mothers, it is often sensationalized in the media. Symptoms of postpartum psychosis include delusions, hallucinations, rapid mood swings, and obsessive thoughts about the baby. Women who have other mental health disorders, such as bipolar disorder, are at higher risk of developing postpartum psychosis.

Seasonal affective disorder (SAD) may also be called winter depression or winter blues. It is characterized by normal mental health throughout the year with an onset of depressive symptoms during the winter months. The prevalence of SAD varies by location, with higher rates occurring in locations that experience longer winters. Although less common, SAD can also occur in the reverse with increased mental distress, most often in the form of increased anxiety, during the summer months. This is referred to as reverse seasonal affective disorder.

## Causes of Depression

There is no single cause for depression, and risk factors can include genetics—specifically having a first-degree relative with depression; sex hormones; and life stress and trauma, such as sexual abuse, assault, domestic violence, and physical illness. Cognitive style can also be a risk factor for depression.

Ruminative thinking, defined as repetitively and passively focusing on the symptoms, causes, and consequences of distress, has also been identified as a risk factor for depression, and is more likely to occur in women. Women are also more likely than men to experience distress over relationships and events in the lives of significant others, and to place their own needs second to others, particularly their children. These interpersonal factors place women at greater risk for depression. Social demands on women through their traditional roles as caregivers and nurturers may increase women's risk for depressive episodes by the increase in chronic stress that is experienced through these roles, as well as the through feelings of inadequacy when women cannot meet the expectations of these roles due to unsupportive and disadvantaged environments.

Poverty, income inequality, and discrimination are all associated with greater incidence of depression, and increase stress among women through a variety of channels—including their decreased ability to successfully fulfill social roles and expectations of women to be "good" mothers, wives, and caregivers. Women, particularly single mothers of young children, are overrepresented among the poor and often suffer from discrimination and negative stereotyping. Poverty also increases the number of uncontrollable and threatening life events that women face—such as violence, ill health, and trauma—which have been found to increase susceptibility to depression. Social relationships and social support networks are also negatively affected by poverty and discrimination, which further increases mothers' risk of both isolation and depression. Family structure can also be a contributing factor in women's depression. Single mothers experience a greater proportion of physical and psychiatric illness than married mothers, including depression, anxiety, and substance abuse, with rates of depression more than doubled for single as compared to married mothers. Family structure as a risk factor is confounded with poverty and discrimination, since single mothers are also more likely to experience social and economic disadvantages than married mothers.

## Depression and Reproduction

Women are at greater risk for depression at certain times in their lives, including puberty, during and after pregnancy, and during perimenopause. Since gender differences in the rates of depression first appear at the age of puberty, and many women report mood disturbances during other times associated with fluctuating sex hormones (oral contraceptive use, menopause, and onset of menstrual cycle), hormonal changes have previously been identified as a casual risk factor. However, research has shown no consistent association between these experiences and major depression. While some women may experience depression while transitioning through menopause, research has found no direct link between menopause and depression. Instead, it appears that stress and negative life events that may be experienced at this time in life are risk factors for depression. Exceptions include women who suffer from severe vasomotor symptoms during the perimenopausal period and/or women who have previously suffered from depression or other affective disorders.

One event that often occurs during the perimenopausal period for mothers is the transition of their children to independent living (the so-called empty nest syndrome). Previously, mothers were thought to be at higher risk for depression due to this event. However, more recent studies have found no negative effects on women's well-being during this transition, and for women who are confident in their children's ability to live independently, an increase in positive affect has been found.

Increases in rates in depression are found, however, during the postpartum period. However, hormonal changes alone are unlikely to cause postpartum depression, since rates within this population are consistently higher among women with a personal and/or family history of depressive episodes. Infertility, miscarriage, and stillbirth are also associated with depression for women as traumatic and uncontrollable life events, as well as through the increased stress of medical intervention—especially in the case of infertility.

### Effects of Maternal Depression on Children

Strong relationships have been found between maternal depression and negative child outcomes. Children of depressed mothers are more likely to suffer from depression themselves than children of nondepressed mothers. Rates of depression among school-aged and adolescent children with depressed mothers range from 20 to 41 percent, and having a depressed mother is the strongest risk factor for depression in adolescence. Children of depressed mothers have other emotional and behavioral problems, including more negative affect, more anxiety, dysregulated aggression, attention deficit disorder, and disruptive behavior disorders. They are also more likely to have lower academic performance and to score lower on tests of intelligence.

Depression affects a woman's ability to care for herself, which may increase the risk of premature birth or delivery of an underweight baby among pregnant women. Depression also affects a woman's ability to parent, and postpartum depression can interfere with mother–infant bonding and attachment. The effects of maternal depression on children are largely due to diminished mother–child interactions that occur because of depression. Depressed mothers are both more withdrawn and more critical in their interactions with their children. Depression also impairs the parenting practices of women. Depressed mothers feel less competent in their parenting, have less energy to devote to parenting, and are less engaged in parenting. Depressed mothers expect negative behaviors from their children and are more likely to perceive their children as being deliberately noncompliant. Children of depressed mothers are also exposed to maternal modeling of cognitions, behaviors, and affect associated with depression.

### Treatment Options

A range of treatment options is available for women suffering from depression, including psychotherapeutic treatments, biological treatments, and pharmacological treatments. Both psychotherapy and antidepressants have been found to be equally effective for mild to moderate depression. Common pharmacologic treatments include tricyclic antidepressants (TRAs), selective serotonin reuptake inhibitors (SSRIs), and serotonin norepinephrine reuptake inhibitors (SNRIs). However, 30–35 percent of the population does not respond to antidepressants.

The use of antidepressant medications during pregnancy or the postpartum period is controversial, and there is no clear consensus on treatment options. Instead, treatment plans are best developed on a case-by-case basis. All antidepressants are secreted into the amniotic fluid and can easily diffuse across the placenta. While SSRIs and SNRIs are the most commonly prescribed medications for perinatal depression, studies have demonstrated contradictory findings with regard to their safety, forcing clinicians to conduct careful risk-benefit analyses for individual cases.

For psychotherapy, interpersonal and cognitive-behavioral interventions have been found to be most effective. Psychotherapy may also be especially helpful at preventing relapse after treatment with antidepressants. Biological and alternative treatments include light therapy, meditation and relaxation, exercise, acupuncture, and herbal agents such as St John's Wort. These alternatives have not been well tested.

There are many barriers for women to seek treatment, including a lack of knowledge—especially regarding postpartum depression—discouragement from family members within cultures where discussing mental health issues outside of the family is unacceptable, access to health care, dissatisfaction with health care providers, fear of addiction to pharmacological treatment, and fear of the side effects of pharmacological treatment—especially among women who are pregnant or breastfeeding. In addition, there is a stigma associated with antidepressant medications, and women may not want to be associated with that stigma.

**See Also:** Drug Abuse; Infertility; Miscarriage; Postpartum Depression; Poverty and Mothering.

**Bibliography**

Avis, Nancy E. "Depression During the Menopausal Transition." *Psychology of Women Quarterly*, v.27 (2003).

Belle, Deborah and Joanne Doucet. "Poverty, Inequality and Discrimination as Sources of Depression Among U.S. Women." *Psychology of Women Quarterly*, v.27 (2003).

Dennerstein, L., E. Dudley, and J. Gutherie. "Empty Nest or Revoving Door? A Prospective Study of Women's Quality of Life in Midlife During the Phase of Children Leaving and Re-Entering the Home." *Psychological Medicine*, v.32 (2002).

Goodman, Sherryl H. "Depression in Mothers." *Annual Review of Clinical Psychology*, v.33/107 (2007).

Kessler, Ronald C. "Epidemiology of Women and Depression." *Journal of Affective Disorders*, v.74 (2003).

Tracy R. Nichols
University of North Carolina at Greensboro

# DES Mothers

DES, short for diethylstilbestrol (or stilbestrol), known as the "grandmother of synthetic estrogens," was the first in a long line of synthetic estrogens. First synthesized in 1938 to prevent menstrual disorders, it quickly became prescribed widely to prevent miscarriages and enhance pregnancies. However, what was supposed to be a miracle drug became a medical nightmare, as it was the first known drug to cross the placenta during pregnancy. Women who took diethylstilbestrol during pregnancy became known as DES mothers; their exposed offspring are known as DES daughters and DES sons.

DES was never patented because funds for its discovery, received from the British government, required that all discoveries it funded be freely available to the world for production; this made it widely available. Although it was undertested and its efficacy and safety subject to debate, it was produced by more than 300 pharmaceutical companies under many brand names, and was prescribed to millions of pregnant women around the world for over 30 years.

Unfortunately, as some researchers had argued as early as the late 1930s, DES was not effective in preventing miscarriage or enhancing pregnancy. Although it was finally contraindicated for pregnancy in 1971, it continued to be used well into the 1980s. When DES was no longer saleable in privileged parts of the world, it was "dumped" into some third world countries for over-the-counter use during pregnancy. Ironically, while DES was an old reproductive technology erroneously used to support pregnancy, it was also used to decrease breast-milk production after pregnancy, and later reappeared as a postcoital pregnancy preventative in the Morning-After pill.

## A Sinister Link Emerges

In the late 1960s, young females began to be diagnosed with a rare and often fatal form of vaginal and cervical cancer known as clear cell adenocarcinoma, previously seen only in postmenopausal women. While physicians were puzzled, it was a mother who was prescribed DES while pregnant who first suggested a connection between her exposure and her daughter's unusual cancer. DES was usually prescribed in the earliest months of pregnancy, when the fetal reproductive tract develops; therefore, it caused cellular and structural abnormalities to the reproductive tracts of the developing fetuses. In a bitter irony, in addition to an increased risk of clear cell adenocarcinoma, DES daughters also have increased risks of infertility, miscarriage, and preterm labor, as well as some autoimmune disorders and breast cancer. DES mothers have an increase in their lifetime risk of breast cancer; other health consequences to DES mothers are suspected and being studied. DES sons are also at an increased risk of reproductive health problems.

This legacy of reproductive woe lives beyond even a second generation. The hoped-for babies of DES daughters that are never conceived, or that die or because of an increased risk of miscarriage or preterm birth, represent a lost part of the third DES generation. Those who survive a premature birth are at risk for both short- and long-term effects of their early exit from the womb; and it is their mothers (DES daughters) and grandmothers (DES mothers) who mourn their loss, tend to their needs, and together experience this intergenerational tragedy.

In a study of DES mothers and daughters, four mother–daughter links in their exposure to DES have been noted. Mothers and daughters explained that they were bound together by their exposure, were both affected in their reproductive capacities, both had increased risk of health consequences due to their co-exposure to DES, and were tied together in their difficulty accomplishing motherhood or grandmotherhood.

Many DES mothers experienced guilt after learning that their daughter's cancers, deaths, and reproductive maladies were consequences of their best intentions to maintain their pregnancies and protect their developing fetuses. Many DES mothers were by their daughter's sides during their illnesses, reproductive challenges, and losses. Some DES mothers even acted as gestational surrogates for their daughters who were unable to carry their own children.

Feelings of mother guilt turned into anger, and anger into political activism for many DES mothers. In the late 1970s, Pat Cody, a DES mother, founded the grassroots group DES Action USA; in the early 1980s in Canada, DES mother Shirley Simand and DES daughter Harriet Simand began DES Action Canada. Both groups spawned a worldwide network of DES activists. The work of DES mothers continues today through their passionate and persistent voices, most currently against the toxic bioaccumulation of other environmental estrogenic substances.

**See Also:** Adoption; Activism, Maternal; Becoming a Mother; Daughters and Mothers; Environmentalism and Mothering; Fertility; Grandmothers and Grandmothering; Grief, Loss of Child; Infertility; Intergenerational Trauma; Miscarriage; Mother Blame; Motherhood Denied; Pregnancy; Reproductive Technologies; Technology and Motherhood.

## Bibliography

Bell, Susan. "A New Model of Medical Technology Development: A Case Study of DES." *Research in Sociology of Health Care*, v.4/1 (1986).

Bell, Susan. "Gendering Medical Science: Producing a Drug for Women." *Feminist Studies*, v.21/3 (1995).

Braun, Margaret Lee. *DES Stories: Faces and Voices of People Exposed to Diethylstilbestrol*. New York: Visual Studies Workshop Press, 2001.

Cody, Pat. *Voices: From Anger to Action*. Self-Published on Lulu.com, 2008.

Centers for Disease Control and Prevention (CDC). "Patients Prescribed DES While Pregnant." www.cdc.gov/des/hcp/information/women/index.html (accessed May 2009).

Davidson, Deborah. "Woe the Women: DES, Mothers and Daughters." In *Gender, Identity & Reproduction: Social Perspectives*, Sarah Earle and Gayle Letherby, eds. New York: Palgrave Macmillan, 2003.

Seaman, Barbara and Gideon Seaman. *Women and the Crisis in Sex Hormones*. New York: Bantam, 1983.

Deborah Davidson
York University

# Dialectics of Reproduction

The concept of the dialectic of reproduction refers to the contradiction in perspectives and experiences on the processes of human reproduction between the genders, as well as referencing conflicting concepts on subjectivity, including essentialism and constructivism. Theories of subjectivity that are dialectical and significant to reproduction hold that essentialism reduces and rationalizes the experiences of the person or subject to their biology—in particular, the expression of their gender.

The notion of essentialization holds that male and females are naturalized in their gender roles and that biology determines the expression of these roles. For example, essentialism would hold that females are good at nurturing, which is why they often prefer to play with dolls or care for babies; and males are aggressive, which is why they enjoy competitive sports or are better suited as breadwinners. Constructivism, on the other hand, holds that gender roles are not inherent, but are constructed as a result of socialization. Accordingly, the roles of males and females are influenced by exposure to particular cultural rules and norms. Constructivist theory asserts that gender roles are produced discursively and politically, and that people learn what it means to be male or female by performing the social prescriptions for normal behavior; otherwise, they risk marginalization, exclusion, and/or being labeled as deviant.

## The Politics of Reproduction

Mary O'Brien, midwife and author of *The Politics of Reproduction*, analyzed the dialectical, historical, and material aspects of the reproductive process. She argued that the physical labor involved in women's reproductive experiences affirms women's connections with their children and integration into the human species, whereas men's discontinuous experiences negate such connections and integration.

Patriarchy enables the reconciliation of this negation for men, by allowing them to claim ownership of the products of women's reproductive labor. O'Brien believed that men and women perceive the world differently because men and women have differing reproductive consciousness as a result of patriarchy. Women's experiences of reproduction are shaped by their location; women worldwide are still lobbying for legal abortion, maternal and child health, childcare, and security for themselves and their families. In a strictly patriarchal society, women are all but absent from most decision-making positions; they are particularly vulnerable to abuses in reproductive technologies.

O'Brien suggests social theory that accounts for women's experience must begin with the process of human reproduction, which is mediated by the intersections of biology, culture, and politics. O'Brien finds the material base of male domination in the separation of male sexuality from reproduction. While maternity is confirmed in the act of giving birth, paternity can be an abstract and uncertain knowledge. O'Brien suggests that men's domination of women arose through the discovery of the link between sexuality and reproduction. In her 1978 article "The Dialectics of Reproduction," Mary O'Brien argues that women's physical experience of bearing children automatically affirms their connection with their children, while male consciousness of the reproductive process is necessarily discontinuous because they do not experience pregnancy and childbirth. Paternity remains an abstraction about which there will always remain some uncertainty, because in the process of conception, men ejaculate their semen into the woman's body (what she calls "the alienation of the seed") without knowing if one of their sperm (or that of some other man) will result in a child.

Reproductive processes are dialectically structured because they are contradictory instances of separation, unification, and transformation. O'Brien asserted the female biological reproductive experience includes menstruation, ovulation, copulation, conception, gestation, labor, birth, appropriation, and nurturing. These moments are symbolically important in the development of female universality; thus, these moments must be considered in the elaboration of the dialectics of reproduction. Women's cultural, sexual femininity requires that they be both dependent and inactive, whereas their biological motherhood feminine identity requires that they be active, aggressive, and competent. The biological manifestations of the material oppositions in reproduction between males and females signal a need for men and women to address these oppositions in a sociological, historical way. From either a practical or abstract perspective, reproduction, in the biological sense, is necessarily social.

## A Philosophical Response

Reproduction has been regarded as quite different from other natural functions. Eating, sexuality, and dying are biological functions with theoretical and philosophical frameworks; yet, there are no comparable philosophies of birth. The understanding of reproduction as merely biological, and the biological as natural, justifies philosophical neglect and the regulation of the reproducing body to the narrow perspectives of the natural and medical sciences. The dialectic of reproduction begs a philosophical response.

Some radical feminists believe that reproductive technologies could be liberating to women if they were controlled by women and used in women's interests. Reproductive technologies that aim to duplicate natural reproduction are potentially disruptive to patriarchal ideology. At first, women hoped that reproductive technologies would offer more choice; however, reproductive and genetic technologies serve many levels of social ordering and control.

Feminists have argued that the opposition between private and public realms works to silence or diminish the concerns of those who give birth and raise children. Unpaid labor in the home forms the invisible foundation on which the public economy operates and depends. Reproductive technologies displace reproduction from the private to the public sphere, which does not actually liberate birthing women, but can subject them to increased medical and social surveillance, as well as decreased authority over the legal and political significance of their pregnant bodies.

## Personal Versus Political Realm

Human reproduction is not often thought of as political; rather, childbirth and its surrounding events usually are construed as individual, biological events, rather than being socially significant. Relegating reproductive activities to the personal realm demonstrates how reproduction has been marginalized in both mainstream and feminist theory, simply by virtue of its designation as biological by conventional social and political philosophies.

Feminist theories analyze how power relationships shape social relationships and channel the direction of social change. Shifts in power relationships transform the economic, social, and moral dimensions of human behavior. With contraceptive and reproductive technologies, women now face a situation where reproduction is a conscious and deliberate act; therefore, also a moral and political act.

Reproductive work differs from productive work in that is it cyclical rather than linear, it commands time on a compulsory rather than voluntary basis (babies need to be fed when they are hungry), and it is necessarily social rather than socially necessary. Because reproduction is both biological and social, the politics and dialectics of reproduction trouble and explore the separation of morality from desire, the separation of mind and body, the separation of private and public.

**See Also:** Artificial Insemination; Childbirth; Pregnancy; Reproduction; Social Reproduction.

## Bibliography

Fuss, Diana. *Essentially Speaking: Feminism, Nature & Difference.* Abingdon, UK: Taylor & Francis, 1989.

Guenther, Lisa. *The Gift of the Other: Levinas and the Politics of Reproduction.* Albany: State University of New York Press, 2006.

Handwerker, W. Penn. "Politics and Reproduction: A Window on Social Change." In *Births and Power: Social Change and the Politics of Reproduction.* Boulder, CO: Westview Press, 1990.

Harstock, Nancy. "Mary O'Brien's Contributions to Contemporary Feminist Theory." *Canadian Woman Studies,* v.18/4 (1999).

Henig, Robin. *Pandora's Baby.* New York: Houghton Mifflin, 2004.

O'Brien, Mary. "The Dialectics of Reproduction." In *Maternal Theory: Essential Readings,* Andrea O'Reilly, ed. Toronto: Demeter Press, 2007.

Spallone, Patricia. *Beyond Conception: The New Politics of Reproduction.* Westport, CT: Bergin & Garvey Publishers, 1989.

Thiele, Bev. "Retrieving the Baby: Feminist Theory and Organic Bodies." *Canadian Woman Studies,* v.18/4 (1999).

Tornes, Kristen. "Reproduction Politics." *Acta Sociologica,* v.26/2 (1983).

Treichler, Paula. "Feminism, Medicine and the Meaning of Childbirth." In *Body/Politics: Women and the Discourses of Science*, Mary Jacobus, Evelyn Fox Keller, and Sally Shuttleworth, eds. New York: Routledge, 1990.

Joani Mortenson
University of British Columbia

# Dinnerstein, Dorothy

Dorothy Dinnerstein (1923–92) was an American feminist scholar and activist whose best-known study *The Mermaid and the Minotaur: Sexual Arrangements and Human Malaise* (1976) argues that, because child rearing is an essentially female occupation, it is responsible for the creation and the maintenance of gender inequalities. Thus, Dinnerstein viewed the unbalanced responsibility between genders in parenting not simply as a symptom of social oppression of women, but as the very cause that continued to perpetrate such oppression. To Dinnerstein, the fact that the responsibility of taking care of children is primarily assigned to the mother eventually causes a rejection of women and of responsibilities falling into the female sphere.

Dorothy Dinnerstein was born in New York City on April 4, 1923, into a Jewish family of Russian and Polish descent. Dinnerstein grew up in a Jewish neighborhood in the Bronx, and her parents' radicalism soon became an inspiration for her own political commitment to socialism. Dinnerstein's adolescence was marked by the Depression; her father, an architectural engineer, lost his job and died before the recession was over. Dinnerstein graduated from Brooklyn College in 1943 and was a graduate student at Swarthmore College, working under Wolfgang Kohler, father of Gestalt psychology, and Max Wertheimer.

She completed her Ph.D. in Psychology at the New School for Social Research under the supervision of Solomon Asch, a prominent social psychologist. Dinnerstein spent most of her teaching and academic career at Rutgers University in Newark, New Jersey, where she cofounded the Institute for Cognitive Studies.

In *The Mermaid and the Minotaur*, Dinnerstein combined Freudian psychoanalysis and Gestalt psychology to trace the marginalization of women in society to motherhood. Because the child has an almost exclusive contact with the mother, he or she tends to see her as both a nurturer and a disciplinarian, an ambivalence they retain through adulthood. Because children are so dependent on their mothers, they come to view her as a threat to their identity and associate her with a state of dependency that, once adults, they do not want to reexperience. To her children, the mother represents an individual with power of life and death over them; because of this, she becomes an object of fear and is rejected in the children's adult lives.

Both sexes experience this sense of rejection toward the mother. Males turn this rejection in a consolidation of their masculine identity, which is tinged with sadistic attitudes toward women. Females equally feel this sense of rejection against their mothers, but because of their gender, they also tend to identify with such a figure. Thus, according to Dinnerstein, they turn their rage against the mother toward themselves in a masochistic attitude. The sole responsibility of child rearing assigned to a female figure conditions the future relationship of the adults with their mothers and fathers, as well as their sex lives and the way they interact with nature. Dinnerstein traces the abuse of "mother nature" to gender inequalities. The language of *The Mermaid and the Minotaur* thus conceives motherhood in almost apocalyptic terms, and the study marks a departure from Dinnerstein's early books, which were written in the tradition of empirical psychology.

In her later works, Dinnerstein combined her interest in feminism with her growing environmental interest and her militancy for nuclear disarmament. She was an active participant of peace camps and campaigned against what she saw as an increasingly unavoidable nuclear holocaust. At the time of her death after a car accident on December 17, 1992, Dinnerstein was working on a project called *Sentience and Survival*, which explored human's inability to prevent world destruction.

**See Also:** Feminist Theory and Mothering; Freud, Sigmund; Psychoanalysis and Motherhood.

**Bibliography**

Gottleibe, R. "Mothering and the Reproduction of Power: Chodorow, Dinnerstein and Social Theory." *Socialist Review*, v.14/5 (1984).

Haaken, J. "Freudian Theory Revisited: A Critique of Rich, Chodorow, and Dinnerstein." *Women's Studies Quarterly*, v.2/4 (Winter 1983).

Snitow, A. "Thinking About *The Mermaid and the Minotaur.*" *Feminist Studies*, v.4/2 (June 1978).

Luca Prono
Independent Scholar

# DiQuinzio, Patrice

The Associate Provost for Academic Services at Washington College, in Chestertown, Maryland, Patrice DiQuinzio earned a bachelor's degree from Villanova and a Ph.D. from Bryn Mawr. As an author of several books and articles on mothering and feminist theory, DiQuinzio is a well-written scholar on motherhood.

Describing and illustrating the difficulty of embodying the totality of the ideal mother in U.S. society, which tends to reward perfection and the achievement of an ideal type of woman, while at the same time tending to fault others who fail to succeed, DiQuinzio contends that the United States provides little to no material or social support to mothers and children. This is the difficulty inherent in mothering, as described by DiQuinzio her 1999 book *The Impossibility of Motherhood*.

DiQuinzio often examines how well feminist theory is able to explain or conceptualize motherhood, finding it often lacking. In *The Impossibility of Motherhood*, feminist theory is touted to be able to describe a unified and all-inclusive account of the experiences of pregnancy and motherhood, which DiQuinzio argues are inherently individualistic and subjective accounts of a singular individual's understanding of life. Feminism as a predominantly social theory, DiQuinzio contends, would have to recognize that conception, pregnancy, childbirth, and mothering are individualist in nature and need to be theoretically and conceptually comprehended as such in scholarly work.

Essentially, DiQuinzio suggests that in order to be most useful and able to incorporate the lived experiences of mothering, motherhood, pregnancy, and childbirth, new concepts of feminist theory must be formed to account for the inherently individualistic nature of these social and individual events.

**See Also:** Becoming a Mother; Childbirth; Family Values; Feminist Theory and Mothering; Mothering Versus Motherhood.

**Bibliography**

DiQuinzio, Patrice. "Exclusion and Essentialism in Feminist Theory: The Problem of Mothering." *Hypatia*, v.8/3 (Summer 1993).

DiQuinzio, Patrice. *The Impossibility of Motherhood: Feminism, Individualism, and the Problem of Mothering*. New York: Routledge, 1999.

Valerie R. Stackman
Howard University

# Disabled Mothers

The term *disabled mother* includes any woman living with a disability who also parents children. However, "disabled mothers" cannot be understood as a stable category, but instead as a set of changing definitions and attitudes with regard to both disability and mothering. What constitutes disability varies across cultures and history and greatly depends on material and social conditions and ideological beliefs and values at a given moment in human history.

From Classical antiquity to the current postmodern era, a range of meanings has been ascribed to disability—from a sign of divine glorification or punishment, or later an outward mark of inner moral character, to a common condition of the poor and an index of social position, to biological and then medicalized definitions that led to a therapeutic model of correction or restoration, and then to critiques of medicalization, and the social and political models of disability.

Efforts to characterize "disabled mothers" are further complicated by androcentric histories, which report elite male achievements of state and war. The few available representations of everyday life often generalize lived realities and overlook the lives of women or the disabled as particular and not universal. As a result, it is difficult to know the numbers of mothers with disability or what they would have experienced in daily life. Certainly, women with disability did bear and parent children; disease and illness and their effects would have been common in earlier ages.

However, ascertaining the number of women born with disability surviving to reproductive age proves impossible. The outright discouraging of women with disability from bearing children probably did not occur until the eugenics era of the early 20th century. Such prohibition is no longer overt, but its legacy remains in genetic and popular discourses and in the lack of social supports for mothers with disability.

Histories of disability argue that perceptions about disability fell into two categories in antiquity: disability as a sign of the gods or an omen, both requiring interpretation. Individuals bearing visible anomalies of the human form could be read as monstrous or as signs of special powers, e.g., as an omen of future events or a sign of the ability to prophesize. Intellectual disabilities or mental illness could be read as signs of demonic power. Alternately, disability was seen as illness or weakness brought on as punishment from the gods or fates.

In both categories, disability was understood as interpretable, as either divine or malign. Unlike later perceptions of disability, both positive and negative, there was no sense that disability was an inheritable or a general human condition. Given the prevalence of disease and illness among men and women, and disfigurement resulting from war, famine, and epidemics, the experience of a weakened or impaired body was likely widespread; however, much of what today might be marked out as *disability* may have gone unremarked. Extant texts and visual depictions suggest that the while the disabled were not excluded from public life, most women were confined to the private sphere of children, slaves, and chattel. No doubt there were mothers with disability, but high infant and maternal mortality made their survival even more difficult than for nondisabled women.

## Middle Ages and Early Modern Period

During the Middle Ages and early modern period in the Christian era of Western Europe, disability came to be seen increasingly through a framework of religious and moral imperatives as punishment for sin. Disability scholarship indicates that disabilities could be read as a visible sign of God's retribution for violations of moral, ethical, or religious laws. Thus, rather than viewing disability as a sign of special power, this perspective suggested a causal relationship between sin and disability.

However, histories of disability also suggest that disability was probably a very common situation for the poor, and that impairment resulting from plague or disease meant that communities typically contained members with disabilities. One's position in society dictated one's lived experiences and living conditions. For example, members of the aristocratic class with a disability might have been taken care of in a convent or abbey, whereas serfs or peasants remained enmeshed in the fabric of the working community. For the poor, disability resided in family and community spaces and women with disabilities likely bore children and/or cared for children of larger family groupings. In sum, a woman's position in society was more important than disability in terms of reproductive possibilities or limitations.

## Enlightenment

The Enlightenment ushered in a scientific orientation to disability. Studies in anatomy and physiology, especially through autopsies, led physicians to connect behaviors and functions to specific sites in the body and to view the disabled body as an object for scientific scrutiny. Under the scientific gaze, disability became biological rather than mystical or supernatural. Medical advancements brought greater specificity to descriptions of disability and to the classification of disease, empowering physicians to diagnose and treat disability.

This new emphasis on disease and treatment led to fears of contamination, which in turn prompted the creation of institutions and specialized hospitals to sequester the disabled. As a result, disability disappeared from community spaces as fewer individuals were cared for at home. Many hospitals and institutions also sponsored rehabilitation or restoration of the disabled to a "normal" state, implying that people could be made whole again and reintroduced into society. Thus, institutionalization also led to the belief that the disabled were "abnormal," a move that mutually constituted non disabled people as "normal."

For the poor and lower classes, sheltered workspaces were developed for people with disabilities, but members of the upper classes were also given work. For example, an aristocratic woman with disabilities might serve as a family caretaker who would at once be taken care of in the family and would also care for younger members of the family. Elite women with disabilities may have had opportunities to care for disabled children in charity hospitals run by religious groups. During this period, women with disabilities may have had fewer opportunities or encouragement to bear their own children, but they may well have helped raise children in the larger family group.

## Early 19th Century

During the late 18th and early 19th centuries, motherhood came to represent the culmination of a woman's role in white, middle-class society; specifically, mothers were to educate children in society's norms. In addition, disability was increasingly deemed abnormal. Thus, being disabled called into question whether a woman could properly perform the mothering role.

The ideology of the domestic sphere also presented powerful cultural scripts for women and mothers. Prescriptions for femininity and appropriate maternal performance equated the physical body with moral strength. Conversely, the disabled body came to represent either sexlessness, indicating that the woman was unfit to mother, or sexually deviancy, marking her as unfit for marriage. As the child's first educator, good mothers inculcated in their children society's rules and norms, including correct speech, proper manners, independence, and self-reliance. Embedded in this education was a fear of disability as deviant and unpresentable, due in large part to associations with abnormality, dependency, and the institutionalization of people with disabilities. Ironically, such reasoning aligned mothers with the disabled; even as they instructed their children in correct speech and independence, moth-

ers were supposed to be dependent, quietly mute, and apart from the public sphere.

As a result, marital prohibitions increased in the first half of the 19th century under the reasoning that if the mother was not "normal," then she could not adequately fulfill the role of inculcating normalcy in her children. These prohibitions increased during the second half of the century as disability became redefined as an inheritable condition.

## Late 19th, Early 20th Centuries

The eugenics movement of the late 19th and early 20th centuries produced a substantial shift in attitudes about disabled mothers. Eugenics rested on the belief that the human species could be improved through reproductive engineering. Although some eugenicists espoused "positive eugenics" by encouraging reproduction of people believed to have superior traits, most favored "negative eugenics," which discouraged reproduction by individuals presumed to have genetic defects and other undesirable characteristics. Under the influence of eugenics, disabilities were considered not only genetic but also moral, cultural, or behavioral deficiencies or defects that could be purged from humanity through selective breeding.

In 1927, the U.S. Supreme Court ruled in favor of compulsory sterilization of the so-called "feeble-minded," a flexible category used to label any number of abnormally defined traits or social ills including poverty, presumed mental defects, psychoses, and illegitimacy. The case against Carrie Buck, an 18-year-old woman from Virginia, rested on her family's social standing and history. Prosecutors described Buck's birth and the later birth of her daughter as illegitimate and resulting from the expression of a permanent, hereditary flaw that could be passed down from generation to generation. The case of Carrie Buck embodied the fears about the degeneration of the nation circulating during the early 20th century.

Buck was categorized as defective and in need of institutionalization and treatment. As a woman of childbearing years, she came to represent a greater threat in the minds of American eugenicists worried about America's "good stock." When Justice Oliver Wendell Holmes handed down his now infamous decision, arguing "Three generations of imbeciles are enough" (*Buck v. Bell*), the U.S. Supreme Court upheld the existing Virginia State Supreme Court ruling that permitted the eugenic sterilization of the feeble-minded.

## Late 20th, Early 21st Centuries

Emphasis on a return to normalcy after World War I made the open acknowledgment of disability shameful. Technologies, such as prosthetic advances, were designed to enable the disabled to overcome their disabilities and return to normal. Scientific management ruled the day. Regulations on disabled mothers that emerged during the eugenics movement did not disappear but were instead reconfigured and represented as self-directed, scientific mothering.

Handbooks, magazine articles, courses in home economics, and later television offered women best practices for raising a child. However, the medical profession wielded ultimate authority and pressured mothers to send disabled children to institutions for expert care and to protect the normal development of nondisabled children. Though many institutions were little more than warehouses for the disabled, research suggests that within them older disabled women sometimes had opportunities to mother younger children.

In place of overt prohibitions, women were encouraged to internalize regulations for reproductive health by spacing and limiting births. A related hygienic goal was to reduce the number of children born with disability, as for example in March of Dimes campaigns. Twentieth-century women were discouraged from becoming pregnant after age 35 because of the increased risk of Down syndrome. Women with disabilities received little encouragement to reproduce for fear that they could pass their "bad genes" on to their children.

At the turn of the 21st century, opportunities for women with disability to mother grew but so did the demand for genetic normality. Scrutiny of genetic health increased with the advent of advanced reproductive technologies. For example, embryos for in vitro fertilization (IVF) were regularly screened for "defects." Genetic testing of a fetus and selective abortion became another tool for eliminating "defective" fetuses. The rise of social movements in the 1970s—the women's movement, disability rights movement, and Stonewall (later gay-lesbian-

bisexual-transgender-queer [GLBTQ])—led to a denaturalizing of mothering, making it possible for those, heretofore not otherwise able, to mother, and also led to the deinstitutionalization movement. Women with disability sought to live in the least restrictive environment.

The advent of the Americans with Disabilities Act (ADA) in 1990 highlighted the importance of accessibility and accommodation and increased opportunities for women with disability to mother. For example, the ADA raised awareness of the need for wheelchair-accessible examining tables for gynecologists. At the same time, 21st-century medicine now mandated prenatal screening for all women, not just those over 35, thereby reifying normality and making it necessary to decide whether or not to move ahead with a pregnancy. Advanced reproductive technologies thus continued the trend of scientific self-regulation.

Disability studies and feminism as fields for scholarship and activism promoted new analytic models that revealed the social and political dimensions of gender and disability identity, and new theories of interdependent relations that allowed for more complex understanding of disability as part of the wider human condition of vulnerability. Activists and academics studied and contested stigmatizing and oppression and examined the unstable and shifting intersections of identity, thereby revealing the linkages, for example, between mothering and disability, not just for mothers with disabilities but for all women who mother.

**See Also:** Fertility; LBGTQ Families and Motherhood; Maternal Mortality; Reproductive Technologies; Scientific Mothering; Surrogate Mothering.

## Bibliography

Albrecht, Gary L., Katherine D. Seelman, and Michael Bury. *Handbook of Disability Studies*. Thousand Oaks, CA: Sage , 2001.

Davis, Lennard, ed. *The Disability Studies Reader*. New York: Routledge, 2006;

Davis, Lennard. *Enforcing Normalcy: Disability, Deafness, and the Body*. New York: Verso, 1995.

Fine, Michelle, and Adrienne Asch, eds. *Women With Disabilities: Essays in Psychology, Culture, and Politics*. Philadelphia: Temple University Press, 1988.

Kevles, David. *In the Name of Eugenics: Genetics and the Uses of Human Heredity.* New York: Knopf, 1985.

Kudlick, Catherine J. "'Disability' and 'Divorce': A Blind Parisian Cloth Merchant Contemplates His Options in 1756." In *Gendering Disability*, Bonnie G. Smith and Beth Hutchison, eds. New Brunswick, NJ: Rutgers University Press, 2004.

LaCom, Cindy. "Female Disability, Sexuality, and the Maternal in the Nineteenth-Century Novel." In *The Body and Physical Difference: Discourses of Disability*, David T. Mitchell and Sharon L. Snyder, eds. Ann Arbor: University Michigan Press, 1997.

Lewiecki-Wilson, Cynthia and Jen Cellio, eds. *Disability and Mothering: Liminalities of Cultural Embodiment.* Toronto: Demeter Press, 2010.

Pernick, Martin. "Defining the Defective: Eugenics, Aesthetics, and Mass Culture in Early Twentieth-Century America." In *The Body and Physical Difference: Discourses of Disability*, David T. Mitchell and Sharon L. Snyder, eds. Ann Arbor: University of Michigan Press, 1997.

Stiker, Henri-Jacques. *A History of Disability.* William Sayers, trans. Ann Arbor: University of Michigan Press, 1999.

Trent, James W., Jr. *Inventing the Feeble Mind: A History of Mental Retardation in the United States.* Berkeley: University of California Press, 1995.

Cynthia Lewiecki-Wilson
Miami University
Jen Cellio
Northern Kentucky University

# Discipline of Children

According to the classic work of Diana Baumrind, there are different parenting styles: authoritative, authoritarian, and permissive—a typology based on a two-factor model of control (how demanding parents are) and warmth (parental responsiveness). She noted that permissive parents are high on acceptance/responsiveness, but low on control; authoritarian parents are low on responsiveness and high on control; and authoritative parents are high on both responsiveness and control.

The style believed and shown to have the most positive results on children is authoritative or democratic parenting, which sets and enforces limits; sets expectations that are age appropriate; and involves monitoring, support, affection, encouragement, and appropriate participation by children. In the study, authoritarian parents were the most likely to use corporal punishment or more punitive types of discipline. Classic and more recent studies found social class variations in parenting styles, with working-class parents more likely than others to use more punitive approaches. Some studies found that family poverty and its related stresses, resulting from chronic adverse conditions, also increase the likelihood of parents using a reactive socialization style that often includes harsh, inconsistent, and punitive physical punishment. That said, many parents in poor economic circumstances do not use corporal punishment, and child maltreatment in middle- and higher-income homes is not uncommon. The line between mild and harsh discipline is often difficult to draw, but easy to cross.

## Corporal Punishment

For a time, in the West, corporal punishment was seen as a way to civilize, moralize, educate, and correct "bad" behavior in children. For some, corporal punishment continues to be seen as the duty of good parents and teachers, and part of proper household governance. Some continue to believe that corporal punishment is an effective tool in correcting bad behavior, reinforcing respect and obedience, protecting children from harm, teaching life lessons, and preparing them for life's challenges, and is a sign of caring. Opponents of corporal punishment have argued that spanking is immoral, potentially abusive, demoralizing, and ineffective in correcting misbehavior. The Coalition on Physical Punishment of Children and Youth, a national coalition of organizations concerned with the well-being of children and their families, has noted that there is no clear evidence of any benefit to using physical punishment with children, and that it is linked to weaker internalization of moral values. There is also evidence that it places children at increased risk of physical injury.

A study conducted in the United States and Canada noted that most parents want more information on child rearing, including discipline, but few pediatricians discuss it. The study found that 38.4 percent of parents reported using the same discipline that was used when they were children, while 54.2 percent did not. Parents who experienced spanking or yelling in their childhood were more likely to use those techniques on their own children. One-third viewed their disciplinary efforts as ineffective.

In the *Joint Statement on Physical Punishment of Children and Youth,* coauthored by Joan Durrant, Ron Ensom, and The Coalition on Physical Punishment of Children and Youth, recommends that parents receive more and better parenting education, as studies have shown that parents with knowledge of child development are less likely to interpret a child's drive for independence and testing as bad behavior. In contrast, a parent whose sense of control is believed to be threatened by a child's behavior or who sees the child's behavior as an intentional challenge to parental authority is more likely to use physical punishment. Increased education on child development may help parents feel less frustrated, and less likely to respond emotionally to a child's misbehavior. Some studies have shown that physical punishment often results in short-term compliance and, potentially, longer-term, negative behavioral outcomes.

A Statistics Canada study of parenting styles found a link between more punitive parenting practices and more aggressive behavior for girls and boys, for low-income and higher-income households, and across regions of residence. The study found that when nonpunitive parenting was used at ages 2–3 to ages 8–9, children had low aggressive behavior scores at age 8–9. When punitive parenting was used at ages 2–3 to 8–9, children were reported to score high in aggressive behavior at ages 8 and 9. While this does not prove there is a causal link between punitive parenting and aggressive behavior in children, this is consistent with earlier research showing that harsh or punitive parenting practices often lead to increased aggressive behavior in children.

Durrant and Ensom also suggest that children be afforded the same rights and protection from physical assault that other citizens, and a growing number of children in countries around the world, are receiving. They ask that Canada join a growing list of countries that have prohibited the use of physical punishment against children, including Sweden (1979), Finland (1983), Norway (1987), Austria (1989), Cyprus (1994), Denmark (1997), Latvia (1998), Croatia (1998), and Israel (2000), even though this represents only about 2.4 percent of the world's children.

Proponents of corporal punishment are concerned over the erosion of parental control over children. Opponents of the use of corporal punishment have argued that adult/parental power and children's powerlessness are precisely the problem that needs to be eradicated. Some of these argue that it is a human rights violation and runs counter to the United Nations Convention on the Rights of the Child. Controversy in Canada continues to focus on section 43 of the Criminal Code, enacted in 1892: "Every school teacher, parent or person standing in the place of a parent is justified in using force by way of correction towards a pupil or child, as the case may be, who is under his care, if the force does not exceed what is reasonable under the circumstances."

A number of organizations have fought unsuccessfully for years for the repeal of this section of the Criminal Code, on the grounds that it violates children's right to protection from assault, and because what are deemed to be "reasonable force" and "by way of correction" are left to individual judges to interpret and determine. Recently, the Canadian Foundation for Children, Youth and the Law challenged the constitutionality of section 43 in an Ontario Court on violations of section 7 (on the security of persons) of the Canadian Charter of Rights and Freedoms. In 2000, the Court upheld section 43, with the judge dismissing the application. The Foundation turned to the Ontario Court of Appeal, and again the Court upheld the constitutionality of section 43. The case was taken to the Supreme Court of Canada. In a 6–3 decision, the Supreme Court ruled that section 43 does not violate the constitutional rights of children, but narrowed the definition of who may use physical punishment; on what ages, body parts, and capacities of children; with what force; and under what circumstances.

The Court interpreted "reasonable force" as "minor corrective force" that is short-lived and not harmful. It set limits on what would be considered reasonable force to help reduce the risk that courts will make arbitrary or subjective decisions. It also ruled that "teachers may reasonably apply force to remove a child from a classroom or secure compliance with instructions, but not merely as corporal punishment." It ruled out the use of force stemming from the caregiver's frustration, loss of temper, or abusive personality. The latter use of force would be considered abuse.

**See Also:** Care Giving; Child Abuse; Child Custody and the Law; Childhood; Child Poverty; Children; Poverty and Mothering; Violence Against Mothers/Children.

## Bibliography

Ackerman, B., E. Brown, and C. Izard. "Continuity and Change in Levels of Externalizing Behaviour in School of Children From Economically Disadvantaged Families." *Child Development*, v.74 (2003).

Baumrind, Diana. "Child Care Practices Anteceding Three Patterns of Preschool Behaviour." *Genetic Psychology Monographs*, v.75 (1967).

Canadian Broadcasting Corporation/CBC News. "Spanking Parents Refused Custody." http://www.cbc.ca/news/story/2001/07/09/spanking_parents010709.html (July 9, 2001). (accessed July 2009).

Conger, R, X. Ge, G. Elder, F. Lorenz, and R. Simons. "Economic Stress, Coercive Family Process and Developmental Problems of Adolescents." *Child Development*, v.65 (1994).

Davis, Phillip. "The Changing Meaning of Spanking." In *Families in Transition*, A.S. Skolnick and J. Skolnick, eds. New York: HarperCollins, 1997.

Greenspan, Stephen. "Rethinking 'Harmonious Parenting' Using a Three-Factor Discipline Model." *Child Care Practice*, v.12/1 (2006).

Kohn, Melvin. *Class and Conformity: A Study of Values*. Chicago: University of Chicago Press, 1977.

Lareau, Annette. 'Social Class and the Daily Lives of Children: A Study From the United States." *Childhood*, v.7/2 (2000).

Lareau, Annette. *Unequal Childhoods*. Berkeley: University of California Press, 2003.

Mansager, Erik and Roger Volk. "Parents' Prism: Three Dimensions of Effective Parenting." *Journal of Individual Psychology*, v.60/3 (2004).

McLoyd, Vonnie. "Socioeconomic Disadvantage and Child Development." *American Psychologist*, v.53 (1998).

Pettit, G., J. Bates and K. Dodge. "Supportive Parenting, Ecological Context and Children's Adjustment: A Seven-Year Longitudinal Study." *Child Development*, v.68 (1997).

Smith, Judith and Jeanne Brooks-Gunn. "Correlates and Consequences of Harsh Discipline of Young Children." *Archives of Pediatric and Adolescent Medicine*, v.151 (1997).

Thomas, Eleanor. "Aggressive Behaviour Outcome for Young Children." *Statistics Canada*, 2004.

Patrizia Albanese
Ryerson University

# Displacement

The term *displacement* refers to a situation in which individuals are uprooted from their homes involuntarily and moved either to another country or to a different location within their own country. Persons displaced globally across international borders are defined as refugees and asylum seekers. People who have been obliged by forces beyond their power to give up their usual home, and seek refuge elsewhere within their own country, are defined as internally displaced persons (IDPs).

## Reasons for Displacement

The major causes of external and internal displacement are natural disasters, ethnic and civil conflicts, major development projects, human rights violations, and political persecution. Around the world, there are approximately 33 million displaced people (12 million refugees and 21 million IDPs). The international community is under legal obligations via the United Nations 1951 Refugee Convention to assist refugees, but not IDPs, except in the case of an invitation or submission of the national government. Although national governments are, in the first instance, responsible for the protection of their own people, not all governments have been willing or able to help their own IDPs. In many cases, the national governments themselves have been involved in the displacement, and thus, have hindered international assistance and intervention. Additionally, even in cases where the local governments allow international aid, there are common obstacles such as closed borders, land mines, and front-line battles that might prevent the proper help from reaching the displaced people.

## Vulnerability of Mothers and Children

In comparison with the general population, both refugees and IDPs suffer from higher rates of malnutrition, exposure to disease, and lack of access to proper housing, education, and health care. It is not uncommon for displaced people to suffer from posttraumatic stress disorder and other mental health problems. Displacement breaks peoples' links to livelihoods and traditional support mechanisms. Vulnerability to disease is exacerbated by high exposure rates resulting for overcrowded living conditions and poor health care.

Women and children comprise between 70 and 80 percent of the displaced population. Displaced women are at a specific risk of being sexually exploited and victimized. Children are particularly vulnerable, since displacement interrupts their education, ruptures their families, often separates them from their parents, breaks their communities, and destroys traditional norms. The war in Bosnia, for instance, was characterized by massive displacement and disruption, as well as loss of life, relatives, and property. Following the war, there was a high rate of depression and an overwhelming loss of perceived power and self-esteem among women and children. Similarly, the costs of civil wars in Africa have impacted women intensely. There has been a substantial increase in the rates of female poverty, sexual assaults, and rape. Displacement is particularly difficult when mothers are separated from their children. Some displaced mothers, as is the case of migrant labor mothers, move from impoverished parts of the globe, mainly from Asia, Africa, the Caribbean, and Latin America, to postindustrial economies to serve as nannies, domestic workers, and unskilled hotel and restaurant workers. These women are separated from their children, and much of their personal mothering work relies on the support of other women. Grandmothers, sisters, older daughters, and female neighbors and friends assist with daily mothering of the children who are left behind.

The stringent immigration and refugee policies of most Western countries compel many refugee mothers to continue to be separated from their children for long periods, which perpetuates uncertainty and poses several risks to these mothers and their children. When and if they are reunited, the pain of the absence, the lack of shared family memories, and the obvious drifts between these mothers and their children all have to be overcome in the process of reestablishing continuity. In few cases, however, displacement may erode patriarchal arrangements and thus enhance women's power. Gender roles may become more egalitarian when fathers assume the duties of the missing mothers. In these instances, displaced women contribute to their families' livelihood, earning them a right to voice their opinion on household issues. Another important outcome of relative financial independence is that women are less likely to tolerate abusive relationships.

When the spatial separation of mothers from their children is perceived as an act of patriotism in times of national emergency, women are sometimes glorified for sacrificing their families and children's needs for the advancement of national goals. For example, in the context of Israeli mothers who served as emissaries in Europe during World War II, women and motherhood were reconceptualized to accommodate the national struggle against the Nazis. Another example can be seen in the case of women from the Philippines, who, by traveling and working in highly industrialized countries and sending home remittances, assist in the national effort to pay off a huge foreign debt.

Case studies suggest that the effect of displacement on mothers' lives is both negative and positive. As their material, social, and psychological worlds collapse, their lengthy separation from their children results in a lifelong sense of trauma and loss. In other cases, by mobilizing other women to assist them, they may increase their earning power and feel a sense of enhanced freedom.

**See Also:** Maternal Absence; Migration and Mothering; Nannies; Other Mothering; Race and Racism; Refugee Mothers; Transnationalism; War and Motherhood.

## Bibliography

Gibson, E.C. "The Impact of Political Violence: Adaptation and Identity Development in Bosnian Adolescent Refugees." *Studies in Social Work*, v.73/1 (2002).

Hinton, D.C., V. Pich, S. Safren, M. Pollack, and R McNally. "Anxiety Sensitivity in Traumatized Cambodian Refugees: A Discriminant Function and Factor Analytic Investigation." *Behavior Research and Therapy,* v.43/12 (2005).

Norwegian Refugee Council, Internal Displacement Monitoring Centre. *Internal Displacement: Global Overview of Trends and Developments in 2005.* New York: United Nations, 2006.

Ogbonna-Nwaogu, Ifevinwa Maureen. "Civil Wars in Africa: A Gender Perspective of the Cost on Women." *Journal of Social Sciences,* v.16/3 (May 2008).

Riley, Robin. "Women and War: Militarism, and the Practice of Gender." *Sociology Compass,* v.2/4 (July 2008).

Rosenberg-Friedman, Lilach. "The Nationalization of Motherhood and the Stretching of Its Boundaries: Shelihot Aliya and Evacuees in Eretz Israel (Palestine) in the 1940s." *Women's History Review,* v.17/5 (November 2008).

Rousseau, Cecile, Marie-Claire Rufagari, Deogratias Bagilishya, and Toby Measham. "Remaking Family Life: Strategies for Re-Establishing Continuity Among Congolese Refugees During the Family Reunification Process." *Social Science & Medicine,* v.59/5 (September 2004).

Witmer, T., et al. "Trauma and Resilience Among Bosnian Refugee Families: A Critical Review of the Literature." *Journal of Social Work Research and Evaluation,* v.2/2 (2001).

Rina Cohen
York University

# Divorce

Divorce is a legal process that leads to the termination of a marriage; that is, the separation of husband and wife that confers on the parties the right to remarriage under civil and/or other provisions, according to the laws of the country. These vary considerably around the world, and divorce is not permitted in some countries, such as Malta and the Philippines, though annulment is permitted. The wide variation in the legal provision for divorce also affects the incidence of divorce, which is relatively low in countries or areas where divorce is difficult to obtain. Levels of divorce are also affected by the ability of husbands and wives to meet administrative and court cost, and likewise by religious beliefs worldwide. Statistics consistently show that Guatemala has the lowest divorce rate in the world, with 0.1 divorces as a percent of marriage. In 2002, Sweden had the highest rate, with 54.9 percent followed by Belarus at 2.9 percent. A separation can be obtained in many countries, but this usually only comprises the first part of divorce.

## The Principles of Divorce

The divorce process usually also involves consideration of child custody and residence, as well as spousal and child maintenance and the distribution of property and assets. This is usually the case if there is disagreement between the parties, and if amicable arrangements are made, the legal system may only be used to grant the divorce itself. These areas are complex and are often subject to dispute.

Divorces are based on the principles of "fault" or "no fault" of the husband and/or wife, depending on the country's legal system. Australia has a no-fault system that has been in place since 1975, but in the United Kingdom, couples must wait for two years if a no-fault divorce is to be granted. Adversarial proceedings about fault or other issues can be an expensive and stressful experience to those involved, and particular attention is paid to children in such circumstances by sociologists as well as governments.

There is increasing focus on introducing less adversarial proceedings and mediation processes, although these have had mixed success internationally. For example, the United Kingdom's 1996 Family Law Act intended to make a 12-month "cooling off" period and mediation compulsory, but pilots were unsuccessful, and that part of the Act was not implemented. In Portugal, however, since March 2008, if spouses agree to divorce and associated terms, they can have an electronic divorce, which can also be issued by a nonjudiciary administrator. Parenting plans are compulsory in the United States, and these set out child and parent contact in some details.

## History and Demographics

Divorce has existed as far back as there are historical records, and in Roman times, attitudes toward divorce relaxed over time to the extent that either spouse could divorce the other, although this remained to some extent culturally taboo. The issue of divorce as taboo is seen in many cultures for many reasons, including associations between lone parenting and poverty, religious beliefs, social standing, and negative labeling. Religion in particular has affected the divorce rate, and by the 10th century after the growth of Christianity, divorce rates were lower due to marriage being seen as a lifetime promise to God and therefore only possible to dissolve by God.

Over time, marriage became to be accepted as a civil contract, over which civil courts could preside. This is variously described as progressive rejection of the Christian marriage doctrine. Divorce only increased slowly, however, And divorce was allowed in Switzerland in 1531 on such grounds as abandonment, leprosy, "whoreishness," and insanity. Henry VIII declared his own divorce from Catherine of Aragon in 1533 and later broke away from the Catholic Church in Rome to become head of the new Church of England. Before the enactment of the world's first no-fault divorce law in 1792, Pierre-Frangois Gossin demanded legal divorce as the logical fulfillment of the French Revolution: "After having made man again free and happy in public life, it remains for you to assure his liberty and happiness in private life." On the eve of the Russian Revolution, Lenin wrote: "One cannot be a democrat . . . without demanding full freedom of divorce."

The issue of fault became more important, and as governments were concerned about rising divorce rates, particularly in the Western world, courts applied stringent fault rules, without evidence of which couples were not allowed to divorce. The concepts of guilt or innocence were therefore tied to divorce proceedings in many countries. In the medieval Islamic world, divorce (known as *talaq*), was seen as acceptable and was more common than in the modern-day Middle East, where rates of divorce are low and still considered undesirable by many.

## Statistics

The top 10 world divorce rates in 2002 were Sweden, 54.9 percent; Belarus, 52.9 percent; Finland, 51.2 percent; Luxembourg, 47.4 percent; Estonia, 46.7 percent; Australia, 46 percent; United States, 45.8 percent; Denmark, 44.5 percent; Belgium, 44 percent; and Austria, 43.4 percent. The bottom 10 rates were Guatemala, 0.13 percent; Sri Lanka, 0.15 percent; Libya, 0.24 percent; Armenia, 0.3 percent; Mongolia, 0.38 percent; Georgia, 0.40 percent; Bosnia and Herzegovina, 0.40 percent; Chile, 0.42 percent; Mexico, 0.48 percent; and El Salvador, 0.49 percent.

## Child Support and Residence

There is much controversy over the arrangements made for children after divorce. Ex-spouses often find it difficult to agree on financial maintenance and frequency of contact between parents and children, which can be complicated by legal systems and parents linking the two. In around 10 percent of cases in Europe, parents who cannot agree on the terms of divorce in respect to their children use the court systems to make a decision for them. It is usually the case that such courts will settle living and visiting arrangements of children before coming to decisions about property division and maintenance.

Some child support systems, such as the United Kingdom Child Support Act of 1991, reduced the amount of maintenance payable to the parent with residence of the children if the children stayed more than two nights a week with the nonresident parent. Many studies showed that this resulted in problems with the ongoing relationship between the parents and children, and this association was removed in 2005. Other child support systems impose sanctions if maintenance is not paid, such as money deducted from the absent parent's source of income to withholding passports or even curfews.

Some countries encourage a "clean break" divorce, which is intended to make each spouse self-sufficient as soon as possible. For example, a husband may be required to maintain his ex-wife only while she acquired a qualification or was retrained in order to improve her earning capacity. It is usually considered, however, that even if any maintenance payable to an ex-spouse is temporary, the nonresident parent has an obligation to their children that should last until they are adults.

It is also possible in some countries for a child to divorce their parents, providing they can present sufficient evidence and are considered capable enough of instructing legal counsel or representing themselves. Grounds include those of neglect or abuse.

## Divorce and Poverty

Around 70 percent of all divorces are instigated by women, although this varies over time and place. After divorce, most women's income goes down and most men's goes up. This is the result of most divorces where children are resident with the mother rather than the father. Lone fathers occur in around 10 percent of cases in Europe, but many of these are due to the death of the spouse rather than divorce. Mothers do not always gain residence of their children, however; for example, in Iran, the ongoing care of the children is seen as the responsibility of the father.

In cases where women do gain custody of their children, they then become responsible for their general day-to-day care and have to fit employment and other responsibilities around them, depending on family support and the availability and cost of childcare. Poverty rates among lone mothers are higher than in families with two parents. Feminists argue this is part of widespread feminization of poverty, and during the 1986 divorce referendum in Ireland, one woman remarked: "A woman voting for divorce is like a turkey voting for Christmas."

## Effects of Divorce on Children

There is much discussion in the fields of psychology and sociology about the effects of separation and divorce on children. Older children are more likely than younger children to live in a household without one biological parent. There is some evidence that children from separated and divorced families do less well in their educational achievements, but this depends on many variables such as age, gender, the cirumstances of their parents' separation, and the ongoing relationship between parents and children. Younger children can become unsettled and "clingy," while older children can blame themselves for one parent leaving the family home.

In the United Kingdom, nearly 50 percent of divorced fathers lose touch with their children completely 12 months after divorce, and this also occurs in other countries. Fathers may find other partners or find it difficult to accept a part-time relationship with their children, or their ex-spouse may make contact difficult. Many of these effects are similar to a bereavement, which divorce is often likened to. Over a 12–18-month period, children can also experience stages of bereavement, starting with

shock and disbelief, anger, and profound sadness, before moving to a stage of recovery.

There are also potential problems with lower self-esteem, truancy, health problems, and problems forming long-term relationships themselves later in life. Loss of a male role model may be significant to children, particularly boys, but there is evidence to support the argument that if other male role models are available in the family, these effects can be alleviated. For some children, divorce may be a release from some of the negative aspects of their parents' relationship; for example, domestic violence or frequent arguments. The bond in particular between daughters and mothers can become stronger after divorce. If children see their parents happier after separation and perhaps in new, happier relationships, this can have a positive effect. After divorce, the most positive outcomes for children are seen where the onging relationship between parents is amicable.

For those who go on to remarry, the rates of subsequent divorces are higher, which usually reflect the fact that second divorces often involve children, perhaps from two families, complicating relationships in families with stepparents and stepsiblings.

## Making Divorce Easier or Harder

There is much debate over whether rising divorce rates are naturally occurring due to society and no action should be taken to change this, or whether governments should reinforce the sanctity and permanence of marriage.

Some see the increase in divorce as a change in people's expectations, moving away from marriage as an economic and child raising cooperation to wanting emotional fulfillment. Emotionally unfulfilled spouses may want to get out of the marriage; however, if divorce is made more difficult, it may result in spouses making more efforts to stay together. This in turn may result in fewer social security payments in countries that support lone parents, creating an economic and political benefit.

The influence of religion on marriage and divorce rates is still important in some countries. In addition, increased financial equality, equal opportunities, and equal pay legislation in many international labor markets over the last century means that some women are more economically able to manage after divorce. There are still many differences in the way divorce is perceived worldwide, along with variations in process.

**See Also:** Child Custody and the Law; Child Poverty; Children; Lone Mothers; Marriage.

**Bibliography**

Gillespie, G. "When the Bough Breaks." *Family Law* (July 2002).

Goody, J. *The European Family.* Oxford: Basil Blackwell, 2000.

Phillips, R. *A History of Divorce in Western Society.* Cambridge, UK: Cambridge University Press, 1988.

United Nations Statistics Division. http://unstats.un.org/unsd/default.htm (accessed May 2009).

U.S. Census Bureau 2008. www.census.gov (accessed May 2009).

Wasoff, F. and I. Dey. *Family Policy.* London: Routledge, 2000.

Gill Gillespie
University of Northumbria

# Domestic Labor

Domestic labor refers to the maintenance of private homes and the care of those living within them. Domestic workers typically perform a wide array of jobs, such as shopping, cooking, cleaning, and laundry, as well as tending to the sick, elderly, young, and disabled. Such labor draws on emotional resources and physical strength. Engagement in house and caring work, or employment of others to perform it, can denigrate or enhance one's social status. Despite the high cultural and theoretical values placed on the home, cleanliness, and caring for others, domestic labor receives low to no compensation, similar to motherhood.

Since the early 19th century, some feminists activists have moved to either heighten the value attributed to such labors by collectivizing them, advocating government payment for them, or attempting to leave them for paying jobs. While the first two met with only short-term successes, the third—the movement of women into the labor force—has encountered a stalled revolution in which gainfully employed women continue to remain primarily responsible for the maintenance of their own homes and families despite their jobs outside the house. To fulfill both their personal and professional obligations, women draw on three different arenas: the family, the state, and the market.

## The Family

The family is vital to the performance of domestic labor. Wives, husbands, parents, siblings, and children all pitch in to complete housework and care for family members. According to data since 1965 from time diaries and the National Survey of Families and Households, women in the United States have reduced time spent on housework (with the exception of shopping and childcare) by 12 hours per week, cutting their time almost in half; men have nearly doubled their housework, increasing their contributions by five hours per week. Despite such shifts, women still perform at least twice as much

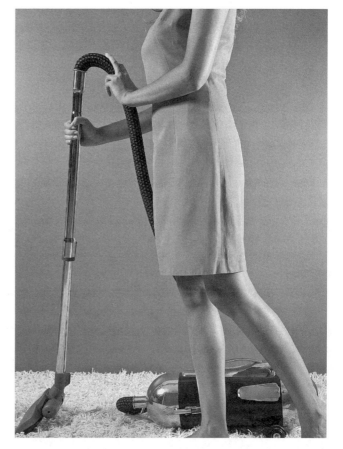

*Since the 1940s, tax deductions for domestic work have been proposed; womens' housework has been cut in half since 1965.*

housework as men. Their domestic obligations are furthered by the rise of a sandwiched generation responsible for the maintenance of both young children and elderly parents. The rise of intensive mothering, in which mothers devote themselves almost exclusively to their children's physical, psychological, emotional, and intellectual well-being, has also expanded the boundaries of domestic labor.

## Economic Consequences for Women

The unequal sharing of domestic labor within families plays a central role in restricting women's participation in paid labor. As long as women remain the primary domestic laborers within families, their second shift of housework and family obligations limits the extent to which they can devote themselves to paid employment. Although working-class women can rarely afford to drop out of the labor market, many of them reduce their hours or change jobs to accommodate the demands placed on them by caring work. Within the corporate and professional worlds, single-minded allegiance to work, necessitating long hours and travel, often conflicts with domestic responsibilities. In this environment, double standards hinder women's career advancement. Professional women who marry and have children appear less committed professionally, whereas men who follow the same trajectory enhance their opportunities for promotion. Scaling back work in the paid labor market because of domestic labor has short-term as well as long-term financial consequences. Frequently, such reductions remove women from health benefits and lower their retirement incomes.

## The State

In some countries more than others, the state attempts to close the caring gap. Governments can provide paid parental leave to help parents manage when children are born, adopted, or sick. They can offer visiting nurse assistants and stipends to those who care for the sick and disabled. Furthermore, the state can supplement domestic obligations by supplying services such as free daycare, public schools, health care, tax incentives, food stamps, and recreational programs. European welfare states, such as Sweden, the Netherlands, and France, are more likely to provide such services as a universal benefit available to all of their citizens, whereas countries such as the United States tend to provide services based on financial need.

In the United States, even seemingly universal benefits, such as Social Security, historically excluded those who performed house and caring work. Although legislative changes have expanded Social Security to almost all workers, domestic laborers often still remain outside of its purview either because of their legal standing—many are illegal immigrants—or because of their financial status, since employers often evade tax payments by paying domestic laborers "off the books." The international reduction of social welfare programs in the last 25 years has further lessened government support for domestic labor and increasingly encouraged women and families to turn to the labor market to fulfill their domestic needs.

## The Market and Global Migration

Outsourcing housework and caring responsibilities has become a central way for women who work outside the house try to meet their continuing domestic obligations. Middle- and upper-class women from industrialized nations often hire, manage, and compensate women from third world nations to maintain their domestic lives. Such paid laborers include domestics, live-ins, nannies, childcare providers, home health aides, nurses, maids, housekeepers, house cleaners, dry cleaners, gardeners, and restaurant workers. Over the past 25 years, domestic laborers have grown increasingly international, with domestic workers coming from southeast and south Asia, Central and South America, and eastern Europe.

Performing house and caring work in the domiciles of industrialized nations, paid domestic laborers meet with varying conditions depending primarily on their immigration status and their living arrangements. Those who are citizens and live outside of where they work predictably maintain a greater degree of autonomy than noncitizen laborers who live where they work. Domestic workers can suffer further as a result of isolation, lack of labor regulations, and sometimes abuse by their employers.

## Feminist and Ethical Issues

Although outsourcing domestic labor to low-paid, third world women may benefit middle-class and affluent female employers in industrialized nations, it also presents ethical and feminist challenges. It highlights inequalities among women based on race, class, and nationality. If paying others to perform domestic labor frees well-off women in industrialized nations to avoid conflicts with their partners over housework and caring responsibilities and to replicate masculine patterns of employment, sometimes it does so by exploiting female migrant workers, many of whom leave their own children in their countries of origin to care for their wards in first world homes. Paid domestic laborers are vulnerable to exploitation both because of the privatized and isolated nature of housework, and also because of the legal issues associated with it. Given such circumstances, some activists advocate increased government regulation of domestic labor and worker protection to improve the care of children as well as the working conditions of their caretakers.

**See Also:** Care Giving; Carework; Housework; Maternal Practice; Second Shift/Third Shift; Unpaid Work.

**Bibliography**
Anderson, Bridget. *Doing the Dirty Work? The Global Politics of Domestic Labour.* London: Zed Books, 2000.
Cowan, Ruth Schwartz. *More Work for Mother: The Ironies of Household Technology From the Open Hearth to the Microwave.* New York: Basic Books, 1983.
Hochschild, Arlie Russell. *The Second Shift.* New York: Avon Books, 1989.
Parrenas, Rhacel Salazar. *Servants of Globalization: Women, Migration, and Domestic Work.* Palo Alto, CA: Stanford University Press, 2001.

Sharon Ann Musher
Richard Stockton College of New Jersey

# Doula

Coming from the Greek word meaning "a woman who serves," a doula is a female companion who provides nonclinical support to women before, during, and after childbirth. Doulas recognize the importance of the birth experience for women and work to foster the most positive experience possible. Doulas are experientially and/or formally educated in understanding and meeting women's needs for personalized, empathic, and emotional support; comfort care; nonmedical information; and advocacy during pregnancy and during and after childbirth. While doulas were originally women who were had experiential knowledge but no formal training, professional or paraprofessional certification is becoming increasingly common for doulas specializing in antepartum, birth, and postpartum care.

Doula care is often misunderstood as midwifery. Midwives, however, are trained and licensed to provide antepartum, childbirth, and postpartum medical care, while doulas are not. Doulas work as part of a team that also includes physicians and nurses who provide pregnancy, prenatal, and childbirth care. The doula's role is as a coach or companion, providing emotional and practical support, physical comfort, and information, but not to provide clinical skills or medical advice. There is a suggested link in the rise in demand for doula care to the increasing medicalization of pregnancy and childbirth by midwives. As well, doula care is often a precursor to becoming a licensed midwife.

## Benefits of Doula Care
Doula care has been demonstrated to have many positive benefits for women and babies. Births supported by doulas have been documented to show considerable reductions in caesarean rates, duration of labor, epidural requests, the use of oxytocin and analgesia, and forceps delivery, as well as higher Apgar scores for newborns. After birth, mothers who had doula care were shown to have less postpartum depression and anxiety, be more confident with their baby, and be more satisfied with their partner. Doula care is also more likely to result in breastfeeding.

There are three types of doulas, although one doula can perform all or some of the related care. Antepartum doulas provide various types of care and support prior to birth. They might demonstrate relaxation techniques; help around the house, including with other children; and run errands. More likely to be professionally trained, birth doulas provide encouragement, reassurance, and support during childbirth, enabling the birthing woman and her partner to relax

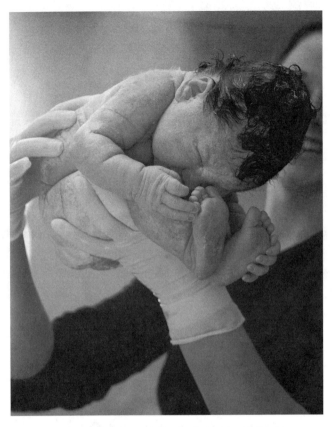

*It is becoming more common for doulas to specialize in antepartum, birth, and postpartum care.*

and focus on birthing as the labor progresses. Like birth doulas, postpartum doulas also provide breast-feeding support. They are also likely to be trained to provide various kinds of after-delivery care such as assistance with housework and childcare.

Isolating birthing women from their female support network marks a profound change in childbirth practices beginning in the 20th century, although doula care has remained a common practice for First Nations families. While women who share their experiential knowledge have continued to assist pregnant and birthing women in developing countries, it is interesting to note that in developed countries, where pregnancy and childbirth have become more medicalized and technologized, there has been an increased demand for doula care. Given that a highly technologized provision of pregnancy and childbirth care has decreased human interaction in care, it is not surprising that the care provided by doulas has helped to counter the distancing affects of technology during pregnancy and childbirth.

Doula training is provided by various local, national, and international organizations and involves intensive seminars on all aspects of doula care. Certification may involve apprenticeship, observation, and exams. When choosing a doula, consideration is based on the doula's training and experience, fee schedule and references, personal comfort with her style of communication, her comfort level with the mother's choices, her availability, and whether or not she works alone or as part of a team.

The doula movement has inspired the growth of supportive and comfort care tailored to the needs of the dying and their families. These death doulas, or thanadoulas (*thana* is the Greek word for death) work primarily through hospices and homes. Sometimes called death midwives, death doulas recognize how the life cycle relates birth to death.

**See Also:** Becoming a Mother; Childbirth; Midwifery; Postpartum Depression; Pregnancy; Prenatal Health Care; Technology and Motherhood.

**Bibliography**
Abramson, Rachel. "The Critical Moment and the Passage of Time: Reflections on Community-Based Doula Support." *International Journal of Childbirth Education*, v.194 (2004).
Anon. "Childbirth Improved With Doulas." *Herizons*, v.20/2 (2006).
Davidson, Deborah. "A Technology of Care: Caregiver Response to Perinatal Loss." *Women's Studies International Forum*, v.31 (2008).
Dona International. www.dona.org (accessed June 2009).
Klaus, Marshall H. *The Doula Book: How a Trained Labor Companion Can Help You Have a Shorter, Easier and Healthier Birth*. New York: Perseus Books, 2002.
Koumouitzes-Douvia, Jodi, and Catherine A. Carr. "Women's Perceptions of Their Doula Support." *The Journal of Perinatal Education*, v.15/4 (2003).
Pascali-Bonaro, Debra. "Childbirth Education and Doula Care During Times of Stress, Trauma, and Grieving." *The Journal of Perinatal Education*, v.12/4 (2006).

Deborah Davidson
York University

# Dove, Rita

With her third collection of poetry, *Thomas and Beulah*, in 1987, Rita Dove became the second African American to win the Pulitzer Prize, after Gwendolyn Brooks. In the span of 25 years, Dove has published her first book of poetry, *The Yellow House on the Corner* (1980); over eight poetry collections; a short story collection, *Fifth Sunday* (1985); a novel, *Through the Ivory Gate* (1992); and a play, *The Darker Face of the Earth* (1994). Appointed in 1993, Dove served as the U.S. Poet Laureate for two years and was reappointed as Special Consultant in Poetry to the Library of Congress in 1999 for its bicentennial celebration. Her poetry encompasses a range of themes, from slavery and civil rights to ballroom dancing, and most overtly, motherhood in the collection *Mother Love*.

Born in Akron, Ohio, in 1952 and raised in a middle-class neighborhood, Dove demonstrated a love for reading and writing at a young age. She graduated from Miami University of Ohio with a degree in English, spent two semesters as a Fulbright scholar in Germany, and later enrolled in the Iowa Writer's Workshop and received her Master's of Fine Arts degree in 1977, the same year her volume *Ten Poems* appeared. With the Pulitzer for *Thomas and Beulah*, a series of poems inspired by the lives of her grandparents, Dove gained national attention and stature with subsequent literary honors, such as fellowships from the National Endowment for the Arts and the Guggenheim Foundation. In 1990 and 1996, she received the Literary Lion medals from the New York Public Library, and in 2000 she received its Library Lion medal.

## Dove's Style and Mother Themes

In her poetry, Dove is known for a tight, lyrical style that embraces a diversity of form, from free verse to more traditional forms such as the sonnet. Trained in playing the viola and cello, Dove frequently uses music as both subject and metaphor, as in the collection *American Smooth* (2004), which features such poems as "Fox Trot Fridays," "Samba Summer," and "Blues in Half-Tones, ¾ Time."

As comfortable with classical allusions as she is with music, Dove references many of the more well-known figures of biblical and ancient literature, such as Herodias's daughter in "The Seven Veils of Salomé," portraying the story from multiple perspectives, including Salomé, whose dancing seduces King Herod and persuades him to grant her John the Baptist's head.

The Greek myth of Demeter and Persephone takes center stage in Dove's collection *Mother Love*, which features the voices of a late-20th-century daughter abroad in Paris, her artist lover, and her worried mother. The poems in *Mother Love*, many of which are sonnets, evoke the kidnapping of Persephone by Hades, the Greek god of the underworld, and the onset of fall and winter that results from the goddess of agriculture's grief for her abducted daughter.

In the collection *Grace Notes*, her poem "After Reading Mickey in the Night Kitchen for the Third Time Before Bed" also explores the relationship of a mother and daughter, though in this instance the poet-speaker depicts a moment when her 3-year-old daughter discovers "her vagina:/hairless, this mistaken/bit of nomenclature/is what a stranger cannot touch/without her yelling." In other poems, such as "Genetic Expedition," Dove explores the experience of interracial marriage and her daughter's biracial identity: ". . . My child has/her father's hips, his hair/like the miller's daughter, combed gold./Though her lips are mine, housewives/stare when we cross the parking lot/because of that ghostly profusion."

The collection *On the Bus With Rosa*, nominated for the National Book Critics Circle Award in 2000, includes poems that depict her mother's experience, as in one titled "My Mother Enters the Work Force," as well as the experience of Rosa Parks and other African American women who spearheaded the Civil Rights Movement with their work to desegregate public transportation. Dove served as editor for the *Best American Poetry 2000*. A recipient of over 20 honorary doctorate degrees, Dove taught creative writing at Arizona State University from 1981 to 1989. Currently, she holds the chair of Commonwealth Professor of English at the University of Virginia in Charlottesville, Virginia. She also serves as chancellor of the Academy of American Poets.

**See Also:** African American Mothers; Demeter, Goddess; Literature, Mothers in; Poetry, Mothers in.

**Bibliography**

Dove, Rita. *American Smooth*. New York: W.W. Norton, 2004).

Dove, Rita. *The Darker Face of the Earth*. Ashland, OR: Story Line Press, 1994.

Dove, Rita. *Fifth Sunday*. College Station, TX: Callaloo Fiction Series, 1985.

Dove, Rita. *Grace Notes*. New York: W.W. Norton, 1989.

Dove, Rita. *Thomas and Beulah*. Pittsburgh, PA: Carnegie Mellon University Press, 1986.

Dove, Rita. *Through the Ivory Gate*. New York: Pantheon, 1992.

Dove, Rita. *The Yellow House on the Corner*. Pittsburgh, PA: Carnegie Mellon University Press, 1980.

Rita Dove Homepage. http://people.virginia.edu/~rfd4b (accessed January 2009).

Justine Dymond
Springfield College

# Dramatic Arts, Mothers in

Until recently, mother characters have almost exclusively been the creation of male playwrights and actors in the dramatic arts. Many societal factors, both practical and moral, have kept mothers from public expression through performance. The types of mother roles that have traditionally been presented have often been very limited, two dimensional, and generally fall into certain categories that are repeated over and again. Once actual mothers and women began creating mother characters for the stage, these characters emerged as more complex and became central, rather than merely supporting, roles in the dramas. Still, mere inclusion for mothers in the theater has not been viewed as sufficient by theater practitioners and scholars, who instead, advocate for the creation of an entirely new theatrical model better suited to the experience and preferences of mothers and women. By examining the lives of prominent mothers in the theater, evolutions in the theater in regards to mothers, both positive and negative, can begin to be understood.

Outstanding mothers as portrayed in Western theater include Euripedes's Medea, who in the Greek Classical tragedy, *Medea,* kills her own chil-

dren to avenge her husband's betrayal. There is also William Shakespeare's Gertrude, who in the Elizabethan tragedy, *Hamlet,* marries her brother-in-law nearly before the leftovers had been eaten from her husband's funeral. Another is Henrik Ibsen's Nora, who in the modern realistic play, *A Doll's House,* abandons her role as mother to find herself as a woman. Yet another is August Wilson's Bernice in the American drama, *The Piano Lesson,* who comes to terms with her African heritage through the spirits roused by the playing of her family's piano.

One common feature of all of these mothers is that they have been imagined and written by male playwrights. Indeed, it could be said that the dramatic works of men still tend to dominate our collective sense of theatrical history. In addition, actual female performers have only been performing the roles of mother characters (or any others) on the stage for the last few centuries, a relatively short time given the span of theatrical history. Not only is this true for the Western tradition, but also worldwide, where male performers have dominated the stages of India, Japan, and China; in African theatrical masked performances; Native American theater; Aztec performance; and beyond. Clearly, the dramatic representation has not been thought of as the domain for women, let alone mothers.

## Limiting Factors for Mothers in the Theater

There have been many historical factors that have kept mothers from participating in the dramatic arts. In a practical sense, the life of the theater was often far too demanding for mothers who often had to provide supervision over dependent children, gather food and wood, keep house, and cook. An extreme and rare exception to this was found in India for a traditional classical dancer, or *devadasi,* who was often a mother. These women were symbolically married to a temple and were provided for by the sponsorship of a high-caste man with whom she had relations as a sacred expression. Resulting children were cared for by the temple, leaving her free to pursue the rigorous training required of a Bharata Natyam performer. Throughout Java and Bali there have been a few instances of mothers performing as puppet masters in the *Wayang Kulit,* a traditional shadow puppet theater, but it has not occurred often or lasted for many women, since it is cited that her life demands kept her from being able to pursue a performing career. Here we find no social or moral obstacles, just practical ones.

Far more common, however, are the moral codes in societies that restrict mothers from public expression. In China, Confucianism clearly disapproves of women and men interacting in the public realm, which has resulted in mothers and women not being included in their theatrical traditions until nearly a century ago, when ideas of communism and gender equity were adopted. In patriarchal societies, women and mothers have historically been denied access to public expression. There is also a pervasive association with theater, or entertainment in general, and prostitution. This fact has kept women, and especially mothers—often the holders of the family honor—from being involved in theater, and arguably, to some degree until today.

Historically, mothers have tended to be cast in supporting roles, such as the nurturer of a male son whose life actions are something of consequence. At times, the mother is either a dutiful, nagging, cuckolding, or saintly wife to a husband who is the focus of the drama. Certain types of mother characters seem to emerge over and again. One prominent type is the silent, suffering nurturer who, particularly in countries dominated by the Catholic faith, is often modeled on the Virgin Mother Mary. The Irish play *Riders to the Sea* (1904), by John Millington Synge, is an example of this. Another prominent type is the stepmother who comes to motherhood through marriage, and never develops an authentic attachment to the children she mothers, but rather expresses her attention in some evil or perverse way, such as in *Senca* or Racine's *Phaedra*, or Eugene O'Neill's *Desire Under the Elms*.

## Expectations for Mothers

Strong messages are communicated through these plays regarding the expectations for a mother's behavior in society. Many times, patriarchal expectations of mothers are reinforced through these dramas. In most cases throughout history, dramatists have been either in service of the king or some other governmental leader, or at least dependent upon their support or approval. Therefore, it is no surprise that the dramas and characters they would create would reinforce the values and expectations of the

ruling class. For actual mothers, this has meant that the mother characters created and performed in the theater have been held up either as the model by which mothers should measure their own worth, or as cautionary tales warning against any transgression to motherly expectations. Theater is the oldest media through which the world has witnessed portrayals of mother. Though current theater cannot be said to have the same broad-scale influence that it once held, it is notable that movie and television programming inherited the theatrical tradition that enormously informs its presentation.

## Women and Mothers as Playwrights

Once actual women, and sometimes mothers, began to write for the theater productions, the mother characters tended to become more complex and nuanced. Rachel Crothers, a U.S. playwright who wrote at the beginning of the 20th century, created nonbiological mother characters who questioned the expectations and restrictions placed on motherhood in plays such as *A Man's World* (1910). Playwright Ama Ata Aidoo, from Ghana, explores issues of intercultural marriage and how it influences expectations of motherhood in her play *The Dilemma of a Ghost* (1964). Critiques of patriarchal mothering (mothering styles that perpetuate the patriarchy and work to mold their daughters in service of the status quo) begin to emerge where daughters speak out and act in defiance against expectations of motherhood, as seen in plays such as *Real Women Have Curves* (1990) by Josefina Lopez.

## Unsatisfied Feminists

Although many feminists have felt that simply having women author dramatic work has not been sufficient, and advocate for a new form of theater better suited to women's and mother's stories and tastes, it is recognized that it is problematic and reductive to assume all mothers share the same tastes and preferences. Some theater scholars felt betrayal rather than triumph when female playwrights, such as U.S. writers Wendy Wasserstein and Marsha Norman, became critical successes on Broadway in the 1980s as they molded themselves to male archetypes of theater rather than forging a new model of feminist theater.

Better regarded by these scholars are theater groups that have creating their own theaters in order to investigate effective and innovative ways of dramatizing women's and mother's stories. Feminist collectives such Split Britches in New York, founded in the early 1980s; the Native American women's theater troupe, Spiderwoman Theater; and Fortaleza de la Mujer Maya (FOMMA) in Chapas, Mexico, are regarded as both demonstrating the increased presence of women in theater; but, more importantly, as evolving new forms of theater for women. However, sometimes even the new forms of theater generated by women artists are thought to be "off the mark" by scholars. At the Foot of the Mountains, a feminist theater collective in Minneapolis, created a work entitled *The Story of Mother (1977)* and *The Story of Mother II* in 1987, largely a multicultural revision of the first. This revision was criticized for advancing what many scholars thought of as universalized notions of femininity and views toward mothers and mothering as necessarily positive, leaving no room for alternative views.

## Two Italian Mothers

By examining the lives of two Italian mothers separated in time by a half a millennium, but influenced by the same lineage, we can see how much and how little has changed. Isabella Andreini (1562–1604) is regarded as the first serious professional actress in all of Europe. She brought charm, grace, and dignity to a profession hitherto thought to be the domain of prostitutes and lowbrow entertainers. She began at the age of 16, then named Isabella Canali, for the commedia dell'arte company of the Gelosi. With her husband, Francisco Andreini, who was also an actor with the same troupe, she refined and uplifted the form of commedia. The commedia stock character, Isabella, is named in her honor.

As a poet and published writer, she successfully introduced set speeches in the plots of the otherwise improvised performances. Isabella had seven children in all: four girls, who according to some historians, all joined the convent; and three boys, one of whom pursued a life in the theater as a writer, actor, and director. At the age of 42, Andreini died. Her husband was inconsolable and left the theater completely. She was buried with pomp and circumstance, and all Lyons mourned her passing. As the first actress of Europe, she won position, glory, and

renown and set an example for as a mother of virtue who also excelled at her art.

The descendant of a commedia family of actors, The Italian theater artist Franca Rame is also a prominent actress and mother who has shaped the theater of her day in Italy and beyond. Her stage debut occurred when she was 8 days old as a baby in her mothers arms. Like Andreini was, Rame is also married to her partner in art, Dario Fo. Their collaborative work can be seen to largely resemble the commedia formula, as it is sketch comedy that retains immediacy even when scripted. In response to the governmental corruption they perceived in their time, much of their work is created to expose the atrocities committed, dramatize the hypocrisy of the officials responsible, and to give voice to the poor and the oppressed who suffered beneath this rule. For this effort, Rame was not awarded accolades; rather, in 1973 was abducted, tortured, and raped by a fascist group largely thought to be commissioned by a high-ranking official in the Italian military police. Remarkably, she was back on the stage within months. For their collective work, Dario Fo was awarded the Nobel Prize for literature in 1997. Though they have consistently generated their works collaboratively, he alone received the award.

In Rame's solo work, also created with Fo, she has bravely dared to speak out about restrictive attitudes toward mothers and unrealistic and unfair expectations placed on mothers by patriarchal society. Her one-woman performance, *All Home, Bed, and Church* (1977), she hilariously yet poignantly enacts the absurd oppression under which mothers attempt to function in their everyday lives. In her one-woman performance of *Sex? Thanks, Don't Mind If I Do* (1994), she speaks as a mother responsible for openly discussing sexuality. It was her own experience as a mother of a teenaged boy, her only child, that led her to create this performance/lecture aimed particularly for secondary schools. This performance was temporarily restricted to students over the age of 18. She has expanded the very notion of what a mother can say on the stage, how she can present herself, her right to be funny and brazen, and to whom she can present her work. Though she is highly regarded as a theater artist, her name often still appears in association with her husband's and, tellingly, after his.

There are a world of mothers presently asserting their voices through the dramatic arts, though their voices still lack some amplification, attention, and recognition. Performance artist and mother Michelle Ellsworth presents multimedia works throughout the United States, such as *All Clytemnestra on the Western Front: A Techno Feminist Reconstruction of the* Iliad, in which she gives voice to the mother in the story, Clytemnestra, and enacts the story of the *Iliad* from her perspective. Activist performer and cofounder of Mothers Acting Up, Beth Osnes, performs her one-woman show, *(M)other,* in cities throughout North America to invigorate communities to act up and speak out on issues of social justice, especially as they effect children and mothers.

As mothers claim access to public expression through the dramatic arts, there is great potential for attitudes and opportunities in theater and society to expand for mothers. For audience members, there is a chance to reimagine an expanded variety of roles mothers can perform both on the stage and off.

**See Also:** Art and Mothering; Celebrity Motherhood; China; Clytemnestra; India; Italy; Work and Mothering.

**Bibliography**
Aston, Elaine and Geraldine Harris, eds. *Feminist Futures? Theater, Performance, Theory.* New York: Palgrave, 2006.
De Gay, Jane and Lizbeth Goodman, eds. *Languages of Theater Shaped by Women.* Portland, OR: Intellect, 2003.
Gilder, Rosamond. *Enter the Actress: The First Women in the Theater.* New York: Theater Arts Books, 1961.

Beth Osnes
University of Colorado, Boulder

# Drug Abuse

Drug abuse is generally considered to be the use of psychoactive or performance-enhancing drugs for nonmedical or therapeutic purposes. Drug abuse may occur with both legal (e.g., alcohol, cigarettes, prescription, and over-the-counter [OTC] medication) and illegal (e.g., cocaine, heroin, marijuana) substances. The abuse of drugs can lead to both psychological and physical addiction, with the degree of physical addiction depending upon the properties of the drug. Due to metabolic differences between the sexes, women are more susceptible to the effects of drugs, particularly alcohol, and are more likely to become addicted than men. A woman's entry into drug use may begin after experiencing a traumatic event, and women are more likely to use drugs to ease emotional pain from abuse, grief, and/or guilt than men. Since women are more likely to be prescribed mood-altering substances for emotional and psychological symptoms, they are more susceptible to addiction to prescribed medications.

Although overall rates of drug use are still higher among men than women, the gender gap has been decreasing, especially among younger age groups and with regard to specific drugs, such as tobacco and the nonmedical use of prescription drugs. Research has also begun to highlight health disparities in the consequences of drug use for women, with women demonstrating greater health consequences at the same level of behavior as men. Female alcoholics have a greater number of drinking problems and higher death rates than male alcoholics, and women are more susceptible than men to brain damage, cardiac problems, and liver disease as a result of their drinking. Women are also significantly more likely to develop dependence on nonmedical uses of psychotropic drugs, such as sedatives and tranquilizers, than men. Women may become addicted sooner than men but also seem to seek treatment sooner, causing womens' drug use experiences to be more compressed than men's.

## Prenatal Drug Abuse

Women's drug use also has several unique costs to both the individual and to society, given their role in reproduction. The highest prevalence of use among women, regardless of substance, occurs during the childbearing years. In fact, alarming numbers of adult women and teens continue to use alcohol, tobacco, and other drugs during pregnancy. Substance abusers often have multiple addictions, and approximately half of all pregnant women who use illicit substances also smoke and drink. Since approximately half of all pregnancies are unintended, women may be using substances, especially cigarettes and alcohol, throughout the first trimester of pregnancy without knowing they are pregnant.

Drug abuse during pregnancy increases a woman's risk for a number of negative outcomes such as poor fetal growth, premature rupture of membranes, placental complications, premature delivery, and miscarriage. Likewise, the negative effects of smoking, alcohol, and other drug use on infants born to drug-using mothers are well established, and include low birthweight, preterm birth, fetal alcohol syndrome, a variety of birth defects, learning disabilities, and developmental delays. In addition, prenatal maternal smoking has been found to be associated with adolescent children's smoking, and this effect is stronger for daughters than for sons.

Risk factors associated with prenatal drug abuse include being single, unemployed, having less than a college education, relying upon public aid, being or having been a victim of physical or sexual abuse, and living with a substance abuser. Pregnant women who abuse drugs tend to be single mothers with limited access to support systems, including financial, social, and childcare. In addition, up to 20 percent of pregnant women have experienced abuse, which may begin or intensify with pregnancy.

## Causal Factors

Drug abuse and addiction is caused by a variety of comingled factors. Studies have shown that having a history of physical and sexual abuse is more common in female drug users than in males. Concurrent mental health issues with substance abuse are higher for women than men, and mental health issues are more likely to precede substance use issues. This is due, in part, to the greater likelihood of women substance abusers to have experienced abuse or trauma at some point in their lives. Depression is a common comorbid condition among female drug abusers.

Women are often introduced to drugs through male partners, and drug-abusing women may trade sex for drugs, thereby increasing their risk for sexually transmitted disease (STD) infections, including human immunodeficiency virus (HIV). Women are also more likely to use drugs to manage emotions and reduce stress. Women have been found to self-medicate with a variety of drugs to relieve anxiety, depression, and fatigue in order to meet societal role

demands of caregiving and nurturance. In addition, associations between body image and drug use are more prevalent for women than men, given the pressures women face to fit societal expectations of beauty. Unfortunately, much of the research on women and drug use has been conducted with drug-dependent women in treatment. Consequently, very little is known about women who abuse legal substances and/or do not seek treatment. Significant barriers exist for accessing and receiving treatment, making it possible that women overcome these barriers only when their difficulties are extreme.

## Mother–Child Interactions

Prenatal drug exposure can compromise mother–child interactions. Interactions are affected by the mother's drug use, as in her altered perceptions of her child's behaviors as well as temperamental difficulties experienced by infants who are exposed to drugs prenatally. Since high rates of both physical and sexual assault have been found among substance-abusing mothers, mental health issues associated with abuse can also affect mother–child interactions.

Drug-addicted mothers are more likely to exhibit parenting deficits than nonaddicted mothers. Their parenting styles juxtapose overly involved, harsh,

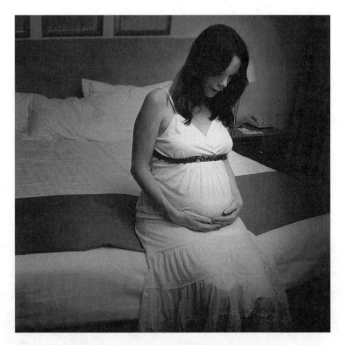

*Pregnant women ages 15–17 have a higher rate of drug use than women of the same age who are not pregnant.*

and authoritarian behaviors with permissive and neglectful behaviors. Substance-using mothers are more likely to display role-reversals with their children, lack an understanding of basic child development issues, and show poor sensitivity and lack of responsiveness to their children's emotional cues than mothers who do not abuse drugs. As a consequence, children of drug-abusing mothers are more likely to use drugs themselves; to become romantically involved with a drug abuser; and to suffer a variety of social problems, such as school dropout, teen pregnancy, and aggressive/violent behavior.

Strong parent–child bonds can serve as a protective factor for children's substance use, as well as other deviant behavior among families of nonusers. Among drug-using families, however, this association is either nonexistent or serves to increase children's risk of problem behaviors, especially drug use. Mechanisms of intergenerational transmission of substance use can include modeling of the behavior as well as transmission of pro-drug use norms and attitudes. Other parenting behaviors, such as inconsistent discipline and lack of monitoring of children's whereabouts, have also been found to increase children's risk of engaging in socially deviant behaviors.

The use of drugs by women, and particularly by pregnant or parenting women, is an emotionally charged issue, and societal reactions to drug dependent mothers, particularly mothers dependent upon illicit substances, is severe. Societal expectations of women to fulfill caregiving and nurturing work as wives and mothers may create greater discrimination against women who abuse drugs. The abuse of legal substances, such as prescription drug use, is far less visible and therefore does not carry the same stigma as illicit drug addiction. Illicit drug use among women is also tied to the sex industry, and both place women at increased risk for HIV infection. Much of the stigmatization of drug-dependent mothers focuses on their children as innocent victims and the mother's perceived inability to effectively parent. Since HIV can be transmitted from mother to child, this increases the perception of the drug-using woman as a "bad mother," as her child is subjected to a double risk.

The media's portrayal of "crack babies" in the 1990s increased the stigmatization of drug-dependent mothers. Pregnant and parenting women who used crack were seen as uncaring, neglectful, and/or abusive mothers. More recent and nuanced studies have found no significant differences between "crack babies" and children born into disadvantaged circumstances. The relationship between drug use and neglectful and/or abusive parenting is complex, with characteristics of the household and the mother being more important than effects of illicit drug use. Since many drug-dependent women are or have been victims of violence and are often economically disadvantaged, it is difficult to disentangle the effects of household and mother characteristics with the effects of drug use. Some research has shown socioeconomic disadvantage to be as important, if not more so, than drug use for negative child outcomes.

Women who use drugs while pregnant suffer from a double stigma—for abusing their own bodies and for abusing the fetus. This stigma increases both denial of a drug abuse problem and decreases the chance that a pregnant woman will seek treatment. Other barriers to seeking treatment include fear of losing custodial privileges for the child they are carrying as well as born children. In addition, recent societal responses to prenatal drug use has been to increase mandatory drug testing, prosecution, and incarceration. Although no U.S. states have existing laws against substance use during pregnancy, 250 women have been prosecuted. Charges have included fetal abuse, child abuse and neglect, delivering drugs to a minor, corruption of a minor, assault with a deadly weapon, and manslaughter. All but one of the 250 convictions has been overturned. Opponents of this approach argue that fear of incarceration and/or losing their children leads to decreased use of prenatal services and medical care and, ultimately, greater harm to children.

**Perspectives of Substance-Abusing Mothers**
Studies are just beginning to address the perspectives of substance-abusing mothers themselves. When drug-dependent women are given a voice to convey their experiences, they articulate the ways their mothering practices fit into the larger social construction of the "good mother." Contrary to the larger public's negative stereotypes of drug-using mothers, mothers who use drugs are able to convey more complex descriptions of their mothering practices. While drug-dependent mothers recognize and feel guilt over

the harm their children are exposed to through their drug use, they also perceive their actions as falling into the realm of "good mothering." Specifically, the positive practices they identify are: their use of harm reduction strategies; their ability to provide for the physical and structural needs of their children; and their ability to provide alternative care, even if alternative care means relinquishing custody when they are not able to meet their children's needs.

## Treatment

Treatment opportunities in the United States and other developed countries are limited in general, and this is especially true for pregnant and/or parenting women. Only 5–10 percent of pregnant, substance-abusing women receive treatment in the United States. Women access treatment services at about one-third the rate of men, even though they approximate men's drug use problems. Children can serve as both a barrier and catalyst to accessing treatment for women. Many drug-dependent women do not have acess to childcare while undergoing treatment, as most drug treatment facilities do not provide any support for children. Also, the fear of losing custody of their children can lead some women to forgo seeking help. Since drug-addicted mothers are more likely to lose their children to foster care than mothers who are not dependent upon drugs, this fear is not unfounded.

Families in general and children in particular are important factors in women's drug treatment. While the negative stigma attached to women who use drugs—especially to pregnant or parenting drug users—can keep women from even admitting they have a drug addiction problem, many drug-using mothers report that their mothering role serves as a protective factor in their drug use. Drug-addicted mothers share the same attitudes and values toward mothering that nonaddicted mothers hold, and it is because of their concern for their children's well-being that some women seek treatment. Women may also seek treatment in an attempt to regain their children once they have lost custody. In addition, some studies have found that women who retain custody and/or are able to keep their children with them in treatment are more likely to stay in treatment.

Women seeking drug treatment may have a number of comorbid conditions or issues that need to be addressed, including a history of self-harm and/or suicide attempts, polydrug use, personality disorders, eating disorders, physical health problems, experiences of violence and abuse, posttraumatic stress disorder, and affective disorders such as depression and anxiety. Drug abuse treatment approaches for women are most effective when they include parenting skills, address comorbid factors, and address factors to overcome barriers for accessing and receiving services, such as childcare and stigma. Studies have shown excellent outcomes when gender-specific treatment has been provided to pregnant and parenting women, with rates of negative child outcomes among treated women comparable to women without drug abuse problems.

Gender-specific treatment programs have also shown positive mother outcomes, such as abstinence, decreases in criminal arrests, and improved indicators for interpersonal relationships and economic well-being. Components of gender-specific treatment include programs that are based on theories of women's psychological development, use methods designed to empower women, recognize the importance of women's relationships and interpersonal connections, and address the social context of women's lives. However, few such programs exist.

**See Also:** Alcoholism; Child Custody and the Law; Fetal Alcohol Syndrome; Poverty and Mothering.

## Bibliography

Baker, Phyllis L. and Amy Carson. "'I Take Care of My Kids': Mothering Practices of Substance-Abusing Women." *Gender & Society*, v.13 (1999).
Boyd, Susan C. *Mothers and Illicit Drugs: Transcending the Myths*. Toronto: University of Toronto Press, 1999.
Klee, Hilary, et al. *Drug Misuse and Motherhood*. New York: Routledge, 2002.
National Center on Addiction and Substance Use at Columbia University [CASA]. *Women Under the Influence*. Baltimore, MD: Johns Hopkins University Press, 2006.
National Institute on Drug Abuse. "Drug Abuse Among Pregnant Women in the U.S." (May 2009). http://www.drugabuse.gov/tib/prenatal.html (accessed September 2009).

Tracy R. Nichols
University of North Carolina at Greensboro

# Earth Mothers

The concept of an Earth Mother, Mother Goddess, or Great Goddess derives primarily from the Greeks. The Romans worshipped her as Tellus, or *Terra Mater*, whom Varro (116–27 B.C.E.) called the Great Mother. Largely suppressed during the beginnings of Christianity, period, she emerged again in the 18th century, when references were made to the Earth as Mother Goddess.

Interest in the Earth Mother and the Great Mother increased significantly in the 19th century. In classical Greek mythology, Gaia was the Earth Goddess. Another manifestation of the Earth Goddess or Earth Mother is the Greek Goddess Demeter, one of the deities that people in Greek society prayed to for a bountiful harvest. She was tied to the underworld; symbolizing the cycle of life, birth, death, and rebirth. Demeter is often connected with the Earth, as *meter* is the Greek work for mother. Modern scholars of religion and archaeology have also contributed to the dissemination of the belief in the existence of a once-universal goddess.

The mother archetype is symbolized by the primordial mother, or Earth Mother of mythology, and by Eve and Mary in Western traditions. The Great Mother archetype is seen to reflect early childhood feelings about the primacy of the mother. While Freudians consider goddess imagery to be founded in experiences of the personal mother, Jungians believe the archetype of the mother is based in the collective unconscious. Some scholars link societal ambivalence toward the Mother/Goddess with the cultural evaluation of uncontrolled female sexuality as dangerous and disruptive. In patriarchal societies, control is often expressed and experienced as oppression of the feminine.

## Metaphor and Concept

The Earth Mother is a metaphor for creative energies. The female principle is recognized in many cultures as the pervading cosmic force, as radiant and auspicious; the Mother is identified with Earth. The Earth Mother/Goddess can be interpreted as expressing ideas of autonomy and primacy in the widest sense. The Earth Mother conveys not so much the idea of physical motherhood, but a worldview in which the creative power of femininity is central; the Mother/Goddess mediates between life and death and contains the promise of regeneration and rebirth.

## Ecofeminist Link

Closely aligned with concepts of the Earth Mother is the theory and practice of ecofeminism. According

*The notion that women are closer to the environment has been very influential in certain development circles such as donor agencies and nongovernmental organizations that seek to promote both environmental and certain forms of feminist activism.*

to Vandana Shiva, the symbolism of Terra Mater as the Great Mother who is creative and protective has been a shared symbol across cultures. Shiva believes ecology movements in the West are inspired by the recovery of the concept of Gaia, the Earth Mother/Goddess. In ecofeminist thought, there is a link between the abuse of the Earth and the oppression of women through a destructive, dualistic ordering of the world, where the masculine is superior to the feminine, the heavenly to the earthly, and the spiritual to the material.

Ecofeminists argue that women and nature have been subjected to a shared history of oppression by patriarchal institutions and dominant Western culture. Ecofeminist arguments have fueled a large range of social and environmental movements. These include specific forms of grassroots activism, such as socially and politically transformative practices as the Women's Environmental Network, which has promoted issues such as green consumerism.

Some feminists, such as Simone de Beauvior, reject the woman/nature connection because emphasizing women's natural procreative capacities emphasizes reproduction, which often excludes them from cultural production. Radical feminists, such as Mary Daly, affirm the women/nature connection and form the dominant group of ecofeminists. While radical feminists acknowledge that patriarchal culture emphasizes the woman/nature connection in order to exploit them both, writers like Susan Griffin assert women's difference from men and suggest reclaiming their natural creativity, intuition, emotion, and spirituality. Socialist feminists argue that the concept of nature, like woman, is historically and socially constructed.

Some scholars contend these notions of "women as nature" and Earth Mother are essentializing fables used to justify the cultural and political appeal of global environmental sisterhoods. This critique casts women's relationships with the environment as emerging from the social context of dynamic gender relationships, and thus challenges notions that women have a naturalized relationship with the environment. While ecofeminism suggests that hope for an environmentally sustainable future lies in the recovery of the principle of the Earth mother, critics take issue with the vagueness and generality in which nature is defined.

**See Also:** Demeter, Goddess; Earth Goddess; Ecofeminism; Gaia; India; Myths, Mothers in.

### Bibliography

Dwivedi, O. and Lucy Reid. "Women and the Sacred Earth: Hindu and Christian Ecofeminist Perspectives." *Worldviews*, v.11 (2007).

Ganesh, Kamala. "Mother Who Is Not a Mother: In Search of the Great Indian Goddess." *Economic & Political Weekly*, v.25 (1990).

Jayakar, Pupul. *The Earth Mother*. New York: Penguin, 1980.

Jung, Carl. *The Collected Works of C.G. Jung*. Princeton, NJ: Princeton University Press, 1981.

Leach, Melissa. "Earth Mother Myths and Other Ecofeminist Fables: How a Strategic Notion Rose and Fell." *Development & Change*, v.38/1 (2007).

Rose, Ellen. "The Good Mother: From Gaia to Gilead." *Frontiers: A Journal of Women Studies*, v.12/1 (1991).

Shiva, Vandana. *Staying Alive: Women, Ecology, and Development*. London: Zed Press, 1988.

Stuckey, Johanna. "Ancient Mother Goddesses and Fertility Cults." *Journal for the Association of Research on Mothering*, v.7/1 (2005).

Witcombe, Christopher. "Women in Prehistory: Venus of Willendorf." (2005). http://witcombe.sbc.edu (accessed January 2009).

Joani Mortenson
University of British Columbia

# East Timor

This former Portuguese colony, occupied by Indonesia from 1975 until 1999, had a population of 1.12 million in 2005, with a female life expectancy rate of 68.7 years. It has a birth rate of 27 per 1,000 population, and an infant mortality rate of 45.9 per 1,000 live births.

During the period of Portuguese colonial rule, outside Dili, the administrative capital, tribal society was largely unaffected. These societies involved clans who lived in villages, where women were responsible for traditional chores, including bringing up children, preparing food, and tending crops. The clinics established in Dili were essentially for the Portuguese, expatriates, and the local elite. In Tetun (or Tetum) society, a dowry—known as bride wealth—was paid by the bride's family. The newlywed couple then lived in their own house, where the wife gave birth and brought up children with help from both her and her husband's extended family.

Xanana Gusmao, East Timor's former guerilla leader and later president, wrote of his mother raising him and his siblings, but otherwise included very little in his autobiography about his mother. Gusmao's second wife, the Australian-born Kirsty Sword Gusmao, expressed herself in her memoirs on the role of women bringing up children in East Timor. After East Timor's independence, she wrote about her attempt to achieve normalcy in their home while tumultuous events were rocking the nation.

During the Indonesian occupation, there was an expansion of health services, this time beyond the city of Dili. Many clinics were built, which were particularly important for midwives. This allowed for improved birthing and child-rearing techniques, leading to a reduction in infant mortality rates. However, after the East Timorese voted for independence in 1999, pro-Indonesian militia destroyed many of these facilities, especially in rural areas. Since then there have been attempts to rebuild the health services. Foreign governments, nongovernmental organizations (NGOs), and charities have improved health care, although there is no provision of social security for mothers.

**See Also:** Autobiographies; Conflict Zones, Mothering in; Indonesia; War and Mothers.

### Bibliography

Brandewie, Ernest and Simon Asten. "Northern Belunese (Timor) Marriage and Kinship: A Study of Symbols." *Philippine Quarterly of Culture and Society*, v.4/1 (March 1976).

Gusmao, Kirsty Sword. *A Woman of Independence: A Story of Love and the Birth of a New Nation*. New York: Macmillan, 2003.

Gusmao, Xanana. *To Resist Is to Win! The Autobiography of Xanana Gusma*. Santa Fe, NM: Aurora Books, 2000.

Hicks, David. "*La Compensation Matrimonial chez les Tetum*" [Tetun Bride Wealth]. *L'Homme*, v.15 (1975).

Hicks, David. *A Maternal Religion: The Role of Women In Tetum Myth and Ritual*. DeKalb: Center for Southeast Asian Studies, Northern Illinois University, 1984.

Justin Corfield
Geelong Grammar School, Australia

# Eating Disorders

According to the National Eating Disorder Information Center, eating disorders primarily affect women of childbearing age, with an estimated 5–7 percent of this population experiencing an eating disorder. While the research findings are inconclusive, an estimated 1–9 percent of pregnant women develop an eating disorder. Disordered eating during childbearing years is not an area widely researched, and knowledge about the relationship between eating disorders and conception, pregnancy, and postpartum is limited.

### Eating Disorders in General

It is roughly estimated that 3 percent of women will experience an eating disorder in their lifetime. Females between the ages of 15–64 are at risk for developing an eating disorder, with an even greater probability for younger women. The most recent *Diagnostic and Statistical Manual of Mental Disorders* outlines definitions of bulimia nervosa (BN), anorexia nervosa (AN), and eating disorders not otherwise specified (EDNOS). BN is defined by recurrent episodes of binge eating compensated by purging behavior, including vomiting, misuse of laxatives or other medications, and/or excessive fasting or exercise. The compensatory behaviors occur at least twice weekly for a period of three months.

AN is defined as the refusal to maintain a minimally normal body weight for one's age and height, coupled with an intense fear of gaining weight or becoming overweight. Often, with AN, a denial of the seriousness of current weight exists, as well as a distorted view of the body; and, in women of childbearing age, the absence of at least three consecutive periods.

EDNOS encompasses several conditions, and is the most prevalent of all eating disorders. This category includes individuals meeting the same criteria as AN, except in females there is a continuation of regular menstrual cycles, or, despite significant weight loss, their weight is in normal range. On the other hand, the individual may match all the criteria for BN, except that binge eating and compensatory behaviors are less frequent than twice weekly for three months. Other criteria for EDNOS include regular use of compensatory behavior in an individual of normal body weight after consuming small amounts of food, and/or repeatedly chewing and spitting out large amounts of food without swallowing.

While the DSM-IV classifications of AN, BN, and EDNOS are widely accepted as standard within the medical community, this type of categorization fails to take into account broader cultural influences on a woman's body and the etiology of disordered eating issues. In congruence with the personal is the political facet of feminist theory, which is that disordered eating symptoms can be viewed as coping mechanisms in response to internalized societal oppressions. It is notable that disordered eating and body image dissatisfaction are not exclusively a pandemic for white, Anglo-Saxon girls and women, as is often the public portrayal. Women of color, older women, impoverished women, pregnant women, disabled women, and lesbian women are left out of the media attention and public understanding of eating issues, which is a result of the demographic of girls and women included in the majority of disordered-eating and body-image research. Disordered eating theorists staunchly advance that disordered eating issues are not mere signs of self-absorbed vanity and obsession with oneself, but rather ways that women cope with untenable life situations. In this view, the body can be a symbolic representation of traumas, and is manifested in eating patterns and extreme dissatisfaction with appetites and body shape. Indeed, traumatic experiences may underlie many female eating problems, as they often disrupt an intact sense of one's body; however, not all women with eating issues are coping with trauma.

Increased rates of dieting, weight preoccupation, eating disorders, and cosmetic surgeries are associated with society's portrayal of the thin female ideal. These images promote unrealistic standards that are impossible to achieve for the average woman, and social comparisons with these standards are highly correlated with body dissatisfaction. Nevertheless, pressure for thinness, exhorted as the primary culprit for disordered eating issues, centers the problem on a woman's obsession with obtaining a thin body, and may reinforce demeaning notions of a young, naïve woman controlled by media image. This perspective also fails to capture the complexity of girls' and womens' embodied experiences and the wide range of etiological factors influencing body regulation practices of diverse girls and women. Issues of globalization, immigration, acculturation, modernization, transition, and identity along dimensions of gender, race, class, ability, and sexual orientation may play a more significant role in contributing to eating issues and body image dissatisfaction.

## Eating Disorders and Pregnancy

From a detection and treatment perspective, women with eating disorders tend to be extremely secretive, and many remain within the ranges of normal weight during the preconception period and throughout pregnancy. As such, health care providers may be completely oblivious to the fact that their pregnant patient is afflicted with an eating disorder, particularly since nausea and vomiting are within the norm of pregnancy symptoms. Being unaware of such a condition, a health care provider could exacerbate negative attitudes. For example, women with disordered eating may experience a worsening of body image with having to be weighed and measured during each prenatal visit.

## Maternal Body Image

Researchers have suggested that women who have previously been concerned about their shape, weight, and eating habits prepartum have more negative psychological reactions to being pregnant, and

report higher levels of body image dissatisfaction, than mothers who have not had such concerns.

Conversely, some mothers with a history of body image issues actually experience a lessening of negative attitudes during pregnancy, with a return to pre-conception levels in the postpartum period. Some researchers propose that this relaxation in attitudes toward weight gain during pregnancy, and their improvement in eating behaviors, result from the desire to take better care of themselves and their unborn child. Additionally, the increase in support systems such as family and friends, and the lowering of societal expectations of weight and shape during pregnancy, also contribute to overall improvement in eating disorders during pregnancy.

Reflecting the improvement in eating disorder symptoms experienced by some women during pregnancy, many women take pleasure in the changes their bodies undergo throughout this period. For instance, many women experience positive feelings, including pride at their weight and shape changes, while others view pregnancy as an excuse to not worry about weight and shape. Many women experience pregnancy as positive and report an alleviation of a sense of responsibility for body weight during pregnancy. In general, it appears that attitudes regarding weight gain and body shape are positively impacted during pregnancy. The realization that weight gain is not only accepted, but expected, appears to alleviate the stress surrounding physical changes for the majority of expectant mothers. Nonetheless, research findings are contradictory regarding maternal reactions to changing pregnant bodies, especially for woman with past disordered eating symptoms.

## Eating Disorders and Pregnancy Outcomes

For women with a history of body image issues, pregnancy may exacerbate their symptoms toward a full-blown eating disorder. While women with BN generally remain within their expected weight range, the emphasis they place on weight as a measure of self-worth makes pregnancy weight gain quite difficult. Likewise, pregnancy can be an extremely stressful time for women suffering from AN. For those who are obsessed with losing more weight, and already consider themselves "fat," the requirement to gain 20 to 30 pounds during the course of normal pregnancy can be particularly traumatic. Eating disorder symptoms and behaviors during the preconception, pregnancy, and postpartum periods can have effects on the course of pregnancy and fetal outcomes.

## Impacts of Pregnancy on Symptoms

The intensification of the negative body image that parallels weight gain during pregnancy in women with eating disorders does not necessarily lead to an escalation of symptoms. While elimination of previous eating disorder behaviors is rare, some researchers have indicated a reduction in behaviors that are considered potentially harmful to the fetus during pregnancy, such as binge eating, purging, use of laxatives, and dieting. Researchers have commonly found that the number of women binge eating and vomiting decreases successively during each trimester of pregnancy, which may result from a woman's motivation to avoid harming the fetus. However, disordered eating symptoms often return in the postpartum period, as the body image issues prevalent during the preconception period return to varying degrees.

## Impacts of Eating Disorders on Pregnancy

Research into the effects of eating disorders on pregnancy has revealed some potential complications and fetal impacts, which appear to be intensified by the severity of the symptoms, and are also related to whether the woman is actively symptomatic or in remission at the time of conception. For example, some researchers have reported a slightly lower live birth rate, higher therapeutic abortion rate, and higher level of spontaneous abortion in women with a history of eating disorders compared to the average population. Furthermore, there may be a significantly higher incidence of miscarriage and premature births in women with AN. Weight-controlling behaviors such as dieting, vomiting, laxative abuse, and excessive physical exercise has been linked to undernourishment and possible contributors to impaired growth in the fetus. Additionally, researchers have suggested that the excessive drug use in the form of laxatives, diuretics, and appetite suppressants in some women may disturb fetal growth and development. Some studies have found that women with eating disorder symptoms are at greater risk for delivering infants of lower birth weight, and that pregnant women with AN may impact fetal growth due to intrauterine malnutrition.

Expected maternal weight gains, higher birth weights, and better Apgar scores were found in women who were in remission from an eating disorder at the time of conception, compared to women with disordered eating symptoms at the time of conception. The evidence suggesting a link between disordered eating and fetal outcomes is extremely inconclusive; however, women with current or past eating disorders need to be aware of the possible link between disordered eating and fetal outcome.

## Eating Disorder Impacts: Postnatal Period

There is often an increase in disordered eating symptoms and negative body image postpartum. Many BN study participants experienced worse symptoms postpartum than preconception. Women suffering from BN have been shown to sustain the reduction in the severity of their symptoms nine months postpartum, while the AN group experienced a return to pre-pregnancy symptom levels typically by six months postpartum. Women with active BN during pregnancy were also three times more likely to develop postpartum depression. In addition, women with active AN or BN at the time of conception appeared to have more difficulty with breastfeeding than those in remission from eating disorders. Likewise, significantly fewer women with a history of an eating disorder breastfed their babies than those without a similar history. Those with an eating disorder in their history who did breastfeed tended to cease breastfeeding earlier than mothers without eating disorders.

In addition to breastfeeding issues, mothers with a history of eating disorders have been found to exhibit other eating-related behaviors toward their children. In examinations of mealtime interactions, mothers with a history of eating disorders tended to have fewer positive comments about food than mothers without a history of eating disorders, and were less likely to eat with their children. While the research results remain mixed in regards to the impact of disordered eating on the pregnant woman, the fetus, and postpartum experiences for the mother and the child, it is an area pending further further attention and investigation.

**See Also:** Body Image; Breastfeeding; Emotions; Postpartum Depression; Pregnancy; Prenatal Health Care.

**Bibliography**

American Psychiatric Association. *Diagnostic and Statistical Manual of Mental Disorders, 4th Edition.* Washington, DC: American Psychiatric Association, 1994.

Cohen, Lee. "Eating Disorders. (Drugs, Pregnancy, and Lactation)." *Family Practice News* (January 2003).

Costin, Carolyn. *The Eating Disorders Sourcebook: A Comprehensive Guide to the Causes, Treatments, and Prevention of Eating Disorders.* New York: McGraw-Hill, 2006.

Wellsphere. "Dying to Be a Good Mom: Eating Disorders in Pregnancy." (July 2008). http://www.well sphere.com/brain-health-article/dying-to-be-a-good -mom-eating-disorders-in-pregnancy/24073 (accessed July 2009).

Gina Wong-Wylie
Athabasca University

# Ecofeminism and Mothering

Ecofeminism and mothering are deeply interconnected in Western ideological constructions of both nature and gender. Ecofeminism as a set of principles emerged in the 1970s with the increased awareness of the connections between women and nature. Françoise d'Eaubonne established the Ecology-Feminisme Center in Paris in 1972, and in 1974 she first used the term *ecofeminisme*. D'Eaubonne addressed the need for an ecological revolution lead by women, which she claimed would establish equality of gender relations and bring an end to the power of one group over another—including the domination of humans over nature. D'Eaubonne linked environmental degradation with patriarchal culture, and believed that a social structure based on *feminisme* would prevent the destruction of human beings and the planet. D'Eaubonne's *feminisme* was based upon the principles of complete equality and the absence of all oppression; in effect, no one gender group or species would have power over the other.

## Woman and Mother Exploited

Ecofeminism, as it has developed further through the work of such theorists as Carolyn Merchant, Karen J. Warren, Charlene Spretnak, Ynestra King, Judith Plant, and Val Plumwood, among others, locates the domination of women and the domination of nature as interrelated and overlapping. As posited in Merchant's *The Death of Nature*, women and nature both suffer under patriarchal domination, as they historically have been treated as objects to be exploited, consumed, controlled, subdued and tamed. The Earth is depicted (both currently and historically) in feminized terms, and the descriptive language is complex and fraught with ambivalence: nature is portrayed as fertile, nurturing, and protective (stereotypically maternal); sexualized and seductive (as observed and possessed by men); and wild, dark, and dangerous (needing to be tamed and civilized). According to ecofeminist theory, this complex representation of female nature as simultaneously alluring, nurturing, and dangerous justified the patriarchal domination and exploitation of nature throughout history—particularly with the advent of new science, colonization, and the industrial revolution in European cultures. Within this mechanistic and masculinist discourse, nature-woman is constructed as needing and deserving of being possessed, penetrated, and domesticated by the more rational and civilized white male, as depicted within Western ideology.

According to ecofeminist theorists, this system of patriarchal domination negatively impacts all living beings—including nature, women, indigenous people, and the poor. In this sense, ecofeminism overlaps with environmental justice theory, which argues that the racial, social, and economic underclasses are most negatively impacted by environmental pollution and degradation because they lack the economic and political power to protect their communities. Ecofeminist and environmental justice theorists argue that the exploitation of nature, women, and people of color takes place because the rights of the individual (man) come before those of the community (all living things). An solution offered by ecofeminists is the "partnership ethic" advocated by Merchant in *Reinventing Eden*. In this work and elsewhere, Merchant promotes a "moral ethic of care," similar to the belief system of many Native American tribes, in which human beings live in a balanced and equitable relationship with all living things. In a partnership community,

*African activist Wangari Maathai (center) planting trees as part of the Green Belt Movement in Kenya.*

no group or species holds power over the other, and interdependence replaces individualism.

**Expanding Field of Study**

Ecofeminism is an expansive field of study with numerous branches: liberal, social, socialist, and cultural. It also has multiple applications, including scientific, philosophical, historical, literary/artistic, psychological, and spiritual. A significant aspect of ecofeminism is political activism; ecofeminist writers, academics, and scientists work to protect and preserve environmental rights. The so-called "mother" of American environmentalist movement was Rachel Carson, author of the acclaimed *Silent Spring*, which exposed the dangers of dichlorodiphenyltrichloroethane (DDT); Carson's research demonstrated the deeply negative impact of toxics and chemicals on the environment, animals, and humans.

In Africa, Wangari Maathi founded The Green Belt Movement to help restore denuded land in her country, enlisting poor African women to help plant millions of trees to stop the soil erosion and improve soil quality, food production, water quality, and economic prosperity. In India, Vandana Shiva founded Navdanya, an organization that works to preserve the biodiversity of seed and food, as well as what it calls the "democracy" and "sovereignity" of water. Winona LaDuke, a Native American author and environmental activist and founder of the Indigenous Women's Network, White Earth Land Recovery Project, and cofounder (with The Indigo Girls) of Honor the Earth, fights to protect the environmental rights and land of Native American communities throughout North America. Petra Kelly cofounded the Green Party Movement in Germany and fought against the use and creation of weapons of mass destruction. In her work and writing she claimed connections between sexism, war, and environmental degradation.

**Nature and Earth as Mother**

In her forthcoming *Polluting Mama: Ecofeminism, Literature, and Film,* Heidi Hutner argues that the relationship between mothering and nature is crucial to ecofeminist theory and ecofeminist activism on linguistic, spiritual, political, and ideological levels. Hutner claims that the very way in which nature is constructed in language is inextricably bound with culturally constructed concepts of motherhood, such as the expressions "mother nature" and "mother Earth," which are embedded so deeply in Western culture that it would be impossible to detach them. Hutner suggests that there are deeply complex ideological, feminist, and ecological ramifications inherent in this linguistic construction of mother-as-nature-as-Earth.

**Spiritual Branches**

Some spiritual branches of ecofeminism are tied to mothering through the belief in Earth-goddess worship. Starhawk, for example, holds that a human return to the mother goddess is "Mother Earth, who sustains all growing things" and will heal the deep ideological rifts between men and women, humans and nature, God and the human world within our Western cultural identity. For spiritual ecofeminists, then, the mother Earth or mother goddess is the center of all spiritual life.

Alice Walker, a self-proclaimed paganist (and womanist) follows a similar spiritual path in her work and discussions about *The Color Purple*. In her poem, "The Earth Is Our Mother," Walker articulates a distinctly ecofeminist spiritual connection to the mother Earth—linking the nature body of the Earth with a human mother's body—and this mother Earth connects all living things in her loving "embrace."

## Female Reproductive Biology and Ecofeminism

There is a historical relationship between mothering and environmental and peace activism; according to Hutner, many women have felt the "call" to fight against environmental degradation to protect their families from environmental toxins, pollution, nuclear waste, and disaster.

The impact of toxics and pollution on female reproductive biology plays an important part in the connections between mothering and ecofeminism, according to Hutner. In *Having Faith*, Sandra Steingraber examines the delicate relationship between the mother's body with the developing fetus and young nursing child, and points to the effect of environmental pollution on the placenta and breast milk. Embryos, fetuses, infants, and children are especially sensitive to environmental damage in their early stages of neurological and hormonal development. As mother's bodies transfer poisons and unwittingly and adversely impact their young, they may be rendered infertile as a result of environmental pollution.

Ecofeminist theory allows for an analysis of the highly charged and complex concepts of the mother's womb—which can be made toxic through pollutants—as a sacred and protected space. Hutner argues that in an environmentally degraded world, mothers are both at fault for polluting their own children (or for being infertile), and they are viewed as responsible for cleaning up the world. A novel such as Margaret Atwood's *Handmaid's Tale* warns of the potential impact of such reasoning. In the fictional nation of Gilead, a land so polluted that human reproduction has diminished significantly, women are forced to procreate for the "good of the nation," are blamed for their inability to conceive, and are punished when they give birth to "monsters."

## Critics of Ecofeminism

Some critics argue that ecofeminism goes too far in embracing the woman and nature connection, which idealizes the female-as-natural and reifies the position that women are not capable of functioning as rational thinkers. Ecofeminism has also been charged with setting men up as inherently outside of any real connection with the natural world. In other words, by idealizing the female-nature connection, some ecofeminists may be accused of recreating the very dualities it seeks to erase. Despite these claims, ecofeminists claim to move out of these binaries and include men, women, children, the elderly, and people of all races, cultures and classes in their theories.

**See Also:** Atwood, Margaret; Demeter, Goddess; Dinnerstein, Dorothy; Environments and Mothering; Paganism (New Paganism) and Mothering; Wicca and Mothering.

## Bibliography

Atwood, Margaret. *Handmaid's Tale*. New York: Random House, 1998.

Carson Rachel. *Silent Spring*. New York: Fawcett Crest Books, 1964.

Hutner, Heidi. *Polluting Mama: Ecofeminism, Mothering, Literature and Film*. Forthcoming, 2011.

Kelly, Petra. *Fighting for Hope*. Cambridge, MA: South End Press, 1999.

King, Ynestra. "The Ecology of Feminism and the Feminism of Ecology." In *Healing the Wounds*. Gabriola Island, BC: New Society, 1989.

LaDuke, Winona. *All Our Relations: Native Struggles for Land and Life*. Cambridge, MA: South End Press, 1999.

Maathi, Wangari. *The Greenbelt Movement*. Brooklyn, NY: Lantern Books, 2003.

Plumwood, Val. *Feminism and the Mastery of Nature*. New York: Routledge, 1994.

Shiva, Vandana. *Earth Democracy*. Cambridge, MA: South End Press, 2005.

Starhawk. *The Earth Path*. New York: Harper One, 2005.

Steingraber, Sandra. *Having Faith: An Ecologist's Journey to Motherhood*. New York: Perseus, 2001.

Walker, Alice. *The Color Purple*. New York: Harvest, 2003.

Walker, Alice. "The Earth is Our Mother." In *We Are the Ones We've Been Waiting For: Inner Light in a Time of Darkness.* New York: The New Press, 2006.

Warren, Karen J. *Ecofeminism: Women, Culture, Nature.* Urbana-Champaign: University of Illinois Press, 1997.

Heidi Hutner
State University of New York, Stony Brook

# Economics of Motherhood

The beliefs that motherhood should be highly valued and that those who have primary responsibility for rearing children should be adequately rewarded are popularly held; however, there is disagreement on how to appropriately compensate parents and caretakers (mothers, fathers, grandparents, and childcare workers). In lieu of a paycheck, some question if there is another way to ensure that the responsibility of child rearing is valued.

## A Mother's Work

The last century has witnessed the evolving concept of how to compensate those who undertake parenting. With the onset of industrial revolution, the home ceased to be the main site of work. Both women and men were pushed to work long hours outside of the home, and with that came the dilmena of who would care for the children. Solutions have included mothers (and more recently fathers), older siblings, grandparents, childcare centers (sometimes connected to work sites), preschools, co-ops, and a community of support. However, mothers still assume most responsibility.

Though many women have held jobs through the ages, their wages have consistently been lower than men's, which meant that women were often the obvious choice to assume primary responsibility for child rearing. Women were (and still are) often paid less on the premise that their incomes were secondary, and because they were more likely to be clustered into female-dominated (and undervalued) professions, including teaching, caretaking, and domestic work. Because of this, some feminists argue that having mothers care for the children

with the men more focused on their jobs emerged more as a consequence of economics than gendered instincts. In the early 1970s, this issue galvanized feminists to question why women were expected to primarily undertake childrearing responsibilities. As a result, many women took jobs outside the home and sought to popularize the notion that every mother is a working mother. However, their looming question remained unanswered: why is the responsibility of child rearing so undervalued, both emotionally and financially?

## The Price of Motherhood

In her 2001 book *The Price of Motherhood,* Ann Crittenden argues that motherhood and child rearing imposes many hidden costs on women, which she refers to as the mommy tax. Some are obvious (no compensation for caring for your own children) and some are not (child rearing does not qualify women for social security). Women often take time off from work to raise children, inhibiting their career growth and diminishing their incomes. Child rearing is valuable to society, but is not compensated as such, Crittenden states, and the cumulative effect is that women are far more likely than men to be poor.

## The Value of Mothering

In 1972, in order to determine life insurance policy payouts, Chase Manhattan Bank determined "the replacement value of the mother," by considering all of the responsibilities that go into parenting (such as being a maid, chauffeur, food buyer, dishwasher, nurse, and seamstress) and concluded that a mother's work was worthy of an equivalent annual salary of $13,391 ($60,000 in 2008). These calculations were primarily based on what mothers would have to pay in order to get the job done using outside assistance.

With the increasing use of assisted reproductive technologies (ART) and the employment of surrogate mothers, women's reproductive labor is attaining some value; however, some fear that if ART is left unregulated, some surrogates will be taken advantage of. While compensating outsourced work is one issue, paying mothers directly challenges many assumptions about a mother's worth.

In 1983, the late economist John Kenneth Galbraith advocated for including a mother's responsibilities in the Gross National Product (GNP). This calculation was designed to ensure that mothers were valued, and to boost a nation's GNP by including work that was previously unremunerated. In 1994, Saskatchewan homemaker Carol Lees refused to list her work hours as "zero" in the Census Canada forms simply because she did unpaid housework at home. In the ensuing lobbying effort, concerted in part by the Ottawa-based group Mothers Are Women, Statistics Canada found that women undertake two-thirds of the 25 billion hours of unpaid work in Canada. As a result, three new census questions concerning caregiving hours were eventually included in the Canadian forms.

## The Dilemma of Paying for Mothering

There is an assumption that women primarily value their worth through a salary. There are emotional considerations as well. Wealthier women are financially able to stay home and may experience cultural pressures if they decide to take a job, whileless wealthy women are motivated to work outside the home, in part to avoid social criticism for being lazy or for not contributing to the family finances.

While putting a price tag on motherhood may be intended to honor the choice to be mothers, paying for "women's work" creates another difficulty. Who is paying, and how much is paid? As Charlotte Perkins Gilman pondered more than 100 years ago, "Are we willing to consider motherhood as a business, a form of commercial exchange? Are the cares and duties of the mother, her travail and her love, commodities to be exchanged for bread?"

Some feminists question whether men would be paid more than women if they took on the responsibilities of home and childcare. The prospect of a "mothering" income begs another question: if motherhood was paid, would more women (or men) commit themselves to full-time parenting? Workers in professions that are comprised of more than 70 percent females are compensated less than professions dominated by men—even if the required skills and training are comparable.

## Government Incentives and Compensation

In Europe, where both parents can take up to 36 months of empolyment leave, much of it paid, there are limitations based on the assumption that the home is women's responsibility. In Germany, for example, public health care is free for stay-at-home mothers, but only if the father works. When parents care for their own child, there is a monthly stipend for childcare, but not if outside help is retained. Russia currently offers a "baby salary," and a similar child tax credit has been proposed in the United States. Japan and Germany have a similar system, with eligibility based on one parent working.

Mexico has pioneered Oportunidades, a program that gives cash to poor mothers as an incentive to keep their children in school, and for the mother to participate in school functions and meetings, and attend doctor's appointments. Each task is attributed a different value. Thirty countries (the majority in Latin America) and the U.S. state of New York have pioneered similar programs. The *New York Times* described this evolution in government funding: "The nanny state offered unconditional love;

This 1891 lithograph titled "The Growing Field of Women's Work," reflects women's arrival into the public sphere.

the new paternalism is tough love, directly aimed at smashing the culture of poverty."

With the exception of the New York example, the United States lags far behind when it comes to financial validation for child rearing. Of 168 countries studied, the United States is one of only five nations that does not have a standardized maternity leave program. In Minnesota, an At-Home Infant Care Program allows working parents who meet the income eligibility (a household income under $20,000)—to receive funds to care for children younger than 1 year of age at home. The state of Maine, during the initial stages of welfare reform, changed attending school to a "work" designation, and subsidized parents who were getting an education.

The long-term challenge with mothering work is the concept that it remains unvalued and unnoticed, leaving women insecure about making this life choice. A woman's ability to stay home and care for children often makes it possible for her partner to work. Just how to place an economic value on a mother's worth—such as mandating maternity leave—is a debate that is unlikely to fade.

**See Also:** Childcare; Consumerism and Motherhood; Daycare; Domestic Labor; Economy and Motherhood; Gilman, Charlotte Perkins; Mexico; Russia (and Soviet Union); Stay at Home Mothers; Surrogate Motherhood.

**Bibliography**
Collins, Patricia Hill. *Black Feminist Thought: Knowledge, Consciousness, and the Politics of Empowerment.* New York: Routledge, 2008.
Edin, Kathryn, and Maria Kefalas. *Promises I Can Keep: Why Poor Women Put Motherhood Before Marriage.* Berkeley: University of California Press, 2005.
Foroohar, Rana. "Myth & Reality: Forget All the Talk of Equal Opportunity—European Women Can Have a Job but Not a Career." *Newsweek* (February 27, 2006).
Gilman, Charlotte Perkins. *Women and Economics: A Study of the Economic Relation Between Women and Men as a Factor in Social Evolution.* Amherst, NY: Prometheus Books, 1994.
Heyman, Jody, Alison Earle, Stephanie Simmons, Stephanie M. Breslow, and April Kuehnhoff. *The Work, Family, and Equity Index: Where Does the United States Stand Globally.* Boston: The Project on Global Working Families, 2004.
Kome, Penney. "A Woman's Work Is Never Counted." *Ottawa Citizen* (May 9, 1997).
Rosenberg, Tina. "A Payoff Out of Poverty." *The New York Times Magazine* (December 21, 2008).
Waring, Marilyn. *Counting for Nothing: What Men Value and What Women Are Worth.* Toronto: University of Toronto Press, 1999.

Amy Richards
Independent Scholar

# Economy and Motherhood

In both their direct mothering and nonmothering work, mothers engage with the economy through transactions, labor, and enterprise. Much of mothers' economic contributions go unrecognized in standard accounting systems, which generally capture economic contributions. Although the United Nations System of National Accounts tries to account for all production in the national economy, including household production, it still excludes activities like childbearing, childcare, elder care, cooking, cleaning, and breastfeeding from the economic activity category.

## Transactions

In developed nations, mothers control a significant proportion of their household's spending (up to 80 percent in the United States) and are assumed to contribute to the economy primarily as consumers in free market exchanges. In developing economies, mothers' economic transactions as consumers and traders often occur in less formal markets, according to a form of social commensurability—goods may be bartered directly, or a mutually agreed price is dependent on relationship, need, and bargaining skill.

In addition, mothers engage in many daily economic transactions that are primarily incommensurable, such as breastfeeding, where a valuable transaction occurs between mother and child. In the 1990s, economist Julie Smith estimated Australian mothers' milk to be worth $2.2 billion Australian dollars annually, and placed the economic costs of declining breastmilk production at $5.7 billion per annum—purely in terms of children's health care and excluding environmental or developmental considerations. Feminist economist J.K. Gibson-Graham lists many other equally incommensurable transactions such as intra-household flows, gift-giving, and gleaning. Economist Nancy Folbre asserts that non-market transactions such as flows of money, time, and gifts within the family are essential to the economy.

## Labor and Compensation

Most discussions around mothers' economic contributions converge around labor and compensation. Time-use surveying confirms that mothers' daily labor is much more than what is generally included in national accounting systems. In most countries, women's total work hours are longer than men's. Globally, women's unpaid labor is approximately twice that of men's—in Japan it is nine times greater. Some estimates state that globally, unpaid labor is worth about $11 trillion annually, of which mothers' labor is likely to be a large proportion. Statistics often merely distinguish men's and women's labor, which is ultimately unhelpful because there are large fluctuations over a woman's life cycle. Mothers of small children have the heaviest workloads, whereas single women in developed countries have equal workloads to men. In a recent Australian time-use study, mothers with babies averaged 70 hours of work per week. In developing countries, the United Nations Development Programme (UNDP) estimates that only 34 percent of women's total working time is spent in paid economic activities—leaving 66 percent of women's work unpaid. Internationally, most part-time jobs are held by women: in Australia and Chile, it is 82 percent; Japan, 72 percent; the United Kingdom, 77 percent; and the United States, 68 percent.

Mothers' labor is compensated through direct payment of wages for full-time and part-time work, through in-kind payments or government parenting payments, and through nonmonetary compensation. In Australia and New Zealand, families may receive compensation through government parenting payments, baby bonuses, and maternity leave payments. In Hong Kong, domestic worker-mothers from the Philippines often get accommodation, food, and a daily allowance as part of their alternative compensation package; their monetary wages are sent home

for the care of their own children. In semi-subsistence rural economies, food is produced by mothers and consumed directly by herself and her household. In many kinship-based societies, such as China, investment in the emotional and physical labor of raising children is partly compensated by the obligation of children to care for their mother in old age.

## Enterprise

Mothers are involved in many economic enterprises: as employees, shareholders, owner–operators, and volunteers in both profit-making and community-owned enterprises. One in 11 adult women are entrepreneurs in the United States, and research in Atlanta shows that 37 percent of women business owners plan to hand their business over to their daughters (while only 19 percent of men planned to hand it to their sons)—showing that even in the world's largest capitalist economy, mothers' business decisions are complexly interlinked with nonmarket considerations.

In fact, women the world over are much more likely to be involved in less formal street-, home-, and market-based enterprises that require low startup costs and allow for maximum flexibility. In Nepal, 77 percent of the female labor force are own-account workers, while only 13 percent are employees and 4 percent are employers. Likewise, in Zimbabwe, 63 percent are own-account workers, compared to 38 percent of males. Mothers may also be involved in community-owned enterprises such as the New Zealand cooperative Playcentre organization, where mothers take turns as childcare workers; women's community savings groups in rural Philippines; or school-based vegetable gardens in urban Australia.

## Mothers in the Economy

Mothers interact with the economy in diverse ways, many of which are unable to be measured with national, male-based economic accounting systems of industrialized nations. Because mothers' transactions are more likely to be incommensurable and informal, their labor unpaid or even uncompensated, they provide the ultimate challenge to any economic model. The challenge to make mothers' valuable and variable contributions more visible may ultimately contest and retheorize the understanding of what constitutes the economy.

**See Also:** Breastmilk; Capitalism and Motherhood; Domestic Labor; Economics of Motherhood; Employment and Motherhood.

**Bibliography**
Folbre, Nancy. *The Invisible Heart: Economics and Family Values*. New York: The New Press, 2001.
Gibson-Graham, J.K. *A Postcapitalist Politics*. Minneapolis: University of Minnesota Press, 2006.
Smith, Julie. "Mothers' Milk and Markets." *Australian Feminist Studies*, v.19 (2004).
United Nations Development Programme (UNDP). "Human Development Report Statistics." http://hdrstats.undp.org (accessed February 2009).
Waring, Marilyn. *Counting for Nothing: What Men Value and What Women Are Worth*. Wellington, New Zealand: Bridget Williams Books, 1989.

Kelly Dombroski
Australian National University

# Ectogenesis

Ectogenesis (from the Greek *ecto*, outer, and *genesis,* origin) is artificial reproduction outside the body. An 1883 biology text on pathogenic anatomy introduced the term to describe bacteria that reproduce outside the body. In 1924, J.B.S. Haldane coined the term for human reproduction in his essay, *Daedalus: or, Science and the Future.*

Haldane's close friend, Aldous Huxley, made ectogenetic reproduction the central theme in his famed 1932 novel, *Brave New World*. Radical feminist theorist Shulamith Firestone embraced ectogenesis in her 1972 treatise on women's equality, *The Dialectic of Sex*, arguing that elimination of pregnancy is the only route to women's equality. Images of so-called "babies in bottles" have frequently appeared in advertisements, magazines, and book covers, and ectogenesis continues to be a central theme for many contemporary feminists and science fiction writers.

## Ectogenetic Research
Research in several areas suggests that ectogenesis might be realized, and perhaps soon. Embodied (in vivo) human gestational length continues to decrease from both ends of pregnancy with advances in neonatology and embryology. Increasingly, neonatologists can sustain barely viable, severely premature infants, using sophisticated incubators to support fetal oxygen transmission and lung maturation. Such developments in preemie preservation impinge on the 24-week viability line that many previously considered unyielding. The length of embodied gestation for human fetuses has also narrowed from conception. Achievements in embryology, originating primarily from in vitro fertilization (IVF) research, have extended science's ability to conceive and maintain embryos outside the maternal body. Successes in these two areas of reproductive technology combine to contract the span during which human reproduction still requires in vivo gestation. The implications of such technologies for full ectogenetic reproduction are monumental.

Other ectogenetic research includes work by Japanese researcher Dr. Yoshinor Kuwabara, who in 1997 artificially gestated a 17-week-old goat fetus removed from its mother's uterus. The transplanted goat fetus gestated artificially for three weeks before Kuwabara terminated the experiment. The artificial uterus Kuwabara designed supported the fetus in tanks filled with amniotic fluid, and hoses connected to the umbilical cord to regulate the animal's intake of nutrients and the output of its body wastes.

In 2002, Cornell University researcher Hung-Ching Liu, Ph.D., cultured donated uterine cells that were then implanted with human embryos. Liu stopped the embryo growth after six days in compliance with U.S. laws governing IVF, but she anticipates extending the growth time to 14 days. Her research, if successful, could allow transplantation of an artificially grown, new uterus, along with any implanted embryos, back into the body of a donor or other woman. It could also one day result in the growth of a fully ectogenetic uterus to permit complete human reproduction outside the body. Interspecies gestation among animals offers the possibility that nonhuman animals might one day gestate human fetuses. In response to the dwindling panda population, Chinese researchers implanted hybridized rabbit-panda embryos (made from panda DNA inserted into rabbit egg casings) into rabbit uteruses. They finally achieved a panda-rabbit embryo pregnancy with an embryo implanted in a cat uterus.

Some researchers look to interspecies reproduction for full ectogenetic human reproduction.

## Challenging Ethics

Ectogenesis is controversial. Supporters argue that ectogenetic reproduction would free women from the burdens of pregnancy; allow infertile women to have children; provide an alternative gestational environment for women with endangered multiple pregnancies; permit men to "have" children (either with or without a female partner); and support reproduction by gay, lesbian, and other nonheterosexuals. Pro-life advocates and some theologians foresee the possibility of ectogenetic fetal transfer as the end to abortion. Finally, some military enthusiasts note the potential for growing "super soldiers," whose personal identification would be with their incubator brethren, rather than a gestational family.

There are also serious concerns about the dangers of reproducing humans outside of women's bodies, as presaged by Mary Shelley in her 1818 novel *Frankenstein: or The Modern Prometheus*. Class-conscious scholars warn of further commodification of conception, pregnancy, and children by the commercial world. Pointing to recent insurance coverage denials for people with certain demonstrated genetic proclivities, some argue that artificial womb technology would allow total environmental control and thereby create a preference or requirement that all pregnancies occur in vitro in order to guard against environmental contamination or other threats posed by "irresponsible" pregnant women.

Liberal feminists point out that employers and governments could vacate all maternity benefits and demand that workers use ectogenesis to create their children. Others argue that ectogenesis might snap the mother–child bond they claim to be essential to healthy human biological and social development. Countering the pro-ectogenetic military idealists, others reject the idea of a disconnected, endlessly replicable class of warriors that could be unleashed upon populations with whom they have little in common. Some theologians express grave concern at the idea of human/animal hybrids and manufactured "babies in bottles," pointing to a divine design for human reproduction. Finally, the most radical thinkers express alarm at the possibility that self-reproductive men might eliminate women as a class altogether.

**See Also:** Abortion; Artificial Uterus; Ectopic Pregnancy; Interspecies Gestation; In Vitro Fertilization; Lesbian Mothering; Miscarriage; Pregnancy; Premature Birth; Transpecies Hybridization; Uterine Transplant; Women's Health (General).

## Bibliography

Alghrani, Amel. "The Legal and Ethical Ramifications of Ectogenesis." *Asian Journal of WRT & International Health Law and Policy*, v.2/1 (2007).

Aristarkhova, Irina. "Ectogenesis and Mother as Machine." *Body Society*, v.11/3 (2005).

Firestone, Shulamith. *The Dialectic of Sex*. New York: Bantam Books, 1972.

Gelfand, Scott and John R. Shook, eds. *Ecotgenesis*. Amsterdam: Rodopi, 2006.

Haldane, J.B.S. *Daedalus: Or, Science and the Future*. Delivered at Cambridge (February 4, 1923). Transcribed by Cosma Rohilla Shalizi. www.cscs.umich.edu/~crshalizi/Daedalus.html (accessed June 2009).

Huxley, Aldous. *Brave New World*. New York: Harper Modern Classics, 1998.

Karp, Laurence E. and Roger P. Donahue. "Preimplantational Ectogenesis: Science and Speculation Concerning In Vitro Fertilization and Related Procedures." *The Western Journal of Medicine*, v.124/4 (1976).

Klass, Perri. "The Artificial Womb Is Born." *New York Times* (September 29, 1996).

McKie, Robin. "Men Redundant? Now We Don't Need Women Either." *The Observer* (February 10, 2002). www.guardian.co.uk/world/2002/feb/10/medicalscience.research (accessed June 2009).

Rosen, Christine. "Why Not Artificial Wombs?" *The New Atlantis: A Journal of Technology & Society*, v.3 (2003).

Smajdor, Anna. "The Moral Imperative for Ectogensis." *Cambridge Quarterly of Healthcare Ethics*, v.16 (2007).

Squier, Susan M. *Babies in Bottles*. New Brunswick, NJ: Rutgers University Press, 1994.

Welin, Stellan. "Reproductive Ectogenesis: The Third Era of Human Reproduction and Some Moral Consequences." *Science and Engineering Ethics*, v.10/4 (2004).

Deirdre M. Condit
Virginia Commonwealth University

# Ecuador

Located in South America, south of Colombia and north of Peru, and east of the Pacific Ocean, Ecuador claimed 25 years of civilian governance in 2004. This period, however, experienced sociopolitical instability. In 2007, the election of a Constituent Assembly to draft a new constitution marked the 20th time Ecuador has dealt with such an event since their independence. In addition to the political situation in Ecuador, religion serves as a central influence on the social issues related to motherhood, sexuality, and family, as 95 percent of the population is Roman Catholic. In contrast to all of Latin America, Ecuador's public health expenditure is one of the lowest. Spanish is the official language, and Ecuador has a literacy rate of 92.3 percent for men and 89.7 percent for women. Thus, public health expenditure and educational levels are inextricably linked and differ greatly across rural and urban areas; in rural areas, limited access to health care, education, and economic resources result in many adolescents not having access to contraceptives; thus, one in 10 adolescents give birth each year.

## Abortions and Health Care

The 1971 Penal Code of Ecuador prohibits abortion—except to save the life or health of the mother, or if the pregnancy is the result of the rape of a mentally incompetent woman—and the 1984 Constitution guarantees the protection of life from conception. In September 2008, Ecuador approved a new constitution, which some religious leaders charged could lead to legalized abortion; however, this interpretation is refuted by the current president, Rafael Correa.

In an effort to curb the rate of unsafe abortions and unintended pregnancies, the Ecuadorian government recently began a comprehensive sexual and reproductive health education program in secondary schools throughout the country. In addition to this program, the Planned Parenthood Federation of America (PPFA) has been involved with organizations in Ecuador since 1974. PPFA claims to have increased access to sexuality education, contraception, and postabortion care. In January 2007, PPFA and their Ecuadorian partner, the Centro Médico de Orientación y Planificación Familiar, started a project for adolescents that is designed to address the reproductive health of rural, indigenous youth in Chimborazo province. PPFA is particularly interested in changing the landscape of this province, as the area has an especially high risk of unwanted pregnancy for adolescents.

Almost two-thirds of health care in Ecuador is privately funded, resulting in limited access for the poor, and financial hardship when they do seek care.

Of its approximately 13.9 million people, Ecuador has a fairly young population. The median age for males is 23.7 years of age, with the median age for females being 24.7 years; 62.7 percent are between 15 and 64 years of age, and 5.2 percent are 65 years and over. The total fertility rate of Ecuador is 2.59 children born to every woman. This figure denotes a steady decrease since 2003, when the total fertility rate was as high as 2.99 children per woman. While Ecuador is slowly changing, caring for and raising children continues to be a central role for women, while men continue to occupy less active roles in the area of childcare. Further, daughters are treated differently than sons, wherein they are portrayed as beings that need protection, and are expected to behave differently than boys as they transition to womanhood. Given the high rate of unwanted pregnancies among adolescents, young girls are likely to bear the heaviest burden when they become young mothers.

**See Also:** Childbirth; Childcare; Children; Domestic Labor; Education and Mothering; Family Planning; Fertility; Reproduction; Rural Mothers.

## Bibliography

Central Intelligence Agency. *The World Factbook: Ecuador.* www.cia.gov/library/publications/the-world-factbook/print/ec.html; www.plannedparenthood.org/about-us/international-program/ecuador-country-program-19002.htm (accessed June 2009).

Eggleston, Elizabeth, et al. "Unintended Pregnancy and Low Birthweight in Ecuador." *American Journal of Public Health,* v.91 (2001).

Torre, Carlos de la and Steve Striffler, eds. *The Ecuador Reader: History, Culture, Politics.* Durham, NC: Duke University Press, 2009.

Danielle Antoinette Hidalgo
University of California, Santa Barbara

# Edelman, Hope

Hope Edelman is an American writer and author. She is the author of five books on motherhood: *Motherless Daughters: The Legacy of Loss* (1994), *Letters From Motherless Daughters: Word of Courage, Grief, and Healing* (1995), *Mother of My Mother: The Intricate Bond Between Generations,* (1997), *Motherless Mothers: How Losing a Mother Shapes the Parent You Become* (2006), and her memoir, *The Possibility of Everything* (2009). Edelman lost her own mother in 1981 to breast cancer. Edelman, who was 17 at the time, has drawn on that experience for her books.

Edelman grew up with her two younger siblings in Spring Valley, New York, about 30 minutes from her maternal grandparent's home in Mount Vernon, New York. She graduated from Northwestern University's Medill School of Journalism in 1986. She was educated in researching, interviewing, and editing for newspapers, but found that the inverted pyramid of newspaper journalism was of interest to her. A professor suggested she try magazine writing, which places more emphasis on facts and details. Edelman earned a master's degree in expository writing from the University of Iowa's nonfiction writing program.

While in college, Edelman interned at the Chicago-based *Outside* magazine. She later worked for three months writing for the *Salem Statesman-Journal*, where she wrote news and feature articles. Once she graduated, Edelman went on to work for Whittle Communications in Knoxville, Tennessee, for three years. Edelman began writing *Motherless Daughters* while she was a student at the University of Iowa, after Professor Mary Swander encouraged Edelman to dig into and write about her feelings surrounding her mother's death. In the book, Edelman explorers her own inability to grieve her mother's death for years, as well as the experiences of other daughters who lost their mothers. She was 29 when it was published in 1994, and it became a *New York Times* bestseller within two months, having since been published in eight languages. Her second book, *Letters From Motherless Daughters*, published a year later, contains letters from readers who had lost their mothers and were touched by Edelman's writing in her first book. She organized the letters by how long it had been since their mother had died.

Edelman's third book, *Mother of My Mother* (1997), explores the relationships between women, their mothers, and their grandmothers, many of whom Edelman interviewed and surveyed, while dismissing paternal grandmothers. Critics reviewed the book as a mix of scientific findings and memoir with an uneven presentation. It was published in 1999, three years after Edelman's grandmother passed away.

In Edelman's fourth Book, *Motherless Mothers*, she explores how women who have lost their own mothers draw on that experience when mothering their own children. She has said that the idea for the book came to her while she was pregnant with her second child and on bed rest. In an interview with LiteraryMama.com, she said that had her mother been living, she would have phoned for help in day-to-day house upkeep and care of her then four-year-old daughter. However, she was forced to find other ways to cope. The book took three years to write, in part due to Edelman's desire not to leave her children motherless while she wrote. Further, her father passed away while she was writing, and Edelman took time off from the book to spend with him during his final months.

Her fifth book, *The Possibility of Everything*, is a memoir, and was published in late 2009.

Edelman has also written for a variety of print publications, including the *New York Times*, the *Chicago Tribune*, the *San Francisco Chronicle*, the *Washington Post*, the *Dallas Morning News*, *Glamour*, *Child*, *Parenting*, *Seventeen*, *Real Simple*, *Self*, the *Iowa Review*, and the *Crab Orchard Review*. She also contributed to the anthologies *The Bitch in the House*, *Toddler*, *Blindsided by a Diaper*, and *Always Too Soon*.

In addition to writing, she has taught classes for the master of fine arts program at Antioch University Los Angeles. She teaches workshops in memoir and personal essay writing at the Iowa Summer Festival. She also sits on the board of several organizations dedicated to helping children who have lost their mothers.

Edelman is married and has two daughters, Maya and Eden.

**See Also:** Daughters and Mothers; Life Writing and Mothers; Maternal Mortality; Motherless Daughters.

**Bibliography**

Edelman, Hope. "Hope Edelman: Biography." www
.hopeedelman.com/bio-edelman.htm (accessed June
2009).

Edelman, Hope. *Motherless Daughters: The Legacy of
Loss.* New York: Da Capo Press, 2006.

Edelman, Hope. *Mother of My Mother: The Intricate
Bond Between Generations.* Peaslake, UK: Delta,
2000.

Olen, Helaine. "Profiles: An Interview With Hope
Edelman." http://www.literarymama.com/profiles/
archives/001288.html (accessed June 2009).

Rosenberg, Merri. "Salving the Lingering Sting of
Death." *New York Times* (December 3, 1995).

Sarah Caron
Independent Scholar

# Edison, Thomas, Mother of

Nancy Matthews Elliott Edison (1810–71) was born in Chenango County, New York, to Revolutionary War hero Ebenezer Matthews Elliott and his wife, Mercy Putnam. She mothered seven children, including prolific American inventor, Thomas Edison. Edison, who held 1,093 patents during his lifetime, including those for the phonograph and incandescent lightbulb, credited his mother for his success: "My mother was the making of me. She was so true, so sure of me, and I felt I had some one to live for, some one I must not disappoint." Nancy Edison indulged her son's curiosities, encouraged his experiments, and homeschooled her son when teachers described him as too "addled" to learn.

As a young woman, Nancy received some formal education, and worked as a teacher. Following the American Revolution, the Elliott family, like other war refugees, fled the newly independent colonies to settle in Ontario, Canada. There, Nancy met Samuel Edison, and they married in 1828.

Samuel Edison's family was very different from his wife's. The Edison family had remained loyal to the British government during the American Revolution and subsequently fled to Canada several years before the Elliott family. The young couple started a family, and within a decade, was raising four children: Wallace, William, Harriet, and Carlisle. Politically minded Samuel was active in the unsuccessful Papineau-MacKenzie Rebellion of 1837, and like his father during the American Revolution, was afterwards forced to flee Canada. Samuel later left his family in Canada to prepare a home for them in the United States.

Nancy Edison moved her children to Milan, Ohio, to join Samuel in 1839. Now a small coastal town along the shore of Lake Erie in northwest Ohio, Milan during the 19th century was a major port. Samuel Edison established a business manufacturing roof shingles. Nancy purchased a small plot of land in 1841, and Samuel designed a home. Today, that home is a national historic site maintained by the Edison Birthplace Association. Following the move to Ohio, Nancy gave birth to three more children: Samuel, Eliza, and Thomas. Young Thomas Edison was often ill and was a terrible student. There is evidence that Edison was partially deaf as a result of scarlet fever and multiple, untreated ear infections. Classroom learning was difficult for Thomas.

Fed up with unsuccessful teachers, Nancy began schooling her son at home. Many of her lessons came from R.G. Parker's *School of Natural Philosophy* and the Cooper Union. Nancy encouraged her son to read books, for which he was always grateful: "My mother taught me how to read good books quickly and correctly, and this opened up a great world in literature; I have always been thankful for this early training." In 1854, the Edison family moved to Port Huron, Michigan, the easternmost point of land in the state along Lake Huron. Nancy gained a reputation as a caring neighborhood mother, baking for many of the local children. She died in 1871 after struggling for years with mental illness. At the time, Thomas Edison was 24 years old, and about to marry his first wife, Mary Stilwell. Though Nancy Edison sowed the seeds for her inventor son's success, she did not live to see him reap the benefits.

**See Also:** Lincoln, Abraham, Mother of; History of Motherhood: 1750 to 1900; Michigan; Ohio.

**Bibliography**

National Park Service. "Thomas Edison National Historical Park." http://www.nps.gov/edis/index.htm (accessed June 2009).

Rutgers University. "The Thomas Edison Papers." http://edison.rutgers.edu (accessed June 2009).

Stross, Randall. *The Wizard of Menlo Park: How Thomas Alva Edison Invented the Modern World.* New York: Three Rivers Press, 2008.

Tiffany Willey
American Bar Association

# Education and Mothering

Education, like mothering, is a constant yet always changing presence in women's lives, historically and socially defined. Each historical period defines good education and good mothering differently from the previous one. Education and mothering are social constructs, used unproblematically in ordinary ways of speaking, yet meaning different actions in different settings, and changing over time. Mothers participate in education through their practical and supplementary educational work in the home, as teachers and administrators in educational settings, as students at all levels of schooling, and as home schoolers.

What is defined as education and what is taught to children varies from one locality to another. In hunter-gatherer societies, a child's education would include the gender-specific tasks of the group, for example hunting, planting, or harvesting. In industrial and postindustrial societies, children's education is less gender-specific, and is formalized in schools and systems that set the rules and regulations for children's learning. This institutional form, called *schooling*, is the current form of children's education today. Mothers are involved in every aspect of this education as educators, teachers, school administrators and nonteaching staff, daycare workers, students, and school volunteers.

## Mothers as Teachers

Mothers are sometimes described as their child's first teacher. From birth onward, mothers teach their children how to speak, put on clothes, eat, play with others, name colors, and draw pictures. The list is endless. The everyday work of mothers is essential for teaching the child the local culture of family and neighborhood. Within the family, mothers' everyday educational work with children draws from—and at times acts in opposition to—their own experiences of being mothered: media articles devoted to mothering, advice literature for mothers, religious or spiritual beliefs, and watching other mothers at community or play groups. As the social themes that define an historical period wax and wane, so do the particularities of mothering work.

Mothers' educational work is always done in a local, embodied context. The work depends on the biography of the mother and the social relationships of the family, as well as the social and educational resources she has available.

Mothers' educational work with children is central to the child's future participation in schooling. Learning language within the family teaches children a way of speaking that, in the context of education, becomes a marker for school achievement. Similarly, when mothers have time, space, and resources to spend with their children doing such activities as painting, drawing, or going to museums and plays, children's knowledge of their social world expands to support future participation in schooling.

Research on families and children's language use showed that working-class mothers spoke less frequently to their children, and often used simpler sentence structures than did mothers with more education and family resources. To offset this educational disadvantage, community groups such as Home Instruction for Parents or Preschool Youngsters (HIPPY) work in poor communities, showing mothers with few resources how to teach their children in ways that support the child's educational growth.

## The Development of Learning

Mothers' educational work is also informed by articles in newspapers and magazines, and by television and radio. These sources are full of information about different ways to interact with children. Most parent-oriented media stories and advice literature draw their notions of children's educational needs from the research literature on children's development, in which children's development is conceived of as consecutive stages. Learning is based on a mix of individual capacities and engagement in learning through the teachings of others—nature and nurture.

As they grow, children become increasingly able to think about and act in their social world. That is, children learn how to engage with their world through their interactions with others, such as naming a particular color blue, deciding whether to look an adult in the eye when being introduced, and taking turns in conversations. A child's intellectual, emotional, and social growth requires that caregivers (mothers, fathers, grandparents, extended family, daycare staff, foster homes, and so on) actively teach children how and what to learn from the world. This staged model of children's development makes claims to universality across cultures and historical periods.

## The Modern Concept of Schooling

Social groups, including nuclear families, textended families, classroom teachers, and the workplace have ideals and expectations for children's maturation. Historically, schooling was done in the homes of families who could afford to hire a teacher. In the late 19th and early 20th centuries, mass compulsory schooling was instituted in many industrial societies. Schools as we know them today have been developed and continue to change based on their mandate to teach children "reading, writing, and arithmetic," as well as ways of thinking, problem solving, and sociality. Schooling was initiated for many reasons, including teaching children how to behave, and preparing children for a labor market that required literacy: schools teach subjectivities as well as subjects. Mass compulsory schooling coincided with a developing middle class and a professional class whose paid employment required literacy and social skills. Urbanization and the union calling for a "living wage" meant that the family economy did not require mothers to work outside the home in order for the family to survive, allowing mothers' work to therefore be used to support children's school achievement. This period is an important turning point in the relationship between mothering work in the home and the child's participation in schooling.

During the same period, psychology and education became intertwined disciplines. The conception of the developmentally staged child became the basis for curriculum standards by Ministries or Boards of Education, as well as becoming part of the curriculum at teachers' colleges. This conception of children's learning requires the participation of mothers as supplementary educators. Middle-class mothers were anxious to participate in the new scientific ways of raising children to reach their potential.

Children who have a wide knowledge of the social world—such as urban children who have been to a farm, children observing that putting the yellow paintbrush back in the yellow paint pot will preserve the paint colors, children who know how to hold a pencil—are often described as "school ready." This is a concept that references the often-invisible educational work of mothers in the home and family. Today, many mothers who are not working outside the home become the mainstays of school support through volunteering in schools, tutoring their own and others' children, and supplementing children's educational activities. Mass compulsory schooling, with mothers working invisibly in the background, became one avenue to financial success. Currently, education and mothering are inextricably intertwined. Mothers are often the primary organizers of their children's participation in both education and schooling.

## Conforming to the School Schedule

When children reach the age of formal schooling—Kindergarten to high school graduation—mothers' educational work becomes oriented to the requirements of schooling. In most countries with compulsory schooling, the school day is legislated to begin and end at the same time on most days, and does not conform to the hours of the parents' and caregivers' paid employment. In those families with both parents working, after and/or before school care must be arranged. Where parents do shift work, childcare arrangements that match work hours are difficult to find. Other family members, neighbors, or part-time sitters are often involved in maintaining the relationship between parents' educational work, employment, and children's schooling.

Mothering work for schooling extends beyond the legislated school day. School-appropriate clothes and school supplies must be bought. School forms must be filled in and returned. Books must be taken back and forth to school based on the school schedule. Homework must be supervised and returned to the classroom. Typically, mothers and some fathers monitor their children's school activities and orga-

*Preschool children whose mothers interact with them in problem-solving tasks demonstrate greater skills performance.*

tary educational work required of parents, which is done primarily by mothers, has intensified. This trend can be traced to a number of social influences, including a decline in educational funding, the loss of entry-level jobs for skilled labor, the increase in global competition for jobs, and the success of mass compulsory schooling. While social class has always been a strong indicator of future success, as teaching and learning have improved, schooling credentials are also predictors. And as schools have become more equitable, the mothers' supplementary education activities have become more important for ensuring the child's future in a competitive labor market. Thus, intensified mothering work, or the ability to buy those services (for example, tutoring), has changed the work that mothers do to support their children's schooling.

Some parents do not have the time, resources, education, or interest to do supplementary educational work. Parental support is necessary, although sometimes not sufficient, for the child's school success. Unless the child is intellectually very able, the lack of parental support may translate into school difficulties. Extensive research on school success and social class consistently shows that parents' education and parental involvement, as well as the family's economic resources, are positively correlated with school success. A mothers' time, energy, access to resources, and educational background is central to the child's success in the school setting.

nize academic, social, and interpersonal activities in order to repair school-generated difficulties. For example, tutoring services might be sought or other family members consulted about difficult school assignments. Highly educated mothers describe reading through their children's textbooks in order to put in place the supplementary education required for success. Parents with little formal education speak about learning along with their children as they attempt to support their children's homework and school assignments.

## Supplementary Educational Work

Today's mothering work has been called *intensive mothering*, which highlights the historical character of mothering for schooling today. Unlike previous educational eras, the amount of supplemen-

## Mothers as Teachers and Administrators

School teaching is historically known as a woman's field of employment. From the early years of mass compulsory schooling, women have dominated the early school years, while male teachers have been concentrated in the higher grades. Although the gender balance of teachers in schools is less dramatic today, the gendered division of teaching still remains.

Many women teachers are mothers. As teachers, they are familiar with the institutional and academic organization of schooling. As mothers, they often use that knowledge to support their children's participation in schooling. Whatever the familial arrangement, these mothers bring a far-reaching academic resource to their work with their own children as well as others. Women teachers have an educated understanding of the conceptual frames that underpin education—for example, children as developmental learners. Typically, their mothering work for education draws on those conceptual frames in their everyday, educational, home-based activities with their children. At the same time, their classroom experience mediates their mothering work in unique ways. Teacher mothers, as all mothers, sort through the available knowledge about children's learning in order to develop their unique mothering style.

The intricacies of the relationship that a mother teacher or mother administrator has with their children are increased when both are at the same school. For some children, the effect is minimal, while for others it is not. However, little research has been done in this area.

## Mothers as Students

Mothers are students at a wide range of educational institutions. Pregnancy and childcare are the primary reasons for women dropping out of high school. Mothers who are able to maintain their student enrollment are much more likely to graduate. Teen mothers are often without economic and social resources, including daycare; once they drop out, they rarely return. In a few high schools, for example in Newfoundland, daycare is available in the school for mothers who are students. However, daycare services within high schools are rarely available.

Many mothers return to secondary or postsecondary education when daycare or family supports are available, or after their own children begin school. A few welfare programs will support mothers who attend short-term programs. Historically, welfare programs were available to women who wanted to attend longer-term programs such as university or college. With changes in welfare, however, mothers are are no longer subsidized to attend extended programs. It has subsequently become more difficult for mothers on welfare to return to education. University or college students who are single are not eligible for welfare benefits in any province in Canada or in the United States; most of these students rely on family support and many work part time. Single mothers who are students often must choose between continuing their education and feeding their family, and they take longer to complete college or university programs simply because of the demands on their resources and time.

Colleges and universities have an increasing population of mothers who are students; some are single, but many are not. As with single-mother students, mothers from two-parent families draw on a range of supports such as family resources, scholarships, and bursaries, as well as part-time work. Many of the graduate students in female-dominated professions such as education, social work, and nursing are mothers. As with all working mothers, their time is stretched between family, work, and schoolwork, and student mothers often take longer to complete their degrees. However, most student mothers complete their college or university programs unless family matters or their children's needs become overwhelming.

## Mothers as Home Schoolers

Home schooling has become more popular over the past two decades. Typically, mothers who choose to home school are married and live with another adult who is responsible for the family income. Mothers who home school do so for a number of reasons, often a fundamental disagreement with the mandated school curriculum. Home schooling mothers come from a variety of backgrounds: some have been public school teachers, some are involved with religious groups that oppose public schooling; and still others are not religious but are opposed to public schooling. Home schooling mothers may create some parts of their educational curriculum, use their school district's standard curriculum, or adopt custom materials from home schooling associations. Some mothers home school their children until the high school years, while others do so until the child is old enough to apply to a university. Where formal education is in the home schooling plan, mothers pay careful attention to the mandated curriculum so their children can take standardized tests, such as the SAT, that are required to qualify for university entry.

**See Also:** Academe and Mothering; Advice Literature for Mothers; Anthropology of Motherhood; Care Giving; Class and Mothering; Edison, Thomas, Mother of; Employment and Motherhood; Family; History of Motherhood: 1900 to Present; Intensive Mothering;

Lone Mothers; Mothering as Work; Single Mothers; Teachers as Mothers; Teen Mothers.

**Bibliography**

André-Bechely, L. *Could It Be Otherwise? Parents and the Inequities of Public School Choice*. New York: Routledge, 2005.

Bourdieu, P. and J.C. Passeron. *Reproduction in Education, Society, and Culture*. Newbury Park, CA: Sage, 1990.

Brantlinger, E. *Dividing Classes: How the Middle Class Negotiates and Rationalizes School Advantage*. New York: Routledge, 2003.

Caputo, V. "She's From a 'Good Family': Performing Childhood and Motherhood in a Canadian Private School Setting." *Childhood*, v.14/2 (2007).

Epstein, J.L. *School, Family, and Community Partnerships: Preparing Educators and Improving Schools*. Boulder, CO: Westview Press, 2001.

Freund, L.S. "Maternal Regulation of Children's Problem Solving Behavior and Its Impact on Children's Performance." *Child Development*, v.61 (1990).

Griffith, A.I. and D.E. Smith. *Mothering for Schooling*. New York: Routledge, 2005.

Lareau, A. *Unequal Childhoods: Class, Race and Family Life*. Berkeley: University of California Press, 2003.

McLaren, A.T. and I. Dyck. "Mothering, Human Capital, and the 'Ideal Immigrant.'" *Women's Studies International Forum*, v.27/1 (2004).

Richardson, T.R. *The Century of the Child: The Mental Hygiene Movement and Social Policy in the United States and Canada*. Albany: State University of New York Press, 1989.

Walkerdine, V. "Developmental Psychology and the Child Centred Pedagogy." In *Changing the Subject: Psychology, Social Regulation and Subjectivity*, J. Henriques, et al., eds. London: Methuen, 1984.

Alison I. Griffith
York University

# Egypt

The past few decades have seen significant changes for women's reproductive health in Egypt, due in large part to a recent government program to improve women's and children's health. Still, marriage and motherhood remain key components of the identity of Egyptian women.

In Egyptian Arabic, girls (*bint*) become known as women (*sitt*) only when they have sex following their marriage ceremony; unmarried women are known as "girls" their whole lives. The Arabic phrase *umm-il ghayyib*, mother of the missing one, refers to infertile women.

The family is a basic part of Egyptian life. Mothers often nurse their children for at least two years and depend upon mothers or mothers-in-law for childcare. Children usually live at home until their marriages, even when they are well into adulthood. Egyptian parents traditionally have a strong preference for boys.

Egypt is primarily Muslim (90 percent) with some Coptic Christians, while the government is officially secular. Unlike its Persian Gulf neighbors, Egypt is a poor country, with poverty rates above those in sub-Saharan Africa but below much of the Middle East.

The fertility rate is 2.9 percent, while the adolescent fertility rate (the annual number of live births born to women aged 15–19 years of age per 1,000 women in the same age group) for 2005–10 is estimated to be 39. The infant mortality rate (the number of children dying before 1 year of age per 1,000 live births) is estimated to be 29 in 2005–10. In 2000, the maternal mortality rate was 84 out 100,000 live births, a marked decrease from 174 in 1992–93. The improvement in maternal health is linked to an increase in the use of hospitals and clinics (from 6 percent in 1976 to 49 percent in 1998) and increased training of health care workers, following the government's media campaign. In 2005, 59 percent of married or partnered women used contraception, 57 percent of which United Nations Educational, Scientific, and Cultural Organization (UNESCO) defines as modern methods. Women in Egypt are entitled to 90 days of maternity leave at full wages, paid for by their employer or social security. Upper Egypt (in the south) lags behind the rest of the country in all areas.

UNESCO has estimated that 61 percent of Egyptian women are literate, compared to 84 percent of men, and that 94 percent of girls were enrolled in primary school in 2007, a marked increase from 2002, when only 78 percent were enrolled.

In 1995, 97 percent of Egyptian women had experienced female genital cutting, with higher rates in rural areas, though this is in decline throughout the country following a *fatwah* from Muslim religious authorities and after being outlawed by the government. Famous mothers from Egypt include Jochebed, the Hebrew mother of Moses, and Thermuthis, his adoptive mother from the Egyptian royal family (Pharaoh's daughter in the Christian Old Testament and Jewish Torah; Pharoah's wife in the Qu'ran); Isis, the mother goddess, mother of Horus; and Cleopatra. Notably for Christians, biblical tradition holds that Mary and Joseph fled to Egypt with Jesus following his birth.

**See Also:** Bible, Mothers in the; Family Planning; History of Motherhood: Ancient Civilizations; Islam and Motherhood.

**Bibliography**
Asdar Ali, Kamran. *Planning the Family in Egypt: New Bodies, New Selves.* Austin: University of Texas Press, 2002.
Central Agency for Public Mobilisation and Statistics, Arab Republic of Egypt. www.capmas.gov.eg (accessed June 2009).
Inhorn, Maria C. *Infertility and Patriarchy: The Cultural Politics of Gender and Family Life in Egypt.* Philadelphia: University of Pennsylvania Press, 1996.
United Nations Children's Fund (UNICEF). *The Situation of Egyptian Children and Women: A Rights-based Analysis.* New York: UNICEF, 2002.

Joan Petit
Portland State University

# Einstein, Albert, Mother of

Pauline Einstein (1858–1920) was the mother of the well-known physicist Albert Einstein. She was born Pauline Koch in Cannstatt, Württemberg (now Baden-Württemberg), Germany on February 8, 1858, into a Jewish family, and had one older sister and two older brothers. Pauline's father, Julius Koch, was successful and attained a considerable fortune in the grain business, as well as serving as a

purveyor to the Royal Württemberg Court. In 1876, 18-year-old Pauline married Hermann Einstein, a merchant who at the time was living in Ulm, Württemberg (a city in situated on the River Danube). After the marriage, Hermann and Pauline lived in Ulm, and Hermann was employed as a joint partner in a bedfeathers company. Their first child, Albert, was born on March 14, 1879, in Ulm.

A year after Albert's birth, Hermann's bedfeathers business failed, and the family moved to Munich. There, Hermann's brother, Jakob, owned a gas and electrical supply company, for which Hermann provided salesmanship skills and Pauline provided loans from her family to aid the company. In November 1881, Pauline and Hermann had a second and final child, a daughter named Maria (who went by the name Maja). Albert and Maja were very close throughout their lives. Pauline settled with her family into a Munich suburb for what was an upper-class existence. Albert displayed signs of learning disabilities as a young boy, and Pauline used her passion and talent for music to teach Albert discipline. Although he rebelled at first, Albert later became an accomplished violinist and used it as a way to relax.

In 1894, Hermann Einstein's utility company also failed. At this time, Pauline moved with Hermann, Maja, and Hermann's brother Jakob to northern Italy—first Milan and then Pavia—where their Italian business partners thought there would be an opportunity for a smaller firm. Albert stayed behind with relatives to finish his last three years of school. However, Albert quit school and in late 1894 joined his parents in Italy with the intention of gaining admission to Zurich Polytechnic. However, Albert was not accepted, and instead went to a high school in Switzerland to finish his education.

## Distress and Arguments

From 1895 to 1897, Albert had a relationship with Marie Winteler, the daughter of one of Albert's high school teachers in Aarua, Switzerland. Albert lived with the Wintelers while he was finishing his high school education. When Albert left Aarua to finally go to Zurich Polytechnic, he at first carried on a long-distance relationship with Marie, but eventually ended the relationship. In 1899, Pauline's relationship with Albert began to erode due to a new love interest in his life—Mileva Maric, a Serbian woman he met at Zurich Polytechnic. Pauline did not approve of the relationship because she considered Mileva to be too old, sickly (Mileva suffered from a limp), plain looking, and unsuccessful as an intellectual. Albert's relationship with Mileva caused Pauline much distress and resulted in many fights with Albert. Albert eventually married Mileva and had several children with her before divorcing in 1918 after many years of separation.

In October 1902, Hermann Einstein's health began to fail and he passed away on October 10, 1902. Pauline moved back to Germany to live with her sister Fanny and her husband Rudolf Einstein (Pauline's sister married Hermann Einstein's brother) in Hechingen, Württemberg, Germany. Pauline had unfortunately inherited Hermann's debts, and had no income to pay them. She lived with her sister and brother-in-law for most of the next decade, including moving with them to Berlin in 1910.

In 1911, Pauline moved to Heilbronn to work as a housekeeper for a widowed merchant, and then back to Berlin in 1914 to take care of her widowed brother Jakob. In 1918, Pauline was diagnosed with stomach cancer and stayed briefly in a sanatorium until moving in with Albert and his second wife, Elsa, at the end of 1919. Pauline died as a result of stomach cancer on February 20, 1920, in Berlin at the age of 62.

**See Also:** Edison, Thomas, Mother of; Germany; Music and Mothers; Sons and Mothers.

**Bibliography**
Brian, Denis. *Einstein: A Life*. New York: John Wiley & Sons, 1996.
Folsing, Albert and Ewald Osers. *Albert Einstein: A Biography*. New York: Penguin, 1998.
Goldsmith, Donald and Marcia Bartusiak. *E=Einstein: His Life, His Thought and His Influence on Our Culture*. New York: Sterling Publishing, 2007.
Highfield, Roger and Paul Carter. *The Private Lives of Albert Einstein*. New York: Macmillan, 1994.
Isaacson, Walter. *Einstein: His Life and Universe*. New York: Simon & Schuster, 2007.

Jill Mahoney
Murray State University

# Eleanor of Aquitaine

Eleanor of Aquaitaine was born in 1122, and grew up in Provence, France in the era of the troubadours. She became the Countess of Poitou and Duchess of Aquitaine and Gascony at the age of 15, in an era when female leadership was exceptional. She first became Queen of France and then Queen of England; even when her son Richard was king, she continued to call herself queen and was actually queen regent during his reign, making many of Richard's key decisions.

During her marriage to her distant cousin, Louis VII of France, they went on crusades to the Holy Land together, but she had a limited scope for leadership. Having only given birth to two daughters after 15 years of marriage, they considered that their marriage might not be blessed because of their close degree of sanguinity, so they sought a papal annulment. She married Henry of Anjou and Normandy, who became Henry II of England, while retaining her counties of Aquitaine and Poitou. They were crowned in England in 1154. Eleanor had eight children from this second marriage, including the kings Richard the Lionheart and John, of Magna Carta fame.

Her daughters married European royalty and spread their rich southern culture, making Eleanor virtually the grandmother of crowned Europe. Eleanor brought her Provençal culture to England with her; as granddaughter of the first troubadour, William IX, she patronized the troubadour Bernard de Ventadour at her court in Poitiers, and he wrote under her inspiration. The courts she controlled became centers of chivalry and troubadour culture; legend describes her as leading a veritable court of love. Such chivalric cultures were significant in fostering reverence for women, together with the gentler arts of poetry and literature, in an age of physical violence and brute force.

Endless fighting between the crowned heads of Europe over territory entered her family life, as well as her public life. After the martyrdom of Thomas à Becket, and later estranged from Henry, Eleanor spent more time in her continental domains, which she kept under her own control through both her marriages. She eventually joined her French overlord Louis VII in rebellion against Henry in favor of her sons, which resulted in Henry virtually imprisoning her for 15 years. Finally released by his death, and becoming Richard II's regent at the age of 67, she was able to rule with the vast experience and wisdom accrued over many years in more than two kingdoms through Richard's reign, which he had spent largely abroad. Her popular measures included releasing prisoners, moderating and codifying various laws, and regulating weights and measures, as well as founding hospitals and religious houses.

She toured the land indefatigably, having officials swear oaths of loyalty, and used great diplomacy and sagacity in dealing with officials, knights, and rulers—including her sons, who spent years in rivalry against each other—to bring peace and prosperity to the people. She brought to bear her extensive aquaintance with many leaders of Europe in making shrewd judgments and arranging marriages, and her enlightened methods were so successful they were copied by Philip VIII of France. Richard's death brought her last son John to the throne, although he managed to lose most of his continental territories in a few years. She died in 1204 at the age of 82.

Eleanor was a highly respected ruler when female rule was rare, a powerful wife and mother, as well as mother-in-law, and a significant humane influence on politics and patron of the arts. Much maligned but also highly praised, Eleanor was clearly an exceptional woman for any time.

**See Also:** History of Motherhood: Middle Ages; Royal Mothers; United Kingdom.

**Bibliography**
Boyd, Douglas. *Eleanor: April Queen of Aquitaine.* Phoenix Mill, UK: Sutton Publishing, 2004.
Meade, Marion. *Eleanor of Aquitaine: A Biography.* New York: Penguin, 1991.
Miller, David. *Richard the Lionheart: The Mighty Crusader.* Phoenix, AZ: Phoenix Press, 2005.
Turner, Ralph V. *Eleanor of Aquitaine: Queen of France, Queen of England.* New Haven, CT: Yale University Press, 2009.
Weir, Alison. *Eleanor of Aquitaine.* London: Pimlico, 1999.

Gillian M.E. Alban
Dogus University, Turkey

# Elizabeth, "Queen Mum"

Elizabeth Bowes Lyon, or Queen Elizabeth the Queen Mother (1900–2002), was the wife (Queen Consort) of George VI, King of Great Britain. The "Queen Mum," as she was known in later life, was mother to Queen Elizabeth II and Princess Margaret. Queen Elizabeth was an iconic figure of 20th-century Western motherhood and grandmotherhood.

Elizabeth was born in England and grew up in Scotland, mostly at her family home in Glamis Castle. She was the ninth of 10 children. Her father became the Earl of Strathmore and Kinghorne, and as a child she played with the children of nobility, but technically, she was a commoner. She was educated mostly at home by French and German tutors. Ironically, World War I began on her 14th birthday, and Glamis Castle was converted into a hospital. Elizabeth served notably in the hospital, helping to care for injured service members. This service foreshadowed her future role as a dignified, service-oriented role model for the country.

When she was in her early 20s, Albert, the Duke of York and son of King Edward V, proposed to her four times. Elizabeth was reluctant about accepting the responsibility, even after she received a visit from the queen. In 1923, Elizabeth finally agreed to marry Albert and became the Duchess of York. In 1926, she gave birth to Elizabeth II, the first of two daughters. When baby Elizabeth was 8 months old, the Duke and Duchess embarked on a four-month journey to Australia and New Zealand, leaving the child behind. This was not an uncommon practice, and Elizabeth II was lovingly cared for by nannies and relatives.

Elizabeth and Albert welcomed their second daughter, Margaret, in 1930. Although busy with official duties, the Royal Family was said to have a close-knit, loving relationship. In fact, the quality of Elizabeth and Albert's marriage would later be a crucial factor in determining their destinies. Although there were many surrogates such as nannies and tutors present in their children's' lives, the two parents spent as much time as possible with the girls. One of the Royal Family's favorite events was the annual Christmas pantomime, staged by the children for the parents.

## Unexpectedly the Queen

In 1936, King George V died, making Albert's brother Edward the King of England. However, Edward had already decided he wanted to marry a twice-divorced American named Wallis Simpson. When it became clear that Edward could not marry Wallis and remain King, he abdicated his throne to Albert. This was an enormous trauma for Albert and Elizabeth; it is said that Albert wept upon hearing the news, and Elizabeth was enraged at Edward's selfishness. It is also believed that Elizabeth constantly coached her husband to relieve his shyness and stuttering. Albert accepted the crown and became King George VI, making Elizabeth Queen Elizabeth. At this point Elizabeth's role enlarged; she was becoming a maternal figure for the country, and would soon play a critical role in the most important event of the 20th century.

During World War II, Queen Elizabeth famously refused to leave England. She and King George VI worked every day at Buckingham Palace, and every evening they joined their daughters at Windsor Palace. When asked to flee to Canada, she said, "The children won't go without me. I won't leave the King. And the King will never leave." Queen Elizabeth and her family endured numerous bombings of the palace, and frequently visited bomb-ravaged sections of London. In so doing, Queen Elizabeth became an almost-mythic figure of courage and inspiration; Hitler called her "The most dangerous woman in Europe."

After the war, the royals traveled to South Africa, along with numerous escorts. During the trip they celebrated Elizabeth II's 21st birthday, and upon her return she announced her engagement to Phillip Mountbatten. They were married in 1947. When the King died in 1952, his eldest daughter became queen, and Elizabeth became Queen Mother. It was then that she began engaging herself as a behind-the-scenes supporter of her daughter, and became known as the Queen Mum. She spoke to her daughter by phone every day, and strove to support worthy causes in the public eye.

When the Queen Mother became a grandmother, she became a frequent companion for her grandchildren during their parents' absences. She was particularly fond of Prince Charles, and provided emotional support during difficult times. Diana Spencer,

Prince Charles's first wife, lived with the Queen Mum before she married Charles. The Queen Mum was similarly close to her great-grandchildren, as she completed her final role as the longest-lived royal in British history.

Queen Elizabeth led a quietly influential life, even though she never gave a public press conference after 1926. During her life, the Royal Family was repeatedly rocked by scandalous divorces and marriages, including the one that propelled her to power. Even though she never publicly criticized her family members, she made it clear that she only approved of the monogamous model she had followed.

At the age of 101, the Queen Mum died on March 30, 2002, seven weeks after her younger daughter, Princess Margaret, died of an illness at age 71. Throughout her life, the Queen Mum publicly personified the dignity and strength of a traditional mother.

*Their Majesties King George V and Queen Elizabeth photographed in 1939 at the Parliament buildings.*

**See Also:** Mary, Queen of Scots; Royal Mothers; United Kingdom.

**Bibliography**
Forbes, Grania. *Elizabeth: The Queen Mother: 1900–2002*. London: Anova Books, 2004.
The Illustrated London News. *Her Majesty Queen Elizabeth the Queen Mother: The Life That Spanned a Century 1900–2002*. London: Macmillan UK, 2003.
Kindersley, Dorling. *Queen Elizabeth the Queen Mother: Commemorative Edition: The Story of a Remarkable Life 1900–2002*. London: Penguin UK, 2003.

Jacqueline Ciccio Parsons
Independent Scholar

# El Salvador

El Salvador, the smallest country in Central America, is on the Pacific coast, with the Gulf of Fonseca to its southeast. El Salvador borders Guatemala and Honduras, and its geographic limits have not been officially established. With an area of approximately 32,000 square miles and a population of about 7 million, El Salvador is the most densely populated nation in Central America. The Spanish legacy of colonialism includes Catholicism and a patriarchal system, and were significant forces in shaping the gender inequalities in El Salvador. Women continue to be disadvantaged relative to men with respect to employment and leadership roles.

The mother–child relationship is central to family functioning and the actualization of *respeto* (respect), the high regard granted to a person because of age or position. Mothers are equated with self-denial and abnegation. When exhausted, they may become upset or nervous, or they may quietly suffer, but they are not expected to take time off or to demand cooperation from family members. In return for their sacrifice and dedication, mothers usually receive great respect and obedience from their children. Within the larger community, mothers are accorded higher status than unmarried women and childless women.

Female purity is reinforced as an ideal from childhood onward. Girls and young women usu-

ally have strict curfews. They are discouraged from going away to college and are generally constrained from exploring their sexuality before or outside marriage. For the most part, women are taught to repress their sexuality and to rely on men to teach them about sex in the context of marriage. They are encouraged to emulate the Virgin Mary in terms of purity and sacrifice. Women are viewed as the nurturers of the family and are expected to subjugate their own goals for the well-being of their families.

Birth control and abortion are still illegal in El Salvador. It is difficult to estimate childbirth rates, mortality rates, and the number of women living in poverty, as no census information is available after 1992. The results of the latest (2006) census are being contested and have not been publicized.

## Ravaged by Civil War

El Salvador was engaged in a long and bloody civil war between 1980 and 1992. The Salvadorian Army unleashed a wave of "death squads" as a way to stop the suspected communist leaders of the popular movements. Between 1980 and 1982, almost 70,000 noncombatant civilians were assassinated by death squads or killed in military attacks on villages alleged to be sympathetic to revolutionary groups. An additional 7,000 people "disappeared." More than 1 million fled the country. In addition, about 70,000 internal refugees were displaced from their homes as a result of the violence, and about 1,000 individuals were incarcerated as political prisoners. Overall, the country experienced a period of horrendous violence and destruction.

For the most part, people who were able to leave the country sought refuge in Mexico, Costa Rica, the United States, and Canada. Salvadorians arriving in countries of asylum brought with them psychological wounds due to a long and violent civil war. These traumatic experiences have impacted their acculturation in the settlement countries.

**See Also:** Costa Rica; Mexico; Patriarchal Ideology of Motherhood; War and Mothers.

**Bibliography**
Boland, Roy C. *Culture and Customs of El Salvador*. Westport, CT: Greenwood Press, 2000.

Peñate, Oscar, ed. *El Salvador: Historia General*. El Salvador: Nuevo Enfoque, 2007.

Peñate, Oscar, ed. *El Salvador: Sociologia General*. El Salvador: Nuevo Enfoque, 2007.

Mirna E. Carranza<br>McMaster University

# Emecheta, Buchi

Buchi Emecheta was born in Lagos, Nigeria, in 1944 and moved to London in 1960, where she started a family and worked in a library. She became a student at London University in 1970, and later became a community worker. Her writing explores the intersecting issues of race, gender, and class, and focuses in many cases on the struggles of young, poor, black, and often single mothers.

Emecheta is a formidable voice in African women's literature, and a prolific one as well. She has written more than 11 novels, an (official) autobiography, two children's books, four juvenile novels, and four plays. Besides this, she has written numerous personal and critical essays and is a regular contributor to the *New Statesman*, the *Times Literary Supplement*, and *The Guardian*, and runs her own publishing house with her son. Not only is her writing widely read and acclaimed, it also provided a living for her and her five children while they were growing up. In fact, all of her children were born prior to the publication of her first book, which was published before she even finished her bachelor's degree.

## The Joys of Motherhood

*The Joys of Motherhood* (1979) concerns a Nigerian village woman who believes her purpose in life was to bear and nurture children. She escapes a barren marriage and flees to Lagos, where she bears and raises children only to see them grow up and move away. She thus misses out on the "joys of motherhood" she anticipated: growing old among her children and grandchildren. The novel, set in the 1930s, is a critique of colonialism as well as traditional Nigerian society.

Emecheta is credited for successfully integrating her personal and intellectual life with her role as a mother and a woman, and is able to write characters who are also able to integrate many roles. Her writing explores Igbo culture, both before and after colonialism's impact. She also writes (fictionally) about her experiences of immigrating to London during the early years of her marriage. She exposes the problems of sexism, racism, and poverty, and proposes solutions; but above all, she challenges. She critiques both Igbo traditional culture and the fragmentation that colonialism caused within it.

Critics often call her a feminist, implying the Western meaning of that term by claiming that if she exposes or challenges problems in the Igbo system, she has changed allegiances from Nigeria to the West. It is easy for a Western reader to see Emecheta's criticisms as an indictment of an entire culture, but Emecheta commends what is good in Igbo tradition, especially those characteristics of tradition that give women power. Therefore, the importance of African feminism is a force in her works. Specifically, Emecheta seems to show her characters relying especially on the African feminist tenets of adaptability, networking, and survival strategies in her novels.

Furthermore, her novels, especially as evidenced in *The Joys of Motherhood* (1979), are complex, in the same way that colonial and postcolonial cultures and subjects are complex. The women in her novels navigate many problems within and without their traditional cultures, often utilizing African feminism as a positive force in their lives. Therefore, Emecheta challenges both patriarchy and colonialism/imperialism. Emecheta was named one of 20 Best of Young British Writers by the Book Marketing Council in 1983. She has been a visiting lecturer in the United States and Nigeria, and earned an honorary doctorate from Farleigh Dickinson University. A recent novel is called *The New Tribe* and was published in 2000.

**See Also:** African Diaspora; Literature, Mothers in; Mother/Daughter Plot (Hirsch); Postcolonialism and Mothering; Race and Racism.

## Bibliography

Christian, Barbara. *Black Feminist Criticism: Perspectives on Black Women Writers*. Oxford, UK: Pergamon, 1985.

Christian, Buchi Emecheta. *Double Yoke*. New York: George Braziller, 1982.

Christian, Buchi Emecheta. *The Family*. New York: George Braziller, Inc., 1989.

Christian, Buchi Emecheta. *The Joys of Motherhood*. New York: George Braziller, 1979.

Christian, Buchi Emecheta. *In the Ditch*. Portsmouth, NH: Heinemann, 1972.

Christian, Buchi Emecheta. *The Rape of Shavi*. New York: George Braziller, 1983.

Christian, Buchi Emecheta. *Second-Class Citizen*. New York: George Braziller, 1974.

Christian, Buchi Emecheta. *The Slave Girl*. New York: George Braziller, 1977.

Fishburn, Katherine. *Reading Buchi Emecheta: Cross-Cultural Conversations*. Westport, CT: Greenwood Publishing, 1995.

Nicole L. Willey
Kent State University

# Emotions

Emotions define the way we respond to our social, built, or created environment and involve a way of understanding the world. Our understanding of emotion is gendered, and there are gendered emotional expectations. The experiences of both motherhood and nonmotherhood are infused by emotion and emotional expectations, which necessitates the management of emotions by mothers and nonmothers. In addition, those who support women through these experiences—family members, friends, and health and social care professionals—are also more likely to be women themselves, and they too engage in emotion work and management.

### Gender Differences

The understanding of emotion is gendered in that they are connected to beliefs about what is typical, natural, or appropriate for women and men. Historically, particular emotions have been associated with women and with femininity. Women have been characterized as sensitive, intuitive, and immersed in personal relationships; but also as naturally weak and easy to exploit, submissive, passive, docile, dependent, and so on. From this perspective, women are considered more like children than adults in that they are immature, weak, helpless, and subject to emotional display. Yet, despite these negative connotations, women who adopt and display these characteristics are considered to be well adjusted. There have been fewer corresponding descriptions of the typical man, not least because throughout history, men have been commonly considered to be rational rather than emotional.

Most current research findings suggest very few gender differences when men and women and boys and girls are asked what they know about emotion, but the less information that is made available about a person, the more both sexes will rely on emotion stereotypes. Such stereotypes are an important part of learning the practice or performance of gendered behavior. It emerges, then, that when emotion and gender are intertwined, stereotypical speculations of masculine/ feminine emotions are explored. Thus, exploring shared beliefs about emotions is one way to understand what gender means and how it operates and is negotiated in human relationships.

Groundbreaking work by Arlie Russell Hochschild highlighted the hard work associated with the regulation and management of one's own emotions and the emotions of others. Hochschild differentiated between emotional labor (the management of emotion within paid labor) and emotion(al) work (the management of emotion in personal and intimate relationships). Emotional labor and work then is performed in order to conform to dominant expectations in a given situation, and many authors suggest that in both the workplace and the home, it is women who engage in this activity more than men.

### Motherhood and Emotion

Because motherhood is such a key identity for women, both the experience of motherhood and nonmotherhood is an emotional one. These are both experiences where the emotions that women feel may be judged by others and at times defined as appropriate or even denied. Feminists have demonstrated that many women feel discrepancies between how they experience the world and the official or expert definition of their identity, and the experience of nonmotherhood can result in guilt, fear, anxiety, and feelings of ambivalence and exclusion.

## Involuntary and Voluntary Childlessness

Although a common experience, individual women often find miscarriage both unexpected and traumatic. This is compounded by the (sometimes) medical and social response, which suggests that the experience is a trivial one and all that the woman needs to do to get over it is to get pregnant again. This denies the often strong emotions that women feel, and supposes that miscarriage is always followed by another successful pregnancy—which is not always the case. For some—such as teenagers, single women, and women with many children—miscarriage is considered even less of a concern, perhaps even a relief, which again denies individual feelings. The emotions of those who experience late miscarriage, stillbirth, or infant or child death will likely be taken more seriously, and women will be allowed to grieve in a way in which those who experience early miscarriage are not. Yet, grief is still stigmatized as taboo, morbid, and abnormal in many cultures, and others may attempt to distract the bereaved from her feelings. Anthropological evidence from different cultures and different historical periods suggests that the management of grief can be handled in a way that makes the experience less distressing. In some cultures, for example, miscarried babies are treated as human beings in their own right and mourned in the same way. Not surprisingly, there is even less support for the distress that women who choose a termination may feel, despite the various social, medical, and material reasons that lead to this choice.

The experience of involuntary childlessness, similarly to other reproductive losses, may be difficult to manage within an intimate relationship, and women sometimes turn to others who have had a similar experience—perhaps within a support group—to vocalize their feelings. In this situation (and following miscarriage, termination, stillbirth, and so on), a woman may manage her feelings and put on a brave face so that others will not be embarrassed by her distress. On occasion, the status of involuntary childlessness becomes a dominant, defining characteristic, and a childless woman is therefore defined by others as incomplete and desperate. This denies the possibility of ambivalent feelings for involuntary childlessness, which would mean for others that she is not as concerned to become a mother as she

*A mother's awareness of her own sadness is significantly correlated with her awareness of the emotion in her child.*

suggestions. Conversely, the voluntary childless are often believed to be ambivalent, despite assurances to the contrary. Here again, women's emotions are denied and/or defined differently by others.

## Emotions in the Transition to Motherhood

A lack of preparation for birth and motherhood can make these experiences more frightening and challenging. Mothers are often unprepared, not least because sex education generally focuses on prevention of pregnancy and prevention of disease, rather than on relationships, and because they are encouraged by professionals and the media not to listen to the "old wives tales" of other women. In addition to the distress this can cause pregnant, birthing, and new mothers, it can also mean that a mother's support network—friends, mothers, midwives, or doctors—also have to engage in emotion work themselves.

Once a woman becomes a mother, she is likely to experience a whole new set of emotions. Mothers report conflicting feelings—of pleasure, delight, anxiety, and distress—but because external definitions often deny the ambivalence of motherhood, these contrary and complex feelings may themselves lead to feelings of guilt. For those who experience antenatal and/or postnatal depression, research suggests that potential outcomes can include a breakdown in the mother's relationship with her baby, her husband, and other children; and delays in the child's cognitive and social development, all of which again will likely lead to extra distress for the mother. A 1998 United Kingdom Department of Health report, *Why Mothers Die*, found that suicide was four times more likely to occur in the nine months after childbirth than during pregnancy. Health visitors and midwives are often the first health professionals to suspect that a woman has postnatal depression, and again this means that part of the job of a female-dominated profession will likely involve the management of the emotions of others.

New mothers who do not experience depression are still likely to experience negative emotions when they are persuaded to think that they are not mothering as well as they should. Added pressure results from the expectations of ideal motherhood, where a mother devotes herself entirely to her child, even at the expense of her own social and emotional needs. One example is the pressure that women can feel to breastfeed their babies, supported by the Breast Is Best message—and even women who try to do "the right thing" can get it wrong. Although women who breastfeed are seen to be doing what is best for their baby, at the same time they are concerned about transgressing other norms and expectations, such as maintaining their modesty and feeding at the appropriate time. This has implications for women's feelings of self-worth with reference to motherhood, as mothers who successfully breast feed are assumed to be better mothers than those who do not. Not surprisingly, women who decide to formula-feed their babies, and women who are unable to breastfeed, often report feelings of failure and guilt. Thus, mothers may experience emotional distress when they feel that they are not doing the expected best.

## Media Influences on Emotion in Motherhood

The portrayal of so-called good and bad mothers in the media also helps to define appropriate behavior and feelings surrounding this experience. Examples of bad mothers include those who leave the family home, and those who are seen to selfishly put the interest of their own careers before the care of their children. In addition to devoting themselves to their children, good mothers are charged with the overall positive emotional development of their children (and the emotional comfort of their partners) as well as for their physical and emotional safety. Thus, mothers are responsible for managing

fear from both external and internal threats, protecting their family from the inappropriate physical and emotional behavior of others.

In meeting gendered emotional expectations, which includes servicing the emotional needs of others, both mothers and nonmothers are encouraged to deny the complexity of their own emotions. Yet, in this area, women themselves have not been completely passive; there is evidence of resistance to the emotional expectations of women within these experiences. Those who experience reproductive loss do find spaces to grieve, expectant mothers do listen to the stories of others who have gone before them, and mothers do challenge the idealized vision of motherhood and mothering.

**See Also:** Ambivalence, Maternal; Breastfeeding; Childlessness; Depression; Hochschild, Arlie; Intensive Mothering; Mothering Versus Motherhood.

**Bibliography**
Ahmed, Sara S. *The Cultural Politics of Emotion*. Edinburgh, UK: Edinburgh Publishers, 2004.
Bendelow, Gillian and Simon Williams, eds. *Emotions in Social Life: Critical Themes and Contemporary Issues*. New York: Routledge, 1998.
de Beauvoir, Simone. *The Second Sex*. New York: Penguin, 1972.
Duncombe, Jean and Dennis Marsden. "'Stepford Wives' and 'Hollow Men'? Doing Emotion Work, Doing Gender and 'Authenticity' in Intimate Heterosexual Relationships.'" In *Emotions in Social Life: Critical Themes and Contemporary Issues*, G. Bendelow and S. J. Williams, eds. New York: Routledge, 1998.
Gottman, John Mordechai, et al. *Meta-Emotion: How Families Communicate Emotionally*. Mahwah, NJ: Lawrence Erlbaum, 1997.
Hochschild, Arlie R. *The Managed Heart: Commercialization of Human Feeling*. New York: Berkeley, 2003.
Hochschild, Arlie R. and Anne Marchung. *Second Shift: Working Families and the Revolution at Home*. New York: Viking, 1989.
Hunter, Billie. "Emotion Work and Boundary Maintenance in Hospital-Based Midwifery." *Midwifery*, v.21/3 (2005).
Letherby, Gayle and Catherine Williams. "Non-Motherhood: Ambivalent Autobiographies." *Feminist Studies*, v.25 (1999).

Lupton, Deborah. *The Emotional Self*. Thousand Oaks, CA: Sage, 1998.

Nathanson, Jessica and Laura Camille Tuley. *Mother Knows Best: Talking Back to the "Experts."* Toronto: Demeter, 2008.

United Kingdom Department of Health. "Why Mothers Die: Report on Confidential Enquiries Into Maternal Deaths in the United Kingdom, 1994–1996." (November 16, 1998).

Gayle Letherby
University of Plymouth

# Employment and Motherhood

Balancing motherhood with employment is a developmental challenge that is unique to each working mother. The experience of combining motherhood with employment is a co-coordinating process, which examines the impact of earlier and later experiences on working mothers' ability to bridge the two roles, which ultimately affects the emotional well-being of these mothers. As a result of these internalizations, working mothers think about combining motherhood with employment in particular ways. It is critical to examine the qualitative experience of working mothers in order to understand how the balancing of motherhood and employment operates. Research on the lived experience of working mothers, which includes how they think about balancing motherhood with working, how they manage the two, and the effect of their past and present experiences, have expanded upon the more quantitative works, which examined the number of hours engaged in housekeeping and involvement with children.

## Reconciliation

If circumstances were ideal, such as availability of adequate daycare, effective support systems, and flexibility of hours, it might appear easier to effectively balance motherhood with employment. The empirical literature on maternal employment focused on the effects of employment on mothers by examining variables such as the type of family structure under which employed mothers live, support systems for employed mothers, spillover effects between work and home as related to feelings of well-being, and the relationship between separation anxiety and maternal employment.

The facilitators and barriers, which would include the ability to coordinate the two roles and the ability to manage one's time, however, do not account for all of the sources of conflict that working mothers describe. The underlying dynamics of the working mother need to be examined in order to understand why the manipulation of external factors do not explain the entire phenomenon. There is an intricate relationship between the underlying dynamics and present and past environmental conditions.

## Conflicting Thoughts

The earlier phenomenological/clinical works on maternal employment explored, through their own accounts, how working mothers viewed themselves as mothers and workers, and how they experienced their work and its personal meaning in the context of the rest of their lives. The success of the working mother's efforts to work outside the home depended upon external variables such as status within the organization, flexibility regarding hours of employment, availability of daycare, and the attitude of the spouse, as well as personality attributes shaped by motives, values, and attitudes, along with social and economic influences. In these works, the most common and recurring themes were the crossing of boundaries between a working mother's personal and work life where they balance, blend, integrate, and separate work from her personal life, as well as maintaining a satisfactory balance between her needs and her children's; the balance between the desire for connection, as well as autonomy; work conflicts as reflecting conflicting early mother–daughter relationships; and the role of work in the development of a woman's sense of self and its loss, as equated with work success.

Working outside the home appears to give a woman a sense of autonomy and competence, while offering her social contact with other adults to offset the isolation of being at home with a child. The prevailing literature on this subject, focusing on maternal subjectivity, asserts that a woman's experience as a mother is the product of a complex set of social, political, cultural, biological, and psychological factors. A woman's experience of motherhood is affected by the degree of support she receives from her spouse, family, friends, employers, and the community.

In examining the lived experience of working mothers, there have been conflicting ways of looking at this issue. Some of the literature, which conceptualizes maternal employment as a conflicting experience, may be adding to the discord that working mothers feel. With ideologies such as ideal mothering, which prioritizes mothering above all else; and intensive mothering, with an emphasis on "being there" on all levels, mothers have, nevertheless, still continued to participate in the workforce.

On the other hand, there have been opposing views that maintain that women should work, at all costs, to keep them in the loop as an important contributor to society. The response has been that working mothers can simultaneously maintain a working and motherhood identity, and that both can be a compatible and pleasurable combination. Based on interviews with working mothers and documenting their lived experiences, research explores how to effectively manage and maintain such a balance.

## Mothers' Ways of Thinking About Balance

Research suggests that there are three types of working mothers—the Splitting Working Mother, the Integrating Working Mother, and the Transitional Working Mother. There will be times and situations when the Splitting Working Mother will need to split the experience of motherhood and employment, where one will take precedence over the other. This is a coping mechanism for the mother to deal with the separation between the two domains. When working mothers split, it is temporarily easier to cope because one mode is really not aware of the other's existence.

At other times, the Integrating Working Mother might be able to integrate the two experiences, not losing sight of either. In the process of integrating the experience of working and motherhood, it becomes apparent that it is a difficult experience to balance, in that the working mother has to retain a picture of both at the same time.

Bridging is a helpful tool in achieving this integration in the use of telephone, e-mails, and reminders such as pictures in the place of employment.

Occasionally, another option for the working mother, the Transitional Working Mother, is to

accompany her child to after-school programs and do some work while her child is engaged in the activity. Guilt is most prevalent in this mode, since the transitional working mother is beginning to manage through feelings of loss and separation, anger over feeling so torn, and, ultimately, sadness for being in that position and wishing it was different. Guilt is a reminder of motherhood when the working mother is at work. On the other hand, the reverse also occurs in this transitional space—the spilling over of positive influences, as well as stresses, from one milieu to the next. The same tools and strategies are often used in each domain, with multitasking in both areas.

At times, work is in the forefront and motherhood in the background; at other times, the reverse is true. The comfort level is in equilibrium when the working mother can operate in a place between the two, an intermediate space between working and motherhood.

Another split occurs between the needs of the mother versus the child, and how to reconcile this polarity. Working mothers struggle with balancing their needs with their children's, which often seem diametrically opposed. This is not surprising, particularly given the different perspectives presented by the early childhood education, women's studies, and child psychology disciplines, each operating in a compartmentalized fashion that rarely acknowledges the existence of the other. In contrast, feminist mothering teaches children how to be autonomous beings, promoting egalitarian relationships in ways that encourage collaborative learning and empowerment. This independent thought process, interspersed with connectedness rather than dependence, supports the latest child and parenting research, which discourages "smothering mothering."

Finally, there exists a split between research and therapy in this field, which calls for a end to pathologizing the working mother's experience instead respecting their experience of combining motherhood with employment in a balanced fashion.

## Paternal Involvement, Maternal Employment

Fathers have a role in the balancing of motherhood with employment, as do other support systems. In examining paternal involvement and maternal employment, it becomes clear that fathers choose to be involved with their children of their own accord, rather than as a prerequisite or a result of their partners' employment. Many fathers are influenced by their own fathers' behaviors and perceptions regarding maternal employment. In many cases, fathers model their mothers' roles in their involvement with their children. Paternal involvement may be a way for fathers to rework unresolved issues of their childhood, which is being reactivated in their present parenting status.

In examining paternal involvement, it is interesting to examine some of the feelings of envy, expressed by both mothers and fathers. Working mothers may not want to share the mothering role with their partners because of the significant way in which defines them, while fathers may envy the bond that the mother and child have and feel excluded from that special relationship, the one that he feels he once had with his partner.

## Working Mothers' Feelings

It is equally important for working mothers to feel accepted for the difficulties they have in balancing motherhood with employment, as well as rejoicing in accomplishing an effective balance, which works in a different way for each working mother.

In balancing motherhood with employment, prioritizing becomes a theme. Most working mothers say that motherhood is the priority. However, for women whose mothers worked out of financial necessity, they acknowledge that, even though work is a necessity, it is not necessarily a priority. In balancing work with motherhood, some working mothers are able to combine both, while others temporarily give up certain activities. Where there is no longer a choice to be made and working mothers feel powerless to choose, anxiety is expressed. Subsequently, the balance is knocked out of equilibrium.

This results in a sense of feeling frazzled, torn, tired, depressed, and guilty. Sometimes, upon experiencing these feeling, the working mother is unable to remember, connect, and retain information. The anxiety reflects a conflict between work and motherhood, and guilt expresses the frustration associated with that ambivalence. One way of coping with these unpleasant feelings, according to some working mothers, is to focus on her external appearance in order to convince herself that she is more

together than she feels, working from the outside in. It becomes apparent, though, that it is important for working mothers to also work from the inside out in order to understand the dynamics of these processes, rather than manipulating external factors in the hope of creating a state of equilibrium.

## Internalized Messages of Working Mothers

The working mother has been influenced by her parents' feelings about mothers working. The story is heard from two perspectives—primarily, the mother's and daughter's voices in the past and the present time. Both voices have been interwoven into a whole, as the daughter, now the working mother, has internalized a representation of what a mother should be and draws upon this in her maternal role. Some mothers have idealized versions of mothering, while others have more realistic perceptions.

These internalized working models can change if the working mother is aware of these internalizations and chooses to connect with supportive others, such as a colleague or mentor, who models alternate ways of being a working mother. Daughters sometimes have to work through their fears of surpassing their mothers; of ambivalence regarding identifying with mothers they perceive as victims of a patriarchal society; and of not feeling good enough with the split role, as a result. The solution may lie in appreciating the generational differences between daughters and their mothers. Ultimately, basic security when working mothers realize they need not be perfect—which is unattainable—but rather, good enough.

The voice of the father is not to be underestimated. Daughters also internalize their fathers' messages that are communicated regarding women, mothers, and mothers working. When a working mother's father has made it clear to her that he encourages women and mothers working, yet offers an opposite perspective for his partner, ambivalence prevails; the struggle begins for the daughter when she is faced with the task of balancing motherhood with employment.

## Dependency and/or Independence

There is an intricate, developmental interaction between states of independence and dependence that becomes apparent in combining motherhood with employment. The self has both aspects of separateness and connectedness, which operate in conjunction. These two lines of development move along the continuum of time; the aim is for the working mother to bring the self into a state of psychic equilibrium, or integration. The environment, both past and present, acts upon this process and subsequently affects the state of balance. When the equilibrium is disrupted, this is reflected in the working mother's inability to balance work with motherhood, as it likely does in other areas as well.

Historically, women were socialized to be dependent, usually on fathers, husbands, and male models. However, a new model emerged, whereby women had the option to be independent and to their own choices in regard to to balancing motherhood with employment. The task then became one of politically reshaping and redefining motherhood for mothers, their children, and the family. Whereas previously women were strongly encouraged to stay at home, presently women are strongly encouraged to work. However, there are no choices in either scenario.

As a result, with this new wave of feminism, mothers are struggling to work with two models, one of dependence and one of an independent being with individual choices. This raises the question of whether there is a problem with balancing motherhood with employment, or a discomfort with the opposing models that mothers are struggling to integrate.

Working mothers may also be trying to comprehend and incorporate the motto that "if you cannot do things fully, then don't do them at all." Balancing motherhood with employment requires giving fully to both commitments, which is an incredible feat. Support systems such as employment benefits, flexible schedules, and accessible and affordable daycare eases these commitments, as does meaningful paternal involvement where fathers take active responsibility for their children. Feminists have called for education for parents regarding attitudes toward work and parenthood; informative early childhood education for parents and employers; and inclusive changes in the workplace, government, family and the community to improve conditions for mothers and their children.

The choice to work or not will entail different priorities at different points in time. The working-mother experience is a rich tapestry of all mothers from all walks of life, respecting class, culture, sexual orientation, and different structures of the family.

**See Also:** Ambivalence, Maternal; Idealization of Mothers; Maternal Thinking; Mommy Track; Mothering Versus Motherhood; Myths of Motherhood; Second Shift/Third Shift; Work and Mothering.

**Bibliography**
Crittenden, Ann. *The Price of Motherhood.* New York: Henry Holt, 2001.
Ennis, Linda. *On Combining Motherhood With Employment: An Exploratory Study.* Toronto: University of Toronto Press, 1997.
Ennis, Linda. "Paternal Involvement and Maternal Employment: Who Is the Man We Call Father?" *Women & Work,* v.1 (Spring 1999).
Ennis, Linda. "Working Mothers' Guilt, Ambivalence and Blame." Lecture, Mothering and Work/Mothering as Work Conference, Association for Research on Mothering. Toronto: York University, 2003.
Green, Fiona. "Feminist Mothering: A Site of Ongoing Political and Social Activism." Lecture, Mothering and Work/Mothering as Work Conference, Association for Research on Mothering. Toronto: York University, 2003.
Hirshman, Linda. *Get to Work.* New York: Viking, 2006.
Maher, JaneMaree. "Skills, Not Attributes: Rethinking Mothering as Work." *Mothering and Work/Mothering as Work, York University Publication,* v.6/2 (Fall/Winter 2004).
O'Reilly, Andrea. "Mothering Against Motherhood: Exposing and Deconstructing the Hegemonic Discourse of Natural–Intensive Motherhood." Lecture, Mothering and Work/Motherhood as Work Conference, Association for Research on Mothering. Toronto: York University, 2003.
Schindler, Toni Zimmerman. *Balancing Family and Work: Special Considerations in Feminist Therapy.* London: The Haworth Press, 2001.

Linda R. Ennis
York University

# Empowered Mothering

Empowered mothering is a counternarrative to the proscribed mainstream ideals and approaches to motherhood that are entrenched within Western contemporary society. Andrea O'Reilly began using the term *empowered mothering* in the early 2000s to refer to the theory and practice of mothering that recognizes that women, children, and society at large, benefit when women live their lives as mothers from a position of agency, authority, authenticity, and autonomy.

## Patriarchal Concepts of Mothering

Feminists argue that current ideals and expectations of motherhood are socially constructed as a patriarchal institution that demands all mothers be "good" mothers and that all mothers parent in very specific ways. In this construct, all mothers are expected to be the primary caregivers of children due to their supposed innate capacity to provide such care. They are to spend copious amounts of quality time with their children, and their mother/child interactions are to be informed by the discourse of professional experts to ensure that mothers foster the best physical, emotional, psychological, behavioral, and intellectual development in their children. Mothers are expected to find true fulfillment in mothering, to happily sacrifice their own needs and wants for the good of their children, and to find mothering more important than paid employment.

Within this patriarchal discourse of intensive mothering, work and mothering are seen to be incompatible and in conflict with each other. Therefore, women working in the paid labor force often feel inadequate about themselves as mothers, because they are still solely responsible for children. Mothers who work for pay outside the home are not the only ones to feel inadequate; patriarchal motherhood sets all mothers up to fail because it assigns them the responsibility for mothering without any real power from which to mother. Furthermore, its proscribed standard is fictitious and, thus, unattainable. Perceiving that they are being policed by the gaze of others, mothers often feel evaluated according to this imaginary ideal and judged to be deficient, which further disempowers them and the motherwork that is entailed in raising the next generation of citizens.

## A Confrontation

Empowered mothering directly confronts and counteracts patriarchal motherhood by presenting an alternative approach to mothering that is designed to empower women, mothers, children and others. Also known as authentic, lesbian/queer, radical, gynocentric and/or feminist mothering, empowered mothering is concerned with envisioning and realizing, through conscious action, a view and practice of mothering that is empowering rather than oppressive to women and children. Parenting by African American mothers that is practiced through community-based mothering and other-mothering—an acceptance of responsibility for a child not one's own—are other examples of empowered mothering. By interrupting, destabilizing, and rewriting the socially sanctioned patriarchal script of motherhood, empowered mothering weakens the grip normative patriarchal discourse has on the meaning and practice of mothering.

In emphasizing the authority that women have as mothers and crediting the agency they have in their own right, empowered mothers redefine motherhood as a political site where they can enact social change. Such transformative practices may include providing alternative ways of socially sanctioned parenting by mothering outside of heterosexual relationships, raising children in same-sex or transgender parenting partnerships, living apart from the father and mothering alone, rejecting the role of wife that is expected of mothers, renouncing the belief that mothers are totally responsible for the care and character of the child, or challenging the assumption that mothers will raise their children according to patriarchal or mainstream expectations.

Other practices may entail modeling—for their children and others—ways of mothering by challenging public school systems when they reproduce sexual discrimination, sexism, and heterosexism in their pedagogical and administrative practices; or by revealing these issues in the legal system regarding lesbian and co-mother rights to custody, access, and child support. Empowered mothers disrupt the concept of patriarchal motherhood by socializing their children to recognize and dispute current patriarchal systems of power, by resisting traditional patterns of gender acculturation in their parenting, and by encouraging their children to develop who they are without necessarily adhering to gender stereotypes. Empowered mothering is alive in nonpatriarchal family models; in community and other mothering; and in nonauthoritative, antisexist, antidiscriminatory, and antiracist ways of parenting. Proponents of empowered mothering emphasize that this approach fashions a dynamic place where mothers, children, and other family members can become more themselves. As maternal activists, empowered mothers are mindful and deliberate in their approaches to mothering that counter those of mainstream society; they consciously redefine and actively engage in motherwork that is a socially and politically infused practice through which cultural, social and political change is made possible.

**See Also:** Association for Research on Mothering; Demeter Press; Feminist Mothering; Intensive Mothering; Maternal Authenticity; Mothering Versus Motherhood; Patriarchal Ideology of Motherhood.

### Bibliography

Edwards, Arlene. "Community Mothering: The Relationship Between Mothering and the Community Work of Black Women." In *Mother Outlaws: Theories and Practices of Empowered Mothering*. London: The Women's Press, 2004.

Green, Fiona. "Feminist Mothers: Successfully Negotiating the Tensions Between Motherhood as 'Institution' and 'Experience.'" In *Mother Outlaws: Theories and Practices of Empowered Mothering*, Andrea O'Reilly, ed. London: The Women's Press, 2004.

Hays, Sharon. *The Cultural Contradictions of Motherhood*. New Haven, CT: Yale University Press, 1996.

Horwitz, Erika. "Resistance as a Site of Empowerment: The Journey Away From Maternal Sacrifice." In *Mother Outlaws: Theories and Practices of Empowered Mothering*, Andrea O'Reilly, ed. London: The Women's Press, 2004.

O'Reilly, Andrea. "Introduction." In *Mother Outlaws: Theories and Practices of Empowered Mothering*, Andrea O'Reilly, ed. London: The Women's Press, 2004.

O'Reilly, Andrea. *Rocking the Cradle: Thoughts on Feminism, Motherhood, and the Possibility of Empowered Mothering* . Toronto: Demeter Press, 2006.

Fiona Joy Green
University of Winnipeg

# Empress Matilda

Matilda of England (1102–67), was the daughter of Henry I of England and granddaughter of William the Conqueror; her first marriage to the German Henry V made her Holy Roman Empress in 1114. Widowed and childless in 1125, Matilda returned to England. After her brother William perished in the wreck of the White Ship, her father named Matilda his heir to the English throne and the Duchy of Normandy, forcing all the Anglo-Norman barons and clergy to swear fealty to her. He then arranged her marriage to Geoffrey of Anjou, by whom she had three sons, Henry (later Henry II), Geoffrey, and William.

On the death of her father she was in Anjou, and Henry I's nephew Stephen of Blois seized the throne; Matilda invaded England in 1139. The civil war that followed was bitter and prolonged, with neither side prevailing. In 1148, Matilda returned to Normandy, but her son Henry took over the campaign for England, and in the 1153 Treaty of Wallingford, Stephen acknowledged Henry as his heir. Matilda spent her final years in Normandy presiding over the duchy in her son's absence. She died in 1167 and was buried in the abbey church of Bec-Hellouin.

Matilda was the first female ruler of the Kingdom of England, although she ruled only briefly and remained uncrowned. Matilda had dynastic claims to the English throne from both sides as the only living legitimate child of Henry I and his wife, Matilda of Scotland. Her failure to secure that throne for herself can be attributed to a number of factors. Her father obtained oaths of allegiance to his daughter from all his bishops and magnates in 1127 to defend her against all others if she outlived her father and he left no legitimate son. However, many reneged on these oaths when Stephen presented himself as an alternative. The Church (including Pope Innocent II), nobles, and people believed only a male ruler could reestablish authority.

Furthermore, the popular view of women as "daughters of Eve," promoted by the church of medieval Europe as part of a tradition stretching back to the Greeks and Romans, was that women were "bearers of evil," rebels, treacherous, and vindictive. The chroniclers paint a picture of Matilda as keenly conscious of her high status as empress, and as behaving autocratically. Although the same could be said of both her father and her eldest son, in her this aroused more hostility because of the "feminine softness" it was said she lacked. She made some crucial errors of judgement, but she did not act arbitrarily or alone. Once she accepted what was possible for a woman claimant to the throne of England in the feudal society of the 12th century, when rules of inheritance were in flux and the success of a putative heir depended on quick action and armed force, she worked with a courage and fortitude that were praised even by her enemies to secure the throne for her son. Medieval society was held together by gendered hierarchies that placed women of all social classes outside the formal and public realms of royal politics and government. Much greater leeway was granted to a royal mother, and it was in that role, rather than on her own behalf, that Matilda finally triumphed.

**See Also:** Class and Mothering; Eleanor of Aquitaine; History of Motherhood: 1100 to 1500; History of Motherhood: Middle Ages; Sons and Mothers.

**Bibliography**
Beem, Charles. *The Lioness Roared: The Problems of Female Rule in English History*. New York: Palgrave Macmillan, 2006.
Chibnall, Marjorie. *Anglo-Norman England 1066–1166*. Oxford, UK: Blackwell, 1986.
Chibnall, Marjorie. *The Empress Matilda: Queen Consort, Queen Mother and Lady of the English*. Oxford, UK: Blackwell, 1991.
Duby, Georges. *Women of the Twelfth Century*. Queensland, Australia: Polity Press, 1998.
Carmi Parsons, John and Bonnie Wheeler, eds. *Medieval Mothering*. London: Garland, 1996.

Sue Kentlyn
University of Queensland, Australia

# Empty Nest

The term *empty nest* refers primarily to a feeling of loneliness, depression, sadness, and grief that parents, especially mothers, feel when one or more of their children leave the childhood home, either temporarily or permanently. This feeling may result in a loss of purpose and crisis of identity for the parents, especially the mother.

## The Separation-Individuation Process

The clinical definition of separation and individuation is the emotional ability to form one's own sense of self, with one's own opinions, thoughts, and feelings, and to keep emotional boundaries in relationships. The separation part of the process indicates that an individual needs to experience himself/herself as distinct from his/her parent. A problem sets in when the mother has not successfully completed her own separation process from her mother. This incomplete emotional separation, then, is played out in the next generation's failure to do so in the form of an insecure attachment between mother and child.

The mother or father's reaction to the separation is reflective of his/her own separation issues, as well as the child's reaction to it. If the child has not experienced small, successful separations along the continuum of development in the form of such activities as sleepovers and summers away at camp, for example, this will be an issue when he/she ultimately leaves home either temporarily or permanently. If the parent has modeled that it is unsafe to separate or communicates a sense of abandonment, the child will internalize this insecurity toward being on their own away from the parents. On the other hand, if the parent has communicated that their relationship is more of an egalitarian friendship, the separation will feel harsh and wrenching because, in fact, they are each losing their best friend.

If the parent is divorced, separated, or widowed, the separation between parent and child may be more difficult for the child and alternatively, the empty nest feelings on the part of the parent may be strong, especially if the child has been reflecting the parent's needs; when he/she leaves the nest, there will no longer be a mirror left behind to reflect the parent's needs. However, on the other hand, if the parent has established new connections with friends, family, and colleagues, the separation may also be a smooth one. A great deal depends on the nature of the original separation and how it was handled as a family.

## Empty Nest and Mommy Track

The mommy track refers to the choice made by either the mother or her employer to place the mother on an alternate career path, one that is compatible with motherhood. This route focuses on motherhood and often results in narrowing the working mother's career path. If this decision led to an expectation of motherhood that is all-encompassing or a form of hyper-parenting, it will ultimately limit the time and energy for employment, not withstanding the difficulty in making the leap back onto the fast track. If such a mother finds herself in this situation, the empty nest syndrome would come into play when the child leaves home. The focus from employment to motherhood has resulted in the mother's sense of self to be inextricably involved in this commitment.

## Balancing the Self With Motherhood

For many women, their value as a person becomes stronger and clearer when they become a mother. They may feel more focused and self-confident about themselves. Having said this, when the time comes to separate from their children, there may be a fear that these positive attributes that she possesses may also be lost. Having "a room of one's own," or a space the mother can call her own apart from mothering entails relationships with friends and other family members, as well as interests the mother can call her own. If the focus, however, is on the mother's need to immerse herself in her child's life excessively for the purpose of forgetting herself, the nest will feel very empty when the child ultimately moves on.

## Missed Motherhood Experiences

If the motherhood experience has been missed, either in the past or present relationship, there will be anguish in the empty nest. Many mothers opt or have to work lengthy hours when the children resided at home, and later return to the nest when it is almost time for the children to leave home. Other mothers attempt to re-create and repair in their present relationships with their children what was missed when they, themselves, were children and their mothers were absent or otherwise preoccupied. With so much at stake and so much effort at bringing back the ideal mother, it may feel as if the loss of the child is even greater had this not have been the case.

## More Freedom

Recent research has indicated that while parents do feel a sense of loss when their nests are empty, they also have found that this time can also be one of increased satisfaction and new or improved relationships. In addition, it also appears that fathers may find the empty nest harder than mothers do, perhaps because they were less prepared for the transition and less engaged when the children were at home. Nevertheless, the latest research indicates that most parents enjoy greater freedom, a reconnection with their spouses, and more time to pursue their goals and interests.

**See Also:** Ambivalence, Maternal; Employment and Motherhood: Idealization of Mothers; Mommy Track; Myths of Motherhood; Work and Mothering.

**Bibliography**

Bennetts, L. *The Feminine Mistake*. New York: Hyperion, 2007.

Ennis, L. *Combining Motherhood With Employment: An Exploratory Study*. Toronto: University of Toronto, 1997.

Ennis, L. "Paternal Involvement and Maternal Employment." *Women and Work*, v.1 (Spring 1999).

Fingerman, K. *Mothers and Their Adult Daughters: Mixed Emotions, Enduring Bonds*. Amherst, NY: Prometheus Books, 2002.

Poulter, S. *The Mother Factor*. Amherst, NY: Prometheus Books, 2008.

Stabiner, K. *The Empty Nest*. New York: Hyperion Books, 2007.

Warner, J. *Perfect Madness: Motherhood in the Age of Anxiety*. New York: Riverhead Books, 2005.

Linda R. Ennis
York University

# Environments and Mothering

The relationships between environments and mothering practices are quite variable and complex. A survey of the anthropological and sociological studies that focus on mothering (or caregiving, since mothering may be performed by females other than the child's biological mother, as well as males) quickly reveals that practices around the world are diverse and are very much influenced by geographical, sociohistorical, and economic environments.

Most of the discourse that focuses on the relationships between motherhood (caregiving) and the environment can be grouped into two major categories: first, the historical/sociocultural studies that include analyses of environmental variations in mothering practices and their subsequent effects on the socialization of children; and second, the impact of economic environments upon mothering practices.

## Sociocultural Environments and History

One of the major debates surrounding the relationship between mothering and sociocultural environments has centered upon how much of mothering behaviors (or lack thereof) can be attributed to biological as opposed to social influences (the so-called "maternal instinct"). The scholarship and research on the subject tend to center upon three focal questions: Are women naturally and biologically endowed with a "maternal instinct," or are mothering behaviors simply learned through socialization—mothers are not born, but are made? Why do women appear routinely as the primary caregivers in societies worldwide (or, alternatively, why do men as a group not usually engage in such behaviors) and how does this social arrangement contribute to women's oppression? Should mothering/caregiving be taken out of the private realm and placed in the public one?

## Biological Versus Social Motherhood

Although the word *mother* is one of the oldest found in languages around the world, the term *motherhood* is of comparatively recent creation (the earliest reference is found in the *Oxford English Dictionary* in 1597), with many authors such as Ann Dally arguing that the institution of motherhood is a fairly new invention. Even so, there is general agreement that caregiving is a universal institution established in all societies as a mechanism for ensuring the survival of humanity.

The basic goals of caregiving in societies are to make sure that the young are protected, their growth is fostered, and they adhere to social norms even as they are taught to listen to their own consciences. There is disagreement, however, in the distinction between the practice of mothering as a "natural" and biological imperative, as opposed to the varying social construction(s) of the institution of mothering as found in different cultures and historical periods.

Arguments have gone as far to assert that biological motherhood is simply a myth constructed to assure the continuity of patriarchy, evidenced by systematic subordination of women in societies or institutions where the rule of the father is supreme in families and clans, mothers and children are legal dependents of males, and lines of descent and inheritance pass solely through males. Under such a system, all women are expected to have a natural desire to become mothers, mothers need their children, and children need their mothers.

In their deconstruction of this line of thinking, some researchers and scholars have made three counterarguments. First, they argue that the so-called "maternal instinct" is not a biological one, but a state that arises from the way that girls are socially and culturally conditioned to be mothers.

Second, they argue that women possess no such thing as a "maternal instinct," citing studies such as a group of first-time breastfeeding mothers, where researchers observed that few of the women knew how to nurse their babies unless they had previously seen other females engaged in breastfeeding. Furthermore, they cited observations that most women who abuse or neglect their children have been abused or neglected when they were children themselves.

Finally, with respect to the claim that children need their mothers, they frequently mention the studies of children reared collectively in Israeli *kibbutzim* (whom researchers claim are as happy and socially adjusted as children reared solely by their biological mothers in U.S. suburbs). To counter assertions that the maternal instinct is an intrinsic biological force, they also refer to cross-cultural variations in maternal/care giving behaviors as exemplified by such practices as the *couvade* (a practice in some societies where, when the mother goes into labor, the father simulates bearing the child, then observes any fasting or purification rituals and taboos associated with childbirth) and the *Lakou* (a group living system in Haiti where multiple women traditionally shared in the care of young children, prior to the advent of economic globalization).

## Biological Motherhood and Oppression

For some feminists such as Shulamith Firestone, natural reproduction and biological motherhood are the root causes of women's oppression under patriarchy. In order to liberate women from such oppression, she proposed that women seize control of the means of reproduction in order to rid society of its need to differentiate between the sexes on the basis of their reproductive capacities. To that end, she advocated the use of reproductive technology (in vitro fertilization and the gestation of embryos in environments other than women's bodies when the technology becomes available) and collective child rearing as possible ways of leveling the playing field between women and men.

For others such as Adrienne Rich, however, biological motherhood (i.e., the potential relationship that may exist between a woman and her reproductive abilities and her children) is not necessarily oppressive in and of itself. Rather, biological motherhood as it currently exists under patriarchy is oppressive and restrictive to women because patriarchal societies have convinced most women that mothering should be their sole job. She also writes that women have been kept from rearing children to become people in their own right, as opposed to sons who will simply serve as extensions of their male progenitors and daughters who will faithfully reproduce the male lineage.

## Private Versus Public Mothering

Another major question broached by writers on mothering/parenting and environments has been whether children benefit more from care given in private realms such as the child's home, where they are attended by parents and relatives, as opposed to more public institutions such as daycare, where

*A mother in Mozambique surveys a cassava field with her child. The environment of strict gender roles in some African regions has prevented men—who are generally more educated—from being involved in nurturing. Changing these norms is a difficult process.*

they have increased contact and interaction with their peers. Much of this literature focuses on determining the subsequent impact of public and private environments upon children's social, emotional, and intellectual development. In many of these studies, researchers have found that the outcome is largely dependent on the skill and quality of the care being given, rather than the environment in which the work is done. A few other studies, however, have expressed dissent, finding that children reared in their own home environments tend to outperform their peers on all developmental measures even when children cared for in the public realm are placed in the best of situations.

## Economic Environments and Mothering

Friedrich Engels was one of the first theorists to speculate about how changes in people's economic and material conditions affect family structures. In his work *The Origin of the Family, Private Property and the State* (1845), he expressed the belief that early societies were matrilineal (i.e., inheritance and lines of descent were traced through the mother). As men's work and production began to take on greater importance in the establishment of capitalism and during the process of industrialization, however, what he calls "mother right" was overthrown and women's personal and economic status began to decline. In order to emancipate women, he and others such as Karl Marx proposed that women's work be reconstituted in the public realm (as opposed to their positions as unpaid workers in the home) and that housework and child rearing be socialized.

After the Communist Revolution in Russia in 1917, there was much hope that new economic conditions would allow women to participate on an equal footing with men in the workplace. However, it was still found that socialist women did not do as well as socialist men in the public realm due to the second shift of domestic work they had to perform at the end of the workday. Thus, even in the wake of major economic and societal changes, neither the general attitudes toward gender roles nor the distribution of care giving burdens among males and females became as egalitarian as many expected under the Soviet regime. In other cases, though, researchers have found that certain economic initiatives supported by some countries (such

as Scandinavian countries' daycare and maternity leave) have had some positive impacts on equalizing the amount of care work done by both sexes. Consequently, the pressure of balancing personal and professional lives still remains a pressing concern for the majority of mothers around the world.

Currently, researchers have found that economic globalization is having a profound impact on mothering practices around the globe. One of the major findings is that the gap in income between wealthier and poorer women has grown, and is only expected to increase over time. Due to such disparities, researchers have devoted much time to analyzing phenomena such as transnational mothering (care arrangements for children whose mothers must leave them in their home countries in order to emigrate for work) and global care chains (the emigration and employment of women from poorer countries so that they may care for the children of women in wealthy nations).

Another major impact of current economic globalization on mothering practices that is becoming an area of concern centers upon debates about the uses of reproduction-aiding technologies and their subsequent impact on the phenomenon of surrogate (on contracted) motherhood, where a third party is usually hired and paid to bear a child that will be reared by another person. In Kalindi Vora's work on Indian transnational commercial surrogacy and the disaggregation of mothering, for example, she focuses on how the growing trend of the use of Indian surrogates by clients from wealthier nations is transforming traditional assumptions about what it means to be a parent, what value societies currently attach to mothering and children, and finally, what moral and ethical implications these reproductive technologies themselves pose for the future of mothering and caregiving practices.

**See Also:** Anthropology of Motherhood; Care Giving; Class and Mothering; Economics of Motherhood; Social Construction of Motherhood.

## Bibliography

Barker, Drucilla K. and Susan F. Feiner. *Liberating Economics: Feminist Perspectives on Families, Work, and Globalization.* Ann Arbor: University of Michigan Press, 2004.

Crittenden, Ann. *The Price of Motherhood.* New York: Metropolitan Books, 2001.

Dally, Ann. *Inventing Motherhood: The Consequences of an Ideal.* New York: Schocken Books, 1983.

Doucet, Andrea. *Do Men Mother?: Fathering, Care, and Domestic Responsibility.* Toronto: University of Toronto Press, 2006.

Edmond, Yanique M., Suzanne M. Randolph, and Guylaine L. Richard. "The Lakou System: A Cultural, Ecological Analysis of Mothering in Rural Haiti." *The Journal of Pan African Studies,* v.2/1 (November 2007).

Ehrenreich, Barbara and Arlie Russell Hochschild, eds. Global Woman: Nannies, Maids, and Sex Workers in the New Economy. New York: Henry Holt, 2004.

Smith, Jeremy Adam. *The Daddy Shift: How Stay-at-Home Dads, Breadwinnings Moms and Shared Parenting Are Transforming the American Family.* Boston: Beacon Press, 2009.

Vora, Kalindi. "Indian Transnational Surrogacy and the Commodification of Vital Energy." *Subjectivity,* v.28/1 (September 2009).

Danielle Roth-Johnson
University of Nevada

# Equatorial Guinea

Mothers in Equatorial Guinea face extreme deprivation. Women have occupied an inferior position within the country, which is noted for human rights abuses and for being one of the most corrupt governments in the world. Equatorial Guinea is a least developed country (LDC) with a high total fertility rate (5.9) and a low ranking on indices of human development. In 2007, Save the Children's Mothers' Index ranked Equatorial Guinea 20th out of the 33 among the LDCs. The government has not viewed high fertility as a problem, and does not provide any support for contraceptive use. Abortion is illegal except to preserve the life or health of the woman. High fertility relates to lack of access to contraception and high infant mortality. In 2004, infant mortality was 123 per 1,000 live births and neonatal mortality was 40 per 1,000 births. Maternal mortality was 880 per 100,000 live births. Life expectancy in 2004 was 42 years for men and 44 years for women. Despite legal equality between men and women, the reality is that men make family decisions. Until 1990, women who were divorced, widowed, or abandoned could be imprisoned for failure to repay their dowry. This remains a problem in isolated rural areas.

**Economic Status**

Since the mid-1990s, the international status of Equatorial Guinea has been enhanced by its emerging oil industry, yet the impact on the general population has been negative. Increased international interest has been accompanied by less criticism of governmental corruption and human rights abuses. Oil revenues provide military security for the elite and have increased the authority of Teodoro Obiang Nguema Mbasogo, who has ruled for 30 years. Gross Domestic Product (GDP) has increased, but wealth is concentrated in the hands of a few. Oil production creates relatively few jobs and the laborers are often foreign immigrants. Inflation, urban migration, and underdevelopment of the economy make life difficult for the vast majority who live by subsistence agriculture. The country depends on imported foodstuffs and the cost of basic necessities is very high. Prostitution has increased with urbanization and the influx of oil workers, further putting women at risk. In 2002, human immunodeficiency virus (HIV) and acquired immunodeficiency syndrome (AIDS) was the leading cause of death, accounting for 17 percent of deaths. Some indicators point to improvements in health and educational status; however, levels are still well below those of countries with comparable per capita GDP. Equatorial Guinea spent 1.23 percent of government expenditures on health between 1997 and 2002; during the same period, Nigeria spent 5.95 percent and South Africa 12.1 percent. Recent government efforts include training centers for adult women and increased education among the young.

**See Also:** Globalization and Mothering; Patriarchal Ideology of Motherhood; Postcolonialism and Mothering; Poverty and Mothering; Prostitution and Motherhood.

**Bibliography**
BBC News. "Country Profile: Equatorial Guinea." http://news.bbc.co.uk/2/hi/africa/country_profiles/1023151.stm (accessed February 2009).

Frynas, J.G. "The Oil Boom in Equatorial Guinea." *African Affairs*, v.103/413 (2004).

United Nations Committee on the Elimination of Discrimination Against Women. *Periodic Reports: Equatorial Guinea.* 31st session. (July 23, 2004).

United Nations Department of Economic and Social Affairs. *Contraception 2003: Equatorial Guinea.* (April 25, 2003). www.un.org/esa/population/publications/ (accessed June 2009).

World Health Organization. *Country Health System Fact Sheet 2006: Equatorial Guinea.* www.afro.who .int/home/countries/fact_sheets/ (accessed June 2009).

Margaret J. Weinberger
Bowling Green State University

# Erdrich, Louise

Award-winning poet, fiction writer, memoirist, and children's book author, Louise Erdrich is one of the most renowned and prolific figures in contemporary American letters. The mother of seven children, with over 20 books to her credit, Erdrich has an impressive literary output as the result of disciplined work habits and an abiding, spiritualized belief in the saving power of story. Part German American and part (on her mother's side) Chippewa, Erdrich helped foment what has been called the Native American Renaissance in literature, drawing attention to the virtues and vices, losses and loves of a fractured but resolute people.

She writes with charged lyricism about the fraught, familial tensions and passions among the Native and European inhabitants of a fictional North Dakota locale—very like the place in which she spent her own childhood. Erdrich and her part-Modoc anthropologist/writer husband, Michael Dorris (1946–97) became a celebrated literary couple, intensively immersed in each other's writing projects while raising their six children, until the dissolution of their 15-year marriage and Dorris's eventual suicide.

## Love and Tragedy

Karen Louise Erdrich, the oldest of seven children, was born in 1954 and grew up in a warm, story-loving home near the Turtle Mountain Reservation, where her French Ojibwe (Chippewa) mother, Rita, was born and where her grandfather was tribal chair. Her often-retold story of being given a nickel for each story she wrote shows how her early creative ambition was fostered by her parents, who were both teachers at a Bureau of Indian Affairs school. In *The Blue Jay's Dance: A Birth Year* (1995), her meditative chronicle of her pregnancies and motherhood, Erdrich describes her own mother—an artist—as supremely patient and child-centered, venting any frustrations through sewing or canning tomatoes. Erdrich was an avid reader and absorbed the oral stories of tribal life and settlement from her elders. She traveled east to college, earning an M.A. in writing from Johns Hopkins after completing her B.A. at Dartmouth, where she met Michael Dorris, a founder and first chair of the college's Native American Studies Program. Erdrich has two sisters, Heid and Lise, who are also writers.

When Erdrich and Dorris married in 1981, he was already the single father of three adopted Native American children, all of whom suffered, to varying degrees, from the debilitating effects of fetal alcohol syndrome. Erdrich formally adopted Reynold Abel, Jeffrey Sava, and Madeline Hannah; the couple subsequently had three more daughters, Persia, Pallas, and Aza. *The Broken Cord* (1989), Dorris' influential and controversial memoir (with a forthright and moving forward by Erdrich), won the 1989 National Book Critics Circle Award for nonfiction and helped spur legislation to warn of the dangers of alcohol consumption during pregnancy. *The Broken Cord* recounts the anguish of raising a child (called Adam in the book) with severe impairments and indicts the alcoholic mothers who knowingly compromise their unborn children's development. Reynold Abel was struck by a car and killed in 1993.

The Erdrich/Dorris union seemed an almost preternaturally intimate one, with both authors planning, composing, and editing each other's work in their child-filled New Hampshire farmhouse. The extent of their collaborations isn't public knowledge, but each has credited the other with being catalyst, support, and muse. Two works carry both their names: a novel, *The Crown of Columbus*

(1991) and a collection of travel essays, *Route Two* (1990). Their partnership ended tragically and very publicly amidst sensational allegations of child abuse. They unsuccessfully sued Jeffrey Sava for extortion; both Madeline and Jeffrey Sava accused the couple of child abuse. Two of his biological daughters accused Dorris of sexual abuse as well.

## Novels and Short Stories

The history of North Dakota's Pembina region is revealed in Erdrich's cycle of interwoven Argus tales, which unfold throughout 11 novels and many short stories. Erdrich's celebrated first novel in this series, *Love Medicine*, won the 1984 National Book Critics Circle award for fiction. It was reissued in expanded form in 1993.

*Little No Horse*, her fictional Objibwe reservation, and the North Dakota town of Argus, somewhere on the Red River near the Minnesota border, have been likened to William Faulkner's Yoknapatawpha County in Mississippi. Both authors enliven their places with the relational dynamics of families whose stories and destinies meld and collide dramatically over time. Erdrich's region is home to the Lamartine, Pillager, Morissey, and Kashpaw families, as well as to Father Damien Modeste; Sister Leopolda; the trickster figure, Nanapush; and other memorably idiosyncratic characters. Other works in the series include *The Beet Queen* (1986), *Tracks* (1988), *The Bingo Palace* (1994), *Tales of Burning Love* (1996), *The Last Report on the Miracles at Little No Horse* (2001), *The Master Butcher's Singing Club* (2003), and *A Plague of Doves* (2008).

Erdrich currently resides in Minnesota, where she owns BirchBark Books, a specialized book and native arts store and community center. Being a mother, she says, has helped hone her creative instincts. She credits a strong community of women—helpers, friends, and family members—for permitting her to keep pace with her writing while actively mothering. All women, even those without children, help teach each other to mother, she writes in *The Blue Jay's Dance*. The spirited, opportunistic blue jay is an emblem for maternal audacity, for mothers as adaptive survivors. When she was 46, Erdrich gave birth to another daughter, Azure. Her latest book, *The Red Convertible and Other Stories,* was published in 2009.

**See Also:** Fetal Alcohol Syndrome; Native Americans; North Dakota.

## Bibliography

Beidler, Peter G. and Gay Barton. *A Reader's Guide to the Novels of Louise Erdrich.* Columbia: University of Missouri Press, 2006.

Erdrich, Louise. *The Blue Jay's Dance: A Birth Year.* New York: HarperCollins, 1995.

Erdrich, Louise. "A Wedge of Shade." In *Mothers and Daughters: An Anthology*, Alberto Manguel, ed. San Francisco: Chronicle Books, 1998.

Hansen, Elaine Tuttle. "What If Your Mother Never Meant To? The Novels of Louise Erdrich and Michael Dorris." In *Mother Without Child: Contemporary Fiction and the Crisis of Motherhood*, Elaine Tuttle Hansen, ed. Berkeley: University of California Press, 1997.

Reynolds, Susan Salter. "Playing to Her Strengths." *Los Angeles Times.* http://articles.latimes.com/2001/may/16/news/cl-63904 (accessed June 2009).

Tharp, Julie. "'Into the Birth House' With Louise Erdrich." In *This Giving Birth: Pregnancy and Childbirth in American Women's Writing*, Julie Tharp and Susan MacCallum, eds. Whitcomb, OH: Bowling Green State University Popular Press, 2000.

Tharp, Julie. "Women's Community and Survival in the Novels of Louise Erdrich." In *Communication and Women's Friendships: Parallels and Intersections in Literature and Life*, Janet Doubler Ward, et al., eds. Madison: University of Wisconsin Press, 1993.

Wong, Hertha D. "Adoptive Mothers and Thrown-Away Children in the Novels of Louise Erdrich." In *Narrating Mothers: Theorizing Maternal Subjectivities*, Brenda O. Daly and Maureen T. Reddy, eds. Knoxville: University of Tennessee Press, 1991.

Kate Falvey
New York City College of Technology

# Eritrea

Eritrea, situated in the Horn of Africa (in the northeastern part of the continent), was an Italian colony from 1890 until World War II, after which it was federated with Ethiopia, separated in 1993 and become an independent nation. It has a population of 4.4 million, and has a female life expectancy of 60.6 years. The birth rate in the country is 34.3 per 1,000, and there is an infant mortality rate of 46.3 per 1,000 live births. During the period of colonial rule, there was little attempt to improve the life of the vast majority of the population. Women continued to live as homemakers and tend to crops, as well as taking part in grinding corn. Abeba Tesfagiorgis, in her book *A Painful Season—A Stubborn Hope* (1992), helped provide details on the women of Eritrea during the Ethiopian occupation.

After the 1975 Communist Revolution in Ethiopia (which included Eritrea), the Revolutionary Ethiopia Women's Association was established to improve the education of women. Since independence in 1993, there have been increased efforts to widen the coverage of the health services, but many problems remain, including the prevalence of female genital mutilation in some areas. A spiritual cult called the Zar still exists in Eritrea, and still practices ancient customs, including spiritual healing.

Australian writer Thomas Keneally became interested in events in Eritrea, and his novel *Towards Asmara* (1989) was one of the few bestsellers written about the country before independence. It highlights the problems many girls faced with female genital mutilation, and the fact that so many mothers had to bring their children to refugee camps to seek aid from foreign donors. Unlike in neighboring Djibouti, where many women are involved as market traders, few women do such work in Eritrea.

## Abortion, Health Care, and Births

Abortion is legal in Eritrea only to save the life or physical or mental health of the mother. Forty-nine percent of women receive prenatal care, and 28 percent of births are attended by skilled medical personnel. The maternal mortality ratio in 2000 was 630 per 100,000 live births, in part due to an early age of marragie in the country. Many children are orphaned young from the effects of diseases, including human immunodeficiency virus (HIV) and acquired immunodeficiency syndrome (AIDS), starvation, and complications during birth. Currently, some 70 percent of all births take place at home, with only 28 percent taking place in the presence of a medically trained professional, such as a qualified midwife.

In 2003 the life expectancy at birth for women was 61 years, and 47.6 percent of the female population age 15 and older was literate.

**See Also:** Ethiopia; Infant Mortality; Poverty and Mothering; Violence Against Mothers/Children.

**Bibliography**

Ferryhough, Anna. "The Traditional Role and Status of Women in Imperial Ethiopia." *Journal of the Steward Anthropological Society.* v.13/2 (1982).

Keneally, Thomas. "Eritrean Medicine." *Medical Journal of Australia.* v.153/5 (September 1990).

Keneally, Thomas. *Towards Asmara.* London: Hodder & Stoughton, 1989.

Tesfagiorgis, Abeba. *A Painful Season—A Stubborn Hope.* Trenton, NJ: Red Sea Press, 1992.

Turbiana, Joseph. "Zar and Buda in Northern Ethiopia." In *Women's Medicine: The Zar-Bori Cult in Africa and Beyond,* I.M. Lewis, ed. Edinburgh, UK: Edinburgh University Press, 1991.

Wilson, Amrit. *The Challenge Road: Women and the Eritrean Revolution.* Trenton, NJ: Red Sea Press, 1991.

Woldemicael, Gebremariam. *Teenage Childbearing and Child Health in Eritrea.* Working paper of the Max Planck Institute for Demographic Research. www.demogr.mpg.de/papers/working/wp-2005-029.pdf (accessed May 2009).

Justin Corfield
Geelong Grammar School, Australia

# Essentialism and Mothering

As a philosophy, essentialism believes that the true essence of any person or thing is established prior to its existence and determines what shape that existence will take. In practice, mothering is the individual approach a woman brings to the experience of being a mother. Essentialism has had a tremendous impact on political, cultural, and social visions of what good mothering should be, because essentialist thinking has largely based that image on the notion that all women naturally possess innate female qualities that drive them to pursue maternal goals above all others. These essentialist notions go beyond the obvious biological fact that women physically give birth, and assume that women are genetically destined to be responsible for childcare and, by extension, most domestic duties. Nonessentialist views of mothering argue that women are no more physiologically configured to change diapers, tend to children's needs, and perform domestic services than men are. An intense form of essentialist mothering in mainstream Western society works against nonessentialist views, which posits that the extent of a woman's biological, natural involvement includes carrying the fetus through the gestational period, giving birth to the child after a period of labor, and providing the child's infant nourishment in the form of breastmilk. Everything else associated with mothering is a social and cultural construct, subject to individual interpretation and community scrutiny.

## Essentialism Versus Existentialism

Essentialism has deep roots in Western civilization: many consider the Greek philosopher Plato, with his concepts of ideal forms, to be the first essentialist. Essentialism is the opposite of existentialism, a theoretical development that grew out of the work of 19th-century philosophers Søren Kierkegaard and Friedrich Nietzsche. As theoretical tools, the philosophies of essentialism and existentialism are often used to examine human life. Existentialism postulates that free, rational, responsible individuals develop themselves according to their will: people become who they are by what they do, not through essential physiological structures. By contrast, essentialism presupposes that people's lives are lived according to what they are, not what they learn.

Both theories developed in strongly patriarchal social orders. Essentialism has been applied to expectations of both femininity and masculinity. However, when the existentialism movement became prominent in the early 19th century, its ideas applied primarily to men. In 1949, Simone de Beauvoir did much to initiate a change in thinking with her famous comment that women are not born, but created by culture and society. In 1976, Adrienne Rich expressed the essentialist foundations of motherhood when she described that institution as a structure of patriarchal social orders.

## Essentialist Views of Motherhood

The life opportunities open to women have been widely understood through essentialist mainstream thinking that is rooted in biology and supported by the social and political needs of male-dominant cultures. Essentialist views of motherhood assume that women want to be mothers and that women should be mothers; however, nonessentialists argue that this approach denies women individual autonomy. In essentialist thinking, women who do not become mothers are often seen as somehow unnatural or abnormal. In this type of thinking, women are assumed to be mothers first and foremost.

Because essentialist views of womanhood focus on the notion that natural female capacities determine that women are primarily motivated to bear children and nurture them to adulthood, essentialism not only shapes notions of mothering, but also of femininity: women's feminine nature leads women to selflessly devote themselves to mothering their children or nurturing others. In this way, essentialist thinking sees femininity as self-sacrificing: women derive emotional satisfaction from mothering, and their sexual drives are supported with the idea that they will become mothers. Thus, a subtext of essentialist thinking is that natural female sexuality is heterosexual.

The essentialist influence on mothering has economic consequences: Western society accepts that mothering includes unpaid work, a feminine labor of love. Since its onset after the industrial revolution, capitalist societies have benefited from the free labor provided by mothers as part of their so-called natural roles. As women overcame workforce barriers, even professions deemed appropriate for women (nursing, teaching, social work) grew out of the motherly roles women filled. In the professional world, these female-dominant professions are still among the lowest paid. Women in male-dominant professions often struggle to find a balance between their maternal duties and those of their profession. The notion of the mother omnipresent in her child's life often results in women being sidelined in their careers while men who become fathers do not face these repercussions.

Today's version of essentialism and mothering has combined to create a role with duties ranging from meeting simple needs to arranging elaborate rounds of activities, play dates, and workshops. As mothering practices are integral to social structures, mothers must work to reinforce these structures, even as they simultaneously encourage their children to find their free autonomous selves.

**See Also:** de Beauvoir, Simone; Family; Idealization of Mothers; Rich, Adrienne; Social Construction of Motherhood; Sociology of Motherhood.

**Bibliography**

Di Quinzio, Patrice. *The Impossibility of Motherhood: Feminism, Individualism, and the Problem of Mothering.* New York: Routledge, 1999.

Hays, Sharon. *The Cultural Contradictions of Motherhood.* New Haven, CT: Yale University Press, 1996.

O'Reilly, Andrea. *From Motherhood to Mothering: The Legacy of Adrienne Rich's Of Woman Born.* Albany: State University of New York Press, 2004.

Myrl Coulter
University of Alberta

# Estonia

Estonia is a former Soviet Republic that gained independence in 1991 and joined the European Union in 2004. It is a parliamentary democracy with a population of about 1.3 million, of whom 14.9 percent are age 14 or younger and 17.6 percent age 65 and older. The population growth rate is negative (minus 0.632 percent), with 10.28 births per 1,000 population, 13.4 deaths per 1,000, and a net migration rate of minus 3.26 per 1,000. The total fertility rate (an estimation of the average number of children per woman) is 1.42. Life expectancy at birth is 67.4 years for men and 78.5 years for women. The population is about two-thirds Estonian and one-quarter Russian, with the remainder mostly coming from other former Soviet republics. It is a secular state and the population has a low degree of religious affiliation: about a third of Estonians belong to a Christian denomination, and most of the remainder are unaffiliated. Literacy is quite high and is equal (99.8 percent) for both men and women.

Estonia has a modern market economy, and its Gross Domestic Product (GDP) per capita ($21,200 in 2008) is one of the highest in central Europe and 44th out of 223 countries included in the *CIA World Factbook*. The population enjoys a high standard of communications: there are more mobile phones in use than there are people living in the country, and with Internet access commonly available (online voting was first used in local elections in 2005).

Maternal and child health services are provided on a par with western European countries. Per capita total expenditure in 2002 was $263, and the government provides over 75 percent of the total expenditures for health care. Major childhood immunization rates are near 100 percent, almost all births are attended by skilled personnel, and 56 percent of women use modern contraceptive methods. There are about 12,000 live births annually; the maternal mortality rate is 38 per 100,000 live births, the stillbirth rate in 5 per 1,000 total births, and the neonatal mortality rate 6 per 1,000 live births. In the rankings by Save the Children, an international organization devoted to serving the needs of children around the world, Estonia ranks 17 for maternal health (by comparison, the United States is ranked 26). The index is based on a number of categories, including female life expectancy, female education, child mortality, maternal mortality, modern contraceptive use, and participation in national government.

**See Also:** European Union; Maternal Health; Russia (and Soviet Union).

**Bibliography**

Koupilova, I., et al. "Social Determinants of Birthweights and Length of Gestation in Estonia During the Transition to Democracy." *International Journal of Epidemiology,* v.29/1 (2000).

Save the Children. *State of the World's Mothers 2007.* http://www.savethechildren.org/publications/ mothers/2007/SOWM-2007-final.pdf (accessed April 2009).

Tulviste, T., L. Mizera, B. De Geer, and M.T. Tryggvason. "Child-Rearing Goals of Estonian, Finnish and Swedish Mothers. *Scandinavian Journal of Psychology,* v.48/6 (2007).

Sarah E. Boslaugh
Washington University School of Medicine

# Ethics, Maternal

Virginia Held, Sara Ruddick, and Caroline Whitbeck are feminist philosophers advocating the concept of maternal ethics, or the idea that the majority of human relationships are held between unequal persons. Rather than building ethics on the idea that there is no substantial difference between one persona and another, these three philosophers claim that ethics needs to fit life, and that the relation between a mother and a child forms the essential basis for an ethics. Several criticisms of this approach to morality exist, including the idea that the theory idealizes motherhood and that not all mothers behave in an ethical manner toward their children (i.e., cases of neglect or abuse).

## Sara Ruddick and Maternal Ethics

In Ruddick's article *Maternal Thinking* in the journal *Feminist Studies*, she sets out the task for others of constructing an ethics based upon what she calls "maternal practices." Upon having a child, three maternal interests begin with the unselfish emotion of love. The first of these interests is rooted in preservation of the life of the child. The mother cares for the child, protecting her from potential harm. The second of these interests is fostering the growth of the child. This growth is physical, emotional, and intellectual. The final maternal interest is the ability of the child's peers to accept her child into their society upon the age of majority. It should be noted that these three interests sometimes conflict with one another. Perhaps an adventurous child wishes to skateboard with friends (growing a sense of independence) but the mother is afraid the child will face harm (the interest in preserving the child's life).

Because of this, various maternal practices arise, which coincide and respond to the unique interests. With the interest of preservation, the mother must avoid falling into the path of being fearful and controlling of the child. To avoid this (which is harmful to the growth and community acceptance of the child), the mother must practice humility (the idea that there are events beyond our control) and cheerfulness (a sense of humor in the irony of life). The second maternal interest, growth, coincides with the maternal practice of fostering the child's

growth. To do this, the mother will raise her child in a way that understands a child and her changing realities. Finally, the mother must take on the values exhibited by the culture she lives in to help her child gain acceptance into the peer group. This leads to the mother exhibiting obedience to the dominant societal values.

Finally, love and attention ground maternal practices. Ruddick pulls her notion of attention from French philosopher Simone Weil. Ruddick calls "attention" a capacity and "love" a virtue. This couplet has a tendency to undermine the final maternal practice, obedience, because they call into question who their children really are. If a mother blindly practices humility, obedience, cheerfulness, fostering, etc., then she will not know who her child is and may misguide her. By being attentive and loving, she then exhibits a knowledge of who that child is and can better rear the child to adulthood and acceptance.

## Virginia Held's Maternal Ethics

Unlike Ruddick, who argues that maternal ethics should extend into the public domain, Held posits that maternal ethics should govern private relationships. She claims that when brought into the moral realm, mothers and children exhibit an unequal relation. She also believes that this relationship should not stretch to cover all other relationships—in fact, Held believes that different relationships require different individual moral constructions to govern them. Her claim is that the history of ethics has been biased because a universal ethics attempts to cover too many situations being ambiguous about important questions of justice. Held critiques Ruddick's ethics for appearing to hold that maternal practices are unique to mothers—signaling for Held that mothers and nonmothers have different value systems.

It is precisely because of the inequity between mother and child that Held rejects the notion of extending maternal practices into the wide community. She believes that basing all ethics on a fundamentally skewed relationship would be detrimental to society. Mothers must apply discipline, she says, in order to avert the conflict that is inconsistent with the goals of parenting. While mothers should aim for peacefulness, some are violent, and the relationship is fundamentally an oppressive one. The main objection here is not the capacity for violence in unequal relationships, but rather Ruddick's wish to stretch maternal thinking to cover all potential relationships.

## Caroline Whitbeck and Others

Caroline Whitbeck emphasizes the physical, biological aspects of motherhood over the emotional aspects. In her thinking, the mother pays attention to details that men otherwise neglect. The reason for this is that the biological experience of giving birth creates a feeling of helplessness that men do not experience.

Eva Feder Kittay has another take on maternal ethics. She believes, much like Ruddick, that dependency relations are the fundamental starting point for formulating an ethic. This is because we can extract the notion of "our child" to "some mother's child" and apply this to each person we meet. By extending the maternal practices to any other situation where one needs to be cared for, a morality can be derived for equality. Naturally, this is contrary to Held's perspective. Kittay argues that maternal practice requires instructions for care to adapt to the child. Because the person receiving the care is vulnerable, then the caregiver can relate to a time when they were also vulnerable, and extend a hand to help. This position argues for a more universal view of ethics beginning with the mother and ending in social responsibility.

Cynthia Willett takes maternal ethics in a different direction, citing Hegel when she calls it a "slave morality." She uses this approach to demonstrate, with Hegel, the way that one can be moral while holding onto relationships. The master–slave relationship is one where the slave is dependent upon the master for a livelihood. However, Hegel turns this fundamental relationship on its head—calling attention to the idea that it is not just that the slave who is dependent upon the master, but the master is dependent upon the slave. Every time the master breaks bread at the dinner table, he is enjoying the fruits of the slave's labor. Through this intersubjective relationship, the two realize they have a mutual dependency. The master cannot exist without the slave.

The child–mother relationship is similar. The mother cannot be without a child and the child cannot be without the mother. The infant calls to the mother who must take care of it (becoming the slave to the master). At the same time, as that infant grows, he must respond to the mother's discipline and her attempts to mold the child into an adult. In that sense, the child is the slave and the mother is the master. Because of the inequality in the relationship, it is never the case that both child and mother are slave or master in relation to one another. The goal, according to Willett, is to have the child reach a point of self-mastery, where the mother no longer directs the life of the child. She takes this maternal ethic and applies it to developing countries and issues of social justice, arguing that those who are assisted should be able to reach a point where they can be masters of their own lives.

## Criticisms of Maternal Ethics

There are several criticisms of maternal ethics. First, it appears tenuous that one relationship (and a relationship of inequality) can form the basis for all other moral relationships, such as applying the same principles for relating to a child toward a husband. However, by abstracting each virtue—humility, fostering, and so forth—it becomes apparent that they are important components of any meaningful human relationship, the field is leveled.

A second possible criticism of maternal ethics is that the mother–child relationship has been idealized, and in the real world, mothers may abuse or neglect their children. This criticism also falls short, because it would apply to any ethical theory; ethics are not invalid simply because some people exhibit poor choices and do not live ethical lives. Similarly, virtue ethics, which forwards the exhibition of various virtues such as kindness, temperance, charity, are not any less virtuous simply because there are mean, gluttonous, or miserly people in the world. This argument can apply to defend maternal ethics as well.

A further criticism of maternal ethics is that men are left out of the equation. The argument follows the logic that many men (and adoptive or foster mothers) may be better parents than their biological counterparts. By claiming that maternal practices and ethics are the ideal, these important persons are left out. However, with the exception of Whitbeck, the rest of the theorists might hold that the reason these virtues are mother-centered is that our society is structured in such a way that mothers are associated with children and fathers are associated with work. If our society were set up in a different way, they might suggest, then fathers might have similar values and practices.

Regardless of whether one accepts maternal ethics as a universal theory for how we ought to govern our moral relationships with others, this branch of ethics is making headway along with ethics of care in feminist moral theory. By seeing the various aspects of motherhood as giving room for virtue, some theorists believe we can not only behave in ways that are ethical toward children, but also solve problems of development ethics, equal rights, and more, using the principals governing one of the fundamental life relationships.

**See Also:** Bad Mothers; Caregiving; Care Work; Daughters and Mothers; Ethics of Care; Feminism and Mothering; Feminist Mothering; Feminist Theory and Mothering; Idealization of Mothers; Maternal Practice; Maternal Thinking; Ruddick, Sara.

**Bibliography**

Brennan, Samantha and Robert Noggle. Taking Responsibility for Children. Waterloo, ON: Wilfrid Laurier University Press, 2007.
Held, Virginia. *Feminist Morality: Transforming Culture, Society, and Politics*. Chicago: University of Chicago Press, 1993.
Held, Virginia. *The Ethics of Care: Personal, Political, and Global*. New York: Oxford University Press, 2006.
Kittay, Eva Feder. *Love's Labor*. New York: Routledge, 1999.
Ruddick, Sara. "Maternal Thinking." *Feminist Studies*, v.6/2 (Summer 1980).
Ruddick, Sara. *Maternal Thinking: Toward a Politic of Peace*. Boston: Beacon Press (1989).
Tong, Rosemarie, and Nancy Williams. "Feminist Ethics." *Stanford Encyclopedia of Philosophy* (November 29, 2006). http://plato.stanford.edu/entries/feminism-ethics/#MatAppEth (accessed June 2009).
Willet, Cynthia. *Maternal Ethics and Other Slave Moralities*. New York: Routledge, 1995.

Ronda Lee Levine
Independent Scholar

# Ethics of Care

Early or traditional care perspectives viewed what is referred to as women's "ways of knowing"—how women perceive themselves and approach the world—as emerging from both women's care giving of and attentiveness to others, especially tending to the physical needs of children.

## Articulations of the Ethics of Care

Feminist scholars have articulated the ethics of care, particularly in Carol Gilligan's 1982 book *In a Different Voice: Psychological Theory and Women's Development*; Mary Field Belenky, Blythe McVicker Clinchy, Nancy Rule Goldberger, and Jill Mattuck Tarule's 1985 book *Women's Ways of Knowing: The Development of Self, Voice and Mind*; and Nel Noddings's 1984 book *Caring: A Feminine Approach to Ethics and Moral Education*. All three publications focus on "women's ways of knowing" and the subsequent moral decisions that follow. Feminist scholars argue that this way of knowing creates an "ethics of care" that values care giving of others and the practice of relating to and maintaining a connection with others.

## Characteristics of Ethical Caring

The characteristics most associated with caring as an ethical perspective are responsiveness, sensitivity to others, acceptance, and relatedness. Responsiveness to others includes responding to others to acknowledge, value, and affirm them, while also being careful to listen to and observe others to understand their behavior. Sensitivity to others means taking care to identify and attend to others' needs, desires, and perspectives, which is fundamentally about validating others. Acceptance entails allowing people to feel "psychologically safe" or free to communicate their wants, feelings, needs, and beliefs. Finally, relatedness emerges from a caregivers' view of the self as connected to or interdependent with others. This sense of interdependence requires a caregiver to act cooperatively or in relationship with others.

## Alternative to Moral Reasoning

In terms of moral reasoning, an ethics of care offers an alternative to moral reasoning grounded in justice, explained most notably Lawrence Kohlberg's work. Kohlberg argued that ethics of justice requires people to engage in moral decision making by carefully considering the abstract rights of the people involved and choosing the solution that seems to harm the least number of people. As a result, moral decision makers focus on an abstract, universal approach to moral decision making that seeks autonomy, fairness, and equality. Feminists argue that this is a masculine or male-biased mode of reasoning that is most often associated with "men's ways of knowing." Gilligan argued that she heard a "different voice" or way of knowing when she interviewed girls and young women about their moral decision making. Primarily based on her interviews with 29 women in their abortion decisions, Gilligan argued women ground moral reasoning via particular cases and in their relationships and responsibilities to others, rather than on universal principles. As such, Gilligan argued a care perspective is grounded in a context-based approach that works to maintain connections with others and prioritizes nurturing, caring relationships.

*As mothers are primary caregivers, feminists have argued that traditional ethics subjugates women into a nurturing role.*

## Critiques of Tradition

The traditional ethics of care was critiqued for its essentialism (the belief that there is a real, true essential nature for women or a biological femininity), the failure to attend to power issues embedded in caring, and its exclusion of men. In response, contemporary care proponents retain the characteristics of the traditional care perspective, but now suggest that ethics of care arises out of women's location as subordinates in culture, as well as that care arises out of particular, material, social, and historical conditions of women's subordinate positions in patriarchal culture.

Initial criticisms of traditional ethics of care focused on four key issues. First, from the beginning, feminist scholars argued that continuing to link care giving as primarily a feminine practice in the private sphere reinforced rather than challenged gender roles that subordinate women. As a result, feminists also argued the ethics of care excluded men from care giving and continued to dichotomize women and men and the care and justice perspectives. Second, feminist scholars also critiqued Gilligan's work and method in *A Different Voice*. Specifically, some feminists argued Gilligan

relied on very limited data—both a small number of participants and women who were fairly homogeneous in terms of race, class, and sexual orientation. Consequently, many believed Gilligan's generalizations from the data were unwarranted and too broad. Third, and related to the first and second concerns, many feminists were concerned that Gilligan's work (and other feminist care ethicists' work) was essentialist in that she generalized for all women the ways of knowing and thinking of a specific group of homogeneous women.

Fourth and finally, from its inception, feminists argued that when care ethicists grounded their work in the emotional dimensions of interpersonal relationships, this ethics of care focused too little on the social and political institutions that construct and constrain emotions and relationships. As such and related, by primarily focusing on women's emotional lives, feminists argued that care ethicists also seemed to suggest rationality, reasoning, and argumentation are somehow antithetical to caring. By doing so, care ethicists also seemed to reinforce patriarchal views of women as the "emotive gender" who do not or cannot employ reasoning because of those emotions.

## A Feminist Response

As feminist scholars began to respond to the criticisms of the care perspective, they began to ground caring in women's subordinate location in patriarchal culture. Unlike traditional care perspectives that tend to view women's ways of knowing as emerging from women's nature, more contemporary work views women's ways of knowing as emerging from women's subordinate location in patriarchal culture. Specifically, contemporary work argues that caring originates and emerges from power relations that position those with less power to care for or be attentive to those with higher status and power. This position continues to be primarily occupied by women, which means that caring continues to be a primary component of women's subordinate location. As a result, most contemporary feminist thinkers now view the ethics of care as arising out of particular, material, social, and historical conditions of women's subordinate positions in culture.

One significant implication of viewing caring in this way is that men are no longer precluded from showing care. Because contemporary understandings view gender differences, knowledge, and privilege as grounded in power relations that are socially constructed, all can be both learned and unlearned. As a result, knowledge and privilege can be unlearned, and perspectives of subordinates can be learned. Consequently, contemporary understandings of the ethics of care is argued to be more inclusive than the traditional perspective because it provides a theoretical rationale for viewing caring as arising from a social position that all people can learn and utilize. Moreover, when caregivers are situated within their social, historical, economic, and political realms, the foundations of moral reasoning and argumentation are also socially located in historical contexts.

## Using All Modes of Understanding

Several significant implications emerge as a result. First, the Enlightenment separation of reasoning from emotions and everyday contexts is rejected. Instead, such a reformulated view encourages the use of all modes of understanding: reasoning, emotions, narratives, argumentation, and empathy. As a result, both masculine and feminine modes of knowing and caring are encouraged. In this perspective, caregivers can simultaneously use reasoning and emotions, argumentation and empathy, and/or argumentation and narratives when they make moral decisions. Thus, more contemporary understandings of the ethics of care as grounded in women's subordinate position refuses to perpetuate and enact the separation of reasoning and argumentation from emotions and narratives that pervaded traditional views of caring.

**See Also:** Care Giving; Essentialism and Mothering; Maternal Thinking (Ruddick).

### Bibliography

Belenky, Mary R., Blythe Clinchy, Nancy Goldberger, and Jill Tarule. *Women's Ways of Knowing: The Development of Self, Voice, and Mind.* New York: Basic Books, 1986.
Gilligan, Carol. *A Different Voice: Psychological Theory and Women's Development.* Cambridge, MA: Harvard University Press, 1982.
Noddings, Nel. *Caring: A Feminine Approach to Ethics and Moral Education.* Berkeley: University of California Press, 1984.
Tong, Rosemarie. *Feminine and Feminist Ethics.* Belmont, CA: Wadsworth, 1993.
Wood, Julia T. *Who Cares? Women, Care, and Culture.* Carbondale: Southern Illinois University Press, 1993.

D. Lynn O'Brien Hallstein
Boston University

# Ethiopia

Ethiopian mothers are primarily rural and traditional. Commonly seen in Ethiopia are women carrying their babies on their backs, though sometimes a young girl may substitute for her mother and carry a younger sibling in the same manner. Ethiopian woman are responsible for the children, animals, and home, while the men generally have more freedom. Many Ethiopian women face daily challenges of poverty and disease: human immunodeficiency virus (HIV), malnutrition, and lack of access to clean water and quality health care are major problems in this east African country, the result of which is that many women suffer from poor maternal health. Just 10 percent of women give birth with a trained attendant, and the maternal mortality rate is a high 850 per 100,000 live births. Stillbirths are common, while the infant mortality rate in 2006 was 77 (down from 122 in 1990). The fertility rate is 5.3 percent, while the adolescent fertility rate is 94 per 1,000 girls. A low 15 percent of women in 2005 used contraception.

According to a report by Wairagala Wakabi in *The Lancet* in 2008, many girls are forced into marriage before they are 16. The result of this early marriage, combined with the resulting prolonged labor during childbirth, abuse, and female genital mutilation, is obstetric fistula—a hole in the vagina or rectum—which afflicts 9,000 girls and women each year. One bright spot for maternal health care in Ethiopia is improved treatment for fistula in dedicated hospitals and branches throughout the country.

## Maternity Leave, Health Care, and Beliefs

The government formally allows for 90 days of maternity leave with full wages paid by the employer, but many rural women cannot claim these benefits.

Many Ethiopian children are without mothers. According to United Nations Educational, Scientific and Cultural Organization (UNESCO), over 4 million Ethiopian children are orphans, which represents 12 percent of the entire population of children in Ethiopia, with over 2 million having lost their parents to HIV and acquired immunodeficiency syndrome (AIDS). 1.5 million people in Ethiopia are HIV positive, about 4.4 percent of the population. Of children under five who die in Ethiopia, about half die because of malnutrition and 20 percent because of diarrhea from contaminated water.

Ethiopian women also suffer from a lack of education, with a low literacy rate of 23 percent, compared to 50 percent for men. In 2007, 68 percent of girls were enrolled in primary school, but only 19 percent in secondary school. About 40 percent of Ethiopians are Muslim, and about half are Ethiopian Orthodox Christian. The government is secular but dominated by Christians.

The Ethiopian foundation myth holds that the Queen of Sheba, Ethiopia's monarch, visited King Solomon of Israel, a union that resulted in Mene-

lik I, the first king of Ethiopia, who, according to tradition, later traveled to Israel and stole the Ark of the Covenant from King Solomon to avenge his mother. Menelik brought the Ark of the Covenant back to Ethiopia, where, tradition says, it remains to this day, hidden within a monastery in Axum in northern Ethiopia.

**See Also:** AIDS/HIV and Mothering; Child Poverty; Eritrea; Family Planning.

### Bibliography

Taffa, Negussie and Francis Obare. "Pregnancy and Child Health Outcomes Among Adolescents in Ethiopia." *Ethiopian Journal of Health Development*, v18/2 (2004).
United Nations Children's Fund (UNICEF). "Ethiopia." http://www.unicef.org/infobycountry/ethiopia_12162.html (accessed January 2009).
United Nations Educational, Scientific and Cultural Organization (UNESCO) Institute for Statistics. "Ethiopia." http://www.uis.unesco.org/template/pdf/scb/DiagnosticReports/Ethiopia_Diagnostic_E.pdf (accessed January 2009).
Wakabi, Wairagala. "Ethiopia Steps Up Fight Against Fistula." *The Lancet*, v.371/9623 (May 2008).
Wax, Emily. "A Crushing Choice for Ethiopia Mothers With HIV." *The Washington Post* (February 19, 2005).
World Health Organization. "Ethiopia." http://www.who.int/countries/eth/eth/en (accessed June 2009).

Joan Petit
Portland State University

# Ethnic Mothers

The term *ethnic* is often used to describe members of a nonwhite cultural/racial group. An ethnic group applies to people who share a common racial background. As such, ethnic mothers are nonwhite women who comprise this group. The word ethnic has also historically been used to connote difference to a dominant cultural/racial group. Ethnic mothers may also be referred to as women of color, racial ethnic women, or minority women.

## Factors That Influence Experience

To better understand the experiences of ethnic mothers, feminist scholars of color have argued that one must take into account factors such as race/ethnicity, social class, sexuality, and gender, which will impact how a woman mothers her children. For ethnic women, gender alone does not form the basis of their identity; rather, it is a combination of race/ethnicity, gender, and socioeconomic status that affects their experiences and the process of identity formation, as numerous scholars have argued. Different meanings and values are associated with mothering and motherhood in any given racial-ethnic group. According to scholars, an ethnic woman from a working-class or poor background who lives in a country where a dominant racial group is established will mother her children as she experiences this life.

To study this group of mothers, their race, gender, sexuality, and socioeconomic background must be analyzed as inextricable from each other. These scholars have noted that the majority of motherhood studies have omitted ethnic mothers from their work, leaving much theorizing to be done in this area. They claim that many studies of motherhood are framed from the perspective of Anglo, middle-class mothers and do not take into account the vast differences between mothers. Feminist scholars of color, however, have made great strides to discuss the complex interplay between ethnicity, gender, and socioeconomic background in their studies on motherhood.

In a great majority of ethnic cultures, mothers are tasked with the responsibility of the caretaking and socializing of their children. Mothers in many ethnic cultures, such as Mexicans and other Latinos, are seen as cultural transmitters and preservers of the family and its cultural ideals. Ethnic mothers will go to lengths to teach their children how to live and survive in an environment that may be harsh to children of color, as feminist scholars have noted. In some cases, ethnic mothers may encourage their children to assimilate to the dominant culture in order to "fit in" and ease the acculturation process. Not all ethnic mothers encourage their children to assimilate, however. For some ethnic immigrant mothers, preserving cultural traditions, even those considered to be patriarchal and oppressive to women, is viewed as a way to combat racial and economic oppression. Many factors determine whether an ethnic mother will encourage assimilation or resistance to the dominant culture, including ethnicity, social condition, form of worship, and region.

## Ethnic Mother–Daughter Relationship

Feminist scholars of color have shown an increased interest in the relationship between ethnic mothers and their daughters and the myriad issues that affect this maternal bond. For ethnic women, the mother is the most important figure in a daughter's quest for identity formation. In many ethnic cultures, the mother is viewed as her daughter's role model, as she aids her daughter in the rather difficult process of self-identity.

The mother may be a source of comfort for a daughter who is alienated by racism and sexism in the outside world, or in some cases she may be an obstacle and a source of added conflict. Tension and resentment may arise between mothers and daughters when ethnic mothers within patriarchal cultures teach their daughters that subservience to men and patriarchy is their female duty and obligation. Research indicates that daughters of these mothers may choose to rebel against their mothers in favor of the dominant culture's views, which they perceive as more liberal and favorable to them as women. Daughters of ethnic mothers who encourage obedience see their mothers as complicit with sexism. The mother–daughter relationship has been described as conflicted by a number of researchers who examine the ethnic mother's struggle in raising a daughter who refuses to abide by cultural beliefs that encourage female passivity and obedience to male authority.

Mothers in patriarchal ethnic cultures may reinforce oppressive views and pass them on to their daughters. Cultures that regard daughters as less valuable or worthy than sons will often make mothers responsible for the gendered socialization of children. Ethnic mothers of sons will reinforce their superiority and privilege, while teaching daughters to accept their subordinate position. This is especially the case with ethnic cultures that are heavily influenced by religions that place great emphasis on moral behavior in women. Many social scientists have suggested that the Catholic Church has some influence on Latina mother–daughter relations because of the strict value placed on female modesty and virginity, attributes Latina mothers are expected to pass on to their daughters.

However, some scholars have noted that not all ethnic mothers socialize their daughters to be passive receptacles of male domination. Certain ethnic mothers, such as African American women, for example, have been shown to teach their daughters how to resist oppression by men within their culture as well as how to fight racial oppression from the dominant culture. Although long deemed as traditional by some social scientists, Latina and Asian mothers have also been shown to teach their daughters the necessary tools to fight various forms of oppression. Thus, it is impossible to state that ethnic mothers raise their daughters in one universal way. Some ethnic mothers will teach daughters complicity with racism and sexism as a mode of survival, while other ethnic mothers show their daughters how to protect themselves by fighting back.

## Meanings of Ethnic Motherhood

In a great deal of ethnic cultures such as the African American, Latino, and Native American cultures, the caretaking of children is a combined effort, wherein nonbiological members of the community and/or extended family will assist the biological mother. Termed *other mothers* by some scholars and theorists, these nonbiological women help to raise children in their racial-ethnic community when biological mothers work long hours away from home, become ill, or are otherwise unable to attend to their families. Motherwork for some ethnic cultures is community-oriented, and the care of a child is viewed as the responsibility of all. Ethnic mothers throughout the United States and abroad rely on these extended-support networks to help care for their children. Ethnic mothers living in cities with large immigrant populations have created social networks not only to share childrearing responsibilities, but also to provide information or even advice to mothers in their community.

Some ethnic cultures view motherhood as central to the overall survival and well-being of the family, community, or tribe. Certain indigenous groups in the Americas, for example, value motherhood and maternity, granting mothers a high degree of

agency and power within their respective groups, and often rely on mothers for wisdom and leadership. Motherhood within African American communities has also been viewed by scholars and theorists as a mode of empowerment for black people as a whole. In this light, it is possible to see the ways in which meanings of motherhood and mothering vary greatly among ethnicities and cultures.

## Economic Status

Statistics have shown that a larger percentage of ethnic mothers comprise a working-class economic background and tend to work outside the home in greater numbers than white women. For many ethnic mothers, work is not a male-only responsibility, but is deemed as a necessary part of a mother's responsibility to ensure her family's survival. Because of their historical working-class and poor economic background, paid employment for ethnic mothers has for the most part been a fact of life. There is also a higher rate of women-headed, single-parent households among ethnic women than white women. Several studies show that many, but not the majority, of African American women are single mothers.

Poverty persists among ethnic women who head households. Statistics have reported that ethnic women such as Latinas in the United States tend to have a higher fertility rate than white women, African American women, and Asian American women. Social scientists have noted that ethnic women in the United States on average have lower educational levels and comprise a great deal of the lowest-paid, lowest-skilled jobs in the country. Asian women in the United States tend to have higher-paying, professional careers and higher educational levels, particularly among Japanese, Chinese, and Filipino women, than other ethnic women. Ethnic women remain among the most economically disadvantaged groups in the United States, which may be a long-term, residual effect of slavery for African American women, according to some historians and social scientists. Similarly for Latinas and Native American women, the takeover of their lands throughout the 18th and 19th centuries by Anglo settlers and the United States government has had a long-lasting impact on the economic status of these women.

## Health Issues

There are also health disparities that must be considered when examining the lives of ethnic mothers. Statistics have reported that Mexican American women tend to have double the chance of having cancer by age 44 than white women. Latina women, particularly Mexican American women living in the United States, tend to be uninsured, have less access to health care and preventive care, and have higher mortality rates. Undoubtedly, the economic status of ethnic mothers influences their likelihood of having health insurance and access to health care. Ethnic mothers living in poverty face numerous challenges, economic and health disparities being among the most significant. Language barriers are also a factor in accessing preventive care, especially among non-English-speaking women. Women who do not speak English have a much more difficult time finding medical and health services for themselves and their children. Ethnic mothers in low-paying jobs may not have access to health insurance through their employers. When researching and examining the socioeconomic conditions of ethnic mothers, it is clear that the issue of health disparities is one area that significantly affects quality of life and mothering patterns.

## Racial and Sexual Discrimination

In addition, scholars have noted that although ethnic mothers have distinct lives and experiences, many ethnic mothers share a history of racial and sexual discrimination in countries where white, Anglo dominance has prevailed. For example, in the early half of the 20th century in the United States, Chinese and other Asian women were often stereotyped as "cold" mothers who did not nurture or love their children. It was quite common for newspapers of that era to depict ethnic mothers as "bad" women who were responsible for high rates of crime and violence in cities. Ethnic mothers were also depicted as sexually promiscuous, irresponsible mothers. African American mothers were simultaneously portrayed as stereotypical "Mammy" figures on one hand, while overbearing and exceedingly proud on the other. Latin American mothers, particularly Mexican mothers, were often described by early social scientists as extremely passive, obedient, martyr-like figures.

As contemporary scholars have argued, these stereotypes of ethnic mothers as bad, cold, or passive served to reinforce strict racial and gender divisions. Stereotypes of bad mothers were used to rationalize and justify gender and racial hierarchies. To this day, ethnic mothers have been among those blamed by media outlets for issues ranging from gang violence to mental illness. Thus, ethnic motherhood has historically been deemed to be in direct contrast to idealized, white motherhood. While white motherhood was often romanticized in the early half of the 20th century by Anglo journalists and writers, ethnic motherhood was harshly criticized by the media and social scientists of that time.

A 1965 report written by Daniel Moynihan, for example, used the supposed matriarchal structure of black families as the basis to explain the poverty rates among African Americans. black mothers were blamed for pathological traits that he said existed among African American families, in addition to other societal ills such as crime, unwed pregnancy, violence, and high dropout rates. Numerous studies conducted on Latino families in the United States by Anglo scientists argued that Latina mothers were weak-minded, obedient, and resistant to assimilation and change. Many ethnic mothers in early studies were presumed to be victims of emotional and physical abuse from their husbands and fathers, who were also stereotyped as violent and excessively domineering toward women.

As contemporary feminist historians and other social scientists have examined, this ongoing criticism of ethnic mothers was clearly demonstrated during the early 1970s in the United States in what is now known as *eugenics*. During this time, the federal government authorized and sanctioned the sterilization of numerous African American, Latina, Native American, and poor white women, usually without their knowledge and/or consent. Because ethnic mothers were depicted as having unusually large families and being overly reliant on federal programs such as welfare and Medicaid, sterilization was seen as a solution to limit the increasing number of children born to these women. Ethnic mothers were labeled by doctors, practitioners, and government representatives as undesirable or unfit mothers. Feminist scholars of the eugenics movement point out that factors such as race/ethnicity, economic background, and number of children would determine whether a woman was deemed fit or not to be a mother.

## The 1960s: Starting to Fight Back

The racially and politically turbulent years of the 1960s, however, would brought about an active response by ethnic women and mothers to the racialized, sexualized representations of them made by the media and social scientists. The participation of black women in the Civil Rights Movement of this decade eventually contributed to the passage of the 1964 Civil Rights Act, which prohibited racial discrimination in the workforce. This Act granted black women much-needed security in the workforce in order to better provide for their families. The Chicano Movement of the 1960s also witnessed participation from women, many of whom were mothers. One segment of the movement, the farmworkers' strike in Delano, California, was led by César Chávez and Dolores Huerta, who was a mother of 11 children. Huerta contributed a maternal presence to the farmworkers' movement, as she discussed the substandard working conditions forced upon pregnant and nursing migrant farmworking women. Huerta pressed for better working conditions for all farmworkers, particularly Mexican women.

The 1960s was a decade of increased political consciousness among Native American as well, with many women, including mothers, creating the American Indian Movement and other organizations to protest unequal treatment of Native American people. Yet, feminist scholars have examined how women participating in racial protest movements such as the Black Power Movement, Chicano Movement, and American Indian Movement faced sexism among their male ethnic counterparts. Women in these movements were often relegated to secondary tasks such as cooking and cleaning for male activists. Ethnic activist women thus vocalized gender politics that were in play in these movements that ultimately viewed race and social class as more pressing factors of oppression rather than gender.

## Challenging Maternal Myths and Stereotypes

The 1981 publication of the groundbreaking anthology *This Bridge Called My Back,* edited by

Gloria Anzaldúa, Cherríe Moraga, and Toni Cade Bambara, attested to the ambiguous place occupied by ethnic woman. Contributors to this anthology, many of whom were mothers, discussed the racism faced in dominant society, in addition to the sexism experienced within the private home and racial-ethnic community to which they belonged. Ethnic mothers voiced their experiences with this triple oppression of being ethnic and working-class women in an Anglo-dominant culture. Some ethnic women, including Cherríe Moraga, offered her own critique of Mexican/Chicana motherhood, arguing for a dismantling of the myth of suffering motherhood in favor of a strong, politicized bond between mothers and daughters of color. The ethnic mothers featured in *This Bridge* anthology and others of that decade and in later years began to challenge maternal myths and stereotypes that existed in the dominant culture and their own respective racial-ethnic groups. In challenging these maternal myths, ethnic mothers attempted to construct their own maternal theories free from racist, sexist undertones. Ethnic mothers have challenged ideals of womanhood and motherhood that do not account for the many differences among women.

## Ethnic Mother Activism Worldwide

There is an extensive history of mother activism outside the United States as well. Ethnic mothers within the United States and abroad have used their motherhood as a mode of activism to protest living conditions in their community at the grassroots level, while some mothers have become activists on a much higher scale in order to protest oppressive governmental policies and practices. Feminist scholars have increasingly discussed the ways motherhood has been a site of political resistance and mobility for ethnic women. Ethnic mothers have protested wars as well as fought for reproductive rights, improved housing, better access to health care and education for their children, and improved economic conditions for their communities and families.

In one of the most well-known examples of a maternal protest movement in Latin America, mothers in Argentina became known as Las Madres de la Plaza de Mayo (Mothers of the Plaza de Mayo) for protesting the military dictatorship that controlled

*African American mothers and their children participate in one of the 1965 civil rights marches in Alabama from Selma to Montgomery. These marches were part of the voting rights movement, started by Amelia Boynton (1911– ) and her husband Bill.*

the country between 1976 and 1983. The Argentine military dictatorship was responsible for the disappearance of thousands of Argentineans who were labeled as subversive and threatening to the regime. The mothers of these disappeared Argentines stand on the Plaza de Mayo facing the presidential palace as a means to protest the loss of their children, many of whom remain missing. To this day, many Madres continue this weekly vigil.

In Ciudad Juárez, Chihuahua, Mexico, hundreds of mothers have spoken out and have marched weekly to raise awareness of the thousands of young girls and women who have been raped, beaten, and killed along this Mexican border city located just feet away from El Paso, Texas. They have formed groups such as *¡Ni Una Más!* (Not One More) and Nuestras Hijas de Regreso a Casa (Return Our Daughters Home) for mothers of dead or missing daughters. The mothers have also continued to criticize what they perceive as the inadequacy and

unwillingness of the Mexican government and local police's to solve the murders and stop the killing of women. The mothers have remained vocal despite the danger involved in pointing out the possibility of police corruption and involvement in the killings of their daughters.

Women in Israel have also used their motherhood as a basis to organize peace efforts in the 1980s, a time of war and conflict in that country and the neighboring region. Dubbed the Mothers Against Silence by the Israeli media, mothers in this movement began to protest as concerned mothers of their military sons following the country's invasion of Lebanon. Mothers in this movement received much media attention for using motherhood as a mode of political mobilization. Mother activism in Palestine was visible during wartime as well, most notably following the occupation of the Gaza Strip. Motherhood was seen as an appropriate, acceptable way to politicize their concerns.

## Visibility of Ethnic Mothers

The subject of motherhood continues to be a significant theme addressed by ethnic women today. The visibility of ethnic mothers has especially been prevalent in the arts, government, politics, and even sports. The election of Barack Obama as President of the United States in November 2008 has made his wife Michelle perhaps the most well-known African American mother in the world. Ethnic women who are mothers have also been elected and appointed in a number of high-ranking governmental positions throughout the globe, forging a union between politics and motherhood that has been unheard of in previous decades and centuries before.

Motherhood as a literary theme has been incredibly visible in fiction written by women of color, many of whom happen to be mothers as well. Chicana literature by prominent writers and mothers such as Ana Castillo, Alma Luz Villanueva, and Helena María Viramontes use motherhood and maternity as a central theme in order to shed light on the contemporary Chicana mother's struggle to create her own concept of mothering. Women writers of color, including Amy Tan, Maxine Hong Kingston, Toni Morrison, and Alice Walker, have constructed complex mothers in their works that sharply contrast and belie the stereotypical portrayals of mothers that dominated early 20th-century newspapers and social scientific literature. In addition to fictional works, ethnic motherhood and maternity have been popular subjects of literary criticism by scholars of color. While ethnic motherhood is still considered to be an underinvestigated area, women scholars of color have made major contributions to scholarship on motherhood. Scholars now view motherhood as an institution that cannot and should not be examined as universal, but rather, as socially and culturally constructed and ever-changing across generations and time.

**See Also:** Activist Mothering; African American Mothers; Chicana Mothering; Class and Mothering; Literature, Mothers in; Myths of Motherhood: Good/Bad; Working-Class Mothers.

### Bibliography

Anderson, Karen. *Changing Woman: A History of Racial Ethnic Women in Modern America*. New York: Oxford University Press, 1996.

Bell-Scott, Patricia, et al. *Double Stitch: Black Women Write About Mothers & Daughters*. Boston: Beacon Press, 1991.

Castillo, Ana. *Massacre of the Dreamers: Essays on Xicanisma*. New York: Plume, 1994.

Collins, Patricia Hill. "Shifting the Center: Race, Class, and Feminist Theorizing About Motherhood." In *Mothering: Ideology, Experience, and Agency*, Evelyn Nakano Glenn, et al., eds. New York: Routledge, 1994.

Glenn, Evelyn Nakano, et al. *Mothering: Ideology, Experience, and Agency*. New York: Routledge, 1994.

Ho, Wendy. *In Her Mother's House: The Politics of Asian-American Mother-Daughter Writing*. Lanham, MD: AltaMira Press, 1999.

Jetter, Alexis, et al. *The Politics of Motherhood: Activist Voices From Left to Right*. Lebanon, NH: University Press of New England, 1997.

*Journal of the Association for Research on Mothering*. Mothering, Race, Ethnicity, Culture, Class [special issue], v.9/2 (Fall/Winter 2007).

Zinn, Maxine Baca and Bonnie Thornton Dill. *Women of Color in U.S. Society*. Philadelphia: Temple University Press, 1994.

Cristina Herrera
California State University, Fresno

# Eugenics

Eugenics refers to a theoretical perspective developed in the late 19th century by a English mathematician named Sir Francis Galton. The theory posited that in order to create a human population without flaws, humanity could be preserved through selective breeding and the discouragement of reproduction from those humans perceived to have undesirable traits. Selective breeding and infanticide have both been terms associated with eugenics and motherhood. The term and the definition were heavily accepted by the upper and middle classes, primarily in the United States. Application of the theory was attempted in the early 20th century within the United States and later adopted by Adolf Hitler, demonstrated through eugenics experiments during World War II.

## Eugenics Movement's Impact on Motherhood

The Eugenics Movement that took place in the early 20th century in the United States as well as many historically British protectorates, including South Africa and India, strongly influenced certain women to become mothers, primarily upper-middle-class Caucasian women. In certain circles in the United States, the Eugenics Movement was viewed as an awakening of the power of women. Upper- and middle-class women were told they were now responsible for the future of mankind. They were advised to find suitable matches to provide offspring that were of acceptable and appealing demeanor, who had a higher genetic makeup than lower-class individuals—primarily referring to immigrants. Those who came from a northern European background were considered to be of the highest genetic makeup. Laws were created in numerous states that forbid interracial marriage; certain races were not considered genetically sound. At this juncture in history, many women were willing to be cast as heroines, responsible for proliferation of a better society; they were able to now choose their mate and afforded a power not attainable prior to this period in history.

Due to the Eugenics Movement, women were considered to be essential to the procreation of the perfect race and were validated as the essential gender, enabling the destiny of the human population. The eugenics message implied that women needed to stay home and be mothers for the benefit of society. The message was circulated at houses of worship and meeting houses, and written about in articles in local newspapers.

Changing social factors during the early 20th century in the United States helped to catapult men to advocate for the Eugenics Movement. During industrialization, women were beginning to seek opportunities for themselves, the birth rate declined, upper-middle-class women were seeking to attend colleges, a greater incidence of abortions (though illegal) was documented, and the use of birth control increased. Women were engaging in more dominant behaviors; this indicated upheaval for a male-dominated society and a need to repress female independence.

Many feminists were quiet regarding the issue of eugenics, as it did afford some choice for certain populations of women. Yet, a small group of American feminists of the early 20th century, mostly those who engaged in the Suffragette Movement, were opposed to the eugenics philosophy. Feminists recognized that the "positive" aspect that enabled certain women to choose their mate for procreation at the same time disenfranchised women of lower-class status. Lower-class women were expected to choose not to procreate for the sake of creating a pure race. For early feminists, the Eugenics Movement repressed all women by not encouraging, nor permitting, women to be independent, work outside of the home, or have an influence on their own outcomes in life. It also established a mechanism for keeping women out of the workplace as well as diminishing the likelihood of the ability of individual groups—such as immigrants, African Americans, and Native Americans—to gain employment that would take jobs away from Anglo male populations.

Additionally, women who were deemed to have inferior traits were made to believe that they should not have the right to procreate. Individual states sought laws to sterilize certain groups of women. Young women with disabilities were often taken by their parents to be sterilized so as to preclude any possibility of continuing an inferior bloodline; those parents were looked upon as upstanding citizens within the society. Some women with physical disabilities engaged in self-sacrifice by selecting to be sterilized, and were considered to be "champions of society." Children who were found to have disabilities or uncharacteristic traits were often hidden in their homes by their mothers for fear of reprisal from being an unfit mother; motherhood was not to be celebrated unless the mother produced an offspring of promising genetic attributes. Some researchers believe that eugenics still exists in a more subtle form today.

**See Also:** Eugenic Ideology; History of Motherhood: 1900 to Present; Reproductive Morality; Selective Reproduction; Sterilization; Voluntary Motherhood.

**Bibliography**
Kline, W. *Building a Better Race: Gender, Sexuality, and Eugenics From the Turn of the Century to the Baby Boom.* Berkeley: University of California Press, 2001.

Robb, G. "Eugenics, Spirituality, and Sex Differentiation in Edwardian England: The Case of Frances Swiney." *The Journal of Women's History*, v.10 (1998).

Sanger, A. "Eugenics, Race, and Margaret Sanger Revisited: Reproductive Freedom for All?" *Hypatia*, v.22/2 (2007).

Selden, S. *Inheriting Shame: The Story of Eugenics in America*. New York: Teachers College Press, 1999.

Barbara Schwartz-Bechet
Bowie State University

# European Union

The European Union (EU), as a unique political body, can be said to be committed to promoting gender equality in a supranational environment, and this includes concern for enabling women and men to reconcile their occupational and family responsibilities arising from the care of children. While EU member states share a broad legal framework and have signed up to the same social standards in relation to motherhood, much variation is still to be found between them as a result of historical, cultural, and continuing institutional difference.

Some countries, particularly those with a pro-natalist history such as France and Sweden, have extensive legislation facilitating the combining of work and family life for mothers. Others, such as Austria, the Netherlands, and Germany, offer large financial supports to mothers to promote their remaining out of the labor market for longer periods. Other countries, such as Ireland and the United Kingdom, often only comply with minimum standards (often unpaid provisions) set by EU legislation and largely see provision of childcare as a matter of private responsibility. There is some evidence in the recent Organisation for Economic Co-operation and Development (OECD) publication *Babies and Bosses* that some member states with effective reconciliation policies for both women and men have not only higher fertility rates, but also a higher female labor force participation rate and thus higher employment rates. Despite this, on average, fertility rates remain below replacement level across the EU.

## Impact on Motherhood

Membership of the EU impacts motherhood in a number of ways. A series of legally binding directives concerning maternity demand compliance from member states. The existing EU law, which dates from 1992, provides for a minimum of 14 continuous weeks of maternity leave, including two compulsory weeks before the birth. At the time of writing, there are plans to extend this to 18 weeks. This length of time is considered appropriate to help the worker to recover from the immediate effects of giving birth, while also making it easier for her to return to the labor market at the end of her maternity leave.

Mothers (and fathers) are also granted a minimum of three months unpaid parental leave under the Parental Leave Directive of 1996. EU law specifies minimum requirements and many member states exceed these. For example, the duration of maternity leave varies from 14 weeks in a small number of member states to 28 weeks in others, and in certain circumstances up to 52 weeks, not all of which is paid. EU law also lays down requirements on health and safety at the workplace to protect pregnant workers and workers who have recently given birth or are breastfeeding.

A woman cannot be dismissed during maternity leave. A woman has the right, after her maternity leave, to return to the same or an equivalent post. According to the same provision, less favorable treatment of a woman related to pregnancy or maternity leave constitutes discrimination.

## EU Composite and Social Model

The EU consists of 27 member states, and this number is likely to increase. The original members dating from 1958 are Belgium, France, West Germany, Italy, Luxembourg, and the Netherlands. Membership increased to 12 members by 1995, and also included Denmark, Ireland, and the United Kingdom (1973); Greece (1981); Portugal and Spain (1986); and Austria, Finland, and Sweden (1995). In 2005, Cyprus, Czech Republic, Estonia, Hungary, Latvia, Lithuania, Malta, Poland, Slovakia, and Slovenia joined the EU. In 2007, Romania and Bulgaria became the newest members. Croatia, Macedonia, and Turkey are official candidates.

While there has been some considerable debate on the extent to which there is a common European social model, centralizing institutions of the EU such as the European Commission have expressed their commitment to promoting gender equality; the issue has been firmly on the agenda of the European Community since the 1980s.

There are also many examples of ways, as discussed by Linda Hantrais, in which a legal commitment to equality can be traced even further back to the early years of the European Economic Community.

There are strong arguments that the EU has promoted gender equality in countries that otherwise would not have had the issue on their domestic agendas. However, female control over fertility and access to reproductive technologies still varies widely between member states. There is no common abortion policy in the EU, although an EU citizen denied an abortion in her own country can freely travel to a member state where it is legal. Abortion is illegal in Ireland, Poland, and Malta.

## Demographics of the EU

Official EU statistics are provided by its official statistics agency, Eurostat. The birth rate in Europe is currently below replacement rate. On average, European women have fewer than two children. The average age of women giving birth for the first time was 28 years in 2007. The trend is for women and men to marry later; in 2003, the average age of first marriage for women in the EU as a whole was 27.4 years.

A growing percentage of live births are outside marriage. In the EU, this trend has been increasing in almost every country, and in some, mostly in northern Europe, it already accounts for the majority. Southern European countries are less affected by this phenomenon. Much of this is linked to an increase in cohabitation, but lone motherhood is common in many countries. Women living with a dependent child are especially vulnerable to being at risk of poverty, except those living in the three Nordic countries.

With regard to female labor market participation, the proportion of men of working age in employment exceeds that of women across the EU. In 2006, 57 percent of women aged 15–64 were in paid employment, as compared with 72 percent of men in the same age group. However, the proportion of women of working age in employment varied in the EU, from 73 percent in Denmark and 71 percent in Sweden, to just over 46 percent in Italy and only 35 percent in Malta. European time-use studies confirm that women across the EU spend more time than men on all domestic work except gardening and household maintenance, particularly on cooking, washing, and cleaning as well as childcare.

**See Also:** Employment and Motherhood; Fathers and Fathering; Fertility; Maternity Leave; Pronatalism; Sweden; United Kingdom.

**Bibliography**

Eurostat. *The Life of Women and Men in Europe—A Statistical Portrait.* Luxembourg: Eurostat Statistical Books, 2008.

Hantrais, L. *Social Policy in the European Union.* Basingstoke, UK: Macmillan, 2000.

Lanzieri, G. "Population in Europe 2007: First Results." *Population and Social Conditions: Eurostat Statistics in Focus,* v.81 (2008).

McCormick, John. *The European Union: Politics and Policies.* Boulder, CO: Westview Press, 2007.

Organisation for Economic Co-operation and Development (OECD). "Babies and Bosses: OECD Recommendations to Help Families Balance Work and Family Life." Policy Brief. Paris: OECD, 2008.

Organisation for Economic Co-operation and Development (OECD). "Balancing Work and Family Life: Helping Parents Into Paid Employment." *Employment Outlook* (2001).

Smith Koslowski, A. *Who Cares? European Fathers and the Time They Spend Looking After Their Children.* Saarbrücken, Germany: VDM Verlag, 2008.

Alison Smith Koslowski
University of Edinburgh, Scotland

# Fairy Tales, Mothers in

Fairy tales represent the full range of loving and caring mothers, from those who protect, nurture, and sacrifice themselves for their children, to those acting carelessly, irritably, or with favoritism. They usually teach morality and life lessons, although at times the mother sets herself up as a rival beauty to her daughter. Alternate mother figures, particularly stepmothers, are frequently shown, since mothers often died early, especially in childbirth. Any orphaned child left in the care of the father's second wife was not preferred over her own children; similarly, mothers-in-law often show little fondness for their charges. The stark simplicity of folk tales exposes people's weaknesses, whether they protect or exploit the person closest to them, such as stepchild or sister's child.

## Sociological Representations of Mothers

Ordinary mothers seldom appear in fairy tales. More common are stepmothers (often wicked) and fairy godmothers (usually benevolent). The stepmother embodies the threat or challenge which the heroine must overcome. For instance, in *Cinderella*, the father's second wife treats Cinderella like a servant while favoring her own daughters and providing them with an entry into privileged society.

The fairy godmother is a type of donor figure who offers the hero or heroine of the story magical assistance to allow them to complete their quest or fulfill their destiny. The fairy godmother in *Cinderella* provides Cinderella with beautiful clothing, servants, and a coach so that she may attend the ball and meet the prince whom she will marry.

Many scholars believe similar fairy tales exist in many cultures because they treat basic facts about human existence and allow contemplation of aspects of human behavior, which are too horrifying to consider realistically. It is interesting to note that in early versions of some fairy tales, the mother, rather than the stepmother, was the villain, but this was changed to make the stories more acceptable for children.

## Themes of Protection, Sacrifice, and Wisdom

In the Scottish folktale *The Stolen Bairn and the Sidh*, when a mother seeking water for her child falls over a cliff, she is saved, but her child is taken by the fairies. In order to retrieve him, she makes a "white cloak of Nechtan" and a "golden stringed harp of Wrad" from materials on the beach and her own hair, braving the fairies and clinging to these barter goods until she has her son back. In the Iroquois folktale *The Vampire Skeleton*, a vampire emerges

*The fairy tale* The Old Woman in the Shoe *may have referred to Queen Caroline, wife of King George II, who had eight children.*

from his cedar coffin and eats the father, although the mother had warned him not to sleep there, and she desperately escapes with her child to the next village. In the Irish folktale *The Horned Women*, when witches possess a woman's house, she saves her family and breaks the witches' spells by having her family eat the cakes made with their own blood and by blocking the house against the witches' further entry. Another mother in the Korean tale *The Tiger and the Coal Peddler's Wife* rises from her own birthing to open the door to a tiger, to whom she throws two newborn puppies; but taking pity on her dog's last puppy, she wraps a burning coal and throws that to the tiger as food, thereby destroying him.

In *The Three Spinners*, the Brothers Grimm (German), when the mother is asked why she is beating her lazy daughter, the mother lies to cover her daughter's laziness, saying she spins constantly, whereupon the daughter is taken off to the palace to work.

The Grimm's *Looking for a Bride* shows the mother's sound advice in helping her shepherd son choose a bride by observing the way the girls eat cheese. In another Brothers Grimm tale, *The Twelve Brothers*, the mother is unable to prevent the father from sacrificing their 12 sons for the new daughter, warning the youngest son of their fate and showing him the prepared coffins. When the daughter learns of her brothers, she goes out to save them, but inadvertently turns them into ravens by picking their flowers. She marries the king, and endures being mute and not laughing for seven years in order to save them from this transformation, while the king's mother condemns her to death. The allotted time completed, she finally defends herself against the "wicked stepmother," her mother-in-law, as her brothers are restored to human shape.

The Grimms' *Snow-White and Rose-Red* features a poor widow bringing up her two daughters in an exemplary fashion, teaching them to navigate the wood independently, and encouraging them to share with the friendly bear as well as the rude dwarf who is the bear's master, thereby enabling the bear's transformation back into a prince. When the girls marry, their old mother shares their home happily for years. There have been several varients of *Little Red Riding Hood*, but French writer Charles Perrault's 1697 version shows a caring mother: ". . . beyond reason excessively fond of her, and her grandmother yet much more . . ." who advises her daughter caution before she walks through the woods to grandmother.

The Grimms' version, *Little Red Cap*, has the girl help the huntsman fill the predatory wolf's stomach with stones, and later the grandmother helps her learn crisis management after her initial mistakes of wandering off the path and talking to strangers or wolves, as they trap the wolf down the chimney on a subsequent attack. In the Spanish folktale *The Singing Sack*, a daughter is trapped in a sack by a man who asks her to sing as he carries her along. When she sings out her own story, her mother learns her daughter's fate, and rescues her by showing the man hospitality. She then cunningly replaces her daughter with a cat and dog in the sack while he is sleeping, earning him a scratched and bitten face.

In *The Story of the Female Shaman*, the mother is divided between her duties for another sick child and her own son, who dies while she visits the other boy, but she determinedly pursues her son into death and outwits the monster who has taken him until she restores both her child and herself to life. In *The Woman, Her Husband, Their Children and the Dodo*, the Nigerian mother successfully brings home fowl, fish, and corn, but each time her husband tries to help her, he spoils her goods, requiring her to find new resources. When he foolishly brings home the *dodo* or ghoul with him, she gains the help of a mouse in outmaneuvering and escaping from the dodo, defending them all safely from attack.

In most versions of *Cinderella* the dead mother returns to protect her child after her own death, for example, in the Grimms' version the mother returns as a bird to grant her wishes. In the Lang version, she comes as a calf to supply her needs, but the stepmother butchers her in order to weaken Cinderella, although her mother continues to help her.

In the Grimms' *The Goose Girl*, a loving widowed queen sends off her daughter with one servant to marry in another kingdom. The mother gives her a handkerchief containing drops of her blood, but when the princess has to dismount to drink water, she loses the magical handkerchief, thereby falling into her servant's power, who replaces her.

The refrain of both handkerchief and her beheaded horse, Falada, is: "If this your mother knew, her heart would break in two," which enables her to maintain her morale until she eventually regains her rightful position through oblique remarks to the king.

When the father in the Grimms' *The Girl Without Hands* carelessly promises a stranger whatever is behind their mill, the horrified mother understands he has gambled away their daughter, who also loses her hands. Her adventures take her to an orchard where a king falls in love and marries her. When the king has to travel, the girl's mother-in-law cares for her lovingly; however, when the devil switches the letters stating that she has borne a monster and should be killed, the mother-in-law does not obey, but enables her to escape. The younger queen also becomes an exemplary mother, teaching her child to care for the father who had outlawed them.

## Mothers of Great Leaders

Some fairy tale mothers go on to produce exemplary children. In *The Shepherd of Myddvai*, a Celtic lake woman marries a man on condition that he will not strike her three times without cause, and they have three children. When he does finally strike her for her incongruous behavior three times, she takes her animals back down into the lake with her. When she returns later to award her sons the gift of healing, they became the physicians of Myddvai. Another otherworldly mother is *Melusine*, who promises to marry Raimondin if he agrees not to observe her on Saturdays. In this French fairy tale, when he sees her transformed into a snake below the waist, he betrays her secret. She leaves him as a dragon, but returns to suckle her last two sons, and all 10 sons grow up to be great leaders.

## Mothers and Stepchildren

The contrast between a mother's behavior to her own child and a stepchild is shown in several tales. In the many variations of *Diamonds and Toads* or *The Fairy*, the stepmother does not love the good child, but loves her own bad daughter to distraction; Perrault omits mention of the stepmother theme, merely stating that one was like the father and the other like her mother.

In *Snow White and the Seven Dwarves*, Grimms' describe the stepmother as a beautiful woman who cannot bear her daughter's beauty to surpass hers. The Celtic *Gold Tree and Silver Tree* relates the older version with the true mother unable to bear her own daughter's beauty, and the father saves her by marrying her to someone far away. The mother pursues her to destroy her, poisoning her through a keyhole. In this version, the second wife twice revives the first wife, offering to leave her husband to his first wife, but he keeps them both.

In the Grimms' *The Three Little Men in the Wood*, the stepmother first promises to wash the girl in milk and give her wine if she marries her widowed father, but soon becomes her bitterest enemy, sending her out for strawberries in winter wearing a paper dress. When she shares her crust of bread and sweeps the floor for three little men, she is rewarded with beauty, marriage with a king, and gold dropping from her mouth as she talks. When the mother sends her sister out in a magnificent fur coat with bread and butter and cake in attempting to produce the same results, she refuses to share her food or do any work, and grows ugly, has toads falling from her mouth, and is doomed to die in misery. The stepdaughter marries the king and has a baby, but her stepmother and sister throw her into a stream, where she becomes a duck, managing to return in her old form to nurse her baby. The wife finally regains her position through an observant kitchen scullion, when the king has the others decide their own punishment, which is to be rolled away in a barrel of nails. In the *Mother Holle* version, the stepdaughter is made to jump into the well to retrieve her shuttle; she succeeds by helping all who ask for her aid, returning covered in gold. When the lazy sister attempts the same journey, she returns covered in pitch.

In the German fairy tale *One Eye, Two-Eyes, and Three-Eyes*, the mother loves her abnormal daughters, while both mother and sisters cannot stand the normal girl with two eyes, driving her out hungry. She earns her fortune from a woman who sees her weeping, later sharing her bounty with her sisters. In the Grimms' *Sweetheart Roland*, the stepmother kills her stepchild when her own child wants her sister's pretty apron, declaring she "has long deserved death," but the victim overhears the plot and evades death by swapping places, whereupon the mother cuts her own daughter's head off and the stepdaughter escapes with her lover. In the Japanese tale *The Mirror of Matsuyama*, the mother believes her mirror reflects her soul, and while dying she advises her daughter to gaze into the mirror to recover her lost mother. The stepmother later suspects the girl of witchcraft in this secretly repeated action, but when she and the father understand the girl has been using the mirror to "meet" her dead mother, they are ashamed and reconcile with her.

*The Children of Lir* tells the Irish story of the king's wife's sister marrying him when his wife dies after bearing four children. Her affection for the children turns to jealousy when she sees how much he loves his children, having them sleep in his room. She turns the children into swans who sing their story for 900 years.

In the Celtic *Smallhead and the King's Sons,* when two of a woman's daughters kill their own mother, the mother speaks through a cat to her eldest daughter, telling her to treat her halfsisters properly in spite of what they have done to her. Smallhead then brings her sisters through many misfortunes until they each marry a prince.

## Marriage Themes

Mothers finding suitors for their daughters is a common theme in fairy and folk tales. In the Grimms' *The Six Swans,* a witch releases the king from the forest on condition that he agrees to marry her beautiful but weird daughter; however, after they marry she turns his six sons into swans. Their untransformed sister becomes mute to recover her brothers, even under the accusations of her mother-in-law, who nearly succeeds in killing her.

Another Grimm fairy tale features a sorceress in *The Six Servants,* who uses the lure of marriage with her daughter to have suitors perform impossible tasks, trying to prevent one of lowly birth gaining her daughter, while the girl eventually learns to appreciate her mate.

## Cruel and Foolish Mothers

Mothers acting foolishly are subjects of punishment and retribution in some fairy tale themes. At times, children must overcome or suffer the consequences of the poor choices of their mothers. In the Grimms' *Donkey Cabbages,* a beautiful girl's mother uses magic to steal the huntsman's wishing-cloak and his bird's heart, which lays gold. He finds cabbages that transform him into an ass and back again, and returns to transform the thieving mother and daughter into asses, having the mother beaten; the daughter asks forgiveness for the evil that her mother forced upon her.

In the French *The Yellow Dwarf,* a widowed queen left with one daughter spoils her child, who becomes so proud at 15 that she is unable to marry anyone. The mother becomes trapped in the power of the yellow dwarf, who makes her promise her daughter to him. Mother and daughter attempt to escape the dwarf by the girl marrying the King of the Golden Mines, and the girl learns through experience to value her suitor and his suffering for her, a lesson her indulgent mother could not give her. Finally, she dies for the King of the Gold Mines rather than marry the Yellow Dwarf without love.

The Grimms' spin more tales of mothers who are foolish or careless, and the children suffer. *The Raven* shows a queen so infuriated with her naughty child that she finally wishes her to be a raven and fly away so she can have some rest; when her wish is granted, the girl suffers considerably before she is restored to human shape. A careless mother in *Fundevogel,* or *Bird-Foundling,* falls asleep under a tree and a bird of prey steals her child.

The mother of the two sisters in the Grimms' version of *Cinderella* is so determined for her daughters' feet to fit the slipper and marry the prince that she presents them with a knife, telling one to cut off her toe, the other her heel, since as a princess she would no longer need to walk.

*Hansel and Gretel* shows a particularly cruel mother, while a later Grimms' version softens the account by having the stepmother persuade the father to leave their children out in the forest to starve, with their subsequent adventures with the witch who wishes to cook them. However, in *The Hut in the Forest* it is the mother who grieves that her children are sent out into the forest and lost.

## Restoration and Vindication

Mothers endure unfairness and cruelty, but eventual reclamation, in themes of loss and restoration. When three German sisters marry brothers in *The Three Little Birds,* the two who remain childless throw their sister's children away, causing their mother to be imprisoned for her presumed guilt, until the children are restored. Chaucer's *Patient Griselda* lives her life without her children as an exemplary mother who accepts her cruel husband killing them and replacing her with a young wife, and they are only restored when they are grown up. In the Welsh *Powel, the Prince of Dyfed,* Rhiannon's child is stolen and she has to bear the people on her back like a horse for seven years, until her child is restored.

The loving parents of Perrault's *Sleeping Beauty* remain alive when she pricks her finger at 15, but the entire court sleeps for 100 years. In the sequel, the prince's ogre mother tries to eat her grandchildren, while their mother, Sleeping Beauty, is ready to die in order to reach her lost children. They are all saved by the cook; the ogre grandmother ends up in the tub of toads and vipers she had prepared for her own grandchildren.

## Themes of Tragedy

Sometimes, a tale seems unresolved, ending in tragedy with dead children or dead mothers. Others reflect unspeakable horror. A servant steals the beloved child in the Grimms' *The Pink* because this child has the power of wishing, causing the mother to be blamed for the lost child and her incriminating bloody apron, and she is locked in a tower to starve. Doves feed her until she is vindicated, when she dies happily within three days.

In the French tale *Hop o' My Thumb* or *Little Poucet,* the mother has seven boys within four years because she "went quick about her business," bearing them efficiently as twins. They are left out in the forest only after much persuasion by her husband, since she cannot bear to see them die of hunger.

A Palestinian woman in *Tunjur Tunjur* is so keen to have a child she is prepared to have one as a cooking pot, and the magical pot goes out and brings back honey, meat, and jewels. After the third foray, the mother advises her pot "daughter" they have gained enough, but when the daughter disobeys and goes out for one last trip, she is used as a toilet.

The Grimms' *The Juniper Tree* starts with the mother praying night and day for a child, but she dies in delight when the child is born. The second wife loves her own daughter but not her stepson, finally beheading him by closing a chest on his head, and then transferring the blame onto her own daughter by telling her to hit him after she has carefully balanced his head on his shoulders. Stepmother and weeping sister make black puddings from the boy, and the father is encouraged to eat what is his own. The boy's bones reincarnate into a bird, which crushes the stepmother with a millstone, leaving the family to live without her in peace.

In the Grimms' *Allerleirauh,* or *Donkeyskin,* it is the mother's insistence before her death that her husband only marry a woman as beautiful as herself which causes him to attempt incest with his own daughter, since no one else possesses her mother's beauty.

**See Also:** Carework; Childcare; Literature, Mothers in; Poetry, Mothers in; Stepmothers.

**Bibliography**
Grimm, Jakob and Wilhelm Grimm. *The Complete Grimm's Fairy Tales.* New York: Pantheon Books, 1944.
Jacobs, Joseph, ed. *Celtic Fairy Tales* and *More Celtic Fairy Tales.* Twickenham, UK: Tiger Books, 1994.
Opie, Iona and Peter Opie. *The Classic Fairy Tales.* New York: Oxford University Press, 1974.
Ragan, Kathleen. *Fearless Girls, Wise Women and Beloved Sisters.* New York: Norton, 1998.
Yolen, Jane and Heidi Stemple. *Mirror, Mirror.* New York: Penguin, 2000.

Gillian M.E. Alban
Dogus University, Turkey

# Family

There are differences and debates about definitions of the family, which vary with time, context, and geography. Theorists do not always agree on a common definition. The traditional or nuclear family is widely used to describe a group consisting of two parents and their children living together as a unit. A family may, however, be described as a group of people related by blood or marriage and even one that comprises all the descendants of a common ancestor. It is therefore necessary to identify relevant contexts when reviewing what the family is perceived to be, as this differs greatly worldwide. It is also important to examine definitions, as these affect people's lives and the choices they make and that are made for them. The study of families is difficult because some academic commentators believe that either "the family" does not exist, or that it is in decline because family forms are diverse and fluid in contemporary societies.

## Definition and Developments

In 1949, G.P. Murdock defined the post–World War II Western family as "a social group characterized by a common residence, economic cooperation, and reproduction including adults of both sexes, at least two of which maintain a socially approved sexual relationship, and, one or more children, own or adopted, of the sexually cohabiting adults."

An example of a very different type of family around that time was that of the Nayar in India. A wife could take up to 12 husbands, who would visit her at night one at a time, none sharing residence with the woman. A man could also have an unlimited number of wives. When a woman became pregnant, therefore, any one of up to 12 men could be the father. The men did not assist in raising children or staying with the women, who were supported by brothers, sisters, and children. In this family, the eldest male was the leader of each kin group. There are many other examples of polygamy (where husbands have more than one wife) and, more rarely, polyandry (where wives have more than one husband).

## Functions of the Family

Many sociologists argue that the male breadwinner form of family is the best way to socialize children, as well as being most efficient for modern industrialized societies. The popularity of this type of family decreased, however, in the 1960s, as birth control methods increased choice for women about when to start a family. In addition, the demand for female labor grew, which was accompanied by a second wave of feminism demanding equal rights in the workplace and in the home.

Perhaps the most important development with regard to families after industrialization into the 1960s in Western societies was the emergence of companionate marriage. Companionate family or marriage is the idea that marriage is a relationship, rather than an economic institution. This meant equal but different roles within the family; for example, that the man would be the breadwinner and the woman would be the carer and stay at home and look after the house and children.

In 1955, sociologists Talcott Parsons and Robert F. Bales contended that the nuclear family provided the most efficient and functional division of labor, with preindustrial extended families performing religious, political, educational, and economic functions. Parsons believed these obligations came before father–mother–child relationships and employment responsibilities.

Parsons and other sociologists (called structural functionalists) believe that the family has declined due to increasing paid employment of mothers, and the weakening of paternal authority. Other viewpoints center around the fact that families are becoming more diverse due to increases in choice for parents as well as changing negotiations about what roles men and women should play within their families; for example, whether they should have an equal role in employment and raising their children.

Another function of the family that has been put forward by theorists is the legitimization of sexual activity. For example, most societies have norms relating to sexual relationships, where incest is taboo between close relatives. In some cultures, it is also not acceptable to have sexual activity unless its purpose is procreation.

### Negative Functions of the Family

Feminist thought, led by sociologist Ann Oakley, argues that the family can carry out negative functions, particularly for women. For example, it argues that women's work in the home is unpaid and demeaning, and so is motherhood. It also says that the family gives men more power and control over women with regard to finances and sexual behavior; in many societies, men believe they are entitled to conjugal rights, and women may be punished for refusing. Feminists also argue that women are kept in the private sphere of the family, which is regulated by men. One example is that in Great Britain, where rape within marriage was not made illegal until 1989. Others argue that women are repressed by being subjected to some religious edicts that declare their lives have half the value of men.

### Religion and Differences

In western Europe, the decline in Christian religious beliefs, along with the decline of stigma related to differing family types such as lone parents, has arguably resulted in less personal need for men and women to create just one type of traditional family; it is more socially accepted for individuals to have more choice in partners, choosing to remarry or partner, become single parents, or live in a same-sex family. This is not necessarily the case, however, in other geographical areas such as the Middle East, where relationships outside marriage are still often frowned upon due to Islamic religious tenets. Many religions, such as Judaism and Islam, encourage their followers to have many children.

Although the usual basis for households in Britain and the United States has been the nuclear family, in many Eastern societies such as China and Japan, the family is based on a paternal stem of three generations: an older married couple, one of their sons, and his wife and children. Alternatively, there are many joint families, in which all the married sons and the unmarried sons and daughters reside with their parents until the death of the parents.

### Family Members

Members of the nuclear family tend to be as follows: mother: a female parent; father: a male parent; son: male child of the parent; daughter: a female child of the parent; brother: male child of the same parent; sister: female child of the same parent; grandfather: father of a father or mother; and grandmother: mother of a father or mother. Half brothers or sisters are those who share only parent with another child of the family, and the terms *stepbrother* or *stepsister* refer to their new relationship with one another when one of their biological parents marries one of the other child's biological parents.

The same applies to stepmothers or stepfathers, where any person other than the biological parent of a child marries the parent of that child, and they become the stepparent of that child. Children may also be adopted into a family, where they are not biologically related to either of the adults (or occasionally the one adult) who has adopted them. Other family relationships, such as brother-in-law or mother-in-law, are created by marriage.

### Support for the Family

The way in which governments view the family influences their policies toward different types of families. For example, the nuclear family in the West has been supported in various ways such as providing tax incentives to married couples but not for those cohabiting, or not allowing single people or single-sex couples to adopt children. Governments may also label types of families as social problems, such as single parents, and introduce rigorous means testing for those who need state assistance.

Another example is the one-child policy in China, where about 35 percent of the population have been restricted since 1979 to one child per family in order to reduce the population. There can also be punishments for those who have relationships outside of marriage; Since 1979 in Iran, wives can be stoned to death for committing adultery.

The state can also support certain family types—such as, the nuclear family—by making divorce difficult; for example, limiting the grounds on which men and women can divorce and allowing high costs for divorce. They can also discriminate against families, such as same-sex couples, by not legally recognizing their relationship through a civil ceremony.

## Industrialization, Development, and Family

Family structures and roles are, and continue to be, influenced by industrialization, or the move away from agriculture to manufacturing industries. Large extended families that were self-supporting and acted as units of production evolved through industrialization into the more isolated nuclear family, which was small, mobile, and well suited to a more contemporary society. Other functions that were previously performed by the extended family, such as education and health care, were largely removed from the sphere of the family.

Contemporary family roles are characterized in many ways, such as organizational diversity (families with two wage earners, a father who stays at home to care for children, and shared childcare); cultural diversity; class and economic diversity; life course diversity; and cohort diversity (due to the variation of wider social and historical events). When a husband and wife share housework and leisure, this is termed *joint conjugal role relationship*. When they perform separate tasks and have different leisure pursuits, sociologists describe their relationship as a *segregated role relationship*.

## International Families

In India, most women are under the authority of fathers, brothers, husbands, or husbands' families, and are often considered property. In Saudi Arabia, wives are often divorced (or second wives taken) if the wife fails to produce sons. In the Middle East, families tend to be multicultural, multiracial, and multiethnic.

One important factor that varies between Middle Eastern regions and determines views of the family is religion, which depends on which party is in power. After the 1979 Islamic Revolution in Iran,

the Muslim family was declared the center of the nation. The family is often thought of as a patriarchal pyramid, and what befalls one member is thought to bring honor or shame to the entire family. The Family Rights Act (1978) that had fixed the minimum age of marriage at 18, banned polygamy, and made divorce and child custody subject to the courts was repealed. Mothers lost custody rights to their children and could be punished to death by stoning if found guilty of adultery. The spread of Islam, even in contemporary times, is therefore extremely important in understanding many Eastern societies. In Islam, a Muslim man can marry a non-Muslim, but women, are not allowed to marry a man who is not Muslim.

The traditional Iranian family is patriarchal. Fathers are considered the dominant force and completely control the family. No one questions his authority over his wife, children, and grandchildren. When the father dies, the eldest son inherits the authority and accepts responsibility for his mother and any unmarried siblings.

In China's traditional family, a new wife spends most of her time in the service of her mother-in-law. A wife can also be divorced if she fails to bear children and has no property rights after a divorce. The prime authority within Chinese families is the most senior male, and it is expected that a newly married couple should live with the groom's family, although for practical reasons this is not always the case. The possessions, income, and expenses of all family members are pooled, and decisions are made through the patriarchal authority structure of the family.

## Emergence of the Nontraditional Family

Over the last 30 years, the definition of *family* has been broadened from that of the nuclear family (two married parents and their biological children) to include any group of people fulfilling the core function of a family, which is caring and providing for each other. This includes single-parent households, blended families (including children from previous marriages), multigenerational families, unmarried partners, and same-sex couples. Sometimes the legal definition of family has been updated to include such arrangements, for instance by extending employer-based health insurance benefits to unmarried and same-sex domestic partners and their children. The 2000 U.S. Census identified over 160,000 households that included same-sex couple and children. The 2006 Current Population Survey estimates that there are 12.9 single-parent families in the United States, of which about 80 percent are headed by women.

## Contemporary Issues and Controversies

Despite the tremendous diversity of family structures and types, there are some debates that are central to most discussion of the family. Should families have the right to genetically select their children—for example, deselecting certain genes that are prone to cancer, choosing the child's gender, or cloning children to be healthy matches for other children who are ill? How are birth rates ethically raised or lowered? How can less developed countries be more effectively educated in contraception, the problems with human immunodeficiency virus (HIV), and how to manage resources for their families? In addition, should families be public or private, and to what extent should they be encouraged to support themselves or expect support from society and states when they need help? Finally, what are the ongoing issues associated with inequalities between men, women, and children's rights within families?

**See Also:** Adoption; Birth Rates; Feminism and Mothering; Islam and Motherhood; Marriage.

## Bibliography

Alavi, N. *We Are Iran*. London: Portobello Books, 2005.

Benokraitis, N.V. *Marriages and Families: Changes, Choice and Constraints:* Upper Saddle River, NJ: Prentice Hall, 1996.

Bernardes, J. *Family Studies: An Introduction:* London: Routledge, 1997.

Bochel, H., et al. *Social Policy: Issues and Developments*: Upper Saddle River, NJ: Pearson Education, 2005.

Ebadi, S. *Iran Awakening:* New York: Random House, 2006.

Esposito, J.L. and J.J. Donohue. *Islam in Transition: Muslim Perspectives*. New York: Oxford University Press, 1982.

Finch, J. and Summerfield, P. "Social Reconstruction and the Emergence of Companionate Marriage 1945–59." In *The Sociology of the Family*. Oxford: Blackwell, 1999.

Fredman, S. *Women and the Law:* New York: Oxford University Press, 1997.

Gough, E. "Is the Family Universal? The Nayar Case." In *A Modern Introduction to the Family*, N.W. Bell and E.F. Vogel, eds. London: Collier-Macmillan, 1959.

Harris, J. and S. Grace. *A Question of Evidence? Investigating and Prosecuting Rape in the 1990s*. London: Home Office, 1999.

Hills, H. et. al., eds. *Making Social Policy Work:* Bristol, UK: Policy Press, 2007.

Jordan, D.K. "Filial Piety in Taiwanese Popular Thought." In *Confucianism and the Family*, W.H. Slote and G.A. DeVos, eds. Albany: State University of New York Press, 1998.

Morgan, D. "Ideologies of Marriage and Family Life." In *Marriage, Domestic Life and Social Change*, D. Clark, ed. New York: Routledge, 1991.

Muncie, J., et al, eds. *Understanding the Family:* Thousand Oaks, CA: Sage, 1997.

Murdock, G.P. *Social Structure:* New York: MacMillan, 1949.

Oakley, A. *The Sociology of Housework:* New York: Pantheon, 1974.

Parsons, T. and R.F. Bales. *Family Socialization and Interaction Process*. Glencoe, IL: Free Press, 1955.

Sasson, J. *Princess*. London: Bantam Books, 2004.

Steel, L. and W. Kidd. *The Family:* London: Palgrave Macmillan, 2000.

Stockman, N., et al. *Women's Work in East & West*: London: UCL Press, 1995.

Gill Gillespie
University of Northumbria

# Family Planning

The idea of motherhood planning represents a major aspect of the social construction of pregnancy and motherhood in today's world. It expresses the concretization of women's right to their own bodies: by allowing for women's sexuality and sexual pleasure not to remain solely connected to reproduction. As such, it has been a claim of all feminist movements as a basis for real emancipation. Access to contraception and abortion are both part of family planning, its third dimension being the prevention of sexually transmitted diseases.

## Ancient Beginnings

Techniques of birth control, abortion, and contraception were not discovered by modern medicine. Since the ancient times, all societies have developed extended knowledge of, as well as social rules pertaining to, reproduction and its management. Instructions to prepare contraceptives have been found in ancient Egyptian monuments. Local and especially women's knowledge everywhere in the world has been rich in abortive and reproductive recipes and rules. Before the contraception pill, for instance, the *United States Practical Receipt Book* (1844) mentions, among its many cooking recipes, various ways to prepare formulas to avoid pregnancy or provoke an abortion.

## State Power and the Women's Movement

In the last two centuries, the development of the contemporary Western state has been characterized by what French philosopher Michel Foucault called *biopower*, power over physical bodies—also known as the state's power to make live and let die: giving birth and allowing death. Such deployment of state power corresponded to a new social concept, *population*, and organized state action around it. Public health and reproduction issues became essential to the monitoring and management of the population, which were also recognized as a strategic interest of the state. This feature of the modern concept of state power runs across the east–west divide, spreading around the socialist countries and also influencing underdeveloped countries.

Accordingly, population control expressed itself through legislation and national initiatives regarding matters of public health, family policies, and social policies. Medicine—and the development of modern science in general—legitimized and gave content to such state powers. This development of the public power over reproduction has also been at the core of the women's movement. Feminist and women's groups have organized to reclaim the right to decide over their own bodies, against public,

social, and moral norms. Family planning is a part of, and stems from, such societal shifts.

## Malthusianism

One of the most influential modern scientific theories in matters of public control of reproduction is Malthusianism. According to the English reverend Thomas Malthus, writing at the end of the 18th century (1798), the Western world was approaching a food and economic crisis, due to population growth. Malthus suggested marriage postponement, sexual abstinence, and cessation of relief for the poor as remedies against poverty, the economic crisis, and even war, arguing that less numerous populations would render war more difficult. During the end of the 19th century, a revival of neo-Malthusianism birth control was supported by economists and politicians adverse to social assistance for the poor and favoring population containment as a supposed means of combating poverty. Practical contraceptive methods were publicized and spread, communicating the idea that poverty is a matter of sexual behavior and could therefore be fought through public education, especially focusing on working-class and rural women. Depending on the national gender gap and the particular welfare state model, these would make more or less explicit reference to the heterosexual family.

## The Spread of Family Planning

From the Western countries, family planning ideology has spread to almost all world countries, propagating information regarding reproduction and sexuality in general and directly assisting and advising women undergoing abortion or giving birth in matters of health. The family planning movement stems out of the will to configure pregnancy as a planned event, both as a public health objective and as a sexually emancipated attitude to sexual behavior. To refer to motherhood as a planned event implies that men should subordinate their desire for fatherhood to women's desire for motherhood, yet also that they would find it difficult to deny their paternity.

Family planning has two main components. First, it addresses women's right to their own bodies, articulated as a women's right to choose pregnancy, including access to contraceptives and abortion. Second, it concerns reproduction in socioeconomic

*Since the 1980s, there have been significant changes in patterns of family development. For example, more women are waiting until their 30s to begin families, family size is decreasing as employed women have fewer children, and the total fertility rate is declining.*

terms and its normalization. In this sense, it is frequently formulated as a matter of public interest in economic terms. This second approach includes, for example, the stigmatization of teenage pregnancies and of single motherhood.

The difficulty in interpreting family planning data stems from the fact that the decisions concerning giving birth and sexual behavior are complex and are not taken by women simply based on the availability of contraception methods or abortion. Feminist critiques of family planning programs therefore address the latter's objectives of imposing demographic trends instead of women's fulfillment and health.

Family planning has been criticized as trying to promote a socioeconomic rationale over women's

bodies and lives, or imposing a prescriptive image of motherhood and child rearing, legitimized by medical authority and joined by various moral and social rules, which links motherhood to the image of an economically and otherwise stable heterosexual couple and reinforces the sexist gender division in child rearing.

## Access to Abortion and Contraception

During the 19th and 20th centuries, feminist movements have strongly reclaimed the right to freely decide about one's body, especially concerning access to abortion. Throughout the 20th century, extreme right-wing movements and parties opposed this, promoting pro-natal policies. What these have in common is an opposition to abortion; some also uphold an ideology of motherhood as a national duty—such as during the Fascist dictatorship in Italy, the Vichy regime in France, or most recently the Ceausescu regime in Romania. In the 1970s, many countries around the world legalized abortion, as well as access to oral contraception for women.

Family planning structures helped in diffusing information and assistance in effectively rendering these rights. But in spite of pro-abortion battles and claims, abortion has been authorized restrictively, generally at the beginning of pregnancy, with the specifics varying from country to country. Nowhere in the world has abortion yet been granted completely as a women's right. On the contrary, its limitations range up to its complete prohibition in several countries, as for instance in Ireland and Poland.

Furthermore, even among the countries where abortion is legal, it is continuously fought by strong antiabortion lobbies and family planning units with it, particularly among some political and religious groups. Of these is notably the Catholic Church, which frequently reiterates the opposition of Catholicism to abortion, as well as to all contraceptive methods including the use of condoms instead promoting sexual abstinence. Advocates for access to contraception and abortion argue that banning these measures causes clandestine abortions, which are very dangerous and frequently claim women's lives, and runs the risk of spreading sexually transmitted diseases.

Where abortion is allowed, public health structures or women's organizations work as referents for the population, helping women and couples to prevent and manage unwanted pregnancies by advising on the most appropriate contraception measures. The contraceptive pill, the morning-after pill, the condom, and sterilization are all alternative yet not equivalent contraceptive methods. Family planning therefore consists in spreading the information regarding the advantages and limits of each contraceptive method, in relation to sexual practices and to the risks of sexually transmitted diseases.

## Feminist Perspective on Family Planning

Feminist perspectives on family planning are differentiated: liberal feminists may focus on the availability of family planning services, with a limited critique of the broader women's sexuality and reproduction issues; for radical feminists, a critique of reproduction is at the core of women's liberation politics. For the latter, it is therefore essential to feminism to have an extensive critique of violence against women and real women's control over their bodies. By criticizing male domination and the spread of heteronormative structures and institutions, they are more likely to criticize heteronormativity as part of the practices and information provided by family planning units.

Socialist feminist critique of family planning originates, on the one hand, from the special attention paid to women's socioeconomic position, and on the other hand from the questions of gender labor division and of social relations arising from the systems of production and reproduction. Ecofeminist critique of family planning focuses on the north-south divide in family planning programs, which asymmetrically limit fertility of the populations worst affected by the international division of labor and neocolonialist exploitation. In addition, ecofeminists point out that international institutions responsible for these family planning programs are presenting them to the countries of the global south as a condition of the process of industrialization, and that they impose certain social reproductive models as a solution to the problems of poverty, instead of critically engaging with the changes in the capitalist mode of production necessitated by the local environment.

## Sterilization Campaigns

The most obscurantist interpretation of birth control and family planning was articulated, on both a national and an international level, along class and racial lines: through secret mass sterilizations. Such practices, which were organized through national or international public health programs, were directed toward the poorest and most discriminated-against segments of the population, in order to secure the socioeconomic status quo and prevent revolt. Nonconsensual sterilizations were performed on the poorest women and men in many parts of the world: India, Bangladesh, Brazil, Africa, the Aboriginal peoples in Australia, Indians in Latin America, and the Native American and black women populations in Canada and in the United States. In the United

States, 25 percent of Native American women aged from 15 to 44 years were sterilized during the 1970s; in a large majority of the cases using forced and unclear practices or pressure. During the 1970s, several scandals in the United States revealed the spread of the sterilizations, performed with the help of federal funds. In 1972 alone, the number of sterilizations in the United States has been estimated to range from 100,000 to 200,000, of which the majority were black and Native American women and men. A very high number, especially if compared to the 250,000 sterilizations performed in Germany during Hitler's regime against the Jewish and Gypsy populations, as well as against homosexuals and the disabled.

One of the largest present-day population containments is the one-child policy of the Chinese government. In a context of strong sexist beliefs, statistically at least 1 million girls appear to be lacking, as Chinese families prefer to have a boy as an only child. Infanticide and abandoned baby girls are a consequence of the one-child policy, which results in China's uneven gender ratio and in mental trauma to the mothers involved. This strictly enforced policy—with its awards and severe penalties—comes at the cost of high invasion of women's autonomy and privacy. The imposed procedures, with and without a mother's consent, include intrauterine devices (IUDs), sterilization, and abortion. Contraception is distributed free of charge, yet in practice is not accessible for many. Birth control in China has largely been targeted toward women: 48 percent use IUDs and 33.9 percent have undergone sterilization, compared to 10 percent of males using condoms.

## Birth Strikes as Sociopolitical Strategy

Birth strikes are a practice of women's collective resistance against societal functioning. French women anarchists initiated a birth strike in 1848. At that time, it was intended as a refusal of love, marriage, and contribution to what they perceived as the militarization of society through marriage and reproduction. Spreading to Germany in the 1913, the birth strike became a refusal of motherhood, interpreted as a means of promoting public health, as well as a means of class struggle and allowing working-class families to have more time for political involvement.

It was again used as a socioeconomic protest during the reunification of East and West Germany following the 1989 fall of the Berlin Wall. In more recent times, East German women voluntarily underwent sterilizations in order to protest against the skyrocketing of female unemployment; the new labor market system made it suddenly impossible for women to jointly achieve economic independence and motherhood.

## Global Family Planning

Family planning developed globally in the framework of international governance, through both national and nongovernmental structures, with the help of funding coming from states, intergovernmental institutions, or philanthropic institutions. In 1965, the International Conference on Family Planning took place in Geneva, with the support of the Ford Foundation and the Population Council. During this conference, J.D. Rockefeller declared that population containment was necessary to the well-being of humanity. In 1994, another international conference reunited 179 state delegations, aiming to further develop the concept of family planning. The public discourse of global family planning thus turned toward the enhancement of reproductive health and the movement for reproductive rights.

Initially limited to issues of mothers' and children's health, contraceptive methods, and fighting sexually transmitted diseases, the concept of family planning has extended globally to include women's reproductive health and rights, as well as women's right to reproductive information and services. During the last decades, within the scope of family planning services, almost half of the total amount of funding has been spent on programs aimed at combating and curing acquired immunodeficiency syndrome (AIDS).

Among the trends observed in 2008, the use of modern contraceptives has increased from 10 percent in the 1960 to 60 percent in 2000. The demand for modern contraception is still on the rise, especially among young women in the countries of the global South. Since 1965, the average number of children born per woman in these countries has also declined, from six to less than three. In spite of the spread of family planning, the World Health Organization still estimates that in 2008, 120 million couples are not using any modern contraceptive methods, in spite of their willingness to space out childbearing. Reports on modern contraceptive use also show that once the cultural shift has happened, couples tend to turn from public and nongovernmental organization sources of contraceptives to the market, thus increasing the interests of the pharmaceutical industry and further extending the commodification of the global South.

**See Also:** Abortion; Birth Control; China; Poverty and Mothering; Pronatalism; Pregnancy; Public Policy and Mothers; Reproductive Justice/Rights Movements; Rural Mothers; Sexually Transmitted Diseases: Vaginal Diseases; Women's Health.

**Bibliography**
Acharya, Keya. "Sterilization in India." *Contemporary Review*, v.279/7 (2001).
Davis, Angela. *Women, Race and Class*. New York: Vintage, 1982.
Folbre, Nancy and Michael Bittman. *Family Time: The Social Organization of Care*. New York: Routledge, 2004.
Hardee, Karen, Z. Xie, and B. Gu. "Family Planning and Women's Lives in Rural China." *International Family Planning Perspectives*, v.30 (2004).
James, Stanlie M., P. Abena and A. Busia. *Theorizing Black Feminisms: The Visionary Pragmatism of Black Women*. New York: Routledge, 1993.
Lawrence, Jane. "The Indian Health Service and the Sterilization of Native American Women." *Inamerican Indian Quarterly*, v.24 (2000).
LeMoncheck, Linda. *Loose Women, Lecherous Men: A Feminist Philosophy of Sex*. New York: Oxford University Press, 1997.
Matuchniak-Krasuka, Jacqueline Anna. *L'avortement en Pologne: La Croix et la Bannière*. Paris: Editions l'Harmattan, 2002.
McFarlane, Deborah R. and Kenneth J. Meier. *The Politics of Fertility Control: Family Planning and Abortion Policies in the American States*. Chatham, NJ: Chatham House Publishers, 2001.
Nadine, Lefaucher. "Les Familles Monoparentales." In *La Famille: Etats des Savoirs*, François de Singly, ed. Paris: La Découverte, 1992.
Paxson, Heather. *Making Modern Mothers: Ethics and Family Planning in Urban Greece*. Berkeley: University of California Press, 2004.
Seltzer, Judith R. *The Origins and Evolution of Family Planning Programs in Developing Countries*. New York: Rand, 2002.
Sinding, Steven W. "What Has Happened to Family Planning Since Cairo and What Are the Prospects for the Future?" *Contraception*, v.78/4 (October 2008).
Stetson, Dorothy Mcbride. *Abortion Politics, Women's Movements, and the Democratic State: A Comparative Study of State Feminism*. New York: Oxford University Press, 2001.

Elisabetta Pernigotti
Université Paris 8, Saint-Denis

# Family Values

The term *family values* has been used with both positive and negative connotations. When used negatively to comment on the current state of society and individuals, it refers to a lack of family values, which is seen to contribute to the breakdown of not only the family itself, but ethical behavior in society more generally. This leads to a call for the return of family values. The term is also intended more positively as a political and social belief that hold the nuclear family—a father, mother, and their children living together—to be the essential, ethical, and moral unit of society.

This concept of the ideal family is promoted in legal, social, religious, and economic systems in that it is reflected in advertising, government, and housing and social policy. This in turn reinforces the view of this type of family form as normal, natural, and inevitable, and leads to discrimination against those who are not part of families who meet this ideal. Thus, assumptions are made concerning how a particular type of family best serves the interest of its individual members and of society in general. Although it is the responsibility of all family members to adhere to these ideals, the moral value of society is judged, in part, by the behavior of women.

There appears to be a bipartisan political consensus concerning the family, with political parties of all leanings across the world claiming to be the party of the family. But it is conservative politicians who have most often used the term *family values* in their critique on issues such as increased rates of teenage pregnancy, and in their call for the traditional (nuclear) family.

## Family Values Promoted by Legislation

Since 1980, the U.S. Republican Party has promoted family values. Among other things, their reading of the term includes the promotion of traditional marriage and opposition to adultery; opposition to same-sex marriage; support for pro-life policies, which encourage adoption over abortion; support for abstinence eduction for young people; and support for behavior identified as traditional or moral, such as respect, discipline, attentiveness, and religious observance. In addition, there were nostalgic references to the golden age of the family, which some historians have suggested never existed. Similarly, in Britain, the Conservative government elected in 1979 and led by Margaret Thatcher reacted to what it saw as the permissiveness of the 1960s and also argued for the return of the traditional family, when children respected their parents, women were devoted to the care of their children, and fathers modeled standards of behavior. Opponents argued that the patriarchal family then was the one being advocated, pointing to the high levels of poverty, disease and household abuse that characterized the patriarchal period in history.

In the 1980s and 1990s, various governments created laws or attempted to create laws to support their family value vision. For example, in the United States, Republicans wanted to provide a $1,000 tax exemption on the birth or adoption of a child, but only for married couples.

## Retaliation Against Section 28

In Britain, Margaret Thatcher spoke of "the right of a child to be brought up in a real family" which referred to one headed by a heterosexual couple. This was made explicit in Section 2A of the 1988 Local Government Act, which stipulated that local authorities should not "promote the teaching in any maintained school of the acceptability of homosexuality as a pretended family relationship." However, reaction from of the legislation by opponents was swift and retaliatory. Baroness Jill Knight of Collingtree, speaking in Parliament in 1999, warned that support of Section 28 would incur verbal and physical wrath:

"On one occasion, opponents of Section 28 attacked me outside my constituency office and tried to turn my car over with me inside it." Her support for Section 28 was, ironically, in large part based on the demonstrations of those opposing family values: "At that time I took the trouble to refer to their [Gay Liberation Front] manifesto, which clearly stated: 'We fight for something more than reform. We must aim for the abolition of the family.'" Knight explained that her intent was to protect young children, and "was certainly not my intention at any time to try to marginalize or be unfair to those who choose the homosexual way of life."

Similar arguments and concerns have also been dominant in the politics of other conservative governments in countries such as Singapore and Australia.

There are legacies of the late-20th-century concern with family values today. One example is the 1977 *Webster's American Family Dictionary,* which is promoted as a lexicon that reflects common ethical, moral, religious, social, and civic values of mainstream Americans. Sometimes the term has caused embarrassment for politicians when they themselves are seen to be behaving in a less-than-appropriate, traditional way, such as having extra-marital affairs.

Family values is also used more positively to advocate support for the values of love and support found in families and for valuing all types of families. In a recent speech focusing on the banks and financial markets, Gordon Brown (British Prime Minister, Labour Party) called for the adoption of family values where parents do not encourage their children to seek short-term gratification at the expense of long-term success.

**See Also:** Christianity and Motherhood; Intensive Mothering; Lesbian Mothering; Marriage; Religion and Motherhood; United Kingdom.

### Bibliography

Abbott, Pamela, Claire Wallace, and Melissa Tyler. *Introduction to Sociology: Feminist Perspectives.* New York: Routledge, 2005.
Barlow, Anne and Rebecca Probert. "Regulating Marriage and Cohabitation: Changing Family Values and Policies in Europe and North America—An Introductory Critique." *Law and Policy,* v.26/1 (2004).

Coontz, Stephanie. *The Way We Never Were: American Families and the Nostalgia Trap.* New York: Basic Books, 1992.

Coontz, Stephanie. *The Way We Really Are: Coming to Terms With America's Changing Families.* New York: Basic Books 1998.

United Kingdom. *Section 28 of the Local Government Act.* 1988.

*Webster's American Family Dictionary.* New York: Random House, 1977.

Gayle Letherby
University of Plymouth

# Fathers and Fathering

In the past few decades, research and writing on fathering/fatherhood has burgeoned into a major field of theoretical and empirical inquiry. This scholarship has been multidisciplinary, cross-cultural, and diverse in terms of theoretical underpinnings and methodological approaches. Research on fathering has occurred within psychology, social work, family studies, sociology, feminist studies, and economics. The diverse theoretical perspectives that have underpinned this research have included feminist theories, theories of masculinities, symbolic interaction, family systems theories, role theory, poststructuralism, and varied versions of critical theory (informed by Karl Marx or Michel Foucault). Studies on fathering have employed multiple methodologies, including both qualitative and quantitative methods, as well as a range of theoretically informed methodological approaches (such as grounded theory, narrative analysis, and varied versions of ethnography).

The proliferation of interest and research on fathers and fathering has arisen partly out of the profound social changes in women's and men's lives over the past 40 years, particularly within North America, Scandinavia, Australia, and New Zealand, and much of Europe. Such changes include men's declining wages; increasing male unemployment; a downward turn in traditional, male-dominated employment fields; sustained growth in women's labor force participation, especially mothers of pre-school children; the decline of the nuclear family; a rise in divorce rates; increased incidences of step-fathering and nonresident fathering; and changing ideologies and discourses associated with men's and women's roles and identities.

These have been combined with a strong social emphasis on men's involvement in the domestic sphere and fathers' active participation in all aspects of child rearing. Furthermore, these large socioeconomic and structural changes have been accompanied by an interest in how active or engaged fatherhood can lead to positive and generative results for men, women, and children, as well as by a concern about the effects of fatherless families on childrens' well-being. In short, researchers of diverse political and theoretical orientations have increasingly turned their critical gaze to understanding fathering/fatherhood.

## Dimensions of Fatherhood Research

Across disciplines and cultures, social science researchers have explored the changing dimensions of fatherhood at both personal and sociopolitical levels, while political, legal, social, and feminist theorists have theorized dramatic changes in men's and women's lives, and the structural and policy frameworks that enable and constrain those lives. That is, there has been a close relation between fathering as an experience, identity, and practice, and fatherhood as an institutional (social, legal, policy, ideological, and discursive) expression. Another way of thinking about the difference and interconnections between fathering and fatherhood is to draw on Adrienne Rich's (1986) distinction between experience and institution, with fathering thus being more closely related to how men perceive, live out, and enact practices of fathering within larger political, social, cultural, symbolic, ideological, and discursive institutions of fatherhood.

Parallel to early developments in feminist research on women and mothers, initial investigations into fathering were mainly focused on the experiences of white, middle-class men. From the 1990s onward, however, scholarship on fathering/fatherhood has become increasingly multidisciplinary, cross-cultural, and diverse in terms of theoretical underpinnings, methodological approaches, and samples of fathers being studied. There is now a large library of fathering studies that focus on how class, ethnicity, sexualities, age, culture, and ability/disability matter profoundly to the ways in which fathering is understood, experienced, and enacted. The importance of attending to diversity in fathering was underlined at the 2008 International Conference on Fathering in Toronto, Canada. Sponsored by the Canadian Father Involvement Research Alliance (FIRA), the conference highlighted a wide diversity of fathering experiences while also drawing on the seven strands of FIRA's work, which include gay fathers, fathers of ethnic minorities, separated and divorced fathers, new fathers, fathers of children with disabilities, aboriginal fathers, and teen fathers.

## Relations of Fatherhood to Motherhood

A large further area of research attention in the study of fathering/fatherhood has focused on comparisons and relationships to mothering/motherhood. As the field of fathering grew across the social sciences, feminist researchers began to assert that fathering can only be understood through recognizing the intricate coexistence between mothering and fathering as both collective and individual experiences, and as social institutions. Under this umbrella of research, which is often referred to as gender relations or gender divisions of domestic labor/care research, researchers have highlighted several key differences between mothering and fathering, including differing social expectations of men as primary earners and women as primary care givers; distinct moral identities for mothers and fathers; maternal gatekeeping from wives or female partners; co-constructed processes of "doing gender" by both mothers and fathers; gender ideologies and discourses of fatherhood and motherhood; gender differences in embodiment and habitus; and the impact of policy regimes.

## Gender Divisions of Work and Care

Most researchers across disciplines and cultures argue that today's fathers are more involved in their children's lives than fathers of previous generations. Qualitative and quantitative studies have pointed to increases in the time allotted to fathering as well as in the gender balance of childcare tasks. Women, however, still largely do the lion's share of house-

work. There seems to be, however, a link between women's earning power and housework help: a recent Canadian study shows that in households where women have higher wages, housework help is sometimes brought in. Researchers have also concurred that little has changed in the responsibility for children and domestic work.

That is, gendered responsibilities have not shifted, even where women have equal participation in paid employment. Nevertheless, there is some evidence that when men parent without women, as single fathers or as gay fathers, they do take on these responsibilities. Such research points to the importance of considering complex gendered negotiations in parenting and domestic life. Moreover, recent Canadian research has also pointed to how men are increasingly taking on some of the worry and fatigue associated with family–work balance, thus indicating a lessening of gender differences between mothering and fathering in relation to paid employment.

*There is evidence that when men parent as single fathers or as gay fathers, they take on so-called female responsibilities.*

## Fathers' Rights

While this subject area of gender relations and gender divisions of work and care in relation to mothering and fathering has received a high degree of attention in the past three decades, it is also one of the most politically and ideologically charged areas of study within the larger fields of fathering/fatherhood research. Specifically, there have been tensions between feminists and fathers' rights groups. On the one hand, there are agreements between these two sets of large and internally diverse groups in relation to the losses and imbalances that occur for both women and men when men do not participate in childrearing. On the other hand, some fathers' rights advocates are in conflict with feminist goals in that some of them have been labeled by feminists as explicitly antifeminist, antiwoman, or even misogynist.

While differences can be noted between fathers' rights movements and feminist approaches to fathering, there are also differences within each of these wide groupings. Some fathers' rights movements, for example, have promoted discourses of equality and gender-neutral parenting to reinforce their claims in child custody cases for greater access to children. On the other hand, fathers' rights organizations, such as the Promise Keepers and sections of the Fatherhood Responsibility Movement, assert a kind of fathering that emphasizes natural differences between women and men and the view that fathers are primary breadwinners while mothers are primary caregivers. In a related way, there are fathers' groups who act as "moral entrepreneurs," advocating involved fathering as a path toward bolstering a specific model of the family, which includes heterosexuality and marriage.

## Feminist Division on Fathering

Feminists are also divided in their views on fathering. First, many feminists support active fathering because it can lead to gender equality in home life, which can, in turn, support women's equality in the work force. Informed implicitly by liberal feminist assumptions, there is now a large body of feminist work on families and gender divisions of domestic labor, which argues that gender equality between mothers and fathers is desirable and possible and, furthermore, that mothering and fathering are interchangeable identities and

practices. Others have questioned the possibility of achieving equality in domestic life and have argued for spaces and contexts where gender differences can be present, where gendered embodiment can matter, and for an approach that straddles both equality and differences in domestic and community parenting while also interrogating where differences turn into disadvantages.

Another strand of feminist thinking on fathering is found in the work of scholars and policy advocates who focus on how gender differences in caring for children should translate into an argument for gender differences in divorce and child custody cases, and ultimately, differential treatment of mothers and fathers.

## International Spotlight

Over the past two decades, there has been a great deal of international focus on how policies matter to fathers and fathering. Researchers have highlighted how fathering involvement can be dramatically improved through family-friendly policies aimed specifically at men. Parental leave policies, for example, have been one means of encouraging fathers of infants and young children to take time off to care for their children. Nordic countries, notably Sweden and Norway and, more recently, Iceland, have come up with innovative ways of encouraging leave by fathers; two of the most unique measures include "daddy days" (leave reserved exclusively for fathers, as is the case is Sweden and Norway) and the equal division of parental leave between mother, father, and both parents (e.g., Iceland). Parental leave is still taken mainly by women, both in terms of numbers of women in comparison to men and the amount of time taken by mothers. What is notable, however, is that while mothers continue to take more leave than fathers in all countries, leave entitlement set specifically for fathers does lead to an increase in fathers' use of leave from work to care for their infants.

Social and scholarly understandings of fathers have shifted enormously over the past few decades. Discussion and debate have focused on a wide variety of fathers as well as diverse expressions and articulations of fathering and fatherhood. This diversity is present in current terminology that appears in much recent research on fathering. These include, for example, fathers as both providers and carers, resident and nonresident fathers, stepfathers, men as father figures, deadbeat dads, stay-at-home dads, single fathers, sole custody or joint custody dads, "daddy days" or "daddy weeks" in relation to parental leave, vulnerable dads, teen dads, and shared or primary care giving fathers. The field of fathering as a site of research, policy developments, and activism continues to grow. The rapid international rise of fathering Internet sites and "daddy blogs," along with academic and popular books, conferences, research initiatives, and the creation of an academic journal entitled *Fathering*, are good indications of the interest in fathers by academic and laypeople alike.

**See Also:** Care Giving; Child Custody and the Law; Divorce; Fathers Rights Movement; Iceland; Institution of Motherhood; Marriage; Norway; Rich, Adrienne; Sweden.

**Bibliography**

Allen, S.M. and Hawkins, A.J. "Maternal Gatekeeping: Mothers' Beliefs and Behaviors That Inhibit Greater Father Involvement in Family Work." *Journal of Marriage and the Family,* v.61 (1999).

Boyd, S.B. *Child Custody, Law and Women's Work.* Don Mills, New York: Oxford University Press, 2003.

Deutsch, F.M. *Halving It All: How Equally Shared Parenting Works.* Cambridge, MA: Harvard University Press, 1999.

Dienhart, A. *Reshaping Fatherhood: The Social Construction of Shared Parenting.* Thousand Oaks, CA: Sage, 1998.

Doucet, A. "Dad and Baby in the First Year: Gendered Embodiment." *The Annals of the American Academy of Political and Social Sciences,* v.624 (2009).

Doucet, A. *Do Men Mother?* Toronto: University of Toronto Press, 2006.

Doucet, A. "Estrogen-Filled Worlds: Fathers as Primary Caregivers and Embodiment." *The Sociological Review,* v.23 (2006).

Doucet, A. "Gender Equality and Gender Differences: Parenting, Habitus and Embodiment." *Canadian Review of Sociology,* v.46 (2009).

Dowd, N.E. *Redefining Fatherhood.* New York: New York University Press, 2000.

Hearn, J., et al. "Critical Studies on Men in Ten European Countries: The State of Research." *Men and Masculinities,* v.4 (2002).

Hochschild, A.R. *The Second Shift.* New York: Avon Books, 1989.

McMahon, M. *Engendering Motherhood: Identity and Self-Transformation in Women's Lives.* New York: Guilford Press, 1995.

Palameta, Boris. "Who Pays for Domestic Help." *Perspectives on Labour and Income,* v.15 (2003).

Rich, A. *Of Woman Born: Motherhood as Experience and Institution.* New York: W.W. Norton, 1986.

Ruddick, S. "The Idea of Fatherhood." In *Feminism and Families,* H.L. Nelson, ed. New York: Routledge, 1997.

West, C. and R. Zimmerman. "Doing Gender." *Gender & Society,* v.4 (1987).

Andrea Doucet
Carleton University

# Fathers' Rights Movement

In the 1990s, the Fathers' Rights Movement (FRM) evolved in response to feminism. Proponents of FRM believe that male domination is a myth and that women are unfairly advantaged by family law. It represents a number of different movements that arose in reaction to changes in family law and changes in family structure, namely, the increase in unwed childbearing and divorce.

## Unprecedented Rate of Fatherless Families

The current separation of U.S. fathers from their children is historically unprecedented. In the United States in 1960, father-absent families numbered 10 million. In 2008, it stood at 24 million. The divorce rate doubled between 1965 and 1980; an estimated 40 to 50 percent of all marriages now end in separation or divorce, affecting over 1 million children annually. Births to unmarried parents have now overtaken divorce as the primary cause of father absence. Unwed childbearing, after remaining below 5 percent for decades, rose 600 percent from 1960 to 2000. Single-mother families now comprise 7 percent of all households and grew at a rate five times faster than nuclear families during the 1990s. Rates of unwed births have begun to plateau at record annual highs of 1.3 million and 33 percent, respectively. Research suggests that unmarried fathers, through divorce or unwed fathering, tend over time to become financially and psychologically disconnected from their children.

## Goals of the FRM

The FRM fights for legal changes that support equal rights for fathers, including major reforms in divorce, support, and custody laws. The FRM frequently argues that single-parent families produce child poverty, delinquency, and crime. Solutions suggested for solving the problems of single-parent families include ending no-fault divorce laws, extending waiting periods for divorce, and promoting covenant marriages. Additionally, in an effort to make a divorce more difficult to obtain, many FRM members want to link Temporary Assistance to Needy Families (TANF) to marital status, arguing that in order to qualify for welfare benefits, recipients should be married. FRM attempts to use both the legal system and the legislative process to meet these ends.

One goal of the FRM is to dismantle the U.S. child-support apparatus as it exists today. They want to cut guidelines for minimum child support payments and exempt fathers from paying child support when joint custody is awarded, even if children live with their father less than 50 percent of the time. Other goals include reversing the requirement that they register their employment in court documents and have automatic wage garnishment; have child support arrearages that allow for unemployment, layoffs, and illnesses, among other reasons for nonpayment; and reverse recourse to imprisonment, suspension of professional licensing, and the suspension of driver's licenses for nonpayment of child support, claiming that it is a violation of their constitutional rights. The FRM are also against the use of private collection agencies in the collection of child support and the use of data-sharing computer systems that track people who owe child support.

The FRM supports presumptive joint physical custody and actively fights against the primary caretaker rule. The FRM purports that the gender-neutral "primary caretaker" theory is fixated on mothering and ignores fathering. Currently, the FRM is fighting against: (1) interpretations of the "best interest" standard that excludes the biological father; (2) children's visiting centers that are used to marginalize fathers; (3) weight given to children in custody determinations; and (4) the obligation to employ a lawyer for divorce proceedings.

The FRM is in favor of settling family conflicts outside of court, using mediation rather than adversarial means; balanced access to both parents; protected child exchanges; free access to genetic testing to determine paternity; and the "permission to move" law, which redefines relocation as a change in the principle residence of a child "30 miles or greater from the child's current principle residences." Many FRM members argue that the spouse filing for divorce must be considered the one willing to abandon the children to the other parent. It is a common argument from the FRM that false accusations of child or spouse abuse should be punished with imprisonment for felonious perjury. The FRM also considers some elements of the Violence Against Women Act and the Child Support Enforcement Act to be unconstitutional and primary weapons in the "war against fathers."

## Fears and Criticism

Within the FRM, there have been arguments that because men lack the right to make abortion decisions, they should be able to have their own form of "male abortion" (absolution from paying child support). This approach purports the concept that removing laws requiring child support from men who do not want children does not disproportionately place burdens on women, because women who cannot afford to have children can have abortions.

This argument claims that men's bodies are at risk in pregnancy just as women's are, because men must work in order to support children, and work involves the surrender of the body. Feminists have argued that FRM presents children as property, but not as the product of women's labor, and exploits the vocabulary of rights and duties to make men appear disadvantaged in the status quo.

Some have argued that the strategy of the FRM has succeeded in taking away legal protections available to mothers who are victims of violence, and lessened the legal sanctions imposed on violent fathers by discrediting mothers who make accusations of domestic violence or child abuse in divorce and child custody hearings. The National Fathers' Resource Center (NFRC) and Fathers for Equal Rights (FER) has responded to this charge by stating "it is adamant in its belief that domestic violence cannot be tolerated," and further goes on to point out that "domestic violence is an equal problem for both genders," citing statistics from the Office of Violence Against Women that shows 34 percent of domestic violence is against men.

Nevertheless, critics of the FRM fear that if fathers are able to gain more legal rights, violence against woman will increase, and women's and children's economic positions will suffer. Conservative estimates suggest that 2 million women in the United States are victims of domestic violence by husbands or other male partners annually. Further, studies link violence against women with child abuse. The number of female-headed families in poverty increased to 3.6 million in 2002 from 3.5 million in 2001.

According to the U.S. Department of Labor, in 2002, families maintained by women with children under 18 have the highest probability of living in poverty—a rate of 21.9 percent. For children under age 6 living in families with a female householder where no spouse is present, 48.6 percent were in living in poverty, five times the rate of their counterparts in married-couple families (9.7 percent). Mothers with custody of children are 44 percent more likely to live in poverty than custodial fathers. Many feminists interpret FRM rhetoric as an anti-woman, antiequality message and fear that the goals of ending domestic violence and winning gender equality are in direct conflict with the FRM.

The rhetoric of the FRM has emphasized fathers' emotional responsibilities to their children, but some argue that it needs to be clearer about their financial ones. Over the last decade, the FRM has successfully purged the phrase *deadbeat dad* from public discourse by arguing that it was demoralizing. The facts, however, are less forgiving. Approximately 60 percent of poor children in the United States do not get child support that is owed them, and approximately 85 percent of those who do not pay are fathers.

**See Also:** Child Custody and the Law; Child Poverty; Co-Parenting; Divorce; Family Values; Lone Mothers; Poverty and Mothering; Single Mothers; Violence Against Mothers/Children.

**Bibliography**
Arrendell, Terry. *Fathers and Divorce*. Thousand Oaks, CA: Sage, 1995.
Blankenhorn, David. *Fatherless America: Confronting Our Most Urgent Social Problem*. New York: Basic Books, 1996.
Clatterbaugh, Kenneth. "Literature of U.S. Men's Movements." *Signs*, v.25/3 (2000).
Collins, Kristen. "When Fathers' Rights are Mothers' Duties: The Failure of Equal Protection in *Miller v. Albright*." *Yale Law Journal*, v.109/7 (2000).
Fineman, Martha. *The Illusion of Equality: The Rhetoric and Reality of Divorce Reform*. New York: Routledge, 1994.
Griswold, Robert. *Fatherhood in America: A History*. New York: Basic Books, 1994.
Mason, Mary Ann. *From Father's Property to Children's Rights: A History of Child Custody in the United States*. New York: Columbia University Press, 1999.
Mincy, Ronald, and Hillard Pouncy. "There Must Be Fifty Ways to Start a Family." In Wade Horn, et al., eds. *The Fatherhood Movement a Call to Action*. Lanham, MD: Lexington Books, 1999.
National Fathers' Resource Center. "Fathers for Equal Rights." www.fathers4kids.com (accessed June 2009).
Shanley, Mary. "Unwed Fathers' Rights, Adoption, and Sex Equality: Gender Neutrality and the Perpetuation of Patriarchy." *Columbia Law Review*, v.95/1 (1995).
Stacey, Judith. *In the Name of the Family: Rethinking Family Values in the Postmodern Age*. Boston: Beacon Press, 1996.

Lynn Comerford
California State University, East Bay

# Feminism and Mothering

Feminists are often criticized as being antimotherhood, but while this may apply to a few radicals of the 1960s, scholars such as Lauri Umansky argue that while some emphasized the oppressive nature of motherhood in society and preferred to forgo the experience themselves, organizations such as the National Organization for Women emphasized the importance of mother-friendly practices, such as affordable daycare, as part of women's liberation. Others feminists advocated that women should taking back control of the birth process—from what they saw as a male-dominated, overly technological medical profession—through means such as midwifery and the Lamaze technique. By the 1980s, many feminists were writing about their experiences as mothers and using it as motivation for their activism; by the 1990s, the concerns of mothers and children occupied a central place on many feminist agendas.

The relationship between feminism and mothering is a dynamic one, with feminism advancing and pulling back at various times from positions of honoring motherhood, critiquing it, and using it as a platform for securing a host of rights, both those related to mothering directly and those related to other political and social arenas. As with feminism more generally, feminist approaches to the study of mothering have focused in more concentrated ways on dissecting issues confronting white and middle-class families than on a broader, more inclusive view of families, though it continues to evolve its analysis to increasingly address mothering issues in an expansive, cross-cultural context, and to center race and class in its analyses. The links between feminism and mothering can be categorized in three ways: social power and agency, the body and reproductive control, and mothering as a platform for activism.

At their core, feminist approaches to the study of mothering attempt to challenge taken-for-granted assumptions about women's natures and desires, children's needs, power in the family, and power in the larger society. Such approaches also attempt to redistribute power so that all mothers' agency—the ability and resources to act in accordance with their own personal and maternal needs, desires, and convictions—is unimpeded and even facilitated. Feminist motherhood studies have interrogated ways that constructions of motherhood are linked with perceptions of appropriate femininity and assumptions of the domestic realm as women's domain, and how these are valued differently from assumptions about men, and between or across cultures and subcultures. As home is a primary site for mothering activity, or motherwork, expectations about women's roles in the home have been intricately interwoven with assumptions about mothering.

## Clarifications on Feminist Mothering

Despite feminism's pointed efforts to facilitate women's agency in myriad arenas, much has been made in public discourse about feminism being "antimother." As is often the case with mediated and other popular discussions of feminist goals and activities, the actual goals and activities linking feminism to mothering often have been misread, and such discussions are directed by media icons, religious authorities, and other disinvested groups, rather than feminists themselves. Some feminist individuals and groups have clearly indicated their position that mothering is oppressive for women and that there is little or no hope for women's emancipation from it or within it—such as Ti Grace Atkinson and The Feminists in the 1970s, who critiqued the institutions of marriage and motherhood as part of a larger countercultural effort to entirely reconfigure the institution of family; and Jeffner Allen in the 1990s, who proposed a complete "philosophy of evacuation" from motherhood. These positions are certainly part of the larger body of feminist thought on mothering, but they are much more complex than the epithet "antimother" or "mother-hating" would suggest, and in any case represent a minority view.

A majority of feminist writing and activism has looked at mothering differently. In the main, feminist explorations of mothering have critiqued the ways that mothering is socially constructed in an effort to envision more empowering configurations of it for women, and the ways that dominant views about mothering are race and class biased in an effort to envision new constructions that both honor cultural variability and function as emancipatory for marginalized peoples and families.

## Feminist Counterviews

Some feminists have critiqued what they call "pronatalist" views of families and society—views that focus so sharply and in such narrow-scoped ways on children that considerations of women's self-determination, economic conditions, the impact of race and sexual orientation, and the sociopolitical climate are excluded from consideration. Pro-natalism presumes and applauds a universal posi-tive impact of babies on families. Other feminists have worked to challenge and reform what gets to count as a family, as valuable mothering, and as "women's work," as well as the responsibility of government and of parents in families and commu-nities, among other variables. They have critiqued dominant assumptions about children's needs, par-ticularly the idea that children must have constant oversight and meticulous attention provided by the child's biological mother; theories of childhood are intertwined with theories of motherhood. Still other feminists have worked to honor the fact that moth-ering impacts a majority of women and represents a significant part of most women's lives—whether "significant" refers to amount of time, degree of relational engagement and/or emotional intensity, or the importance of mothering as a source for women's identities. A critical component of feminist analysis in general is the effort to illuminate wom-en's experiences and perspectives, and to pay tribute to the lives women have lived and the cultures they have created—not just physically through birth, but relationally and creatively as well.

## Power and Agency

A primary focus for feminist work is on analyzing issues of power in an effort to break down inequita-ble structures and to build up and strengthen equi-table ones. In other words, it examines how power is distributed among women and men, and among different groups of women, and works to redistrib-ute various forms of power so that all women are afforded the authority, resources, and status that allow them to live in self-determined ways. Focus-ing a feminist lens on motherhood directs atten-tion to several critical issues, which, if effectively addressed, would result in more authority, bet-ter resources, and higher social status for women. Given the widespread and firmly entrenched assumptions about women as primarily bearers and raisers of children—and more narrowly, that it is in some circles considered neither a responsibility to be shared with others nor one among many inter-ests or responsibilities a woman may have—femi-nism has argued that dominant assumptions about women's relationship to children ought be informed

by the more marginalized understandings held by many women of color. That is, several feminists and other women advocates have argued for the com-munal rearing of children—which communities of color have long known and practiced—rather than the dominant, white, middle-class notion that women are solely responsible for the day-to-day care of their own children with limited help from fathers or community members, which they argue is not in the family's, the community's, or the larger society's best interest.

## Deciding When and If to Mother

A starting place for women's agency lies in their right to decide for themselves whether or not to be a mother. Feminism has argued that women's liberty to decide against mothering should not be impeded. Such liberty implicates not only issues of contraception and abortion, but also of creat-ing cultures that allow multiple sources in which women might ground their sense of identity, includ-ing work or career, art and creative activity, good health and physical activity, education and continu-ous learning, and meaningful relationships with other adults. For such women, the right to decide when to mother and how many children to mother should be preserved and valued; women need to be able to decide for themselves how many children to have or to mother and at what points in their lives they want to have, adopt, or otherwise take in each child. These decisions also implicate access to and ability to afford contraception and abortion as well as other sources of identity and fulfillment, no less than it does for women who decide against mother-ing altogether. Feminism also holds that women's liberty to choose how to mother, to ground their identities in mothering practices and in relation-ships with their children, and to find fulfillment in mothering and managing home and community should also not be impeded. Feminists have argued on behalf of women's rights to not mother, and to choose when and how to mother.

## Issues of Fulfillment

Beyond issues of whether and when to mother, and the relationship between identity and motherhood, feminism has explored women's maternal agency in other arenas. Purporting that cultural mantras that suggest mothering is "the most important job in the world" are not backed by the social programs, community support, financial compensation, and relationship power that such a classification might suggest, feminists have worked to assign greater cultural value to mothers and to the work and activities of mothering, and to alter and improve the conditions in which women mother so that their ability to make decisions on behalf of their children, their families, and themselves is facilitated rather than impeded. Issues of childcare represent one category of feminist effort in this area. Recognizing that most mothers working outside the home do so out of financial necessity, feminism points to many other women who find work an important source of creativity, identity, and fulfillment. Not all research supports claims that mothers' working outside the home is necessarily detrimental to children's development, but does show that low-quality care for children while their mothers work is problematic. Therefore, as children, communities, and societies benefit when women are fulfilled and self-sustaining, feminism has argued that more affordable, higher-quality childcare should be central to national political agendas.

## Labor and Health Care Issues

A second category of feminist action to improve the conditions in which women mother has addressed issues related to labor, whether paid or unpaid. Feminism has recognized, called attention to, and worked to mediate the direct links between economic resources and ability to mother in self-determined ways; between unfulfilling, undercompensated work and disillusionment with workforce participation; between undercompensated work and membership in poor, working-class and/or racial ethnic groups; between the unpaid labor of home and childcare and lack of economic and social power; and between women's compromised capacity to live fully sovereign lives and the unattainable goals many women feel compelled to meet in order to be culturally endorsed as a good mother.

A third category of feminist effort in this area is that of health care as a critical variable in maternal agency. Feminists have fought toward ensuring the right to high-quality health care for all families. This includes recognizing the relationships between women's health and their ability to mother in ways that benefit their own and their children's lives; between quality prenatal care and the subsequent health and well-being of both mothers and children; and between affordability of adequate health care and the quality of life that women and their families experience.

Feminism has channeled much effort into critiquing the ways in which mothering can function as oppressive, particularly if the conditions in which they mother do not facilitate their well-being and self-determination, and if the cultural value assigned to motherwork is not affirming and supportive. Feminism has worked to break down the ways that oppressive structures of motherhood are normalized and to facilitate women's ability to transgress and extract from those structures. It also has sought to illuminate the ways in which mothering can be a gratifying, creative experience and a potentially empowering context for developing one's identity. In Adrienne Rich's distinction between the patriarchal institution of motherhood and the woman-centered experience of mothering, feminists began to see not only the potential constrictions of motherwork for women, but also and simultaneously the potential for the rearing of children to tap a store of imaginative, creative, and life-affirming ways of living in the world; for mothering and family care to offer refuge from the world of industry; and to be a place where, as black feminist author and theorist Gloria Watkins (a.k.a. bell hooks) suggests, marginalized families can develop and celebrate strategies of resistance to dominant ideology.

## The Maternal Body and Reproductive Control

The long-standing feminist effort to maintain women's right to bodily integrity has particular poignancy in motherhood studies. Nineteenth-century perspectives on the tensions between reproductive and intellectual function, for example, shaped arguments about women's participation beyond mothering and the domestic sphere. It was often assumed in the past that the human body could only direct its energies to either intellectual development or reproduction, but not both. Women's presumed primary responsibility as bearers of children and fear of their educated minds interfering with reproductive physiology were used to keep them from pursuing education.

Early feminist voices speaking on behalf of women as mothers or potential mothers called for "voluntary motherhood." In the 19th century, an Anglo-American and British notion of *coverture* presumed that a woman's selfhood, through marriage, was covered under that of her husband. Under this principle, women owed sexual and reproductive service to their husbands, on his demand, without legal recourse to refuse. The call for "voluntary motherhood" was a rally for wives to insist on the right to abstain from sexual relations in their efforts to limit the number of resulting pregnancies and births. At the turn of the century, birth control advocates, led by pioneers such as Emma Goldman and Margaret Sanger, among others, also invoked the idea of voluntary motherhood, this time in reference to the use of contraception.

Around the middle of the 20th century, feminists argued for women's rights to decide whether, when, and how often to have children, advocating for wider availability of contraception and access to abortion. Women activists around the world have demanded reproductive control; most have defied cultural conventions in order to make contraception and/or abortion procedures available to women. After World War II, for example, Japanese midwife Miyoshi Oba spearheaded family planning campaigns to redress the problem created by ready availability of abortion within a context of the absence of contraception for women in Japan. In the late 1940s, Constance Goh Kok Kee founded the Singapore Family Planning Association, which provided contraceptive devices and information, as well as abortion services. In the 1950s, Sylvia Fernando brought family planning concepts and services to Sri Lanka; in less than 15 years, Sri Lanka was serviced by 85 family planning clinics. In the 1960s and 1970s, Tewhida Ben Sheikh of Tunisia was an active family planning advocate who trained doctors in abortion procedures. Zahia Marzouk founded Egypt's first family planning association in the 1960s.

Reproductive justice movements continue to work toward change on behalf of women's agency in motherhood. Feminist advocates of reproductive control argue for contraception and abortion rights, and against the coercive use of dangerous contraceptive drugs and sterilization abuses, which are most often imposed on women of color and poor women. Groups such as the National Latina Institute for Reproductive Health; SisterSong, a women of color reproductive health collective; and the radical feminist group INCITE! Women of Color Against Violence are U.S. examples of currently active reproductive control advocates. The Association for Improvements in Maternity Services and the Association of Radical Midwives in the United Kingdom advocate on behalf of better prenatal care and more empowering, less medicalized childbirth practices. Women's ability to exercise maternal agency through family planning and reproductive control has been a critical point at which feminism and mothering intersect.

## Motherhood as a Platform for Activism

An important link between feminism and motherhood lies in the ways in which women's advocacy, a primary feminist goal, as been launched from the platform of motherhood. Sometimes, instead of feminism fueling responses to motherhood, motherhood has fueled responses to other social problems. In the United States and Europe, for example, appeals to women's perceived, innate maternal sensibilities were used not only to direct women's attention to address social issues, but also to direct women's and men's attentions to the weakening of the public sphere when women's nurturing and moral qualities were kept from it. Women's rights activists who held that women have innate differences from men argued that women's "mother heart," their natural ability to see the plight of those who are needy or afflicted, is a necessary voice in politics and community, and that confining women to the home is done to the detriment of the larger society. This argument was used to position women in the slavery abolition movement.

Jane Addams was among those who argued against confining female qualities to the home. Addams was the first American woman to win the Nobel Peace Prize, and though she was not a mother herself, she did funnel what she saw as her maternal capacity into creating better conditions for mothering among poor immigrant women and families in Chicago in the late 1800s, through the development of settlement houses. In the late 1800s and early 1900s, members of black women's clubs saw their roles as mothers to be inextricably linked with their leadership of racial uplift in their communities. Comprised largely of members of the middle class, and led by primary figures such as Mary Church Terrell and Anna Julia Cooper, club women practiced forms of social motherhood, grounded in the idea that to take care of black women was to take care of the race.

More currently, many social activism campaigns have emerged from women's efforts to care for their children and other community members; environmental justice movements are often rooted in this way. In Argentina between 1976 and 1983, the Mothers of the Plaza de Mayo violated social convention and demanded that the brutal military dictatorship bring back alive their children who were abducted, tortured, and disappeared. They came to view themselves as the mothers of all the disappeared, not just their own children, creating an international spectacle on behalf of torn families and tormented mothers. The Mothers Milk Project, initiated through the work of Mohawk activist Katsi Cook, focuses on assessing the level of nuclear toxicity in mothers' breastmilk and agitates for toxic cleanup on behalf of Native mothers and their families and communities.

## Motherhood Studies and Current Activism

Motherhood studies emerged as a distinct academic pursuit in the last decade of the 20th century. The first organization devoted to promoting research of motherhood was the Association for Research on Mothering (ARM), founded in 1998 at York University in Toronto; they publish the scholarly *Journal of the Association for Research on Mothering*. Politically focused motherhood organizations include MomsRising (www.momsrising.org), founded in 2006 to support causes relevant to mothers and children, including paid maternity and paternity leave, flexible work hours, universal child health care, and affordable childcare. Mothers Acting Up (www.mothersactingup.org) was founded on Mother's Day in 2002 to advocate for the well-being of the world's children. The International Mothers Network is an international consortium of organizations (over 50 as of 2009) concerned with promoting motherhood and includes both scholarly and advocacy organizations.

**See Also:** Activism, Maternal; Activist Mothering; Anti-Racist Mothering; Economics of Motherhood; Employment and Motherhood; Feminist Mothering; Feminist Theory and Motherhood; Future of Motherhood; hooks, bell; Institution of Mothering; Maternal Feminism; Mothering Versus Motherhood; Mothers of the Plaza de Mayo; Patriarchal Ideology of Motherhood; Pronatalism; SisterSong; Sterilization; Unpaid Work; Work and Mothering.

**Bibliography**
hooks, bell. *Yearning: Race, Gender and Cultural Politics.* Cambridge, MA: South End Press, 1990.
Huston, Perdita. *Motherhood by Choice: Pioneers in Women's Health and Family Planning.* New York: The Feminist Press, 1992.
Jeffner, Allen. "Motherhood: The Annihilation of Women." In *Lesbian Philosophy: Explorations.* Palo Alto, CA: Institute of Lesbian Studies, 1986.
Jetter, Alexis, Annelise Orleck, and Diana Taylor. *The Politics of Motherhood: Activist Voices From Left to Right.* Lebanon, NH: University Press of New England, 1997.
*Journal of the Association for Research on Mothering.* Mothering and Feminism [special issue], v.8/1–2 (2006).
Kinser, Amber E. *Motherhood and Feminism.* Jackson, TN: Seal Press, 2010.

Amber E. Kinser
East Tennessee State University

# Feminist Mothering

Feminist mothering is a political act that takes place in the everyday lives of mothers and children. It entails the practical integration of feminism and mothering, whereby women consciously draw upon their feminist theorizing, philosophies, and worldview as they engage in the motherwork of rearing children. Feminist mothers challenge the effects of patriarchal power and privilege in their own lives, in the lives of their children, and in the lives of people in their communities and the world at large.

While feminism is composed of numerous perspectives and positions, most feminists view the majority of—if not all—cultures as patriarchal and, thus, award power, advantages and prestige to men and the masculine. They recognize that this privileging of males over females is produced, maintained, and perpetuated through gender discrimination. To ensure this imbalance of power between women and men, patriarchy depends upon the oppression, and often the disparagement, of women and the feminine. Feminists are committed to challenging and transforming gender inequity in all of its forms, whether it is expressed culturally, economically, politically, philosophically, socially, ideologically, or in other ways. Most feminists strive to dismantle other hierarchical binary systems, such as race and racism, sexuality and heterosexism, economics and classism, gender discrimination, and ability and abilism.

Feminists refuse to intentionally pass along sexist and patriarchal values to others. Feminist mothering is an act of maternal activism that makes the personal political, dislocates patriarchal essentialist notions of motherhood, and disrupts traditional gender relations. It is primarily concerned with (1) the empowerment of mothers, (2) the empowerment of children, and (3) bringing about far-reaching social change. Feminist mothering is an effective strategy for challenging patriarchal ideological motherhood, thwarting sexist child rearing practices, and fostering critical awareness in children, others, and the world at large.

## Mothering Against Motherhood

Feminist mothering is a revolutionary strategy that seeks to empower mothers. A primary characteristic of feminist mothering is its emphasis on maternal autonomy, which aims to achieve and sustain women's selfhood outside of and beyond mothering. By maintaining a mother-centered focus, rather than a child-centered focus demanded by most conventional approaches to parenting, feminist mothers mother against, rather than with, motherhood. This mother-centered approach actively troubles and counters the unrealistic rules and expectations proscribed by the patriarchal ideology of motherhood. The primary position taken by this unattainable, idealized motherhood is that all mothers instinctively and unconditionally love their children. A good mother is altruistic, patient, selfless, and happily devoted to nurturing her children without complaint. In essence, her life is her children. Yet,

retaining a sense of self often necessitates renouncing these practices of intensive mothering perpetuated by segments of society and the media in some societies. Indubitably, feminist mothers love their children; however, they also recognize the necessity of having an identity outside of mothering. Being true to oneself as a feminist mother means parenting in ways that invariably upset and actively disrupt this unrealistic and idyllic image of mother and concepts of motherhood. For instance, feminist mothers may choose to conceive through medical or other alternative insemination methods, with a number of different men, or with another woman. They may decide to become a mother, either alone or partnered, through surrogacy, adoption or othermothering. Mothering against motherhood may entail deciding not to practice the latest type of child-centered mothering proscribed by child development experts, such as Natural or Alternative Parenting, Attachment Parenting, or the Resources for Infant Educators (RIE) Approach.

It may mean creating equalitarian heterosexual relationships and sharing equitable childrearing practices with men. Some feminist mothers prefer to raise children outside of a relationship or within a same-sex, queer, or other type of relationship rather than being limited to a socially approved heterosexual marriage. They often trust partners, friends, family members, community, and nonfamilial caregivers to engage in co-parenting. Working outside the home, and possibly placing their interests, careers, or employment before the needs of their children and families are other ways in which feminist mothers practice their autonomy and also challenge the mainstream model of motherhood. By questioning motherhood, rather than accepting it as normal, natural, and instinctive, feminist parents illuminate the restrictions placed upon mothers.

## Dismantling Gendered Socialization Practices

Feminist mothers not only resist patriarchal motherhood to make the experience of mothering more rewarding for themselves, their children, and other family members, they also recognize that privileging males over females is enacted and enabled through the patriarchal ideology/institution of motherhood directly through sexist childrearing practices. Thus, they refuse to raise children in sexist environments and consciously work to dismantle traditional gender socialization practices that favor boys over girls. Feminist mothering defies these patriarchal directives by confronting gender inequalities in familial relationships and teaching children how to recognize and think critically about gender hierarchies. Feminist mothers frequently incorporate nonsexist child rearing practices into their everyday relationships with their children.

For example, they regularly provide nonsexist books, gender-neutral toys, and nonsexist games for their children. Feminist mothers engage children in direct conversations in an attempt to acknowledge, understand, and challenge incidences of sexist language, images, and acts that are depicted in popular culture, literature, speech, and daily life. They try to use respectful and specific language during their interactions and to encourage and foster relationships based on trust. These strategies work toward creating alternative and new egalitarian possibilities for women, children, and men in families.

## Nonjudgmental Support for All Mothers
Feminist mothering acknowledges that all mothers require nonjudgmental support for their motherwork. Parenting from a place of agency and authority, they seek to ensure that the vital work of mothering is recognized, valued, and sustained. Feminist mothering is critical of the isolation, guilt, and frustration many mothers experience, and the lack of recognition and support for the work involved in parenting children.

Feminist mothering also draws attention to the chastisement mothers often endure for not staying within the bounds of the prescribed, yet unrealistic, ideal of the patriarchal institution of motherhood. For instance, they confront the so-called "mommy wars" that pit mothers against each other and judge which type of mother is better: the mother who stays at home full time with her children, or the mother who works in the labor force. Stay-at-home mothers are viewed as lazy, boring, and unproductive because they do the invisible and devalued work of caring for children at home, whereas mothers who work in the public sphere are questioned about their simultaneous commitment to their children and their jobs or careers.

Feminist mothering acknowledges that mothers, regardless of their social standing or ability to parent, are often inevitably blamed for their children's inadequacies. Mother-blaming occurs when the cause of a problem the child is experiencing is viewed as the responsibility of the mother, and when a mother is said to damage her child by being either overbearing, over- or underprotective, neglectful, smothering, naïve, suspicious, poor, queer, weak, ineffective, domineering, employed, unemployed, over- or undersympathetic, wealthy, or disabled. While mothers who are financially disadvantaged, underemployed, living below the poverty line, on social assistance, or without a permanent address are at greatest risk of having their children taken away from them by the state, most mothers fear having their children removed from their care for being judged a bad mother.

Feminist mothering brings attention to the unrealistic and mythical expectations of patriarchal motherhood used to judge mothers, and how they can be effectively challenged. Feminist organizations, such as Mother Outlaws and the Association for Research on Mothering, as well as publications like *Demeter Press*, *Mothers Movement on Line*, and the *Journal for the Association for Research on Mothering* provide research, resources, and a supportive community for feminist mothers. Feminist mothering, then, offers a feminist model of how mothers can live self-determined lives, dispute oppressive conditions of patriarchal motherhood, raise children with a nonsexist approach, and demand empowered mothering.

**See Also:** Association for Research on Mothering; Intensive Mothering; *Journal for the Association for Research on Mothering*; Mommy Wars; Mother Outlaws (Group); Patriarchal Ideology of Motherhood.

## Bibliography
Green, Fiona. "Feminist Mothering: Challenging Gender Inequality by Resisting the Institution of Motherhood and Raising Children to Be Critical Agents of Social Change." *Socialist Studies*, v.1/1 (2005).
Green, Fiona. "Living Feminism Through Mothering." *Journal for the Association of Research on Mothering*, v.1/1 (1999).
Lad-Taylor, Molly, and Lauri Umansky, eds. *"Bad" Mothers: The Politics of Blame in the 20th-Century America*. New York: New York University Press, 1998.

O'Reilly, Andrea, ed. *Feminist Mothering*. Albany: State University of New York Press, 2008.

O'Reilly, Andrea, ed. *From Motherhood to Mothering*. Albany: State University of New York Press, 2004.

O'Reilly, Andrea, ed. *Mother Outlaws: Theories and Practices of Empowered Mothering*. London: The Women's Press, 2004.

Fiona Joy Green
University of Winnipeg

# Feminist Theory and Mothering

In the 19th and early 20th centuries, assumptions about women's innate maternal capacity went relatively unchallenged, as did assumptions about the relationship between identity and motherhood, societal structures that impeded or facilitated mothers' self-determination as mothers, and the relationships between race and class bias and the variable value of motherwork. In the 1970s, Jessie Bernard's discussions of motherhood as a social institution rather than merely biological fact in her *The Future of Motherhood,* then Adrienne Rich's distinction between the patriarchal institution of motherhood and the women-centered experience of mothering in her influential work *Of Woman Born,* helped to direct feminist critical analyses into issues related to motherhood specifically.

In particular, it helped feminism to consider ways that mothering can function as both oppressive and emancipatory, and to destabilize the former functions while securing and supporting the latter. Some feminists focused on challenging whether mothering held any possibility for women's liberation at all, given male-dominant cultures' valuing of men's lives over women's, their consequent devaluing of women's knowledge and experiences, and their failure to consider women's personhood beyond motherhood. Most feminist theorizing about motherhood, however, has considered the following: how to improve the conditions in which women mother; how to increase the cultural value of motherwork, particularly given that the vast majority of women do mother and that such work comprises a sizable portion of their lives; and how to reconfigure the institutions of family, work, and government so that women and their motherwork, in all of their variety, are supported. The greater majority of feminist theory about motherhood has emerged since Rich's distinction, and can be broken down into three primary categories: motherhood as institution or ideology; mothering as experience or role; and mothering/motherhood and identity or subjectivity.

## Waves of Feminism

The primary concerns of the first-wave feminists were political, in particular the right to vote. But they also addressed issues relating to motherhood: for instance, Elizabeth Cady Stanton (who had seven children) argued that women should control the marital sexual relationship (and thus the number of children born).

Second-wave feminists were concerned with many issues relating to motherhood, including a woman's right to control her fertility and access to childcare. Some, such as Shulamith Firestone, argued that motherhood was inherently oppressive; and the Redstockings, who asserted that liberation meant women were free to choose any lifestyle, including motherhood. Third-wave feminists broadened their demands for societal support of motherhood, including maternity leave and flexible work schedules and challenged essentialist views of gender differences.

## Mothering as Institution or Ideology

Feminist and other critical theorists have worked to articulate the particular ways in which the ideas of motherhood that flourish in political and personal understandings function in oppressive ways. Their goals are to question and challenge beliefs and practices that are normalized and taken for granted about women, mothers, families, and children; to show that current definitions and practices of mothering, such as those emerging from dominant ideology, are not inherently more valuable, natural, or inevitable than an array of other possibilities; and to foster a variety of different or new ideas that could function as more liberating for women, children, and larger societies.

Sharon Hays argued that motherhood is largely dictated by the ideology of intensive mothering, which holds that mothering necessarily should be time and labor intensive, child-centered, emotionally draining, expensive, and guided by experts. Hays argued that our current constructions of motherhood set women up to pursue forms of mothering that are unattainable, and wholly out of sync with the realities and challenges confronting families today. Many women are, as a result, exhausted, demoralized, and convinced of their failure at being good mothers.

Susan Maushart explained that because the image of effective motherhood is so unattainable at the same time that it is presented as natural and inevitable, women respond to the dilemma by pretending, wearing a "mask of motherhood" that allows them to appear as if their motherwork is derived authentically and from their own convictions, and flows effortlessly from them. Susan Douglas and Meredith Michaels have identified the links between the institution of motherhood and a media-generated new momism, which they identify as a descendant of Betty Friedan's 1960s "feminine

mystique." The new momism seemingly celebrates and glorifies motherhood, but in fact promotes and ennobles standards of perfect motherhood that are impossible to reach, thus failing to honor, value, and support what women are actually doing and needing in motherwork, and impeding the possibility of mothering that functions as a source of fulfillment or identity development.

Ann Snitow, Nancy Polikoff, and others have critiqued the centering of pronatalism not only in the institution of motherhood but also within feminist theory itself. They suggest that feminism has neither adequately critiqued women's decisions to have children nor supported other women's decisions to not have children. Lesbian women who have children, Polikoff argues, in order to help loosen heterosexually oriented norms of motherhood, ought to publicly and frequently defend lesbian women's choice not to have children. Feminist theory has worked to articulate these characteristics of a patriarchal institution of motherhood in an effort to work away from their frequently oppressive outcomes and to

*Women like this single mother with a mixed-race child employ their own modes of mothering as a way to push back against and refuse white, heterosexual, middle-class values and models for mother–child relationships and family life.*

envision possibilities for mothering experience that are woman-centered and grounded in the family realities currently confronting women, to envision what Andrea O'Reilly has called a "mothering against motherhood."

Adrienne Rich made a distinction in her 1986 book *Of Women Born: Motherhood as Experience and Institution* between the oppressive patriarchal institution of motherhood, which includes loss of control over fertility and the birth process, and the empowering, female-defined, woman-centered experiences of motherhood. These two aspects of motherhood these are often in conflict when mothers are within societies that dispense rewards and punishments to women according to how well they meet institutionalized expectations.

## Mothering as Experience and Role

While the distinction between the institution of motherhood and experiences of mothering is a critical one, feminist theory has also typically acknowledged that mothering can scarcely take place outside the institution, and so is always informed by or shaped by it in some way. Sharon Hays, Rickie Solinger, Evelyn Nakano Glenn, and other feminist thinkers have critiqued the faulty distinction between public and private spheres, noting the ways in which what is experienced in the supposed private domain of the family is always shaped in the public domain—through schools, courts, laws, the institutions of medicine, education, government, and media, among other forces.

Much feminist work, therefore, has explored the tension between experiences of mothering and the institution of motherhood. Women of color theorists have taken issue with a blanket view of mothering as oppressive, given the ways in which mothering is often differently valued in their communities—that home and family have historically been one of the sites where many women of color are afforded value and agency; and that institutionalized racism and classism are more primary oppression concerns for them than motherhood. Activist Gloria Watkins, a.k.a bell hooks, has noted that around the world, for example, black people have been systematically deprived of the opportunity to make a "homeplace"; therefore, doing so within white, dominant cultures has political significance for black women. hooks

argues, consistent with other writers such as Baba Copper, Alice Walker, Cherríe Moraga, and Audre Lorde, that the making of home and family functions as a powerful source and form of resistance; women employ their own modes of mothering as a way to push back against and refuse white, heterosexual, middle-class values and models for mother–child relationships and family life. For mothers from marginalized communities, then, mothering often functions as a source of resistant power, and motherhood is rarely the primary oppressive institution against which they are fighting.

## Three Themes for Ethnic Mothers

Patricia Hill Collins has identified three themes in which racial ethnic mothers' empowerment is grounded: having the children they choose (not being forced to produce children through slavery or rape, forced to stop producing children through sterilization, or restricted from reproductive control through limited access to contraception); keeping their children (not having their children forcibly removed from them and sold to slavery or sent to assimilation schools, or not being told that their nonwhite methods of mothering render them unfit parents); and raising their children in self-determined ways (not having their children castigated for speaking their native tongue, or having their histories erased by white emphases in schools and public arenas, or having their cultural values denigrated when white culture is normalized).

Feminist thinkers have explored other ways to consider mothering experience from the perspective of mothers. Philosopher Sara Ruddick articulated responses to the presumption that women possess a maternal instinct, and alternatively argued that the attentive and knowing behavior we often observe in mothers emerges not from biological traits, but rather from maternal thinking. Through everyday mothering practices and mindfulness, they learn and adopt particular ways of viewing the world and navigating their own and their children's ways through it. Unlike maternal instinct, maternal thinking is a discipline that is consciously practiced.

## Identity and Subjectivity

Feminist maternal theory has examined the relationship between mothering and identity/subjectivity in two ways. First, it has explored how mothering shapes maternal identity for the mothers themselves. Writers like Jane Lazarre focused feminist attention on this in the 1970s; Cherríe Moraga's 1990s work has focused attention on queer mothering and on reinventing *familia* in terms of Chicana lesbian identity; Patricia Hill Collins's work has focused attention on racial ethnic mothers' efforts to foster their own and their children's racial identity and teaching children to both fit into and resist racist social systems.

Collins also extended feminist thinking about mothering identity in her work on other-mothering, which argued that in Afrocentric communities, the boundaries distinguishing biological mothering from community and shared mothering are fluid, and that the mothering functions served by nonbiological mothers, or other-mothers, is a central component of black motherhood.

Second, feminist maternal theory has explored how mothering shapes identity in children. Psychoanalytic sociologist Nancy Chodorow offered explanations, based on a model of women as predominately at-home, primary caregivers, for how girls grow up to mother in her claims that girls identify with and emulate their mothers, seeing their own identity as interwoven with their mothers. Given the primary importance of the mother–child relationship, girls come to see all their relationships as marked by such interdependence, which then translates into mothering practices. Boys, in contrast, link identity development with separation from the mother, and therefore base all later relationships on a model of separation or independence from others.

Other feminist theorists from the psychoanalytic tradition, such as Jessica Benjamin, Miriam Johnson, and Dorothy Dinnerstein, have worked to develop theories of identity development and its grounding in mother–child relations. Some have grounded male dominance in presumptions about the awe and envy men have for women's maternal capacity; others ground it in the infant's fear of its overwhelmingly dependent relationship with its mother as primary care giver. While some of these theorists have suggested that infantile or adult male fear and envy can be mediated by altering childcare arrangements, others have argued that male misog-

yny and mother–child relations are much more complex than this solution suggests. Still other theorists critique what they assume is the underlying white and middle-class premises of each of these approaches—that there is an at-home, biological mother caregiver for most children, and therefore take issue with its failure to explain misogyny and differences in female and male identity development in families that are working class or that utilize communal rearing of children.

**See Also:** Chodorow; Nancy; Essentialism and Mothering; Feminist Theory and Motherhood; Feminist Mothering; Hays, Sharon; Homeplace; hooks, bell; Intensive Mothering; Institution of Mothering; Lazarre, Jane; Maternal Feminism; Maternal Thinking; Moraga, Cherríe; Mothering Versus Motherhood; Other Mothering; Patriarchal Ideology of Motherhood; Pronatalism; Rich, Adrienne; Ruddick, Sarah; Solinger, Rickie; Sterilization; Walker, Alice.

## Bibliography

Abbey, Sharon. *Mothers and Daughters: Connection, Empowerment, and Transformation.* Lanham, MD: Rowman & Littlefield, 2000.

hooks, bell. *Yearning: Race, Gender and Cultural Politics.* Cambridge, MA: South End Press, 1990.

Kinser, Amber E. *Motherhood and Feminism.* Jackson, TN: Seal Press, 2010.

Kinser, Amber E., ed. *Motherhood in the Third Wave.* Toronto, Demeter Press, 2008.

Moraga, Cherríe. *Waiting in the Wings: Portrait of a Queer Motherhood.* Ann Arbor, MI: Firebrand, 1997.

O'Reilly, Andrea, ed. *Maternal Theory: Essential Readings.* Toronto: Demeter Press, 2007.

O'Reilly, Andrea. *Motherhood at the 21st Century: Experience, Identity, Policy, Agency.* New York: Columbia University Press, 2010.

O'Reilly, Andrea. *Rocking the Cradle: Thoughts on Feminism, Motherhood and the Possibility of Empowered Mothering.* Toronto: Demeter Press, 2007.

Pollack, Sandra, and Jeanne Vaughn, eds. *Politics of the Heart: A Lesbian Parenting* Anthology. Ann Arbor, MI: Fireband Press, 1987.

Amber E. Kinser
East Tennessee State University

# Fertility

Fertility has acquired radically different meanings throughout history. Currently, fertility is used as a key word for both male and female contribution to reproduction. Women's fertility peaks between the ages of 19 to 24, and miscarriages and risks increase after 30. In men, erectile dysfunction with age, while increases while semen volume, sperm motility, and sperm morphology also decrease. However, fertility declines more slowly in men than in women. Women's fertility also changes within the menstrual cycle: It is actualized with ovulation, which usually occurs in the middle of the cycle.

## Fertility and Fecundity

Demographers attribute grave importance to the difference between fertility and fecundity. In this distinction, fertility is the actual number of children born in a population, and fecundity is the potential for reproduction. Fertility awareness techniques are personal negotiations between fertility and fecundity. They consist of information; for example, that the ovule is fertile for 48 hours and that once sperm is inside the uterus, it survives for two to three days. Yet, fertility-related technologies such as contraceptives, birth control methods, and infertility treatments are wiping out the lines between fertility and infertility.

The term *fertility* is commonly used in further terms such as fertility decline, fertility/demographic transition, and fertility rate, which are all interconnected. It is also used in the definition of fertility cults, which is the subject of a mythographic history rather than demography. However, recent research connects the two and depicts, for instance, ancient Rome as a time and place where contraceptives were used and a certain fertility transition was experienced. It is argued that female healers and the gendered knowledge they embodied disappeared by the Renaissance. Thus, everything they knew had to be learned again, resulting in the cultivated ignorance on fertility that prevailed in the West thereafter.

These developments that point to transformations in the history of fertility perception also require the pursuit of this history in different geographies, which are grouped here as Christian and non-Chris-

tian, developed and underdeveloped, and Communist and non-Communist countries. Whereas the first group refers to a division on abortion, the second group is divided on the usage of eugenics and systematized family planning programs in relation to the regulation of fertility. The last group is divided on the visibility of both the direct effects of fertility regulations on women and the direct relationship between fertility rates and female employment. All these divisions make sense in relation to the increasing importance of population in the forming of nations. Fertility regulation is one of the main pillars of modernization.

## Fertility Cults and Goddesses

The definitions of fertile periods as well as fertility and infertility have a background as old as the history of humanity, throughout which the meaning of fertility has changed radically. The earliest examples of discussions of fertility cults, mother goddesses, and earth mothers are the Woman of Willendorf (24,000–22,000 B.C.E.) and clay female figurines giving birth (7400–6000 B.C.E.) in Çatalhöyük. Fertility goddesses from different cultures around the world followed these ancient figurines. They were partially absorbed by Abrahamic religions and their reinventions in neo-paganism.

The discussions of modernism and the evaluations of women's fertility in terms of fertility rates followed. Going back to fertility cults became a strategy for women to release themselves from the established connections between fertility rates, the maternal body, and the modern state: The case of the feminist reconnection and reaction to fertility cults is one such reinvention. Whereas the reinvention of the past, both in the popular arena and the academic world, always has a historical and political context, going back to the goddesses points to the loss of agency related to modernist politics of reproduction and the need to reassociate with the maternal body in a "higher" level.

In the case of Çatalhöyük, goddess tourism now attracts neo-pagan women from different parts of the world. The figurines that give birth in a sitting position, with wild animals under each arm, have begun to be related to goddesses in this context. Yet, the academic-political understanding of this location is as multilayered as the settlement itself. The figurines in the context of the settlement, stripped from their goddess identities, point to fertility as the products of a far-distant culture that reminisced fertility as a part of their daily lives. This way, the centrality of fertility in human life is defined as a catalyst for unprecedented creativity. These local historical productions that reflect the interests of people from a distant past also reflect the means of expression that were available in that geography at that time.

## Modernist Politics of Reproduction

Continuities are interpreted to exist between Çatalhöyük and early Greek sites of cultural artifacts, despite the large time gap—most significantly, that agriculture was introduced into Greece and the rest of Europe through Anatolia. However, the equation of women's fertility to that of the soil also comes with the territory: The modernist politics of reproduction, which rooted itself in ancient Greek concepts, also took over the ancient Greek definitions of women's wombs as mere receptacles. This transfer of meaning that influenced modernist practices on the levels of statistics, medicine, and education suggests that transitions are experienced not only in the field of demographics, but also in the meanings attributed to fertility.

The first transition occurred when the knowledge of female healers and oral forms of medical knowledge were transferred from women to men and written forms of knowledge. Thus, ancient Greek philosophy constitutes one such area of transition. The second transition occurred when this conception was transferred to the West. The melting of female forms of knowledge in Hippocratic texts led to distorted conceptualizations of women's fertility in Abrahamic religions. In this perspective, the fertility goddesses of ancient Greece and Rome should be viewed as embodiments of these transfers. The relations of these figures to daily life requires questioning of how women's expressions of their fertility transformed, as well as of the mechanisms through which power was derived from suppressing these expressions.

An extensive knowledge of contraceptives and abortifacients still existed in ancient Rome, but this feminine body of knowledge about fertility control had been lost by the early modern period. Physicians did not have sufficient information about the female body, as they were not allowed to touch women, and women were not allowed in the profession. Thus, solutions for women were less represented in the medical arena from then on. The existing literature on women's role in the perception of fertility deals with Judaism as a women-centered religion, and Christianity as prolonging fertility via Mary. However, the philosophy of Islam is usually treated in a reduced manner.

The continuities between ancient Greek philosophy and the philosophy of Islam are easily disregarded by Western feminist scholarship. In fact, Greek medicine and ideas about fertility control not only influenced Rome, but also the Islamic civilizations in Anatolia. The different geographies and histories of Islamic culture were also influenced via Anatolia. For example, during the Middle Ages, where Europe held the Aristotelian view on reproduction where women were seen as the lesser sex, the Ottomans took over the Galenic view that acknowledged women's central role in reproduction.

While the scientific discoveries of the Enlightenment brought material evidence to this view, the value given to expertise, which broke the ties between female oral traditions and medicine in the first place, accelerated. As hospitals turned into medical shrines that also became tools for the social state to help the poor, women in increasing numbers started to give birth in hospitals. By the end of the 19th century, professionals gained more authority over fertility, leaving women less space to celebrate such developments in the perception of their fertility. In fact, what was left for women from this newly regained acknowledgment of their role in reproduction was twofold: First, they gained central roles in the eugenic reproduction of the white race as well as the prevention of the reproduction of nonwhites. Second, poor women, women of different races, and third world women were increasingly blamed for giving birth to unwanted populations. Thus, pronatalism, the desires and actions of centralized powers for a higher birthrate, and antinatalism coexisted in the context of eugenics.

## Fertility as Political and Cultural

Pronatalism has been an aspect of the modern state since the 16th century, where more territorialized populations meant more power. The fertility transition made antinatalism another tool to achieve higher levels of development. By the early 20th century, development began to be measured by the ratio of the population to productivity. Fertility was now negatively correlated with better education for women and more women in the workforce. With the new scientific developments that paralleled the developments in governance, fertility became as much a tool for decreasing population as it had once been for increasing population.

The development of family planning programs transformed the meaning of the use of contraceptives in the preceding cultures: Whereas women previously exercised individual use of family planning methods by means of family planning programs, these methods became systematic and widespread. The quest for measuring sustained that these programs was fed from and rephrased eugenic discourses on fertility, which told women that development was going to be calculated in terms of falling fertility rates. The demographic transition paradigm was put forward in the 1930s, when England captured low birth and death rates. As a result, low birth and mortality rates became the champion of development.

In contrast, in countries like India, high birth and mortality rates resulted in low population rates, but also low development rates. Family planning practices were developed for those countries that had falling mortality rates coupled with high birth rates. This demographic transition influenced China, Egypt, India, and South America. As a result of this paradigm and its resulting policies, China and India established birth control policies by the mid 1950s. Even in countries like Iran, where population was not a problem, power elites desired a healthier population that indicated development.

Throughout the 20th century, underdeveloped countries were distinguished in terms of their rising population, despite these policies. Meanwhile, the local practitioners of these policies developed a variety of methods to establish widespread birth control. Associating unwanted fertility with a far-distant history was one such method. For example, in the late 1960s and early 1970s, public health officials in Turkey argued that ignorant women continued to be fertile figures like the female figurines that

were found in Çatalhöyük 9,000 years ago. Fortunately, the trivialization of women's bodies ceased to be the center of these policies throughout the 20th century. Informing women on methods took center stage, but the aim of reducing fertility for the sake of development prevailed.

In Latin American countries as well as Greece, where Christianity was an important cultural factor, these discourses were formed more in terms of avoiding abortion. Yet bans on abortion still constitutes grounds for never-ending debate.

In communist countries throughout the 20th century, fertility regulations were more visible, and female employment became as important as motherhood. Whether fertility rates were sought to be decreased, as in Maoist China—or increased, as in Ceausescu's Romania—women's fertility has been used as a direct tool for state policies. Like elsewhere, women had to delegate control over their bodies. In other words, the importance of population in nation formation and national success was maintained through maternal bodies, regardless of ideological and religious differences.

**Reproduction Techniques and Technologies**
Works like *Fertility Transitions, Family Structure and Population Policy* provide a contextualized comparison of different countries, yet the place of women as actual and potential mothers is unproblematic. The new literature on reproduction techniques, well exemplified by Sama-Resource Group for Women and Health, develops a similar contextualization but better analysis. Sama-Resource Group for Women and Health from India has emphasized that new technologies do not free women from the regulated fertility roles designed by the social state—on the contrary, they rivet women to these roles. Thus, while fertility transitioned into government territory, the new transformation from the regulation of fertility to the treatment of infertility still takes place in this territory.

For example, cloning, while seemingly attributing more power to the female sex, promises to leave less authority to women, as it is under the total control of science. Previous experiences with assisted reproductive technologies (ART) have demonstrated that even when donor men are sought for reproduction, the invisible agency of the husband gets stronger in the permission he admits to his wife. Likewise, the history of fertility has shown that as the collaboration between the state and the medical profession gets more invisible, its interference on women's bodies increases: stem cell and embryo transfers require women's bodies, the integrity of which are easily overlooked in the discussions of such transfers.

Thus, the previously existing problems related to fertility and its regulation, such women's loss of control over their maternal bodies, are not left behind as infertility becomes a new context in which to study fertility. On the contrary, these problems become more intense with the illusion that they are left behind. These developments also point a more acute need for women to associate with their maternal bodies in more creative ways.

**See Also:** Artificial Insemination; Birth Control; Birth Goddesses; Childbirth; Earth Mothers; Family Planning; Infertility; Reproductive Technologies.

**Bibliography**
Agyei, William K.A. *Fertility and Family Planning in the Third World*. London: Croom Helm, 1988.
Bogdan, Janice. "Losing Birth: The Erosion of Women's Control Over and Knowledge About Birth, 1650–1900." In *Changing Education: Women as Radicals and Conservators*, Joyce Antler and Sari Knopp Biklen, eds. Albany: State University of New York Press, 1990.
Caldwell, John C. "Fertility Control in the Classical World: Was There an Ancient Fertility Transition?" *Journal of Population Research*, v.21/1 (2004).
Davin, Anna. "Imperialism and Motherhood." *History Workshop*, v.5 (1978).
Hodder, Ian and Craig Cessford. "Daily Practice and Social Memory at Çatalhöyük." *American Antiquity*, v.69/1 (2004).
Sama-Resource Group for Women and Health. "Assisted Reproductive Technologies: Autonomy or Subjugation? A Case Study From India." *Women's Studies International Forum*, v.31 (2008).
Ze'evi, Dror. *Producing Desire: Changing Sexual Discourse in the Ottoman Middle East*. Berkeley: University of California Press, 2006.

Elif Ekin Aksit
Ankara University, Turkey

# Fetal Alcohol Syndrome

Fetal alcohol syndrome is one of a group of birth defects commonly grouped together as fetal alcohol spectrum disorders (FASD), also known as fetal alcohol effects. These disorders include a range of effects that can occur or develop in individuals whose biological mother drank alcohol during pregnancy. These effects can include physical, mental, behavioral, and/or learning disabilities, with possible lifelong implications. The umbrella term *FASD* includes FAS, partial fetal alcohol syndrome (PFAS), alcohol-related birth defects (ARBD), and alcohol-related neurodevelopmental disorder (ARND).

## Causes and Symptoms of FASD

Alcohol use during pregnancy is the leading known preventable cause of mental retardation and birth defects in the United States. Because alcohol easily passes through the placental barrier and the fetus is less well equipped to physically process and eliminate alcohol than its mother, the fetus tends to receive a higher concentration of alcohol than its mother; alcohol also lingers longer in the fetus's body than it does in the mother's.

It is unclear how much alcohol is too much, partially because different women process alcohol differently. Full-blown FAS is the result of chronic drinking during pregnancy; FASD and ARND may occur with only occasional or binge drinking. Alcohol consumption during the first trimester is particularly problematic; during these months, many women do not yet realize they are pregnant, and so may feel safe drinking alcohol. However, alcohol interferes with the normal development of the brain during these months, and thus women who drink during the first trimester of pregnancy often have children with the most severe problems. The embryonic brain and central nervous system develop most rapidly during the final trimester of pregnancy, and drinking during these months is linked to growth retardation and other effects. Because there is no clear understanding of "how much is too much," drinking at any time during pregnancy is generally discouraged by medical professionals.

Outcomes of FASD vary among individuals, but can include low birth weight; small head circumference; facial abnormalities, including smaller eye openings, flattened cheekbones, and indistinct philtrum (an underdeveloped groove between the nose and upper lip); epilepsy; growth deficits; heart, lung, and kidney defects; behavior problems such as inability to concentrate, social withdrawal, impulsiveness, and anxiety; attention and memory problems; poor coordination and motor skill delays; difficulty with judgment and reasoning; and learning difficulties and disabilities, such as poor language comprehension and poor problem-solving skills. The outcome for infants with FASD varies depending on the extent of symptoms, but almost none have normal brain development.

ARND, a recently recognized category of prenatal damage, refers to children who exhibit only the behavioral and emotional problems of FAS/FASD without any signs of developmental delay or physical deficiencies. Because these children may score well on intelligence tests and exhibit few or none of the physical characteristics considered typical of FASD children, they are frequently undiagnosed, misdiagnosed, or underdiagnosed. This makes treatment for the child, as well as support for the family and other caregivers (such as teachers), particularly challenging.

### Prevalence of FAS/FASD
Medical experts consider the incidence (number of new cases each year) of FAS and FASD to be significantly underreported. Worldwide, the incidence is estimated at about 1.9 per 1,000 live births. There are an estimated 40,000 cases of FASD each year in the United States, with wide racial disparity: 0.3 per 10,000 births for Asian Americans; 0.8 per 10,000 births for Hispanics; 0.9 per 10,000 births for whites; 6.0 per 10,000 births for African Americans; and 29.9 per 10,000 births for Native Americans.

FAS is the most severe and least common effect under the FASD umbrella; it is estimated that each year in the United States, 1 in every 750 infants is born with a pattern of physical, developmental, and functional problems associated with FAS. These problems tend to intensify as children move into adolescence and adulthood.

Increasing education around alcohol consumption as well as improved prenatal screening and support for pregnant women who drink alcohol are credited with slightly lowering the incidence of FAS over the last decade. Support is available for the parents of children diagnosed with FASD. The National Organization on Fetal Alcohol Syndrome (NOFAS) is based in the United States; FASWorld is an international organization of parents and medical professionals available for support and resources.

**See Also:** Alcoholism; "Bad" Mothers; Drug Abuse; Infant Mortality; Prenatal Health Care.

### Bibliography
Centers for Disease Control and Prevention. "Fetal Alcohol Spectrum Disorders." www.cdc.gov/ncbddd/fas (accessed January 2009).

Clark, M.E. and W.B. Gibbard. "Overview of Fetal Alcohol Spectrum Disorders for Mental Health Professionals." *Canadian Child and Adolescent Psychology Review*, v.12/3 (August 2003).

Stratton, K., et al., eds. *Fetal Alcohol Syndrome: Diagnosis, Epidemiology, Prevention, and Treatment.* Washington, DC: Institutes of Medicine, 1996.

Barbara Gurr
University of Connecticut

# Film, Mothers in

Motherhood has provided subject matter for many movies. Not surprisingly movie directors usually prefer dramatic stories with lots of conflict and tales of illegitimacy, abandonment, maternal cruelty, and the like provide more exciting material than happy families living ordinary lives.

So while no one should take the portrayals of mothers in movies as representing the truth about the real state of motherhood in any particular time and place, movies are fascinating cultural documents which can offer a window into a particular historical era by telling us what representations of motherhood people were willing to pay to watch on the big screen. The content presented in films has also been affected at times by censorship such as that imposed by the Motion Picture Code in the United States and the British Board of Film Censors in Great Britain.

## The Idealized Mother

Saintly mothers appear on screen beginning with the earliest feature films. A good example is D.W. Griffith's *Intolerance* (1916) which intertwines stories from four historical periods—the Fall of Babylon, the early Christian era, the French Renaissance, and early 20th-century America—to portray man's cruelty to his fellow man. In contrast to the of intolerance of these stories Griffith presents a recurring image of a mother rocking her baby in a cradle, representing the maternal love which has allowed life to continue.

The heroically self-sacrificing Jewish mother appears again and again in Yiddish films as well as English-language films set among recent immigrants to the United States. Typically the mothers represent the culture of the old world in contrast to the assimilationist ambitions of their children. For instance *Hungry Hearts* (1922) juxtaposes saintly mother Hannah who lives only for her family with her daughter Sara who has ambitions to "become a somebody" and move beyond her mother's narrow world. *The Jazz Singer* (1927), well known as the first "talkie" or movie with synchronized sound, also provides a good example of this character. The film focuses on the conflict between the desire of Al Jolson's character to pursue a career as a jazz singer and his father's wish that he become a cantor. Jolson's mother mediates between the two men: she loves both her husband and son unconditionally and is able to heal the rift between them. The "Yidishe Mama" became a common American cultural type which spread beyond movies and other cultural products aimed at a Jewish audience; it's still seen and understood by audiences today in popular works such as the musical *Fiddler on the Roof*. Gertrude Berg created one of the most successful characters of this type in Molly Goldberg, who was featured on popular radio and television programs as well as the 1950 film *The Goldbergs*.

A different take on the trope of the saintly mother recalls the Victorian ideal of "the Angel in the House" which demands that women create an ideal home environment and selflessly meet all the needs of their husband and children. This trope was particularly popular in films set during World War II when women not only kept the home fires burning but were also idealized as embodying the values the war was being fought to preserve. The title character of the 1942 William Wyler film *Mrs. Miniver* (1942) epitomizes this wartime paragon. Mrs. Miniver (Greer Garson) is a suburban London housewife during the Blitz who despite the bombs falling manages to keep a beautiful home, tend her garden, supervise her children and disarm a German soldier while simultaneously expressing sympathy for him.

Wartime films about Americans families also had their "Angels in the House." A well-known example is the character of Mary Hatch (Donna Reed) in Frank Capra's *It's a Wonderful Life*. Her role is confined to creating a cheerful and loving home filled with children while her husband struggles with the world outside, but she also represents the ideal to which Stewart returns after his brush with suicide. The character played by Myrna Loy in *The Best Years of Our Lives* (1946) represents a similar character: the eternally patient and absolutely competent wife who kept the household running and raised the children while her husband was serving in the Pacific.

Big families ruled by idealized mothers also provided material for many sentimental popular films. In *Life With Father* (1947) Irene Dunn artfully manages a 19th-century American household full of children, visiting relatives, and servants as well as her ill-tempered husband with grace and charm. She even manages to exert her feminine influence long enough to convince her husband that he must be baptized, demonstrating that her husband may bluster but she's the real heart of the family. Dunn played a similar role in *I Remember Mama* (1948) in which she held together a large Norwegian immigrant family in the early 20th-century San Francisco through financial hardship and medical emergencies. *Meet Me in St. Louis* (1944) offers a nostalgia-drenched look at life in a large family in the turn of the century Midwest. Mary Astor plays the wife of a successful businessman who gracefully manages a large household of daughters, servants, assorted relatives and suitors while also remaining entirely supportive of her husband's career.

## Representatives of Civilization

Mothers in western films often appear as symbols of civilization (in contrast to the wild and untamed spirit of the west) as well as aspects of life which the men are fighting to protect or desire but are not sure how to embrace. In *Angel and the Badman* (1947) Irene Rich plays the mother of a Quaker family who nurses the gunslinger Quirt Evans back to health after he is wounded in a gunfight. He becomes attracted to her peaceful ways as well as her beautiful daughter and is forced to examine the conflict between his aspirations and his current life.

In *Shane* (1953), Jean Arthur's mother character represents the nurturing force of the family which is pitted against the violence of gunslingers as well as unattached drifters such as Shane. The same story was adapted for *Pale Rider* (1985) in which Clint Eastwood plays the preacher, a Shane-like character who protects a group of homesteaders against a predatory mining coming. The sexual undercurrent of attraction between the mother and Shane in the original film is transferred to her daughter and Shane in the remake: in both cases the women are attracted by the wild and untamed force he represents which is missing in their settled lives.

Australian films include a substantial number of films about pioneer and rancher life, and as with American westerns mothers generally appear as supporting characters. *The Chant of Jimmie Blacksmith* presents three different images of motherhood: the racist Heather Newby, the sluttish Gilda Marshall, and the supportive Mrs. McCready. In *Dusty*, the main story is about a man and his half-wild dog who retain some of the untamed spirit of Australia while the female characters, including the mother of the family for whom Tom works, are firmly within the settler class and represent the attempt to bring settled life and European culture to the outback.

Maternal characters play a similar role in the many Australian "growing up" films of the 1970s and 1980s. It doesn't matter whether the characters coming to maturation are male, as in *Gallipoli* (1981, but set in the 1910s) or female as in *The Getting of Wisdom* (1978, but set in the 1880s) and *My Brilliant Career* (1979, but set in the 1890s): mothers are portrayed as part of the established society against which the central characters are rebelling.

## Mothers as Martyrs

Many popular films have been built around the story of a mother who sacrifices everything for her family but receives only rejection and rebuke for her pains. In Josef von Sternberg's *Blonde Venus* (1932), Helen Faraday returns to her singing career in order to pay for medical treatments for her husband; in the process she attracts the attention of a millionaire who also gives her money. Not understanding her motivations her husband divorces her and takes their child, and the family is only reunited when he comes to realize that his wife was acting in his interest.

In *Imitation of Life* (1934; remade in 1959), racial politics are added to a tale of maternal martyrdom. African American housekeeper Delilah Johnson works for a white woman, accepting low wages in return for having a home for her daughter Peola to grow up in. Peola is much lighter-skinned than her mother and when she becomes an adult decides to try passing for white. This involves cutting off all contact with her mother and turning her back on the African American community. Delilah remains devoted to her daughter and mourns her absence, but Peola sees the light too late, breaking down at her mother's funeral and begging for forgiveness.

*Stella Dallas* (1937) incorporates class rather than racial barriers in a similar tale of maternal sacrifice. Working-class Stella marries the wealthy Stephen Dallas and gives birth to Laurel who through her father has the opportunity to associate with children of other rich people and thus becomes far more sophisticated than her mother. Stella becomes an embarrassment to Laurel and decides to step out of her life so as to not impede her advancement into society.

The final scene hammers on the extent of her sacrifice by showing Stella standing in a rainstorm watching through a window as Laurel gets married to a wealthy young man. A similar story is told in *Mildred Pierce* (1945): Mildred leaves her ineffectual husband and raises her daughters alone, working as a waitress, then founding a successful chain of restaurants. She showers money and gifts on her older daughter Veda, who responds with ingratitude, but even Mildred can't cover up a murder committed by Veda.

Maternal melodramas are also popular in Japan, where they are called *Haha-mono* or "mother films." An example is Keisuke Kinoshita's *A Japanese Tragedy* (1953) that centers on the efforts of widow Haruko Inoue to provide for her children's education through a variety of enterprises including working as a bar hostess and selling goods on the black market. Her efforts come to nothing as her son tries to get himself adopted into a wealthy family and her daughter squanders the money provided for her tuition.

The 1939 film *Mutterliebe* (Mother Love) is an example of a maternal melodrama created during the Nazi regime. It tells the story of Marthe Pirlinger, a widow with four sons who sets up a laundry and takes in a lodger in order to support them. At first her efforts are not rewarded: one son impregnates an employee at the laundry, two others carry on affairs with married women, and one goes blind. But the story ends happily as Marthe donates a cornea to restore one son's sight and the other sons reform their behavior: in the final scene the family is happily reunited in a celebration of Marthe's 60th birthday.

## The Monstrous Mother

Some films delight in portraying monstrous mothers who are as extreme in their evil as the saintly and martyred mothers are in the goodness. A famous example is *Mommie Dearest* (1981), a biopic about Joan Crawford based on the bestselling tell-all memoir written by her adopted daughter Christina which portrays Crawford as an alcoholic, mentally unstable woman who is so self-centered that she adopts four children in order to further her career. She's also a child abuser: the "No wire hangers!" scene in which Crawford beats Christina for the sin of hanging clothes on wire hangers is legendary among devotees of camp.

Mothers in films sometimes exert evil influence through their sons. The gangster film *White Heat* is a good example: gang leader Cody Jarrett relies greatly on the counsel of his ruthless mother and goes to her rather than his wife for emotional support. The film's final scene suggests that his entire career was an attempt to impress his mother: battling police atop a gas storage tank which is about to explode Jarrett's final words are "Made it, Ma! Top of the World!" Claude Rains's character in Alfred Hitchcock's *Notorious* (1946) is equally dominated by his mother, who opposes his marriage and treats his wife coldly. When Rains discovers that he has

*Actress Joan Crawford's real life as a mother was depicted as notorious in the film* Mommie Dearest.

married an American spy, it is his mother who comes up with the solution of slowly poisoning her so it will appear she died of natural causes; the film lingers on her coldly smoking a cigarette (a behavior not usually associated with mothers in films) as she works out these plans.

The stage mother seems monstrous because she reverses societal expectations by putting her own needs ahead of those of her children. An early film based on this trope is *Stage Mother* (1933) in which the widow Kitty Lorraine channels her own repressed desires to perform through her daughter. She pushes the girl to success on the stage and breaks up an engagement which would interfere with that success. Tennis stardom rather than show business is the ambition of Clair Trevor's character Milly in *Hard, Fast and Beautiful* (1951): she pushes the girl to accept money under the table and breaks up

Florence's romance with a local boy while trying to marry her off to a wealthier man.

The most unforgiving look at a stage mother, and also one of the best known, is the Broadway musical *Gypsy*, which was filmed in 1963 as *Gypsy: A Musical Fable*. Although the film considerably softens the story compared to the original Broadway presentation, it still presents a portrait of a woman who forces her daughters to perform on the vaudeville circuit to satisfy her own crazed ambition. This mother is so caught up in pursuing success that she can't see that she is pushing away both her children and the man who loves her, although in the film there is a suggestion that she may reconcile with her youngest daughter. Sometimes mothers are falsely accused of behaving monstrously: such stories give filmmakers a chance to examine how quick some people are to judge mothers who seem to not measure up to their ideal. An example is the Australian docudrama *A Cry in the Dark* (1988), which examines the case of Lindy Chamberlain who was accused of killing her nine-week-old daughter. Chamberlain claimed the child was stolen from the family campsite by a dingo (wild dog) and was eventually cleared of the charges, but not before she had been harshly judged in the court of public opinion.

## Unwed Mothers

Unwed motherhood has been a film staple from the earliest features onward, perhaps because it allowed filmmakers to touch on issues of high emotional impact while making the story socially acceptable by presenting it as a cautionary tale. Until the late 20th century, unmarried mothers were generally shown to suffer for their actions and often the film includes an explanation (such as deception on the man's part) for how the woman came to be pregnant. In D.W. Griffith's *Way Down East* (1920), Lillian Gish's character is tricked into a fake wedding by a man who abandons her when she becomes pregnant. Her baby dies and she gets a job, but when her employer learns of her previous child he throws her out of the house during a snowstorm and she nearly perishes while crossing a frozen river in a scene which recalls another fugitive, the escaped slave Eliza in stage versions of *Uncle Tom's Cabin*. Similar trickery is behind a pregnancy in *Forbidden* (1932): Lulu has an affair with a man she does not realize is married. When she bears his child he offers to adopt it but not acknowledge his paternity, an offer she accepts out of desperation.

Charlie Chaplin's first feature film *The Kid* (1921) is framed with a story of unmarried motherhood and parental abandonment. The film opens with a mother leaving a charity hospital: to underscore the pitiful nature of her plight scenes of her carrying her baby are intercut with scenes of Christ carrying His cross. Unable to care for the child, she leaves it in a limousine with a note begging that it be cared for. Chaplin's character takes the child home and raises him and after many twists and turns of fate mother and child are reunited. In *Torch Singer* (1933) unmarried Sally Trent has a baby which she cannot support, so she gives it up for adoption. Feeling her life is now ruined, she pursues a career as a torch singer in grimy bars. Then she becomes a host on a children's radio program and uses the show to contact her lost daughter, which gives her the hope necessary to abandon her dissolute lifestyle.

The *Sin of Madelon Claudet* (1931) offers an interesting combination of the mother as sinner and the mother as saint. Madelon (Helen Hays, who won an Oscar for the role) becomes pregnant by an artist who refuses to marry her, setting her up for a career path which runs from kept woman to prison to prostitute and petty thief. But she sends money anonymously to pay for her son's education through medical school and they are reunited as she is near death.

The social disruption of war was used as an explanation for unwed motherhood in several Hollywood films. In *Only Yesterday* (1933) Mary Lane becomes pregnant by Jim Emerson who shortly thereafter leaves to fight in World War I. She moves in with a liberal-minded aunt and raises her son there. After the war, realizing that Jim does not remember who she is, she settles down to raising the child without him. Twelve years later Mary has become ill and she writes Jim about his son: he regrets his behavior toward her and vows to support the child, despite the fact that most of his wealth has been wiped out in the stock market crash. Bette Davis is caught in a similar situation in *The Old Maid* (1939): her character Charlotte becomes pregnant by her fiancé, but he is killed in the Civil War. To prevent a scandal Charlotte raises the child (Tina) as one among a group of orphans whom she cares for. Several years later, she is engaged to another man who leaves her after learning that she already has a daughter, and only on her wedding day does Tina learn that her mother endured a life as an old maid rather than give up her daughter.

In more recent films single motherhood is often treated as a fact of life rather than a disgrace, even when the film is set in an earlier historical period. For instance *Dancing at Lughnasa* (1998) presents the story of five unmarried sisters living in a small Irish village in the 1930s. One has an illegitimate child (who is narrating the story as an adult), but although there is an undercurrent of sadness as the sisters' household is on the verge of economic collapse, neither the son nor his mother are shown to suffer unduly for the circumstances of his birth.

*Juno* (2007) offers a modern take on illegitimacy in which a high school student becomes pregnant and decides to give the baby up for adoption to a couple she has selected. The screenplay by Diablo Cody won an Oscar and the film was praised for its low-key look at teen pregnancy and the fact that the girl took charge of her own fate, but was also criticized as seeming to present a pro-life position and an unrealistically rosy picture of the girl's experience (only occasional references are made to the social stigma or discomforts of pregnancy).

**See Also:** Celebrity Motherhood; Mothers in Dramatic Arts; Idealization of Mothers; Popular Culture and Mothering.

**Bibliography**
Antler, J. *You Never Call! You Never Write! A Social History of the Jewish Mother.* New York: Oxford University Press, 2007.
Basinger, J. *A Woman's View: How Hollywood Spoke to Women 1930–1960.* Boston: University Press of New England, 1995.
Byars, J. *All That Hollywood Allows: Re-Reading Gender in 1950s Melodrama.* Chapel Hill: University of North Carolina Press, 1991.
Fischer, L. *Cinematernity: Film, Motherhood, Gender* Princeton, NJ: Princeton University Press, 1996.

Sarah E. Boslaugh
Washington University School of Medicine

# Finland

Motherhood and early childhood are firmly secured by the Finnish welfare state. Mothers have free access to special advisory and health care services during pregnancy and after giving birth. The services attend to the general health of mothers and their babies, and provide guidance in motherhood skills. The state also provides every expectant mother with a maternity package containing basic care necessities and clothes for care of the newborn child.

An earnings-related maternity benefit (about 70 percent of salary) is paid for 105 days, and a parental leave allowance is paid for a further 158 days. Parental leave can be taken by either parent, but it is typically the mother who stays at home. Fathers are entitled to a paternity leave of about three weeks. Every child in Finland under school age has the right to daycare, and a child of 6 years of age is entitled to preschool education. The availability of daycare is one of the most significant factors enabling mothers to work. After maternity/parental leave, mothers have a legal right to return to their previous jobs. The rate of employment of mothers with children aged 9 or older is as high as that of fathers. Most Finnish mothers work full time. During their compulsory education, children are provided with school meals, general health care services, and dental care paid for by the government.

On average, Finnish women are 30 years old and men 32 when they marry. Before they marry, a couple may live together for several years and have their first child. In 2006, half of all women giving birth to their first child were not married. Of second children, a third of all women were married; and of third children, a quarter of all children were born to mothers who were not officially married. Common-law marriages have become an increasingly typical family arrangement in Finland.

In 2007, 20 percent of families with children 0–17 years of age were single-parent families. The majority of single parents were women; only one in 10 were male. Motherhood is taking on increasingly different forms in Finnish society. About every tenth child is born to a mother who does not live in a permanent relationship. The number of such mothers has slightly increased over the past few years. Some mothers live in a registered partnership; in 2007, there were 146 same-sex couples with children in Finland.

For a western European country, the fertility rate in Finland is high. Since the late 1980s, it has continuously been above 1.7; in 2007, the figure was 1.83. The average number of children in a Finnish family is 2.2. The typical family has two children, followed by families with at least three children. A number of women remain childless for various reasons; of those women who are nearing the end of their childbearing age, 16–17 percent are childless.

Advanced maternal age is defined as an increase in the age at which women give birth to their first child. First-time mothers in Finland are on average 28 years old. Part of the reason for women postponing motherhood is their high level of education. Other reasons are employment insecurity, lifestyle preferences, and difficulties finding a suitable partner. In 2007, 10 percent of first-time mothers were aged 35 or above, and this tendency is expected to grow. Postponing motherhood may affect fertility. Fertility treatments have increased; today, 3 percent of children in Finland are artificially conceived.

**See Also:** European Union; Single Mothers; Welfare and Mothering.

**Bibliography**
Nikander, Timo. *Fertility and Family Surveys in Countries of the ECE Region*. New York: United Nations, 1998.
Ryan, Lorna. *Working Families: A Comparative Study of Economic Activity Amongst Lone Parents in Ireland and Finland*. Dublin, Ireland: Parents Alone Resource Centre, 1997.
Tilastokeskus. "Gender Statistics." http://www.stat.fi/index_en.html (accessed January 2009).

Kaisa Kauppinen
Finnish Institute of Occupational Health

# Firestone, Shulamith

Radical feminist theorist, activist, and artist, Shulamith Firestone was born in 1945 in Ottawa, Ontario, Canada. Though she eventually disengaged from feminist group politics, Firestone was a key figure in the emergence of the second wave women's movement. She cofounded several American feminist organizations, including its first women's liberation group in 1967, the Chicago West side feminists; as well as Radical Women, also in 1967; Redstockings in 1969; and the New York Radical Feminists that same year. She has also published several key texts, including *Notes From the First Year: Women's Liberation* (edited with Anne Koedt, 1968), *Redstocking* (1969), *Notes From the Second Year: Radical Feminism* (with Koedt, 1970), *Notes From the Third Year: Women's Liberation* (with Koedt, 1971), and *Airless Spaces* (1998), a book of short stories.

Firestone is perhaps best known, however, for her book *The Dialectic of Sex: The Case for Feminist Revolution* (1970), a classic of the second wave written before she was 25 years old, which examines the unequal division of reproductive labor between the sexes and the institutions, especially the nuclear family, which this unequal reproductive labor made possible. Key to Firestone's analysis are her critique of love (because love is not possible between those who are unequal) and the prediction that advances in reproductive technology would make the biological family, biological motherhood, and the sexual distinction between women and men, increasingly irrelevant.

## Sex Class Versus Economic Class

In *Dialectic's* controversial text, Firestone adapts Marx and Engels's dialectical materialist framework to argue that the original class distinction was that of sex class, rather than economic class—that Marxism failed to realize it was the relations of reproduction that underlie the relations of production, and not production that had been the driving force of history. So "deep as to be invisible," sex class for Firestone is, therefore, the fundamental social inequality; what is required to understand women's subordination, she argues, is a biological explanation that emphasizes the different and unequal roles of the sexes in reproduction, and the concomitant oppression of women that is their direct result. Within such an arrangement, women's liberation could only come from a feminist revolution, but not of the strictly economic sort that Marx and Engels envisioned. Whereas Marx and Engels predicted that the working class would seize control of the means of production, thereby eliminating economic inequality and class distinction, Firestone insists that the elimination of sex class could only come through women's seizing control of the means of reproduction, whereby distinct reproductive roles for women and men would no longer be necessary for reproduction.

Such a feminist revolution would turn on the emancipatory potential of reproductive technology. Contraception and artificial insemination were already in use at the time of Firestone's writing; as she put it, with choice of sex and test-tube fertilization "just around the corner" by then, development of the artificial placenta or even parthenogenesis were, as far as Firestone was concerned, real possibilities for the future as well. Once extra-uterine reproduction were to be achieved, gender parity and an androgynous society free of sex classes or distinctions based on biological sex would be inevitable.

These pioneering ideas about what is natural versus what is humanly possible have since been a source of much debate among feminists. In articulating a feminist version of historical materialism, Firestone underscores the important oversight in Marxist theory that even in a classless state, women's oppression on the basis of their sex would remain. However, as socialist feminist Zillah Eisenstein demonstrates, in declaring women a sex class, Firestone artificially separates the sexual and economic spheres, replacing capitalism with patriarchy as the oppressive system, when in fact both are in play simultaneously.

Mary O'Brien, also arguing from a radical feminist perspective, contends that giving up the capacity for biological reproduction could in fact mean giving up women's only power under patriarchy. Firestone and other radical feminists could also be criticized for reducing women's oppression to the functions of their bodies, when in fact women's oppression is a more complex ideological problem in society. Finally, it could be said that Firestone was naive about the future of reproductive technology and the likelihood that women's interests could ever drive developments in this area, given that science and medicine were and still are male-dominated fields.

**See Also:** Artificial Insemination; Dialectics of Reproduction; O'Brien, Mary; Reproduction; Reproductive Labor; Reproductive Technologies.

**Bibliography**
Eisenstein, Zillah. *Capitalist Patriarchy and the Case for Socialist Feminism.* New York: Monthly Review Press, 1979.
Firestone, Shulamith. *The Dialectic of Sex: The Case for Feminist Revolution.* New York: Farrar, Straus and Giroux, 2003.
O'Brien, Mary. *The Politics of Reproduction.* New York: Routledge, 1981.

Shelley Zipora Reuter
Concordia University

# First Nations

First Nations is a term that refers to more than 600 groups of indigenous peoples in North America exclusively, and does not refer to indigenous peoples on other continents. The term *First Nations* can be somewhat misleading. Collectively, First Nations includes Métis and Aboriginal peoples. There is not complete agreement about including Inuit people in the definition of First Nations.

## History of the First Nations

First Nations people have not seen themselves as a nation. However, they were identified as the first inhabitants of North America by the European explorers who migrated in the mid- to late 1800s to what later became known as North America. When Europeans settled in North America, trading occurred between the early settlers and the First Nations people. At that time, the governments of Canada and the United States designated reserved lands, to which the First Nations groups were relocated. These state-sanctioned lands were referred to as reservations (or reserves). This meant that First Nations people were given land, not of their choosing, to live together in colonies apart from the rest of the population. Many communities are still organized by this model.

Governing bodies were later developed, and First Nations people were allowed to vote as early as the 1920s in the United States, and in parts of Canada as late as the 1960s. Some First Nations communities were still hunters and gatherers when they encountered the European migrants. Some treaties still exist to provide special privileges to First Nations people to hunt and fish for food and cultural purposes.

## Cultural Values and Traditions and Their Loss

Despite the diversity among First Nations groups, some cultural values are held in common. These values include respecting elders and maintaining connections with one's history or heritage. In addition, there has typically been an emphasis on the importance of caring for children, looking after extended family members, and nurturing respectful community relations. There is also an emphasis on spirituality, religion, and storytelling in First Nations cultures as ways of expressing values and teaching people how to interact respectfully. Many First Nations traditions link individual health with community wellness. Collective wellness is also linked to environmental well-being, as many First Nations people consider themselves the keepers of the earth and animals. In many First Nations cultures, time was understood as flowing and related to nature's seasons, moon cycles, and celebrations for community members at different life stages. Humor and fun are also important values in parenting and maintaining positive community relationships.

Expression of spiritual traditional ceremonies and medicinal elder ceremonies were illegal in much of North America until the late 1900s; some ceremonies are still illegal in certain locations. Compulsory education programs frequently separated children from their parents by taking children to residential schools in locations away from their communities.

These legal policies created a two-tiered North American society, which has had long-lasting effects often referred to by scholars as the colonization of First Nations peoples. Some of the negative results of colonization are losses of First Nations languages and cultural traditions, including food, traditional clothing, celebrations, and spiritual ceremonies. Other losses for First Nations people include health inequities and lack of educational and employment opportunities. These inequities have resulted in higher mortality rates for First Nations people in North America compared to the rest of the population. Life expectancy is shorter for First Nations people and has been linked to lack of access to

healthy food and adequate medical care. Lack of equal opportunities for children and youth have also been linked to higher rates of youth suicide in First Nations communities. Higher poverty rates have been linked to colonization effects. Other losses that have occurred for First Nations people are the loss of oral history and indigenous knowledge. Generally, scholars agree that North American educational systems have promoted European values and culture over indigenous values, effectively projecting negative images of First Nations peoples.

## Opportunities for Youth

Some efforts are being made to eradicate inequitable practices. However, First Nations allies argue that First Nations people are continuing to experience inequity in school systems and other public and private institutions like child welfare organizations, universities, medical services, and social services. Many First Nations communities have developed independent governance systems to reclaim positive First Nations identity, healing, and economic opportunities for First Nations children, youth, and adults. Some First Nations communities sponsor their youth to attend university programs. First Nations allies recognize that numerous social changes must occur for equitable access to medical, educational, and economic opportunities.

**See Also:** Aboriginal Mothering; Community Mothering; Native Americans; Race and Racism; Residential School and Mothers/First Nations.

## Bibliography

Brubacher, Maurice. *Coming Home: The Story of Tikinagan Child and Family Services*. Sioux Lookout, Ontario, Canada: Tikinagan Child and Family Services, 2006.

Felt, Marvin D., John S. Wodarski, and Hilary N. Weaver. *Voices of First Nations People: Human Services Considerations*. New York: Routledge, 1998.

Lavell-Harvard, D. Memee and Jeannette Corbiere Lavell, eds. *Until Our Hearts Are on the Ground: Aboriginal Mothering, Oppression, Resistance And Rebirth*. Toronto: Demeter Press, 2006.

Carolyn J. Peters
University of Manitoba

# Florida

Florida was occupied for thousands of years by the indigenous Native Americans before the Europeans first arrived in 1513, starting settlements later in the 16th century. It was put under English control in 1763, but was regained by Spain 20 years later; it finally ceded to the United States in 1819 and gained statehood in 1845. The 2008 population estimate stood at 18,300,000. The state's birth rate is 13.1 and the fertility rate is 2.09 children per woman, only very slightly lower than the rate for the entire country, and significantly lower than many other nearby states.

## Population and Politics

The makeup of the population of Florida changed dramatically during the 19th and 20th centuries. Prior to the American Civil War, there was a large Spanish-speaking population with connections to parts of the Spanish Caribbean, along with a slave-owning plantation society. Both of these were effectively eliminated by the war and Reconstruction.

In the second half of the 20th century, Florida's climate invited a building boom that brought many northerners there in search of good weather and a better and less expensive lifestyle. Gradually, Florida became home to more and more retirees. Beginning in the late 1950s, a large Cuban population also settled in Florida, fleeing their Communist government.

There is much wealth in the state, but also extreme poverty, which is reflected in the state's health system—the hospitals are among the best in the world, but are out of reach for those unable to afford treatment or insurance. Some hospitals charge a minimum of $300 for emergency room treatment. The result is that many mothers without insurance avoid the hospital system, which has resulted in the proliferation of clinics that can handle non-life-threatening medical conditions at a lower price.

The median income in the state is about 20 percent lower than the national average, due in part to 12.1 percent of the population living below the poverty line (as compared to a national average of 13 percent). Since the 1970s, there have been many changes in laws and regulations. The abortion laws in Florida were amended in 1972 to reflect the American Law Institute Model Penal Code. A recent study has shown that after the Medicaid income eligibility threshold was raised in 1989, and the rate of low birthweights for infants fell from 69.7 per 1,000 to 61.8 per 1,000 for those who did not have private insurance. For those with insurance, the figures were unchanged. The maternity mortality rate is low, but there are still cases such as in 2004, when Miami singer Nadine Shamir died the morning after the birth of her first child from complications that arose after the delivery.

Compulsory education for all children aged between 6 and 16 years of age was introduced in 1915. Later programs of family planning and contraception were also introduced, as well as education for expectant mothers about maternity care.

Judge Marilyn Milian, who appeared on *The People's Court*, a nationally syndicated television series, places the credit for her success on her mother, who ensured that she was able to fulfill her career aspirations. Her home upbringing was very matriarchal, with her mother helping her through school and college, and ensuring that the family remained multilingual. Columba Bush, the wife of Jeb Bush, governor of Florida 1999–2007, has also spoken of a similar upbringing by her mother, albeit in Mexico.

**See Also:** Abortion; Cuba; Ethnic Mothers; Georgia; Maternal Health.

## Bibliography

George, Paul S., ed. *A Guide to the History of Florida.* Westport, CT: Greenwood Press, 1989.

Green, Elma C., ed. *Looking for the New Deal: Florida Women's Letters During the Great Depression.* Columbia: University of South Carolina Press, 2007.

Harrison, Ellen R., Steve Long, and M. Susan Marquis. *The Effects of Florida's Medicaid Eligibility Expansion for Pregnant Women.* Washington, DC: Rand, 1996.

Jahoda, Gloria. *Florida: a History.* New York: W.W. Norton, 1984.

Perez-Brown, Maria. *Mama: Latina Daughters Celebrate Their Mothers.* New York: Rayo/HarperCollins, 2003.

Justin Corfield
Geelong Grammar School, Australia

# Forcey, Linda Rennie

Linda Rennie Forcey joined the faculty in the School of Education and Human Development at the State University of New York at Binghamton in 1978. Her academic interests included peace and conflict resolution studies, women's studies, American politics, and international relations. She also won a University Award for Excellence in Teaching for the 1983–84 academic year. She published one monograph, *Mothers of Sons: Toward an Understanding of Responsibility*; and, among other publications, coedited *Mothering: Ideology, Experience, and Agency* with Evelyn Nakano Glenn and Grace Chang.

## Commonalities of 100 Mothers

*Mothers of Sons* is a study of what 100 mothers of sons themselves say about their mothering, which she uses to uncover some potential commonalities among real mothers of sons—unlike those suggested by mythology, literature, or psychoanalysis—while always acknowledging every mother's uniqueness. Forcey begins by criticizing some feminist scholars, such as Nancy Chodorow and Carol Gilligan. For instance, Forcey explains that Gilligan, by effectively blaming mothers of sons for raising them to behave differently from daughters, thereby adds another component to the assignment to mothers of primary physical, psychological, and material responsibility for their sons—or what Forcey calls "the mothering myth," which she acknowledges that other feminists have criticized before her.

However, despite that criticism and the "overwhelming evidence of maternal unhappiness and incompetence," Forcey finds that the biggest real commonality among the mothers in her study is their sense of mea culpa, or responsibility toward their sons, along with their inability to fulfill it. She explains that the reasons for the persistence of that myth are that mothers, like everyone else, find this assignment of responsibility difficult to criticize due to popular impressions of mothers' inherent ability to offer unconditional love and of their lifelong culpability for their children's feelings, as well as ambiguous notions of good mothering.

Another real commonality that Forcey finds is that, contrary to what Sigmund Freud and Simone de Beauvoir claim, mothers of all classes and races do not invariably have high expectations for their sons. In fact, mothers with both grown sons and daughters expect far more from their daughters instead. That even applies, she finds, to mothers who encourage their sons to join the military, whom she claims are doing so because they feel that the military will help their sons with the economic and psychological responsibilities they feel unable to fulfill for their sons. This chapter exploring mothers' advocacy of military enlistment is ultimately the one that other academics most discuss from her book.

Forcey also finds that mothers tend to play the role of peacemaker or mediator between fathers and sons, feeling it their "responsibility 'to make it better' so that sons can learn to identify with fathers," even though mothers dislike the fathers' communication patterns that they are thereby encouraging in their sons. Mothers also feel it is their responsibility to not lean on or burden their sons with difficult discussions, such as those related to health problems or divorce. However, that can be particularly dangerous for sons dealing with substance abuse, as their mothers' consequent denial of the problem often makes them the primary enablers of the behavior.

One more expectation of mothers to sons that Forcey's work belies is that mothers would be jealous of their sons' sexual partners; in actuality, they usually admire their sons' (female) partners and worry that each of their sons "won't treat her right and they will break up." In fact—and not surprisingly, in light of Forcey's earlier revelations—some mothers identify with their sons' female partners as they do with their daughters, in ways they cannot with their sons.

## Three Approaches to Feminism and Peace

Forcey seems to reconsider at least one of these interpretations later. Besides coediting *Mothering*, she also contributed the final chapter, "Feminist Perspectives on Mothering and Peace." In this essay, which repeats some aspects of her earlier works, she outlines three approaches to both feminist and peace studies: the essentialist position (that women should be celebrated for being inherently more peaceful and nurturing than men), the poststructuralist critique of essentialism (for endorsing gender stereotypes), and "the need to move beyond the debate with a finely tuned appreciation for a variety of approaches, a tolerance for ambiguity, and more than a little theoretical untidiness." Forcey thereby acknowledges that she has come to recognize the limitations of the essentialist position, but she calls for simultaneous recognition of "the special, mothering, peacemaking skills of many women (and men) while questioning impulses to universalize them." She also acknowledges that some women "choose to be a part of their country's political and military conflicts," despite her refusal to consider that possibility when interpreting mothers' encouragement of their sons joining the military in *Mothers of Sons*.

After its publication, *Mothers of Sons* received mixed reviews in *Contemporary Sociology* and *Journal of Marriage and the Family*; the major criticism in both pieces was the selective nature of her literature review. The book later received more favorable treatment from feminists. *Mothering*, however, was nearly universally reviewed in a positive light, particularly for its diverse and interdisciplinary perspectives on motherhood in the United States, in such journals as *Contemporary Sociology*, *Current Anthropology*, *The British Journal of Sociology*, *Gender and Society*, and *Signs*.

**See Also:** de Beauvoir, Simone; Chodorow, Nancy; Freud, Sigmund; Peace and Mothering; Peace Movement and Mothers; Sons and Mothers.

**Bibliography**

Condon, T.F. "Review." *Contemporary Sociology*, v.17/3 (May 1988).

Fabes, Richard A. "Review." *Journal of Marriage and the Family*, v.49/4 (November 1987).

Forcey, Linda Rennie. "Feminist Perspectives on Mothering and Peace." In *Mothering: Ideology, Experience, and Agency*, Evelyn Nakano Glenn, et al., eds. New York: Routledge, 1994.

Forcey, Linda Rennie. *Mothers of Sons: Toward an Understanding of Responsibility*. Santa Barbara, CA: Praeger, 1987.

Hays, Sharon. "Review." *Contemporary Sociology*, v.24/3 (May 1995).

Ross, Ellen. "New Thoughts on 'the Oldest Vocation': Mothers and Motherhood in Recent Feminist Scholarship." *Signs*, v.20/2 (Winter 1995).

Jessica B. Burstrem
University of Arizona

# Foster Mothering

Foster mothering refers to the process whereby a woman who is not the biological mother of a child raises a child outside of the biological mother–child dyad. Children placed with a foster mother may be removed from biological parent/s and formally placed in the custody of a foster mother by the state authority, or alternatively, the process may be voluntary in nature. Foster mothering is normally a short-term option most frequently followed by longer-term alternatives in the form of legally binding and permanent adoption, reunification with biological parents, or placement in longer-term guardianship.

Guardianship is the norm in cases in which reunification with biological parents is not feasible, and formalized adoption is deemed unsuitable. Foster mothering differs from adoption. In legal adoptions, the child's rights to the biological parents are ceded, and vice versa, and the child instead assumes the same rights as a biological child in the newly constituted family unit. In the case of foster mothering, the child retains all previous rights to inherit from the biological parents, and the biological parents retain rights to veto decisions taken by the foster parents. In cases of state-endorsed fostering, the foster mother does not assume the status of the child's custodian. Instead, custodianship is retained by the state responsible for placing the child in foster care, and the state may at any time remove the child from the foster mother if reunification with the biological family is considered possible. With adoption being a permanent and legally binding category of child-care, any threat of removal is remote.

Studies indicate that the most common motives for women to become a foster mother include maternal desire, often a result of not being able to conceive; the will to help and provide a safe haven for children in need; and a strong identification with deprived children as a result of similar childhood experience. In these instances, the foster mother has usually experienced resilience and developed coping strategies, which she wishes to impart to children in need.

Research further suggests that factors influencing satisfaction of foster mothers and the resulting retention of foster children include feeling significantly competent to handle children placed in their care, the ongoing willingness to provide a home to children who need loving parents, the age of the foster mother, having no regrets about the investment in foster children, and social workers providing adequate information and displays of approval.

## Requirements for Foster Parenting

No formal training is required prior to applying to foster, but formalized state preparation, guidance, and instruction is frequently granted, and foster parents are expected to offer the fostering service while remaining in close contact, and cooperating with, a host of state officials. Legal requirements for becoming a foster mother vary from country to country and between states or provinces within countries, but there is regularly a judicial contract between the municipality ordering the fostering and the foster mother. State-ratified foster mothering is also remunerated by the state in order to assist the foster mother in meeting the needs of any children in her care. Reimbursement rates are also prescribed and codified by law, and vary from country to country and within countries. Given that formalized foster mothers receive specialized training and reimbursements, foster mothering is regarded by some scholars as a profession.

In short-term, state-induced fostering, foster mothers are legally bound to provide childcare in the form of fostering, and ensure that the child receives an education. At the initial stage of fostering, the foster mother frequently assumes the primary role of a caregiver and nurse. However, longer-term placements frequently involve emotional investments in the child on the part of the foster mother and often transpire into long-term fostering, guardianship, or adoption. In such cases, the fostered child, like the adopted child, is drawn into a network of nonbiological kinship that is modeled on biological ties, and begins to identify the foster mother (and foster father, if one exists) as his or her parent. As attachment and affection for the new family unit strengthens, studies indicate that children begin to distance themselves emotionally and identify less rigidly with biological parents. As this occurs, it is not in the child's best interests to be detached from the embedded, fictive kinship tie in an attempt to reassert or assimilate biological ties. Such a move is likely to trigger a sentiment of lost identity and a feeling of being rootless, and may

*When a foster child in the United States reaches her teens, those with a history of trauma have a higher risk for pregnancy.*

result in sporadic childcare between the biological child dyad and the fictive-kinship child dyad.

## Global Models

In many Western countries, the foster mothering norm is state induced, and children are most often placed in foster care as a result of the child being taken into state custody following removal from birth parents. In other parts of the world, such as South America, Asia, and Africa, children are frequently fostered on a voluntary basis. In such instances, the child is fostered outside of the biological parents' home without any official state intervention. In these cases, children are frequently cared for by relatives while maintaining a strong emotional and social bond with their parents. Extending from precolonial times through to the present, many children on the African continent have been informally fostered over extended periods of time through a culturally sanctioned, informal fostering arrangement. This fostering system has historically allowed for acquisition of skills, offers of labor, companionship, enhanced kinship ties, educational opportunities, and economic resources that are more widely spread within the lineage. However, until the advent of human immunodeficiency virus (HIV) and acquired immunodeficiency syndrome (AIDS), the majority of children fostered informally did not remain in the care of foster parents for an indefinite period.

With the emergence of HIV/AIDS, the number of children being absorbed into households on a more permanent basis has increased dramatically, placing tremendous social and economic strain on households. The cultural norm of purposeful voluntary fostering has been replaced by crisis fostering, as traditional, voluntary caregivers succumb to the effects of disease, the pool of potential caregivers are reduced, and increasing care demands are placed on foster mothers. The fundamentals of foster mothering differs significantly from one social and cultural context to the next, and are constantly being re-negotiated in response to changing sociocultural and economic conditions. At present, foster mothering continues to rest on three central premises: the child does not reside in the care of the biological parents, the foster mother receives some form of reimbursement for meeting childcare demands, and rights over the child are not legally transferred to an alternative, socially sanctioned parent.

**See Also:** AIDS/HIV and Mothering; Anthropology of Motherhood; Care Giving; Maternal Desire; Other Mothering; Social Construction of Motherhood.

**Bibliography**
Campbell, Claudia and Susan Whitelaw Downs. "The Impact of Economic Incentives on Foster Parents." *Social Science Review*, v.61/4 (1987).
Dando, Isabel and Brian Minty. "What Makes Good Foster Parents?" *British Journal of Social Work*, v.17/4 (1987).
Denby, Romona, Nolan Rindfleisch, and Gerald Bean. "Predictors of Foster Parents' Satisfaction and Intent to Continue to Foster." *Child Abuse and Neglect*, v.23/3 (1999).
Dozier, Mary K., Chase Stovall, Kathleen E. Albus, and Brady Bates. "Attachment for Infants in Foster Care: The Role of Caregiver and State of Mind." *Child Development*, v.72/5 (2001).
Fonseca, Claudia. "Orphanages, Foundlings and Foster Mothers: The System of Child Circulation in a Brazilian Squatter Settlement." *Anthropology Quarterly*, v.59/1 (1986).
Isomaki, Veli-Pekka. "The Fuzzy Foster Parenting—a Theoretical Approach." *The Social Science Journal*, v.39/4 (2002).
Jones, Sean. "Children on the Move: Parenting, Mobility and Birth-Status Among Migrants." In *Questionable Issue: Illegitimacy in South Africa*. New York: Oxford University Press, 1992.
Oleke, Christopher, Astrid Blystad, and Ole Bjorn Rekdal. "When the Obvious Brother Is Not There: Political and Cultural Contexts of the Orphan Challenge in Northern Uganda." *Social Science and Medicine*, v.61/12 (2005).
Walmsley, Emily. "Raised by Another Mother: Informal Fostering and Kinship Ambiguities in Northwest Ecuador." *Journal of Latin American and Caribbean Anthropology*, v.13/1 (2008).

Thenjiwe Magwaza
Susan Elizabeth de la Porte
University of KwaZulu-Natal, South Africa

# Fox, Faulkner

Faulkner Fox is an American author and feminist who teaches creative writing at Duke University. Her first book, *Dispatches From a Not-So-Perfect Life*, deals with aspects of new motherhood, such as fear and isolation.

Fox was raised in West Point, Virginia, a small mill town. She received her bachelor's degree from Harvard University, graduating magna cum laude in 1986. While in college and also after college, Fox held a variety of jobs including peer contraceptive counselor, high school French teacher, and tour guide at New Orleans's The Voodoo Museum. She has also researched housing and treatment for the mentally ill as well as women's alternative spiritual practices, a subject for which she was issued a grant from Radcliff College to pursue. Fox also earned a master's degree in American Studies from Yale University in 1989 and a master of fine arts degree in poetry from Vermont College. After receiving her M.F.A. in 1997, Fox taught poetry workshops at the University of Texas at Austin.

An award-winning poet, Fox won *Prairie Schooner's* Bernice Slote Award for the best work by an emerging writer in 1998. She's also performed her poetry in Austin and also at Frontera Fest. Her *Sex Talking Mama* piece was particularly popular, and was performed in the United States and Canada as well as featured on public television in Texas.

Fox became interested in capital punishment after being struck by the growing number of executions in Texas. She joined the anti-death-penalty movement and also began writing about racism and capital punishment. She currently volunteers with NARAL Pro-Choice North Carolina.

In 1999, Salon.com published her article on motherhood, *What I Learned From Losing My Mind*, which received a tremendous response from readers. The piece detailed Fox's overwhelmed mind-set that caused her to whittle away time making mental lists of what she should be doing, rather than actually doing. It goes on to tell how Fox arranged to take a six-day trip alone to an *ashram* in Colorado to clear her head and regroup. An *ashram* is a peaceful, secluded place, often in the mountains, where a group resides in spiritual harmony. Following the retreat, Fox says she was more at peace with herself and her life. The piece was so well received that Salon re-ran it twice. Fox says that the response helped her to realize she wasn't the only woman feeling the way she did—conflicted.

Fox's book, *Dispatches From a Not So Perfect Life*, is a memoir of motherhood that talks about her own unhappiness, despite having most of the things she'd always dreamed of, including the house, dreamy husband, and sweet child. She talks openly about the pressures she and other American mothers feel, as well as about the scrutiny she felt from everyone around her—from doctors to friends to strangers. It further delves into inequality in the distribution of housework and other domestic situations. Further, Fox shares her realization that the reality of mother-

hood cannot be like her childhood fantasy. Critics called the book intelligent and refreshing, but several female editors rejected the book before Fox found a publisher, which solidified her resolve to finish and publish the work. Ironically, although the book delves into the divvying up of housework when her children were very young, and specifically about the uneven distribution of work between herself and her husband, Fox's husband shouldered most of the child-rearing and housekeeping duties while she completed *Dispatches From a Not So Perfect Life*.

Fox was married in 1994 and lives with her family in Durham, North Carolina. She teaches creative writing at Duke University and is currently working on a book of creative nonfiction that details people in the South whose religions compel them to work for social and economic justice. It is titled *Good People*.

**See Also:** Feminism and Mothering; Feminist Mothering; Feminist Theory and Mothering; Overwhelmed Mothers; Motherhood Memoir; Work and Mothering.

**Bibliography**
Fox, Faulkner. "About Faulkner." http://www.faulknerfox.com/about.htm (accessed June 2009).
Fox, Faulkner. *Dispatches From a Not So Perfect Life*. New York: Three Rivers Press, 2004.
Fox, Faulkner. "What I Learned From Losing My Mind: How a Week at a Yoga Retreat Saved Me From the Perfect Parenting Frenzy." http://www.salon.com/life/feature/1999/01/12feature.html (accessed January 1999).
Hartman, Joanne Catz. "Profiles: An Interview With Faulkner Fox." www.Literarymama.com (accessed June 2009).

Sarah W. Caron
Independent Scholar

# France

The word motherhood in French is *maternité*; the French hold the idea of motherhood in the highest regard, even though for years many have disputed the role of mothers. Throughout the history of France, these changes in the roles of motherhood have been caused by external forces, including philosophical ideas, the aristocracy, religion, and government.

Before the Enlightenment, motherhood was a necessary burden that many women endured. They often felt that the duties of being a mother encroached on their lives at home, at the salon, and at court. The affluent sent their young ones to wet nurses, often in the country; these children did not return to the home manor until they were 5 years of age. The lack of motherly care took its toll; the infant mortality rate was exceptionally high prior to the onset of the French Revolution.

## Enlightened Ideas on Mothering

The earliest notion of ideal motherhood in the nation-state of France appeared just prior to the French Revolution. During the Enlightenment, the ideals about motherhood changed dramatically from the burdened mother to the "happy mother." Although the Enlightenment started in England, it soon caught on in France, and the nation became a focus for continual, modern philosophical and political thought. Men and women spent hours discoursing over the latest political trends of thought at local coffee houses, social groups, and salons. Many of the discussion groups were led and hosted by women. Numerous discussions in Paris centered on the state of the nation and the displeasure with the French monarchy, Louis XV, and the traditional ideology of the Catholic Church. Ideas from John Locke, Isaac Newton, and other political philosophers circulated around these social groups, and their ideas became very powerful. Some of the more famous individuals included Baron de Montesquieu, Voltaire, and Denis Diderot, all of whom were on the lips of many of the new philosophical elite.

One of these influential philosophers, Jean-Jacques Rousseau, published a book that changed the ideas about motherhood in France. His work, *Emile*, stressed the importance of the mother as the primary caretaker and nurturer of her child. His ideas gained popularity and became known as the *Cult of Motherhood*. This new mode of thought on motherhood enthralled the aristocracy and became the main focus of the ideal mother well into the 20th century. Rousseau advocated that

a woman's natural role was motherhood; it was their business to bear children and shoulder the responsibility of both care and education for the child. He encouraged the education of women in order to produce stronger citizens of the state. His ideas were also reinforced by the French Revolution, which stressed the importance of the mother's role on her children.

The French Revolution and the Enlightenment ignited women to become more active in their community by promoting organizations to educate mothers on proper child rearing. In 1788, the Society for Maternal Charity was founded in Paris; this organization promoted its conception of motherhood on national and provincial levels and helped to shape the celebration of civic motherhood during the 19th century. The organization was supported by the state, encouraging elite women to become role models for poor women.

By 1789, the society in Paris had 193 members and 64 benefactors, including the queen herself, Marie Antoinette. She was named patroness of the society and attributed an annual credit of 24,000 *livres* to the society. The organization paid for expenses such as home birth and pensions to allow women to stay home and nurse for two years following the birth of her child. Even with good intentions, the tumultuous Revolutionary government was unable provide charity to the poor, even the Church was unable assist mothers because they had been deprived of their lands and tithes.

## Mothers as the Linchpin of the Family

During the Third Republic, the Rousseau Law was enacted, which restricted the wet nurse industry and created a social advocacy for poor children. Napoleon supported the education of mothers; he implied that the education of women was designed to create "mothers for their children." During the Napoleonic era, charitable societies reemerged when the imperial government realized they could not provide sufficient aid to the poor. The Society of Maternal Charity reorganized in 1801; several additional provinces followed. The two main goals of the organization included the preservation of children and the encouragement of the maternal role; they realized that care from a good mother was essential to bringing up strong, healthy children, who in turn would become future citizens. Mothers were seen as the key to an orderly family and social life; she was ultimately the linchpin of the family.

During the 19th century, women became the focus and authority of the domestic sphere. Unlike previous generations, the mother became the nurturer, ensured a proper education for her children, and became the role model for proper moral and religious training. Transversely, men conducted the family business, financial, and political affairs for the family, leaving the home to women to run. During this period, attitudes about nursing began to change; no longer were infants sent to a wet nurse, but women were encouraged to nurse their own babies. These ideas grew out of Rousseau's *Emile* along with the medical advancement that promoted better health through a mother's milk. The Société Protectrices de l'Enfance, created to protect and promote the well-being of children, educated women on the importance of nursing and health care for children. This campaign even reached lower-class women; charitable groups known as *crèches* were created in industrial cities to help women care for their young children, even requiring employees to give mothers breaks during the day to nurse their children.

## Contraception History in France

Birth control in France has a long history; dating back to the pre-nation-state, women used various means to control unwanted pregnancies. Although infanticide and abortion were both outlawed in the 18th and 19th centuries, both practices were heavily documented in both court records and newspapers; therefore, the practice was most likely widespread. French women used homemade abortifacients as a form of post-coital birth control, such as worm fern, also known in France as "prostitute root." In the 19th century, the conservative government, supported by the Catholic Church, ordered the suppression of manufacturing and producing contraceptive devices as well as repression of abortion. Even with the attempt to boost the population during this period, this measure failed miserably; the low birth rate during this time strongly suggests that French women were utilizing contraception methods. In 1896, when Paul Robin founded the Ligue de la Regeneration Humane, the sale of contraception and dissemination of pamphlets to the general population were allowed without repercussion from the government.

Before and during World War I, there were several contraception manufacturers, and production was high; France became the one of the European leaders in birth control. Margaret Sanger, a famous birth control advocate in the United States, traveled to France in 1916 to become educated in the methods of French contraceptives.

## The 20th Century's Stringent New Motherhood

The 20th century ushered in an era of regimented motherhood and reproduction. By the end of World War I, the ideology of the "Cult or Motherhood," which lasted over a century, lost its luster; the state stepped in and acted in loco parentis where public health doctors made house calls. The government stopped funding maternal organizations such as the Society of Maternal Charity; instead, *crèches* opened clinics for women to receive fresh cow's milk, bottles, and subsidies. Additionally, women were advised not to coddle their children, but rather give them strong discipline and a regimented schedule based on scientific research. The "Cult of Motherhood" was now replaced by a more scientific approach to child rearing.

The Ignace Law of 1920 became a major focus of the time period, setting the stage for women's maternal issues in the first half of the century. The law was a result of long years of debate on the best way to respond to depopulation, which was to encourage fatherhood or regulate motherhood. Those caught producing, advocating, or selling contraceptives were fined heavily and threatened with prison terms. The push for the conservative turn was due to the fact that the French feared the rising population growth of the Germans; this fear had roots back to their defeat in the Franco-Prussian war. The government focused on reducing abortion and birth control; the more liberal side's insistence on women's reproductive rights was defeated by the masculine bourgeois, the Catholic Church, and a conservative society that insisted it was a French woman's patriotic duty to bear numerous children. Women were directly blamed for the depopulation problem; therefore, regulations were needed for abortion and birth control. The continuation of the militant policy on birth control and abortion continued after World War II, and numerous laws were passed prohibiting contraception and making abortion not only an individual crime, but a crime against the state. Individuals were tried and punished accordingly. Even with the continued push to prevent contraception and abortion, it is clear from the records that many French women did participate in preventing or eliminating unwanted pregnancies.

## Fertility in Modern Times

While politicians were enforcing contraception laws, they simultaneously supported motherhood, offering many incentives for women to continually conceive and produce large families. These incentives have continued even through the 1960s, when women increasingly saw motherhood as a role that could be accompanied by paid employment. As women built identities as mothers and workers, changes to benefits were made to fit the new ideal mother. Generous maternity leaves allowed up to 16 weeks—six weeks before and 10 weeks after the birth—with multiple births adding weeks to the leave policy. This type of subsidy from the French government has given rise to an increased fertility rate in France. In 2000, the fertility rate was second only to Ireland, followed closely by Norway for western European countries. Both young and old women have attributed to this rise in fertility in France.

In the early 21st century, the continued social programs for mothers have become a burden on the French pocketbook. The family-friendly measures, including long maternity leaves, child support payments, public funding for toddlers, and nanny subsidies have come with a heavy price tag for taxpayers, especially since France has overtaken Ireland as Europe's most fertile nation. French women have an average of more than two children each, while the rest of the continent continues to battle the decline in birthrate and an increase in elderly population. While politicians scan for cuts in the budget, no one in France, either conservative or liberal, has proposed reducing expenditures to promote childbearing.

**See Also:** Abortion; Birth Control; England; Germany; Republican Motherhood; Social Construction of Motherhood; Welfare and Mothering; Wet Nursing.

## Bibliography

Abrams, Lynne. *The Making of a Modern Woman.* Upper Saddle River, NJ: Pearson, 2002.

Accampo, Elinor. *Blessed Motherhood, Bitter Fruit: Nelly Roussel and the Politics of Female Pain in the Third Republic France.* Baltimore, MD: Johns Hopkins University Press, 2006.

Adams, Christine. "Contructing Mothers and Families: The Society for Maternal Charity of Bordeaux, 1805–1860." *French Historical Studies* (Winter 1999).

Allen, Ann Taylor. *Feminism and Motherhood in Western Europe.* New York: Palgrave Macmillan, 2005.

Fagnani, Jeanne. "Family Policies in France and Germany." *Work & Family* (February 2007).

Grayzel, Susan R. *Women's Identities at War: Gender, Motherhood, and Politics in England and France During the First World War.* Chapel Hill: University of North Carolina Press, 1999.

Meade, Teresa A. and Merry E. Wiesner-Hanks, eds. *A Companion to Gender History.* Oxford, UK: Blackwell Publishers, 2006.

Pedersen, Jean Elisabeth. *Legislating the French Family: Feminism, Theater and Republican Politics, 1870-1920.* Brunswick, NJ: Rutgers University Press, 2003.

Rousseau, Jacques. *Emile, or On Education.* Sioux Falls, SD: NuVision Publications, 2007.

Wilson, Stephen. "The Myth of Motherhood: The Historical View of European Child-Rearing." *Social History* (May 1984).

Michele Hinton Riley
St. Joseph's College

# Freud, Sigmund

Sigmund Freud, the founder of psychoanalysis and a prolific author of numerous volumes on the subject, was born on May 6, 1856, in Freiberg, Moravia. Freud was the third child of Amalia and Jacob, a wool merchant; originally named Sigismund Schlomo, he grew up in a large middle-class Jewish family of 10 children and spent nearly all of his adult life in Vienna. He obtained his medical degree from Vienna University, where he studied from 1873 to 1881, then spent several years working as a laboratory researcher under Professor Ernst Wilhelm von Brücke at the Physiological Institute of Vienna from 1876 to 1882. With poverty as his prime motivator, Freud reluctantly went on to work as a physician specializing in neuropathology at the Vienna Central Hospital from 1882 to 1885. From 1886 until 1938, he held an appointment as a professor of neurology at the University of Vienna, in addition to opening his own private psychiatric practice specializing in nervous diseases.

After a four-year engagement, he married Martha Bernays. The couple had six children, including the youngest, Anna, who became a respected child psychoanalyst. During his early medical career, Freud's interests shifted from neurology to psychopathology of the mind, and eventually to the groundbreaking idea that neurotic behavior was the manifestation of repressed, unconscious libidinal desires—desires that could only be revealed and resolved (in however limited a fashion) through talk therapy involving free association. Importantly, he posited that these desires developed in deeply gendered ways inextricably tied to the sexual dynamics of family life, the patient's childhood relationship with each parent, and in particular how they, especially fathers, fit into the child's process of sexual maturation. Most notable among Freud's writings are his *The Interpretation of Dreams* (1900), which was based largely on his own self-analysis; *The Psychopathology of Everyday Life* (1901); and *Three Essays on the Theory of Sexuality* (1905). Following Hitler's invasion of Austria and the Nazis' seizure and destruction of his publications, Freud escaped to London in 1938. He died there of cancer at the age of 83 on September 23, 1939.

## Freud's Shift in Focus

Freud's interests shifted from neurology to psychopathology when, prior to setting up his private practice, he undertook a year of study with Jean-Martin Charcot at the renowned Paris hospital for nervous diseases, the Salpêtrière. There he began to explore the use of hypnotic suggestion, eventually following his close friend Josef Breuer in using hypnosis for the treatment of hysteria and working from the premise that hysteria reflected a forgotten psychic trauma that needed to be recalled in order to achieve catharsis. Over time, finding hypnosis to be an unreliable

technique, Freud parted ways with Breuer, gradually replacing hypnosis with the technique of free association based on a controversial system of ideas better known today as psychoanalysis. Introducing the term in 1896, Freudian psychoanalysis was premised on key assumptions he held about childhood sexuality; his theory of the unconscious; and the related repression therein of unresolved conflicts, traumas, and affects, and transference between analyst and patient to aid of reliving past trauma in a safe environment to achieve a different outcome. Freud's examinations of internal conflicts—conflicts between civilized social mores and the primary physical instincts that give rise to sexual or sometimes destructive desires—led to Freud's formulation of an Oedipal stage of sexual development in children.

## Oedipus and Electra

Positing that a vibrant sexual inner life beginning at infancy, Freud contended that all children were born with a sexuality that was "polymorphously perverse." By this he meant that children's sexualities went beyond the narrow categories of homosexuality or heterosexuality, but rather spanned a range of sexual orientations, proclivities, and preoccupations, at least until passing through the stages of sexual maturation on their way to becoming "normal" heterosexuals. These stages included the oral stage, when the infant receives pleasure from nursing and sucking her/his thumb; the anal stage (ages 2–3), when the child finds pleasure in controlling her/his bowel movements; the phallic stage (ages 3–5), when the child finds the pleasure potential from the genitals, and when s/he works through the critical Oedipus and castration complexes.

These precede the stage at approximately age 6 that marks the beginning of a period of sexual latency that lasts until puberty, at which time the genital stage begins and the child's sexual impulses return. Providing that the previous stages have unfolded "successfully," the teenager's sexual energy—the libido—will be directed toward a member of the opposite sex, leading ultimately to psychic peace, or rather, normal unhappiness. The Oedipal stage in boys, referred to sometimes as the Electra stage in girls, is particularly prone to going awry, however, and alleged by Freud to be the main culprit in understanding his adult patients' neuroses. At this critical developmental stage, the child becomes sexually attracted to her/his opposite-sex parent, giving rise to a destructive rivalry with the same-sex parent to whom the child relates as a competitor and an obstacle.

In boys, the Oedipus complex derives from the child's natural attachment to his mother, an attachment that turns into sexual desire as the child grows older. He comes to see his father as standing in the way of his ability to be with his mother sexually, which transforms into a feeling of fear that his father will castrate him should he act upon his desire for his mother. Out of this fear, known as the castration complex, the boy child painfully represses his desire; as a trade-off for giving up this love for his mother, he identifies with his father and the promise of a woman of his own later, developing what Freud referred to as the superego, or that component of the individual psyche that has internalized sociocultural values. The psyche has three parts; thus, the superego functions alongside the id, or that part of the self that is unconscious and includes the instinctive impulses, and the ego, or that part of the psyche that is conscious and deals with external reality, and mediates between the id and the superego. Thus the superego is for all intents and purposes our conscience—that part of us that follows social rules. In this instance, the rule being followed is that which mitigates against sexual relations between mother and child.

In girls, about whom Freud wrote comparatively less, the experience of the Oedipus (or Electra) and castration complexes is quite different. Like the boy child, a girl's first love object is her mother, because mothers nurse children. But unlike boys, in "normal," heterosexual development a girl child has to shift her desire from her mother to her father, and later in life to men who represent her father. Freud notoriously argued that this shift in desire from a female to males begins as soon as the girl realizes that she does not have a penis, in other words, that she has already been castrated. Perceiving this missing penis as a lack, the girl experiences penis envy, and blames her mother for having failed to provide her with one. At this point, the girl child turns to her father as a love object, that is, out of resentment for her mother. Part of this turning to the father means also identifying with the mother and her position relative to the father; in other words, the girl wants to take her mother's place in her father's life. The resentment she feels toward her mother evolves not only from her desire for a penis, but also from the competition she perceives for her father's affections and the opportunity to have his baby, which in her mind would make up for this lack.

Where the fear of castration in boys can lead to a resolution of the Oedipus complex and the development of a superego, in girls there is no threat of castration. What this means, according to Freud, is that girls fail to develop a strong superego, or a social conscience, as they are not nearly so motivated (by fear) as boys to internalize the social values required to become moral, civilized adults.

## Forming Gender Identity

In sum, Freud's insights into this stage of psychosexual development suggest that gender identity is the product of a complex process of sexual maturation. How children turn out as adults is tied to their anatomical differences, and is a direct outcome of how they deal with the pressures of this particular phase as well as family and societal expectations.

The radical nature of Freud's writings and a certain amount of anti-Semitism prevented Freud's theory from being well received initially. His ideas were highly controversial, not least because they flew in the face of Victorian assumptions about childhood sexual innocence. However, these ideas remain controversial in many circles. Within feminist thought they have had a mixed reception: responses have ranged from outright rejection of his biological determinism in his arguments about penis envy, to more forgiving readings such as those by Nancy Chodorow and Juliet Mitchell that suggest Freud's theory described rather than prescribed the gendered sexual politics and subordinate femininity of Victorian Vienna. Feminists such as Elizabeth Abel and Michèle Barrett have argued for further pluralism, challenging the normative heterosexuality and familialism of his framework, as well as his focus on the white, middle-class experience, this being an argument for expanding the theory to account for how we become raced and classed.

**See Also:** Chodorow, Nancy; Freud, Sigmund, Mother of; Psychoanalysis and Motherhood; Psychology of Motherhood; Sons and Mothers.

## Bibliography

Abel, Elizabeth. "Race, Class and Psychoanalysis? Opening Questions." In *Conflicts in Feminism,* Marianne Hirsch and Evelyn Fox Keller, eds. New York: Routledge, 1990.

Barrett, Michèle. *The Politics of Truth: From Marx to Foucault.* Queensland, Australia: Polity Press, 1991.

Chodorow, Nancy. *The Reproduction of Mothering: Psychoanalysis and the Sociology of Gender.* Berkeley: University of California Press, 1978.

Freud, Sigmund. *Freud on Women: A Reader.* Elisabeth Young-Bruehl, ed. New York: W.W. Norton & Company, 1990.

Gay, Peter. *Freud: A Life for Our Time.* New York: W.W. Norton, 1988.

Mitchell, Juliet. *Psychoanalysis and Feminism.* New York: Pantheon, 1974.

Strachey, James. "Sigmund Freud: A Sketch of His Life and Ideas." In *The Interpretation of Dreams*, Angela Richards, ed. New York: Penguin Books, 1953.

Shelley Zipora Reuter
Concordia University

# Freud, Sigmund, Mother of

Amalia Nathanson, sometimes called Amalie, was born in 1835 in Brody, Galicia, and died in 1930, possibly of tuberculosis. The September 22 issue of *Time* that year identified her as the wife of Jacob, reporting: "Died: Frau Jacob Amalia Nathanson Freud, 95, mother of famed Neurologist Sigmund Freud; of old age, at Vienna." She was descended from Nathan Halévy Charmatz of Brody, who was a famous Talmudic scholar in the 18th century. At age 20, she became either the second or third wife of Jacob Freud, a textile dealer who was 20 years her senior. Emmanuel (or Emanuel), one of the children from Jacob's first marriage, was older than Amalia and had children when Amalia and Jacob had their first child. That child, whom they named Sigismund Schlomo (Schlomo being a Yiddish name given by the Freuds in keeping with Jewish tradition), was born on May 6, 1856, in what has been described as "a rented room over a blacksmith's shop in Freiberg in Moravia, a small town in what is now a part of the Czech Republic, 50 miles north of Vienna." Sigismund later changed his name to Sigmund and became known as the father of psychoanalysis.

After Sigismund's birth, Amalia gave birth to Julius, whom she named after her recently deceased, younger brother. She then had five daughters—Anna, Rosa, Maria, Esther Adolfine (called Dolfi), and Paula (or Pauline)—and finally a son, Alexander.

Amalia and her husband were not very religious but did observe Purim and Passover.

In 1859, the family moved to Vienna after Jacob's father's business failed, and he went bankrupt. During the next 15 years, the family was extremely poor, according to Sigmund's granddaughter, Sophie, and lived in a succession of six apartments in what had been the Jewish ghetto. Jacob never again had full-time work, instead being supported by relatives.

*Freud's mother, Amalia, was either Jacob Freud's second or third wife, and was 20 years younger than him.*

An early biographer of Sigmund (Helen Walker Pruner) described Amalia as intelligent, pretty, slender, and possessed of great vitality: "She cooked, she baked, she tended the child; she was alert, sharp-witted and gay." Sigmund at age 70 described himself as having been a happy child of a youthful mother. The fame of Sigmund, and what has been called the androcentrism, misogyny, and mother-blame that characterized much of his work has also pervade historical commentary about Amalia, making it difficult to discern what she was really like in certain respects.

Sigmund claimed that he was his mother's indisputable favorite, but what is unknown is whether or not Amalia agreed. On the positive side, her love and support (she called him her golden Sigi) seem to have given him great self-confidence. It appears that she considered him brilliant and special and did, for instance, stop her daughter Anna's piano lessons when Sigmund complained that the noise interfered with his studying. However, the dilemma of a mother raising children with competing needs in a male-centered time and place likely helped determine such behavior. While Sigmund was growing up, Amalia, Jacob, and the other children shared three rooms, but Sigmund had his own; but again, what is unknown is who chose and implemented that arrangement.

As an adult, Sigmund is said to have visited Amalia every Sunday for lunch and brought her flowers. Commentators have said that Amalia was beautiful, vivacious, and had a strong personality, and that she and Sigmund had a close relationship. However, where some have said that Sigmund benefited from her praise and devotion, his granddaughter Sophie Freud said that he had stomachaches on those Sunday visits, and Peter Gay opined that Amalia was dictatorial and that Sigmund was a little afraid of her. Whatever benefits Sigmund derived from his relationship with his mother, they did not keep him from casting mothers—and females in general—as in many ways inferior to fathers and males. What remains unknown is how Amalia felt about what her son wrote about mothers and other women.

Amalia suffered the tragedy of the death of her younger son, Julius, in his first year of life from an intestinal infection. After her death, four of her daughters were killed in the Nazi Holocaust: Rosa, Maria, and Pauline at Treblinka or Maly Traustinec, and Dolfi, who starved to death at Theresienstadt.

**See Also:** Einstein, Albert, Mother of; Freud, Sigmund; Hitler, Adolf, Mother of; Jefferson, Thomas, Mother of; Lincoln, Abraham, Mother of; Psychoanalysis and Motherhood; Psychology of Motherhood.

### Bibliography

Gay, Peter. *Freud: A Life for Our Time*. New York: W.W. Norton, 1988.

Public Broadcasting System. "Family: Mother." In "Young Dr. Freud: A Film by David Grubin." http://www.pbs.org/youngdrfreud/pages/analysis_guilt.htm (accessed July 2009).

Puner, Helen Walker. *Sigmund Freud: His Life and Mind*. New York: Grosset & Dunlap, 1947.

Strachey, James. "Sigmund Freud: A Sketch of His Life and Ideas." In *The Interpretation of Dreams*, Angela Richards, ed. New York: Penguin Books, 1953.

Paula J. Caplan
Harvard University

# Friedan, Betty

Born in Peoria, Illinois, on February 4, 1921, Betty Friedan made a long-lasting and critical impact on the second wave of feminism with her publication of *The Feminine Mystique* (1963) and her tireless work as a feminist activist. In this major publication, she charts the "problem that has no name," arguing that the assumed happiness that women feel as domesticated wives and mothers is a farce; according to Friedan's study, writing, and activism, women were not allowed to live out their full potential as they did not have the choice of living beyond domesticity. The "feminine mystique," therefore, served as a highly constraining social practice wherein women were expected to be happy wives and mothers; if they failed to successfully manage either of these roles, they were failed women. Friedan's work, therefore, enabled millions of women to see how the taken-for-granted roles they played as wives and mothers were not the only roles they necessarily had to play. From the time she published her first book, she worked tirelessly to challenge the feminine mystique and shift the paradigm that continued to constrain women, men, the family, and American society at large. Additionally, she also argued that men were confronted with the masculine mystique wherein their efforts to nurture, be sensitive, and engage in other assumed feminine behaviors and practices were not deemed appropriate or acceptable.

## Accomplished Author

In addition to her relentless work as a feminist activist, she published a number of books both about her life and her theoretical insights and activist work. She wrote these books to legitimate her work and to continue conversations with her many opponents. In 1976, she published *It Changed My Life: Writings on the Women's Movement*. In response to the transitions of the women's movement, she published *The Second Stage* (1981), where she queried where the women's movement needed to move in the future. Since the publication of *The Feminine Mystique*, women had made huge transitions out of the home and into the public sphere.

However, in addition to these major transitions, women's work had largely doubled in that women were still expected to do the vast majority of work in the home while also honing a career outside of the home. Essentially, men's positions both in and outside of the home had not shifted very much, while the positions of women shifted drastically, resulting in a *superwoman syndrome*. Unlike radical feminists at this time, Friedan contended that rather than completely removing family from women's lives, family needed to be rethought, positioning men and women in far more equal roles as parents. Interestingly, Friedan often conceived family in a highly heterosexual way, thus offering a rethinking of a particular kind of family. For example, given the many debates around gay marriage and lesbian, gay, and queer families, her rethinking would only account for heterosexual families.

Approximately 10 years later and in an effort to better understand the "mystique of age," she published *The Fountain of Age*. In this project, she used the same methods for conducting research on *The Feminine Mystique*: collecting, organizing, and analyzing scientific studies, anecdotal evidence, interviews with active seniors like herself, personal experiences, and popular culture images and constructions of old age. She found American society was dealing with another mystique that was far more pervasive than the feminine mystique, because it was an idea that became a self-fulfilling prophecy. Further, she noted how those who were constructed as old were feminized, often described as weak and helpless. Her solution, she claimed, was to shift the ideas surrounding old age or shift the paradigm, both on an individual and collective level. However, as Friedan was often criticized in her feminist activism, her liberal arguments often failed to account for the structural dimensions of social life and inequality.

The feminine mystique, for example, was not a process of inequality that affected all women in the same way. As Friedan quickly realized via her activism, the solution to the feminine mystique—that women needed to move beyond the home and have the opportunity to work in the same jobs as men—was not necessarily a viable option for many women. White, middle-class, highly educated women such as Betty Friedan failed to see how their solutions to a better life and happiness did not necessarily solutions make any sense for, nor were attractive to, some members of marginalized groups such as women of color, particularly across class and sexuality.

Betty Friedan died of congestive heart failure on February 4, 2006, at the age of 85.

**See Also:** Childcare; Domestic Labor; Economy and Motherhood; Employment and Motherhood; Full-Time Mothering; Hochschild, Arlie; Housework; LGBTQ Families and Motherhood; Marriage; National Organization for Women; Psychology of Motherhood; Second Shift/Third Shift; Unpaid Work; Work and Mothering.

## Bibliography

Friedan, Betty. *It Changed My Life: Writings on the Women's Movement.* Cambridge, MA: Harvard University Press, 1976.
Horowitz, Daniel. *Betty Friedan and the Making of the Feminine Mystique.* Amherst: University of Massachusetts Press, 1998.
Sherman, Janann, ed. *Interviews With Betty Friedan.* Jackson: University Press of Mississippi, 2002.

Danielle Antoinette Hidalgo
University of California, Santa Barbara

# Full-Time Mothering

Full-time mothering is a term used to describe a childrearing approach in which a woman organizes her daily life so that caring for her children is prioritized over paid employment. Full-time mothering is culturally defined as the ideal approach to childrearing; yet, full-time mothering has declined over time due to historical, social, and economic forces.

Full-time mothering is synonymous with stay-at-home mothering; however, some women prefer the moniker *full-time mother,* as it draws from job-like terminology and diverges from the image of the traditional homemaking mother that is often invoked with the term *stay-at-home mother.* Full-time mothering is not economically compensated in the United States; however, popular media commonly imagines what a full-time mother is worth. In 2007, the salary of a full-time mother, if she were to be paid, was estimated to be $134,121 a year, after breaking down the work of a full-time mother into distinct categories of housekeeper, cook, counselor, daycare teacher, and others. Nevertheless, women who engage in full-time mothering must be attached to a wage earner.

Economic and social forces have influenced women's decreased participation in full-time mothering, as most mothers today work for pay. The movement of women into paid work has risen from a 20 percent participation rate for those 16 and older in 1940, to 60 percent today. By 2001, 71 percent of childrearing women were employed, a steep incline from the 31 percent of mothers who participated in the labor force in 1976. According to the U.S. census, there are currently 5.6 million full-time mothers today.

## Emergence of Full-Time Mothering

The child-rearing approach known as full-time mothering emerged in the United States as the economy transitioned from agrarian to industrial. Prior to the industrialization of the U.S. economy in the late 18th and early 19th centuries, there was no distinction between the public world of work and the private realm of the home. Work and family were intricately connected as the entire family engaged in the work necessary for the survival of the family, including children who took up tasks as soon as they were able. Childhood as we know it today did not exist; the prevailing view of the time was of children as miniature adults. Children were not considered a separate category from adults; therefore, there was no need for full-time mothering. Child rearing was not a distinct set of tasks; it was performed by parents as they did their daily work. Though mothers and fathers performed separate tasks, they both participated in the care of children and trained them in gender-specific work at young ages.

With the industrial economy emerged the distinction between the private sphere of the family and the public sphere of work. In 1900, men made up over 80 percent of the paid workforce, leading to the social definition of work as masculine and the home as feminine. As work and family evolved into separate spheres, childhood was redefined as a distinct developmental stage. Children were viewed as necessitating a full-time caregiver, a role for which women were viewed as naturally suited. This new definition of childhood justified the existence of the private family and established full-time mothering as the gold star standard for proper child rearing.

## The Golden Age of Full-Time Mothering

Full-time mothering became fortified as the ideal child-rearing approach in the 1950s, when economic and social conditions converged so that women were encouraged to take on full-time mothering. Experiences of World War II left many individuals hungry for a haven, and willing to try family in new ways than previous generations. This era was a time of high rates of birth and marriage, at relatively young ages. Between 1940 and 1957, fertility soared 50 percent, creating what is referred to as a baby boom. The U.S. economy enjoyed a strong manufacturing sector, which enabled many men to earn a wage that could easily support a family.

Further supporting families, low-interest loans were widely available to acquire homes, and veterans were able to take advantage of the G.I. Bill that offered low-cost college education to its beneficiaries. Television airwaves were dominated by shows that depicted full-time mothering, such as *Leave It to Beaver* and *Father Knows Best.* Their popularity cemented full-time mothering as the standard for which all women were expected to strive. However, full-time mothering was more easily achieved by the white middle class and far less attainable for racial-ethnic, low-income, and single mothers who either did not have access to a breadwinner's wages or were coupled with partners who were unable to earn a family wage that supported full-time mothering. Even for those who were able to achieve the ideal of full-time mothering, it was not always experienced with the bliss and contentment that was represented in the widely circulated sitcoms.

## Feminist Thought

While the wider culture viewed women's role as full-time mother as natural, notable feminist Betty Friedan challenged that cultural belief in her book *The Feminine Mystique*. She asserted that women's confinement to the domestic sphere was oppressive and that women must participate in the public realms of work and politics in order to achieve social equality. Her monumental work struck a chord with thousands of women who shared similar feelings of discontentment and unhappiness with full-time mothering. Friedan's work is widely viewed as providing the impetus for the inception of the contemporary women's movement, of which the family, particularly mothering, is viewed as the linchpin of gender inequality.

Feminist thought is not a unitary set of ideas, but a diverse approach to examining gender inequality. Liberal feminists like Betty Friedan advocate for women's equal access to jobs and politics so that their options in life extend beyond full-time mothering. Radical feminists of the 1960s and 1970s viewed the family and mothers' work within it as the root cause of women's oppression and sought to abolish the private family. Marxist and socialist feminists approach women's inequality through mothering as well, concentrating on how women's unpaid work in the home supports capitalism, especially as they reproduce the workforce. In addition, Marxist and socialist feminists point to the economic dependence of full-time mothers on a male wage earner as central to women's social inequality. Multicultural feminists criticized liberal feminists in the 1960s and 1970s as addressing women's inequality too narrowly. Racial-ethnic, immigrant, poor, and working-class mothers have often combined motherhood with paid employment, unable to experience full-time mothering. Multicultural feminists point out that full-time mothering should be viewed as a privilege of which many women have been excluded. Especially for racial-ethnic women struggling against not only gender but also racial oppression, family is less a source of oppression, and more of a source of comfort and power.

## Full-Time Mothering Today

The number of women engaging in full-time mothering continues to be impacted by economic and social forces. The transition of the U.S. economy from industrial to postindustrial has changed the nature of work so that fewer families are able to survive with one wage earner. In this new era, male wages have decreased substantially, signaling the end of the "family wage" that enabled many men to support their families in the 1950s. Jobs in the postindustrial economy offer less financial stability, flexibility, and fewer benefits than did the manufacturing jobs that characterized the industrial economy. Thus, full-time mothering is less common than in previous generations, as many women have been pushed into the labor market as a household survival strategy.

Women have experienced a pull away from full-time mothering for reasons other than economic. Many seek not only economic freedom, but also personal fulfillment through paid work, especially middle- and upper-class women who often do not work out of economic necessity. For some, the decision to engage in full-time mothering is guided by religious conviction. Evangelical Christians are strong proponents of women limiting their work outside the home; the nearly 40 million Americans who identify with evangelical Christianity comprise a small, yet politically active segment of the Republican Party. Integral to the evangelical community is the prominent, nonprofit organization Focus on the Family, led by James Dobson. Focus on the Family actively promotes conservative social policies.

Other women choose full-time mothering in response to social pressure to fulfill the dictates of intensive mothering. Despite increasing demands on women to participate in the workforce, social standards of good mothering have intensified, and children's needs have increased. Good mothering is defined as exclusive, child-centered, emotionally painstaking, and time-consuming. Children are identified as individuals in need of an attentive caretaker who can unearth their unique possibilities, tastes, and interests. Women who identify with the mothering style known as attachment parenting view their decision to engage in full-time mothering as a radical departure from the mainstream culture of careerism. Followers of attachment parenting immerse themselves in the role of full-time mother and organize their lives around the needs of their children in a way that follows more "natural living." This may include home births, extended breastfeeding, homeschooling, and co-sleeping.

Due to the lack of taxpayer-funded family social policies in the United States, work and family are often experienced as contradictory spheres in the lives of women. Employers often expect women, as they do men, to perform work as if they have no parenting responsibilities. Although outdated, the breadwinner-homemaker model of family continues to structure social policy in the United States.

The lone policy to allow workers time for caregiving in the United States is the 1993 Family and Medical Leave Act, which requires large employers to provide 12 weeks of unpaid family or medical leave to workers. Many workers are not covered by this initiative, while others cannot afford to take an unpaid leave. Therefore, balancing both paid and unpaid work continues to be challenging, to the point that many women give up paid employment and take on full-time mothering. Even as workers, women are expected to be the primary caregiver of children as well as perform the majority of housework when at home, resulting in a "second shift" that most men do not experience. Often, full-time mothering becomes the most viable option for a woman when faced with inflexible job requirements, a "second shift" of work when they arrive home, and the scarcity of affordable-quality childcare. Sometimes women will engage in full-time mothering for a limited time, while children are young and their needs are most demanding. Women confront a dichotomy of motherhood when making work and family decisions.

## Mommy Wars

In opposition to the full-time mother is the working mother. Popular media strengthens this dichotomous view of motherhood by portraying full-time mothers

and working mothers as rivals in the mommy wars. Full-time mothers are depicted as harshly judging working mothers as selfish and career-oriented, whose children are raised by daycare centers. Similarly, media depicts working mothers as criticizing full-time mothers as not making real contributions to society. Nonetheless, social science research demonstrates that the mommy wars are less relevant in the lives of women than the ideological work mothers undergo in justifying their difficult, multifaceted decisions regarding work and family. Full-time mothering is but one of the many ways in which women may balance life's demands.

**See Also:** Attachment Parenting; Employment and Mothers; History of Motherhood: American; Intensive Mothering; Mommy Wars; Social Construction of Motherhood; Stay-at-Home Mothers.

**Bibliography**
Bobel, Chris. *The Paradoxes of Natural Parenting.* Philadelphia: Temple University Press, 2002.
Collins, Patricia Hill. *Black Feminist Thought.* New York: Routledge, 2000.
Coontz, Stephanie. *The Way We Never Were: American Families and the Nostalgia Trap.* New York: Basic Books, 1992.
Hays, S. *The Cultural Contradictions of Motherhood.* New Haven, CT: Yale University Press, 1996.
Friedan, Betty. *The Feminine Mystique.* New York: Norton, 1965.
Mintz, S. and S. Kellogg. *Domestic Revolutions: A Social History of American Family Life.* New York: Free Press, 1998.

Melissa A. Freiburger
University of Kansas

# Future of Motherhood

When considering the future of motherhood, it is important to first acknowledge the multiple meanings the term *motherhood* may invoke. Definitions of motherhood typically include the state of being a mother, maternity, the character or qualities of a mother, and mothers collectively.

Within the developed world, the increasing emergence of a range of nontraditional family structures and technologically mediated motherhood are increasingly challenging traditional understandings of the term, including giving birth, adoption, intercountry adoption, and fostering. Blended families, same-sex partnerships, technologically assisted and biologically controlled parenthood, surrogacy, and gamete donation continue to stretch the definition and use of the term *motherhood*. The term may be equally bestowed upon any person undertaking the parenting tasks of developing kinship, providing nurture, and offering guidance and love in biological and nonbiological relationships with the children in their care. As the capacity for technological intervention in regulating and controlling fertility increases, the gendered construction of the term *motherhood* may also become increasingly open to challenge in the future.

In the developed world, the pathway to becoming a mother is strewn with an ever-increasing array of parenting options, socially achievable possibilities, and technologically mediated choices. In addition, the dwindling fertility rates across the Western world have been met in many countries with a range of pronatalist government policies, which seek to encourage more women to proactively choose motherhood and have more children. In the developing world, however, a different picture of motherhood is evident, with high fertility rates still being observed (although generally trending downward), and government support often limited. The future of motherhood is considered against this backdrop of social determinants; of simultaneous population growth in certain regions and marked decline in others; and the expansion of technological intervention (although this is likely to remain inaccessible to much of the world's population), which will arguably redefine and reshape the future essence, processes, expectations, and experiences of motherhood.

## Demographic Trends and Predictions

According to recent Organisation for Economic Co-operation and Development (OECD) and the United Nations Children's Fund (UNICEF) reports, birth rates in OECD countries have declined markedly over the past few decades. The current average fertility rate is now reported to be 1.6 children per woman, significantly below the average of 2.1 children per woman needed to maintain current population levels. This decline in total fertility rate (TFR) is, in part, attributed to the trend observed in the West of postponing childbirth. For many women, higher levels of education, improved employment prospects and earning capacity, and changes in family structure have all contributed to the changed expectations that younger women may adopt toward accepting the traditional role of mothering in society. The statistics reveal that women with paid jobs, higher education and income, and who are not married have a lower number of births than other women, with an increasing number of women in developed nations mothering only one child. Furthermore, the ability to control fertility has created higher expectations for managing the terms and timing of childbearing for women.

The higher frequency of childlessness among women in their 30s and 40s is now a recognized risk factor for some health problems, while the increasing age of maternity brings statistically associated health risks for the child. Evidence of a widening gap between women's desired and observed fertility rates does not suggest a rejection of the desire to embrace motherhood per se, but rather is a reflection of the complex combination of a range of broader social and economic factors impacting upon the individual woman's capacity to choose motherhood.

While this trend toward older mothers with fewer children is being observed in developed nations, the gap between the numbers of teenage pregnancies and numbers of older mothers continues to widen. Data from the UNICEF Report on Child Welfare reports that "on average across 13 countries of the European Union, women who gave birth as teenagers are twice as likely to be living in poverty.

Moreover, when assessed against five different indicators of disadvantage, including poverty, unemployment, and school failure, those who gave birth as teenagers are far worse-off than those who gave birth later on." The impact of teenage motherhood in terms of reduced social opportunity, with its associated negative impact on child poverty, health, and education, flags this emerging trend as one that may prove increasingly socially divisive and damaging in the future.

*A mother and her two children waiting to be seen at a health care clinic in M'banza Congo, in the Zaíre province. Access to health care is improving in sub-Saharan Africa, although it is still unequal to care provided in more developed nations.*

The declining population levels in the Western world are increasingly raising social and political concerns for the future. As the population ages, the workforce becomes less adaptable, and fewer young adults may be able to provide care for the elderly or generate enough taxation to contribute to public spending on pensions and health care. The currently observed declining fertility rates may, therefore, have significant, long-term economic consequences.

In response to this negative trend in population growth, many OECD/European countries have implemented a range of policies to stem the tide of decreasing fertility rates. These include a range of tax credits, cash benefits, and care support to help families meet their childcare costs and reduce the direct cost of children. However, it is suggested that childcare availability and leave provisions have the potential to promote motherhood. Cross-country analysis suggests that total fertility rates are higher in OECD countries with more accessible childcare availability, lower direct costs of children, higher part-time availability, and longer leaves. As the efficacy of such government policies varies widely across countries, their future impact on women's choices and desire to become mothers is difficult to predict.

In contrast, many developing nations, particularly in the Middle East and sub-Saharan Africa, are experiencing strong population growth, with the overall global trend in population growth being positive. Estimates to date note a global growth of approximately 200,000 people per day, which translates to almost 80 million per year. This global figure is offset by death rates, which are continuing to decline as mortality rates decrease with improving, although still unequal, access to health care.

In summary, current demographic trends in motherhood in developed nations suggest that TFR will continue to remain below the 2.1 children per mother needed to stabilize population levels, and the age of maternity will generally continue to rise. The widening gap between the health and social opportunities of teenage mothers and their children remains a significant problem in the Western world. While birth rates remain relatively high in developing countries, current trends are moving toward a decreasing number of births per woman; however, overall global population growth is expected to remain positive.

**Trend Toward Technological Intervention**
In the West, motherhood has become increasingly facilitated, constructed, and defined in terms of technological interventions. For example, it is now estimated that up to 90 percent of women in the Western world engage in some form of prenatal intervention, such as having an ultrasound to detect fetal abnormalities, throughout the course of their pregnancy. The number of women seeking fertility treatments has been steadily rising, to some degree a consequence of the increasing age of maternity and the decreased fertility rates that accompany it. In addition, the risk of disability in children born to older mothers increases. The technological tools to detect and prevent the outcome of a child with a disability has subsequently cemented the role of technology in motherhood both as a means of achieving the pregnancy in a biological sense, but also as a means of prenatally screening to assess the health of the child.

As notions of choice become further entrenched into the language and expectations of motherhood, control over the timing of childbirth and numbers of children may extend to include control over the characteristics of these children. As mentioned previously, this may incorporate screening out particular kinds of disabilities, which may extended to include more minor or non-life-threatening conditions, such as poor teeth.

While some social commentators advocate for the genetic enhancement of children to ensure they

have the best possible future, this idea remains ethically contentious. The use of such technology is interpreted as a proactive and positive intervention, and equally as a potentially eugenic form of discrimination and disability prejudice.

Declining fertility rates in the Western world, coupled with the rising age of motherhood and a decrease in the numbers of children born to each mother, will continue to shape the future of motherhood, both as an institution and an experience. In the Western world, increasing access to reproductive technologies will continue to mediate and control biological fertility, but may also become increasingly accepted as a means of regulation and control over the kinds of children that may be born. Ultimately, these expectations are likely to significantly alter the expectations of motherhood, replacing unconditional acceptance with notions of conditional control and choice.

**See Also:** Artificial Insemination; Economics of Motherhood; Employment and Motherhood; Eugenics; European Union; Family; Fertility; History of Motherhood: 1900 to Present; Maternalism; Maternity Leave; Work and Mothering.

**Bibliography**
Aldred, M.J., R. Savarirayan and J. Savulescu. "It's Only Teeth—Are There Limits to Genetic Testing?" *Clinical Genetics*, v.63/5 (2003).
D'Addio, C.A. and M.M. D'Ercole. *Trends and Determinants of Fertility Rates in OECD Countries: The Role of Policies.* www.oecd.org/dataoecd/7/33/35304751.pdf (accessed June 2009).
Economic Community of West African States (ECOWAS)/Organisation for Economic Co-operation and Development (OECD). "Atlas on Regional Integration in West Africa: Demographic Trends." (2007). http://www.oecd.org/dataoecd/8/24/39802965.pdf (accessed March 2009).
Kamerman, S.B., M. Neuman, J. Waldfogel, and J. Brooks-Gunn. "Social Policies, Family Types and Child Outcomes in Selected OECD Countries." http://www.oecd.org/dataoecd/26/46/2955844.pdf (accessed June 2009).
O'Reilly, Andrea, ed. *Motherhood at the 21st Century: Experience, Identity, Policy, Agency.* New York: Columbia University Press, 2010.

Organisation for Economic Co-operation and Development (OECD). "Can Policies Boost Birth Rates?" (2007). http://www.oecd.org/LongAbstract/0,3425,en_2649_34489_39970766_1_1_1_1,00.html (accessed February 2009).

Organisation for Economic Co-operation and Development (OECD). "SF6: Share of Births Outside Marriage and Teenage Births." http://www.oecd.org/dataoecd/62/49/41919586.pdf (accessed February 2009).

Rapp, R. *Testing the Woman, Testing the Fetus. The Social Impact of Amniocentesis in America.* New York: Routledge, 2000.

Savulescu, J. "New Breeds of Humans: The Moral Obligation to Enhance." *Reproductive Biomedicine Online,* v.10/1 (2005).

United Nations Children's Fund (UNICEF). "An Overview of Child Well-Being in Rich Countries. A Comprehensive Assessment of the Lives and Well-Being of Children and Adolescents in Economically Advanced Nations." (2001) http://www.unicef-irc.org/publications/pdf/rc7_eng.pdf (accessed March 2009).

Eleanor Milligan
Griffith University

# Gabon

The country of Gabon, in central Africa, was a French colony until it gained independence in 1960. With a population of 1.5 million (2005 estimate), it has a female life expectancy of 55.8 years. Gabon has a birth rate of 36.2 per 1,000 people, with an infant mortality rate of 54.5 per 1,000 live births.

Many precolonial traditions in Bantu society continue in modern Gabon, with girls marrying very young, sometimes at early as 11 or 12 years of age. This has helped contribute to the high maternal mortality rate of 420 deaths per 100,000 live births. Because of the income brought in by the country's oil boom starting in the 1980s, about 94 percent of pregnant women receive at least some professional prenatal care, with 86 percent of mothers having the help of a trained professional during childbirth.

The country's wealth has enabled the government to provide schools and education for girls, and it has been estimated that a third of females in the country have access to contraception. Abortion is only allowed in exceptional cases, but illegal abortions do take place. In spite of the fact that Libreville, the country's capital, has a well-developed health services system, some 60 percent of the population live in the countryside and rely on agriculture, and 12 percent of the population do not have easy access to clean drinking water. However, the government of President Omar Bongo has done much to improve the situation, and the oil wealth has ensured that conditions in the country remain much better than those of its neighbors; the country has 27 hospitals and nearly 700 clinics. Gabon is one of the few countries in sub-Saharan Africa where there are maternity benefits and family allowances for mothers.

**See Also:** Abortion; Congo; Congo, Democratic Republic of the; Ethiopia; Maternity Leave; Prenatal Health Care.

**Bibliography**

Dupuis, Annie. "Etre ou Ne Pas Etre: Quelques Sociétés de Femme au Gabon" [To Be or Not to Be: Some Women's Societies in Gabon]. *Objets et Mondes,* v.23 (1983).

Larsen, U. "Infertility in Central Africa." *Tropical Medicine and International Health,* v.8/4 (April 2003).

Nguema, Isaac. "Les Voies Nouvelles du Développement de la Femme Gabonaise" [The New Ways of the Development of Gabonese Women]. *Droit et Cultures,* v.1 (1981).

Yates, Douglas A. *The Rentier State in Africa: Oil Rent Dependency & Neocolonialism in the Republic of Gabon.* Trenton, NJ: Africa World Press, 1996.

Justin Corfield
Geelong Grammar School, Australia

# Gambia

Gambia is a small country (over 7,000 square miles, slightly twice the size of Delaware) whose shape follows that of the Gambia River. It is surrounded by Senegal (except for a western border on the Atlantic Ocean) and gained its independence from the United Kingdom in 1965. It has a population of approximately 1.8 million, which is disproportionately young: the median age is 17.9 years of age; 43.6 percent of the population is 14 years of age or younger, versus only 2.8 percent age 65 years or older. The population growth rate is 2.7 percent, with a birth rate of 38.4 per 1,000, a death rate of 11.7 per 1,000, and a net migration rate of 0.3 per 1,000.

Life expectancy at birth is 53.4 years of age for men and 57.3 years of age for women. The total fertility rate (an estimate of the number of children per woman) is just over 5. The population is 90 percent Muslim and comes from several African ethnic groups, of which Mandinka is the largest (42 percent). Literacy rates are low for males (47.8 percent) and even lower for females (32.8 percent), and children are only expected to attend school for seven years.

Gambia is a poor country with limited agriculture and no mineral or natural resources. Poverty and unemployment are high: the per-capita Gross Domestic Product (GDP) is $1,300 and it is unequally distributed with a Gini Index (a measure of household inequality) of 50.2. The Gambian government expends 7.3 percent of its GDP on health, constituting less than half (44.6 percent) of the total expenditures on health: 40.6 percent comes from external sources and the rest from private expenditures.

The per-capita expenditure on health is $18. Preventive care is a priority: child immunization rates are high at over 90 percent for the most common diseases, and 92 percent of pregnant women receive at least one prenatal care visit. However, only 55 percent of births are attended by skilled personnel, and mortality rates are high: in 2000, the maternal mortality rate was 540 per 100,000 live births, the stillbirth rate was 44 per 1,000 total births, and the neonatal mortality rate 46 per 1,000 live births.

Save the Children, an international organization dedicated to improving children's health around the world, places Gambia in Tier III (least developed countries) in terms of health care services, but ranks it fairly highly among its peers (11 out of 33) on the Mother's Index, which takes into account maternal and child health indicators as well as measures of women's equality and participation in society. Gambia is on the Tier II Watch List of the U.S. Department of State for human trafficking, primarily of women and girls for sexual exploitation and domestic servitude.

**See Also:** Child Poverty; Islam and Motherhood; Poverty and Mothering; Slavery and Mothering.

**Bibliography**
Save the Children. *State of the World's Mothers 2007.* https://www.cia.gov/library/publications/the-world -factbook/geos/en.html (accessed April 2009).
Walraven, G., M. Telfer, J. Rowley, and C. Ronsmans. "Maternal Mortality in Rural Gambia: Levels, Causes and Contributing Factors." *Bulletin of the World Health Organization,* v.78/5 (2000).
World Health Organization. "World Health Statistics Report 2008." http://www.who.int/whosis/whostat/ EN_WHS08_Full.pdf (accessed April 2009).

Sarah E. Boslaugh
Washington University School of Medicine

# Genocide and Motherhood

The United Nations (UN) 1948 Convention on the Prevention and Punishment of the Crime of Genocide defines genocide as "acts committed with intent to destroy, in whole or in part, a national, ethnical, racial, or religious group, such as: a) Killing members of the group; b) Causing serious bodily or mental harm to members of the group; c) Deliberately inflicting on the group conditions of life calculated to bring about its physical destruction, in whole or in part; d) Imposing measures intended to prevent births within the group; e) forcibly transferring children of the group to another group." By definition, genocide is integrally tied to the suppression of pregnancy and births; the forcible separation of parents from their children; and mass violence against civilians, particularly women and children. Genocide is closely related to other grave human rights violations, such as crimes against humanity, war crimes, mass killing, ethnic cleansing, politicide, slavery, apartheid, torture, mass rape, and forced displacement. In the 20th century alone, there were dozens of large-scale massacres that qualified as genocide under the UN definition.

## Characteristics of Genocide

Every case of genocide is perpetrated in unique political and social circumstances, but all genocides are characterized by intentional, systematic, and organized state-sponsored violence that targets a specific group of noncombatant men, women, and children. The persecution and massacre of women and children is often central to the genocidal plan. For example, during the Armenian genocide (1915–23), when the Ottoman Empire killed over 1 million Armenian civilians, women and children were raped, massacred, enslaved, and sent on death marches to concentration camps in the Syrian Desert, where many were deliberately starved to death.

During the Holocaust (1933–45), the Nazis and their collaborators murdered 6 million Jewish and Roma men, women, and children in ghettos, mass shootings, concentration camps, and death camps. Jewish children, pregnant women, and mothers with young children were usually killed immediately upon their arrival at the death camps. During the Rwandan genocide (1994), Interahame militia and "ordinary" Hutu civilians hacked to death 800,000 Tutsi men, women, and children in only 100 days. The perpetrators raped hundreds of thousands of Tutsi women and girls, resulting in human immunodeficiency virus (HIV) infection and unwanted pregnancies. Some cases of genocide target only a single gender, such as the massacre of 8,000 Bosniak men and boys during the Srebrenica genocide (1995). Similarly, there were a disproportionate number of male victims in the Bangladesh (East Pakistan) genocide (1971), which was committed by the West Pakistan government.

## Mother and Child Targets

Since the ultimate goal in many cases of genocide is the eradication of an entire national, ethnical, racial, or religious group, perpetrators are usually preoccupied with motherhood and childbirth. They exploit traditional notions of motherhood in nationalist and racist propaganda, and ground their ideologies about racial superiority and inferiority in the pseudoscience of eugenics and celebratory nationalism. Mothers, themselves, have occupied diverse roles in historical cases of genocide, acting as perpetrators, victims, bystanders, and rescuers. As victims of genocide, women have experienced forced sterilization, separation from family, the forcible transfer of their children to another group, internment and enslavement, medical experimentation, mass rape resulting in unplanned pregnancies, and mass killing campaigns where pregnant women and mothers with young children are often specifically targeted for destruction.

Under the 1948 UN Genocide Convention, the 1998 Rome Statute of the International Criminal Court, and the 2005 UN Responsibility to Protect doctrine, the international community has a collective obligation to prevent and punish genocide and other Crimes Against Humanity. In practice, the international community has failed to intervene in almost every modern case of genocide in a timely and effective way to quell the violence.

## Perpetrators, Propaganda, and Motherhood

Genocidal regimes often produce racist and nationalist propaganda, and institutionalize segregation through laws that bar the persecuted group from the full rights of citizenship. Imperatives about marriage, motherhood, and childbearing are central to this exclusionary discourse. For example, in her groundbreaking research on women in Nazi Germany, Claudia Koonz suggests that motherhood was one of the ideological foundations of the Nazi racial state. The Nazis established an extensive, pronatalist program based on the pseudoscientific theory of eugenics, which deemed Aryans racially superior to non-Aryans, such as Jews and Romas. Birth incentives for Aryan Germans included a Marriage Loan program, pro-family propaganda, severe punishments for abortion, increased tax deductions for families with children, eugenics counseling, and a birth control ban. Every year on August 12, Hitler's mother's birthday, the Nazis awarded motherhood medals to German women who bore large numbers of children. Nationalist and racist propaganda was incorporated into all levels of media, government, civil society, schools, and professional associations.

The Nuremberg Laws of 1935 forbade intermarriage between Aryans and Jews, and excluded Jews from participation in most elements of German public life. The combination of dehumanizing hate propaganda, institutionalized anti-Semitism, and the celebration of the German *Volk* and German motherhood, primed the population for genocide. In stark contrast to the glorified images of Aryan Germans, Jewish men were depicted as usurers and child killers, and Jewish women as evil seductresses. Jews living in Nazi-occupied territories were subject to forced sterilization, ghettoization, separation from family, deportation, and massacre.

Likewise, prior to the Rwandan genocide, Hutu extremists disseminated "Hutu-Power" and anti-Tutsi propaganda on the radical radio station RTLM, and in propagandist publications like *Kangura*. The infamous Hutu Ten Commandments, published in *Kangura* in December 1990, condemned Hutus who befriended, married, or employed a Tutsi woman. In addition to demanding that only Hutus occupy government, military, educational, and other strategic positions, the Commandments suggested that Hutu women made better mothers, and that they should "bring [their] husbands, brothers, and sons back to reason." Tutsi women—as wives, mothers, and as potential partners or secretaries—were widely dehumanized as seductive and dishonest before the genocide, paving the way for mass rapes and massacres once the genocide began.

### Forcible Transfer of Children to Another Group

The UN Genocide Convention enumerates the forcible transfer of children from a persecuted group to another group as an act of genocide. In such cases, the bonds of motherhood are violated and parents are involuntarily separated from their children, who are enslaved, interned, or resettled with another family or in a communal living situation. For example, during the Cambodian genocide (1975–79), when Khmer Rouge murdered 1.7 million people and forcibly relocated millions of civilians to collective farms, families were frequently forced apart and children sometimes sent to live on different communes than their parents. During the Armenian genocide, Armenian children were enslaved or given to Kurdish or Turkish families by desperate parents who sought to save their children from death marches.

In cases of cultural genocide, like the enslavement of Africans in the Americas (1607–1865) or the willful destruction of First Nations culture by colonial settlers and subsequent governments, children are also frequently displaced from their families. During the Atlantic slave trade, Africans were kidnapped, transferred to slave fortresses, and forced to endure a horrific journey aboard slave ships bound for the Americas. This "middle passage" from one continent to another marked the willful destruction of the Africans' ties to family, community, culture, and language. Under American and British law, African American slaves were property, not people, which meant that children born into slavery could be sold at auction, and thus, forcibly separated from their mothers.

Some argue that the Canadian Indian residential school system, operated by the Canadian federal government from the late 19th century to the late 20th century under the Indian Act, was a program of forced assimilation. First Nations children were forcibly taken from their families, their communities, and their cultures, and "re-educated" in residential schools that were run by the churches. Victims were not allowed to speak their native languages or practice their spiritual beliefs.

### Mass Rape

Systematic mass rape is frequently an element of genocide campaigns. Genocidaires systematically raped and tortured Armenian women and girls during the Armenian genocide, Indigenous Maya women and girls during the Guatemalan genocide (1981–83), Tutsi women and girls during the Rwandan genocide, and non-Arab Darfurian women during the genocidal counterinsurgency in Darfur (2003–05). During the Bosnian genocide, Serb forces raped tens of thousands of Bosniak women and girls, holding some victims in "rape camps" where they were repeatedly assaulted. For many women, being a genocide survivor also meant being a rape survivor, and, in the aftermath of rape, some these women were blamed and ostracized from their communities.

In some cases of mass rape, like the Serbian rapes of Bosniaks, impregnating the victims with the perpetrators' semen functioned as both ideological and physical erasure of the victims' national or ethnic identities, a forced motherhood in which a generation of "Serbian" babies were born to Bosniak women. Similarly, during the Rwandan genocide, many Tutsi women who survived the rapes and massacres found themselves HIV positive and/or pregnant by Hutu perpetrators. Since abortion was illegal in Rwanda, some women sought abortions in the Congo, pursued illegal abortions in Rwanda, or gave up their newborns to orphanages. Still others kept their babies, but experienced ambivalence about motherhood and vexed feelings about their children. In total, approximately 20,000 children—referred to as *les enfants mauvais souvenirs* or "the children of bad memories"—were born as a result of rapes during the Rwandan genocide.

## Ghettos, Internment Camps, and Mass Killing

Many cases of genocide include internment of the victims in ghettos, concentration camps, or forced labor colonies. Ghettoization means the disruption of normal family life, the seizure of victims' property, and, in some cases, the separation of children from their mothers and fathers. For example, during the Holocaust, the children and the elderly were the first people deported to death camps from ghettos

*Marguerite (left) of Rwanda tells Pascasie Mukamusoni how she lost most of her family during the 1994 Rwandan genocide; her mother then died of HIV in 2004. Before she was helped by USAID, she struggled to mother and support her two young brothers.*

like Lodz and Warsaw, leaving only the young, able-bodied adults to labor in Nazi factories. Conditions in ghettos and camps were horrendous, and genocide victims often died of starvation, disease, and execution. Other forms of displacement included forced collectivization on farms and imprisonment during the Cambodian genocide, death marches and concentration camps during the Armenian genocide, and mass exile into refugee camps and camps for internally displaced persons (IDPs) during the Rwandan and Darfur genocides.

Most cases of genocide are defined by mass killing of civilians, including execution by mobile killing squads, massacres at checkpoints or killing fields, and death camps. The murder of women and children in these mass killings is often considered a defining feature of genocide. During the mass shootings of Jews and eastern Europeans by the Nazi Einsatzgruppen units, mothers were often shot with their babies, or watched their children die before they, themselves, were killed. In the six Nazi death camps—Chelmno, Auschwitz-Birkenau, Majdanek, Treblinka, Belzec, and Sobibor—pregnant women, children, and mothers with young children were gassed to death immediately upon arrival. Pregnant women and children were also the victims of torture at the hands of Nazi doctors, who used them for medical experimentation in the camps. Women who survived internment in concentration camps and death camps reported secret abortions, births, and cases of infanticide to protect pregnant women and new mothers from execution. Most mothers who managed to survive the Holocaust lost their children to the genocide.

## Genocide Survivors and Motherhood
Survivors of genocide suffer from trauma and depression, and have disproportionately high suicide rates. Many women survivors mourn for lost children, spouses, extended family members, and friends. In some cases, like the Nazi Holocaust, there were fewer female survivors, while in other cases, like the Rwandan genocide, there were fewer male survivors. After most cases of genocide, like the Armenian genocide, the Holocaust, and the Darfur genocide, the survivors lived in Displaced Persons (DP) camps and eventually immigrated to new countries as refugees. In other cases, like the Rwandan genocide, Tutsi survivors returned to

their homes and lived alongside the Hutu perpetrators who had killed their families and friends. The years that follow a genocide can sometimes include intense efforts to renew the decimated population through motherhood, such as the quick succession of marriages, pregnancies, and births among Jewish Holocaust survivors in DP camps in Europe and detention camps in Cyprus. In general, there are less survivor testimonies and published autobiographical accounts of genocide by women than by men, and the study of gender, motherhood, children, and genocide is still a developing field of research.

**See Also:** Anti-Racist Mothering; Conflict-Zones, Mothering in; Eugenics; First Nations; Grief, Loss of a Child; Hitler, Adolf, Mother of; Intergenerational Trauma; Jewish Mothers; Nazi Germany; Race and Racism; Slavery and Mothering; War and Mothers.

**Bibliography**
Alpert, J. "Muted Testimony: Rape and Gendered Violence in the Holocaust." *Proteus*, v.20/2 (2003)
Baer, E. and M. Goldenberg, eds. *Experience and Expression: Women, the Nazis, and the Holocaust.* Detroit, MI: Wayne State University Press, 2003.
Des Forges, A. *Leave None to Tell the Story: Genocide in Rwanda.* New York: Human Rights Watch, 1999.
Gellately, R. and B. Kiernan, eds. *The Specter of Genocide: Mass Murder in Historical Perspective.* Cambridge, MA: Cambridge University Press, 2003.
Grossmann, A. "Trauma, Memory, and Motherhood: Germans and Jewish Displaced Persons in Post-Nazi Germany, 1945–1949." *Archiv fur Sozialgeschichte*, v.38 (1998).
Kiernan, B. *Blood and Soil: A World History of Genocide and Extermination from Sparta to Darfur.* New Haven, CT: Yale University Press, 2007.
Koonz, C. *Mothers in the Fatherland: Women, the Family, and Nazi Politics.* New York: St. Martin's, 1987.
Leggat-Smith, R.J.Y. *Rwanda: Not So Innocent: When Women Become Killers.* 1995. www.cranepsych.com/Travel/Rwanda/Innocent895.pdf (accessed July 2009).
Lifton, Robert Jay. *The Nazi Doctors: Medical Killing and Psychology of Genocide.* New York: Basic Books, 1986.
Lindsay, R. "From Atrocity to Data: Historiographies of Rape in Former Yugoslavia and the Gendering of Genocide." *Patterns of Prejudice*, v.36/4 (2002).

Ofer, D. and L. Weitzman, eds. *Women and the Holocaust*. New Haven, CT: Yale University Press, 1998.

Office of the High Commissioner for Human Rights. *Convention on the Prevention and Punishment of the Crime of Genocide*. New York: United Nations, 1948.

Power, S. *A Problem From Hell: America and the Age of Genocide*. New York: Perennial, 2002.

Schiessl, C. "An Element of Genocide: Rape, Total War, and International Law in the Twentieth Century." *Journal of Genocide Research*, v.2/4 (2002).

Smith, R. "Women and Genocide: Notes on an Unwritten History." *Holocaust and Genocide Studies*, v.8/3 (1994).

Totten, S., W. Parsons, and I. Charney, eds. *Century of Genocde: Critical Essays and Eyewitness Accounts*. New York: Routledge, 2004.

Waxman, Z. "Unheard Testimony, Untold Stories: The Representation of Women's Holocaust Experiences." *Women's History Review*, v.12/4 (2003).

Amanda Grzyb
University of Western Ontario

# Georgia

The status of mothers in the U.S. state of Georgia varies widely depending on a woman's age, race, socioeconomic background, and geographic location. The state has a history of racism which has resulted in deep economic disparities between blacks and whites; and conservative government policies, which have resulted in limited subsidies for the poor as well as restricted information and access to abortion and sterilization.

These two factors have made certain populations particularly vulnerable to teen pregnancy, abortion, health complications during pregnancy and childbirth, and the impoverishment of mothers and their children. Young, poor, black women, in particular, are much less likely to have access to quality health care during pregnancy and adequate resources to care for their children once born.

## Vital Statistics and Health Care

In 2006, the number of births per mother was 2.2 in Georgia, above the national average of 2.1.

Georgia's mean age at first birth is 24.5, under the national average of 25. The rate of induced terminations of pregnancy per 1,000 women is 13.5 overall; 8.1 for white women and 23.1 for black women. The percentage of births to unmarried mothers was 42.4 percent overall—25 percent of white mothers, 67.8 percent of black mothers, and 48.6 percent of Hispanic mothers. In 2006, the teen birth rate in Georgia was 54.2 per 1,000 girls aged 15–19, the 10th highest in the nation (the national rate was 41.9). For women who gave birth in 2006, 32 percent were never married (versus 28.4 percent nationally); 27.9 percent were in poverty (compared to 25.2 percent nationally); 58.5 percent were in the labor force (versus 57.3 percent nationally); and 19.2 percent were not high school graduates (compared to 17.9 percent nationally). Despite the fact that 27.9 percent of women who gave birth were in poverty, only 3.5 percent of impoverished women who gave birth received cash public assistance.

The percentage of mothers beginning prenatal care in the first trimester is 83.3 percent overall—89.4 percent of white mothers, 78.9 percent of black mothers, and 73.3 percent of Hispanic mothers. The percentage of mothers with late or no care is 4.1 percent overall—2.3 percent of white mothers, 4.9 percent of black mothers, and 8.1 percent of Hispanic mothers. The rate of fetal deaths for fetuses over 20 weeks gestation per 1,000 fetal deaths plus live births is 8.3, 6.2 for white women and 12.3 for black women. Georgia ranks 46th among states based on the size of the gap in infant mortality by mother's education, when comparing the current overall state rate of 8.1 deaths per 1,000 live births with the lower rate—4.9 deaths per 1,000 live births—seen among infants born to the state's most educated mothers.

## Georgia and the Law

Georgia has a large conservative and religious population with restrictive laws regarding reproduction. Georgia law allows individual providers to refuse women's health services for abortion and sterilization. Although the law requires insurance coverage of contraception, it also allows pharmacists to refuse to dispense contraception. In Georgia, the following restrictions on abortion were in effect as of January 2008: the parent of a minor must be notified before an abortion is provided; a woman must receive state-directed counseling that includes information on abortion and then wait 24 hours before the procedure is provided; and public funding is available for abortion only in cases of life endangerment, rape, or incest. In 2005, 92 percent of Georgia counties had no abortion provider (primarily rural counties) and 62 percent of Georgia women lived in these counties. Georgia requires abstinence-based sex education statewide.

Atlanta is home to a national advocacy organization for incarcerated mothers—Aid to Imprisoned Mothers (recently renamed Aid to Children with Imprisoned Mothers), founded in 1987 by Sandra Barnhill. Also located in Atlanta is SisterSong Women of Color Reproductive Health Clinic, a network of local, regional, and national grassroots agencies representing women of color on issues of reproductive and sexual health and rights. SisterSong was cofounded in 1997 by Loretta Ross.

Famous mothers from Georgia include Lillian Gordy Carter, mother of President Jimmy Carter; and Alice Walker, feminist/womanist activist and author of *The Color Purple*, winner of the Pulitzer Prize for Fiction in 1983.

**See Also:** Incarcerated Mothers; Ross, Loretta; Walker, Alice.

### Bibliography
Georgia Humanities Council. *The New Georgia Guide.* Athens: University of Georgia Press, 1996.
Sullivan, Buddy, and Georgia Historical Society. *Georgia: A State History.* San Francisco: Arcadia Publishing, 2003.
U.S. Department of Health and Human Services. *National Vital Statistics Reports*, v.57/7 (January 2009).

Carrie N. Baker
Smith College

# Georgia (Nation)

Georgia, a country in the Caucasus, was a part of the Soviet Union until it gained independence in 1991. With a population of 4.73 million, it has a female life expectancy of 79.9 years. The birth rate is 10.4 per 1,000, and the infant mortality rate is 18 per 1,000 live births. The 2004 estimated divorce rate was 0.42 divorces per 1,000 marriages.

Traditionally, people married young and had children soon after marriage. Stalin's mother, Ekaterina, was 15 when she wed Vissarion Djugashvili, and was 20 when the future Soviet dictator was born in 1879—her fourth child, the three older children having already died as infants. In Georgian society at the time, few women, and even fewer mothers, had careers. They were involved in looking after the home, bringing up children, preparing meals, and tending the family's vegetable garden. Occasionally some women, such as Stalin's mother, took in laundry to enable them to have a little more money.

During the Communist period from 1917 to 1991, Georgian health services improved dramatically; there was another marked improvement in the 1960s and 1970s, when regional hospitals and clinics were opened in towns and villages. Communist literature of the period highlights these health facilities, midwifery services, and improved work opportunities for women. The Tbilisi State University, established in the Georgian capital in 1918, had a special pediatrics faculty. At the time of the dissolution of the Soviet Union, Georgia had the highest number of doctors per capita within the former Soviet republics, and great efforts have been put into medical care since their independence.

One of the country's important indicators, the fertility rate, has showed a marked decline in recent decades. It has fallen from 2.5 in 1975 to 1.6 in 1999. At the same time, there has been a large increase in the percentage of extramarital births—from 0.2 percent in 1975 to 30.9 percent in 1999, the most dramatic rise in any European country. Part of this has been caused by far less people marrying, rather than a dramatic rise in one-parent families.

**See Also:** Armenia; Azerbaijan; Communism and Motherhood; Russia (and Soviet Union).

### Bibliography
Caldwell, John C. and Thomas Schindlmayr. "Explanations of the Fertility Crisis in Modern Societies: A Search for Commonalities." *Population Studies,* v.57/3 (November 2003).

Deutscher, Isaac. *Stalin*. New York: Pelican Books, 1966.

Suny, Ronald Grigor. *The Making of the Georgian Nation*. Bloomington: Indiana University Press, in association with Hoover Institution Press, 1988.

Justin Corfield
Geelong Grammar School, Australia

# Germany

During the last two centuries, motherhood in Germany has changed drastically from the traditional role of home parenting and taking care of household and children, to a new model of working motherhood that involves sharing housework with a partner. The kindergarten movement and the three waves of feminism have played a role in this process, as have World Wars I and II, during which time the available male population declined drastically and women had to join the workforce.

Motherhood was further defined by the reunification of the opposing political systems in the former Federal Republic of Germany (FRG) and the former German Democratic Republic (GDR). How recent government initiatives—including ad campaigns to make motherhood more attractive—impact motherhood in Germany in the future remains to be seen. In modern Germany, birth rates are declining, the average age at first birth is rising, and state-sanctioned benefits are provided for parents. Unless specified, all statistical information refers to the year 2007.

## Pre- and Post-Reunification

Mothers in the former GDR were fully integrated into the workforce, giving them financial independence from their spouses. At the same time, government family policies tried to promote the ideal family image of three children via financial incentives. Being a mother and a career woman was socially accepted and well supported; for example, with childcare centers. The family politics of the former FRG also promoted a patriarchal family image. Employment of mothers was considered to be a conflict of their duty within the family. The value of giving birth was later recognized through ad campaigns and government-assisted programs, such as maternity leave. Since reunification, new mothers have available to them a similar government support structure. However, many women who became mothers under the GDR and FRG still feel the effects of the differences between these former political systems.

## The Kindergarten Movement

German educator Friedrich Froebel (1782–1852) founded the *Kindergarten* in the 1830s, an institution for the education of preschool children by means of play and guided activities. The term signifies both a garden "for" children, a place where they can observe and interact with nature; and also a garden "of" children, where they themselves can grow and develop free from arbitrary political and social imperatives. Children play with toys for sedentary creative play and engage in games and dances for healthy activity. This institution allows mothers to drop off their children for education and play, so they can pursue a career. The *Kindergarten* model of preschool education has been practiced throughout the world since the end of the 19th century.

## Fertility and Abortion

The overall birth rate in Germany has been declining for the past four decades, and in 2007 was the lowest in Europe. Several factors contribute to this low fertility rate: the political taint and correlation of motherhood with fascism, lengthy education times, consumerism, and the fear of an uncertain future. In addition, German women have had access to an array of birth control methods, which have allowed them to postpone or opt out of motherhood. Through various policies, such as the child benefit plan, the government attempts to encourage women to have more children.

Approximately 117,000 abortions are performed annually, for medical or nonmedical reasons. A woman can get a legal abortion only if she has received counseling regarding her options for a responsible decision at a state-recognized facility; the procedure is performed by a medical doctor; and the woman is no more than 12 weeks pregnant. Abortion beyond 12 weeks is only legal if the pregnancy poses a current or future physical or mental threat to the woman, and the only available solution is to terminate the pregnancy. The diagnosis of fetal abnormalities would be one such circumstance.

## Vital Statistics

30 percent of German women do not have children, according to European Union statistics from 2005, with the figure rising among female university graduates to 40 percent. Women become mothers at an average age of 30.2 years with a trend to start later. This makes them the oldest first-time mothers in Europe. Most women who have children opt to have only one or two. Hence, Germany's birth rate is one of the lowest in Europe, with an average of 1.37 children per woman. Thirty percent of these babies are born outside of marriage, while a total of 144,981 minors are affected by divorce. The annual divorce rate of couples with children is 10.5 percent.

## Prenatal Care

Prenatal care is provided by a gynecological obstetrician. Once the pregnancy has been confirmed, the pregnant woman is given a booklet (*Mutterpass*), in which the progress of her pregnancy is tracked and available to the doctor delivering the baby. There are usually 12 examinations prior to the baby's due date—one per month until the 32nd week, and every two weeks thereafter.

If a pregnancy continues past the due date, a daily examination may be required. Routine examinations include pelvic exams, blood tests, blood pressure, urine tests, and weight analysis, as well as ultrasounds. All of these procedures are conducted in the doctor's office. Near term, the baby's heart rate and any contractions are measured. Upon delivering the baby, mothers stay in the hospital 5–7 days for a vaginal delivery and 7–12 days for a caesarean section.

## Parental Leave and Child Benefits

Working parents-to-be are protected by laws that outline their rights and the obligations of their employers. Employees cannot be terminated or penalized for taking parental leave. Additionally, parental pensions are unaffected by their leave.

Maternity benefits (*Mutterschaftsgeld*) are provided by government-mandated insurance offered by all employers. Employed women receive this maternity allowance during their mandatory maternity leave (*Mutterschutzfrist*), six weeks prior and eight weeks following delivery. The amount of maternity allowance is based on the woman's previous income and consists of a portion from the State Health Insurers, supplemented by the employer (*Arbeitgeberzuschuss*). Those who were receiving unemployment benefits are paid fully by the State Health Insurer. The Maternity Allowance Department (*Mutterschaftsgeldstelle*) provides support for women insured through a private health insurance company, as well as women working part time, and women insured through a family member. Self-employed persons without Sick Leave Insurance (*Krankengeldanspruch*) receive no assistance.

Parental benefits are available to both parents 8 weeks after the child's birth or adoption. These benefits are equal to 67 percent of their income to a maximum of 1,800 euros, for up to 12 months, or 14 months in the case of a single parent. The following months of the parental leave, up to 36 in total, are unpaid. Unemployed parents receive a minimal amount of benefits during this time. If another child is born during parental leave, the periods of parental leave can be served consecutively.

Parents (or guardians) of children under 18 years can apply for government child benefit (*kindergeld*). To qualify, they must live and work in Germany and pay income tax there. The benefit amount is dependant on how many children the parent has and the children's ages. For the first, second, and third child, the parent receives monthly payments of 154 euros per child. For each additional child, they receive 179 euros more. This benefit can be extended to age 25, if a child pursues postsecondary education or an apprenticeship. Additionally, each child living with a parent or guardian is considered a dependant, for which parents can receive a child tax credit (*kinderfreibetrag*) on their income tax.

## The Power of Language

The German language assigns three genders to nouns (masculine, feminine, and neutral). Once the words are in the plural form, they take on the uniform article *die*, incidentally the same article as for feminine singular nouns. This grammar function of the German structure can be construed as a metaphor for a woman, who has the ability to become pregnant and create life within, becoming plural.

Typical German words that include the word *mutter* (mother) are *muttersöhnchen* (a derogatory term for men, who have strong ties to their mothers and/or are very dependent) and *Rabenmutter* (a derogatory term for a mother who neglects or does not care for her children). The German language also contains words that derive from the word "mother" in various languages: alma mater, matrix, material, and *matriarchat (*matriarchy*).*

## Famous German Mothers

Hildegard von Bingen (1098–1179) was a saint, a German abbess, and pioneer in science, philosophy, and music, among other talents. Though in many ways she was before her time, she was also deeply attached to tradition and mindful of her duties to the Catholic Church. She became a mother superior at the age of 38.

Käthe Kollwitz (1867–1945), née Schmidt, was a German painter, printmaker, sculptor, committed socialist and pacifist, and mother of two sons. Her youngest died in World War I. In her works, Kollwitz focuses frequently on the maternal and the mother–child bond, articulating an expressive and often searing account of the human condition and embracing the victims of poverty, hunger, and war.

Ursula Gertrud von der Leyen, born in 1958, is a German politician and mother of seven children. In 2005, she was appointed to Angela Merkel's cabinet as Federal Minister for Family Affairs, Senior Citizens, Women, and Youth.

Luise von Preussen (1776–1810), was the Queen of Prussia and mother of 10 children. She commanded universal respect and affection and was the legendary glorified model of German womanhood.

## German Mothers in Literature

Gretchen, short for Margaret, is seduced by Faust in Johann Wolfgang von Goethe's tragedy *Faust I* (1808). She becomes pregnant, drowns her illegitimate child, and is then condemned to death.

In *Maria Magdalene* (1843), a play by Friedrich Hebbel, the female protagonist becomes pregnant by an arranged partner, her fiancé. Since she is in love with another man, she commits suicide prior to giving birth to her child.

Mutter Courage (Mother Courage) is a character in Bertolt Brecht's play *Mutter Courage und ihre Kinder* (*Mother Courage and Her Children*, 1941). Anna Fierling (called Mother Courage) is torn between protecting her children from the 30 years war and making a profit from the war.

Maid Grusche is a character in the 1944 epic parable by Bertolt Brecht called *The Caucasian Chalk Circle* (*Der Kaukasische Kreidekreis*). She raises an abandoned baby as her own and is willing to give him up to ensure his health and safety.

Wendla Bergmann is a schoolgirl in Frank Wedekind's play *Frühlingserwachen* (*Spring Awakening,* 1891), who becomes pregnant by rape because she has no knowledge of sexual reproduction. Her mother does not provide her with sufficient information and takes her to get an abortion without her knowledge. She dies from complications.

**See Also:** Birth Control; Feminism; Motherhood and Consumerism; Nazi Germany; War and Mothers.

**Bibliography**
Bundesministerium für Familie, Senioren, Frauen und Jugend. www.bmfsfj.de (accessed December 2008).
Bundeszentrale für Politische Bildung. www.bpb.de (accessed December 2008).
European Commision. "Eurostat." www.epp.eurostat.ec.europa.eu (accessed December 2008).
Statistisches Bundesamt Deutschland. "Destatis." www.destatis.de (accessed December 2008).

Sonja M. Allen
Queen's University

# Ghana

Social, cultural, and economic factors contribute to the ways in which motherhood is practiced and perceived in Ghana. Because Ghana is considered a developing country, there is a need to improve infant and mortality rates.

In Ghanaian society, a woman's status is linked to her fertility. The more children she has, the higher her status increases. Infertile women, however, may be socially stigmatized because they are not able to further their lineages. In this context, fertility rates are relatively high in Ghana. The U.S. Census estimates the total fertility rate (number of births per woman) was 4.7 in 1995 and decreased slightly to 3.8 in 2008.

Despite the high fertility rates, Ghana faces several health-related issues that affect mothers and their children. The United Nations Children's Fund (UNICEF) shows a maternal mortality rate ratio of 210 (per 100,000 live births) from 2000 to 2006. This number was adjusted in 2005 to indicate a more accurate number of 560. The 2006 World Health Organization statistics show an infant mortality rate of 68 (per 1,000 live births) and a neonatal mortality rate of 27 (per 1,000 live births). Socioeconomic factors contributing to these rates are: maternal education, disease and health issues (such as human immunodeficiency virus (HIV) and acquired immunodeficiency syndrome (AIDS) and malaria), water and sanitation facilities, and nutrition. UNICEF's 2004 statistics show that one-fourth of Ghana's total population does not have access to safe drinking water, and 18 percent lack sanitation facilities.

Contributing sociocultural factors to infant and maternal health include food taboos and traditional rural practices such as home births. Depending on the ethnic group and context, certain food taboos deprive infants and mothers of vital nourishment. Poverty, illiteracy, and unemployment contribute to women's reduced power in making decisions regarding family planning, contraceptive use, and child-drearing practices. Increasing maternal education is one way of improving infant and maternal mortality rates, but education rates are lower for women. According to the Ghanaian Ministry of Health, in 1993 38.3 percent of females had no education. In 2003 the number decreased to 28.2 percent. United Nations Educational, Scientific, and Cultural Organization (UNESCO) 2006 statistics indicate that adult literacy rates for females (aged 15 and older) were 57.2 percent, and 74.8 percent for female youth (aged 15–24 years). This is compared to adult males at 71.2 percent and male youth at 79.2 percent.

**See Also:** AIDS/HIV and Mothering; Cross-Cultural Perspectives on Motherhood; Globalization and Mothering; Infant Mortality; Maternal Mortality; Poverty and Mothering; Pronatalism; Religion and Mothering.

**Bibliography**

Gyimah, Stephen Obeng. "Cultural Background and Infant Survival in Ghana." *Ethnicity and Health,* v11/2 (2006).

Ministry of Health. www.moh-ghana.org (accessed June 2009).

Oppong, Christine and Katherine Abu. *Seven Roles of Women: Impact of Education, Migration, and Employment on Ghanaian Mother.* Geneva, Switzerland: Geneva International Labour Office, 1987.

Tettey, Elizabeth. *Motherhood: An Experience in the Ghanaian Context.* Ghana: Ghana Universities Press, 2002.

UNICEF. Info by Country: Ghana. http://www.unicef.org/infobycountry/ghana_statistics.html (accessed November 2008).

UNICEF. "The State of Africa's Children 2008." http://www.unicef.org/wcaro/soac08 (accessed November 2008).

World Health Organization (WHO). Statistics Ghana 2008. http://www.who.int/countries/gha/gha/en (accessed July 2009).

Sarah Monson
Minnesota State University

# Gift Economy

The gift economy has been much discussed in European-American academia as an economy of indigenous, pre-capitalist cultures, which do not have money or markets as such, but function on the basis of a triple obligation of giving, receiving, and reciprocating. With a few partial exceptions, these discussions do not distinguish between gift giving and exchange, nor do they accord any particular place to mothering.

Recently, however, women scholars have begun to recognize the mothering aspect of gift economies and the economic aspect of mothering. In contrast to exchange, maternal gift giving can be seen as the unilateral satisfaction of needs, made necessary by the biology of dependent children, who are unable to give back an equivalent of what has been given to them. From this perspective, unilateral giving and receiving is seen as a transitive, bond-creating, communicative process not contingent upon immediate reciprocity. This process is extended in the circulation of gifts.

Unilateral giving constitutes a logical gesture, which is essentially complete but may also be elaborated by variations, including reciprocity and symbolic exchange, and is finally doubled back upon itself as *do ut des*. The logic of exchange is ego-oriented. Giving in order to receive an equivalent cancels the unilateral gift and gives rise to adversarial relations. When women mother, they are practicing an alternative economy.

The structural values of care deriving from this economy form the gift paradigm, as opposed to the values of the exchange paradigm that is derived from the market. In light housework and childcare are nonmonetary gifts, passed through the family to the market. Profit itself can be considered the gift of surplus labor, leveraged from the worker by the capitalist. Exchange is usually considered as occupying the whole category of the economic. By including mothering in the category as a mode of distribution of goods and services directly to needs, the figure of *homo economicus* (economic human) can be diminished by the coexistence of *homo donans*.

## Gift Paradigm

Many initiatives based on the idea of the gift economy have arisen in recent years, from open source software to *Wikipedia*, intentional communities with income sharing, Freecycle, time dollars, Burning Man festivals, and Really Really Free Markets, but in practice as in academia there has been little or no mention of their basis in mothering. International Feminists for a Gift Economy is a network of activists and scholars who try to provide a framework for reclaiming the gift economy as maternal.

The gift paradigm is a radical re-visioning of many areas of academic endeavor and can also be used to assess present policies. For example, foreign aid, which is given with strings attached, is actually an exchange that drains the receiver, creating more profit for the giver. Globalization is the privatization and redirection of the gifts of underdeveloped countries by developed countries, gifts of cheap labor, and such previously free resources as water, seeds, and even air. In this way, underdeveloped countries can be seen as nurturing developed countries, to

their own detriment. Abundance is necessary for gift economies to function without sacrifice.

The market establishes control by directing the gifts of the many to the few and by wars and waste, creating the scarcity necessary for its own type of efficient functioning. The market can be seen as an antinurturing distributive mechanism, deeply influenced by a Western construction of masculinity that requires the male child to reject the nurturing role while nevertheless depending upon mother's, or other's, gifts.

## Matriarchal Gift Societies

Non-Western matriarchal societies like the Iroquois had functioning gift economies in which women were in charge of the distribution of goods to needs. Gifting is also part of the cultural heritage of groups where women are at the center, such as the Minangkabau of Sumatra. The African Khoekhoe maintain the gift economy in their spiritual practices. Recently, women activists in Mali have recognized the gift framework as descriptive of their Dama system, and women's solidarity networks in Kenya are finding it useful for describing and planning their practice. Understanding the logic of the gift economy and proposing its partial or complete restoration as part of the birthright of the maternal human also reveals the gift-based character of contemporary movements for peace and the environment and provides the basis for new coalitions.

**See Also:** Economics of Motherhood; Economy and Motherhood; Ethics of Care; Maternal Feminism; Matriarchy.

## Bibliography

Salleh, Ariel, ed. *Eco-Sufficiency and Global Justice: Women Write Political Ecology.* London: Pluto Press, 2009.

Vaughan, Genevieve. *For-Giving: A Feminist Criticism of Exchange.* Austin, TX: Plain View Press, 1997.

Vaughan, Genevieve, ed. *Women and the Gift Economy, A Radically Different Worldview Is Possible.* Toronto: Inanna Publications, 2007.

Genevieve Vaughan
Independent Scholar

# Gilman, Charlotte Perkins

Charlotte Perkins Gilman (1860–1935) was a feminist writer and lecturer who is best remembered for her autobiographical and semiautobiographical writings, especially *The Yellow Wallpaper*. Born in Connecticut, she was related through her father's mother to the Beecher family, and after her father abandoned the family in poverty, the Beecher sisters were instrumental in young Charlotte's upbringing.

The sisters, Catharine Beecher, Isabella Beecher Hooker, and Harriet Beecher Stowe (author of *Uncle Tom's Cabin)* were all abolitionists and suffragists. Despite the lack of her father in her life, Gilman's autobiography recounts that she was a tomboy as a young woman, with few female friends and little relationship with her mother.

## Postpartum Depression Experience

Her first marriage was to Charles Walter Stetson, an artist, in 1884; she gave birth to their daughter Katharine Beecher Stetson in 1885, and her subsequent case of postpartum depression was dismissed as "hysteria" and "nervousness" by both her husband and her physician. This was typical of the male-dominated profession at the time, which treated women as inherently irrational and unreliable at reporting their own symptoms. The difficult period not only contributed to her separation in 1888 (and divorce in 1894—both were rare in the 19th century, and rarer still when the woman initiated it) but inspired "The Yellow Wallpaper," which she wrote after her divorce and published in *New England Magazine* in 1891.

Presented as a series of journal entries, the short story is that of a woman who has been confined to her bedroom by her physician husband after giving birth. The windows are barred, and a gate at the top of the stairs prevents her from leaving. Confinement, isolation, and postpartum depression contribute to the narrator's descent into psychosis as she becomes obsessed with the patterns in the yellow wallpaper of her prison, eventually imagining women hidden in it, women with whom she belongs.

By conflating her husband and physician, and writing a first-person narrative that drew heavily on her own experience, Gilman later admitted she was trying to reach her own physician and show him the error of his ways. Here she drew on more than just her experience with postpartum depression; in 1887 she fell into chronic depression, for which one of the country's leading doctors prescribed the "rest cure," which called for isolation, bed rest, and fattening up, followed by "as domestic a life as possible—no more than two hours' intellectual life a day, and never touch a pen, brush, or pencil as long as you live."

Readers since have pointed out that the power disparity in 19th-century marriage is condemned as strongly as the power of male physicians over female patients, and that the domestic prison of the bedroom can be read figuratively as the confinement of the domestic sphere—and in particular the way women were expected to so narrowly focus on the task of motherhood based not according to their own judgment, but on that of men who had authority over them.

In 1898, Perkins wrote *Women and Economics*, which attacks the division of social roles considered normal in her contemporary society. She argues that keeping women economically dependent on men and unable to fully participate in public life due to their domestic responsibilities is arbitrary and deleterious to human advancement. She believed public interest would be better served if women hired professional cooks and housekeepers and were thus freed to participate in the paid workforce.

Despite the deterioration of her marriage, Charlotte strongly supported the rights of fathers—which may have been influenced by her own father's attempt to maintain an epistolary relationship with her—and supported her husband's remarriage, eventually sending her daughter to live with the new couple. When she returned to Connecticut in 1895, after her mother's death, she began a romance with her first cousin, Houghton Gilman, which they maintained through letters while she toured as a lecturer on social reform.

They married in 1900; Houghton eventually died in 1934. Having been diagnosed with breast cancer two years earlier, Charlotte committed suicide by overdose of chloroform a year after her husband's death, explaining in her suicide note her support of euthanasia and her choice of "chloroform over cancer."

**See Also:** Autobiographies; Cancer and Motherhood; Economy and Motherhood; Literature, Mothers in; Poetry, Mothers in; Postpartum Depression.

**Bibliography**

Allen, Judith. *The Feminism of Charlotte Perkins Gilman: Sexualities, Histories, Progressivism.* Chicago: University of Chicago Press, 2009.

Davis, Cynthia J. and Denise D. Knight. *Charlotte Perkins Gilman and Her Contemporaries: Literary and Intellectual Contexts.* Tuscaloosa: University of Alabama Press, 2004.

Gilman, Charlotte Perkins. *The Living of Charlotte Perkins Gilman: An Autobiography.* New York: Harper & Row, 1975.

Knight, Denise D. *Charlotte Perkins Gilman: A Study of the Short Fiction.* New York: Twayne Publishers, 1997.

Bill Kte'pi
Independent Scholar

# Girlhood and Motherhood

Girlhood has historically been considered a transition period between childhood and womanhood (as the period preceding motherhood), ending around the time a young woman started menstruating and became able to bear children and get married. Motherhood and girlhood are related in three significant ways: first, in the relations of mothers and daughters; second, in modes of girlish behavior that imitates motherhood and serves as a preparation for it; and third, they intersect in the category of teenage mothers.

## Emergence of Girlhood

Girlhood as a distinct category and set of particular experiences did not emerge until the mid-19th century among the middle and upper classes of the Western world. Up until that point, children were almost exclusively considered miniature adults, and until the age of 6 or so, gender was not as important. In the working classes, gender played only a secondary role throughout early youth. As the primary concern among the rural and urban working classes was survival, both

*By the mid-1800s, young girls were urged to be "good girls" by controlling emotions and remaining chaste.*

male and female children were, from the earliest age, expected to help support the family by working alongside adults, either in industries or on the fields.

The category of girlhood has, over the course of time, acquired characteristics like politeness, deference to authority, and sexual chastity, as well as consumerism. Since approximately the 1950s, and especially since the publication of Vladimir Nabokov's *Lolita*, an ever-increasing amount of attention has being given to girls' sexuality and sexual attractiveness, which is often considered the central part of a girl's identity. These trends have peaked in the late 1990s, with the emergence of concepts like girl power, equating female empowerment with sexual aggressiveness and youthful sex appeal. In light of those events, the meaning of being a girl has broadened extensively. Now, the term can encompass a wide variety of activities and modes of behavior, and is no longer strictly reserved for the teenage years. Thus, *girlhood* serves as an umbrella term encompassing the totality of female experience up to childbirth, substituting, among others, the concept of womanhood. Due to that shift, the gap between a childlike girl and a mature mother is widening.

## Mothers and Daughters in Myth and Culture

The archetypal mother–daughter relationship in Western culture is presented in the Greek myth of Demeter and Persephone. Demeter, the most prominent of the Greek earth mother goddesses, represents the essence of motherhood: she is fertile, caring, nurturing, and extremely protective and possessive toward her offspring. Persephone, on the other hand, performs the dual role of a girl and a daughter, and is defined by her naïveté, innocence, and attachment to her mother. The myth tells the story of Persephone's abduction by Hades, the god of the dead, to his underground domain. The abduction is a clear allegory of marriage, defined here as a violent severing of the girl's ties with her mother and her reappropriation by her husband. Persephone's descent to the underworld is also symbolic of the death of her blissful, sheltered childhood. This type of descent is connected in numerous cultures with a rite of passage into adulthood, which, in the Western construct of girlhood, is synonymous with being removed from her mother's care and coming under her husband's. Demeter mourns the loss of her child and sets out in search of her, to the neglect of all her other duties. Persephone's experience in the underworld, however, has already transformed her, and the exclusive relationship with her husband has taken the place of her attachment to her mother.

The myth of Persephone demonstrates the tendency in Western culture, discussed by various scholars such as Sigmund Freud, Jacques Lacan and Adrienne Rich, to figure femininity as an essential "lack" or incompleteness, which is filled either by a man (in the experience of girlhood and personified by Persephone) or by a child (in the experience of motherhood, personified by Demeter).

The myth of Demeter and Persephone serves as a general model of the cultural expectations and assumptions about girls and mothers. Girls, according to this model, are typically passive, obedient, innocent and vulnerable, while mothers are expected to be protective, nurturing, devoted, and self-sacrificing.

This myth is crucial here, as it is virtually the only existing representation of a mother–daughter relationship in narratives such as fairy tales, myths, and legends of Western culture. In fairy tales of the West, the mother figure is usually absent or dead, and the other prominent female figures are typically depicted as negative: a witch, a wicked stepmother, or an evil queen. It was the second wave feminists of the 1960s who first noticed this tendency and emphasized the need to create, establish, and research the field of daughter–mother relations. They saw fairy tales and other cultural texts and images as models for the socialization of girls. According to the feminists, the danger of such female depictions in stories lies in the fact that, by not presenting positive female mentors, they fail to teach girls how to establish meaningful female–female relationships, especially mother–daughter relations.

## Girls Imitating Mothers

The process of the socialization of girls is not limited to the texts of culture. It is also enacted through the choice of toys, activities, and interests, which are desired to stimulate the girls' interest in motherly things. This would typically mean dolls that look like and imitate the behavior of a toddler; kitchen or house-making sets; encouraging pretend play, such as playing house, the family, or tea party; and discouraging any interests that transcend the boundaries of the domestic sphere, such as excessive physical activity or technical and mechanical pursuits.

As children begin to perceive biological differences between sexes, they begin to identify with the parent or caregiver of their own sex. Girls will therefore typically take their mothers as their primary role model and begin to construct their own gender identity largely by imitating them. Exposure to a wider variety of persons and behaviors, usually starting at kindergarten age, allows girls to observe and acquire models of femininity other than the one represented by their own mothers. This knowledge becomes the basis for a more detailed and nuanced view of societal roles and hierarchies. Consequently, girls begin to perceive the notions of femininity and motherhood as separate and distinct categories.

During their teenage years, children usually begin to question various societal norms, rules, and authorities. Girls in particular are likely to reject their mothers and authority figures and seek out alternative role models and behavioral patterns. Quite often, this repudiation is linked with the onset of matriphobia, the fear of becoming one's mother. When in this state, many young women believe that as long as they avoid repeating their mothers' mistakes in their choice of career, partners, lifestyle, education, or child rearing techniques, their lives will be significantly more fulfilling.

## Teenage Mothers

Annually, there are about 13 million children born to women under 20 years of age worldwide. In the United States alone, it is estimated that a million teen pregnancies occur every year, nearly a third of which end in abortion. Most cases of teen pregnancy occur in Africa and Asia, particularly India, and commonly happen within arranged marriages, to which girls are committed even before their teenage years. In the Western world, however, the majority of teen pregnancies occur out of wedlock, are seen as a social problem, and thus bear a social stigma. Studies show that a disproportionately large percentage of teenage pregnancies occur when the young woman remains in an abusive relationship.

Teen pregnancy is, in fact, a problem, as girls who become pregnant in their teens are more likely to drop out of school, less likely to find employment, and have children who are likely to perform poorly academically. However, the girls who do stay at school reach better incomes by the time they reach their 30s. Some scholars believe that teenage pregnancy carries such a strong social stigma because, in the figure of the teenage mother, the clear-cut divisions into a girl (the object of sexual desire) and a mother (the desexualized caregiver) become blurred, and the transition between girlhood and adulthood (motherhood) is no longer a distinct point. Teenage mothers, therefore, can be said to transgress social categories and encompass, all at once, the experience and notion of girlhood as well as motherhood. This transgression is often seen as threatening and destabilizing to the social order, and the very mention of teenage pregnancy is typically used to imply moral decay. Efforts to alleviate the problem of teen-age pregnancy are usually focused on prevention or elimination (contraception and abortion) rather than aid for the girls who do give birth.

**See Also:** Childhood; Daughters and Mothers; Demeter, Goddess; Fairy Tales, Mothers in; Freud, Sigmund; Matriphobia; Teen Mothers.

## Bibliography

Meaney, Geraldine. *(Un)Like Subjects. Women, Theory, Fiction.* New York: Routledge, 1993.

Rich, Adrienne. *Of Woman Born. Motherhoood as Exerience and Institution.* New York: W.W. Norton, 1995.

UNICEF. "Child Protection From Violence, Exploitation and Abuse." http://www.unicef.org/protection/index _exploitation.html (accessed December 2008).

Vasta, Ross, Marshall M. Haith, and Scott A. Miller. *Child Psychology: The Modern Science.* New York: John Wiley & Sons, 1999.

Agata Wilkins
University of Warsaw

# Globalization and Mothering

Globalization refers broadly to three main forms of worldwide integration: economic, political, and cultural. While globalization's definition as well as its impact is much debated, the term is commonly used to refer to the rise of interdependent national economies that created a global flow of capital, people, goods, and services during the second half of the 20th century. Globalization has undoubtedly created new economic opportunities for women. Since the 1960s, the number of women working for pay in the formal and informal sectors has risen markedly in every region. Women themselves have been beneficiaries of globalization. As wage earners, women are able to choose to delay or refuse marriage, participate in household decisions, and care for themselves and their children. An additional and unexpected benefit of globalization has been the increased ability of women's and feminist groups to form transnational networks.

However, as feminist scholars and activists have documented, globalization has created a several interrelated phenomena relevant to mothers and mothering, including unsafe working conditions, women's labor made cheap through national and international policies, environmental damage, women's transnational migration, and a global care crisis. Although some of these factors follow a historical timeline, others should be considered as happening simultaneously, producing compounded effects.

### History of Mothers and Globalization

Before considering how globalization has affected mothers, it is just as important to ask when globalization occurred, as to ask what globalization is. Although globalization usually refers to more recent historical phenomena, European imperialism and the subsequent industrial revolution began this process. From the 16th century onwards, imperialism involved mothers as European colonizers and as colonized subjects in underdeveloped countries. Globalization might be understood as consisting of several phases including European colonization of much of the globe; the growth of European trade in the 1800s; the contraction of world markets in the wake of World War I and the Great Depression; the imposition of Western ideas of industrialization and development on the underdeveloped countries since the 1950s; concurrent opposition to globalization through the emergence of import substitution policies in parts of Latin America, Africa, and Asia; and a new era of free trade starting in the 1990s.

European women's role in colonial rule is a complex one that encompassed resistance to imperialism, such as their work in the antislavery movement, as well as complicity in its aims. European women (especially those of the middle and upper classes) were often able to assume more power and prestige through their roles as wives and mothers in colonial locations than in their countries of origin. White women worked as missionaries and teachers in the colonies, occupying positions of authority not available to them at home.

White women's support of colonial regimes, the "civilizing mission," and military outposts is a forerunner of privileged women's complicated relationship to the twin powers of globalization and militarization in the present. One consequence of the intersection of reproduction and colonization is the ways in which white, middle-class, heterosexual motherhood was reified, and the mothering performed by women of color, working-class women, and lesbians has been devalued.

Colonized women's social power generally, and mothers' power in particular, was eroded by European colonial rule that sought to impose a Western version of patriarchy with a male breadwinner and a female housewife. This is a surprisingly common feature of European colonial rule, given the different European nations involved (Dutch, English, French, Spanish) and the wide variety of regions colonized: the Americas, the Middle East, Asia, and Africa. Women in regions and colonial regimes as different as French Indonesia, Native Americans in North America, Maori in New Zealand, and British-ruled West Africa all experienced a loss of their traditional rights and cultural power as women and mothers. In early processes of forced migration such as slavery, for example, women taken from Africa and brought to the New World were valued for their labor as much as their ability to reproduce. Sau-ling C. Wong defines the historical phenomena of colonized women and later racialized women taking care of white women's children as "diverted mothering." In this model, time that might be spent on caring for kin is rerouted into the unpaid or poorly paid and low-status carework of white children.

### Women's Working Conditions

Women's movement into paid labor has been precipitated by a number of conditions. Since the 1800s, both men's and women's labor has shifted from agriculture to service and industrial work. After World War II, industrialized nations began to move their factories to less developed countries, largely in eastern Asia, as a means of lowering production costs in order to compete globally. Other underdeveloped nations were encouraged to take out loans to build their infrastructure. International organizations such as the International Monetary Fund and the World Bank then created structural adjustment programs (SAP) designed to cut social service spending, increase resource extraction, and privatize state-owned enterprises in developing nations to facilitate repayment of their debt. SAPs have a negative impact on mothers in countries providing social services, since it is mothers who take up the slack when government spending on welfare, education, and health care is cut.

SAPs also encouraged developing nations to create export processing zones (EPZs) as a means of increasing the nation's production by attracting foreign investment. EPZs are deregulated areas that offer little protection for workers, few environmental regulations, and tax breaks for corporations. Women are often seen as the ideal workers in EPZs, since their labor is considered cheaper than men's and they are perceived as less likely to be organized into labor unions. The majority of workers in EPZs are women, making up to 85 to 90 percent of such workers in places such as Bangladesh, El Salvador, Cape Verde, Nicaragua, and Jamaica.

The creation of globalized economies has meant more women are working in industrialized settings. Women are more likely to hold positions in the skill-intensive service economy. Women now constitute a sizable percentage of the paid workforce globally, making up one-quarter to close to one-half of all formal sector workers. These numbers range from 25 percent in the Middle East, 31 percent in North Africa, 33 percent in Central America, 43 percent in Oceania, 46 percent in North America. These figures leave out women employed in the informal sector, so the number of women working for wages outside the home is likely to be higher. Women's unpaid domestic labor is not counted. Approximately 340 million children under the age of 6 are members of families where all adults work for pay, and 590 million children ages 6 to 14 live in households where all the adults work.

### The Environment, Globalization, and Activism

Increasing industrialization as well as the control over agriculture by multinational agribusinesses has had grave environmental impacts as well as negative impacts on mothers' quality of life. Land where local food was previously cultivated is converted into growing cash crops for export. Women's unpaid labor increases as they take over or perform more subsistence farming as men turn to cultivating cash crops or paid factory work. Women who remain outside industrialized areas often have increased difficulty collecting safe water, fuel, and food to feed

their family due to the corporatization of land and pollution. These economic pressures often encourage women to migrate internally to find paid work, or to emigrate.

Feminist activist groups have made the connection between globalization and the low status and poor living conditions of many mothers. Some focus on the related issues of women's work as farmers and mothers in protecting the environment and biodiversity. Two such groups are Navdanya, created by Dr. Vandana Shiva in India, which holds seminars such as "Grandmother University" for female farmers; and the Greenbelt Movement, founded by Dr. Wangari Maathai in Kenya, which relies on women's local knowledge of the land and soil and their interest in feeding their families to combat environmental degradation through the planting of trees. Other transnational feminist organizations that provide critiques and activism of globalization and development include the Women's Environment and Development Organization (WEDO) and Development Alternatives with Women for a New Era (DAWN). While DAWN and WEDO do not focus exclusively on conditions facing mothers, their activism and policy recommendations recognize the links between women's social roles as caretakers and the effects of globalization.

### Mothers and Migration

Industrialization has resulted in the movement of people, both within national borders during the rise of urbanization, as well as internationally. Many women, then, face the challenges of mothering in diaspora. Women currently make up 49 percent of all internal and transnational voluntary migrants, which does not include women displaced by natural disasters, human rights abuses, or armed conflicts. In 2003, the United Nations estimated that there were 75 million female international immigrants who were long term (resident abroad for over one year), voluntary, and legal. In 2005, approximately 2 million women worked outside their nations' borders as maids. The number of actual immigrant women must of course be higher, due to the uncounted nature of undocumented workers. The wages of these women, many of them single mothers, sustains not only their families, but their nations' economies through remittances sent back home.

The feminization of certain jobs, such as unskilled factory work, home-based work, domestic work, and sex work, has meant that women are in demand for these positions. In particular, mothers' perceived duties within the domestic sphere have meant that they are in demand for home-based manufacturing work. Mothers work in these positions in both the developing and developed world. Third world mothers are recruited for jobs as nannies, maids, and caregivers to the disabled and elderly in first world nations. Mothers' sole responsibilities for their children make them more likely to emigrate from their country in search of better-paying work. One example of this is women being "pulled" to emigrate from the Philippines to industrialized nations such as Italy, Hong Kong, or the United States to become nannies, maids, and elder care workers. Motherhood and poverty makes women more likely to be "pushed" to migrate within their own country to perform work other women might avoid because it is dangerous, such as sex work in the Dominican Republic.

## The Crisis of Care

Whether pulling or pushing, economic forces inducing women to take paid work has created a crisis of care around the world. Women's social roles as caretakers of their families mean that when they enter the paid workforce, others must be found to take over their family responsibilities.

Arlie Hochschild calls this process the "global care chain." Childcare and household responsibilities of mothers in industrialized countries is replaced with the work of women from developing countries. Jody Heyman notes that when leaders are asked who is taking care of their nations' children, they respond that grandmothers and extended family members take on this work. Heyman's study of over 55,000 families in eight nations shows that this is a fiction. In a globalized economy, those who can work for wages do, with the result that children are frequently left with caretakers who cannot work for pay in any other capacity, such as the very elderly and school age children. Women's elder care or childcare labor in developing nations has been replaced with the labor of the extended family, the elders themselves, or older children, or children are being left alone. This crisis of care has resulted in children being taken out of school to care for other

children, increased incidence of developmental or behavioral problems, malnutrition, and physical injuries from lack of adult care and supervision. In Botswana, 53 percent of families with children under the age of 14 reported accidents or emergencies while their parents were at work, while Mexican families reported an accident or emergency rate of 47 percent and Vietnamese families reported a 38 percent rate. Within developed nations, such as Russia and the United States, the crisis of care manifests itself in the large number of school-age children who are left alone after school.

## The Globalization of Mothering

*Transnational motherhood*, a term first coined by Pierrette Hondagneu-Soleto and Ernestine Avila, refers to the experiences of Latina immigrant mothers, although these conditions of mothering can apply to women of other regions. Transnational mothers continue to be involved in their children's lives through long-distance communication and financial support, but do not provide day-to-day care. Mothering from a distance and being the main financial provider do not constitute cultural norms for many of the women who have left their children, or within their host society, leading to cultural contradictions for these mothers about the value of their work and the costs of their distance from their children. This "international division of reproductive labor," as Rhacel Salazar Parreñas terms it, leads to one set of women hiring immigrant mothers to care for their children. Hiring immigrant women is one way that women in developed nations surmount the lack of gender equality in performing household labor and childcare.

Gender inequality in first world nations has links to global gender equality through the ways in which domestic and reproductive labor has become globalized. Immigrant women hire other women in their home country to care for their children. Women's work as childcare providers for their own children, when ensconced in the private, middle-class home has cultural value. Women's work as childcare providers for nonbiological children has become a global commodity, which loses value as it passes down the global care chain—from privileged first world mothers, to hired childcare workers from developing nations, to women caregivers resident in developing nations.

**See Also:** Carework; Immigrant Mothers; Migration and Mothers; Transnationalism; Work and Mothering.

**Bibliography**

Bordo, Michael D., Alan M. Taylor, and Jeffrey G. Williamson, eds. *Globalization in Historical Perspective.* Chicago: University of Chicago Press, 2003.

Clancy-Smith, Julia and Frances Gouda, eds. *Domesticating the Empire: Race, Gender, and Family Life in French and Dutch Colonialism.* Charlottesville: University Press of Virginia, 1998.

Ehrenreich, Barbara and Arlie Russell Hochschild. *Global Woman: Nannies, Maids, and Sex Workers in the New Economy.* New York: Henry Holt, 2002.

Heymann, Jody. *Forgotten Families: Ending the Growing Crisis Confronting Children and Working Parents in the Global Economy.* New York: Oxford University Press, 2006.

Hondagneu-Sotelo, Pierrette and Ernestine Avila. "I'm Here but I'm There: The Meanings of Latina Transnational Motherhood." *Gender & Society,* v.11/5 (October 1997).

Moghadam, Valentine M. "Gender and Globalization: Female Labor and Women's Mobilization." *Journal of World-Systems Research,* v.5/2 (1999).

Morgan, Jennifer L. *Laboring Women: Reproduction and Gender in New World Slavery.* Philadelphia: University of Pennsylvania Press, 2004.

Moss, Barbara A. "Mai Chaza and the Politics of Motherhood in Colonial Zimbabwe." In *Stepping Forward: Black Women in Africa and the Americas,* Catherine Higgs, et al., eds. Athens: Ohio University Press, 2002.

Naples, Nancy A. and Manisha Desai, eds. *Women's Activism and Globalization: Linking Local Struggles and Transnational Politics.* New York: Routledge, 2002.

Parreñas, Rhacel Salazar. *Servants of Globalization: Women, Migration and Domestic Work.* Palo Alto, CA: Stanford University Press, 2001.

Wong, Sau-ling C. "Diverted Mothering: Representations of Caregivers of Color in the Age of 'Multiculturalism.'" In *Mothering: Ideology, Experience, and Agency,* Evelyn Nakano Glenn, et al., eds. New York: Routledge, 1994.

Jocelyn Fenton Stitt
Minnesota State University

# Gore, Ariel

A well-known author and cultural critic, Ariel Gore has spent much of her adult life challenging American stereotypes of the good mother and urging other mothers to do the same. After founding the award-winning magazine *Hip Mama* in 1993 as a project during her senior year of college, Gore garnered a loyal following of women interested in alternative parenting.

She went on to create the Website, www.hipmama.com, and has written, edited, and contributed to numerous books on mothering. Articulating theories that are derived primarily from her own experiences as a single mother, Gore urges mothers to follow their intuition rather than advice manuals, to forgo faulty notions of perfect mothering, and to take the time to nurture both the mother as well as nonmother parts of themselves. Standing in sharp contrast to the parenting advice offered by "experts," Gore's work engages with both the personal and political dimensions of motherhood.

Gore's maternal identity is, undoubtedly, central to her work. For example, in her first book, *The Mother Trip: Hip Mama's Guide to Staying Sane in the Chaos of Motherhood* and *The Hip Mama Survival Guide,* she explores the early years of her maternal self, sharing experiences relating to her pregnancy, the birth of her daughter, and the first decade of her daughter's life. In *Whatever, Mom: Hip Mama's Guide to Raising a Teenager,* Gore describes the challenges and joys she encountered during her daughter's adolescence.

While motherhood is clearly at the heart of her writing, it is equally apparent that she does not define herself solely as a mother. Indeed, part of the appeal of Gore's work stems from her candid descriptions of those struggles she faces as she attempts to balance her mothering self with other parts of her identity: author, daughter, lover, friend, student, woman, human. Attention to this type of juggling act is certainly not uncommon in advice books aimed at mothers. Yet what distinguishes Gore's work is her move away from a romantic, idealized vision of motherhood and toward a more pragmatic, nuanced representation of maternal identity, experience, and emotion. For example, Gore acknowledges not only the funny and wonderful moments that stem from her relationship with her daughter, she also thoroughly describes the recurrent stress, heartache, and exhaustion that are part of that relationship. She describes her mothering successes and her mistakes, the good days as well as the bad ones, the moments when she revels in her role as a mother and those moments when she desperately longs to escape from the constraints of motherhood. Eschewing mandates from so-called parenting experts, Gore advises mothers to trust themselves and their intuition as they find their own path on the journey that is motherhood.

This is not to suggest that Gore believes mothers can or should attempt this journey on their own. On the contrary, a central tenet of her work is the belief that mothers can and should rely not only on their own tuition and experiential knowledge, but also on the wisdom of other mothers, including those in their kin networks and communities (defined broadly to include both immediate social milieus as well as Internet-based and other forms of communities). Indeed, Gore posits that mothers are happiest and healthiest when they are surrounded by a community of supportive "mamas" who help nurture and sustain them in all aspects of their lives. It is within such a community, Gore's work suggests, that mothers are best able to come together across racial, class, cultural, and other boundaries in order to share wisdom with one another, value their unique gifts, share resources, meet their own needs and those of their children, and become fully self-actualized. In this respect, Gore's work is decidedly political, challenging mainstream notions of the self-sacrificing mother in favor of a type of motherhood that is connected, supported, and valued in all of its complicated, wonderful, messy incarnations.

**See Also:** Empowered Mothering; Feminist Mothering; *Hip Mama*; Internet and Mothering; Single Mothers; Unwed Mothers.

**Bibliography**

Gore, Ariel. *Atlas of the Human Heart: A Memoir.* Jackson, TN: Seal Press, 2003.
Gore, Ariel, ed. *The Essential Hip Mama: Writing From the Cutting Edge of Parenting.* Jackson, TN: Seal Press, 2004.
Gore, Ariel. *The Hip Mama Survival Guide.* New York: Hyperion, 1998.
Gore, Ariel. *The Mother Trip: Hip Mama's Guide to Staying Sane in the Chaos of Motherhood.* Jackson, TN: Seal Press, 2000.
Gore, Ariel and Bee Lavender, eds. *Breeder: Real-Life Stories From the New Generation of Mothers.* Jackson, TN: Seal Press, 2001.
Gore, Ariel, with Maia Swift. *Whatever, Mom: Hip Mama's Guide to Raising a Teenager.* Jackson, TN: Seal Press, 2004.

Jillian M. Duquaine-Watson
University of Texas at Dallas

# Grandmothers and Grandmothering

Grandparents have a special significance for their grandchildren, and therefore have an impact on their lives. Relative to what they used to do for their own children, they are often known for spoiling, comforting, mediating, and for being eager to avail time for their grandchildren. They also influence their grandchildren's development. In particular, the grandmother is viewed either as an important source of support, playmate, or caregiver, second only to the mother.

Some households are more likely than others to include both a grandchild and a grandparent. Researchers studying care giving note that since the late 1980s, there has been a dramatic increase in the number of grandmothers taking up the role of a primary caregiver to their grandchildren and great-grandchildren. In particular, the last decade saw further changes with grandparents as young as in their late 30s and adversely affected by human immunodeficiency virus (HIV) and acquired immunodeficiency syndrome (AIDS). It is more common for grandmothers than grandfathers to participate in parental activities. Grandmothers' level of involvement differs; while some provide full-time or part-time care for a grandchild, others do occasional overnight visits, provide daycare, or simply visit grandchildren regularly without any care giving responsibilities.

The extent of grandmother involvement in helping raise their grandchildren also varies across social class, race, culture, and ethnic group, and accord-

*British research found 34 percent of grandmothers looked after their grandchildren while the parents were working or busy.*

ing to generational difference from the mother of the child. Further, grandmothers' involvement in parenting may be determined by family structure or whether they reside with their grandchildren. There is substantial involvement for grandmothers who co-reside with their grandchildren, as well as in instances where the mother is an adolescent. Some studies on child development maintain that a certain family type is crucial in the development and rearing of children. These studies suggest that there is a marked difference between children raised in fully extended families from those raised in nuclear units, or in families where the grandmother assumes the role of a mother. In families where the grandmother is actively involved in parenting alongside parents, the child tends to have a richer childhood and adapt better in a complex social situation.

For example, parents or a mother may have a primary role in setting and enforcing rules, while a grandmother may have a more supportive role, or a role that combines both aspects. In many black communities and families in the South, grandmothers are often an important part of a larger extended family kinship system, and it is common for them to reside with the family. A resident grandmother who is working may contribute economically to the family, which in turn could affect her parenting involvement as well as the quality of life of her grandchildren. Contrary to some studies' contention, in most Southern communities, the grandmother's age or lack of employment does not negatively affect nor limit their parental involvement.

## Mixed Regard and Expectations

The concept and practice of grandmotherhood is culturally constructed and imbued with both good and unfortunate characteristics as well as expectations. In addition to being considered a symbol of love, in some communities she is held in high esteem as a reference source from whom advice is continuously sought. This regard takes into consideration the traditional assumption that grandparents are elderly; at this stage, notions of patriarchy begin to lose their grip as both elderly men and women receive equal respect. In Africa, the grandmother, like her male counterpart, is equally regarded as a walking library and a living heritage, hence the existence of a number of folk stories and sayings alluding to her objectivity and wisdom. In communities where ancestor veneration is widespread, the elderly grandparent—irrespective of gender—is often called upon to communicate and mediate with the ancestors in difficult times. Like her male counterpart, the grandmother is regarded as being closer to the ancestors and therefore in possession of power to intercede on behalf of her children and grandchildren. Consequently, she is commonly referred to as the ancestor. Thus, even in her frail state, residing with her is welcomed, as opposed to placing her in a communal elderly people's facility. She is generally believed to have power to bless those who reside with her or are in her presence.

On the other hand, the demands placed and expected of a grandmother can be enormous, and differentially difficult, compared to her male counterpart. In some families, especially those of Indian origin, grandmothers are extremely overworked as they are expected to carry out household chores for every member of the household with whom she co-resides, as well as, to some extent, for children and grandchildren outside her abode. These responsibilities could include moving from one of her children or grandchildren's house to the next cleaning, supervising cleaning, or cooking or delivering cooked meals.

## Evolving Grandmothering Patterns

About four to five decades ago, co-residence among grandparents and grandchildren used to be a norm in a number of communities, especially those with an emphasis on communal culture. This phenomenon later changed due to urbanization and industrialization. However, since the mid-1990s in some countries, there has been a significant increase in of the skip-generation household, with neither of the grandchild's parents present. Numerous studies list a variety of reasons for the rise of the custodial grandparent.

Cited factors are not only limited to class, race, culture, or ethnic group, but are also along geographical and even poverty lines. For most northern countries, the grandparent would primarily care for the grandchildren due to maltreatment typically associated with substance abuse by one or both parents, mental or emotional problems, teen pregnancy, parental death, divorce, job loss, abandonment, and even incarceration. While these reasons also hold true for the developing countries of the south, human immunodeficiency virus (HIV) and acquired immunodeficiency syndrome (AIDS) deaths are the major contributing factor leading to custodial grandparenting.

## The Impact of HIV/AIDS on Grandmothers

Many grandmothers raise their grandchildren as a result of an AIDS-related death of their children and may be the only or main source of income. In these and other contexts, grandmothering is transformed into mothering. In the developing world, most specifically in southern African countries, HIV/AIDS has adversely affected grandmothers at a time when their income and physical energy are decreasing. In South Africa, for instance, the disease is at times referred to as the grandmothers' disease, as many grandmothers in impoverished communities are largely responsible for both nursing their sick and dying children, as well as being actively involved in co-parenting and raising their orphaned grandchildren. It is reported that two-thirds of people living with HIV/AIDS are cared for by their parents, who are often more than 60 years old. More than 60 percent of orphaned children in southern Africa live in grandparent-headed households.

Many writers and nongovernmental organization (NGO) personnel working with HIV/AIDS-affected communities have pointed out that there is an urgent need to provide support to grandmothers who are adversely affected. A number of organizations have been formed specifically for this purpose. However, grandparents in poorer communities have greater and special needs that go beyond tangible resources, as their circumstances are relatively more dire and substantial.

**See Also:** AIDS/HIV and Mothering; Carework; Foster Mothering; Social Construction of Motherhood.

## Bibliography

Bowers, Bonita F. and Barbara J. Myers. "Grandmothers Providing Care for Grandchildren: Consequences of Various Levels of Caregiving." *Family Relations,* v.48/3 (1999).

Cohler, Bertram J. *Mothers, Grandmothers, and Daughters: Personality and Childcare in Three-Generation Families.* New York: John Wiley & Sons, 1981.

DailyMail.com. "The Important Family Role of Grandmothers." (November 2005). http://www.dailymail.co.uk/news/article-370159/The-important-family-role-grandmothers.html (accessed September 2009).

*Journal of the Association for Research on Mothering.* Grandmothers and Grandmothering [special issue], v.7/2 (Fall/Winter 2005).

Pearson, Jane L., Andrea G Hunter, Margaret E. Ensminger, and Sheppard G. Kellam. "Grandmothers and Multigenerational Households: Diversity in Family Structure and Parenting Involvement in the Woodlawn Community." *Child Development,* v.61/2 (1990).

Pruchno, Rachel. "Raising Grandchildren: The Experiences of Black and White Grandmothers." *Gerontologist,* v.39/2 (1999).

Voland, Eckart, Athanasios Chasiotis, and Wulf Schiefenhövel, eds. *Grandmotherhood: The Evolu-*

*tionary Significance of the Second Half of Female Life*. Brunswick, NJ: Rutgers University Press, 2005.

Susan de la Porte
Thenjiwe Magwaza
University of KwaZulu-Natal, South Africa

# Greece (and Ancient Greece)

Women in ancient Athens were often divided into two main categories: wives and potential wives made up the group with the most expectations and respect; all other women were grouped together, including prostitutes, concubines, and *hetairai* (women who were known for their entertaining and companionship capabilities). Wives had very specific roles to fulfill, namely to produce healthy male heirs to receive the wealth of the father, to weave cloths and other textiles, and to keep a house in order.

Thought to be irrational, have weak minds and to be completely at the mercy of their strong emotions, women were deemed incapable of controlling the vast majority of their own affairs. As a result, women had *kyrios* (male guardians) who would oversee any financial or property transactions that involved the woman, including her marriage partner. *Kyrios* were often the closest male blood-relative or a husband, and were required to accompany a woman in nearly all of her excursions out of the house. Thought to be overwhelmingly seductive to men, women were expected to dress modestly covering their necks, hair, and the majority of their bodies so as to not tempt men.

Outside of birthing, raising and caring for children, respectable women were not thought to have much use in ancient Athens. Women in Athens who were not legitimate citizens (i.e., not born to parents who were both Athenian citizens) had no hope for obtaining citizenry by neither marrying an citizen Athenian man, nor giving birth to a child in Athens.

Births were considered a time for great celebration among Greek women, especially that of a first-born child. Male children were honored with an elaborate naming ceremony approximately a week after birth. In fact, sons were so widely favored over daughters that barren women and women who had multiple daughters sometimes smuggled in sons of their slaves to be passed off as their own legitimate children. In addition, men often performed female infanticide to control the size of the family and to reduce the number of daughters for whom the family needed to provide a dowry.

Further, women who wanted to control their family size had some access to contraceptives, including vaginal suppositories with a type of spermicidal substance like olive oil or vinegar. Women also used abortifacients, such as ingesting toxic potions, or performing strenuous labor.

Ancient Spartan women, however, lead drastically different lives than Athenian women. The nation, not the individual family, was the focus of attention and affection for Spartans. At 7 years of age, Spartan men left their houses to be raised by the state as warriors. At around 30 years old, Spartan men left the army to establish their own households, but returned to the barracks to eat daily. This overwhelming neglect of Spartan women, wives, and mothers engendered a wholly different way of life for Spartan women, who married later, could own property, and both daughters and sons inherited property from their parents. Spartan women were also known for being much more outspoken, opinionated, and bold than Athenian women, a characteristic that was not valued outside of the Spartan city-state.

Marriage in Sparta, similar to Athens, was considered necessary for the production of heirs. In contrast, though, if a man was in need of a son, and his wife had not bore him one, it was not uncommon for that man to ask another man for permission to borrow his wife to bear him a son. In addition, several men may share a wife, who may claim her children as theirs.

## Modern Greeks

Women were first allowed to vote in Greece in 1953, and marriages were still arranged in Greece until the 1970's. While parents and families still have a significant amount of input into the choices of their children's marriage partners, young adults also tend to choose partners that they have some affection toward. Modern Greek women also marry later, now in their early to mid-20s, and some even later, compared with ancient Greek women who married shortly after puberty around the age of 14 or 15.

Still considered to be a formal union between two families, not between two individuals, Greek parents still have a large influence on the interactions between young adults, and both whole families must get along well. It is not uncommon for a mother's displeasure of her son's potential bride to nullify any plans for marriage.

Women are still thought to possess such seductiveness that she is likewise required to dress modestly. It was still commonly held, until recently, that repression and control over men's sexual desires was considered unbearably painful and harmful for men. In 1980, two thirds of Greek murders could be traced to a desire to save a family's honor or to decrease public humiliation.

It was not until the 1983 Family Law that equality between the sexes was legalized, removing a husband's legal right to the status as head of household. This also disallowed him from dispensing her property and wealth as he deemed appropriate, nor could he forbid his wife to work. Now, Greek women struggle to find the same balance between professional careers and their still highly expectant role as mothers that Americans face. Discriminated against in society for their sex, Greek women are lobbying for more equality in the workforce as well as in the household. There have been several notable advancements for women in Greece since ancient times, however, there are still a number of substantial changes that must take place in Greek society for women to occupy the respected role they deserve as equals.

**See Also:** Abortion; Birth Control; Feminism and Mothering; History of Motherhood: Ancient Civilizations; Infanticide; Sons and Mothers.

**Bibliography**
Bauer, Susan Wise. *The History of the Ancient World: From the Earliest Accounts to the Fall of Rome.* New York: W.W. Norton, 2007.
French, Katherine L. and Allyson M. Poska. *Women & Gender in the Western Past: Volume One to 1815.* Boston: Houghton Mifflin Company, 2007.
Humphreys, S.C. *The Family, Women and Death: Comparative Studies.* London: Routledge Publishers, 1983.

Valerie R. Stackman
Howard University

# Grief, Loss of Child

Ultimately, death is unavoidable, a natural part of the life cycle. The death of a child, however, seems like a perversion of nature and is seen as a death out of order. Parents expect to predecease their children, not bury them. Maternal grief is a mother's highly variable emotional, physical, psychological, and social response to the death of her child of any age. Maternal grief is thought to be the most persistent and profound grief; mothers themselves are surprised by its depth and intensity. While there are common maternal responses to the death of a child, experiences of maternal grief are diverse, inconsistent, and change over a lifetime. Male parents also experience grief at the death of a child, but unlike maternal grief, their grief often goes unrecognized and unvalidated.

## Understanding Maternal Grief

To understand maternal grief, it is important to also understand a set of interrelated terms, which are defined variously or not at all in grief and bereavement literature. Grief, in general, is an individual, multidimensional response to a loss. Grief is a normal process that helps the griever adjust to loss. Grief involves somatic, behavioral, and emotional components. Bereavement is the overall experience of grief. Mourning, or the social expression of grief shaped by cultural practices, is a process of coping that includes grieving, rituals, or ceremonial acts to acknowledge and remember the dead. In late modernity, we have fewer culturally accepted rituals for mourning that help others recognize and respond to maternal grief in helpful ways. Mothers want their deceased children, whether their child was not yet born, stillborn, newly born, an infant, an older child, or an adult child, to be acknowledged and remembered. When this does not happen, maternal grief may be exacerbated.

Ideas about what constitutes complicated, pathological, and traumatic grief vary. Generally, these terms describe grief as going beyond what is normally expected, as grief that takes over a person's life in terms of time and intensity. Such grief may become a lasting and dominant part of one's identity. The griever seems to "get stuck" in grief and is not able to feel its intensity lessen. The likelihood of complicated, pathological, or traumatic grief depends, in part, on circumstances around the child's death, other life circumstances including other losses, circumstances related to the grievers relationship with the deceased, other stressors and coping mechanisms, and family and social support.

Theoretically, grief has been described as being a process comprised of stages, phases, or tasks that ideally conclude in a positive way, primarily with what has been described as resolution, reorganization, acceptance, or accommodation. Such steps have been criticized as being too deterministic; when in the reality of experience, the process of grieving is much more complex, multidimensional, and fluctuating. Knowing that grief is a normal reaction to loss, and that it is a process involving somatic, behavioral, and emotional components helps mothers realize they are not "going crazy," and that their early, intensely acute grief will likely diminish eventually. It is widely accepted, however, that while maternal grief changes over time, its course is lifelong.

## Maternal–Child Attachment

Research on maternal–child attachment beginning in the 1950s launched a new understanding of maternal grief. Maternal attachment, it would be learned, begins even before birth, and grief at the death of a child is based, at least in part, on underlying attachment. Further, continuing bonds theory

*Theories hold that mother/child bonds are not broken by death, and mothers develop rituals to remain attached to their children.*

holds that bonds with children are not ruptured in death, but that they are part of the reality of mothers who develop rituals to remain attached to their children. Mothers have developed ways to have their children remembered and included as family. This is similar to a Buddhist tradition, where rituals around disposal of the deceased body ends a physical relationship, but begins a new spiritual relationship with the deceased.

Deceased children continue to be remembered by their mothers. Anthropologist Nancy Scheper-Hughes found that even when children died in circumstances where life was harsh and child death was not uncommon, mothers remembered their dead children and counted them as part of their family; saying, for example, they have a specified number of living children and a specified number of dead children. While photographs taken after death, especially of babies, were typically found on display in homes in the 19th century, this practice lapsed in much of the 20th century, reemerging in the late 20th century with photographs of dying and dead infants. It is not unusual to have mothers memorialize their children in a variety of ways, from major events like scholarships or annual fund-raisers, to small ways such as displaying photographs, including representing their deceased child as a star or heart in family signatures or portraits. What mothers want most is for their child to be remembered and spoken of.

## Grief Across Time and Cultures

The ways grief is experienced and responded to vary by time and culture. Earlier in history, death was not unexpected, and children died frequently. Dying and death were presided over by family and community. Today, in late-modern Western culture, death is medicalized, hidden from view, and often prevented or prolonged by technology. Death as a taboo subject has consequences for how grief is understood and supported. Although in late modernity grief may be, for the most part, limited to the private sphere, broader social issues such as medicine, law, ethics, and the marketplace intervene with private grief. The social expectation of grief is that it is or should be limited to a specific time frame, after which that the griever should "be over it." This expectation, however, does not fit with the experience of maternal grief. Rather than getting over it, mothers learn to live with the death of a child, and over time even incorporate their child's death and their experiences of grief into their lives in meaningful ways. The death of a child is experienced as a deep wound. Mothers say that a vital part of themselves has died along with their child. Healing after the death of a child is a lifelong process; grief changes rather than ends.

## Physical and Emotional Responses to Grief

Not only does maternal grief change over the course of a lifetime, grief changes the griever, both short and long term. Grief at the death of a child, especially when new or acute, is felt in the body as physical symptoms such as tightness in the chest, high blood pressure, reoccurring aches and pains, exhaustion and weakness, weight loss or weight gain, and insomnia. Grief also brings with it behavioral and emotional changes such as short-term memory loss, inability to concentrate, disorientation, distraction, disorganization, anger, alienation, withdrawal, lack of confidence, guilt, blame, anxiety, heightened vigilance over other family members, alcohol or substance abuse, engagement in risky behaviors, and generalized anguish, among others.

Even many years after the death of a child, symptoms of grief may increase around the time of particularly difficult days such as holidays and anniversaries of birth and death. Longer term, bereavement raises questions about the meanings of life and death, good and evil, religion and spirituality. Grief changes the griever, who often reports their child's death was a life-changing event, and that they are not the same person they were prior to their loss. Time becomes measured by before and after, and a new sense of normalcy is being established. Health and vitality are lost in bereavement. Some of these things can be regained, but not easily, not without grief work, a psychological concept meaning the work done by an individual to make sense out of loss.

## Others' Involvement in the Grief Process

Family and friends of bereaved mothers, however, often desire the grieving mother to return to her old self after a brief period of mourning, culturally determined by those who have not experienced child loss. Grieving mothers are put under a time-line, which does not help to assuage their grief. Furthermore, maternal grief, depending on the situation, is subject more or less social recognition and supportive response. Maternal grief at perinatal loss (death in pregnancy or shortly after birth), for example, is not well understood or validated by those who have not experienced it. The erroneous idea is that the mother did not get to know her baby or have investments in her baby's life therefore does not have much to grieve about; she can just have another one to replace her dead child.

This does not accord with the experience of grief at the loss of any baby. Mothers whose babies die of sudden infant death syndrome (SIDS) experience not only a similar lack of validation of their bereavement as well as their babies' short but meaningful lives, they are also subject to police investigation, self-blame, and sometimes harsh judgment by others. Even less acknowledged is that miscarried babies (babies under 20 weeks' gestation) are also grieved. Neither is it well recognized that birth mothers often experience grief at the loss of their adopted babies, as do women who elect to have abortions. The intensity of grief has to do with more than length of life and can be affected, for example, by the degree of investment in the pregnancy, difficulty of becoming pregnant or sustaining a pregnancy, and circumstances surrounding the loss.

While the life span of an infant is often used as consideration for how much one is expected to grieve, when children die as adults, their mother's grief is often not sufficiently validated because, as adults, they are thought of as less a part of their mother's lives. Mothers, however, remain mothers until they themselves die, and in terms of family histories, even after their own deaths. The death of an adult child is still seen as a death out of turn. Mothers whose adult children die report being less included or not included, for example, in their child's funeral arrangements or disbursement of sentimental items, and they fear that contact with grandchildren may be compromised. Maternal grief at the death of an adult child is also in need of social recognition, validation, and support.

## Sudden and Tragic Child Deaths

Mothers of children who die suddenly by violence, through suicide, homicide, in natural disasters, terrorist attacks, or accidents experience grief that is especially traumatic. Thoughts of the terror and pain their children may have felt prior to and in death can be overwhelming. These deaths often leave the grieving mother wondering, but perhaps never being able to answer, why the death happened to her child in this way. The specific circumstances around their child's death may never be known. SIDS deaths and perinatal deaths are both highly unexpected, or come with little warning or explanation, also increasing the trauma associated with death and grief. In the case of prolonged, fatal illness, grieving often begins before death, and mothers have to deal with knowledge of their child's suffering and impending death. Short illnesses that end in death come as an acute shock.

It is important to note, however, that losses should not be weighed, nor should grief. Each loss is unique, as is each experience of grief. It is important to know that maternal grief is profound, and judgment is unwelcome and exacerbates rather than assuages grief. Certain types of comments are unhelpful: the mother of a baby who died did not have as many memories of that child, the mother of an adult child at least got to see her child grow up, or that a child who died while sleeping at least did not suffer. It is important not to assume that bereaved mothers who seem to be doing well, are indeed well; their internal distress may be far greater than they show in public. If they are obviously distressed in public, this does not mean that their grief is pathological.

Common to all maternal grief is its lack of sustained social acknowledgment, validation, and support. Maternal grief is lifelong, and it is exacerbated, not relieved, when well-meaning or judgmental others do not even speak of or make room for mothers to speak of their children. Also common to maternal grief are secondary losses, which include the loss of hopes for the future; loss of routine, companionship, and relationships that may have been attached to the deceased; loss of self and identity; and entitlements attached to being a mother. Bereaved mothers report that their friendships change, as some friends are lost and some are gained. Some friends turn away, while others, often quite unexpectedly, show support. Marital or partner relations often suffer, given the increased stress and different ways of grieving. Partners in same-sex relationships often experience even less validation of their grief.

But dealing with and making sense of and meaning out of loss is not best done alone. Griefwork, as a social science concept, has been described as the work shared by grieving mothers and helpful others to make sense out of loss. Mothers are comforted to know that they are not alone in their experiences of loss.

Helping professionals and peer support groups enable women to share with others who understand the intensity of the experience, and validate each other's losses. It is by walking through grief with others that women can talk, express their feelings, and share strategies for coping without being judged by those who have not experienced child loss, or who have not been closely involved with those who have.

**See Also:** Abortion; Cross-Cultural Perspectives on Motherhood; DES Mothers; Emotions; Family; Maternal Health; Miscarriage; Motherhood Denied; Postpartum Depression; Pregnancy; Stillbirth.

### Bibliography

Auger, Jeanette. *Social Perspectives on Death and Dying*. Toronto: Fernwood, 2000.

Cecil, Rosanne. "Memories of Pregnancy Loss: Recollections of Elderly Women in Northern Ireland." In *The Anthropology of Pregnancy Loss*, Roseanne Cecil, ed. Oxford, UK: Berg, 1996.

*Journal of the Association for Research on Mothering*. Mothering, Bereavement, Loss, Grief [special issue], v.12/2 (Fall/Winter 2010).

Hockey, Jennifer Lorna, Jeanne Katz, and Neil Small, eds. *Grief, Mourning and Death Ritual*. Maidenhead, UK: Open University Press, 2001.

Riches, Gordon and Pamela Dawson. "Lost Children, Living Memories: The Role of Photographs in the Process of Grief and Adjustment Among Bereaved Parents." *Death Studies*, v.22 (1998).

Talbot, Kay. *What Forever Means After the Death of a Child: Transcending the Trauma, Living With the Loss*. New York: Brunner-Routledge, 2002.

Deborah Davidson
York University

# Guam

The Island of Guam is situated in the Pacific Ocean, and is the southernmost and largest island in the Mariana island chain. As the westernmost (unincorporated) territory of the United States. Guam is a truly cosmopolitan community with a unique culture, the core of which is the ancient Chamorro, heavily influenced by the Spanish occupation and the Catholic Church. In addition to the indigenous Chamorros and stateside Americans, Guam boasts large populations of Filipinos, Chinese, Japanese, Koreans, and Micronesian Islanders, as well as a few Vietnamese, Indians, and Europeans. Spanish influence may also be seen in the *mestiza*, a style of women's clothing, or in the architecture of Guam's southern villages.

## Ancient Society

In ancient Chamorro society, the clan leaders arranged marriages. Women did not marry men in their clan, as marriage was a chance to elevate clan status and increase influence in gaining hunting, fishing, and farming rights in other clan districts. Marriages were means of expanding clan relations to elevate clan ranking and to tie clans together. Depending on their needs and resources, clan leaders made marriage pairing decisions. In present-day Guam, most marriages have become Westernized and do not conform to traditional practices.

Guam natives have rapidly become incorporated into the dominant American culture and economy. This accelerated process of modernization has been accompanied by a very sharp fertility decline. One reason for this decline has been the increasing defection of Guam Roman Catholic women from traditional beliefs on birth control. Women reported that the birth control pill was the most common contraceptive used (about 48 percent of women). Guam's birth rate ranges from 18.8 to 25 births per 1,000 population, and the growth rate is estimated at 1.43 percent. The majority of pregnant women receive prenatal care from a trained health care worker during pregnancy. Women, occupying a permanent position, are granted 20 days of maternity leave.

Historical records show that Guam has allowed legal abortions since 1974. There are offices that provide medical abortion, surgical abortion, and the abortion pill. Abortions are legal only when two separate doctors determine that the pregnancy will endanger the mother's life or will seriously affect the physical or mental health of the mother. Contraceptive pills are available free of charge, and the increase in the usage of family planning techniques has resulted in lower birth rates.

## Equality for Women

Women have equal status in society due to the traditional matriarchal culture of Guam, and women play a prominent role in Guam's politics and economy. According to law, at least two females must be appointed to all government boards and commissions. Women have the right to vote as well as the legal right to initiate a divorce. Women play a vital role in family responsibilities as the Chamorro people place great importance on the family. The majority of women have control over the family finances. Women equal men in all levels of schooling, and many women enter universities for higher education. Although they have high educational qualities, women still lag behind men in job opportunities.

**See Also:** Abortion; China; Indonesia; Japan; Papua New Guinea; Philippines.

## Bibliography

Cunningham, Lawrence J. and Janice J. Beaty. *A History of Guam.* Honolulu, HI: Bess Press, 2001.

Department of Chamorro Affairs. "Marriage Traditions." http://www.guampedia.com/category/243-9-marriage/entry/481-marriage-traditions (accessed February 2009)

Workman, A.M., et al. "Abortion on Guam: Demographic Trends and Fertility Data." *ISLA: A Journal of Micronesian Studies, Dry Season,* v.1/2 (1992).

Miranda E. Jennings
University of Massachusetts, Amherst

# Guatemala

The Republic of Guatemala is a former Spanish colony bordered by Mexico to the north and the Pacific Ocean to the southwest, and has a large indigenous population. Fertility rates are high; early union and childbearing are the norm. Divorce is rare. Gender roles have evolved as more women have entered the labor force. The Catholic Church's opposition to birth control has influenced government policies, although there is universal free access to contraception. Use of modern contraceptives is low, however. Many women lack skilled prenatal care and birth attendants. Educational attainment is low. Women's organizations founded during the 36-year civil war work for resolution and justice.

The fertility rate of 4.4 lifetime births per woman and the adolescent birthrate are among the highest in Central America. Fertility is highest in rural areas, among indigenous women, and for young women with no education. Mothers in the formal sector are eligible for 84 days of paid maternity leave. Many women work in the domestic sphere. The very low divorce rate may be due to a religious view of marriage as indissoluble.

More than half of Guatemalans are descended from Mayan ancestry, which attributes birth with cosmic significance and believe fertility is predetermined. Indigenous and mixed (indigenous and European) cultures hold traditional attitudes about gender roles and responsibilities that are evolving with women's increased labor force participation. Social norms encourage early unions and adolescent childbearing, and discourage single motherhood, although one in five families is female headed.

In 1994, the Guatemalan government reversed its support of its reproductive health platform of the International Conference on Population and Development. In 2001, the Social Development Law created the national Reproductive Health Program. A 2006 law stipulated universal and free access to contraception. The use of modern contraceptive methods (40 percent) is on the rise. Complications from abortion, which is illegal except to save a woman's life, is the second most common cause of death in women.

Compulsory schooling is for 6 years. Women lag in educational attainment; 55 percent of girls and 66 percent of boys are enrolled in secondary school.

*Comadronas*, traditional midwives, attend 59 percent of births, 85 percent in rural areas. Although the majority of women attend at least one prenatal care visit, about half of the least educated and indigenous women do not. Mayan beliefs about fertility and childbirth make them wary of Western medical practices and modern maternal health services. Maternal mortality is one of the highest in the region.

Guatemalan women formed several organizations during the 36-year civil war (1960–96), including prominent human rights organizations created by war widows and mothers of persons who disappeared or died. Rigoberta Menchú is a human rights activist and author who won the Nobel Peace Prize for her work on behalf of native Guatemalans.

**See Also:** Activist Mothers for the Disappeared; Religion and Mothering; Spain.

**Bibliography**
Centeno, Lisa-Marí. "Guatemala." In *The Greenwood Encyclopedia of Women's Issues Worldwide,* Lynn Walter, ed. Westport, CT: Greenwood Press, 2003.
Guttmacher Institute. "Early Childbearing in Guatemala: A Continuing Challenge." *In Brief,* v.5 (September 2006).
Tooley, Michelle. *Voices of the Voiceless: Women, Justice, and Human Rights in Guatemala.* Scottdale, PA: Herald Press, 1997.

Keri L. Heitner
University of Phoenix

# Guilt

Because research has demonstrated that guilt, especially if persistent, can result in a sense of ineffectiveness that impacts physical well-being, mental health, and the ability to be productive, it is important to explore guilt within the mothering role. Despite the scarcity of systematic research on mothering and guilt, the notion of "maternal guilt" in the media and in the everyday lives of women is inescapable.

In popular magazines, as well as academic work across disciplines, guilt appears as a natural and common component of motherhood. As Adrienne Rich said of mothers: "the guilt, the powerless responsibility for human lives, the judgments and condemnations, the fear of her own power, the guilt, the guilt, the guilt."

## Contributing Factors to Maternal Guilt

In 1978, Heffner noted that, among other factors, the desire for perfection, the nature of consumerism, and the proliferation of "expert" advice was contributing to frustrations within motherhood. Guilt was noted as the most prominent outcome. Heffner observed that women felt increasingly bad about themselves as mothers, concluding, "The answer is that women are vulnerable to these attacks because feeling guilty is a normal condition of motherhood . . . The functions of mothering induce intense emotional reactions which lead inevitably to guilt." Rankin, while researching employed mothers, found maternal guilt to be one of the eight major stresses reported by mothers. Also, for inner-city women, among the several barriers to their own treatment for substance abuse were lingering and unresolved feelings of guilt and shame in the maternal role, according to Ehrmin.

Ehrensaft found maternal guilt to be related to societal expectations of good mothering. While acknowledging the subtle shifts in child rearing, specifically the increased involvement of fathers, Ehrensaft pointed out that it is the mother who remained "in charge," carrying a greater "mental load" of parenting. She added that for women who leave the home to work, it is difficult for them to relinquish the child rearing to someone else. Ehrensaft argued that women in these egalitarian, shared-parenting situations give up power, "only to find societally induced guilt feelings for not being a 'real' mother, and maybe even for being a 'bad' mother."

Hays described the dynamics of the "guilt gap," in which mothers, as compared to fathers, experience vastly higher levels of guilt—even when both are equally responsible for childcare. Further, Douglas and Michaels not only described women as guilt ridden, but also contend that this guilt co-occurs with and is exacerbated by feelings of inferiority, exhaustion, confusion, fearfulness, and anger.

One of the few works to specifically address maternal guilt and motherhood asked women to describe the experience of and the meanings associated with maternal guilt. In an unstructured interview format, subjects were asked to talk about guilt and mothering. Many of the qualitative themes that Seagram and Daniluk developed for their discussion reflected the cultural expectations of mothering so prolific in other works. For example, Seagram

*In mother surveys, researchers found that the subject of guilt and motherhood was second in interest only to anger.*

and Daniluk described their respondent's sense of responsibility as "an unrelenting and total sense of responsibility for the health, welfare, and development of their children." The women reported feelings of ultimate responsibility for all aspects of a child's needs. This sense of total responsibility captures what Hays called "intensive mothering." Similarly, the sense of inadequacy reported by the respondents reinforce Douglas and Michael's assertions concerning the impact of the media on a woman's sense of self as a mother. Comparing themselves to women on television, or the information in parenting books, these mothers' feelings of inadequacy have led them to believe that they have failed in the quest for good mothering.

## Three Risk Factors

There are three notable factors that may place mothers, as compared to others, at higher risk for experiencing guilt. These factors include labor force participation, role identity, and what is called new momism. First, the increased presence of mothers in the labor force may put them at risk for guilt and shame. In a 10-year period (1993–2003), the percentage of mothers in the labor force, with children under age 6, increased from 58 percent to 62 percent. Women with children over the age of 6 participated in the labor force at a rate of 76 percent, according to 2005 data from the Employment Policy Foundation's Center for Work and Family Balance.

However, even as mothers' labor force participation increases and men begin to participate more fully in home life, mothers remain "in charge" and shoulder a larger burden of childcare. Mothers are more likely to be responsible for a majority of the household tasks from the practical (e.g., feeding, clothing) to the complex (e.g., stimulating intellectual growth). Additionally, when mothers are working in the labor force, it is often difficult for them to relinquish child rearing to others. Not only are mothers worried about the well being of their children, they also fear social disapproval for being away from home. These stressors, worries, and burdens are ripe for the experience of guilt and shame.

Second, a woman's identity in relation to her role as mother may also put her at risk for guilt and its associated consequences. In a well-known study on multiple roles, Simon discovered that 85 percent of her female respondents "felt guilty about combining work and family because they perceive that a consequence of having a job is that they sometimes slight their children and neglect their husbands." Further, as a result of having internalized wife and mother as their principal identities and the subsequent responsibilities associated with those roles, she found that wives carried much more guilt than their husbands did and felt much more responsible for the overall operation of the family. Similarly, other research has suggested that women internalize their perceived inadequacies not as externally mandated or caused, but rather as personal failures, which often occur in tandem with high levels of psychological distress and low perceived control. Unable to live up to standards that have prescribed by societal expectations as well as by themselves, mothers are more likely to experience guilt.

Finally, new momism, a term coined by Douglas and Michael, captures the contemporary ideology of motherhood, which appears to celebrate women and motherhood on the surface, but actually creates standards of unrealistic proportions. All women are expected to crave motherhood, and approach it with instinctual joy and patience. Upon becoming mothers, women find themselves serving as the primary caregiver of children, with the norms of motherhood requiring devotion from all parts of the self—physical, emotional, intellectual and psychological—to the process of mothering. The impossible standards that women face in our culture are a primary source of guilt for women. In this realm, guilt emanates from three main sources: the mothers' experiences with their families, including their families of origin (specifically their mothers) and their families of procreation; observations of other mothers; and the internalization of media images. These sources feed new momism, or the contemporary myth that fulfillment comes to women only in the form of selfless mothering with high expectations. The problem is that these expectations represent ideals that few, if any, women can actually achieve.

## Mothering Road Map

In contemporary Western society, Collins suggested that mothering is most affected by the macro-social environment, wherein women have less social power to determine their own life outcomes. This larger context is characterized by an ideology that motherhood is or should be a goal for women. Furthermore, on behalf of their families, mothers are to sublimate their own needs and desires in order to become models of selfless giving and caring. This type of mothering is not only defined as the proper way for women to perform this role, but also, if done correctly, this behavior is rewarded with self satisfaction and fulfillment. At the same time, some research has noted that the strong ideological demands made on mothers frequently conceal how women themselves construct their roles as mothers, often marginalizing those women who are unable to portray and internalize motherhood as their major aim or priority.

Much of the work on guilt (and shame) reports higher levels of guilt for females than for males. Simon found that these differences had to do primarily with how women experience multiple roles and role meanings. Due to cultural expectations of mothering, women are more likely to feel conflicted when combining work and family, and to feel guilt when they sense they have let their families down in their emotional support role. One of Simon's respondents reported, "Guilt is probably the number one emotion because if I didn't work, that time could be devoted to my kids or my home life . . ." Simon remarked that men, however, reported no response of emotion in terms of combing work and family roles. The sex differences, Simon reasoned, were due to meanings these men and women ascribed to mother, father, and worker. For women, the combination of mother and worker resulted in feelings of guilt.

In *A Mother's Place: Choosing Work and Family Without Guilt or Blame*, Susan Chira wrote, "When I was a child, it was clear to me who the good mother was . . . the bland suburban homemaker mother of Sally, Dick, and Jane. She lived in my television set: Mrs. Cleaver, the ever-aproned, ever-available mother of Wally and the Beaver. She even lived in my house." Chira, a *New York Times* journalist, goes on to describe her process of becoming a mother and adopting this 1950s suburban model of a mother, who was happy to sacrifice and devote herself to her family, never displaying boredom or anger. Unfortunately, when the actual experiences of mothering are not consistent with the good mother model, mothers such as Chira often experience anxiety and guilt. Chira felt frustrated in the early months of her child's life. Rather than the blissful early months at home with her baby, she missed her career and longed to return to work. Reflecting on this period of confusion, she stated: "I still feel a sense of shame, a belief in a secret corner of my heart that my emotions brand me a bad mother, alone amid a tide of rapture."

Chira's account illustrates the power of the mothering ideology to provide a kind of road map for mothers, even as they have difficulty following it. Her experiences reveal that contemporary mothering norms trap her in three ways. First, performing as the ideological good mother contradicts her definition of self as defined by her relationship to work. Second, Chira's guilt and shame in relation to missing her career was grounded her conclusion that working was bad for the child and signaled bad mothering. Third, her experience of shame came as

a result of not following the inflexible road map drawn for her by the ideologies of ideal motherhood. When she attempted a deviation from this powerful ideology, she felt guilty and shameful.

Another road map exists for mothers who have adopted what is known as attachment parenting, which has become an increasingly popular approach to parenting. While contemporary versions of attachment parenting exist (also called *natural mothering*), little has changed from the foundations set forth by Bowlby, whose original method told parents (specifically the mother) that, in order for a child to develop in a healthy manner, the parent should stay in close proximity to the child. Mothers/parents were to accomplish healthy child development by holding or carrying the child when possible, protecting, nurturing, and bonding with the child.

## Collision of Ideologies

As was the case with Bowlby's initial work in 1958, this particular ideological approach to parenting has ramifications that are more significant for mothers than for fathers. It is the mother who will be breastfeeding on baby's demand, and subsequently responding to the baby's cries as quickly as possible. It is also assumed in the community of attachment parenting that spending time with one's baby is also the job of the mothers, who will more than likely be the stay-at-home parent. The assumption in this method of child rearing is that the mother is the best caregiver for her child, irrespective of the quality of daycare or her desire to work outside of the home. A mother embracing attachment parenting while seeing herself as a working mother set the stage for feelings of guilt and shame after the collision of the two belief systems. It also suggests the importance of a mother nurturing her own child is the natural route to take. Villani noted the language of natural mothering in her interviews with mothers. She also quoted those mothers' expressions of guilt when they felt they had fallen short of the image they strove to emulate. One of her participants told her, "I thought I could be more loving . . ."

Buskens's analysis of natural parenting drew attention to the loneliness and social isolation that can accompany this method. Adhering to the attachment parent ideology "requires a home base; however, this 'home base' is often a no-man's land (literally there are very few men here) on the social periphery."

For one young mother, a participant in a focus group conducted in 2005, the ideology of attachment parenting conflicted with the child rearing ideologies promoted by her mother and grandmother. That clash left her confused and feeling even guiltier about which method was correct. She told of her grandmother's fears that she was "creating a monster" through her method of mothering. She said: "I feel bad either way, but I carry him all the time. It makes me feel guilty, answering to my mother or my grandmother—'Maybe you're spoiling him . . . You need to let him soothe himself.'" But, when she abandoned the attachment method and tried the style proposed by her mother and grandmother, she felt as though she had let her son down. "And then, if I do that to him, I feel horribly guilty."

As history documents, the "feminine mystique," as posited by author Betty Friedan, trapped many women in an ideology that for them, proved unhealthy and unreasonable. In *The Feminine Mystique*, Friedan told the stories of women suffering from "the problem that has no name," of women who "slept more than an adult needed to sleep," and took "tranquilizers like cough drops." As Douglas and Michaels warned, "Unless we start admitting to ourselves and each other that it's [mothering] not always a walk in the park, our guilt, anger, fear, and depression will continue to go underground." Guilt and shame, and the ways in which these emotions limit a mother's propensity to meet her needs and affect her abilities to provide care for her children, have serious implications that are being investigated by social scientific research.

**See Also:** Attachment Parenting; Bad Mothers; Intensive Mothering; Natural Mothering; New Momism.

## Bibliography

Barnhill, Julie. *The Guilt That Keeps on Giving.* Eugene, OR: Harvest House Publishers, 2006.

Baumeister, Roy F., Arlene M. Stillwell, and Todd F. Heatherton. "Guilt: An Interpersonal Approach." *Psychological Bulletin,* v.115 (1994).

Bowlby, John. "The Nature of the Child's Tie to His Mother." *International Journal of Psychoanalysis,* v.39 (1958).

Chira, Susan. *A Mother's Place: Choosing Work and Family Without Guilt or Blame.* New York: HarperCollins, 1998.

Chodorow, Nancy. *The Reproduction of Motherhood: Psychoanalysis and the Sociology of Gender.* Berkeley: University of California, 1978.

Collins, Patricia Hill. "Shifting the Center: Race, Class and Feminist Theorizing About Motherhood." In *Mothering: Ideology, Experience, and Agency,* Evelyn Nakano Glenn, Grace Chang, and Linda Rennie Forcey, eds. New York: Routledge, 1994.

Douglas, Susan J. and Meredith W. Michaels. *The Mommy Myth: The Idealization of Motherhood and How It Has Undermined Women.* New York: Free Press, 2004.

Ehrensaft, Diane. "When Women and Men Mother." In *Mothering: Essays in Feminist Theory,* Joyce Trebilcot, ed. Totowa, NJ: Rowman & Allanheld, 1983.

Ehrmin, Joanne T. "Unresolved Feelings of Guilt and Shame in the Maternal Role with Substance-Dependent African American Women." *Journal of Nursing Scholarship,* v.33 (2001).

Hays, Sharon. *The Cultural Contradictions of Motherhood.* New Haven, CT: Yale University Press, 1996.

Heffner, Elaine. *Mothering: The Emotional Experience of Motherhood After Freud and Feminism.* New York: Doubleday, 1978.

Hochschild, Arlie R. *The Second Shift.* New York: Avon Books, 1989.

Rankin, Elizabeth D. "Stresses and Rewards Experienced by Employed Mothers." *Health Care for Women International,* v.14 (1993).

Rich, Adrienne C. *Of Woman Born: Motherhood as Experience and Institution.* New York: W.W. Norton, 1976.

Seagram, Samantha and Judith C. Daniluk. "It Goes With the Territory: The Meaning and Experience of Maternal Guilt for Mothers of Preadolescent Children." *Women and Therapy,* v.25 (2002).

Simon, Robin W. "Gender, Multiple Roles, Role Meaning, and Mental Health." *Journal of Health and Social Behavior,* v.36 (1995).

Warner, Judith. *Perfect Madness: Motherhood in the Age of Anxiety.* New York: Riverhead Books, 2005.

Jean-Anne Sutherland
University of North Carolina, Wilmington

# Guinea

This west African country was a French colony until it gained independence in 1958. With a population of 10.2 million (July 2005 estimate), it has a female life expectancy of 50.7 years. The country's birth rate is 41.8 per 1,000, with an infant mortality rate of 90 per 1,000 live births.

Traditional rural lifestyles have changed little since the arrival of the French, with many of the population still living in small villages. The area received worldwide attention in Camara Laye's book *L'Enfant Noir* (1954), translated into English in the following year. It describes the life of a boy growing up in a village, his jeweler father having been a blacksmith, and his mother bringing him up with tribal customs while becoming a mediator in numerous village disputes. Although Guinea was a colony at the time, the book shows that French culture had no significant influence on village life, although as a boy Laye did attend French elementary and secondary schools. During the French colonial period, a hospital was built in Conakry, the country's capital, but little other change occurred in towns and villages throughout the country.

Although the country has extensive natural resources, Guinea has never prospered; some attribute this to the socialist policies of Sekou Touré, who ran the country for the first 26 years after independence. He was eager to hold a different political stance than France, and this resulted in many companies choosing not to invest in Guinea, and in turn the economy of the country never grew as much as other countries in the region.

## Vital Statistics and Health Care

Life expectancy in Guinea is 51 for males and 53 for females. Literacy for 15- to 24-year-olds in 2003 was 58.7 percent for males and 33.7 percent for females. Labor force participation is high for both females (79.7 percent) and males (87.4 percent) age 15 and older.

Only 4 percent of women reported having used modern methods of contraception. 74 percent of women giving birth reported receiving at least one antenatal care visit, and 48 percent reported four or more. The maternal mortality rate in 2000 was quite high, at 740 per 100,000 live births, relating to the fact that only 35 percent of births were attended by skilled health personnel, and 29 percent of births took place in health care facilities.

Access to abortion is highly restricted (only in cases of saving the mother's live or preserving her physical or mental health), but illegal abortion is believed to be common: one study estimated that half of maternal deaths were due to illegal abortions.

There is a dire shortage of funds for Guinea's health services; the average per capita expenditure is $13, and most of the best facilities are located in Conakry, with few regional hospitals and clinics. There is also a shortage of doctors—0.9 per 10,000 people, and 4.7 nurses and midwives per 10,000.

In 2007 the international organization Save the Children ranked Guinea 16th on the Mothers' Index, 14th on the Women's Index, and 19th on the Children's Index, out of 33 Tier III or least developed countries.

**See Also:** Burkina Faso; Congo; Gambia; Ivory Coast; Maternal Health; Senegal; Sierra Leone.

## Bibliography

Gassain, Monique. "Coniagui Women." In *Women of Tropical Africa,* Denise Paulme, ed. New York: Routledge, 1963.

O'Toole, Thomas, with Janice E. Baker. *Historical Dictionary of Guinea.* Lanham, MD: Scarecrow Press, 2005.

Sow, Diamilatou. "Women Literacy in Guinea." *African Association for Literacy and Adult Education Journal.* v.6/1 (1992).

World Bank. *Guinea: Gender Issues.* Washington, DC: World Bank, 1993.

Justin Corfield
Geelong Grammar School, Australia

# Guinea-Bissau

Located in west Africa, Guinea-Bissau was known as Portuguese Guinea, and was closely linked with the nearby Portuguese colony of the Cape Verde islands until it gained independence in 1974. With a population of 1.586 million (2005 estimate), it has a female life expectancy of 48.8 years. The birth rate is 37.2 per 1,000, and the infant mortality rate is 105.2 per 1,000 live births, one of the highest in the world. The maternal mortality rate at 1.1 per 100 births is also one of the highest in the world.

In tribal society, the role of women was very much seen as homemakers and caretakers of the crops, while men were involved in hunting and animal husbandry. This changed little during Portuguese rule, which started in the 16th century and lasted until 1974. For much of the period of colonial rule, slavery depleted the local population and disrupted tribal societies.

In 1956, an armed rebellion against the Portuguese started, which gradually gained more and more support, until the Portuguese government was forced to concede independence. There had been little development of the country's infrastructure during the 300 years of colonial rule, and after independence, attempts were made to build up health services in this desperately poor country that remained isolated from much of the rest of the world.

## Vital Statistics for Mothers and Children
Guinea-Bissau's total fertility rate is 7.1, the birth rate 36 per 1,000 population, and the population growth rate is 2.9 percent. Life expectancy at birth is 45 years for males and 48 years for females. Sixty-one percent of women and 92.6 percent of men age 15 and over participate in the labor force. Male literacy is estimated at 58.1 percent and female literacy at 27.4 percent, with a schooling expectancy of 7 years for males and 4 years for females.

Guinea-Bissau ranks very poorly on issues of mother's and children's health. Only four percent of women report using modern methods of contraception, and the maternal death rate is one of the highest in the world at 1,100 per 100,000 live births. The stillbirth rate is 43 per 1,000 total births, and the neonatal mortality rate is 48 per 1,000 live births. Two-thirds of women give birth at home, often without medical assistance. Abortion is illegal, but allowed in practice if necessary to save the mother's life. In 2007, the international organization Save the Children placed it 29th on the Mothers' Index, 26th on the Women's Index, and 25th on the Children's Index out of 33 Tier III or Least Developed Countries.

Few women are in the labor force, although some operate as village traders, and others work in menial jobs in factories and as domestics and cleaners. The Uniao Democrático de Mulheres (UDEMU: Democratic Union of Women) was established by the government "to mobilize the mass of women in the struggle for their emancipation," but it has not helped the plight of the majority of women in the country.

**See Also:** Burkina Faso; Cape Verde; Congo; Gambia; Ivory Coast; Maternal Health; Senegal; Sierra Leone.

### Bibliography
Galli, Rosemary E. and Jocelyn Jones. *Guinea-Bissau: Politics, Economics and Society.* London: Frances Pinter Publishers, 1987.
Larsson, Maria, "Preventive Maternal Care Saves Lives in Guinea-Bissau." *Vardfacket,* v.8/21 (November 29, 1984).
Lobban, Richard A. and Peter Karibe Mendy. *Historical Dictionary of the Republic of Guinea-Bissau.* Lanham, MD: Scarecrow Press, 1997.
Sand, E.M. "Norwegian Midwife Leads First Midwifery Education in Guinea-Bissau." *Jordmorbladet,* v.5 (1994).

Justin Corfield
Geelong Grammar School, Australia

# Guyana

Very little is known about family structures, maternal roles, and socioeconomic differences of families in the English-speaking Caribbean. These topics are especially relevant for the country of Guyana, which has one of the poorest economies in the Caribbean.

Situated between Suriname, Brazil, and Venezuela, Guyana has a population of 767,000 people and is roughly the size of Kansas. The population is comprised largely of East Indians, blacks, and a small group of Amerindians. The official language is English; however, four dialects, including Creole and Caribbean Hindustani, are also spoken.

Although rich in natural resources, Guyana is plagued with extreme poverty. Roughly 36 percent of Guyanese live below the national poverty line. Inequality, ethnic disparities, high child and maternal mortality rates, and disproportionate access to health care are some of the issues that affect the people of Guyana. Reported to have an adult literacy rate of 98 percent, there appears to be no difference in functional literacy between males and females. Women, however, are overwhelmingly represented as the working poor and account for 51 percent of the total population. Approximately 25 percent of all households are headed by females, which contributes to the country's high rates of migration and divorce. In comparison to East Indians and Amerindians, which represent 35.2 and 2.6 percent of female-headed households, respectively, black women account for approximately 50 percent of all households headed by women.

Guyanese women have a fertility rate of two children per woman; consequently, the infant mortality rate is 30.4 per 1,000 live births. Likewise, the under-5 mortality rate is relatively high at 64 per 1,000 live births. Though maternal mortality rates remain high, there has been a substantial decline from 133.3 to 115.9 deaths per 100,000 live births between 2000 and 2004. The primary causes of deaths for pregnant women are largely due to hemorrhaging, hypertensive diseases, abortion-related conditions, and complications during pregnancy and/or childbirth. Breastfeeding is an important aspect of motherhood in Guyana. In maternity wards, skin-to-skin contact between mother and child is assured immediately after childbirth. Over 90 percent of mothers begin breastfeeding within the first hour, and 70 percent breastfeed during the first month of life.

Family planning practices used in Guyana include oral contraceptives, followed by condoms, subdermal injections, and intrauterine devices. However, for females 15–49 years of age who are either married or in monogamous relationships, the use of all contraceptive methods is under 40 percent. Abortion laws allow for access to elective abortion services while prohibiting abortion procedures from taking place within public hospitals.

The national health care industry is controlled by the Guyanese government, which oversees health care policies and delivers health care services. Due in part to insufficient administrative resources, about 12.5 percent of the population does not have access to health services. Faced with the challenges of poverty, social inequality, ethnic disparities and inadequate access to health care, the Guyanese government created a National Plan between 2003 and 2007, which aimed to decrease infant and maternal mortality with importance placed on child and maternal health care, including vaccinations, nutrition, and healthy development.

**See Also:** Birth Control; Brazil; Breastfeeding; Poverty and Mothering.

### Bibliography

Hintzen, Percy C. *The Costs of Regime Survival: Racial Mobilization, Elite Domination and Control of the State in Guyana and Trinidad*. Cambridge, UK: Cambridge University Press, 2008.

Peake, Linda. *Gender, Ethnicity and Place: Women and Identities in Guyana*. New York: Routledge, 1999.

World Health Organization (WHO). *Health in the Americas*. Geneva, Switzerland: WHO, 2007.

Nicole T. Branch
Howard University